Sleeping price codes

LL	over US$200
L	US$130-200
AL	US$90-130
A	US$40-90
B	US$20-40
C	US$10-20
D	US$5-10
E	US$2.50-5
F	Under US$2.50

Price codes refer to the cost of two people sharing a double room in the high season.

Eating price codes

♛♛♛	Over US$10
♛♛	US$3.50-10
♛	Under US$3.50

Price codes refer to the cost of a two-course meal for one person, excluding drinks or service charge.

Footprint story

It was 1921

Ireland had just been partitioned, the British miners were striking for more pay and the federation of British industry had an idea. Exports were booming in South America – how about a handbook for businessmen trading in that far away continent? The Anglo-South American Handbook was born that year, written by W Koebel, the most prolific writer on Latin America of his day.

1924

Two editions later the book was 'privatized' and in 1924, in the hands of Royal Mail, the steamship company for South America, it became The South American Handbook, subtitled 'South America in a nutshell'. This annual publication became the 'bible' for generations of travellers to South America and remains so to this day. In the early days travel was by sea and the Handbook gave all the details needed for the long voyage from Europe. What to wear for dinner; how to arrange a cricket match with the Cable & Wireless staff on the Cape Verde Islands and a full account of the journey from Liverpool up the Amazon to Manaus: 5898 miles without changing cabin!

1939

As the continent opened up, the South American Handbook reported the new Pan Am flying boat services, and the fortnightly airship service from Rio to Europe on the Graf Zeppelin. For reasons still unclear but with extraordinary determination, the annual editions continued through the Second World War.

1970s

Many more people discovered South America and the backpacking trail started to develop. All the while the Handbook was gathering fans, including literary vagabonds such as Paul Theroux and Graham Greene (who once sent some updates addressed to "The publishers of the best travel guide in the world, Bath, England").

1990s

During the 1990s the company set about developing a new travel guide series using this legendary title as the flagship. By 1997 there were over a dozen guides in the series and the Footprint imprint was launched.

2000s

The series grew quickly and there were soon Footprint travel guides covering more than 150 countries. In 2004, Footprint launched its first thematic guide: *Surfing Europe*, packed with colour photographs, maps and charts. This was followed by further thematic guides such as *Diving the World*, *Snowboarding the World*, *Body and Soul escapes*, *Travel with Kids* and *European City Breaks*.

2010

Today we continue the traditions of the last 89 years that have served legions of travellers so well. We believe that these help to make Footprint guides different. Our policy is to use authors who are genuine experts who write for independent travellers; people possessing a spirit of adventure, looking to get off the beaten track.

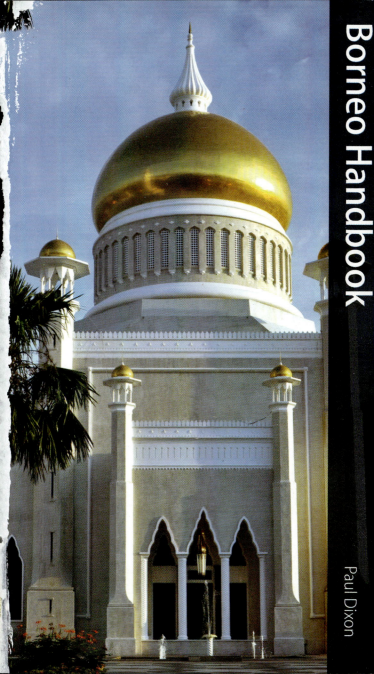

Borneo Handbook

Paul Dixon

The third largest island in the world and surrounded by the Java, Celebes, Sulu and South China seas, Borneo screams adventure. The first foreign settlers battled horrendous waves of cholera, malaria and warfare with local tribes to get their foot in the door of this resource-rich, natural treasure house.

Sarawak, dominated by the snaking crocodile-infested Rejang river, is renowned for its headhunters' trail and Iban, Melanu and Kenyah longhouses. Neighbouring Brunei glimmers with golden-roofed mosques whose calls to prayer ring out over the country's dense and pristine rainforest, filled with proboscis monkeys and lazy pythons, while offshore, flares from oil rigs light up the clouds in the tropical night.

The moody peak of Gunung Kinabalu, Borneo's highest mountain, offers views down through the swirling clouds to Sabah's islands including Pulau Gaya, Layang Layang and Sipadan, which offer unparalleled underwater adventures. Sabah's jungle, though fast making way for endless plantations, still provides stunning jaunts for the hardy in the Maliau Basin, home to elephants, orang-utan and the shy Sumatran rhino.

Few travellers cross into Borneo's greatest portion, Indonesian Kalimantan. The coastal cities are seething with energy, choked with traffic beyond which the jungle is rapidly being consumed by logging concessions. Boat travel is the most rewarding experience here, chugging up the Mahakam on the way to visit Dayak long-houses, or around the vast Tanjung Puting National Park, whose empty riverways still echo with the call of Borneo's untamed beasts.

Borneo highlights

1 The chilled city of Kuching has garish cat statues, Chinese shophouses and colonial splendours. ▶▶ page 94.

2 Speed around Brunei's massive water village, Kampong Ayer, in a water taxi. ▶▶ page 288.

3 Get a closer look at Asia's only great ape at the world's largest orang-utan sanctuary in the Sepilok Reserve. ▶▶ page 247.

4 Tiny craft bump through rapids on Malaysia's longest river, the Rejang, to forest longhouses. ▶▶ page 126.

5 Gunung Kinabalu is Borneo's tallest peak and a most magnificent sight. ▶▶ page 229.

South China Sea

Niah National Park ◆

Bintulu

MALAYSIA

SARAWAK

Belaga

Sibu ✈

Rejang

4 Batu (2012m)

Kapit

Kuching

1

Gunung Penrissen ▲

Bandar Sri Aman

Singkawang

Ngabang

Semitau

Sanggau

Pontianak

Sintang

Nangah Pinoh

Sukadana

Kendawangan

Pangkalanbun ✈

8 Tanjung Puting National Park ◆

Sampit

Java Sea

KUALA LUMPUR

SINGAPORE

Kudat

Kota Belud

Kota Kinabalu

5 Gunung
Kinabalu
(4095m)

Sulu Sea

3 Sandakan

SABAH

Kinabatangan

6

BANDAR SERI
BEGAWAN

Beaufort

Keningau

Lahad
Datu

BRUNEI **2**

Lotung
(1667m)

Magdalena
(1347m)

Ulu Temburong
National Park

Semporna

Tawau

9 Sipadan Island
Marine Reserve

Gunung Mulu
National Park

7

Murudi
(2423m)

Nunukan

Bario

Tarakan

*Celebes
Sea*

Tanjungselor

Tanjung
Redeb

Sangkulirang

Mahakam

10 Long
Iram

KALIMANTAN

Tenggarong

Samarinda

INDONESIA

Balikpapan

Tanahgrogot

Tanjung

Amuntai

N

Banjarmasin

Martapura

Pagatan

100 km

100 miles

6 The Kinabatangan river
is an ideal environment for
spotting Borneo's wildlife.
▶▶ page 249.

7 Explore underground
in the world's largest
limestone cave system in
Gunung Mulu National Park.
▶▶ page 159.

8 See wild orang-utans,
proboscis monkeys,
crocodiles and more in
Tanjung Puting National
Park. ▶▶ page 330.

9 Amorous turtles
delight snorkellers at the
world-class diving site of
Sipadan. ▶▶ page 254.

10 Relax on a boat
and travel slowly up the
Mahakam River past Dayak
villages. ▶▶ page 345.

Top Kuching.

Mid-left Kampong Ayer.

Mid-right Sepilok Orang-Utan Sanctuary.

Above Sungai Rejang.

Right Gunung Kinabalu.

Title page Stunning architecture of the Sultan Omar Ali Saifuddien Mosque, Brunei.

Pages 2-3 Paddle upriver to the Dayak heartland of Central Kalimantan.

Left Sungai Kinabatangan.

Below left Gunung Mulu National Park.

Below right Tanjung Puting National Park.

Bottom Sipadan.

Next page Mahakam River.

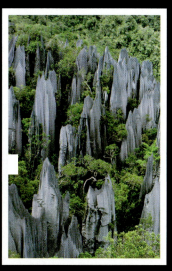

Contents

Contents

Footprint features

Essentials

Planning your trip

Where to go

The Malaysian states of Sarawak and Sabah are by far the most visited regions of Borneo and – along with Brunei – they are the island's most accessible entry points. Kalimantan, despite covering 73% of the Borneo land mass, is less frequented by tourists, and trips deep into its interior are about as adventurous as 'adventure' travel can get. Rivers, rather than roads, are the main arteries in Borneo and, even today, river travel forms the principal means of getting about the island. Borneo can accommodate trips of anything from a couple of days to a month or more; if you intend to head upriver independently and stay in longhouses, the more time you have the better.

Crossing international borders within Borneo is a fairly straightforward process, particularly if you are travelling between Malaysia and Brunei, or vice versa. You should, however, allow time within your itinerary for immigration and custom formalities. Visas are required for entering Kalimantan and these are not universally available at all border crossings. It may be necessary to fly to Jakarta and obtain a 30-day VOA (Visa On Arrival) before picking up a flight to Kalimantan. *See Getting around, page 20, and Visas and immigration, page 47.*

Carefully planning a trip to Borneo is crucial, especially for those with restricted time. Many places have quotas; for example, dive licences on Sipidan and beds on Kinabalu. Slots for visits to the Turtle Islands are often booked weeks in advance. It is therefore important to think in advance about which sights and activities you most want to see and do and then organize them before arrival. This does take some of the spontaneity out of travel, but saves the disappointment of being turned away or sleeping on an icy floor.

Stopover

If you are just passing through, the tiny sultanate of **Brunei** makes a good stopover. Allow a day for the sights around the capital, **Bandar Seri Begawan**, including a tour of Kampung Air (water village) and a proboscis monkey river safari. Those with a few days to play with can head for the **Ulu Temburong National Park**, with its excellent (if daunting) canopy walkway. Longer stays in Brunei could take in **Tasek Merimbun** (Brunei's largest lake) or longboat journeys upriver to Iban longhouses.

Two weeks

Two weeks will fly by in Borneo. The two most popular options for a fortnight would be either to speed about **Sarawak** and **Sabah**, taking in the major highlights – say, **Kuching**, **Bako National Park**, the **Rejang River** and **Gunung Mulu National Park** (in Sarawak); followed by **Mount Kinabalu**, **Sepilok**, the **Turtle Islands** and the **Kinabatangan Wetlands** (in Sabah) – or to stick to one state and explore it in more depth (a week, perhaps, in the tranquil **Kelabit Highlands** and another in the Kuching area; or a week at a beach resort in Sabah, combined with the climb up Mount Kinabalu). A few days in **Brunei** could also be incorporated, especially if this is your point of entry into Borneo. Alternatively, a fortnight would allow sufficient time to explore one of the interior regions of **Kalimantan**. This kind of two-week itinerary allows very little time to solidify travel arrangements and is perhaps best organized through an established ecotourism operator – this would help to make the most of a fairly intense visit.

Packing for Borneo

When packing, remember that most items are available in Borneo's main towns and cities – often at a lower price than in Western countries – and that laundry services are cheap and rapid, so there is no need to bring lots of supplies. You may wish to pack your favourite brand of sun cream or insect repellent, for instance, but even these will be fairly easy to track down in the major department stores, particularly in Brunei, where large shops are as sophisticated as their counterparts in the West. Of course, if you're heading to more remote areas, you will need to stock up in advance, as items may be unavailable or in short supply in local towns and villages.

The following lists provide an idea of what to take with you on a trip to Borneo: bumbag, first-aid kit, insect repellent, international driving licence, passport (valid for at least six months), photocopies of essential documents, spare passport photographs, sun protection, sunglasses, Swiss Army knife, torch, umbrella and phrase book. Those intending to stay in budget accommodation might also include: cotton sheet sleeping bag, money belt, padlock (for room and pack), soap, student card, towel and travel wash. For women travellers: a supply of tampons (although these are available in most towns) and a wedding ring for single female travellers who might want to ward off the attention of amorous admirers. There is a good smattering of camping grounds in Sabah and Sarawak. If you're intending to camp, then all the usual equipment is necessary: a tent, stove, cooking utensils, sleeping bag, etc. Iodine drops – good for purifying water, sterilizing jungle cuts and scratches, and loosening leeches – are difficult to come by in Malaysia but easily obtained in UK camping and outdoor shops. They are distributed by Lifesystems, www.lifesystems.co.uk.

Four to eight weeks

With plenty of time on your hands, you could take in all the major sites of Borneo. Even so, there's only so much jungle trekking and river travel one can endure, so you'll probably want to be choosy about where you go, pinpointing a specific area to explore in detail. In six weeks, you'll be able to cover most of the suggestions detailed below, though, to avoid burnout, it's best to pick and choose between the national parks. Also, bear in mind that journeys deep into the jungle or upriver can be expensive. You might begin in **Kuching**, administrative capital of Sarawak, using this attractive riverside city as a base for forays deeper into the state. Destinations not to be missed in the region include **Bako National Park**, on the tip of the Santubong Peninsula; the **Sarawak Cultural Village**; the **Semenggoh Wildlife Rehabilitation Centre**; and **Gunung Gading**, where giant rafflesia flowers bloom. Also, head up the **Batang Ai River** to stay at a series of Iban longhouses. The mighty **Batang Rejang River** runs through the heart of Sarawak and a journey upriver is a great way to get a feel for the state, passing Iban, Kenyah and Kayan longhouses along the way. You might make a brief visit to the Melanau heartland, **Mukah**, before heading along the coast to the magnificent **Niah Caves**. Inland from here is the **Gunung Mulu National Park**, one of Sarawak's highlights and home to the one of the world's largest caves (the Deer Cave). The **Kelabit Highlands**, meanwhile, offer a laid-back retreat high in the jungled mountains of Sarawak. From here, move on to Sabah via **Brunei**, stopping for a few days in the Brunei capital, with a river trip in search of proboscis monkeys and tasty fare at the *pasar malam*. Then, press on to **Kota Kinabalu**, capital of Sabah, and prepare for the ascent of Mount Kinabalu. Afterwards, rest your limbs at the **Poring Hot Springs**, or jump on a launch to the islands of the **Tungku Abdul Rahman National Park**. Then, cross the state to **Sandakan**, your base for a trip to the idyllic **Turtle Islands National Park** and to the **Sepilok Orang-Utan Rehabilitation Centre**. Next, head for the **Kinabatangan Wetlands** for your best chance of spotting wild elephants, orang-utans and proboscis monkeys. If you've got the time and money, spend a few days in the remarkable **Danum Valley Conservation Area**, which is rich in wildlife. Divers will want to head straight for Semporna to catch a launch out to **Pulau Sipadan**, reckoned by some to be the best dive site in the world. From here, adventurous travellers may decide to head across the border into **Kalimantan**. The east coast city of **Samarinda** is the launch pad for trips up the **Mahakam River**, which winds almost as far as the Sarawak border. Allow at least a week to get the most of a tour upriver. Or strike out north for the **Kutai National Park**. Then move on to **Banjarmasin** in the south, a city dominated by its waterways (and Borneo's largest conurbation). Nearby are the **Cempeka diamond fields**, while further afield, in Kalteng province, is Kalimantan's best known national park, the **Tanjung Puting National Park**, home to a concentration of wild orang-utans. West Kalimantan attracts few tourists, though die-hard travellers may like to venture up the **Kapuas River**, the longest river in Borneo.

When to go

Climate → *See also page 375.*
When planning a trip to Borneo, you'll need to take the rainy season into account. The worst rains are usually from November to February and some roads are impassable in these months. However, the main highways are usually open all year. Travelling during the wet season can have its advantages: hotel prices can be negotiable and resorts that may be excessively crowded at peak times of year can be wonderfully quiet. Conversely, in the dry season some rivers become unnavigable. In recent years, the onset of the wet and dry seasons in Borneo has become less predictable; environmentalists ascribe this to deforestation and/or global warming. So expect rain even in the dry season. It's also worth noting that the sky is often overcast rather than blue.

Festivals and events → *See Festivals and events, page 28.*
Note that in Sabah and Sarawak, school holidays run from mid- to late February, mid-May to early June, mid- to late August and late November to early January. During these periods it is advisable to book hotels in advance. Room rates also increase significantly during these holiday periods. During Ramadan travel can be more difficult and many restaurants close during daylight hours. After dusk many Muslims break their fast at stalls which do a roaring trade, although generally Ramadan is not a period when Muslims eat out, but instead dine at home.

A great time to visit Brunei is the week of the Sultan's birthday celebrations in mid-July. The event is celebrated with parties and fireworks and this is the only time when the palace grounds are open to the public.

What to do

Birdwatching

Borneo is home to hundreds of birds, including many migratory species, and there are great facilities for birdwatchers. Some of the best spots are: Bako National Park, Sarawak, page 108 ; Gunung Kinabalu Park, Sabah, page 229; Gunung Mulu National Park, Sarawak, page 159; Tanjung Puting National Park, Kalimantan, page 330; Tempasuk River, Sabah, page 225; and Ulu Temburong National Park, Brunei, page 296. For organized birdwatching holidays, see www.birdtours.co.uk.

Cookery courses

For those wishing to learn more about Malaysian cuisine, several state tourist boards offer short courses. Enquire at Tourism Malaysia information centres. A wide variety of Malaysian cookery books is available at leading bookshops.

Diving

Sarawak and Sabah Borneo's underwater life is as diverse as anywhere in the world. There are immaculate corals, enormous whalesharks and schools of hammerheads as well as shallow waters, rich in tiny and rare marine creatures. The island is the third largest in the world and its land mass is ringed by the South China, Sulu, Celebes and Java seas. Together they create some of the most varied diving on the planet.

The state of **Sabah** is *the* destination for those who come to Borneo for no other reason than to submerge. Sabah's coastal and offshore reefs are washed by currents that create favourable conditions and better visibility than its more southerly neighbour, **Sarawak**, whose shallow and somewhat murky waters attract less marine life. The island of Labuan, which sits between the two states, has also gained a moderate dive reputation due to four well-known wrecks. Sea and wind conditions vary, so diving can be challenging but there are many places that are suitable for novices. Tourism Malaysia, www.tourism.gov.my, has plenty of diving information on its website.

Sipadan, page 254, is the most famous of Borneo's dive destinations, a tiny spit of land that sits off the eastern tip of Borneo on the Litigan Reefs. It is an all-out magnet for divers. The walls off the island drop to well over 600 m and this unique geography has created a spectacular marine environment. If you're looking for big stuff, this is the place. Turtles are everywhere, so prolific and curious that they will follow you around on a dive. Sharks are easy to spot: white tips snooze on sandy shelves and hammerheads are frequently sighted. On the aptly named Barracuda Point, huge schools of this fish just hang about. There are plenty of small and colourful creatures to see as well. Dive conditions are variable, currents can be strong and dives are done as drifts. A few years ago all resorts were either closed or moved to Mabul Island (see below) or nearby Semporna. This closure was largely due to environmental concerns and now diver numbers in the Sipadan area are limited by a strict permit system. Licences to dive around Sipadan are usually booked weeks in advance; no surprise given its fame. A good website is www.scuba-junkie.com, with descriptions and maps detailing Sipadan and Mabul dives.

Sipadan's nearest neighbour is **Mabul**, page 255, best known as a special place for spotting small creatures. The island is quite large compared to both Sipadan and nearby Kapalai, with a village and several resorts, including **Sipadan-Mabul Resort** ① *Lot A-1-G Block A, KK Times Square, T088-486389, www.sipadan-mabul.com.my*. Offshore is an ugly oil rig, but beneath it is one of the best muck dives in the region. Shore dives are equally spectacular, with seahorses, frogfish and ghost pipefish. Conditions are mostly easy, although occasional currents can restrict dive choices.

Although charted on maps, **Kapalai**, page 256, is only a sand bar remaining from what was once a small island, a short motor from Sipadan. The flat topography extends underwater, yet visibility is reasonable as the reef mounds are washed daily by gentle tides. Corals tend to be low lying to the contours of the landscape and are a great haven for masses of sea creatures. Leaf fish, hawkfish and frogfish appear on virtually every dive. The **Sipadan Kapalai Resort** ⓘ *484 Bandar Sabindo, 91021 Tawau, Sabah, T089-765200, www.sipadan-kapalai.com*, is a water village perched on stilts over an aquarium-like lagoon and the dive from the jetty is superb: resident mating mandarin fish, blue-ringed octopus, batfish and even baby nurse sharks reside within a couple of fin strokes. Diving is year-round and suitable for everyone.

An hour or so by boat from Sandakan into the Sulu Sea, idyllic **Lankayan**, page 244, is ringed by an iridescent white beach and covered in a labyrinth of unruly jungle. The reefs surrounding the island are gently shelving, flat plateaus. A recent survey confirmed high biodiversity but visibility can be low at times, due to the proximity of the mainland and the high concentration of plankton. Diving here is about looking for the animals that thrive in these nutrient-rich conditions. There are plenty, including rare rhinopias and occasional whalesharks. Several shipwrecks ensure good variety, including one straight off the jetty. **Lankayan Island Resort** ⓘ *484 Bandar Sabindo, 91021 Tawau, Sabah, T089-765200, www.lankayan-island.com*, is open all year with easy conditions, making it a great place for trainees or new divers.

An hour north of Kota Kinabalu, **Layang Layang**, page 196, is a tiny, man-made island sitting on a stunning lagoon. Around the edge of the lagoon is a large atoll whose steep-sided walls drop off to unimaginable depths. Strong currents drag nutrients across the reefs, which, in turn, ensures prolific hard coral growth and creates a haven for masses of pelagic life. However, most people come for the curious hammerhead phenomena every Easter, when large schools swarm around Layang for a few weeks. **Layang Layang Island Resort** ⓘ *A-0-3 Block A, Megan Phileo Av II,12, Jln Yap Kwan Seng, 50450 Kuala Lumpur, T03-2170 2185, www.layanglayang.com*, is open March to September.

Pulau Labuan, page 210, is a Malay Federal Territory 8 km off the west coast of Sabah and a short hop from Brunei. The marine park off Labuan's south coast consists of three small islands with pretty beaches, ringed by some shallow reefs that are suitable for snorkelling. However, the real draw is the cluster of accessible wrecks. A couple – the American and Australian wrecks – date from the Second World War, while the Blue Water and Cement wrecks are more recent. This last is suitable for beginners, but the others require more advanced diving experience. Fish and coral growth on the structures are both reasonable, which is a good thing as the local reefs suffer from sediments and low visibility. The best dive season is May to September.

Miri, page 146, the coastal region off northern Sarawak, has a growing dive reputation but is sadly affected by the weather and the coastal marine environment. Miri sits on the mouth of a river that extends seawards as a flat plateau, never dropping far beyond 15 m. The areas can be awash with sediment, caused by both man-made and natural erosion. But arrive on a clear day, when there has been little rain, and the diving can be excellent. Further offshore are some dive sites that reach 30 m and several oil rigs that make great artificial reefs, attracting pelagics like barracuda and turtles. The reefs here are 'undiscovered' but whether you enjoy the diving will depend much on the visibility. Contact **Tropical Dives Miri** ⓘ *Lot 273, ground floor, Brighton Centre, Jln Temenggong Datuk Oyang Lawai, 98000 Miri, T085-415582, www.seridanmulu.com*.

Brunei The incredibly wealthy, oil-rich Sultanate of Brunei is better known for its wealthy capital backed by untouched rainforest than its underwater realm and there is good reason for that. Like Labuan Island just north and Miri to the south, the waters here are never very clear, having been affected by erosion, shipping and industry. Until recently, there wasn't even a dive centre. However, with the establishment of the PADI-affiliated **Scuba Tech Dive Centre** ⓘ *Empire Hotel and Country Club, Jerudong BG3122, Negara Brunei Darussalam, T673-261 1381, www.divebrunei.com*, and access to offshore reefs and the Labuan wrecks (see above), diving here has the potential to develop.

Kalimantan Comprising over two-thirds of Borneo, Kalimantan has much less of a reputation for diving than Sabah and Sarawak. This is simply because there is no easy way to reach the small resorts that hover off the northeast coast. Not far from the Sabah border are Sangalaki, Derawan and Kakaban, among others, and the diving here can be as thrilling and rewarding as the resorts around Sipadan.

Sangalaki is a small, lush island surrounded by a shallow lagoon that extends someway offshore and is completed by a series of patch reefs. This is a protected marine park and as such, the reefs are in good condition. The smaller reefs are rich with all sorts of marine creatures, but what attracts most divers are regular sightings of two much bigger animals: manta rays and turtles. There are several manta cleaning stations just north of the island and encounters are year round. Green turtles also use Sangalaki's lovely beach for nesting. Contact **Sangalaki Dive Lodge** ⓘ *PO Box 16360, 88000 Kota Kinabalu, Sabah, T088-242336, www.sangalaki.net*.

The islands of **Derawan** and **Kakaban** are less than an hour from Sangalaki and can be easily reached on a day trip. Derawan also has a resort, **Derawan Dive Resort** ⓘ *Komp Balikpapan Permai, G1 No34, Jln Jend Sudirman, Balikpapan, T0542-707 2615, www.derawan. com*, with a lovely house reef, an excellent jetty dive and several wall dives, a feature not found further south. Kakaban, however, has one of the most unusual features both in the region and on the planet. When geological forces pushed the atoll upwards, Kakaban's lagoon became landlocked, leaving a completely enclosed, brackish lake. The species that have developed here are unique and include masses of jellyfish that have evolved without the capacity to sting as they have no predators. There is no accommodation on Kakaban but the best diving and facilities can all be accessed from Sangalaki.

Most resorts have shuttle boats running from Berau on the mainland. There are flights to Berau from Banjarmasin and Balikpapan.

Diving practicalities It is hard to be general about diving seasons across Borneo. Although it is warm and humid all year, each state is governed by different wind patterns and currents. No matter what time of year you visit, or what area, the water is invariably warm. Temperatures hover between 25°C and 29°C, but may occasionally drop as low as 23°C.

In terms of equipment, a 3 mm wetsuit is as much as you're likely to need, unless you plan to do more than three dives a day. Almost every dive centre will rent good-quality equipment but bringing your own will considerably reduce costs. Prior to departure, check the baggage allowance with your airline and see if you can come to some arrangement for the extra weight.

While there are highly professional dive operations in Sabah and Kalimantan, the unpredictable nature of the diving in Brunei, Labuan and Sarawak means that the industry and its dive facilities are less developed. It's always worth asking around to find out what's on offer.

If you plan to dive make sure that you are in good health. Check that any dive company you use is reputable and has appropriate certification from BSAC or the **Professional Association of Diving Instructors** (PADI) ⓘ *Unit 7, St Philips Central, Albert Rd, St Philips, Bristol BS2 OTD, T0117-300 7234, www.padi.com.* Should you fall victim to a suspected decompression attack, immediately contact the 24-hr **Malaysian Diving Emergency Hotline** ⓘ *T05-930 4114,* for advice. Recompression facilities are available at the **Labuan Recompression Chamber** ⓘ *Labuan Pejabat Selam, Markas Wilayah Laut Dua, 87007, Labuan, T087-412122,* operated by the Malaysian Navy, and at the **Naval Medicine and Hyperbaric Centre** ⓘ *36 Admiralty Rd, West Singapore 759960, T6750 5632 (appointments), T6758 1733 (24-hr emergencies).* Note that air evacuation services, if available, are extremely expensive and hyperbaric chambers can charge up to US$800 per hour.

Good dive insurance is imperative. It is inexpensive and well worth it in case of a problem. Many general travel insurance policies do not cover diving. Contact **DAN** (the **Divers Alert Network**) ⓘ *www.diversalertnetwork.org,* **DAN Europe** ⓘ *www.daneurope. org,* or **DAN South East Asia Pacific** ⓘ *www.danseap.org,* for more information. If you have no insurance you can join online.

Trekking and climbing

There are numerous opportunities for climbing in Sarawak and Sabah. Most national parks offer hiking trails, but the best are in the parks listed below. Climbing Mount Kinabalu in Sabah, to be at the summit for sunrise, is one of the most popular hikes. New and exciting multi-day hikes are opening up in more remote regions of Sabah and Sarawak, such as the spectacular route between waterfalls in the Maliau Basin Conservation Area, Sabah. There are good treks in Gunung Kinabalu National Park, Sabah, page 229, Gunung Mulu National Park, Sarawak, page 159 and Niah National Park, Sarawak, page 143.

Whitewater rafting

Wild or whitewater rafting is not a well-established activity in Borneo, although there are some good spots to take to the swirl. Tour operators can organize rafting. Some of the best rivers are Kiulu river (Grade II), Sabah, page 205 (under Riverbug/Traverse Tours) and Padas river (Grade III), Sabah, page 206.

Getting there

Air

The majority of visitors will be touching down at one of three international airports: Kuala Lumpur (page 53), Singapore (page 70) or Brunei (page 286). Around 40 international carriers serve Kuala Lumpur and Singapore.

Flights from Europe

Royal Brunei Airlines ⓘ *49 Cromwell Rd, London, SW7 2ED, T020-7584 6660, www.bruneiair.com,* is the only airline that flies direct to Borneo from the UK; regular flights between London Heathrow and Bandar Seri take 16 hours, including a brief stop in Dubai for refuelling, and cost in the region of £650.

Direct flights from Europe to Kuala Lumpur (KL) leave from London Heathrow (12½ hours), Manchester, Amsterdam, Istanbul, Frankfurt, Milan, Moscow, Paris, Rome and

Zurich. From other cities a change of plane is often necessary en route. Many of the best deals can be found on Middle Eastern carriers and involve a brief stopover in the Gulf. Budget airline **AirAsia** (www.airasia.com) has direct flights from London Stansted to KL from where it operates numerous flights to Borneo.

Flights from Australasia
Royal Brunei Airlines ⓘ *BT Tower, 1 Market Sq, Sydney, T02-8267 5300, www.bruneiair.com*, flies direct to and from Australia and New Zealand, with daily flights to and from Auckland and Brisbane and five times weekly to Perth.

You can fly direct to KL from Sydney, Melbourne, Brisbane, Darwin, Perth and Auckland (flights range from five to nine hours). Budget airlines **Tiger Airways** (www.tigerairways.com), **Jet Star Asia** (www.jetstarasia.com) and **AirAsia** (www.airasia.com) connect Singapore and KL with Australasia. From other cities a change of plane is often necessary en route.

Flights from North America
There are no direct flights to Borneo from the USA and Canada. To KL, there are direct flights from Los Angeles, Houston and New York. Many of the North American carriers stop over in Northeast Asia on the way.

Flights from Southeast Asia
The vast majority of tourists heading to Borneo will first fly to KL or Singapore and then transfer flights for the remainder of the journey (see below). There are also flights to KL and Singapore from all the regional centres in Southeast Asia.

Flights from KL and Singapore
Connecting flights from KL and Singapore go to: Bandar Seri Begawan (Brunei); Kuching Bintulu, Miri and Sibu (Sarawak); Kota Kinabalu, Pulau Labuan, Sandakan and Tawau (Sabah). The main airlines serving these destinations are budget ones. **AirAsia** operates flights out of both KL and Singapore, **Tiger Airways** and **Jet Star Asia** both fly to Borneo from Singapore. Full service carriers include **Malaysian Airlines (MAS**, www.malaysiaairlines.com), **Royal Brunei Airlines** and **Singapore Airlines** (www.singaporeair.com). **Silk Air** (www.silkair.com) has daily flights from Singapore to Balikpapan (Kalimantan). There are also flights to Borneo from other Southeast Asian hubs, including Clark (Manila) Jakarta, Johor Bahru, Macau and Penang on **AirAsia**; Hong Kong, Johor Bahru, Cebu, Seoul and Shanghai on **MAS**; Bangkok to Bandar Seri Begawan on **Royal Brunei**, and Jakarta to Balikpapan, Banjarmasin or Pontianak with **Mandala Airlines** (www.mandalaair.com), **Lion Air** (www.lionair.co.id) and **Garuda Indonesia** (www.garuda-indonesia.com).

Discount flight agents

UK and Ireland
STA Travel, 86 Old Brompton Rd, London, SW7 3LH, T0871-230 0040, www.statravel.co.uk. Other branches across the UK and in cities worldwide. Specialists in low-cost student/youth flights and tours and insurance.
Trailfinders, 194 Kensington High St, London, W8 7RG, T0845-058 5858

www.trailfinders.com. Other branches across the UK and in major cities worldwide.

North America
Air Brokers International, 323 Geary St, Suite 411, San Francisco, CA94102, T1-800-883 3273, www.airbrokers.com. Consolidator and specialist on RTW and Circle Pacific tickets.
Discount Airfares Worldwide On-Line, www.etn.nl/discount.htm.

A hub of consolidator and discount agent links.

STA Travel, 5900 Wilshire Blvd, Suite 2110, Los Angeles, CA 90036, T1-800-781 4040, www.sta-travel.com. Branches across US.

Travel CUTS, 187 College St, Toronto, Ontario, M5T 1P7, T1-866-246 9762, www.travel cuts.com. Specialist in student fares and IDs. Branches in other Canadian cities.

Travelocity, www.travelocity.com. An online consolidator.

Flight Centre, 82 Elizabeth St, Sydney, T1-300-733867, www.flightcentre.com.au; 205 Queen St, Auckland, T09-309 6171. Plus other branches.

STA Travel, www.statravel.com.au. Offices across New Zealand and Australia. Good deals on flights, insurance and hotels.

Travel.com.au, 80 Clarence St, Sydney, T02-929 01500, www.travel.com.au.

Getting around

Owing to Borneo's inadequate road network, flying is by far the easiest way to travel around the island, with frequent and inexpensive flights between the main towns. Speed ferries also skirt the island, passing immigration points either en route or at the departure and arrival points. The cheapest (and slowest) means of travelling around Borneo is by bus. When travelling around the island, remember that Sarawak has its own immigration rules (independent to those of Malaysia), with visitors receiving a one-month entry stamp, which needs to be renewed in Kuching for longer stays. Also, travellers heading to Kalimantan should check the latest visa situation before travelling as this can be volatile in Indonesia.

Air

Malaysian Airlines (MAS, www.malaysiaairlines.com.my), its subsidiary **MASwings** and the budget airline **AirAsia** (www.airasia.com) have extensive flight networks in Borneo. Flying is relatively inexpensive but flights get booked up on public holidays (see page 28). **MASwings** offers services to many rural parts of Sabah and Sarawak on its ATRs, Fokker 50s and Twin Otters. Flights get booked quickly so it's best to book online as soon as possible. It serves Ba'kelalan, Bario, Bintulu, Kota Kinabalu, Kuching, Lahad Datu, Pulau Labuan, Lawas, Limbang, Long Akah, Long Banga, Long Seridan, Long Lellang, Marudi, Miri, Mukah, Mulu, Sandakan, Sibu, Tanjung Manis and Tawau. Local **MAS** offices are listed under each town.

AirAsia serves Bintulu, Clark (Manila), Johor Bahru, Kota Kinabalu, Kuching, Pulau Labuan, Miri, Penang, Sandakan, Sibu and Tawau. **Indonesia AirAsia** also connects Jakarta with Kota Kinabalu and Balikapapan.

There is a thrice-weekly flight between Pontianak and Kuching operated by Indonesian carrier **Batavia Air** (www.batavia-air.co.id). In addition, **Royal Brunei Airlines** (www.bruneiair.com) flies from Bandar Seri to Kuching, Kota Kinabalu, although note that it is usually cheaper to fly from Malaysian Borneo into Brunei rather than vice versa.

Flying in Kalimantan often works out cheaper than taking the rough overland option, and is many times faster and more comfortable. In 2007, after a string of high-profile air disasters, the EU blacklisted all Indonesian airlines from entering EU airspace and warned its citizens to avoid flying on Indonesian airlines. Following the ban, the Indonesian government went to great efforts to improve the poor safety records. Better maintenance and newer planes have made the Indonesian skies a much better place to be and 2009 saw the EU blacklist being lifted from four Indonesian airlines: Garuda, Mandala, Airfast Indonesia and Premair. The main airline connecting townships and cities in Kalimantan is **Kal Star** (www.kalstaronline.com), which uses ATRs and Fokkers. A newcomer to the Kalimantan flying scene is **Susi Air** (www.susiair.com) that flies so-called 'Pioneer routes' to remote destinations such as Long Ampung in the Apo Kayan and Melak on the Mahakam using small Cessnas. Other airlines connecting cities on the island and to destinations in Java include **Mandala** (www.mandalaair.com), **Lion Air** (www.lionair.co.id), **Batavia Air** (www.batavia-air.co.id), and **Indonesia Air Transport** (www.iat.co.id).

Note For the best prices, book online as early as possible.

Rail

Trains are not a feasible way of getting around Borneo as the infrastructure is virtually nonexistent and the rolling stock very old. In the state of Sabah, however, there is one railway line, which passes through the spectacular Padas River Gorge (see page 206). However, this line is currently being upgraded and will be out of action until late 2010.

River and sea

There are speedy ferry services to Brunei every day from Limbang and Lawas (Sarawak) and from Pulau Labuan, which in turn has an onward service to Kota Kinabalu in Sabah. Tawau, in Sabah, is the main crossing point between Malaysian and Indonesian Borneo, with ferries leaving for Nunakan and Tarakan.

There are excellent coastal and upriver express boat services in Sarawak and Sabah, where local water transport comes into its own, as lack of roads makes it the only viable means of communication. Express boat services are also the primary means of travelling around Kalimantan. If there is no regular boat it is nearly always possible to charter a local longboat, although this can be expensive. In the dry season the upper reaches of many rivers are unnavigable except by smaller boats. In times of heavy rain, logs and branch debris can make rivers unsafe.

Road

Travel around Borneo via road is not always easy, as the network is limited and some routes are not in a good state of repair. The highway between KK and Sandakan, for example, is occasionally blocked by mudslides after heavy rain. Recently the governments of Sabah and Sarawak have started to counter this situation with extensive investment in road infrastructure; in some places road surfacing has outpaced public transport, which has yet to establish itself in many areas. Air or water transport may be the only choice, or provide at least the more comfortable options.

It is possible to cross overland from Sarawak and Sabah to Kalimantan and Brunei. The main crossing point into Kalimantan is in the west, between Kuching (Sarawak) and Pontianak (Kalimantan), with frequent buses between these two towns. From Miri (Sarawak) there are regular buses to Kuala Belait and Bandar Seri Begawan (Brunei), with an immigration post on either side of the border where passengers disembark briefly for customs formalities. Less regular bus services run between Sipitang (Sabah) to Bangar (Brunei), from where there is a ferry service to the capital.

Bus

Air-conditioned buses connect major towns; seats can be reserved and prices are reasonable, varying according to whether the bus is express or regular, and between companies. (Be warned that the air conditioning can be very cold.) In larger towns there may be a number of bus stops and some private companies may operate directly from their own offices. Beyond the main towns, buses are less reliable and road conditions are poorer. Details of routes, fares and timetables are listed under Transport in the main text.

Car hire

Visitors can hire a car provided they are in possession of an international driving licence, are aged 24 to 65 years and have at least one year's driving experience. In Sabah and Sarawak, car hire costs approximately RM150 to RM250 per day depending on the model and the company. 4WDs are expensive but they are readily available and are de rigueur in Sabah. Cheaper weekly and monthly rates and special deals may be available.

Driving is on the left; give way to drivers on the right. The wearing of seat belts is compulsory for front seat passengers and the driver. Most road signs are international but note that *awas* means caution.

Hitchhiking

It is easy for foreigners to hitch in Borneo, as long as they look reasonably presentable. However, hitching is not advisable for women travelling alone.

Taxi

There are two types of taxi in Borneo – local and 'out-station', or long distance. Local taxis are fairly cheap in Sabah, Sarawak and Kalimantan, but it is rare to find a taxi with a meter, so you will need bargaining skills. Taxis in Brunei are metered.

Out-station taxis connect towns and cities. They operate on a shared-cost basis: as soon as four passengers turn up the taxi sets off. Alternatively, it is possible to charter the whole taxi for the price of four single fares. Taxi stands are usually next door to major bus stations. If shared, taxis usually cost about twice as much as buses but are much faster. For groups, taking a taxi makes good sense.

Maps

Maps are widely available in Malaysia and Singapore. The Malaysian tourist board produces good maps of Kuala Lumpur and a series of not-so-good state maps. The Sabah and Sarawak tourist boards also publish reasonable maps. Soviet-era air charts are often the most detailed maps available, but these must be ordered from a specialist such as Stanfords (see below) with plenty of time to spare. Availability isn't always guaranteed.

In the UK, the best selection is available from **Stanfords** ① *12-14 Long Acre, London WC2E 9LP, T020-7836 1321, www.stanfords.co.uk.* Also recommended is **McCarta** ① *15 Highbury Place, London N15 1QP, T020-7354 1616.*

Country maps

Bartholomew Singapore and Malaysia (1:150,000); **Nelles Malaysia** (1:1,500,000); **Nelles Indonesia** (1:4,000,000). Decent maps of Brunei are more or less impossible to obtain.

Sleeping

Sarawak and Sabah → *See also box, page 24.*

Room rates are subject to 5-10% tax. Many of the major international chains have hotels, such as **Hilton**, **Holiday Inn** and **Hyatt**. Room rates in the big hotels have been fairly stable for the last few years. The number of four- and five-star hotel rooms has also multiplied and this, combined with a generally depressed economy, has helped to keep prices stable. By world standards even the most expensive hotels are good value. It is also worth noting that in tourist resorts, many hotels have two, sometimes three, room tariffs: one for weekdays, one for weekends and, sometimes, a third for holiday periods. Room rates can vary substantially between these periods.

Superb guesthouses and 'flashpacker' boutique hostels are spreading fast across Sabah and Sarawak, with competition stiff in major centres such as Kuching and Kota Kinabalu, these can represent superb value.

It is often possible to stay with families in Malay kampongs (villages) as part of the so-called homestay programme (contact the local tourist office or travel agent for more information) or in longhouses, where rates are at the discretion of the visitor (see page 124). For accommodation in national parks it is necessary to book in advance.

Youth hostels are only available in Kuala Lumpur and Kota Kinabalu. There are not many campsites either but wild camping is easy. In Sabah, you can camp exactly where you want to be, for example at Tunkul Abdul Rahman Marine Park.

Brunei

Brunei has a real dearth of places to stay – though, given its size and population, this should come as no particular surprise – and accommodation is significantly more expensive than in neighbouring Sarawak, Sabah and, especially, Kalimantan. Most of the hotels are functional, business-oriented places, and there are virtually no budget options, apart from the excellent and extraordinarily quiet youth hostel (**D Pusat Belia**, page 302) in Bandar Seri Begawan and the indigenous longhouses, some of which offer homestay programmes. At the top end, Brunei boasts the outrageously decadent six-star **Empire Hotel and Country Club** (see page 303), one of the world's flashiest hotels.

With relatively small visitor numbers, there shouldn't be a problem finding a room, whatever your budget. What's more, the top-end hotels frequently offer promotions.

Kalimantan

Major towns and cities usually have a fair range of accommodation for all budgets. However, visitors venturing off the beaten track may find hotels restricted to dingy, overpriced places catering for local businessmen and officials. Terminology can be confusing: a *losmen* is a cheaper hotel; a *wisma* is a guesthouse.

The star system used in Indonesia can give a rough guide to the price of the establishment. The *melati* (flower) system is for cheaper hotels; while the *bintang* (star) system is for more expensive hotels. All hotels are required to display their room rates on a price list, with rooms on higher floors usually cheaper. Hotels in the middle and lower price categories often have some kind of breakfast included in the room rate. This can vary from sad white toast and tea to scrumptious *nasi goreng* or a hearty noodle soup. In the top-end hotels, a service charge (10%) and government tax (11%) are added onto the bill; they are usually excluded from the advertised room rate, which tends to be quoted in

Sleeping price codes

LL	over US$200	**L**	US$130-200
AL	US$90-130	**A**	US$40-90
B	US$20-40	**C**	US$10-20
D	US$5-10	**E**	US$2.50-5
F	under US$2.50		

Price codes refer to the cost of two people sharing a double room in the high season.

Top-end hotels (LL-A)

Hotels in this top of this bracket are confined to Brunei and Singapore. The rest are beautifully appointed and offer impeccable service and an array of facilities and business services. At the bottom of this bracket, hotels still have a good range of services and facilities, sometimes including a pool, gym and maybe a spa. These are very competitively priced, given the standards of service.

Mid-range hotels (B-D)

Hotels at the top of this bracket provide a basic range of services and facilities including a coffee shop and/or simple restaurant and all rooms should have air conditioning. Places in the **C** category will usually have the option of air-conditioned or fan-cooled rooms and a choice of attached/shared bathrooms. In Sarawak and Sabah, backpacker hostels fall into this category, and usually offer good travel advice, laundry services, breakfast facilities and maybe a communal fridge and kitchen; they can be suitable for families on a budget. Most hotels in the bottom end of this bracket (**D**) are located in town centres; they are often noisy and many are pretty scruffy joints with not much in the way of services or facilities. Rooms may have air conditioning and attached bathrooms, but cheaper ones will have fans and communal bathrooms. Some fine, old, tumbledown colonial relics in this range offer good value for money. Youth hostels fall into this price category.

Budget hotels (E-F)

For this price range you are looking at a simple room with shared bathroom and fan in a lodging house, guesthouse or hostel. Some backpacker places will have simple rooms and dorms in the top end of this bracket. In the lower end, you'll get a space in a dorm at a bottom-of-the-range hostel or a simple A-frame near the beach, if you're lucky. In Kalimantan you'll get a fan-cooled room, often with shared *mandi* (water tank and ladle) and Asian squat toilet. Toilet paper and towels are unlikely to be provided, although bed linen will be. Places can vary a great deal, and change very rapidly. Other travellers are the best source of up-to-the-minute reviews. There aren't any hotels in Singapore in this price category.

US dollars. During the low season, hotels in tourist destinations may halve their room rates, so it's always worth bargaining or asking whether there's a special price.

Baths and showers are not a feature of many cheaper *losmen*, instead a *mandi* – a water tank and ladle – is used. Water is ladled from the tank and splashed over the head.

Some bathrooms will also have a shower attachment, occasionally with hot water although more often not. The traditional Asian toilet is of the squat variety. Water scooped from a *mandi*, or a large water jar, is used to flush the bowl. In cheaper accommodation you are expected to bring your own towels, soap and toilet paper and the bed may only have a bottom sheet and pillow (so bring your own top sheet if you want to keep the mosquitoes at bay).

Camping is not common and, even in national parks, camping facilities are poor and limited. It is possible to camp in Tanjung Puting. Arrange it with a tour operator in Kumai as part of a *klotok* river tour. Operators should be able to provide equipment.

Eating → See also the Food glossary, page 385.

Sarawak and Sabah

Malaysians love their food and the dishes of the three main communities, Malay, Chinese and Indian, comprise a hugely varied national menu. Even within each ethnic cuisine, there is a vast choice; for example, there are North Indian, South Indian and Indian Muslim dishes. Malaysia also has great seafood, which the Chinese do best. You'll also find various tribal specialities. For non-meat eaters, there are numerous Chinese and Malay vegetarian dishes, although it is not unusual to find slivers of meat even when a vegetable dish is specifically requested.

The best **Malay** food is usually found at stalls in hawker centres. The staple diet is rice and curry, which is rich and creamy due to the use of coconut milk. Herbs and spices include chilli, ginger, turmeric, coriander, lemongrass, anise, cloves, cumin, caraway and cinnamon.

Cantonese and **Hainanese** cooking are the most prevalent Chinese cuisines in Malaysia. Some of the more common Malaysian-Chinese dishes are Hainanese chicken rice (rice cooked in chicken stock and served with steamed or roast chicken), *char kway teow* (Teochew-style fried noodles, with eggs, cockles and chilli paste), *luak* (Hokkien oyster omelette), dim sum (steamed dumplings and patties), *bak kut teh* (Hokkien herbal pork stock soup with pork ribs) and *yong tow foo* (beancurd and vegetables stuffed with fish). Good Chinese food is available in restaurants, coffee shops and from hawker stalls.

Indian cooking can be divided into three schools: northern and southern (no beef) and Muslim (no pork). Northern dishes tend to be more subtly spiced, use more meat and are served with breads. Southern dishes use fiery spices, emphasize vegetables and are served with rice. The best known North Indian food is tandoori, which is served with delicious fresh naan breads, baked in ovens onsite. Other pancakes include roti, *thosai* and chapati. Malaysia's famous *mamak* men are Indian Muslims who are highly skilled at making everything from *the tarik* (see below) to rotis.

The Kadazan form the largest ethnic group in Sabah and their **Sabahan** food tends to use mango and can be on the sour side.

The cheapest places to eat are in hawker centres and roadside stalls (often concentrated in or close to night markets) where it is possible to eat well for less than RM5. Stalls may serve Malay, Indian or Chinese dishes and even pseudo-Western (think deep-fried chicken chop, chips and cold baked beans). Next in the sequence of sophistication and price come the ubiquitous *kedai kopi* (coffee shops), where a meal will cost upwards of RM5. Usually run by Chinese or Indian families, rather than Malay, they open at around 0900 and close in the early evening. Some open at dawn to serve dim sum to people on their way to work and they are also the only coffee shops where it is possible to track down a cold beer. Malay-run *kedai kopi* are good for lunch with their *nasi campur* spreads. Hotel restaurants regularly lay

Eating price codes

✓✓✓ over US$10   ✓✓ US$3.50-10   ✓ under US$3.50

Prices refer to the average cost of a two-course meal for one person, not including drinks or service charge.

on buffet spreads, which are fair value at around RM30, often much cheaper than the price of a room would suggest; these are also usually open to non-residents.

Drink Soft drinks, mineral water and freshly squeezed fruit drinks are available. Anchor and Tiger beer are widely sold and are cheapest at the hawker stalls (RM5-7 per bottle). A beer will cost RM8-15 per bottle in coffee shops. The potent Malaysian brewed Guinness Foreign Extra is popular, mainly because the Chinese believe it has medicinal qualities. Malaysians like strong coffee and unless you specify *kurang manis* (less sugar), *tak mahu manis* (no sugar) or *kopi kosong* (black, no sugar), it will come with lashings of condensed milk. Those who want their drinks without milk and sugar should ask for *teh/kopi o kosong*.

One of the most interesting cultural refinements of the Indian Muslim community is the *mamak* man, who is famed for *the tarik* (pulled tea), which is thrown across a distance of about a metre, from one cup to another, with no spillages. The idea is to cool it for customers but it's become an art form; *mamak* men cultivate a nonchalant look when pouring. Malaysian satirist Kit Lee says a tea stall *mamak* "could 'pull' tea in free fall without spilling a drop, while balancing a *beedi* on his lower lip and making a statement on Economic Determinism".

Brunei

The variety and quality of food in Brunei is good, with a medley of restaurants, market stalls and food courts offering a wide range of cuisines from Malay, Chinese and Indian, to Indonesian, Thai and Japanese. Because of Brunei's relative wealth, there isn't the same density of street food as elsewhere in Borneo. Nevertheless, the informal local restaurants and food courts are still the best places to sample good local cuisine – and at great prices.

Drink Brunei is a 'dry' country: sale of alcohol is banned, while consumption is prohibited for Muslims. Certain restaurants will allow non-Muslims to bring their own alcohol to drink with the meal, but always check in advance.

Kalimantan

Indonesians will eat rice – or *nasi* (milled, cooked rice) – at least twice a day. Breakfast often consists of leftover rice, stir-fried and served up as *nasi goreng*. Mid-morning snacks are often sticky rice cakes or *pisang goreng* (fried bananas). Rice is the staple for lunch, served up with two or three meat or fish and vegetable dishes and followed by fresh fruit. The main meal is supper, which is served quite early and again consists of rice, this time accompanied by as many as five or six other dishes. *Sate/satay* (grilled skewers of meat), *soto* (a nourishing soup) or *bakmi* (noodles, a dish of Chinese origin) may be served first.

Foodstalls (*warung*) may be temporary structures or more permanent buildings, with simple tables and benches. In the larger cities, there may be an area of *warung*, all under one roof. Night markets (*pasar malam*) are usually better for eating than day markets.

Feast days, such as Lebaran which marks the end of Ramadan, are a cause for great celebration and traditional dishes are served. *Lontong* or *ketupat* are made at this time. They are both versions of boiled rice – simmered in a small container or bag, so that as it cooks, the rice is compressed to make a solid block.

In addition to rice, there are a number of other common ingredients used across the country. Coconut milk, ginger, chilli peppers and peanuts are used nationwide, while dried salted fish and soybeans are important sources of protein.

Drink Although Indonesia is a predominantly Muslim country, alcoholic drinks are widely available. The two most popular beers – light lagers – are the locally brewed Anker and Bintang brands. Imported spirits are usually only sold in the more expensive restaurants and hotels. There are, however, a number of local brews including *brem* (rice wine), *arak* (rice whisky) and *tuak* (palm wine).

Water must be boiled before it is safe to drink. Hotels and most restaurants, as a matter of course, should boil the water they offer customers. Ask for *air minum*, literally drinking water. Bottled water is cheap. Mineral water – of which the most famous is **Aqua** (*aqua* has become the generic word for mineral water) – can be found anywhere with a significant population. There have been some reports of empty mineral water bottles being refilled with tap water, so always check the seal before accepting a bottle.

Western bottled and canned drinks are widely available in Indonesia and are relatively cheap. Alternatively, most restaurants will serve *air jeruk* – citrus fruit juices – with or without ice (*es*). Ice in many places is fine but in cheaper restaurants and away from tourist areas, many people recommend taking drinks without ice. The milk of a fresh coconut is a good thirst-quencher and a good source of potassium and glucose. Fresh, strong coffee (*kopi*) is usually served sickeningly sweet (*kopi manis*) and black; if you want to have it without sugar, you should ask for it '*tidak pakai gula*'. Tea (*the*), usually weak, is obtainable almost everywhere. If you want tea without sugar, specify *teh tawar*. Hot ginger tea is a refreshing alternative.

Entertainment

Kuching and Kota Kinabalu have a good selection of pubs and clubs and things can get a little wild in the late hours. Miri, Bintulu and Labuan are renowned for their sleazy karaoke bars, catering for booze and lust-filled oil workers fresh off the rigs or Bruneians out for a weekend bender. Larger towns in Sabah and Sarawak have a choice of cinemas showing Hollywood movies, along with local films, Bollywood blockbusters and films from Japan, China and Korea. Note that Bollywood movies and local films are unlikely to have English subtitles.

In a dry country like Brunei, you might expect there to be some replacement entertainment. But come evening everything quietens down. The centre of Bandar Seri Begawan itself is eerily deserted after dark. The suburb of Gadong is probably the busiest place in the evenings, its lively *pasar malam* churning out local food until late at night to an endless stream of Bruneians, who turn up in their 4WDs, pick up their food, then drive home to eat it. If there were tables and chairs laid out at the night market, it might become Brunei's prime hangout; but then that wouldn't be in the spirit of things.

Festivals and events

Islam is the dominant religion in Borneo. The timing of Islamic festivals is an art rather than a science and is calculated on the basis of local sightings of various phases of the moon. Muslim festivals move forward by around nine or 10 days each year. For exact dates of local festivals, see www.tourism.gov.my or www.holidays.net. Chinese, Indian (Hindu) and some Christian holidays are also movable. To make things even more exciting, each state has its own public holidays when shops close and banks pull down their shutters. This makes calculating public holidays in advance a bit of a quagmire of lunar events, assorted kings' birthdays and tribal festivals.

Islamic festivals

Maal Hijrah (Awal Muharram) (public holiday in Malaysia, Brunei and Indonesia) marks the first day of the Muslim calendar and celebrates the Prophet Muhammad's journey from Mecca to Medina on the lunar equivalent of 16 Jul AD 622. Religious discussions and lectures mark the event.
Maulidur Rasul (public holiday in Malaysia), **Maulud Nabi** (public holiday in Brunei), **Garebeg Maulad** (public holiday in Indonesia) commemorates Prophet Muhammad's birthday in AD 571. Koran recitals and processions in most Malaysian towns; public gatherings and coloured lights in BSB. Celebrations in Indonesia begin a week before and last a month, with *selamatans* in homes, mosques and schools.
Israk Mekraj (public holiday in Brunei), **Al Miraj/Isra Miraj Nabi Muhammed** (public holiday in Indonesia) celebrates the Prophet's journey to Jerusalem, led by the archangel Gabriel, and his ascension through the 7 heavens. He speaks with God and returns to earth the same night, with instructions, which include the 5 daily prayers.
Awal Ramadan (public holiday in Brunei) is the first day of Ramadan, a month of fasting for all Muslims. Muslims abstain from all food and drink (as well as smoking) from sunrise to sundown; if they are very strict, Muslims do not even swallow their own saliva during daylight hours. The elderly and pregnant or menstruating women are exempt from fasting.
Nuzul Al-Quran (public holiday in Brunei) is the Anniversary of the Revelation of the Koran. Includes various religious observances, climaxing in a Koran-reading competition.
Hari Raya Puasa/Hari Raya Aidil Fitri/ Lebaran/Eid (public holiday in Malaysia, Brunei and Indonesia) celebrates the end of Ramadan, the Islamic fasting month, with prayers and celebrations. In order for Hari Raya to be declared, the new moon of Syawal has to be sighted; if it is not, fasting continues for another day. It is the most important time of the year for Muslim families to get together. This is not a good time to travel; trains, planes and buses are booked up weeks in advance and hotels are also often full. Malays living in towns and cities return home to their village, where it is open house for relatives and friends, and special local delicacies are served. Hari Raya is also enthusiastically celebrated by Indian Muslims in Malaysia. In Brunei, families keep themselves to themselves on the first day but on the second they throw their doors open. Everyone dresses up in their best clothes; men wear a length of *tenunan* around their waist, a cloth woven with gold thread.
Hari Raya Qurban (public holiday in Malaysia), **Hari Raya Haji** (public holiday in Brunei), **Idhul Adha** (public holiday in Indonesia). Held on the 10th day of Zulhijjah, the 12th month of the Islamic calendar, this is the 'festival of the sacrifice' and marks the willingness of Abraham to sacrifice his son. The festival marks the return of pilgrims from the Haj to Mecca. The Haj is one of the 5 keystones of Islam.
In the morning, prayers are offered and later, families hold open house. Those who can afford it sacrifice goats or cows to be distributed to the

poor. Muslim men who have been on the Haj wear a white skullhat. Many Malays have the title Haji in their name, meaning they've made the pilgrimage to Mecca.

Unlike in neighbouring Islamic states, the cost of a trip to Mecca is affordable for many in Brunei, so there is a large population of Hajis. Every year 4000 Bruneians go on the Haj. If any pilgrim has difficulty making ends meet, the Ministry of Religious Affairs will provide a generous subsidy.

Sarawak and Sabah

Schools in Sabah and Sarawak have 5 breaks in the year, generally falling in Jan (1 week), Mar (2 weeks), May (3 weeks), Aug (1 week), and October (4 weeks). State holidays, which can last several days, may disrupt travel itineraries, so confirm your travel plans in advance. In addition, note that some government offices are closed on the 1st and 3rd Sat of each month.

Apart from festivals celebrated throughout the country – including Chinese New Year, Christmas and Hari Raya – Sabah and Sarawak have their own festivals. Exact dates are available from the tourist offices in the capitals.

1 Jan New Year's Day (public holiday).
Jan/Feb Thaipusam (movable) is celebrated by Hindus throughout Malaysia in honour of their deity Lord Subramanian (also known as Lord Muruga), who represents virtue, bravery, youth and power. Held during full moon in the month of Thai, it is a day of penance and thanksgiving.
Jan/Feb Chinese New Year (movable; public holiday) a 15-day lunar festival. Chinatown streets are crowded for weeks with shoppers buying traditional oranges, which signify luck. Lion, unicorn or dragon dances welcome in the New Year and, unlike in Singapore, thousands of firecrackers are ignited to ward off evil spirits. Chap Goh Mei is the 15th day of the Chinese New Year and brings celebrations

to a close. The Chinese believe that in order to find good husbands, girls should throw oranges into the river/sea on this day. In Sarawak the festival is known as **Guan Hsiao Cheih** (Lantern Festival).
1 Feb Federal Territory Day (state holiday in KL and Pulau Labuan).
Mar/Apr Easter (movable). Good Fri is a public holiday in Sabah and Sarawak.
1 May Labour Day (public holiday).
Kurah Aran is celebrated by the Bidayuh tribe in Sarawak (see page 175) after the paddy harvest is over.
May Kadazan Harvest Festival or Tadau Keamatan (movable; state holiday in Sabah and Labuan). Marks the end of the rice harvest in Sabah; the *magavau* ritual is performed to nurse the spirit back to health in readiness for the next planting season. Celebrated with feasting, *tapai* (rice wine) drinking, dancing and general merrymaking. There are also agricultural shows, buffalo races, cultural performances and traditional games. The traditional *sumazal* dance is a highlight.
May (movable) Miri International Jazz Festival is a well received international jazz extravaganza, which attracts performers from as far away as New Orleans, Cuba, Morocco and Europe. See www.mirijazzfestival.com for the latest on the upcoming treats and more.
May Wesak Day (movable; public holiday except Labuan). The most important day in the Buddhist calendar, celebrates the Buddha's birth, death and enlightenment. Temples are packed with devotees offering incense, joss sticks and prayers. Lectures on Buddhism and special exhibitions are held.
May/Jun Gawai Dayak (movable; state holiday in Sarawak) is the major festival of the year for the Iban of Sarawak; longhouses party continuously for a week. The Gawai celebrates the end of the rice harvest and welcomes the new planting season. The main ritual is called *magavau* and nurses the spirit of the grain back to health in advance of the planting season. Like the Kadazan harvest festival in Sabah (see above), visitors are welcome to join in, but in Sarawak, the harvest

festival is much more traditional. Urban residents return to their rural roots for a major binge. On the 1st day of celebrations everyone dresses up in traditional costumes and sings, dances and drinks *tuak* rice wine until they drop.

Jun Dragon Boat Festival (movable) honours the suicide of an ancient Chinese poet hero, Qu Yuan. To press for political reform and protest against corruption, he drowned himself in Mi Luo River. To try and save him fishermen played drums and threw rice dumplings to try and distract vultures. His death is marked with dragon boat races and the enthusiastic consumption of rice dumplings.

Jun Gawai Batu (Sarawak) is a whetstone feast held by Iban farmers.

3 Jun Official birthday of HM the Yang di-Pertuan Agong (public holiday).

Jul Rainforest World Music Festival (movable). This popular festival takes place just outside Kuching at the superb and aptly green venue of the Sarawak Cultural Village. Indigenous performers, from Borneo and further afield, combine with well-known world music acts to share music, performance skills and their diverse cultures and experiences. Workshops, jamming sessions and talks are a major feature of the multi-day event. For details of the 2010 festival and beyond, see www.rainforest music-borneo.com or contact the Sarawak Tourism Board, Jln Tun Abang Haji Openg, Kuching, T082-410944, www.sarawaktourism.com.

Aug Mooncake or Lantern Festival (movable). This Chinese festival marks the overthrow of the Mongol Dynasty in China; celebrated, as the name suggests, with the exchange and eating of mooncakes. According to Chinese legend secret messages of revolt were carried inside these cakes and led to the uprising. Children light festive lanterns while women pray to the Goddess of the Moon.

31 Aug Hari Kebangsaan/National Day (public holiday) commemorates Malaysian Independence (*merdeka*) in 1957. In Sarawak it's celebrated in a different capital each year.

Aug/Sep Festival of the Hungry Ghosts (movable), on the 7th moon in the Chinese lunar calendar, when souls in purgatory are believed to return to earth to feast. Food is offered to these wandering spirits. Altars are set up in the streets and candles with faces are burned on them.

14 Sep Governor of Sarawak's birthday (state holiday in Sarawak).

16 Sep Governor of Sabah's birthday (state holiday in Sabah).

Oct Festival of the Nine Emperor Gods or Kiew Ong Yeah (movable) marks the return of the spirits of the 9 emperor gods to earth. Devotees visit temples dedicated to the 9 gods. A strip of yellow cotton is often bought from the temple and worn on the right wrist as a sign of devotion. Ceremonies usually culminate with a fire-walking ritual.

Oct/Nov Deepvali (movable; public holiday except Sarawak and Labuan), the Hindu festival of lights commemorates the victory of light over darkness and good over evil: the triumphant return of Rama after his defeat of the evil Ravanna in the Hindu epic, the Ramayana. Every Hindu home is brightly lit and decorated for the occasion.

Nov/Dec Gawai Antu/Gawai Nyunkup/ Rugan (Sarawak) is an Iban tribute to departed spirits. In simple terms, it is a party to mark the end of mourning for anyone whose relative has died in the previous 6 months.

25 Dec Christmas Day (public holiday). Christmas in Malaysia is a commercial spectacle with decorations and tropical Santa Clauses, although it doesn't compare with celebrations in Singapore. Midnight mass is the main Christmas service held in churches.

Other tribal festivals (*gawai*) in Sarawak include **Gawai Burung**, honouring the Iban war god, Singallang Burong; **Gawai Mpijong Jaran Rantau**, celebrated by the Bidayuh before grass cutting in new paddy fields; **Gawai Bineh**, celebrated by the Iban after harvest to welcome back the spirits of the paddy from the fields; and **Gawai Sawa**, celebrated by the Bidayuh to offer thanksgiving for last year and to make next year a plentiful one.

Brunei

1 Jan New Year's Day (public holiday).
Jan/Feb Chinese New Year (public holiday), a 15-day lunar festival.
23 Feb Hari Kebangsaan Negara Brunei Darussalam/National Day (public holiday), processions and fireworks in BSB.
31 May Armed Forces Day (public holiday), celebrated by the Royal Brunei Armed Forces who parade their equipment around town.
15 Jul Sultan's Birthday (public holiday) is celebrated until the end of the 2nd week in Aug. There's a procession, with lanterns and fireworks and a traditional boat race in BSB.
25 Dec Christmas Day.

Kalimantan

1 Jan Tahun Baru/New Year's Day (public holiday). New Year's Eve is celebrated with street carnivals, fireworks and all-night festivities. In Christian areas, festivities are more exuberant .
Jan/Feb Imlek/Chinese New Year (movable) is not an official holiday but many Chinese shops and businesses close for at least 2 days.
Mar Nyepi/Hindu New Year (movable; public holiday).

Mar/Apr Wafat Isa Al-Masih/Good Friday (movable; public holiday).
21 Apr Kartini Day. A ceremony held by women to mark the birthday of Raden Ajeng Kartini, born in 1879 and proclaimed as a pioneer of women's emancipation. The festival is rather like Mother's Day, in that women are supposed to be pampered by their husbands and children, although it is women's groups like the **Dharma Wanita** who are the most enthusiastic. Women wear national dress.
May Kenaikan Isa Al-Masih or Ascension Day (movable; public holiday).
May Waisak Day (movable; public holiday). Marks the birth and death of the historic Buddha; at Candi Mendut, a procession of monks carrying flowers, candles and images of the Buddha walk to Borobudur.
17 Aug Independence Day (public holiday). This is the most important national holiday, with processions, dancing and other merrymaking. Festivities continue for a month.
1 Oct Hari Pancasila commemorates the Five Basic Principles of Pancasila.
5 Oct Armed Forces Day. Anniversary of the founding of army, celebrated with parades.
25-26 Dec Christmas (public holiday). Celebrated by Christians.

Shopping

Except in the larger fixed-price stores, bargaining (with good humour) is expected; start bargaining at 50-60% lower than the asking price. Do not expect to achieve instant results; if you walk away from the shop, you will almost certainly be followed with a lower offer. If the salesperson agrees to your price, you should feel obliged to purchase; it is considered very ill mannered to agree on a price and then not buy the article.

Sarawak and Sabah

The traditional handicraft industry is flourishing in Sarawak (see page 182). Kuching, the state capital, is full of handicraft and antique shops selling tribal pieces collected from upriver; those going upriver themselves can often find items being sold in towns and even longhouses en route. Typical handicrafts include woodcarvings, *pua kumbu* (rust-coloured tie-dye blankets), beadwork and basketry (see page 116).

Larger urban areas may have a Chinatown (with a few curio shops and a *pasar malam*, or night market) and an Indian quarter; these are the best places to buy sarongs, longis, dotis and saris (mostly imported from India) as well as other textiles. Malay handicrafts are usually only found in markets or government craft centres. The island of Labuan has duty-free shopping, and is a good place to pick up cheap textiles from India and Indonesia as well as cheap wine for those lonely nights in Brunei.

Brunei

Compared to Malaysia, Brunei is not up to much when it comes to shopping; the range of goods on offer is limited and the prices much higher. That said, you'll have no trouble finding international branded and luxury items.

Kalimantan

Indonesia offers a wealth of distinctive handicrafts and other products. Best buys include textiles (batik and ikat), silverwork, woodcarving, puppets, paintings, ceramics and local black opals. Early-morning purchases may well be cheaper, as salespeople often believe the first sale augers well for the rest of the day. If you do make the first sale of the day, note how for luck the vendor often brushes the remaining stock with the banknotes you have just handed over.

Responsible travel

"Tourism is like fire. It can either cook your food or burn your house down". This sums up the ambivalent attitude that many have regarding the effects of tourism. It is a major foreign exchange earner and the world's largest single industry, yet many countries would rather tourists stayed at home. Tourism is seen as the cause of polluted beaches, rising prices, decline in moral standards, consumerism and much more.

Most international tourists come from a handful of wealthy countries. This is why many see tourism as the new 'imperialism', imposing alien cultures and ideals on sensitive and less modernized peoples. The problem, however, is that discussions of the effects of tourism tend to degenerate into simplifications, culminating in the drawing up of a checklist of 'positive' and 'negative' effects. Although such tables may be useful in highlighting problem areas, they also do a disservice by reducing a complex issue to a simple set of rather one-dimensional costs and benefits. Different destinations will be affected in different ways; these effects are likely to vary over time; and different groups living in a particular destination will feel the effects of tourism in varying ways and to varying degrees. At no time or place can tourism (or any other influence) be categorized as uniformly 'good' or 'bad'.

Ironically, travellers or backpackers sometimes find it difficult to consider themselves as tourists at all. This, of course, is hubris built upon the notion that the traveller is an independent explorer somehow beyond the bounds of the industry. Anna Borzello in an article entitled 'The myth of the traveller' in the journal *Tourism in Focus* (No 19, 1994) writes that: "Independent travellers cannot acknowledge – without shattering their self-image – that to many local people they are simply a good source of income … [not] inheritors of Livingstone, [but] bearers of urgently needed money." Although she does, in writing this, grossly underestimate the ability of travellers to see beyond their thongs and friendship bracelets, she does have a point when she suggests that it is important for travellers to honestly appraise their role as tourists, because, "Not only are independent travellers often frustrated by the gap between the way they see themselves and the way

How big is your footprint?

The point of a holiday is, of course, to have a good time, but if it's relatively guilt-free as well, that's even better. Perfect ecotourism would ensure a good living for local inhabitants, while not detracting from their traditional lifestyles, encroaching on their customs or spoiling their environment. Perfect ecotourism probably doesn't exist, but everyone can play their part. Here are a few points worth bearing in mind:

- Think about where your money goes and be fair and realistic about how cheaply you travel. Try to put money into local people's hands; drink local beer or fruit juice rather than imported brands and stay in locally owned accommodation wherever possible.
- Haggle with humour and appropriately. Remember that you want a fair price, not the lowest one.
- Think about what happens to your rubbish. Take biodegradable products and a water filter to avoid using lots of plastic bottles. Be sensitive to limited resources such as water, fuel and electricity.
- Help preserve local wildlife and habitats by respecting rules and regulations, such as sticking to footpaths, not standing on coral and not buying products made from endangered plants or animals.
- Don't treat people as part of the landscape; they may not want their picture taken. Ask first and respect their wishes.
- Learn the local language and be mindful of local customs and norms. It can enhance your travel experience and you'll earn respect and be more readily welcomed by local people.
- And finally, use your guidebook as a starting point, not the only source of information. Talk to local people, then discover your own adventure.

they are treated, but unless they acknowledge that they are part of the tourist industry they will not take responsibility for the damaging effects of their tourism."

For suggestions on how to minimize your impact on the country you're visiting and its people, see box above. You could also contact the UK-based charity **Tourism Concern** ⓘ *Stapleton House, 277-281 Holloway Rd, London N7 8HN, www.tourismconcern.org.uk*, and subscribe to their magazine, *In Focus*.

Local customs

Conduct

As elsewhere in Southeast Asia, in Borneo 'losing face' brings shame. Even when bargaining, using a loud voice or wild gesticulations will be taken to signify anger and, hence, 'loss of face'. By the same token, the person you shout at will also feel loss of face, particularly if it happens in public. In Muslim company it is impolite to touch others with the left hand or with other objects – even loose change. You should also not use your left hand to pick up or pass food. Men shake hands in Malaysia but it is not usual for a man to shake a woman's hand, except in Kuala Lumpur. Indeed, excessive personal contact should be avoided. However, Indonesians of the same sex tend to be more affectionate – holding hands, for example. Using the index finger to point at people, even at objects, is regarded as insulting. The thumb or whole hand should be used to indicate something, or to wave down a taxi. Before entering a private home, remember to remove your shoes; it is also usual to take a small gift for the host, which is not opened until after the visitor has left.

Dress

Clothes are light, cool and casual most of the time, but also fairly smart. Some establishments, mainly exclusive restaurants, require a long-sleeved shirt with tie or local batik shirt and do not allow shorts in the evening. For jungle treks, a waterproof is advisable, as are canvas jungle boots, which dry faster than leather. Those heading to the highlands or making an ascent of Gunung Kinabalu should bring some warm, lightweight clothing that dries fast. Dress codes are important to observe from the point of view cultural and religious sensitivities. Women should be particularly careful not to offend. Dress modestly and avoid shorts, short skirts and sleeveless dresses or shirts (except at recognized beach resorts). Public nudity and topless bathing are not acceptable. Remove shoes before entering mosques and temples; in mosques, women should cover their heads, shoulders and legs and men should wear long trousers.

Books

Fiction

Burgess, Anthony Burgess lived in Malaysia between 1954 and 1957, learnt Malay, and mixed with the locals far more than Maugham or Conrad, reflected in a better understanding of the Malay character. After leaving Malaya in 1957, he taught in Brunei until 1960. His books include *Time for a Tiger* (1956), *The Enemy in the Blanket* (1958) and *Beds in the East* (1959), later published together as *Malayan Trilogy* (1996).

Conrad, Joseph *Almayer's Folly* (1895) Vintage. Conrad's first novel, set on the east coast of Borneo.

Godshalk, CC *Kalimantan* (1998) Little Brown. A fictional account of an ambitious Englishman's quest to build his own kingdom on the north Borneo coast in the mid-19th century. It's a superb book, detailing the violence, duplicity, waves of pitiless disease and dark colonial attitudes that epitomized the lives of the first white settlers in Borneo.

Keith, Agnes *Land below the Wind* (1969) Ulverscroft: Leicester. Perhaps the best-known English-language book on Sabah.

Maugham, William *Somerset Maugham's Malaysian Stories* (1969) Heinemann: London and Singapore. Another British novelist who wrote extensively on Malaysia. These stories are best for the insight they provide of colonial life, not of the Malay or Malay life. The *Outstation* (1953) is a novel set in Borneo.

Theroux, Paul *The Consul's File* (1979) Penguin. A selection of short stories based on Malaysia.

History

Barley, Nigel *White Rajah* (2003) Abacus. Extremely readable account of the life and extraordinary achievements of James Brooke, filled with ingenuity and dark, bloody violence.

Chapman, F Spencer *The Jungle is Neutral* (1949). About the British guerrilla force fighting the Japanese in Borneo, not as enthralling as Tom Harrisson's book, but still worth reading.

Harrisson, Tom *World Within* (1959) Hutchinson: London. During the Second World War, explorer, naturalist and ethnologist Tom Harrisson was parachuted into Borneo to help organize Dayak resistance against the occupying Japanese forces. This is his extraordinary account.

Payne, Robert *The White Rajahs of Sarawak* (1960). Readable account of the extraordinary history of this East Malaysian state.

Turnbull, Mary C *A History of Malaysia, Singapore and Brunei* (1989) Allen and Unwin. A very orthodox history of Malaysia, Singapore and Brunei, clearly written for a largely academic/student audience.

Natural history

Briggs, John *Mountains of Malaysia: a Practical Guide and Manual* (1988) Longman: London. He has also written *Parks of Malaysia* (Longman: Kuala Lumpur); useful for those intending to visit Malaysia's protected areas.

Cubitt, Gerald and Payne, Junaidi *Wild Malaysia* (1990) London: New Holland. Large-format, coffee-table book with lots of wonderful colour photos, reasonable text and a short piece on each national park.

Francis, Charles M *Pocket Guide to Birds of Borneo* (1998) WWF/Sabah Society.

Hanbury-Tenison, Robin *Mulu, the Rain Forest* (1980) Arrow/Weidenfeld. The product of a Royal Geographical Society trip to Mulu in the late 1970s; semi-scholarly and useful.

Wallace, Alfred Russel *The Malay Archipelago* (1869). A classic of Victorian travel writing by one of the finest naturalists of the period. Wallace travelled through all of island Southeast Asia over a period of some years. Only 3 out of 20 chapters are on Borneo.

Travel

Bock, Carl *The Headhunters of Borneo* (1988, first published 1881) Graham Brash: Singapore. Bock was a Norwegian naturalist and explorer and was commissioned by the Dutch to make a scientific survey of southeastern Borneo. His account, though, makes much of the dangers and adventures that he faced, and some of his 'scientific' observations are, in retrospect, highly faulty. Nonetheless, this is an entertaining read.

Hansen, Eric *Stranger in the Forest: On Foot Across Borneo* (2000) Penguin. A fascinating account of Hansen's trek through Sarawak and Kalimantan.

Hose, Charles *The Field Book of a Jungle Wallah* (1985, first published 1929) OUP: Singapore. Hose was an official in Sarawak and became an acknowledged expert on the material and non-material culture of the tribes of Sarawak. He was one of that band of highly informed, perceptive and generally benevolent colonial administrators.

King, Victor T (edit) *The Best of Borneo Travel* (1992) OUP: Oxford. A compilation of travel accounts from the early 19th century through to the late 20th. An excellent companion to take while exploring the island.

Mjoberg, Eric *Forest Life and Adventures in the Malay Archipelago* (1930) OUP: Singapore.

O'Hanlon, Redmond *Into the Heart of Borneo* (1985) Salamander Press: Edinburgh. One of the best more recent travel books on Borneo. This highly amusing and perceptive romp through Borneo in the company of poet and foreign correspondent James Fenton includes an ascent of the Rejang River and does much to counter the more romanticized images of Bornean life.

Essentials A-Z

Accident and emergency

Sabah and **Sarawak**: Ambulance and police T999; Fire T994. **Brunei**: Ambulance T991; Police T993; Fire T995. **Kalimantan**: Ambulance T118; Police T110; Fire T113.

Children

Travelling with children in this part of the world is a lot easier and safer than in many other so-called 'developing' countries. Food hygiene is good, bottled water is sold almost everywhere, public transport is cheap (including taxis) and ubiquitous and most attractions provide good discounts for children. Powdered milk and baby food and other baby/child items, including disposable nappies, are widely sold and high chairs are available in most restaurants. Naturally, taking a child to a developing country is not something to be taken on lightly; there are additional health risks for the child or baby and travelling is slower. But it can also be a most rewarding experience. Children are excellent passports into a local culture.

Children in Borneo are rarely left to cry and are carried for most of the first 8 months of their lives since crawling is seen as animal-like. A non-Asian child is still a novelty and parents may find their child frequently taken off their hands; either a great relief (at mealtimes, for instance) or most alarming.

The advice given in the health section (see page 39) on food and drink should be applied even more stringently where young children are concerned. Be aware that some expensive hotels may have squalid cooking conditions; the cheapest street stall can be more hygienic. Where possible, try to watch the food being prepared. Stir-fried vegetables and rice or noodles are the best bet; meat and fish may have been pre-cooked and then left out before being reheated. Fruit is cheap; papaya, banana and avocado are all excellent sources of nutrition and can be peeled ensuring cleanliness. If your child is at the 'put it in mouth' stage, disinfectant wipes are useful. Frequent wiping of hands and tabletops can help to minimize the chance of infection.

At the hottest time of year, a/c may be essential for a baby or young child's comfort when sleeping. This rules out some of the cheaper hotels, but a/c accommodation is available in all but the most remote spots. Guesthouses probably won't have cots but more expensive hotels should (email or phone to check). Be aware that the water could carry parasites, so avoid letting children drink it when bathing.

Public transport may be a problem; trains are fine but long bus journeys are restrictive and uncomfortable. Hiring a car is the most convenient way to travel with a small child. Back seatbelts are fitted in more recent models and you can buy child seats in capital cities or rent them from larger car hire firms. **Checklist** Pack your own standard baby/child equipment and include baby wipes; child paracetamol; disinfectant; first-aid kit; immersion element for boiling water; oral rehydration salts (such as Dioralyte); sarong or backpack for carrying child; Sudocreme (or similar); high-factor sunblock; sunhat; thermometer and powdered or instant food.

Customs and duty free

Duty-free allowance in **Sabah** and **Sarawak** (Malaysia) is 200 cigarettes, 50 cigars or 250g of tobacco and 1 litre of liquor or wine. Cameras, watches, pens, lighters, cosmetics, perfumes and portable radio/cassette players are also duty free in Malaysia. Visitors bringing in dutiable goods, such as video equipment, may have to pay a refundable deposit for temporary importation. It is advisable to carry receipt of purchases to avoid this problem. Export permits are required for gold, platinum, precious stones and jewellery (except reasonable personal effects). Export permits are required for antiques (from the Director General of Museums, Muzium Negara, KL, page 59).

The duty-free allowance in **Brunei** for those over 17 is 200 cigarettes or 250g of tobacco, 60 ml of perfume and 250 ml eau de toilette. Non-Muslims are allowed 2 bottles of liquor and 12 cans of beer for personal consumption. All alcohol must be declared on arrival. There is a yellow declaration form that needs to be presented at a counter along with a valid passport before clearing customs. Trafficking illegal drugs carries the death penalty in Brunei.

The allowance in **Kalimantan** (Indonesia) is 2 litres of alcohol, 200 cigarettes or 50 cigars or 100g of tobacco, plus a reasonable amount of perfume.

Disabled travellers

For travel to this area, it would be best to contact a specialist travel agent or organization dealing with travellers with special needs. In the UK, contact RADAR (**Royal Association for Disability and Rehabilitation**), 12 City Forum, 250 City Rd, London, EC1V 8AF, T020-7250 3222, www.radar.org.uk. In North America, contact SATH (**Society for Accessible Travel & Hospitality**), Suite 610, 347 5th Av, New York, NY 10016, T1-212-447 7284, www.sath.org.

Disabled travellers are not well catered for in Malaysia. Pavements are treacherous for those in wheelchairs, crossing roads is a hazard, and public transport is not well adapted for those with disabilities. This is surprising for a country which in so many other ways presents itself as cutting edge. But it is not impossible for disabled people to travel in Malaysia. For those who can afford the more expensive hotels, the assistance of hotel staff makes life a great deal easier, and there are also lifts and other amenities. Even those staying in budget accommodation will find that local people are very helpful.

Facilities for disabled travellers in **Brunei** are better than those in Malaysia, though still limited by Western standards. Contact **Brunei Tourism**. The top hotels have pretty good facilities for disabled travellers.

Indonesia has almost no infrastructure to help disabled people to travel easily around areas such as **Kalimantan**. Pavements are frequently very high, uneven and ridden with holes and missing slabs. Buildings, including shops and museums, are often accessible via steps only, with no wheelchair ramps. Public transport is usually cramped and overcrowded. However, some Western-owned upmarket hotels provide wheelchair access and facilities for disabled visitors.

Electricity

Borneo's supply is 220-240 volts, 50 cycle AC. Some hotels supply adaptors.

Embassies and consulates

Malaysia
Australia, Malaysian High Commission, 7 Perth Av, Yarralumla, Canberra, ACT 2600, T+61-(0)2-6273 1543.
Brunei, Malaysian High Commission, 61 Simpang 326, Jln Kebangsaan BA 1211 kg. Sungai Akar, PO Box 2826, Bandar Seri Begawan BS8675, T+673-238 1095.
Canada, Malaysian High Commission, 60 Boteler St, Ottawa, Ontario KN 8Y7, T+1-613-241 5182.
France, Malaysian Embassy, 2 bis rue Benouville, Paris, T+33-01-4553 1185.
Germany, Malaysian Embassy, Klingelhoefer St 6, D-10785 Berlin, T+49-030-885 7490.
Italy, Malaysian Embassy, Via Nomentana 297, 00162 Rome, T+39-06-841 5764.
Japan, Malaysian Embassy, 20-16, Nanpeidai-Machi, Shibuya-ku, Tokyo 150, T+81-03-3476 3840.
New Zealand, Malaysian High Commission, 10 Washington Av, Brooklyn, Wellington, T+64-04-385 2439.

Spain, Malaysian Embassy, Paseo de la Castellano 91-10, Centro 23, 28046 Madrid, T+34-915 550684.

Sweden, Malaysian Embassy, Karlavagen 37, PO Box 26053, 10041 Stockholm, T+46-8-440 8400, F8-791 8760.

Switzerland, Malaysian Embassy, Jungfrau-strasse 1, CH-3005 Berne, T+41-031-350 4700.

UK, Malaysian High Commission, 45 Belgrave Sq, London, SW1X 8QT, T+44-(0)20-7235 8033.

USA, Malaysian Embassy, 3516 International Court, NW, Washington DC 20008, T+1-202-572 9700.

For embassies and consulates in other countries check www.kln.gov.my.

Brunei

Australia, 10 Beale Crescent, Deakin, Canberra, ACT 2606, T+61-(0)2-6285 4500.

Belgium, 238 Av Franklin Roosevelt 1050, Brussels, T+32-02-675 0878.

Canada, 395 Laurier Av East, Ottawa, Ontario K1N 6R4, T+1-613-234 5656.

France, 7 rue de Presbourg, 75116 Paris, T+33-01-5364 6760.

Germany, Zentralverband des Deutschen Baugewerbes, 1st floor, Kronenstrasse 55-58, 10117 Berlin-Mitte, T+49-030-2060 7600.

Japan, 5-2 Kitashinagawa 6-Chome, Sinagawa-ku, Tokyo 141, T+81-03-3447 7997.

Malaysia, 19-01 Tingkat, No 19 Menara Tan & Tan, Jln Tun Razak, 50400 Kuala Lumpur, T+60-03-2161 2800.

Singapore, 325 Tanglin Rd, Singapore 24795, T+65-733 9055.

UK, 19-20 Belgrave Sq, London SW1X 8PG, T+44-(0)207-581 0521

For embassies and consulates in other countries check www.mfa.gov.bn.

Indonesia

Australia, 8 Darwin Av, Yarralumla, Canberra, ACT 2600, T+61-02-6250 8600.

Canada, 287 MacLaren St, Ottawa, Ontario, K2P 0L9, T+1-613-236 7403.

Germany, Lehrter Str 16-17, 10557 Berlin, T+49-030-478 070.

Japan, Higashi Gotanda 5-2-9, Shinagawa-ku, Tokyo, T+81-03-3441 4201.

Malaysia, 233 Jln Tun Razak, Kuala Lumpur 50400, T+60 3 2116 4000.

New Zealand, 70 Glen Rd, Kelburn, Wellington, T+64-04-475 8697.

Singapore, 7 Chatsworth Rd, T+65 6737 7422.

UK, 38 Grosvenor Sq, London W1K 2HW, T+44-(0)20-7499 7661.

USA, 2020 Massachusetts Av, NW, Washington DC 20036, T+1-202-775 5200.

Gay and lesbian travellers

Malaysia – officially at least – is not particularly accepting of what might be regarded as alternative lifestyles, and homosexuality remains a crime. (Bear in mind that even Malaysia's former deputy prime minister, Anwar Ibrahim, was charged with sodomy in 1999 and was, at the time of writing, facing a second round of charges after being accused of sodomizing his aide.) However, there is a small gay and lesbian scene in Kota Kinabalu and Kuching. There are 2 good websites for gay and lesbian travellers to the region: www.fridae.com and www.utopia-asia.com. But the site's homepage states: "Gay life in Malaysia is blossoming. However, Muslims, both Malay and visitors, are subject to antiquated religious laws which punish gay or lesbian sexual activity with flogging and male transvestism with imprisonment. Police may arrest and harass any gay person (Muslim or non-Muslim) in a public place (ie cruise spots), so discretion is advised."

As Malaysia, **Brunei** is not a good place to be gay, at least not officially: homosexual sex is illegal and punishable with jail sentences and fines. In reality, things are more easygoing, although it's best not to flaunt your sexuality. See also www.utopia-asia.com.

Indonesia is surprisingly tolerant of homosexuality given that it goes against the tenets of both Islam and traditional indigenous religions. Homosexuality is not illegal; the age of consent is 16 years for men and women. Indonesian men are affectionate in public, which allows foreign gay men to blend in more easily.

Health

See your GP or travel clinic at least 6 weeks before departure for general advice on travel risks and vaccinations. Try phoning a specialist travel clinic if your own doctor is unfamiliar with health conditions in Malaysia and Indonesia. Make sure you have sufficient medical travel insurance, get a dental check, know your own blood group and, if you suffer a long-term condition such as diabetes or epilepsy, obtain a Medic Alert bracelet/necklace (www.medicalert.co.uk). If you wear glasses, take a copy of your prescription.

Vaccinations
Vaccinations for tuberculosis, hepatitis B, rabies and Japanese B encephalitis are commonly recommended for Borneo. The final decision, however, should be based on a consultation with your GP or travel clinic. You should also confirm your primary courses and boosters are up to date (diphtheria, tetanus, poliomyelitis, hepatitis A, typhoid). A yellow fever certificate is required by visitors over 1 year old, who are coming from or have recently passed through an infected area.

Health risks
The most common cause of travellers' **diarrhoea** is from eating contaminated food. In Malaysia and Indonesia, drinking water is rarely the culprit, although it's best to be cautious (see below). Swimming in sea or river water that has been contaminated by sewage can also be a cause; ask locally if it is safe. Diarrhoea may be also caused by viruses, bacteria (such as E-coli), protozoal (such as giardia), salmonella and cholera. It may be accompanied by vomiting or by severe abdominal pain. Any kind of diarrhoea responds well to the replacement of water and

salts. Sachets of rehydration salts can be bought in most chemists and can be dissolved in boiled water. If the symptoms persist, consult a doctor. Tap water in the major cities is in theory safe to drink but it may be worth drinking only bottled or boiled water to be sure. Avoid having ice in drinks unless you trust that it is from a reliable source.

Travelling in high altitudes can bring on **altitude sickness**. On reaching heights above 3000 m, the heart may start pounding and the traveller may experience shortness of breath. Smokers and those with underlying heart or lung disease are often hardest hit. Take it easy for the first few days, rest and drink plenty of water, you will feel better soon. It is essential to get acclimatized before undertaking long treks or arduous activities.

Mosquitoes are more of a nuisance than a serious hazard but some, of course, are carriers of serious diseases such as **malaria**, so it is sensible to avoid being bitten as much as possible. Malaria is present in the Malaysian states of Sabah and Sarawak and in Kalimantan and is making a comeback worldwide. Sleep off the ground and use a mosquito net and some kind of insecticide. Mosquito coils release insecticide as they burn and are available in many shops, as are tablets of insecticide, which are placed on a heated mat plugged into a wall socket. Those travelling to Kalimantan and away from coastal areas of Sabah and Sarawak are advised to speak to a doctor about suitable anti-malarial medication. Malarone is widely available in Europe and can be purchased in Singapore with a doctor's prescription. Doxycycline can be bought from pharmacists in Peninsular Malaysia. Dengue, a disease also carried by mosquitoes, is in the region. Fortunately, travellers rarely develop a severe form of dengue, although fatal cases do occur annually in Malaysia and Indonesia.

If you get sick
Contact your embassy or consulate for a list of doctors and dentists who speak your language, or at least some English. Doctors

and health facilities in major cities are also listed in the Directory sections of this book. Good-quality healthcare is available in the larger centres of Malaysia and Indonesia but it can be expensive, especially hospitalization. Make sure you have adequate insurance.

Useful websites

www.btha.org British Travel Health Association.
www.cdc.gov US government site that gives excellent advice on travel health and details of disease outbreaks.
www.fco.gov.uk British Foreign and Commonwealth Office travel site that has useful information on each country, people, climate and a list of UK embassies/consulates.
www.fitfortravel.scot.nhs.uk A-Z of vaccine/health advice for each country.
www.numberonehealth.co.uk Travel screening services, vaccine and travel health advice, email/SMS text vaccine reminders and screens returned travellers for tropical diseases.

Internet

Malaysia is one of the most forward-thinking countries in Asia when it comes to information technology and the internet. In line with this, internet cafés have sprung up all over the place and every town, however small, down-at-heel and apparently forgotten by the wider world, will have a place offering internet services. Rates are cheap too: RM2-RM3 per hr. Internet cafés geared to tourists are more expensive than those serving the local market, where teenage boys spend hours playing online games. For travellers with laptops, you'll find that guesthouses, hotels, cafés and coffee shops routinely offer free Wi-Fi.

There are plenty of internet cafés in **Brunei**, too, and all the top-end and most of the mid-range hotels offer internet access. Free Wi-Fi is less widely available in Brunei than in Malaysia, but many mid-range cafés and the more expensive hotels offer it.

Internet access is available all over **Kalimantan**, with any town of any size

having a cyber café. Expect to pay around Rp 5000 per hr. Mid-range hotels often offer a voucher scheme for Wi-Fi access, with 24 hrs costing around Rp 55,000. Some shopping malls and cafés have free Wi-Fi access.

Language

Bahasa Melayu (the Malay language, normally shortened to Bahasa) is the national language in **Sarawak**, **Sabah** and **Brunei**. It is very similar to Bahasa Indonesia, which evolved from Malay. All communities, Malay, Chinese and Indian, as well as tribal groups in Sabah and Sarawak, speak Malay, as most are schooled in the Malay medium. Nearly everyone in Malaysia speaks some English, except in remote rural areas. In Brunei, English is widely spoken and is taught in schools. Chinese is also spoken, mainly Hokkien, but also Cantonese, Teochew, Hakka and Mandarin.

The best way to take a crash course in Malay is to buy a teach-yourself book; there are several on the market, but one of the best ones is *Everyday Malay* by Thomas G Oey (Periplus Language Books, 1995), which is widely available. A Malay/ English dictionary or phrasebook is a useful companion too; these are also readily available in bookshops.

The national language in **Kalimantan** is **Bahasa Indonesia**. English is the most common foreign language, and Chinese dialects can be heard in coastal cities, particularly Pontianak. Bahasa Indonesia is a relatively easy language to learn and visitors may have a small but functional vocabulary after just a few weeks. Unlike Thai, it is not tonal and is grammatically straightforward. However, this does not mean it is an easy language to speak well. There are many cheap, pocket-sized Indonesian-English dictionaries available in Indonesia. They are fine for the odd request for a towel or a cleaner room, but for anyone wishing to learn more, they are disappointing. For visitors interested in studying Bahasa Indonesia in more depth, the Cornell course, though expensive, is recommended. English isn't widely spoken in Kalimantan and it helps to know some Bahasa Indonesia.

The basic grammar of both languages is very simple, with no tenses, genders or articles, and sentence structure is straightforward. Pronunciation is not difficult either as there is a close relation between the letter as it is written and the sound. Stress is usually placed on the second syllable of a word. The **a** is pronounced as *ah* in an open syllable, or as in *but* for a closed syllable; **e** is pronounced as in *open* or *bed*; **i** is pronounced as in *feel*; **o** is pronounced as in *all*; **u** is pronounced as in *foot*. The letter **c** is pronounced *ch* as in *change* or *chat*. The **r** is rolled.

For further information, see Useful words and phrases, page 380.

Media

Newspapers

The main English-language newspapers in **Sarawak** and **Sabah** are the *Daily Express* (www.dailyexpress.com.my) and the *Eastern Times* (www.easterntimes.com.my). *Aliran Monthly* (www.aliran.com) is a high-brow but fascinating publication offering current affairs analysis from a non-government perspective. The *Sarawak Tribune* was forced out of business in 2006 in a controversy over the Jyllands-Posten Mohammed cartoons, about which the paper claimed the cartoons had made no impact in Sarawak, and reprinted the cartoon, generating enormous criticism from the pro-Islamic Malaysian government. *The Rocket* is the Democratic Action Party's opposition newspaper, and also presents an alternative perspective. International editions of leading foreign newspapers and news magazines can be obtained at main news stands and bookstalls, although some of these are not cleared through customs until mid-afternoon. One of the most popular online news portals is Malaysia Kini (www.malaysiakini.com), with independent coverage of news and politics.

There are 2 daily newspapers in **Brunei**: the *Borneo Bulletin* (English) and the *Media Permata* (Malay), which cover both local and international news.

The main English-language newspaper in **Kalimantan** is *The Jakarta Post* (www.the jakartapost.com), though this can be difficult to find. One of the outcomes of Indonesia's mad dash to full democracy is the emergence of a more independent media. Of the international papers available, the *Asian Wall Street Journal* and the *International Herald Tribune* is in major cities and tourist centres. *Tempo* (www.tempo interactive.com) and *Inside Indonesia* (www.insideindonesia.org) are magazines on all things Indonesian. Though hard to find in Kalimantan, their websites are worth a look.

Radio

There are 6 government radio stations in **Sarawak** and **Sabah** broadcasting in various languages including English. Radio 1 is in Bahasa Melayu; Radio 2 is a music station; Radio 3 is Malay; Radio 4 is in English; Radio 5, Chinese; Radio 6, Tamil. The BBC World Service is on shortwave; the main frequencies are (in kHz): 11750, 9740, 6195 and 3915.

More likely than not, during your first taxi ride in **Brunei** you'll be confronted with the surreal sound of London's Capital Radio ringing loud and clear across the airwaves. It's the most popular radio station in Brunei. Capital Gold is also broadcast live in Brunei.

Republik Indonesia (RRI) broadcasts throughout **Kalimantan**. News and commentary in English is broadcast for about an hour a day. Shortwave radios will pick up Voice of America, the BBC World Service and Australian Broadcasting.

Television

RTM1 and RTM2 in **Sarawak** and **Sabah** are operated by Radio Television Malaysia, the government-run broadcasting station. Apart from locally produced programmes, some American and British series are shown. Programmes for all channels are listed in daily newspapers. Satellite TV is very popular in

Malaysia and many hotels carry the ASTRO service, which offers HBO, STAR movies, ESPN, CNN, BBC, Discovery and MTV as well as a host of Chinese channels.

The national TV network in **Brunei** transmits local programmes and Malaysian TV. Satellite TV is widespread in Brunei (even remote longhouses have dishes) and virtually all hotels provide a wide range of channels including CNN and the BBC.

Indonesia has put satellites into geo-stationary orbit so that TV pictures can be received anywhere in the archipelago. The vast 'parabolas' outside many houses in **Kalimantan**, including shacks which may not even have piped water, testifies to the power of TV. Televisi Republik Indonesia (TVRI) is the government-run channel. There are also 9 private stations of highly variable quality. Indonesians like their TV like their tea, sugary and light. The airwaves are filled with news, singing contests and *sinetron* (the Indonesian version of a soap opera). Hotels also usually receive satellite TV and if they have foreign clientele they may offer English-language channels. CNN, the BBC, Star, Television Australia and Malaysian, Philippine and Thai television are all received in Indonesia.

Money

Currency

The unit of currency in **Malaysia** is the Malaysian dollar or ringgit (RM), which is divided into 100 cents or sen. Bank notes come in denominations of RM1, 5, 10, 50, and 100. Coins are issued in 5, 10, 20 and 50 sen. The exchange rate in May 2010 was RM3.22 = US$1.

The official currency in **Brunei** is the Brunei dollar (B$), which is interchangeable with the **Singapore** dollar. Notes are available in denominations of B$1, B$5, B$10, B$50, B$100, B$1000 and B$10,000 (about US$6000!). There are 1, 5, 10, 20 and 50 cent coins. The exchange rate in May 2010 was B$1.39 = US$1. Singapore dollars can be used

as legal tender in Brunei with a rate of 1:1.

The unit of currency in **Indonesia** is the rupiah (Rp), which is divided into 100 sen. Denominations are Rp 1000, Rp 5000, Rp 10,000, Rp 20,000 and Rp 50,000 and Rp 100,000. Coins are minted in Rp 100 Rp 200, and Rp 500 denominations. The exchange rate in May 2010 was Rp 9,025 = US$1.

Exchange

Most of the bigger hotels, restaurants and shops in **Sarawak** and **Sabah** accept international credit cards, including American Express, BankAmericard, Diners, MasterCard and Visa. The latter two are the most widely accepted. Cash advances can be issued against credit cards in most banks, although some banks limit the amount that can be drawn. A passport is usually required for over-the-counter transactions. There are ATMs all over major centres in Borneo which accept credit or debit cards. In Malaysia, **Maybank** and **OCBC** will accept both Visa and MasterCard at its ATMs; cards with the Cirrus mark will also be accepted at most banks' ATMs. Traveller's cheques can be exchanged at banks and money changers. Money changers often offer the best rates, but it is worth shopping around.

Brunei banks charge a commission of B$10-15 for exchanging cash or traveller's cheques. Money changers often don't charge a set commission at all, but their rates won't be quite so good. ATMs are widespread in Brunei and many accept debit cards (with Maestro), as well as credit cards. Depending on who you bank with, withdrawing money on your debit card is often free (there are plenty of **HSBC** ATMs around, for instance). Most hotels and many shops and establishments accept credit cards, too.

Banks and money changers outside main centres in **Kalimantan** tend to give poor rates; shop around as there can be great variations between exchange rates. In more out-of-the-way places it is worth making sure that you have a stock of smaller notes and coins, as it can be hard to break larger bills. Major credit cards are accepted in larger hotels, airline offices, department stores and some restaurants, although this method of payment is often subject to a 3% surcharge. Visa and MasterCard are the most widely accepted. Banks such as **BCA**, **Lippo Bank** and **BNI** have ATMs that accept credit cards and debit cards. Traveller's cheques can usually be changed in larger towns and tourist destinations. The US dollar is the most readily acceptable currency. Money changers often give better rates than banks but will occasionally charge a commission – check beforehand. If changing cash, note that banks like bills in pristine condition.

Cost of travelling

It is best not to calculate your budget simply by multiplying the number of days you intend to stay by the figures given below: a couple of days' diving or the need to hire a guide on a trek, for example, would throw such careful calculations right out.

Malaysia is relatively cheap for overseas visitors. However, with the global credit crisis raging, currencies are going up and down. Nevertheless, Malaysia remains an excellent-value destination. It's possible to travel on a shoestring, and getting by on RM60-80 (US$15-20) per day – including accommodation (dorms), meals and transport – is possible if you stay in the bottom-end guesthouses, eat at stalls or in hawker centres and use public transport. Cheaper guesthouses charge around RM40 a night for two (US$10). Dorm beds are available in most budget guesthouses and can be superb value at less than RM25 (US$7). It's possible to find a simple a/c room for RM40-80 (US$10-20). A room in a top-quality, international-class hotel will cost RM300-500 (US$80-130) and in a tourist-class hotel (with a/c, room service, restaurant and probably a pool), RM100-150 (US$26-40). Eating out is also comparatively cheap: a good curry can cost as little as RM4 (US$1). Finally, overland travel is a bargain and the bus network is not only extremely good, but fares are excellent

value. Booking plane tickets well in advance gives superb deals.

Per capita, **Brunei** is one of the wealthiest countries in the developing world, with a GDP not far off that of Singapore. This means that everything, from hotel rates to groceries and transport, is more expensive than in the rest of Borneo. Unless you hire a car, you may have to rely on taxis (the bus network is skimpy at best) and these are not cheap. By Western standards, however, Brunei is not particularly expensive. And, when it comes to local food at market stalls or in *kedai kopi* (traditional coffee shops), prices are only slightly higher than just across the border.

Visitors staying in first-class hotels and eating in hotel restaurants in **Kalimantan** will probably spend over Rp 600,000 (US$60) a day. Tourists staying in cheaper a/c places and eating in local restaurants will probably spend about Rp 250,000 (US$25) a day. Travellers on a shoestring aren't particularly well provided for in Kalimantan, although staying in fan-cooled guesthouses and eating cheaply, one might expect to be able to live on Rp 150,000 (US$15) a day. A meal should cost Rp 10,000 to Rp 20,000 in a simple *warung*, Rp 20,000 to 40,000 in a local restaurant, and Rp 50,000 or more in a swish hotel coffee shop. However, most people don't come to Kalimantan to linger in cities and bask in the exhaust fumes. The majority of tourists visit to head upriver on expensive tours. Solo travellers will often find themselves effectively priced out of the tours unless they are willing to dig deep. Those with less smaller budgets will find the attractions offered in Sabah and Sarawak more affordable, and much better value.

Opening hours

In **Sabah**, **Sarawak** and **Kalimantan**, business hours are Mon-Thu 0800-1245, 1400-1615, Fri 0800-1200, 1430-1615, Sat 0800-1245. Note that offices and banks are shut on the 1st and 3rd Sat of every month.

In **Brunei**, business hours are Mon-Fri 0900-1500, Sat 0900-1100 (banks), but most shopping malls are open daily 1000-2130. For post office opening hours, see below.

Post

Malaysia's post is cheap and quite reliable, although incoming and outgoing parcels should be registered. To send postcards and aerograms overseas costs RM0.50, letters cost RM0.90 (up to 10g) or RM1.40 (up to 20g). Post office opening hours are Mon-Sat 0830-1700 (closed 1st Sat of every month). Fax services are available in most state capitals. Poste restante, at general post offices in major cities, is reliable; make sure your surname is capitalized and underlined. Most post offices have a packing service for a reasonable fee (around RM5). You can also buy **AirAsia** tickets at post offices.

Post offices in **Brunei** are open Mon-Thu and Sat 0745-1630, Fri 0800-1100 and 1400-1600. Most hotels provide postal services at reception. The cost of a stamp for a postcard to Europe is around 50 cents.

The **Kalimantan** postal service is quite reliable, though important mail should be registered. Every town and tourist centre has either a *kantor pos* (post office) or postal agent, for stamps and to post letters and parcels. Poste restante services may also be available; make sure your surname is capitalized and underlined. *Kantor pos* are open Mon-Sat 0800-1400; postal agents have much longer hours, often until 2200 daily.

Prohibitions

The trafficking of illegal drugs into Malaysia and Brunei carries the death penalty. In Indonesia, for trafficking even modest quantities, you can expect a lengthy jail term.

Brunei is a 'dry' country: sale of alcohol is banned, while consumption is prohibited for Muslims. Non-Muslims may consume alcohol that has been declared at customs (2 bottles of liquor or 12 cans of beer; see page 37), but not in public. Certain restaurants will allow non-Muslims to bring their own alcohol, but always check in advance.

Safety

Normal precautions should be taken with passports and valuables; many hotels have safes. Pickpocketing and bag snatching are problems in Kuching. Generally women travelling alone need have few worries – although take the usual precautions like not walking alone in deserted places at night. Drink driving is a problem in Sabah and Sarawak.

Student travellers

Anyone in full-time education is entitled to an International Student Identity Card (ISIC). These are issued by student travel offices and travel agencies across the world and offer special rates on transport and other concessions. See www.isic.org. Students can get discounts on some entry fees and transport, but there is no institutionalized system of discounts for students.

Taxes

There is a 7% GST (Goods and Sales Tax) in Singapore, refundable at the airport for goods bought (over US$300) with receipts. There is no sales tax in Brunei. In Malaysia, sales tax is generally 10%.

Telephone

There are public telephone booths in most towns in **Sarawak** and **Sabah**; telephones take RM0.10 and RM0.20 coins. Card phones are now widespread and they make good sense if phoning abroad. **iTalk** offers the best IDD (international direct dialling) rate. Cards

Telephone information

Numbers are shown as they should be dialled long distance WITHIN the country. If phoning from abroad, dial your country's international access code, the country code for Malaysia, Singapore, Brunei or Indonesia, followed by the area code (minus the initial zero) and then the number.

IDD access codes Malaysia: 00; Singapore: 020 for calls to Malaysia (no country code needed) or 00 for other countries; Brunei: 00; Indonesia: 001/008.

International country codes Malaysia: +60; Singapore: +65; Brunei: +673; Indonesia: +62.

Operator Malaysia: T101; Singapore: T100; Brunei: T113; Indonesia: T100/101.

Directory enquiries Malaysia: T102/103; Singapore: T100; Brunei: T0213; Indonesia: T108/106.

International assistance Malaysia: T108; Singapore: T104; Brunei: T113; Indonesia: T102.

come in denominations from RM10 to RM100 and are available from airports, petrol stations, most 7-Eleven and magazine stalls. International direct calls can be made from any telephone with an IDD facility, including most Kedai Telekom booths in major towns.

You can use your mobile phone in Malaysia if you have a GSM model, but the service will be expensive. Or get a pre-paid SIM card when you arrive, available from most mobile phone shops, with Maxis, Celcom and DiGi offering the widest service. International calls from these are very good value.

There are no area codes in **Brunei**. With a Hallo Kad phonecard (widely available) you can make international calls from any phone. You can also make international calls from some hotel rooms. Coin phones take 10 and 20 cent pieces. Getting a mobile prepaid SIM card is expensive in Brunei and only really worth it if staying longer than a few days.

Indonesia has a comprehensive network of telecommunications. Every town in **Kalimantan** has its communication centre – Warpostel – where you can make local and international calls. Most Warpostels open early in the morning and operate until around 2400. International calls have a cheap rate between 2400 and 0800, and all Sat and Sun; otherwise calls are expensive. There is an

incredible choice of mobile phone operators in Indonesia. Some of the more reputable providers include IM3, Simpati and XL.

Time

Official time is 8 hrs ahead of GMT. Indonesian Borneo is split into 2 time zones: WIB (Waktu Indonesia Barat) and WIT (Waktu Indonesia Tengah) Kalbar and Kalteng are on WIB (GMT+7) and Kalsel and Kaltim are on WIT (GMT+8) .

Tipping

Tipping is unusual in **Malaysia**, as a service charge of 10% is automatically added to restaurant and hotel bills, plus a 5% government tax (indicated by the + and ++ signs). Nor is tipping expected in smaller restaurants where a service charge is not automatically added to the bill. For porters a modest tip may be appropriate. In **Indonesia**, a 10% service charge is added to bills at more expensive hotels (in addition to tax of 11%). Porters expect to be tipped about Rp 1000 a bag. In more expensive restaurants, where no service is charged, a tip of 5-10% can be appropriate. Taxi drivers (in larger towns) appreciate a small tip (Rp 1000).

At times it can seem as though Indonesia is run on tip money, with notes being handed over frequently for road repairs, mosque construction and much more.

Tour operators

In the UK
Audley Travel, New Mill, New Mill Lane, Whitney, Oxfordshire OX29 9SX, T01993-838000, www.audleytravel.com. Tailor-made eco-tour itineraries.

Discovery Initiatives Ltd, The Travel House, 51 Castle St, Cirencester, Gloucestershire GL7 1QD, T01285-643333, www.discovery initiatives.co.uk. Ecotourism provider with a strong conservation focus. Tours in Southern Kalimantan and Sabah, giving a financial contribution to the conservation projects being visited. It directly supports orang-utan rehabilitation in Tanjung Puting National Park.

Exodus, Grange Mills, Weir Rd, London SW12 0NE, T020-8675 5550, www.exodus. co.uk. Wide range of trips including river journeys and caves at the Niah National Park.

Explore Worldwide, Nelson House, 55 Victoria Rd, Farnborough, Hampshire GU14 7PH, T0870-333 4001, www.explore. co.uk. Small group tours, including cultural trips, adventure holidays and natural history tours.

Kuoni Travel, Kuoni House, Dorking, Surrey, T01306-747002, www.kuoni.co.uk. Consistently high-quality tour operator.

Magic of the Orient, 14 Frederick Place, Clifton, Bristol BS8 1AS, T0117-311 6050, www.magicoftheorient.com. Knowledgeable staff specializing in tailor-made holidays.

Realworld-travel, Lower Farm, Happisburgh, Norwich NR12 0QQ, T0709-23322, www.4 real.co.uk. Self-drive tours and rainforest treks.

Regaldive, 58 Lancaster Way, Ely, Cambs CB6 3NW, T0870-220 1777, www.regal-diving. co.uk. Diving tours around Sipadan and Mabul islands on Sabah's southeast coast.

Silk Steps, Compass House, Rowdens Rd, Wells, Somerset BA5 1TU, T01749-685162, www.silksteps.co.uk. Tours of Borneo.

Trans Indus, Northumberland House, 11 The Pavement, Popes Lane, London W5 4NG, T020-8566 2729, www.transindus.com. Tailor-made and group tours and holidays.

Travel Mood, 214 Edgware Rd, London W2 1DH; 1 Brunswick Ct, Bridge St, Leeds LS2 7QU; 16 Reform St, Dundee DD1 1RG, T0207-087 8400, www.travelmood.com. More than 20 years of experience in tailor-made travel to the Far East and specialists in adventure and activity travel.

Trekforce Expeditions, Way to Wooler Farm, Wooler, Northumberland NE71 6AQ, T0845-241 3085, www.trekforce.org.uk. A UK-based charity offering programmes consisting of sustainable projects, language, teaching and cultural experiences.

In North America
Asian Pacific Adventures, T+1-800-825 1680, www.asianpacificadventures.com. Small group, tailor-made and family adventure tours.

In Australia
Intrepid Travel, 11 Spring St, Fitzroy, Victoria, T+61-1300-360887, www.intrepid travel.com.au. Australian company with agents all over the world. Dozens of different tours of Malaysia.

Tourist information

Sarawak and Sabah
Australia, Level 2, 171 Clarence St, Sydney, NSW 2000, T+61-02-9299 4441, mtpb.sydney@tourism.gov.my; 56 William St, Perth, WA 6000, T08-9481 0400, mtpb.perth@tourism.gov.my.

Canada, 1590-1111 W Georgia St, Vancouver, BC, V6E 4M3, T+1-604-689 8899, mtpb.vancouver@tourism.gov.my.

France, 29 rue des Pyramides, 75001 Paris, T+33 -01-4297 4171, mtpb.paris@tourism.gov.my.

Germany, Rossmarkt 11, Frankfurt Am Main, D-60311, T+49-069-283782, mtpb.frankfurt@tourism.gov.my.

Indonesia, Jln HR Rasuna Said, Kavx/6, No 1-3, Kuningan, Jakarta Selatan 12950, T+62-021- 522 0765 (ext 3030), www.tourism.gov.my.

Italy, Via Priviata della Passarella, No 4, 20122 Milan, T+39-02-796702.

Japan, 5F Chiyoda Bldg, 1-6-4 Yurakucho Chiyoda-ku, Tokyo 100, T+81-03-3501 8691, mtpb.tokyo@tourism.gov.my.

Singapore, 01-01B/C/D, 80 Robinson Rd, Singapore 068898, T+65-6532 6321, mtpb.singapore@tourism.gov.my.

South Africa, 1st floor, 5 Commerce Sq, 39 Rivonia Rd, Sandhurst, T+27-011-268 0292, mtpb.johannesburg@tourism.gov.my.

Sweden, Klarabergsgatan 35, 2tr Box 131, 10122 Stockholm, T+46-08-249900, mtpb.stockholm@tourism.gov.my.

UK, 57 Trafalgar Sq, London WC2N 5DU, T+44-020-7930 7932, mtpb.london@tourism.gov.my.

USA, 120 East 56th St, Suite 810, New York 10022, T+1-212-745 1114, mtpb.ny@tourism.gov.my.

Brunei and Kalimantan

For tourist information, contact the relevant embassy in your country (see page 37) or see the websites listed below.

Useful websites

headlines.yahoo.com/full_coverage/ world/malaysia/ An excellent news site for Malaysian current affairs.

www.aseansec.org The Asean Secretariat, the Southeast Asian regional organization of which Singapore is a founder member.

www.brunei.gov.bn The government of Brunei's official website.

www.indonesia-tourism.com The official tourism website for Indonesia.

www.journeymalaysia.com A great web resource that covers most of Malaysia's tourist sites in an entertaining and factual way.

www.jungle-drum.com An expat view on Brunei for visitors and people living there.

www.sabahtourism.com A well-designed but hard-to-navigate site about Sabah by the state's tourism board.

www.sabahtravelguide.com A great travel site with interactive maps, tour agents, up-to-date information and good travel advice.

www.sarawaktourism.com Heaps of information on the state.

www.tourismbrunei.com Brunei's official tourism site.

www.tourismmalaysia.gov.my Tourism Malaysia's website.

www.virtualtourist.com A good website with content by other travellers. Information on hotels, restaurants, things to see and avoid.

Visas and immigration

No visa is required for a stay of up to 3 months in **Malaysia** (provided you are not going to work) for citizens of the UK, the US, Australia, New Zealand, Canada, Ireland and most other European countries. If you intend to stay in the country for longer, 2-month extensions are usually easy to get from immigration offices. Note that Israeli passport holders are not allowed to enter Malaysia.

Visitor passes issued for entry into Peninsular Malaysia are not automatically valid for entry into the states of **Sabah** and **Sarawak**. (The reason for this anomaly is that Sabah and Sarawak maintain control over immigration and even Malaysian visitors from the peninsula are required to obtain a travel permit to come here.) On entry into these states from Peninsular Malaysia, visitors will have to go through immigration and receive a new stamp in their passport, usually valid for a month. If you want to stay for longer, then you must ask the official. Apply to the immigration offices in Kota Kinabalu and Kuching for a 1-month extension; 2 extensions are usually granted with little fuss. There are certain areas of East Malaysia where entry permits are necessary; for example, Bario and the Kelabit Highlands in Sarawak. These can be obtained from the residents' offices (see appropriate sections).

All visitors to **Brunei** must have valid passports, onward tickets and sufficient funds to support themselves while in the country (though the latter is rarely checked). Visitors from the UK, Germany, New Zealand, Malaysia and Singapore do not need a visa for visits of up to 30 days. US nationals can stay for up to 3 months without visas. Visitors from Belgium, Denmark, France, Luxembourg, the Netherlands, Norway, Spain, Sweden, Switzerland, Japan, the Maldives, the Philippines, South Korea and Thailand do not need visas for visits of up to 14 days. Australian passport holders are issued visas on arrival at Brunei International Airport for stays of up to 14 days. All other nationals must obtain visas prior to arrival from diplomatic missions abroad. These visas are normally valid for 14 days, but can easily be extended. For all visitors, getting permission to extend your stay is usually a formality; apply at the **Immigration Department**, Jln Menteri, Bandar Seri Begawan.

For **Kalimantan**, visitors from several nations, including Malaysia, the Philippines and Singapore, are allowed a visa-free stay of 30 days. Visitors from nations including the following are able to get an extendable US$25 30-day Visa On Arrival (VOA) at Balikpapan, Jakarta, Bali and the overland crossing at Entikong between Kuching and Pontianak: Australia, Canada, France, Germany, Ireland, Italy, the Netherlands, New Zealand, Portugal, Spain, the UK and the USA. Check with your embassy. Pay at a booth at the port of entry. These visas are extendable at immigration offices for another 30 days (US$25). Bear in mind this could be troublesome in parts of Kalimantan and tourists who wish to stay more than 30 days will save a lot of hassle and bureaucracy by simply entering on a 60-day visa. Those wishing to stay in the country for more than 60 days will need to leave the country and come back in again, or apply for a B211 60-day visa at Indonesian embassies. These visas can be extended with the help of a local sponsor giving a total stay of 6 months;

enquire at the embassy on application. (They must be extended at an immigration office in Indonesia each month after the initial 60-day visa has expired; take it to the office 4 days before expiry.)

Those wishing to travel into Indonesia by boat from Tawau to Nunukan or Tarakan (these ports do not offer VOA) have to obtain a 60-day visa from Indonesian embassies and consulates around the world (a ticket out of the country, 2 photos and a completed visa form are necessary). Costs vary. To extend the visa in Indonesia, a fee of US$25 is levied and a sponsor letter from a local person is needed. To obtain a 60-day visitor visa in Singapore, a one-way ticket from Batam to Singapore is adequate; purchase it from the ferry centre at HarbourFront in Singapore. 60-day visas are available at Indonesian consulates in Tawau, Kuching and Kota Kinabalu. Do not wear shorts to the consulates or you face being barred from entry.

It is crucial to check this information before travelling as the visa situation in Indonesia is extremely volatile. Travellers who overstay their visa can expect a fine of US$20 a day. Those who over stay long term can expect a fine and jail sentence. See also www.indonesianembassy.org.uk.

Weights and measures

Metric, although road distances are marked in both kilometres and miles.

Women travellers

Unaccompanied women often attract unwarranted attention. Most male attention is bravado and there have been few serious incidents involving foreign female tourists (or male, for that matter). However, remember that all 3 countries in Borneo are mainly Muslim and dress appropriately, avoiding short skirts and vest tops. In beach resorts, clothing conventions are more relaxed but topless bathing remains unacceptable to most Muslims. If swimming outside beach resort areas bear in mind that local women usually bathe fully clothed, so think twice before wearing a bikini. Keep to public transport and travel during the day. Hitching is not advisable for women travelling on their own.

Working in Borneo

For jobs in Malaysia and Indonesia and tips (and links) on working there, see www.escapeartist.com/as/pac.htm. The **Centre for British Teachers** has teaching opportunities for qualified teachers to work in Brunei and Malaysia and offers fairly reasonable recompense, see www.cfbt.com. Occasional lucrative ESL teaching posts are offered in oil camps in Kaltim in Indonesia, see www.tefl.com. The Malaysian government has an incentive programme for foreigners to move or retire to the country called 'Malaysia: My Second Home'. This scheme offers a renewable 5-year multiple-entry visa called a Social Visit Pass. The catch is you need at least RM350,000 banked (depending on age and pension income) in Malaysia and a minimum RM10,000 monthly income. If you are retired, you only need one of these. Apply at Malaysian embassies or **Tourism Malaysia** offices. Check www.mm2h.com for more information. The **Ministry of Human Resources** (MOHR) provides details of labour law and practice in Malaysia, details of which can be found on www.mohr.gov.my.

Contents

Footprint features

Kuala Lumpur & Singapore

Introduction

Kuala Lumpur and Singapore serve as gateways to Borneo, and for many people this provides a good opportunity to stop over for a few days in either of these cities.

In recent decades, Malaysia's capital, Kuala Lumpur, has transformed itself from a scruffy, polluted metropolis into one of Asia's great cities, hot on the heels of Singapore. The mighty Petronas Towers (which for a time held the record as tallest buildings in the world) are fitting symbols of the new KL, a cosmopolitan place where East and West blend on every corner. Highlights include a trip up to the Skybridge on the Petronas Towers; the green, rolling Lake Gardens with its huge bird park; several good museums, including the Islamic Arts Museum; the wonderful blend of colonial and modern architecture; and, of course, the limitless shopping and dining opportunities.

Singapore is often unfairly slated as dull and sterile. Granted, the country's unprecedented climb to prosperity has been achieved at a cost – its populace strait-jacketed by what Western commentators would describe as draconian social policies. But with a more vocal younger generation coming to the fore, things are set to change. Meanwhile, the arts scene has blossomed in recent years, with a commendable line-up of new museums and galleries and, on Marina Bay, a stunning arts centre, the Esplanade - Theatres on the Bay – Singapore's answer to the Sydney Opera House. Singapore's principal lure remains its cuisine – this is a city fully deserving of the designation 'Culinary Capital of Asia' – but there are plenty of other worthy diversions. Don't miss Raffles Hotel, the Asian Civilizations Museum, the immaculate Botanical Gardens and Chinatown.

Kuala Lumpur

In the space of a century, Kuala Lumpur grew from a trading post and tin-mining shanty town into a colonial capital. Today, it is a modern, cosmopolitan business hub and centre of government. The economic boom that started in the late 1980s has caused a building bonanza that has rivalled Singapore's. In downtown Kuala Lumpur, old and new are juxtaposed. The jungled backdrop of the Supreme Court's copper-topped clock tower has been replaced by scores of stylish, high-rise office blocks, dominated by the soaring, angular-roofed Maybank headquarters. The Victorian, Moorish and Moghul-style buildings, the art deco central market, and the Chinese shophouses stand in marked contrast to these impressive skyscrapers. The Petronas Twin Towers offer the most impressive addition to the modern skyline; part of the Kuala Lumpur City Centre (KLCC) development, this is the second tallest building in the world. ▸▸ *For listings, see pages 62-69.*

Ins and outs → *Population: 1,500,000.*

Getting there As befitting Malaysia's capital, Kuala Lumpur (KL) is well linked both to other areas of Malaysia and to the wider world. The international airport, **KLIA** ⓘ *www.klia.com.my*, at Sepang, provides a slick point of entry to the country. Domestic air connections (including to Sabah and Sarawak) also pass through KLIA. Opened in 2006, the **Low Cost Carrier Terminal** (**LCCT**) ⓘ *20 km south of KLIA, www.lcct.com.my*, is dominated by AirAsia but is also used by other budget airlines. Shuttle buses connect KLIA and the LCCT (20 minutes) for RM1.50. Always check your ticket to confirm which terminal you're flying from.

The **KLIA Ekspres train** ⓘ *T03-2267 8000, www.kliaekspres.com, 30 mins, every 20 mins, RM35 (children RM15) one way*, runs between 0500 and 0100 between the airport and **KL Sentral** train station in the city centre.

Alternatively, you can take the **KLIA transit** ⓘ *35 mins, RM35*. It stops at three intermediate stations and leaves between 0550 and 0100. If using the KLIA Ekspres you can check your luggage in at KL Sentral for outgoing flights.

The **Airport Coach Service** ⓘ *T03-8787 3894, 1½ hrs, RM10*, provides an efficient service from KLIA to KL Sentral from 0630 to 2400. For those travelling to or from the LCCT Terminal with budget airlines AirAsia, Tiger Air, etc, there are a couple of excellent bus companies. **Star Shuttle** ⓘ *T03-4043 8811, www.starwira.com/index.htm 1½ hrs, RM12*, has frequent departures from Puduraya Bus Terminal to the LCCT from 0430 until 0145. **SkyBus** ⓘ *T016-217 6950, www.skybus.com.my*, runs from KL Sentral to the LCCT from 0330 to 2200. You can purchase AirAsia tickets on the bus for those in a spontaneous mood.

Bargain hard for a **taxi** to the city. For a taxi from the city to KL Airport expect to pay around RM80-100, the journey takes one hour. Hotels can arrange fares in the RM75 region. Make sure the taxi fare includes the motorway toll for either direction.

Getting around Kuala Lumpur is not the easiest city to navigate, with its sights spread thinly over a wide area. Pedestrians are not very high on the list of priorities for Malaysian urban planners, with many roads, especially outside the city centre, built without pavements, making walking both hazardous and difficult. In addition, with the exception of the area around Central Market, Chinatown and Dayabumi, distances between sights are too great to cover comfortably on foot, both because of the lack of pavements and because of heavy pollution and the hot and humid climate. Kuala Lumpur's bus system is labyrinthine and congested streets mean that travelling by taxi can make for a tedious wait in a traffic jam. Try to insist that taxi drivers use their meters, although do not be surprised if they refuse. The three **Light Rail Transit** (**LRT**), the **Monorail** and the **KMT Komuter** rail lines are undoubtedly the least hassle and provide a great elevated and air-conditioned view of the city.

Orientation   The colonial core is around the Padang and down Jalan Raja and Jalan Tun Perak. East of the Padang, straight over the bridge on Lebuh Pasar Besar, is the main commercial area, occupied by banks and finance companies. To the southeast of Merdeka Square is KL's vibrant Chinatown.

The streets to the north of the Padang – the cricket pitch in front of the old Selangor Club, next to Merdeka Square – are central shopping streets with modern department stores and smaller shops.

To find a distinctively Malay area, it is necessary to venture further out, along Jalan Raja Muda Musa to Kampong Baru, to the northeast. To the south of Kampong Baru, on the opposite side of the Klang River, is Jalan Ampang, once KL's 'millionaires' row', where tin magnates, or *towkays*, and sultans first built their homes. The road is now mainly occupied by embassies and high commissions. To the southeast of Jalan Ampang is KL's so-called Golden Triangle, to which the modern central business district has migrated. In recent years the city's residential districts have been expanding out towards the jungled hills surrounding the KL basin, at the far end of Ampang, past the zoo to the north, and to Bangsar, to the southwest. KL has become a city of condominiums, which have sprung up everywhere from the centre of town to these outlying suburbs. Greater KL sprawls out into the Klang Valley, once plantation country and now home to the industrial satellites of Petaling Jaya and Shah Alam.

The most recent – and grandiose – development is Putrajaya, Malaysia's new administrative capital, which has been hacked out of plantations 35 km south of KL.

Best time to visit   The weather is hot and humid all year round with temperatures rarely straying far below 20°C or much above 30°C. There is no rainy season per se, although you can get rainstorms throughout the year. Try to to be here for one of the festivals (see page 28), particularly the Thaipusam Festival (see page 29), one of the most colourful and shocking. To access an up-to-date weather report, call T1052.

Tourist information

The **Malaysian Tourism Centre** (**MTC**) ① *109 Jln Ampang, T03-9235 4848, www.mtc. gov.my, daily 0800-2200*, is located in an opulent mansion formerly belonging to a Malaysian planter and tin miner, it provides information on all 13 states; money-changing facilities (until 1800); an express bus ticketing counter; reservations for package holidays; a souvenir shop; a tempting chocolate boutique; a Malay restaurant; cultural shows every Tuesday, Thursday, Saturday and Sunday at 1500 (RM5); demonstrations of traditional handicrafts; and 15-minute-long audiovisual shows. There is free internet access bookable in 30-minute blocks.

There is a Visitor Services Centre on Level 3 of the airport's main terminal building. Also try **Tourism Malaysia** ① *Information Centre, Level 2, Putra World Trade Centre, 45 Jln Tun Ismail, T03-2615 8188, www.tourismmalaysia.gov.my, Mon-Fri 0900-1800*. Other useful contacts are **KL Tourist Police** ① *T03-2149 6593*, and the **Wildlife and National Parks Department** ① *Jln Cheras, T03-9075 2872, KM10*.

24 hours in Kuala Lumpur

Begin the day by heading to the Petronas Twin Towers. Queue for a free ticket to the Skybridge (closed Mondays) to survey the city from above. Head back to earth, pick up a copy of the *New Straits Times* and enjoying a leisurely *kopi* before making a foray for the classic Malay breakfast: *nasi lemak (*rice cooked in coconut milk served with prawn sambal), *ikan bilis* (like anchovies), hard-boiled egg and peanuts.

Make your way to Chinatown and discover the two facets of Malaysia's cultural heritage: the Sri Mahamariamman Temple and the Chan See Shu Yuen Temple. For the sake of cultural balance make your way to the Masjid Negara (National Mosque), stopping en route at the art deco Central Market to browse handicrafts and souvenirs.

At midday enjoy a dim sum buffet lunch which you can work off with a walk in the 90-ha Lake Gardens before looking around the Islamic Arts Museum near its southern tip.

Then shake off the past and witness Malaysia's tryst with modernity. Start the evening with a cold beer at the **Coliseum Café** before heading back to Chinatown at around 1930 when the copy-watch sellers and all kinds of other hawkers emerge from their workload.

For dinner, sample another slice of this culinary melting pot in the unique Nyonya cuisine of the Straits Chinese.

While KL doesn't have the liveliest nightlife, there is still a reasonably hot stock of bars and clubs on Jalan Pinang and Jalan P Ramlee, and less touristy options in Bangsar Baru, west of the city centre and near the university of Malaya. If your stomach grumbles after midnight, 24-hour *mamak* canteens are plentiful in Bangsar.

Lie on your bed and reflect on what's in your stomach or in your head: Indian, French, Taoist, Hindu, Chinese, Malay, Muslim and Western. Quite a cultural score for one day.

Many companies offer city tours, usually of around three hours, which include visits to Chinatown, the National Museum, the Railway Station, Thean Hou Temple, Masjid Negara (the National Mosque), the Padang area and Masjid Jamek, and which cost about RM30. City night tours take in Chinatown, the Sri Mahmariamman Temple and a cultural show (RM60). Other tours visit sights close to the city such as Batu Caves, a batik factory and the Selangor Pewter Complex (RM30), as well as day trips to Melaka, Port Dickson, Fraser's Hill, Genting Highlands and Pulau Ketam. Helicopter tours are also available.

Sights

Kuala Lumpur is a bit of a sprawl of a city. The big shopping malls, trendy restaurants and bars are clustered around The Golden Triangle and the KLCC. Here too are the Petronas Towers, once the tallest in the world, and the KL Tower, another mighty spike on the landscape. The ethnic neighbourhoods lie southwest of here – there's Chinatown, a web of bustling streets filled with temples, funeral stores, restaurants and shophouses, and Little India, packed with stores selling Bollywood DVDs, saris and spices. Also here is the colonial core where the remnants of the British empire ring Merdeka Square. You can escape from the hustle a few streets southwest of here in the Lake Gardens which house the fine Islamic Arts Museum and a bird and orchid park.

Kuala Lumpur

Sleeping 🛏
Backpackers Travellers
 Inn 6 D3
Bintang Warisan 1 D5
Carcosa Seri Negara 2 D1
Cardogan 3 D5
Citrus 18 A2
Corus 4 A6
D'Oriental Inn 20 D3
Imperial 5 D5
Mandarin Oriental 7 B5
MiCasa All Suites
 Hotel 8 A6
Pondok Lodge 9 C5
Puduraya 11 D4
Replica Inn 21 C5
Serai Inn 22 C3
Swiss Inn 10 D3
Tune 23 A3

Eating 🍴
Athena 3 C6
Bangles 1 A6
Benkay 5 A6
Bombay Palace 8 B6
Carcosa Seri
 Negara 27 D1

Ciao 7 C6
Coliseum Café 10 C3
Delaney's 9 D6
Esquire Kitchen 11 D6
E'Toile Bistro 12 C5
Formosa Vegetarian 2 D3
Golden Phoenix 12 C5
Kampachi 12 C5
Lafitte 15 B5
Marco Polo 16 C5
Nam Heong 17 D3
Old China Café 18 E3
Oriental Bowl 19 D3
Sakura Café &
 Cuisine 20 D3
Sawadee-Dee Thai
 Kitchen 4 D3
Scalini's 21 B4
Seri Angkasa 22 B4
Seri Melayu 6 C6
Shang Palace 15 C4
Shook! 24 C6
Spices 25 B5
Tarbrush 26 C6
Zipangu 15 B5

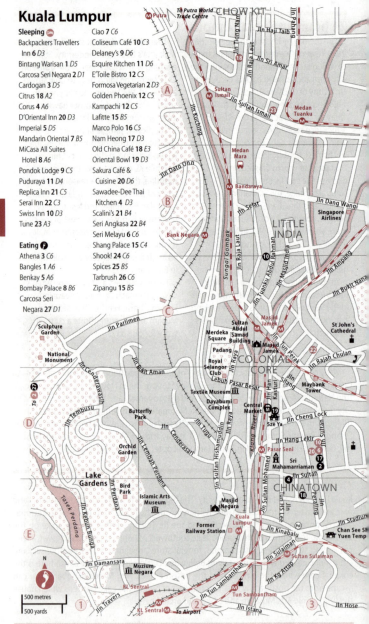

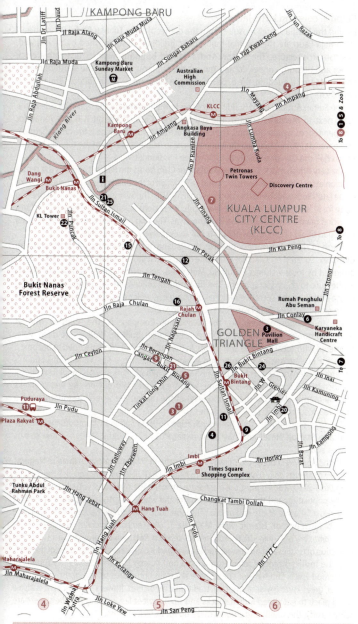

KAMPONG BARU

Jln Dr Latiff

Jln Daud

Jln Raja Alang

Jl Raja Alang

Jln Raja Muda Musa

Jln Sungai Baharu

Jln Yap Kwan Seng

Jln Tun Razak

Jln Raja Muda

Kampong Baru
Sunday Market

Australian
High
Commission

Jln Mayang

Jln Ampang

To 8 1 5 & Zoo

KLCC

Jln Raja Abdullah

Klang River

Kampong
Baru

Jln Ampang

Angkasa Raya
Building

Jln P Ramlee

Jln Limbu Kuda

Petronas
Twin Towers

Discovery Centre

KUALA LUMPUR
CITY CENTRE
(KLCC)

To 8

Dang
Wangi

Bukit Nanas

21 25

Jln Sultan Ismail

Jln Pinang

KL Tower

22

Jln Puncak

15

Jln Perak

Jln Kia Peng

Jln Stonor

Bukit Nanas
Forest Reserve

12

Jln Tengah

Jln Raja Chulan

16

Rajah
Chulan

Jln Nagasari

Rumah Penghulu
Abu Seman

Jln Conlay

6

Karyaneka
Handicraft
Centre

GOLDEN
TRIANGLE

3 Pavilion
Mall

Jln Ceylon

Jln Berangan

Cangat Bukit Bintang

9

21

5

Tinkat Tong Shin

Jln Bukit Bintang

26

Bukit
Bintang

24

Jln W Grenier

Jln Inai

7

To 7

Jln Kamuning

Puduraya

11

Jln Pudu

Plaza Rakyat

3 1

11

9

Jln Imbi

20

Jln Galloway

Jln Eberwein

4

Jln Kampong

Jln Barat

Tunku Abdul
Rahman Park

Imbi

Times Square
Shopping Complex

Jln Horley

Jln Imbi

Jln Hang Jebat

Hang Tuah

Changkat Tambi Dollah

Jln Pudu

Jln 1-777 C

Maharajalela

Jln Maharajalela

Jln Wisma
Putra

Jln Kenanga

Jln Hang Tuah

4

Jln Loke Yew

5

Jln San Peng

6

Colonial core and Little India

Behind the Masjid Jamek mosque, from the corner of Jalan Tuanku Abdul Rahman and Jalan Raja Laut, are the colonial-built public buildings, distinguished by their grand, Moorish architecture. The **Sultan Abdul Samad Building**, with its distinctive clock tower and bulbous copper domes, houses the Supreme Court. To the south of here is another Moorish building, the excellent **Textile Museum** ⓘ *26 Jln Sultan Hishamuddin, daily 0930-1800, free.*

The Sultan Abdul Samad Building faces on to the **Padang** on the opposite side of the road, next to **Merdeka Square**. The old Selangor Club cricket pitch is the venue for Independence Day celebrations. The centrepiece of Merdeka Square is the tallest flagpole in the world (100 m high) and the huge Malaysian flag that flies from the top can be seen across half the city, particularly at night when it is floodlit.

The very British mock-Tudor **Royal Selangor Club** fronts the Padang and was the centre of colonial society after its construction in 1890. Much of the building was damaged by a fire in the late 1960s and the north wing was built in 1970. The Selangor Club is still a gathering place for KL's VIPs. It has one of the finest colonial saloons, filled with trophies and pictures of cricket teams. The famous Long Bar (known as 'The Dog') – which contains a fascinating collection of old photographs of KL – is still an exclusively male preserve.

North of the mosque, back towards the Padang, is the 35-storey, marble **Dayabumi Complex**. Located on Jalan Raya, it is one of KL's most striking modern landmarks. It was designed by local architect Datuk Nik Mohamed, and introduces contemporary Islamic achitecture to the skyscraper era. The government office-cum-shopping centre used to house Petronas, the secretive national oil company, which has since moved to the even more grandiose Petronas Twin Towers (see page 60).

On the opposite bank to the Dayabumi Complex is the **Central Market** ⓘ *www.centralmarket.com.my*, a former wet market built in 1928 in art deco style, tempered with 'local Baroque' trimmings. In the early 1980s it was revamped to become a focus for KL's artistic community and a handicraft centre – KL's version of London's Covent Garden or San Francisco's Fisherman's Wharf. It is a warren of boutiques, handicraft and souvenir stalls – some with their wares laid out on the wet market's original marble slabs. On the second level of the market are several restaurants and a good foodcourt serving regional cuisines.

The fairy-tale Moorish-style **Railway Station** on Jalan Sultan Hishamuddin is now the **Heritage Station Hotel** and has been replaced by the Sentral Station a few streets further south.

To the northwest of the old railway station is the the National Mosque (**Masjid Negara**) ⓘ *open to tourists daily 0900-1230, 1400-1530 and 1700-1830, muslims can visit the mosque from 0630-2200; women must use a separate entrance*, the modern spiritual centre of KL's Malay population and the symbol of Islam for the whole country. Completed in 1965, it occupies a 5-ha site at the end of Jalan Hishamuddin. Close to the National Mosque is the superb **Museum of Islamic Arts Malaysia** ⓘ *Jln Lembah Perdana, T03-2274 2020, www.iamm.org.my, daily 1000-1800, RM10, children RM5*, which provides a fascinating collection of textiles and metalware and is a wonderful oasis of calm in the midst of the city.

Little India's streets – Jalan Masjid India and nearby lanes – echo to the sounds of Bollywood DVDs and hawker cries. There are stalls and stores selling garish gold, saris, fabrics, great *kurta* (pyjama smocks), traditional medicines, flowers and spices. It is also a good place to eat cheap Indian snacks and sip on sweet lassis. Although the streets are fairly scruffy, the smells and colours make up for its lack of gloss.

At the muddy confluence of the Klang and Gombak rivers where KL's founders stepped ashore, stands the **Masjid Jamek** ⓘ *daily 0900-1100, 1400-1600*, formerly the National Mosque (main entrance on Jalan Tun Perak). Built in 1909 by English architect, AB Hubbock, the design was based on that of a Moghul mosque in North India. The mosque has a walled courtyard (*sahn*) and a three-domed prayer hall. It is striking with its striped white and salmon-coloured brickwork and domed minarets, cupolas and arches. Surrounded by coconut palms, the mosque is an oasis of peace in the middle of modern KL, as is apparent by the number of Malays who sleep through the heat of the lunchtime rush hour on the prayer hall's cool marbled floors.

Chinatown

Southeast of the Central Market lies Chinatown, roughly bounded by Jalan Tun HS Lee (Jalan Bandar), Jalan Petaling and Jalan Sultan, a mixture of crumbling shophouses, market stalls, coffee shops and restaurants. This quarter wakes up during late afternoon, after about 1630, and in the evening, when its streets become the centre of frenetic trading and haggling. Jalan Petaling and parts of Jalan Sultan are transformed into an open-air night market, *pasar malam*, and foodstalls selling Chinese, Indian and Malay delicacies, fruit stalls, copy-watch stalls, pirate DVDs, leather bag stalls and all manner of impromptu boutiques line the streets. Jalan Hang Lekir, which straddles the gap between Jalan Sultan and Jalan Petaling, is full of popular Chinese restaurants with their tables set up on the pavement. Off the north side of Jalan Hang Lekir, there is a lively covered fruit and vegetable market in two intersecting arcades.

The extravagantly decorated **Sri Mahamariamman Temple** is south of Jalan Hang Lekir, tucked away on Jalan Tun HS Lee (Jalan Bandar). Incorporating gold, precious stones and Spanish and Italian tiles, it was founded in 1873 by Tamils from southern India who had come to Malaya as contract labourers to work in the rubber plantations or on the roads and railways. Its construction was funded by the wealthy Chettiar money-lending caste, and it was rebuilt on its present site in 1985. It has a silver chariot dedicated to Lord Murugan (Subramaniam), which is taken in procession to the Batu Caves (see page 61) during the Thaipusam Festival, when Hindu devotees converge on the temple. Large numbers flock to the temple to participate in the ritual; this is usually preceded by about half-an-hour's chanting, which itself is accompanied by music.

There are two prominent Chinese temples in the Chinatown area. The elaborate **Chan See Shu Yuen Temple**, at the southernmost end of Jalan Petaling, was built in 1906 and has a typical open courtyard and symmetrical pavilions. Paintings, woodcarvings and ceramic sculptures decorate the façade. It serves both as a place of worship and as a community centre. The older **Sze Ya Temple**, close to the central market on Lebuh Pudu, off Jalan Cheng Lock, was built in the 1880s on land donated by Yap Ah Loy. He also funded the temple's construction and a photograph of him sits on one of the altars. Ancestor worship is more usually confined to the numerous ornate clan houses (*kongsis*); a typical one is the **Chan Kongsi** on Jalan Maharajalela, near the Chan See Shu Yuen Temple.

Lake Gardens and around

Overlooking Jalan Damansara, near the southern tip of the Lake Gardens, is the **Muzium Negara** ⓘ *T03-2282 6255, www.museum.gov.my, daily 0900-1800, RM2, children RM1*, with its traditional Minangkabau-style roof and two large murals of Italian glass mosaic on either side of the main entrance. They depict the main historical episodes and cultural activities of Malaysia. The museum was opened in 1963 and, set on three floors, provides an excellent introduction to Malaysia's history, geography, natural history and culture.

Close to the museum is the south entrance to the 90-ha Lake Gardens (**Taman Tasek Perdana**). Pedal boats can be hired on the main lake, Tasek Perdana, at the weekend. The gardens also house a **Hibiscus Garden** (Taman Bunga Raya), with over 500 species; an **Orchid Garden** (Taman Bunga Orkid), which has over 800 species and is transformed into an orchid market at weekends; as well as children's playgrounds, picnic areas, restaurants and cafés, and a small deer park. At the north end of the Lake Gardens is the **National Monument**. Located at the far side of Jalan Parlimen, this 15-m-tall memorial provides a good view of Parliament House. Below the monument is a **sculpture garden** with exhibits from all the Association of South East Asian (ASEAN) countries.

The showpiece of the Lake Gardens is the **Bird Park** (**Taman Burung**) ⓘ *T03-2272 1010, www.birdpark.com.my, daily 0900-1900, RM28, children RM20.* Opened in 1991 in an effort to outdo neighbouring Singapore's famous Jurong Bird Park, this aviary at 20.9 acres is twice the size of Jurong and is billed as the world's largest covered bird park, and houses more than 2000 birds from 200 species, ranging from ducks to hornbills. Spread out over landscaped gardens, most of the birds are free and very accustomed to being around people. There are bird shows and feeding sessions of eagles, ostriches and hornbills.

The **Butterfly Park (Taman Rama-rama)** ⓘ *T03-2693 4799, daily 0900-1800, RM17,* is a five-minute drive from the main entrance to the Lake Gardens, coming in from Jalan Parlimen. It is a miniature jungle, which is home to almost 8000 butterflies, from 150 species. There are also small mammals, amphibians and reptiles, and rare tropical insects in the park. There is an insect museum and souvenir shop on the site.

To get to the Lake Gardens, take bus 21C or 48C from behind Kotaraya Plaza, or bus 18 or 21A from Chow Kit; get off at the old railway station. Taxis away from the park can be difficult to find – it may be worth either chartering one to wait for you or booking one in advance.

Kuala Lumpur City Centre (KLCC)

The old Selangor Turf Club racecourse, which lies to the southeast of this intersection, has been the focus of extraordinary redevelopment in the guise of the Kuala Lumpur City Centre (KLCC), www.klcc.com.my, a 'city within a city'. High-rise development came late to KL but has rapidly gained a foothold. The city's offices, hotels and shopping complexes are mostly concentrated in the Golden Triangle, on the east side of the city. The complex is one of the largest real estate developments in the world, covering a 40-ha site and including the Petronas Towers, see below.

Petronas Towers

ⓘ *The Skybridge is open to the public Tue-Sun 0900-1900. Visitors must queue for a ticket which gives free access to the bridge. Only a limited number of people are allowed up every day, so it is advisable to get there before 1000.*

The Petronas Twin Towers were designed by American architect Cesar Pelli and the surrounding park by Brazilian landscape artist Roberto Marx Burle. From the Skybridge, which links the two towers on the 41st floor, there are some stunning views. On Level 4, Suria KLCC Petrosains, **The Discovery Centre** ⓘ *T03-2331 8181, www.petrosains.com.my, Tue-Sun 0930-1830 (except Fri 1330-1730), RM12, children RM4,* which is really a petroleum promotion exercise, has rides and hands-on computer games all glorifying this industry, but is actually a great place for children.

Menara KL and the Bukit Nanas Forest Reserve

① T03-2020 5444, www.menarakl.com.my, daily 1000-2200, RM20, children RM10. There is no public transport – take a taxi or walk from one of the surrounding roads.

Near the intersection of Jalan Ampang and Jalan Sultan Ismail atop Bukit Nanas stands the Menara KL (**KL Tower**). This 421-m-high tower is the second tallest telecommunications tower in Asia and the fourth tallest in the world (the viewing tower stands at 276 m). The views from the top are vastly superior to the views from the Skybridge at the Petronas Twin Towers. Characteristically, the tower is the brainchild of former Prime Minister Dr Mahathir Mohammed. There are 22 levels and 2058 stairs, so the lift is recommended! At ground level there are several shops and fast-food restaurants and a mini amphitheatre. Above the viewing platform is the **Seri Angkasa** revolving restaurant. It has excellent Malay cuisine and revolves once every 60 minutes, so diners get to see the whole city between hors d'oeuvre and ice cream.

Combine a visit to the tower with a walk in the surrounding **Bukit Nanas Forest Reserve** *① free*, a beautiful 11-ha area of woodland in the centre of the city with marked trails. KL is perhaps the only city with a patch of rainforest at its heart. There are a couple of entrances into this reserve and various tracks running through it – you can get onto one of these tracks from the road going up to KL Tower. There are also ways in from Jalan Ampang and Jalan Bukit Nanas (off Jalan Raja Chulan); look for signposts. Butterflies, monkeys, squirrels and birds live in the forest. There are warnings about dangerous snakes.

The Golden Triangle

The **Rumah Penghulu Abu Seman** *① T03-2144 9273, www.badanwarisan.org.my, Mon-Sat 1000-1700 (tours at 1100 and 1500, including a video presentation, RM5),* on Jalan Stonor otherwise known as the **Heritage Centre of the Badan Warisan Malaysia**, is to be found in a mock-Tudor building off Jalan Conloy, on the northern edge of the Golden Triangle. In the garden is a reconstructed headman's house made of timber – it displays detailed carvings and is furnished in the style of a 1930s house. Just to the east of the Heritage Centre is the **Komplex Budaya Kraf**, a local handicraft centre offering visitors the chance to dabble in batik or watch artists at work.

One of the newest shopping plazas in the Golden Triangle is **Times Square** on Jalan Imbi, which features a roller coaster, an Imax cinema, and hotel complex as well as the usual retail and dining suspects.

The **Karyaneka Handicraft Centre** (Kompleks Seni Budaya) *① Jln Conlay, T03-2162 7533, daily 0900-1730, RM3, children RM1,* to the east of the city centre, is popular with tour groups. There is a small museum illustrating the batik, weaving and pottery processes. Craft demonstrations are held from 1000 to 1700, and there are crafts on sale from each of the 13 states of Malaysia. To get there, take a minibus or **RapidKL** No 40 from Jalan Tuanku Abdul Rahman.

Around Kuala Lumpur

The most popular day trip from KL is the **Batu Caves** *① 13 km north of KL, open until about 2100, RM1,* around 30 minutes' drive north (one hour by public bus) and a fun day out. This series of caverns, whose entrances are wreathed in mist, is reached by a sweat-inducing flight of steps with colourful Hindu paraphernalia everywhere. To get there take a taxi or bus 11 or 11D from near Central Market or taxi; the caves are a short walk off the main road. This system of caverns, set high in a massive limestone outcrop, was 'discovered' by American naturalist William Hornaby in the 1880s. In 1891 Hindu priests set up a shrine in the main cave dedicated to Lord Subramaniam and it has now become the biggest Indian pilgrimage centre in Malaysia during the annual Thaipusam Festival (see page 29), when over 800,000 Hindus congregate here. The main cave is reached by a steep flight of 272 steps. Coloured lights provide illumination for the fantasy features and formations of the karst limestone cavern. There are a number of other, less spectacular caves in the outcrop, including the **Museum Cave** (at ground level) displaying elaborate sculptures of Hindu mythology. During the Second World War, the Japanese Imperial Army used some of the caves as factories for the manufacture of ammunition and as arms dumps; the concrete foundations for the machinery can be seen at the foot of the cliffs.

◉ Kuala Lumpur listings

Hotel and guesthouse prices			
LL over US$200	**L** US$130-200	**AL** US$90-130	
A US$40-90	**B** US$20-40	**C** US$10-20	
D US$5-10	**E** US$2.50-5	**F** under US$2.50	
Restaurant prices			
▮▮▮ over US$10	▮▮ US$3.50-10	▮ under US$3.50	

See pages 23-27 for further information.

● Sleeping

Most top hotels are between Jln Sultan Ismail and Jln P Ramlee, in KL's Golden Triangle. South of Jln Raja Chulan, in the Bukit Bintang area, south of the Golden Triangle, there is another concentration of big hotels. There are also lots of cheap hotels in the Golden Triangle, particularly along Jln Bukit Bintang, which are convenient for upmarket restaurants, bars and shopping, while the Chinatown area is home to rock-bottom budget places which are looking the worst for wear.

Many of the cheaper hotels are around Jln Tuanku Abdul Rahman, Jln Masjid India and Jln Raja Laut, all of which are within easy walking distance of the colonial core of KL (although these tend to be quite sleazy and run down), northeast of the Padang. Some top hotels drastically reduce their room rates during weekdays.

Colonial core and Little India
p58, map p56

A **Citrus**, Jln Tiong Nam (off Jln Raja Laut), T03-9195 9999, www.citrushotelkl.com. Popular new hotel with excellent discounts, modern rooms with Wi-Fi, cable TV and

electronic safe. Colour schemes follow the hotels refreshing minimalist style. De luxe rooms have great views of the Petronas Twin Towers. Recommended.
B-E **Tune**, 316 Jln Tuanku Abdul Rahman, T03-7962 5888, www.tunehotels.com. Owned by AirAsia's Tony Fernandez, this hotel follows the no-frills budget airline model with clean, bright and functional rooms emblazoned with advertising. Wi-Fi, towels and a/c are available at additional costs on a daily basis. For best rates, book as much in advance as possible (5 months for the cheapest rates). There is a newsagents, **Subway** and shuttle bus service to the airport (RM 75) in the lobby. It's very popular at weekends.

Chinatown *p59, map p56*

A **Swiss Inn**, 62 Jln Sultan, T03-2072 3333, www.swissgarden.com. Fair value lodgings in the heart of Chinatown. Rooms in the new wing are a little on the small side, but feature flat screen TV, good mattress and new, spotless bathroom. Rooms in the older wing come without windows. Free internet access (no Wi-Fi). Breakfast included.
B **D'Oriental Inn**, 82 Jln Petaling, T03-2026 8181, www.dorientalinn.com. Newly renovated hotel with a selection of clean, well-furnished a/c rooms with attached bathroom and free Wi-Fi access in all rooms. Friendly staff. Recommended.
B **Puduraya**, 4th floor, Puduraya Bus Station, Jln Pudu, T03-2072 1000, F2070 5567. Excellent location above the bustling coach

station. This hotel is tired and looks dated but rooms are clean and some have incredible views over the city.

C Serai Inn, Jln Hang Lekiu, T03-2070 4728, www.seraiinn.com. Rooms here are tiny with paper-thin walls, but are kept spotless and all have free Wi-Fi access. Bathrooms are shared, but kept very clean. Pleasant rooftop terrace for smokers, and communal area with TV, internet access and free tea and coffee all day. Recommended.

C-E Backpackers Travellers Inn, 2nd floor, 60 Jln Sultan, T03-238 2473, www.backpackerskl.com. Well-run hotel with attached travel agency and relaxed rooftop bar/café with good views and cheap beer. Rooms are simple and the owner is proactive in the fight against bugs, with each room having bug deterrents and seamless mattress covers. Rooms are small, dark and unattractive but generally clean, ranging from a/c dorm rooms (RM 11 per night), single windowless fan rooms to a/c rooms with facilities. Also available are a book exchange, video, TV and laundry. Wi-Fi access (RM 5 per day).

Lake Gardens and around *p59, map p56*

L Carcosa Seri Negara, Taman Tasek Perdana, T03-2282 1888, www.ghmhotels.com. The former residence of the British High Commissioner and built in 1896, this is now a luxury hotel, where Queen Elizabeth II stayed when she visited Malaysia during the Commonwealth Conference in 1989 and where other important dignitaries, presidents and prime ministers are pampered on state visits. Situated in a relatively secluded wooded hillside and overlooking the Lake Gardens, this is truly fit for royalty. A/c, restaurant and pool. Recommended.

KLCC *p60, map p56*

L-AL MiCasa All Suites Hotel, 368b Jln Tun Razak, T03-2618 8333, www.micasahotel.com. Recently reopened, this place is truly first rate, especially for longer stays. It has 240 suites (which include fully equipped kitchen with utensils and sitting room), an Italian restaurant and a tapas bar. Also has a/c, pool, shopping arcade, hair salon, dentist and doctor, children's pool, jacuzzi, tennis, squash, gym, sauna, children's playhouse and business centre. Recommended.

AL Corus, Jln Ampang, T03-2161 8888, www.corushotelkl.com. Upmarket hotel with some rooms enjoying a great view of the Petronas Twin Towers. It has broadband internet, functional but comfortable rooms, a pool and Chinese and Japanese restaurants.

AL Mandarin Oriental, KLCC (next to Petronas Twin Towers), T03-3380 8888, www.mandarinoriental.com. Luxury chain hotel, with all that you would expect for its prestigious location, including some spectacular views and bookmarks with thought-provoking quotes left on pillows. Several bars and restaurants including the excellent **Pacifica**. There's also a health spa, pool, tennis, sauna and massage rooms.

The Golden Triangle *p61, map p56*

B Bintang Warisan, 68 Jln Bukit Bintang, T03-2148 8111, www.bintangwarisan.com. Well-managed hotel with clean, spacious a/c room with TV and attached bathroom. Most rooms have windows, some have excellent views of Petronas Twin Towers and some have their own garden. The only facilities are 2 small cafés. Price includes breakfast. Recommended.

B Cardogan, 64 Jln Bukit Bintang, T03-2144 4883, www.cardogan.com. A/c rooms are simple and clean but a little old with small attached white tiled bathrooms. There's a coffee house, health centre and business centre.

B Imperial, 76-80 Jln Cangkat Bukit Bintang (Jln Hicks), T03-2142 9048, www.hotelimperial.com.my. Recently revamped, this place offers a/c rooms with attached bathroom and cable TV. It's a good-value Chinese hotel in an otherwise pricey part of town, well located for shopping centres and nearby eateries.

B Replica Inn, Cangat Bukit Bintang, T03-2142 1771, www.replicainn.com. Newish place in a super location for shops and foodstalls. Rooms here are excellent value with good bedding, TV, attached bathroom and window. There's a good Malay café downstairs. Another branch is on Jln Petaling in Chinatown.

C-D Pondok Lodge, 20 Jln Cangkat Bukit Bintang, T03-2142 8449, www.pondoklodge.com. Rooms are simple and comfortable with a/c and free breakfast. What sets this place apart is the rooftop garden, and the funky upper floor lounge area which has a kitchen, big comfy sofas and a breakfast dining area.

Airport

AL Pan Pacific, T03-8787 3333, www.panpacific.com. Linked to the airport via a skybridge. With well over 400 rooms, and plenty of sports facilities and dining options.

A Airside Transit Hotel, T03-8787 4848, airsidetransit@klia.com.my. Located within the airport at satellite A. There are 80 comfortable rooms, a gym, bar and café.

LCCT

B-E Tune, T03-7962 5888, www.tunehotels.com. No-frills comfy and heavily branded lodgings handy for morning departures from the LCCT. Book well in advance for sizeable discounts.

🍴 Eating

Many of KL's big hotels in the **Jln Sultan Ismail/Bukit Bintang** areas serve excellent-value buffet lunches. Recently, **Cangkat Bukit Bintang** and **Tingkat Tong Shin**, a couple of streets sprouting west from Jln Bukit Bintang, have emerged as trendy eating areas.

Foodstalls The best area for foodstalls is **Chow Kit**. On Jln Raja Muda Abdul Aziz there is a food court with great Indian and Afghan food. Jln Haji Hussien has a picturesque collection of superb foodstalls. Walk up Jln Haji Hussien and turn right. The food court on the top floor of The Mall, built like rows of old Chinese shophouses, is run down but has an attractive ambience. The Indian, Malay and Chinese food is all good, but the majority of these eating places close by 2000. It's cheap too: tandoori chicken, naan, dal and drink, all for just RM8. **Jln Raja Alang** and **Jln Raja Bot** stalls, off Jln Tuanku Abdul Rahman, are mostly Malay. Next to Keramat supermarket there is a South Indian stall with good mutton soup. In the alleyway between Keramat supermarket and the Pakistani mosque there are lots of good foodstalls during the day. **Kampong Baru** and **Kampong Datok Keramat** are Malay communities. On the riverfront behind Jln Mesjid India are good Indian and Malay night stalls. **Jln Masjid India**, **Little India**, has many good Indian and Malay foodstalls. **Lorong Raja Muda Food Centre**, off Jln Raja Muda, on the edge of Kampong Baru, has mainly Malay food. The **Sunday Market**, Kampong Baru (main market actually takes place on Sat night), has many Malay hawker stalls.

Colonial core and Little India
p58, map p56

🍴 **Coliseum Café**, 100 Jln Tuanku Abdul Rahman (Batu Rd). Next door to the old Coliseum Theatre, this place has been long-famed for its sizzling lamb and beef steaks, Hainanese (Chinese) food and Western-style (mild) curries, all served by frantic waiters in buttoned-up white suits. During the Communist Emergency, planters were said to come here for gin and curry, handing their guns in to be kept behind the bar; it is easy to believe it. Recommended.

Chinatown *p59, map p56*

🍴 **Oriental Bowl**, 587 Leboh Pudu, T03-2202 5577. A/c restaurant above Chinese spice shop, in a convenient location for the Central Market. It has a rather formal atmosphere and a fascinating array of Chinese herbal soups (very good for stomach problems) as well as some tasty antelope and fish maw dishes.

¶¶–¶ Old China Café, 11 Jln Balai Polis, T03-2072 5915, www.oldchina.com.my. Good, interesting Nyonya and Malay favourites, including *asam* prawns (prawns cooked with candlenuts and tamarind), *mee siam* and plenty of seafood dishes. The walls are covered in old photos of Malaysia and the tables are topped with marble. Lots of olde worlde ambience. A fine choice for a romantic evening out.

¶ Formosa Vegetarian, 48 Jln Sultan. Mammoth menu of fake meats and fish, beancurds and other creative veggie dishes. Recommended.

¶ Nam Heong, 54 Jln Sultan. Open 1000-1500. Clean and non-fussy place specializing in delightful plates of delicious Hainanese chicken rice, but also featuring some wonderful Chinese delights including pork with yam (truly outstanding), *asam* fish and fresh tofu.

¶ Sawadee – Dee Thai Kitchen, G/F Plaza Warisan, Jln Tun HS Lee, T03-2070 4788. Open 0900-2100. Superb value authentic Thai dishes served up in a bright, fresh setting. The seafood fried rice is excellent. Recommended.

Lake Gardens and around *p59, map p56*

¶¶¶ Carcosa Seri Negara, Persiaran Mahameru, Taman Tasek Perdana (Lake Gardens), T03-2282 1888 (reservations). Daily 1530-1800. Built in 1896 to house the British Administrator for the Federated Malay States, **Carcosa** offers English-style high tea (recommended) in a sumptuous, colonial setting and expensive Italian lunches. Dinners are also served in the Mahsuri dining hall on fine china plates with solid silver cutlery.

KLCC *p60, map p56*

¶¶¶ Benkay, Hotel Nikko, Jln Ampang, T03-2161 1111. Japanese restaurant named after a legendary warrior. Seasonal specials, a teppanyaki room and sushi bar.

¶¶¶ Ciao, 428 Jln Tun Razak, T03-9285 4827. Tue-Sun 1200-1430 and 1900-2230.

Authentic, tasty Italian food served in a beautifully renovated bungalow. Recommended.

¶¶¶ Golden Phoenix, Hotel Equatorial, Jln Sultan Ismail, T03-2161 7777. Open 1200-1430. Gourmet Chinese establishment, which has been recently revamped, and with sleek undertones, serving up delicious dishes such as double-boiled bamboo pith with seafood soup and the Shanghainese favourite of sautéed prawns with salted egg.

¶¶¶ Kampachi, Hotel Equatorial, Jln Sultan Ismail, T03-2161 7777. Japanese place with Ginza-trained chefs, private tatami rooms and another winner of Malaysian Tourism award.

¶¶¶ Lafitte, Shangri-La Hotel, 11 Jln Sultan Ismail, T03-2074 3900. Open 1200-1500 and 1900-2300. Excellent French restaurant with an award-winning wine list, but very expensive. Formal dress in the evenings. Recommended.

¶¶¶ Shang Palace, Shangri-La Hotel, Jln Sultan Ismail, T03-2032 2388. Open 1200-1430 and 1830-2230. Sleek, posh eatery famed for its Cantonese cusine, this restaurant often has a superb value dim sum lunch of over 40 varieties – check with the hotel for current promotions.

¶¶¶ Zipangu, Shangri-La Hotel, 11 Jln Sultan Ismail, T03-2032 2388. This Japanese eatery is a regular winner of best restaurant, and has a small Japanese garden. Despite the limited menu, it's highly regarded with a cigar lounge and walk-in wine and sake cellar. Recommended.

¶¶ Bangles, 270 Jln Ampang, T03-4532 4100. This is reckoned to be among the best North Indian tandoori restaurants in KL. It's often necessary to book in the evenings. Recommended.

¶¶ Bombay Palace, 388 Jln Tun Razak, next to the US Embassy, T03-2145 4241. Open 1200-1500 and 1830-2300. Good-quality North Indian food in tasteful surroundings with staff in traditional Indian uniform; the menu includes a vegetarian section. Tourism award winners for several years.

E'Toile Bistro, Basement, Equatorial Hotel, Jln Sultan Ismail. Coffee and pastries with free internet access for all customers. Nice touch. Recommended.

Kapitan's Club, 35 Jln Ampang, T03-2201 0242. Open 1100-1500 and 1800-2230. A spacious Nyonya restaurant decorated with Straits woodwork, with staff in traditional outfits and 'top hats'. The house speciality is a tasty pastry and egg dish and the *kapitan* chicken is popular. Malay dishes are also served.

Seri Angkasa, at the top of the KL Tower (see page 61), T03-2020 5055. A sister restaurant to Seri Melayu. The tower revolves, achieving a full rotation in 60 mins. Good food, booking advisable for the evenings. There is also a good-value buffet lunch.

Spices, Concorde Hotel, 2 Jln Sultan Ismail, T03-2244 2200. Mon-Sat 1130-1500 and 1830-2300. Ironically, considering its name, the food is not overly spicy. Eclectic Asian cuisine as well as traditional Malay. There's a 4-piece band as background music, a/c indoors or poolside seating outdoors. Setengah (a stiff whisky drink popular in colonial times) features on the varied drinks list.

The Golden Triangle *p61, map p56*

There are a number of excellent Middle Eastern restaurants in this area. Also recommended are Zaytoun, Sahara Tent Restaurant and Restoran Lebanese (all around the corner from Tarbush on Jln Sultan Ismail).

Sakura Café & Cuisine, 165-169 Jln Imbi. Excellent variety of Malay, Chinese and Indian dishes including fish-head curry, located in an area with many other good cheap restaurants. Recommended.

Scalini's, 19 Jln Sultan Ismail, just down from the Istana Hotel. Perennial favourite among both expats and locals, this place serves up delightful Italian food. Pasta dishes are excellent, surroundings are trendy and the staff are friendly. Superb wine list. Pricey but recommended.

Shook!, The Feast Floor, Starhill Gallery, Jln Bukit Bintang, T03-2719 8535. Emphasizing seasonal trends, the fusion menu includes Japanese, Chinese, Italian and a Western grill. It's popular with celebrities and features a huge walk-in wine cellar with over 3000 bottles.

Athena, Pavilion Mall, T03-2141 5131. The bright blue and white decor screams Greece and, whilst there are a few Greek dishes on the menu, there is evidence of other Western influences in dishes such as Worcester striploin and nutmeg fish fillet.

Delaney's, Parkroyal Hotel, Jln Sultan Ismail. Open 1200 until late. The manufactured Irish experience available at most cities around the world. There are Asian snacks, hearty pies and a pint of Guinness – you can't go wrong.

Marco Polo, Wisma Lim Foo Yong, 86 Jln Raja Chulan, T03-2142 5595. Open 1200-1400 and 1830-2230. This place, with 1970s-style decor, has an extensive menu. The barbecue roast suckling pig is recommended. It's very busy at lunchtime.

Seri Melayu, 1 Jln Conlay, T03-2145 1833. Open 1100-1500 and 1900-2300 (reservations recommended for groups of 4 or more, although it seats 500). One of the best Malay restaurants in town in a traditional Minangkabau-style building. It is the brainchild of former Malaysian prime minister, Dr Mahatir Mohamad, with a beautifully designed interior in the style of the Negeri Sembilan palace. Don't be put off by cultural shows or the big groups; the food is superb and amazing in its variety, including regional specialities; it's very popular with locals too. Individual dishes are expensive, the buffet is the best bet (with a choice of more than 50 dishes), with promotions featuring cuisine from different states each month. Those arriving in shorts will be given a sarong to wear. Recommended.

Tarbush, 138 Jln Bukit Bintang, T03-4253 4177. Lebanese cuisine served in a simple setting. Locals recommend it for the good service and the authentic Middle Eastern taste with no Malay influence.

Esquire Kitchen, Level 1, Sungai Wang Plaza, Jln Sultan Ismail. Good-value dumplings and pork dishes, and popular Shanghai dishes.

Teahouses
Try the traditional Chinese teahouse opposite **Sungai Wang Hotel** on Jln Bukit Bintang.

🌓 Bars and clubs

Kuala Lumpur *p53, map p56*
Kuala Lumpur now has a vibrant bar scene. Several streets have emerged over the past 5 years or so as hip to be seen in. The **Golden Triangle** is a good place to find bars and clubs – the main bar and club street being **Jln P Ramlee**, but a few bars have begun setting up pumps in **Cangkat Bukit Bintang**, and this area is slated to grow more nightspots. **Bangsar** and **Desi Sri Hartamas** are 2 areas just outside the centre of KL that have developed into popular night spots. Bars, restaurants, coffee shops and *mamaks* stand side by side in a network of streets in these 2 areas. Most stay open until the early hours of the morning.

The Metro section in *The Star* (Malaysia's most widely read English-language daily) is devoted to what's on and where.
Bar Blonde, 50 Jln Doraisamy, Asian Heritage Row, T03-2691 1088, www.barblonde.com.my. Shamelessly contemporary design, cool house grooves and a roof terrace used for occasional moon parties make this a very trendy venue.
Bar Ibiza, 924 Jln P Ramlee, T03-2713 2333, www.modestos.com.my. Open 1600-0300. Trying to capture the laid-back old Ibiza vibes, this intense bar has beams of light shone on walls to look like lava. Podium dancing, drinks promotions. Ladies' night Wed and Sun.
Bed, Heritage Row, 33, Jln Yap Ah Shak, T03-2693 1122, www.bed.com.my. Trying hard to attract the beautiful people, beds are scattered around this venue for the cool to lounge to a backdrop of slick contemporary tunes.

Viper Room, D5 KL Plaza, 179 Jln Bukit Bintang, T03-2148 8471. Attracts an interesting mix of characters for pre-clubbing drinks.
Wine@Nine, Plaza TTDI, 3 Jln Wan Kadir, Taman Tun Dr Ismail, T012-286 1688. Relaxing venue with good wine list, snacks and a couple of new snooker tables.
Zouk, 113 Jln Ampang, T03-2171 1997, www.zoukclub.com.my. Perhaps KL's trendiest nightclub following in the footsteps of Singapore's **Zouk**. A glowing futuristic domed exterior, with changing hue encapsulates the groovy interior. Hosts occasional gay parties. Attracts international DJs such as Tiesto and has a great chillout bar, Velvet Underground. Now expanded, **Zouk** features 3 new clubs with distinct vibes: **Barsonic**, **Phuture** and **Aristo**. Check the website for more details. Recommended.

🎭 Entertainment

Kuala Lumpur *p53, map p56*
Cultural shows
Eden Village, 260 Jln Raja Chulan, T03-2141 4027. Malay, Indian and Chinese cultural performances on Thu, Fri, Sat between 2030 and 2130 (RM55 includes a meal).
Malaysia Tourism Centre (**MTC**), 109 Jln Ampang, T03-2164 3929. Shows on Tue, Thu, Sat and Sun at 1500 to 1545 (RM5).
Temple of Fine Arts, 116 Jln Berhala, Brickfields, T03-2274 3709. This organization, set up in Malaysia to preserve and promote Indian culture, stages cultural shows every month with dinner, music and dancing. The temple organizes an annual Festival of Arts (call for details), which involves a week-long stage production featuring traditional and modern Indian dance (free, since "the Temple believes art has no price"). It also runs classes in classical and folk dancing, and in playing traditional musical instruments.

O Shopping

Kuala Lumpur *p53, map p56*

Many of the handicrafts are imported from Indonesia. The areas to look for Chinese arts and handicrafts are along **Jln Tuanku Abdul Rahman** and in the centre of **Bangsar**. **Jln Masjid India**, running parallel with Jln Tuanku Abdul Rahman, is a treasure trove of all things Indian, from saris to sandalwood oil, from bangles to brass incense burners. For clothes, shoes, bags and textiles try **Jln Sultan** and **Jln Tun HS Lee**, close to Klang bus station. In Petaling St, Chinatown, you can barter for items such as Chinese lanterns, paintings and incense holders.

Batik Corner, Lot L1.13, Weld Shopping Centre, 76 Jln Raja Chulan. Excellent selection of sarong lengths and ready-mades in batiks from all over Malaysia and Indonesia.

Central Market, Jln Hang Kasturi. A purpose-built area with 2 floors of boutiques and stalls selling just about every conceivable craft: pewter, jewellery, jade, wood and ceramics for a start. Stalls sell anything from all kinds of moulds and cutters for baking, to wonderful spices to dried fruits. Downstairs are hand-painted silk batik scarves, while many shops sell batik in sarong lengths.

Jln Melayu is another interesting area for browsing, with Indian shops filled with silk saris and brass pots and Malay shops specializing in Islamic paraphernalia such as *songkok* (velvet Malay hats) and prayer rugs, as well as herbal medicines and oils.

Jln Tuanku Abdul Rahman, Batu Rd. This was KL's best shopping street for decades and is transformed into a pedestrian mall and night market every Sat, 1700-2200.

Kampong Baru Sunday Market (Pasar Minggu), off Jln Raja Muda Musa (a large Malay enclave at the north end of KL). This open-air market comes alive on Sat nights. Malays know it as the Sun market as their Sun starts at dusk on Sat (so don't go on the wrong night), when a variety of stalls selling batik sarongs, bamboo birdcages and traditional handicrafts compete with dozens of foodstalls. However, the Pasar Minggu has largely been superceded by the Central Market as a place to buy handicrafts.

⊖ Transport

Kuala Lumpur *p53, map p56*

Air

KL's international airport (KLIA) and the LCCT (Low Cost Carrier Terminal) are at Sepang (T03-8776 2000), 72 km south of the city. For transport to and from the airport, see page 53.

Bus

RapidKL, T03-7625 6999, www.rapidkl.com.my, has a good system of a/c buses plying the streets. See website for routes. All-day bus tickets start at RM1.

Worth considering if short of time is the **KL Hop-on Hop-off City Tour**, T03-2691 1382, www.myhoponhopoff.com, daily 0830-2030, RM38, a hi-tech variant on the London tour bus theme. Tickets are for 24 hrs and can be bought at hotels, travel agents and on the bus itself, which stops at 22 clearly marked points around town. A recorded commentary is available in 8 languages as the bus trundles around a circuit that includes KLCC, the Golden Triangle, Petaling Street (Chinatown), KL Central Station, the National Mosque and the Palace of Culture.

Car

Car-hire firms have desks at the airport terminal. Arrange a hotel pick-up service in advance or at the office outside the terminal.

Taxi

KL is one of the cheaper cities in Southeast Asia for taxis. There are stands all over town, but you can hail a taxi pretty much anywhere you like. Most are a/c and metered, but it is a challenge sometimes to get the driver to use the meter: RM2 for the first 1 km and RM0.10 for every 150 m thereafter. Extra charges apply between 2400 and 0600 (50%

surcharge), for each extra passenger in excess of two, as well as RM1 for luggage in the boot. Waiting charges are RM2 for the first 2 mins, RM0.10 for every subsequent 45 seconds. During rush hours, shift change (around 1500) or if it's raining, it can be very difficult to persuade taxis to travel to the centre of town; negotiate a price (locals claim that waving a RM10 bill helps) or jump in and feign ignorance.

For 24-hr taxi service try the following: **Comfort**, T03-8024 2727; **KL Taxi**, T03-9221 4241; **Supercab**, T03-7875 5333; and **Teletaxi**, T03-92211011. A surcharge of RM1 is made for a phone booking.

Trains
Within the city there are 5 rail systems spanning the city: 3 LRT lines, the Ampang line (yellow) and Sri Petaling line (lime green and the Kelana Jaya Line (dark green), 2 **KTM Komuter** lines (blue and red), and the new monorail (light blue). There is also the KLIA Ekspres and Transit line running from KL Sentral to the airport. Trains leave every 5-15 mins, and tickets cost upwards of RM1.20. Going from one line to the other often means coming out of the station and crossing a road! All lines except the Sri Petaling and Ampang lines go through KL Sentral. The trains are a great way to see the city as they mostly run on elevated rails, some 10 m above street level.

○ Directory

Kuala Lumpur p53, map p56
Banks Money changers are in all the big shopping centres and along the main shopping streets and they generally give better rates than banks. Most branches of the leading Malaysian and foreign banks have foreign exchange desks, although some (for example Bank Bumiputra) impose limits on charge card cash advances.There are ATMs everywhere that will provide ringgit for cards with Cirrus, Visa, MasterCard, Maestro or Plus.
Embassies and consulates Australia, 6 Jln Yap Kwan Seng, T03-2146 5555, www.australia.org.my. Canada, 17th floor, Menara Tan & Tan, 207 Jln Tun Razak, T03-2718 3333, www.international.gc.ca/missions/malaysia-malaisie/. France, 192-196 Jln Ampang, T03-2162 0671, www.ambafrance-my.org. Germany, 26th floor, Menara Tan & Tan, 207 Jln Tun Razak, T03-2170 9666, www.german-embassy.org.my. Indonesia, 233 Jln Tun Razak, T03-242 1354, www.kbrikl.org.my. Netherlands, Suite 7.01, 7th floor, The Ampblock, 218 Jln Ampang, T03-2168 6200, www.netherlands.org.my. New Zealand, 21st floor, Menara IMC, Jln Sultan Ismail, T03-2078 2533, www.nzembassy.com. UK, 185 Jln Ampang, T03-2148 2122, www.britain.org.my. USA, 376 Jln Tun Razak, T03-2168 5000, www.malaysia.usembassy.gov.
Emergencies Fire T994. Police/ambulance T999. **Immigration** Jln Pantai Bharu, T03 8880 1000, www.imi.gov.uk. **Internet** There are internet cafés everywhere, many open 24 hrs. There are dozens along Jln Bukit Bintang and a handful around Chinatown. The Chinatown internet venues are often packed with gaming schoolboys which can make it very noisy. Many backpacker places will offer internet. Expect to pay upward of RM3 per hr. Many hotels and guesthouses offer free Wi-Fi access for those travelling with laptops.
Medical services Casualty wards are open 24 hrs. Assunta Hospital, Petaling Jaya, T03-7782 3433. Damai Service Hospital, 115-119 Jln Ipoh, T03-4043 4900. Pudu Specialist Centre, Jln Baba, T03-2142 9146. Tung Shin Hospital, 102 Jln Pudu, T03-2072 1655.
Police T999; KL Tourist Police, T03 2163 4422.

Singapore

To some, Singapore has all the ambience of a supermarket checkout lane and has been described as a Californian resort-town run by Mormons and, even more famously, as Disneyland with the death penalty. It has frequently been dubbed sterile and dull – a report in The Economist *judged Singapore to be the most boring city in the world – and for those who fail to venture beyond the plazas that line Orchard Road, or spend their 3½ days on coach trips to the ersatz cultural extravaganzas, this is not surprising. But there is a cultural and architectural heritage in Singapore beyond the one that the government tries so hard to manufacture. Despite its brash consumerism and toy-town mentality, Singapore is certainly not without its charm. It is difficult to fathom, especially from afar, but beneath its slick veneer of westernized modernity, many argue that its heart and soul is undoubtedly Asian. Behind the computers, hi-tech industries, marble, steel and smoked-glass tower blocks, highways and shopping centres is a society ingrained with conservative Confucian values. For those stopping over in Singapore for just a few days, there are several key sights that should not be missed. Many who visit, however, consider that it is far more important to enjoy the food. The island has an unparalleled variety of restaurants to suit every palate and wallet and offers possibly the greatest selection of variety and quality in Asia. Inexpensive hawker centres in particular are a highly recommended part of the Singapore epicurean experience.* ▸▸ *For listings, see pages 80-90.*

Ins and outs

Getting there

Almost all visitors arrive at Singapore's **Changi Airport** ⓘ *www.changiairport.com*. With three main terminals and a budget terminal for low-cost carriers, Changi is the region's busiest and best connected, and most major airlines fly here. Over 80 airlines service the airport, connecting the city state with 116 cities in 59 countries. As well as major long-haul airlines including **British Airways**, **Cathay Pacific**, **Singapore Airlines**, **Qantas** and **American Airlines**, Changi is a hub for cheap budget Asian airlines including **AirAsia**, **Tiger Airways** and **Jet Star Asia** (all of which offer connections to cities in Borneo including KK, Miri, Kuching and Tawau). These airlines also connect Singapore with destinations as far away as India, China and Australia. ▸▸ *See also Transport, page 88.*

The **Budget Terminal** ⓘ *www.btsingapore.com*, lacks the debonair ambience of Changi's three main terminals, but has all necessary mod cons such as free internet, money changers and some dining options. There are taxis and a free shuttle bus service runs to Terminal 2 from where more comprehensive transport options are available. The service runs every 10 minutes 0500-0200 and every 30 minutes 0200-0500.

A number of **buses** run between the airport and nearby bus interchanges. Bus No 36 (0600-2400, S$2) loops along Orchard Road passing many of the major hotels including the YMCA. Another option is the **airport shuttle** ⓘ *0600-2400 every 15 mins, 2400-0600 every 30 mins, S$9, children S$6, booking counters in arrivals halls*. These minibuses will drop off at various destinations, including hotels within the central business district – make sure your hotel is covered by the door-to-door service. Note that if you are in a group of three or four, it is probably cheaper to take a taxi (see below).

The airport is connected to the **MRT underground line**. Trains to the centre of Singapore take around 27 minutes. The fare is S$2.70 inclusive of a refundable S$1 deposit for a single-trip ticket. Trains runs every 12 minutes between 0530 and 2318.

24 hours in Singapore

After a dawn stroll along the beach at the East Coast Park head to Still Road for a breakfast of half boiled eggs and toast washed down with sweet tea at a *kopitiam*. Take some time to wander around Katong and enjoy the beautiful architecture of the shophouses. Shoppers will want to head smartly over to Orchard Road and pick from a selection of Singapore's finest malls including Ion, Ngee Ann City and Wisma Atria, great for window shopping, people-watching and credit-card crunching.

End your shopping spree with a gentle walk around the **Botanic Gardens**. Hop across the river to **Chinatown** for a tour of Singapore's backbone Chinese community, with its traditional medicine shops, funeral stores, antique shops and shuttered traders' homes, now beautifully restored. On nearby Neil Road, enjoy a delicate Chinese brew at the **Tea Chapter**.

It's a few stops on the MRT line to **Little India**, whose muddle of streets are packed with astrologers, tailors, spice sellers, gaudy jewellers, stalls of sequinned fabrics, thumping Bollywood DVD stores and vendors of Hindu paraphernalia.

As dusk falls head to the Singapore Flyer for superlative sunset views over the city before moving on to the **Singapore River**, to enjoy a cocktail followed by dinner at one of the waterside restaurants.

Dinner does not spell the end of the night, however. Take a taxi to Singapore's **Night Safari** for a tour of the zoo in the dark.

The city has tried hard to pump life into its party scene, to some success. If you feel like dancing and you've got the cash, head to **Zouk**, **New Asia Bar** or **The Butter Factory**, all cool spots that attract the glam set.

On your way home, chat to your taxi driver, who, in perfect Singlish, will no doubt praise his clean, ordered city.

Taxis queue up outside the arrival halls. As a general rule, taxi drivers in Singapore are straightforward and honest folk and, unless you're on an incredibly tight budget, they offer the most painless and hassle-free method to find a bed for the night. They are metered but there is an airport surcharge of S$3, which increases to S$5 on Friday, Saturday and Sunday between 1700 and 2400. A trip to the centre of town should cost from S$18 to S$28 – the only exception being a further 50% fee for late arrivals between 2400 and 0600. Most taxi companies operate a **limousine service** (London cab or Mercedes) with a fee of S$16 plus the metered fare. To book a limousine service from your hotel, call **Comfort City Cab**, T6552 1111, or **Comfort Premier Cab**, T6552 2828.

Car hire desks for **Avis** ① *T6545 0 800*, and **Hertz** ① *T6542 5300*, are open 0700 to 2300 at the arrivals hall in all three main terminals.

Best time to visit

There is no best season to visit Singapore and it is hot throughout the year. It gets even stickier before the monsoon breaks in November, while the hottest months are July and August. The wettest months are November, December and January, during the period of the northeast monsoon, when it is also coolest, but even 'cool' days are hot by most temperate people's standards. As one would expect, the hottest time of day is early afternoon, when the average temperature is around 30°C, but even during the coolest time of the day, just before dawn, the temperature is still nearly 24°C.

Tourist information

For a good, free, official guide called the *Visitor's Guide to Singapore* and for brochures and maps, visit a branch of the **Singapore Tourism Board** ① *Tourism Court, 1 Orchard Spring Lane, T1800-736 2000 (24-hr and toll-free in Singapore), www.visitsingapore.com, daily, 0800-2230; also at: Liang Court Shopping Centre, 177 River Valley Rd, Level 1, T6336 2888, daily 1030-2200; Plaza Singapura, 68 Orchard Rd Level 1, T6332 9298, daily 1000-2200. Changi Airport, arrivals halls 1 and 2, daily 0600-0200; The Galleria at Suntec City Mall, T6333 3825, daily 1000-1800 and The Inn Crowd Backpacker's Hostel, 73 Dunlop St, Little India, T6296 4280, daily 1000-2200.* Complaints can also be registered at these offices. The 24-hour Touristline gives automated information in English, Mandarin, Japanese and German. Also useful are the **Indonesian Tourist Board** ① *T6737 7422*, and the **Malaysian Tourist Board** ① *Ocean Building, 11 Collyer Quay, T6532 6351.*

Sights

Singapore is a city state with a land area of around 710 sq km and, as public transport is impeccably quick and efficient, nowhere is exactly 'off the beaten track'.

Singapore is a great place to bring young children. It is clean, safe and efficient, there are good hospitals, you can drink the water and drivers take notice of pedestrian crossings – all in all it is a child-friendly and parent-soothing place to visit. There are also a multitude of places to see.

Colonial core

The **Padang** ('playing field' in Malay) is at the centre of the colonial area. Many of the great events in Singapore's short history have been played out within sight or sound of the Padang. It was close to here that Stamford Raffles first set foot on the island on the morning of 28 January 1819, where the Japanese surrendered to Lord Louis Mountbatten on 12 September 1945, and where Lee Kuan Yew, the first Prime Minister of the city state, declared the country independent in 1959.

Flanking the Padang are the houses of justice and government: the domed **Supreme Court** (formerly the Hotel de l'Europe) and the City Hall. The neoclassical **City Hall** was built with Indian convict labour for a trifling S$2 million and was finished in 1929. Hearings usually start at 1000 and the public are allowed to sit at the back and hear cases in session; you can enter via the lower entrance at the front.

The revamped Raffles Hotel – with its 875 designer-uniformed staff (a ratio of two staff to every guest) and 104 suites (each fitted with Persian carpets), eight restaurants, a culinary academy, five bars, playhouse and custom-built, leather-upholstered cabs, is the jewel in the crown of Singapore's tourist industry. In true Singapore style, it manages to boast a 5000-sq-m shopping arcade and there's even a **museum** ① *daily 1000-1900, free,* of rafflesian memorabilia on the third floor. The **Palm Court** is still there and so is the **Tiffin Room**, which still serves tiffin (a snack/lunch).

West of **Raffles Hotel** is **Fort Canning Park**, which, over the last few years, has evolved into something a little more ambitious than just a park. The **Battle Box** ① *daily 1000-1800, last admission 1700, S$8, children S$5,* opened in 1997, is a museum contained within the bunker where General Percival directed the unsuccessful campaign against the invading Japanese in 1942. Visitors are first shown a 15-minute video recounting the events that led up to the capture of Singapore. They are then led into the Malaya Command headquarters – the Battle Box – where the events of the final historic day, 15

February 1942, are re-enacted. Visitors are given earphones and are then taken from the radio room, to the cipher rooms and on to the command room, before arriving at the bunker where Percival gathered his senior commanders for their final, fateful, meeting. It is very well done with a good commentary, figures and film. The bunker is also air conditioned, a big plus after the hot walk up. Dhoby Ghaut is the nearest MRT.

Above the Battle Box are the **ruins of Fort Canning**: the Gothic gateway, derelict guardhouse and earthworks are all that remain of a fort which once covered 3 ha. There are now some 40 modern sculptures here. Below the sculpture garden to the south is the renovated **Fort Canning Centre** (built 1926), which is the home venue of **Theatre Works** and the **Singapore Dance Theatre**. In front of Fort Canning Centre is an old Christian cemetery – **Fort Green** – where the first settlers, including the architect George Coleman, are buried.

Below Canning Hill, on Clemenceau Avenue, is the Hindu **Chettiar Temple**, also known as the **Sri Thandayuthapani Temple**. The original temple on this site was built in the 19th century by wealthy Chettiar Indians (money-lending caste). It has been superseded by a modern version, finished in 1984, and is dedicated to Lord Subramaniam (also known as Lord Muruga). The ceiling has 48 painted-glass panels, angled to reflect sunset and sunrise. Its gopuram, the five-tiered entrance, aisles, columns and hall all sport rich sculptures depicting Hindu deities, carved by sculptors trained in Madras. This Hindu temple is the richest in Singapore – some argue, in all of Southeast Asia. It is here that the spectacular Kavadi procession of the Thaipusam Festival (see page 29) culminates.

Singapore River and the City

The mouth of the river is marked by the bizarre symbol of Singapore – the grotesque **Merlion statue**, half lion, half mermaid. The financial heart of the city is just south of here – tall towers cast shadows on streets which on weekdays are a frenzy of suited traders, bankers and office workers. The most pleasant area by far is along the river, which offers peaceful walks along its banks. The riverside is punctuated with pockets of restaurants and bars making it a lively place at night. It is inspired by the two ancient (Sanskrit) names for the island: *Singa Pura* meaning 'lion city', and *Temasek* meaning 'sea-town'.

On the north side of the river, opposite the Merlion and looking like a pair of giant metal durians, is the **Esplanade - Theatres on the Bay** ⓘ www.esplanade.com, the centre of Singapore's performing arts scene. Within the complex there's a 1800-seater concert hall, a 2000-seat theatre, and various outdoor performing spaces and, of course, a shopping mall. To get there, walk through the underground CityLink Mall (from City Hall MRT).

A 20-minute walk from the Esplanade along Raffles Avenue is one of Singapore's newer attractions, the **Singapore Flyer** ⓘ *30 Raffles Ave, T6738 3338, www.singaporeflyer.com.sg, daily 0800-2200, S$29.50, children S$20.65, shuttle bus every 30 mins from City Hall MRT*. This rotating wheel, similiar to the London Eye, stands at 165 m above sea level and is currently the largest Ferris wheel on Earth. A ride offers outstanding views over the city, the busy shipping lanes and the islands of Indonesia's Riau province beyond. Rides last around 30 minutes and the capsules are filled with mellow beats. The Flyer has encountered numerous problems since opening, with financial troubles (locals claim it is too expensive) and five breakdowns, including the dramatic incident in 2008 when a short circuit caused the wheel to stop moving, trapping 173 passengers for six hours.

The **Marina Barrage** is an impressive 350-m dam built across the Marina Channel between Marina South and Marina East, completed in 2008. This award-winning project created Singapore's 15th reservoir, forming the new downtown Marina Reservoir out of the Kallang Basin. The dam is made up of nine gates to block the tide. Each 30 m-long gate has a

Singapore

Sleeping
Footprints Hostel **17** B5
Four Seasons **2** B2
Fullerton **11** C5
G4 Station **18** B4
The Gallery **14** C4
Goodwood Park **1** B3
Hangout@MtEmily **19** B4
The Hive **4** A5
Hotel 1929 **13** D4
The Inn at Temple Street **5** D4
Inncrowd Backpackers
  Hostel **12** B5
Keong Saik **6** D4
Naumi **7** C5
Perak **8** B5
The Prince of Wales **15** B5
Raffles **9** C5
Sleepy Sam's **20** B5
Superb Hub **21** B5
YMCA International
  House One Orchard **3** C4
YWCA Fort Canning
  Lodge **10** C4

Eating
1827 **16** C4
Al Dente Trattoria **2** C4
Ananda Bhavan **20** B5
Annalakshmi **14** C4
Au Jardin **1** B1
Blu **3** A2
Brewerkz **6** C4
Capella **13** C5
Cosafe Bar & Restaurant **21** C5
Esmiradas **9** B3
The French Stall **11** A5
Indochine **15** D4
Indochine Waterfront
  Restaurant **17** C5
Inle **12** C4
Kamal's Vegetarian **18** B5
Kinara **19** C4
Komala's Fast Food **12** C4
L'Entrepot Bistro **23** C4
Lei Garden **13** C5
Lei Garden Orchard Road **4** B4
Madras Woodlands **10** B5
Muthu's Curry **9** B5
Newton Circus Food
  Centre **5** A3
Rochor Beancurd **24** B4
Sakura **25** B3

Eating continued
Seah Street Deli **26** C5
Senso **27** D4
Shahi Maharani **22** C5
Song Fa Bak Kut Teh **23** C4

Soup 28 C5
Thanying **19** D4
True Blue Peranakan
  Cuisine **24** C4
Zam Zam **29** B5

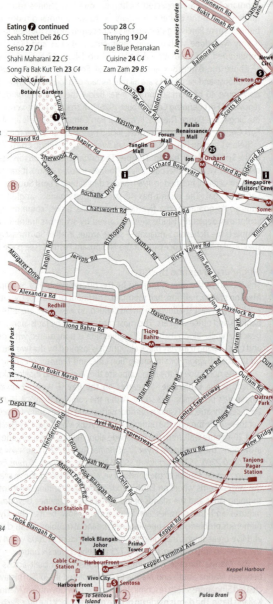

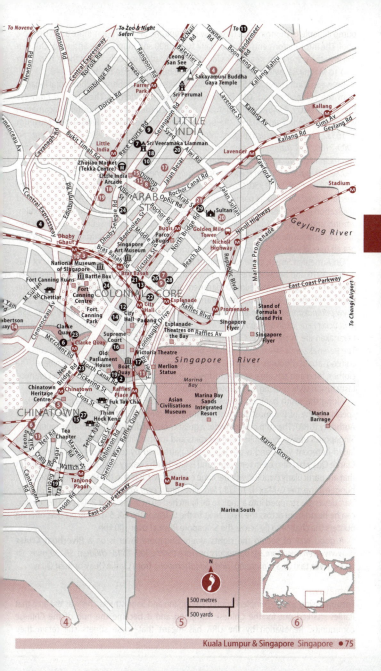

pump capable of pumping out the equivalent volume of water per minute as an Olympic pool. The information centre is open daily 1000-1800 and tours can be arranged. Children will love the water play area with its fountains and paddling pools. To get there, hop on an MRT to Marina Bay where there are free shuttle buses going to the barrage.

Between High Street and Singapore River there are a number of architectural legacies from the colonial period: **Old Parliament House**, the **Victoria Theatre** and **Empress Place**. The latter, a thoroughly confused building, underwent yet another reincarnation when it reopened in 2003 as the second wing of the **Asian Civilisations Museum** ⓘ *T6332 2982, www.acm.org.sg, Mon 1300-1900, Tue-Sun 0900-1900, except Fri 0900-2100, S$8 (admission fees for various exhibitions vary), joint ticket for ACM and Pernakan Museum S$12, under 6s free, over 60s free entry on Mon, reduced entry fee Fri 1900-2100, guided tours in a variety of languages, ones in English Mon 1400, Tue-Fri 1100 and 1400 and Sat-Sun 1330. Check the website for tours in other languages and details of special guided tours*. As its name suggests, the focus of the museum is Asian culture and civilization – 5000 years of it. The 11 galleries explore religion, art, architecture, textiles, writing and ceramics from China to West Asia. It's a superb museum, with interactive features and some superb displays of artefacts from around Asia, and is a good place to get an overall view of Singapore and its history within the regional framework.

On Armenian Street, close to Stamford Road, is a restored school. Tao Nan School was built in 1910 and became one of the first Chinese schools in Singapore. It has been taken over by the Singapore Museums Department and in 1997 opened as the first branch of the Asian Civilisations Museum. The **Peranakan Museum** ⓘ *39 Armenian St, T6332 7591, www.peranakanmuseum.com.sg, Mon 1300-1900, Tue-Sun 0900-1900, Fri 0900-2100, S$6, joint ticket Peranakan Museum and ACM $12, free entry 1900-2100 Fri*, has exhibits describing Peranakan life in the Straits Chinese-dominated cities of Singapore, Melaka and Penang. The Perenakans or Straits Chinese have been one of the region's most important cultures, coming about through centuries of intermarriage between Malays and Chinese. The clothes, food and arts are a wonderful fusion of colours and tastes with gorgeous ceramics, tasty fusion style cooking and colourful fashions.

Along the south bank of the river, facing Empress Place, is **Boat Quay**; commercially speaking, one of the most successful restoration projects of the Urban Redevelopment Authority (URA). The strip now provides a great choice of drinking holes and restaurants for Singapore's upwardly mobile young, expats and tourists, although the area's hipness has faded in recent years and is predominantly patronised by tourists only. Further upriver, **Clarke Quay** has also been renovated and is lined with swanky shops, bars and restaurants that are particularly popular with the large expat crowd. It is also the site of Singapore's first bungee jump, the **G-Max** ⓘ *T6338 1146, www.gmax.com.sg, open 1300-0100, S$45 per ride*. Daredevils are strapped into a chair to be launched 60 m in the air at 200 kph. The screams can be heard from across the river. Next to the G-Max is the **GX-5** ⓘ *S$40 per ride*, offering punters the chance to fly across the Singapore River at over 100 kph.

A good way of seeing the sights along Singapore River is on a **Riverboat Cruise** ⓘ *www.rivercruise.com.sg, bumboats operate 0900-2300, S$13, children $8, 30 mins*. Or take a **river taxi** ⓘ *$1 (morning) and S$3 (afternoon)*, from Clarke Quay or Boat Quay.

Chinatown

Encompassing Smith, Temple, Pagoda, Trengganu and Sago streets, this was the area that Raffles marked out for the Chinese kampong and it became the hub of the Chinese community. Renovation by the URA has meant that these streets still retain their characteristic baroque-style shophouses, with weathered shutters and ornamentation. A good example is the **Thong Chai Medical Institute** on Eu Tong Sen Street, at the corner of Merchant Road. In **Sago Street** (or 'death house alley' as it was known in Cantonese, after its hospices for the dying), **Temple Street** and **Smith Street**, there are shops making paper houses and cars, designed to improve the quality of the afterlife for dead relatives. The English probably gave Sago Street its name in the early 19th century, as Singapore became a centre of high-quality sago production for export to India and Europe. There are also a number of **Chinese medicine shops** in this area and others on Sago Street. On show are antlers and horns, dried frogs and flying lizards, mushrooms and fungi, dried seahorses and octopus, sharks' fins and ginseng. For a full range of Chinese products – from silk camisoles, to herbal medicines, to beaded bags and Chinese tea – visit the **Yue Hwa Chinese Emporium** on the corner of Eu Tong Sen and Upper Cross streets.

As if to illustrate Singapore's reputation as a racial and religious melting pot, the Hindu **Sri Mariamman Temple** is situated nearby at 244 South Bridge Road. The building is dedicated to Sri Mariamman, a manifestation of Siva's wife Parvati. The temple is the site of the annual Thimithi Festival, which takes place at the end of October or the beginning of November.

Also located on Pagoda Street is the **Chinatown Heritage Centre** ⓘ *T6325 2878, www.chinatownheritagecentre.sg, daily 0900-2000, last admission 1900, S$10, children S$6,* which is well worth a visit. The centre evocatively captures the lives of early Chinese settlers with mock-ups of boats, coffee houses, opium dens, and squalid housing through the ages including kitchens, bedrooms, and even a prostitute's boudoir.

Telok Ayer Street is full of shophouses and fascinating temples of different religions and was once one of the most important in Singapore. The city's oldest Chinese temple, the Taoist **Thian Hock Keng** temple, or Temple of Heavenly Happiness, is a gem (notwithstanding the naff fibreglass wishing well in one corner). A little way north of Thian Hock Keng is another much smaller Chinese temple, the **Fuk Tak Chai Temple** ⓘ *76 Telok Ayer St, daily 1000-2200, free,* one of the oldest of Singapore's temples, restored in 1998 and now a museum. It's a little oasis of calm amidst the frenetic life of the city and holds a limited display of exhibits, including some Peranakan jewellery, Chinese stone inscriptions, a pair of porcelain pillows, a model of a Chinese junk and an excellent 'diorama' of Telok Ayer Street, as it must have been in the mid-1850s.

One of Chinatown's more interesting places to visit is the **Tea Chapter** ⓘ *9 Neil Rd, www.tea-chapter.com.sg, daily 1100-2300,* where visitors are introduced to the intricacies of tea tasting in elegant surroundings. You will be invited to remove your shoes, and can choose in one of their special rooms or upstairs on the floor. All in all it's a soothing experience.

Orchard Road and Botanic Gardens

Orchard Road is a long curl of air-conditioned malls, the spine of modern-day Singapore and home to its national pastime: shopping. This glass-fronted materialism is nicely juxtaposed at its western edge with the Botanic Gardens, an elegant park planted with rubber trees, hundreds of orchids, and popular with joggers and stretching tai chi practitioners. There are three MRT stations on, or close to, Orchard Road: Dhoby Ghaut, at the eastern end, Somerset, on Somerset Road, and Orchard station, at the intersection of Orchard Road and Scotts Road. To walk Orchard Road from end to end is quite a slog; from Dhoby Ghaut to the northwestern end of Orchard Road past Scotts Road is around 2.5 km.

At the western end of Orchard Road, on Cluny Road, not far from Tanglin, are the **Botanic Gardens** ⓘ *T6471 9933, www.sbg.org.sg, daily 0500-2400, free.* The gardens contain almost

500,000 species of plants and trees from around the world in its 47 ha of landscaped parkland, primary jungle, lawns and lakes. Every morning and evening the park fills with joggers and tai chi fanatics. The bandstand is used for live music at the weekends. A map can be acquired from the Ranger's office, five minutes' walk into the garden. Lots of buses run past the Botanic Gardens including Nos 7, 77, 105, 106, 123 and 174 (alight at the junction of Cluny and Napier roads, next to Gleneagles Hospital). The Botanic Gardens also house the **National Orchid Garden** ⓘ *daily 0830-1900, last ticket sales at 1800, S\$5, children S\$1*, where 700 species and 2100 hybrids of Singapore's favourite flower are lovingly cultivated. It is billed as the 'Largest Orchid Showcase in the World'. The closest entrance to the Botanic Gardens for the Orchid Garden is on Tyersall Avenue.

Little India

The city's South Asian community has its roots in the grid of streets branching off Serangoon Road. Tourist-spruced handicraft shops are packed into the Little India Arcade opposite the more gritty wet market of the Tekka Centre. The best Indian restaurants lie shoulder to shoulder along Race Course Road, while a bit of exploring will unearth theatres, a Bengali temple and a hand-operated spice mill. Little India **MRT** station on the Northeast line has an exit that opens onto the Tekka Centre market.

The lively **Zhujiao** (or Tekka Centre) **Market**, on the corner of Buffalo and Serangoon roads, is an entertaining spot to wander. Spices can be ground to your own requirements. Upstairs there is a maze of shops and stalls; the wet market is beyond the hawker centre, travelling west along Buffalo Road. Opposite the market on Serangoon Road is the **Little India Arcade**, another Urban Redevelopment Authority (URA) project. This collection of handicraft shops is a great place to pick up Indian knick-knacks: leather sandals and bags, spices and curry powders, incense, saris and other printed textiles. There is also a food court. The closely packed shops in the network of streets house astrologers, framers, tailors, spice merchants, jewellers and pumping Bollywood DVD and Hindi CD shops. Walking up Serangoon Road, take a right at Cuff Road to see Little India's last **spice mill** ⓘ *closed 1300-1400*, at work in a blue and mustard yellow shophouse, owned by P Govindasamai Pillai. It's hard to miss the chugging of the mill and the rich smells of the spices.

The **Sri Veeramakaliamman Temple** ⓘ *Serangoon Rd, closed 1230-1600*, is dedicated to Kali, the ferocious incarnation of Siva's wife. Worshippers and visitors should walk clockwise around the temple hall and, for good luck, an odd number of times. The principal black image of Kali in the temple hall (clasping her club of destruction) is flanked by her sons, Ganesha and Murugan.

Further up Serangoon Road is another Indian temple, **Sri Perumal** ⓘ *daily 0630-1200, 1800-2100*, with its high goporum sculptured with five manifestations of Vishnu. For the best experience of all, visit during the two-day festival of **Thaipusam** – generally held in January – which celebrates the birthday of Murugan, one of Kali's sons.

Further north is the **Buddhist Sakayamuni Buddha Gaya Temple** (Temple of One Thousand Lights) ⓘ *366 Race Course Rd (parallel to Serangoon Rd), daily 0730-1645; remove shoes before entering*. Across the road is the Chinese Mahayana Buddhist **Leong San See Temple** (Dragon Mountain Temple) with its carved entrance (where you don't have to remove your shoes).

Arab Street

The smallest of Singapore's ethnic quarters, Arab Street is a pedestrianized tourist market strip with shops hawking all manner of Middle Eastern and Islamic goods – prayer rugs,

Egyptian perfume bottles, baskets, rattan, silk, velvets and jewellery. There are also great Middle Eastern canteens and the imposing golden-domed **Sultan Mosque** ① *North Bridge Rd, 0900-1300, 1400-1600*, which attracts thousands of the faithful every Friday. Remember to dress modestly. In the maze of side streets around the Sultan Mosque, there is a colourful jumble of Malay, Indonesian and Middle Eastern merchandise. Excellent selections of batik (which is sold in sarong lengths of just over 2 m) jostle for space with silk and Indian textiles (especially along Arab Street), wickerware, jewellery, perfumes and religious paraphernalia. **Bugis Street** is southwest of Arab Street, right across the road from the Bugis Street MRT station. It is packed with stalls selling cheap T-shirts, copy watches and handicrafts, like a street market you may see in Thailand or Malaysia, but something that seems out of place in modern-day Singapore. The whole street has been recreated from a road that was demolished to make way for the MRT in the mid-1980s.

Jurong Bird Park

① *Jln Ahmad Ibrahim, T6265 0022, www.birdpark.com.sg, daily 0830-1800, last admission 1730. S\$18, children aged 3-12 S\$9, 3-in-1 tickets to the bird park, zoo and night safari S\$45, children S\$22.50 (tickets valid for 1 month). There are several bird shows every hour. MRT westbound to Boon Lay then SBS bus No 194 or 251 from Boon Lay Bus Interchange. There is a monorail service round the park for those who find the heat too much, S\$4, children S\$2.*

Situated on Jalan Ahmad Ibrahim, Jurong Bird Park is a beautifully kept 20-ha haven for more than 8000 birds of 600 species from all over the world, including a large collection of Southeast Asian birds. Highlights include the world's largest collection of Southeast Asian hornbills and South American toucans and an entertaining, air-conditioned penguin corner, complete with snow. Another attraction is one of the world's largest walk-in aviaries, with a 30-m-high man-made waterfall and 1500 birds.

Singapore Zoo and Night Safari

① *80 Mandai Lake Rd, T6269 3411, www.zoo.com.sg, daily 0830-1800, S\$18, children aged 3-12 S\$9; tram ride S\$5, children S\$2.50. Boat docks for 20-min rides to attractions S\$5, children S\$2.50. For a 3-in-1 ticket combining the zoo, the night safari and Jurong Bird Park, see the bird park above; combined Zoo and Night Safari ticket, S\$32, children S\$16. Take the MRT to Ang Mo Kio and then bus No 138. A taxi from the city costs around S\$20 and takes 30 mins.*

These zoological gardens have one of the world's few open zoos – with moats replacing bars – making it also one of the most attractive, with animals in environments vaguely reminiscent of their habitats. It contains over 170 species of animals (about 2000 actual animals), some of them rare – like the dinosauric Komodo dragons and the golden lion tamarin – as well as many endangered species from Asia, such as the Sumatran tiger and the clouded leopard. The pygmy hippos are relatively recent newcomers; they live in glass-fronted enclosures (as do the polar bears), so visitors can watch their underwater exploits. Animals are sponsored by companies; Tiger beer, for example, sponsors the tigers and Qantas the kangaroos. There are animal shows throughout the day carrying a strong ecological message: elephants (at 1130 and 1530) and penguins, sealions and manatees at the newly revamped Splash Ampitheatres (at 1100, 1430 and 1700). Animal feeding times are provided upon arrival. There are tram tours for those too weary to walk (S\$5 and S\$2.50), with recorded commentaries, and several restaurants. Overall, it is a well-managed and informative zoo and well worth the trip out there.

Next to the zoo, the unique **Night Safari** ① *www.nightsafari.com.sg, daily 1900-2400, S\$22, children S\$11; with tram ride S\$32, children S\$16, the last tram leaves at 2315, no flash* cameras permitted; 3-in-1 park combination tickets for Night Safari, Zoo and Bird Park (see the bird park on page 79), 2-in-1 combination ticket S$32, children S$16; to get there, see Singapore Zoo, above, has been cunningly converted into a series of habitats, populated with wildlife from the Indo-Malayan, Indian, Himalayan and African zoogeographical regions. The park supports 1200 animals belonging to 110 species, including the tiger, Indian lion, great Indian rhinoceros, fishing cat, Malayan tapir, Asian elephant, bongo, striped hyena, Cape buffalo and giraffe. Visitors can either hop on a tram to be taken on a 40-minute guided safari through the jungle, or they can walk along three short trails at their own pace – or they can do both. The whole affair is extremely well conceived and managed, and the experience is rewardingly authentic. Children especially, love the experience.

◉ Singapore listings

Hotel and guesthouse prices

LL over US$200 **L** US$130-200 **AL** US$90-130
A US$40-90 **B** US$20-40 **C** US$10-20
D US$5-10 **E** US$2.50-5 **F** under US$2.50
See page 24 for further information.

Restaurant prices

♔♔♔ over US$10 **♔♔** US$3.50-10 **♔** under US$3.50.

● Sleeping

Many of Singapore's upmarket hotels are concentrated in the main shopping and business areas, including Orchard and Scotts roads, and near Raffles City and the Marina complexes. Discounts are almost always on offer and few people pay the full rate. Enquire at the airport hotel desk on arrival whether there are any special offers. Singapore offers an excellent choice of hotels in our upper categories, from luxury to tourist class. Though rooms may be more expensive than equivalent classes of hotels elsewhere in the region, they try to make up for this in terms of service. It's rare to stay in a hotel that doesn't offer attentive and professional care. Budget hotels have improved a lot in Singapore over the last decade, from the bed-bug riddled pits of the start of the century to an excellent selection of comfortable, bright and clean guesthouses and hostels, often staffed by cheery and enthusiastic folk. The majority of budget guesthouses are located around Little India, Arab Street and Bugis Junction. Compared to other places in Southeast Asia, Singapore's budget guesthouses and hostels aren't budget at all. Private rooms usually start

at S$55 and a dorm bed costs from S$15. It's imperative to book ahead as the better places fill up fast and walking under the blazing midday sun with a backpack is no fun at all.

Tipping is virtually nonexistent; only tip for special personal services. Most hotels and restaurants add 10% service charge and 5% government tax to bills.

Colonial core p72, map p74

LL Raffles Hotel, 1 Beach Rd, T6337 1886, www.raffleshotel.com. Singapore's most famous hotel and, despite criticisms, it is still a great place to stay if you can afford it. There are 9 restaurants and a Culinary Academy, 5 bars and 70 shops. The 103 suites have been immaculately refurbished, with wooden floors, high ceilings, stylish colonial furniture and plenty of space. Bathrooms are the ultimate in luxury and the other facilities are excellent – a peaceful rooftop pool with jacuzzis (although the gym is small), both 24 hr. Very exclusive. Highly recommended.
L-AL The Gallery, 76 Robertson Quay, T6849 8686, www.galleryhotel.com.sg. Marketed as the 'first hip hotel in Singapore', this Philip Starck-styled hotel provides 222 minimalist rooms, divided between 3 ultra-modern blocks. Brightly coloured cushions provide some light relief from the austerity in the standard rooms (showers only in these rooms). There's free internet access in all rooms, and 'smart wired rooms' have their lighting and a/c controlled with sensors, offering such features as guiding

lights to the bathroom at night without having to press a switch. The 5th-floor pool is certainly different, with glass on all sides. The hotel has chillout lounges and bars including the popular **Liquid Room** club.

AL Naumi, 41 Seah St, T6403 6000, www.naumihotel.com. Gorgeous, intimate boutique hotel with ultra-modern decor and well set up for the business traveller. The executive patio suites are huge and have an outdoor patio area, perfect for an evening drink. There's also a contemporary fitness centre, a rooftop infinity pool with delightful views over the city and a bar and restaurant. Recommended.

Chinatown *p76, map p74*

L Fullerton Hotel, 1 Fullerton Sq, T6733 8388, www.fullertonhotel.com. In a great position at the head of the Singapore River, this is Singapore's 5-star newcomer. It has 399 rooms in Phillipe Starck style, and is very functional and well equipped. Its restaurants are excellent. The infinity pool is stunning, with views over the Singapore River, with the CBD on one side and Boat Quay on the other.

AL Hotel 1929, 50 Keong Saik Rd, T6347 1929, www.hotel1929.com. Tasteful, slick boutique hotel with extremely well-furnished rooms. The owners have used their own collection of retro and designer furniture for this quirkily restored shophouse. The 32 rooms are small, but so chic that size does not matter. There's no pool or gym, but a small rooftop jacuzzi, and small, but excellent restaurant, **Ember**. Highly recommended.

AL The Inn at Temple Street, 36 Temple St, T6221 5333, www.theinn.com.sg. Billing itself as a boutique hotel, the 42 rooms here do have a certain charm. Each is well appointed with safe, cable TV, Wi-Fi access and Peranakan-style furniture and attached shower or bath. On the downside, the rooms are very small; not even the de luxe rooms have space for a desk (except in the few single rooms), which will put off business travellers.

AL-A Keong Saik, 69 Keong Saik Rd, T62230660, www.keongsaikhotel.com.sg.

An intimate little 'business' hotel in a sensitively restored shophouse, with 25 a/c, immaculately presented rooms containing attractive wooden furniture. It is let down by small room size, with little space for anything other than the bed. Standard rooms have no windows or skylights (attic rooms). Wi-Fi in lobby only (chargeable).

Orchard Road and Botanic Gardens
p77, map p74

L Four Seasons, 190 Orchard Blvd, T6734 1110, www.fourseasons.com/ singapore. Hard to beat, this intimate hotel of 254 rooms (and more than 300 staff) provides exceptional personal service. Rooms are elegantly decorated in traditional European style, with feather pillows, writing desks, and spacious bathrooms. The hotel has a unique Asian art collection, with 1500 pieces, including the attractive artwork in all the rooms. There are 2 pools – one is for lengths – and the hotel boasts the only a/c tennis courts in Singapore, a golf simulator and a well-equipped health and fitness centre, with attendants on hand all day. Full spa service with Thai masseuses from their sister resort in Chiang Mai. Restaurants include Cantonese and international cuisine. The weekend brunch at **Jiang-Nan Chun** is a real treat with over 100 dishes to choose from. Although mainly a business hotel, children are well catered for. Recommended.

L Goodwood Park, 22 Scotts Rd, T6737 7411, www.goodwoodparkhotel.com. Apart from **Raffles**, this is the only other colonial hotel in Singapore. The exterior is rakish rather than modern and the lobby area isn't very encouraging, but the rooms are exceptional. Of the 233 rooms, there is a choice of colonial or modern style. The former have ceiling fans and windows that can be opened, with very stylish minimalist decor and lots of space. The modern rooms are slightly smaller, but they overlook the Mayfair pool and some rooms on the ground level lead straight out poolside. All rooms are fitted with the latest electronic equipment. There is a lovely pool area, set in a garden with pagodas, and another larger pool for lengths. It has several restaurants. Recommended.

A-B YMCA International House One Orchard, 1 Orchard Rd, T6336 6000, www.ymca.org.sg. Facilities are well above the usual YMCA standards and include a/c, a restaurant, a rooftop pool, squash, badminton, billiards and a fitness centre. Very clean, efficient and in an unbeatable position at the head of Orchard Rd next to the National Museum. Rooms are minimalist but clean, spacious and light. Good coffee shop, but the constant religious soundtrack can be a bit much. Not cheap, but good value for the location. Recommended.

A-B YWCA Fort Canning Lodge, 6 Fort Canning Rd, T6338 4222, www.nof.ywca.org.sg. Large modern building with 175 plus rooms, a pool, tennis courts and Wi-Fi access in the lobby and café. Despite being a YWCA, it's not your average youth hostel. Dorms available.

Little India p78, map p74

This area offers the best selection of budget digs in town. With some excellent new hostels opening in recent years, this vibrant area is an excellent place to base yourself and has great facilities for those on a shoestring, or those seeking a bit of local style away from the glassy towerblocks.

AL Perak, 12 Perak Rd, T6299 7733, www.perak lodge.net. One of Singapore's better mid-range options, this early 19th-century building has plenty of archipelago flavour, wooden overtones and comfortable rooms with cable TV, minifridge and Wi-Fi access. Some of the rooms are a little dim so ask to see a selection. Friendly atmosphere, excellent buffet breakfast with daily newspapers and good location down a side street in the heart of Little India. There's a pleasant reception area and 2 family suites/apartments make the most of the attic space. Highly recommended.

AL-B Hangout@Mt Emily, 10A Upper Wilkie Rd, T6438 5588, www.hangouthotels.com. Accessed by a steep set of steps and resting on top of a hill, this is prime flashpacker accommodation with comfy, bright modern rooms and dorms with free Wi-Fi access, patio area with games and a chill-out lounge with TV, newspapers and magazines to browse. Excellent range of facilities. Significant discounts available for online reservations. Highly recommended.

A-B G4 Station, 11 Mackenzie Rd, T6334 5644, www.g4station.com. Sparkling new hostel that has taken the Singapore backpacker scene by storm with its spotless dorms and double rooms, friendly staff and superb location on the edge of Little India. Free Wi-Fi, and a handy coin-operated laundry. Recommended.

A-C Footprints Hostel, 25A Perak Rd, T6295 5134, www.footprintshostel.com.sg. Friendly hostel with a range of 6-12 bed dorms and a couple of private doubles. The communal toilets are kept clean and there are enough of them to ensure no leg crossing in the morning. Free Wi-Fi access, breakfast. Friendly staff and communal TV area. Recommended.

B-C The Hive, 624 Serangoon Rd, T6341 5041, www.thehivebackpackers.com. Good-value lodgings near Boon Keng MRT. Rooms here vary a lot from airy and bright to dark and sad, so check a selection. The de luxe rooms, at S\$5 more than the standard ones, are worth the money in terms of extra space and natural light. Beds can be a bit creaky. Free Wi-Fi and internet access, breakfast, loads of travel information and friendly staff.

B-C (dorms **D** pp) **The Inncrowd Hostel**, 73 Dunlop St, T6296 9169, www.the-inn crowd.com. State-of-the-art backpackers' hostel, colourful and welcoming with all the facilities you need: internet, kitchen, communal lounge with TV and plenty of DVDs, breakfast included and a bar next door. Dorms are basic but clean and there are good showers. The only slight problem is its own success, with rooms often booked weeks in advance.

B-C The Prince Of Wales, 101 Dunlop St, T6229 0130, www.pow.com.sg. Prime backpacker lodgings with clean dorms and a few recently renovated doubles in the depths of Little India. There's live music downstairs most nights (fairly noisy). Convivial vibes and friendly staff. Recommended.

Arab Street *p78, map p74*

A-C Sleepy Sam's, 55 Bussorah St, T9277 4988, www.sleepysams.com. Quiet and charming location away from the crowds, these lodgings provides clean, private rooms and dorms (including a female-only dorm), internet access and helpful staff.

B Superb Hub, 144 Arab St, T9669 9990, superbhub@yahoo.com.sg. Whilst rooms are good value and spotlessly clean, they are small and many are windlowless. The place needs an injection of charm, but if it's quiet, simple, safe and clean lodgings you're after, this place is more than adequate. Free Wi-Fi access.

Airport

A Ambassador Transit Hotel Terminal, in transit malls of each of Changi's 3 terminals, T6542 5538, www.airport-hotel.com.sg. Short-term rate quoted (6 hrs). A good place to take a break if you're stuck at Changi for an extended period and don't need to clear immigration. It also provides a 'freshen-up' service including showers, sauna and gym. Excellent budget room rates (shared bathroom and showers). Booking is recommended.

● Eating

Eating is the national pastime in Singapore and is something of a refined art. The island is a tropical paradise for epicureans of every persuasion and budget. Fish-head curry must surely qualify as the national dish, but you can sample 10 Chinese cuisines, North and South Indian, Malay and Nonya (Straits Chinese) food, plus Indonesian, Vietnamese, Thai, Japanese, Korean, French, Italian (and other European), Russian and Mexican. There's a good choice of Western food at the top end of the market, a few good places in the middle bracket, and swelling ranks of cheaper fast-food restaurants and an explosion of pizza outlets.

The best places to eat include **Chinatown**, **Little India** and **Arab St**. In the last few years top-end eateries have burgeoned along **Club St**, all catering for city business people.

For North Indian cuisine, the best option is to the southern end of **Race Course Rd**, where there are 6 good restaurants in a row, all competing for business, including the **Banana Leaf Apolo**, **Delhi** and, most famous of all, **Muthu's**. Some of the best vegetarian restaurants – South Indian particularly – are found on the other side of **Serangoon Rd**, along Upper Dickson Rd. **Arab St** is the best area for Muslim food of all descriptions – Malay, Indonesian, Indian or Arabic.

Colonial core *p72, map p74*

♨♨♨ **1827**, the Arts House, Old Parliament House, 1 Parliament Lane, T6337 1871, www.theartshouse.com.sg. Elegant Thai restaurant on the ground floor of the beautifully renovated Parliament House, also a well-regarded arts venue. Great ambience.

♨♨♨ **Annalakshmi**, 133 New Bridge Rd, Chinatown Point, B1-02, T6339 9993, Annalakshmi. Open for lunch and dinner, until 2130. North and South Indian vegetarian cuisine. Staffed by unpaid housewives, with profits going to the Kalamandhir Indian cultural group. The health drinks are excellent, especially mango *tharang* (mango juice, honey and ginger) and Annalakshmi special (fruit juice, yoghurt, honey and ginger). There's another branch at 104 Amoy St.

♨♨♨ **Capella**, CHIJMES, 01-29, 30 Victoria St, T6334 9927. Large Italian restaurant with earthy copper overtones and sleek modern furnishings. Some excellent pasta and risottos and fair set lunches. Prices are intimidating. Popular Sat-Sun.

♨♨♨ **Cosafe Bar and Restaurant**, 01-11 CHIJMES, 30 Victoria St, T6339 2276. Owned by a Singaporean teen with an obsession with Japanese *Cosplay* (costume play), this place is staffed by young ladies in maid uniforms with impeccable service, and is notable in that it is one of the only *cosplay* cafés outside Japan to have survived more than a few years. The food is a strange mix of Asian and Western, and the novelty factor high. It's a friendly, quirky spot for a light meal or drink.

♨♨♨ **Lei Garden**, 01-24, CHIJMES, 30 Victoria St, T6339 3822. A menu claiming to comprise

2000 dishes. Outstanding Cantonese food: silver codfish, emperor's chicken and regulars like dim sum and Peking duck. Dignitaries, royalty and film stars dine here. Tasteful decor and a 2-tier aquarium displaying the day's offerings. Despite seating 250, you need to book in advance. Worth every cent. Recommended.

Shahi Maharani, 03-21B, Raffles City, 252 North Bridge Rd, T6235 8840. North Indian tandoor, especially good seafood dishes. Live performances during dinner; a cosy place.

True Blue Peranakan Cuisine, 47/49 Armenian St, T6440 0449. Located in a beautifully restored shophouse near the Peranakan Museum, this place offers sensual, colourful Peranakan style in abundance, award-winning chefs and the city's most authentic Nyonya dining. Highly recommended.

Seah Street Deli, ground floor, Raffles Hotel, 1 Beach Rd, T6412 1816. New York style-deli counter with plenty of Americana, gleaming white tiles and some of Singapore's juicest burgers with a range of fillings. Also, sandwiches and salads. Recommended.

Soup, 39 Seah St. A chain of popular Cantonese restaurants serving herbal soups and Guangdong favourites. The steamed chicken is excellent.

Inle, Peninsula Plaza, Basement, Coleman St. One of Singapore's rare Burmese restaurants. Simple canteen style, with Burmese coffee and Shan noodles. There are a couple of other Burmese cheapies down here, with the sour, spicy curries worth a try.

Komala's Fast Food, Peninsula Plaza, Basement, Coleman St. One of Komala's fast-food outlets, serving good South Indian delicacies including thalis, masala dosas and idlis, served at competitive prices; a/c. Next door is the more upmarket **Ganges**, which lays on a superb eat-as-much-as-you-can lunchtime Indian vegetarian buffet spread.

Singapore River and the City *p73, map p74*

Restaurants overlooking the river at Boat Quay (bargains sometimes available), Clarke Quay and Robertson Quay are hugely popular, as much for the river breeze and views as anything else – a casual stroll along the riverbank is as good method as any to find your perfect spot. Boat Quay can get a bit rowdy on weekend evenings.

Al Dente Trattoria, 71 Boat Quay, T6536 5336. Good pizza and lobster pasta. Also has a Holland Village branch and a branch at the Esplanade offering superb views at night.

Brewerkz, Riverside Point, opposite Clarke Quay, T6438 2311. This very popular American-style restaurant and bar provides most of its seating under awnings by the riverfront. Great place for lunch, with a menu of satay, buffalo wings, nachos, burgers, steaks and pizza. Also has a children's menu. However, it's the beer from the mircobrewery that is the stand-out offering here.

Indochine Waterfront Restaurant, 1 Empress Place (next to Asian Civilisations Museum), T6339 1720, www.indochine. com.sg. Delightful decor and Indochinese food. There's plenty of fish on the menu here, from squid to mussels to tiger prawns. The restaurant is filled with the sumptuous hues of the Mekong, Shan antiques and Czech chandeliers. Superb river views at night further enhance the romantic ambience. The restaurant has sister establishments at Wisma Atria on Orchard Rd, Club St and Clarke Quay.

Kinara, 57 Boat Quay, T6533 0412. With distinctive wooden doors at the entrance, this place serves North Indian frontier cuisine. There's a good choice of tandoori-baked meat or vegetarian alternatives and a few good southen Indian offerings too, including the rich Keralan fish curry. Equally atmospheric **Fez** bar upstairs, often quiet and with a big screen showing football matches.

L'Entrepot Bistro, Clarke Quay, Blk E, Unit 01-02, T6337 5585. French-style bistro with a decent wine cellar, hearty fare and dainty wooden tables. It's all a little contrived, but makes for a fun escape from the tropics.

Song Fa Bak Kut Teh, 111 New Bridge Rd, T6533 6128. Small and busy eatery with traditional Chinese decor, alfresco seating

Asian flavours

While Singapore is well known for its three main populations of Indians, Chinese and Malays, there are significant communities of other Asian nationalities that have their own hangout areas. If you want some good authentic Asian cuisine head to **The Golden Mile Complex** on Beach Road for Thai food, **City Plaza** near Paya Lebar MRT for Indonesian fare, **Tanjong Pagar Rd** for hearty Korean food, **Lucky Plaza** on Orchard Road for Filipino cuisine, **Peninsula Plaza** near City Hall MRT for authentic Burmese grub and for Middle Eastern flavours head to **Arab Street**, which has a smattering of Arabic eateries. The Japanese form one of the largest communities of foreigners here and their food can be found all over the city.

and bowls of delicious *bak kut teh* (a Hokkien pork rib herbal soup) and range of Chinese teas. Highly recommended.

Chinatown *p76, map p74*

♥♥♥ **Indochine**, 49B Club St, T6323 0503, www.indochine.com.sg. Sister to **Indochine** at Empress Place. On the ground floor is the **Sa Vanh Bar** (1700-0300), ethnically decorated with a laid-back feel, whilst dining is on the upper floor. Running water on both levels adds to the serene atmosphere, which is undermined by tables being too close together.

♥♥♥ **Senso**, 21 Club St, T6224 3534. An all-Italian experience, with 'neo-classical Italian cooking'. Superb cuisine, great atmosphere, sophisticated London-style joint.

♥♥♥ **Thanying**, Amara Hotel, T6227 7856. A hallmark of Singaporean fine dining, Thanying provides the best Thai food in town, with an extensive menu and superb food (the 15 female chefs are all said to have trained in the royal household in Bangkok). Specialities include deep-fried garoupa, *yam som-o* (spicy pomelo salad), *khao niaw durian* (durian served on a bed of sticky rice – available from May-Aug), as well as such classics as *tom yam kung* (spicy prawn soup with lemongrass). Booking necessary. Recommended.

Orchard Road and Botanic Gardens *p77, map p74*

♥♥♥ **Au Jardin**, EJH Corner House, Singapore Botanic Gardens Visitors' Centre, 1 Cluny Rd, T6466 8812. Situated in the former garden director's black and white bungalow, with only 12 tables, this French restaurant is elegant and sophisticated, with a menu that is changed weekly. Booking essential.

♥♥♥ **Blu**, Shangri-La Hotel, 22 Orange Grove Rd, T62134598. Situated on the 24th floor, **Blu** provides stunning views, great service and excellent Californian food. Recommended.

♥♥♥ **Esmirada's**, corner of Peranakan Pl and Orchard Rd, T6735 3476. Mediterranean food in Spanish-style taverna, good salads, paella, Moroccan couscous. Always packed, reservations recommended. The Mediterranean theme even extends to a Greek plate-smashing ceremony on busy nights.

♥ **Sakura**, 5/F Far East Plaza. Packed restaurant with no pretensions serving halal Thai-Chinese fare. Extraordinarily popular.

Little India *p78, map p74*

♥♥♥ **The French Stall**, 544 Serangoon Rd, T6299 3544. Closed Mon. Charming place owned by a former 5-star hotel French chef who cooks up 'no-frills French cuisine' in a rather Gallic *kopitiam*. The set menu is excellent value and the chocolate mousse rich, heavy and sinful. Recommended.

♥ **Ananda Bhavan**, 95 Syed Alwi Rd, T6297 9522. Pure-veg Indian dishes served in spotless environs with walls covered with information on the benefits of vegetarianism. The food is excellent with a range of fliing thalis, dosai and a selection of *chaat*. Open 24 hrs.

♥ **Banana Leaf Apollo**, 56-58 Race Course Rd. North Indian food, another popular fish-head curry spot, a/c and more sophisticated than the name might imply – although the food is still served on banana leaves to justify the name. Recommended.

†† Muthu's Curry, 138 Race Course Rd, T6392 1722. North Indian food, one of the finest authentic Indian restaurants in town, not catering for bloated expats in search of standard London curries, but Indians on the lookout for contemporary flavours, good presentation and lively ambience. Muthu's fish-heads are famous. Highly recommended. Another branch in Suntec City.

† Kamal's Vegetarian, Cuff Rd. Vegetarian restaurant; excellent paper and masala dosas.

† Madras Woodlands, 22 Belilios Lane. Good vegetarian Indian food, very clean, but staff can be a bit abrupt. Great-value buffet lunch.

† Rochor Beancurd, corner of Middle Rd and Short St. Popular noodle joint.

Arab Street p78, map p74

† Zam Zam, junction of Arab St and North Bridge Rd. Muslim Malay-Indian dishes served in busy and chaotic coffee shop. Very popular and recommended for a taste of the other Singapore: spicy meats, chargrilled seafood, creamy curries.

Hawker centres and food courts

Food courts are the modern, a/c, sanitized version of Singapore's old hawker centres. Hawker centres are found beneath HDB blocks and in some specially allocated areas in the city; food courts are usually in the basement of shopping plazas. Customers claim a table, then graze their way down the rows of Chinese, Malay and Indian stalls. It's not necessary to eat from the stall you are sitting next to.

Lau Pa Sat Festival Market (formerly the **Telok Ayer Food Centre**), Raffles Quay end of Shenton Way in the old Victorian market. Good range of food on offer: Chinese, Indian, Nonya, Korean, Penang, ice creams and fruit drinks. It's best in the evening when Boon Tat St is closed off and satay stalls serve up cheap, tasty sticks of chicken, beef, mutton or prawns washed down with jugs of Tiger beer.

Lavender Food Square, Lavender Rd, north of Little India. One of the best hawker centres.

Newton Circus, Scotts Rd, north of Orchard Rd. Despite threats of closure by the government, this huge food centre of over 100 stalls is still surviving and dishing up some of the best food of its kind. Open later than others so very popular with tourists, and said to be a favourite haunt of celebrated Chinese (now Singaporean) actress Gong Li.

Zhujiao or Kandang Kerbau (KK) Food Centre, corner of Buffalo and Serangoon roads. Wide range of dishes, and the best place for Indian Muslim food: curries, *rotis*, *dosai* and *murtabak* are hard to beat (beer can be bought from the Chinese stalls on the other side).

🍷 Bars and clubs

Singapore p70, map p74

There are lots of bars on **Boat** and **Clarke** quays; those at the former are wilder and less packaged, although the last few years has seen a slight deterioration in quality as locals have moved on and tourists have become the dominant clientele. One of the more dramatic changes over the past couple of years is the development along the riverfront westwards. Both **Robertson's Walk** and **The Quayside** are gradually filling up with shops and restaurants, and the nearby **Mohammed Sultan Rd** has become an extremely popular watering hole; the entire street is lined with bars and clubs. The west side is a row of restored shophouses, whilst the east is a modern high-rise block.

There are several quiet bars on **Duxton Hill**, Chinatown, in a pleasant area of restored shophouses – a retreat from the hustle and bustle of Boat Quay or the city. **Duxton Rd** and **Tanjong Pagar Rd** also have a dozen or so bars in restored shophouses.

Peranakan Place just off Hollywood Rd is home to a string of funky New York-style bars carved out of restored shophouses.

Singapore's newest posh nightlife hub can be found at Dempsey Hill, the quiet and green site of the former British army barracks but now the place to be seen. Places to try include **Red Dot Brewhouse**, 0101 Dempsey Rd, an excellent microbrewery; **Camp**, 8D Dempsey Rd renowned for its cocktails, check out the Tiffin Punch; and **Oosh**, 22 Dempsey Rd, with water features, waiter call buttons and a stern dress code.

There are several options in the famous Raffles Hotel, Beach Rd. The **Bar and Billiard Room** is lavishly furnished with teak tables, oriental carpets and 2 original billiard tables. **The Long Bar**, home to the Singapore Sling, originally concocted by bartender Ngiam Tong Boon in 1915, is now on 2 levels and extremely popular with tourists and locals; gratuitous, tiny, dancing mechanical *punkah-wallahs* sway out of sync to the cover band. Finally there's the **Writers' Bar** (just off the main lobby), in honour of the likes of Somerset Maugham, Rudyard Kipling, Joseph Conrad, Noel Coward and Herman Hesse, who are said either to have wined, dined or stayed at the hotel. Bar research (ie bookcases and mementoes) indicates that other literary luminaries from James A Michener to Noel Barber and the great Arthur Hailey have also sipped Tigers at the bar.

Café Del Mar, Siloso Beach. Located on the beach, this cousin of Ibiza's renowned chill-out bar also plays mellow beats in stylish bar with dipping pool. Also worth checking out at Sentosa are **KM8** on Tanjong Beach and **Club Islander** on Palawan Beach.

Insomnia, CHIJMES, 30 Victoria St. Popular late-night drinking den with live music, top 40 hits and a fairly wild crowd. Packed Sat-Sun.

Loof, Odeon Towers Rooftop, 331 North Bridge Rd, 03-07. Individualistic lounge bar with unique seating plan, gorgeous rooftop garden with superb city views and chilled beats soundtrack. This place is popular with the well-heeled artsy set and is a good spot to meet some of Singapore's less conventional types. Range of promotions include 2-for-1 when it rains and free flow of satay on Mon.

New Asia Bar, atop **Swissotel Stamford**. S$25 admission of Fri, Sat after 2100, including 1 drink. Suave drinking locale with a good happy hour and ice-cold cans of Caffreys. As the bar is on the 71st floor, the real reason to come here is for the stunning views over the city. It's possible to come here during the day for a coffee and to snap some pics, but don't expect to be let in wearing flip flops.

Nihonshu, 33 Mohamed Sultan Rd. Japanese bar with over 100 different types of sake to choose from. Worth a visit for something a little different.

Paulaner Brauhaus, Time-Square@Millenia Walk, 9 Raffles Blvd. Microbrewery serving a huge range of freshly brewed German beers to expat Teutons and merry boozers from around the planet. German sausage and other Teutonic delicacies such as fatty pork knuckle. The weekly Sun brunch is excellent value and great fun.

Penny Black, 26 Boat Quay. A stylized English Victorian London pub, with some classic English food. This is the place to go to watch Premiership matches at weekends.

St James Power Station, HarbourFront. Located in Singapore's first coal-fired power station, the coal has now well and truly gone and been replaced by this mega complex of bars and sophisticated clubs. Places worth a look include Cuban- inspired **Movida**, **Dragonfly** for Mandarin pop music, commercial dance at mega club **Powerhouse** and live music in the **Boiler Room**.

Siam Supperclub, UE Square, 207 River Valley Rd. A tastefully decorated place (with a reputed 56 Buddha images on display), spirit mixes such as 'Buddha jumps over the wall'.

Tivoli Beer Bar, Robertson Walk, 11 Unity St 01-23. Friendly Danish-themed bar with plenty of big TVs for football fans, alfresco seating. Be warned: Liverpool games take priority.

Velvet Underground, 17 Jiak Kim St (off Kim Seng Rd), next door to **Zouk** and under the same management. Tue-Sat 2100-0300. Small nightclub playing contemporary dance music. Those in the mood for some summer of love vibes will want to drop in on Thu for the club's Balearic night. Cover S$25-S$30. Often has gay or lesbian parties. Recommended.

Yard, 294 River Valley Rd. The Singaporean version of a London pub, with darts, dominos, fish 'n' chips and Newcastle Brown Ale.

Zouk, 17 Jiak Kim St, opposite the **Concorde Hotel**. Huge quirky club, with a fun design. The place for hard clubbing. Attracts big-name international DJs. Hosts one of Singapore's most popular nights on Wed, Mambo Jambo. Ladies free Wed.

O Shopping

Singapore *p70, map p74*

Singaporeans have taken shopping to their hearts and to new heights. While the city is not the bargain basement place it was, it is still a great place to browse and buy with care. It doesn't take long to get the feel of where you can bargain and where you can't. Department stores are fixed price, but most smaller places – even those in smart shopping malls – can sometimes be talked into discounts; 20-30% or more can be knocked off the asking price.

The best area for window shopping is **Scotts Rd** and **Orchard Rd**, with many big complexes and department stores. This area comes alive after dark and most shops stay open late. The towering **Raffles City Complex**, **Parco** at Bugis Junction, **Suntec City** Ion@Orchard, Vivo City and **Marina Sq** are the other main centres. Serangoon Rd (or **Little India**), **Arab St** and **Chinatown** offer a more exotic shopping experience.

▲ Activities and tours

Singapore *p70, map p74*

MegaZip Adventure Park, Sentosa, T6884 5602, www.megazip.com.sg. Daily 1400-1700. S$10-60. Take blue line bus to Imbiah Lookout from where it is a 3-min walk. New adventure park much loved by thrill seekers, Megazip consists of 4 rides. The most fun is the 450-m long Megazip flying fox which is the steepest in Asia and gets up to speeds of 50 kph. The ClimbMax features climbing obstacles 40 m

above the jungle floor with superb views over the shipping lanes (for those without vertigo). **Ski 360**, 1206A East Coast Parkway, T6442 7318, www.ski360degree.com. Daily 1000-2200. S$32 per hr Mon-Fri, S$42 per hr Sat-Sun. Singapore's first cable ski park, with participants tied to a cable and pulled around a lake at speeds of up to 58 kph on skis or a wakeboard. Brilliant fun and considerably cheaper than hiring a boat and skis or board. Try and visit Mon-Fri, when you're likely to have the park to yourself. Weekends can be hellish here.

⊖ Transport

Singapore *p70, map p74*

To discourage Singaporeans from clogging the roads with private cars, the island's public transport system was designed to be cheap and painless. Buses go almost everywhere, and the Mass Rapid Transit (MRT) underground railway provides an extremely efficient subterranean back-up.

Call **TransitLink**, T1800-2255 663, daily 0800-1800 or check www.transitlink.com.sg, for bus, MRT and LRT information. A useful guide to Singapore's transport system is the *TransitLink Guide* (S$2), listing all bus and MRT routes and stops and available at news outlets, bookshops, MRT stations and many hotels.

An **Ez-link card**, www.ezlink.com.sg, costs S$15 (S$10 stored value and S$5 non-refundable card deposit) from MRT stations and TransitLink ticket offices (for locations, see www.transitlink.com.sg). It can be used on buses, the MRT and LRT, some taxis and 7-Eleven stores. It's worth buying if you plan to use public transport extensively.

Air

For Changi International Airport, see page 70.

Bus

For anyone visiting Singapore for more than a couple of days, the bus is a great way to get to the spots not yet covered by the MRT. SBS (**Singapore Bus Service**), T1800-287 2727, www.sbstransit.com.sg, is cheap, efficient and convenient. Fares range from 80¢ (non a/c) to S$1.80 (cheaper with an ez-link card). Buses run daily with a Nite Owl service operating after 2400. Nite Owl buses charge a flat rate of S$3. **SMRT** buses, www.smrt buses.com.sg, have fares from 80¢ to S$1.80. It runs a Night Rider service S$3 flat rate. Routes for all buses are listed (with a special section on buses to tourist spots) in the aforementioned *Transit Link Guide*. Tourists can get the useful **Singapore Tourist Pass** (T6223 2282, www.thesingaporetourist pass.com), giving unlimited travel on Singapore buses and MRT lines. The passes are valid for up to 5 days and can be topped up at a Transit Link Office. The pass costs S$8 per day, excluding a one-off refundable S$10 card rental fee.

Note For new arrivals, make sure you have the correct change in coins for buses. Bus drivers don't give change from notes!

Car
Car hire from **Avis** (T6545 0800) and **Hertz** (T6542 5300) desks open 0700-2300 at the arrivals hall in all 3 main terminals.

Mass Rapid Transit (MRT)
Singapore has one of the most technologically advanced, user-friendly light railway systems in the world; about a third of the system is underground. The designer stations of marble, glass and chrome are cool, spotless and suicide-free, thanks to the sealed-in, a/c platforms. 9 of the underground stations serve as self-sufficient, blast-proof emergency bunkers for Singaporeans. Smoking is strictly banned on all public transport; transgression is punishable by a large fine. Eating or drinking inside stations is also strictly forbidden.

There are 4 MRT lines: the North-East line runs from HarbourFront through Chinatown and Little India to Punggol in the northeast. The North-South line runs from Jurong East (for the Singapore Science Centre) in a loop north passing Kranji (for buses to Johor Bahru in Malaysia) and down to Marina Bay passing through Orchard Rd, City Hall and Raffles Place. The East-West line runs from Joo Koon in the west through City Hall, Bugis and onto Changi Airport. The circle line was only partially open at the time of writing, from Marymount to Dhoby Ghaut via Bras Basah. When this line is completed it will run through central and southern Singapore from HarbourFront to Dhoby Ghaut. The main interchanges are at Outram Park, Raffles Pl, Dhoby Ghaut, and City Hall. The MRT's 106 fully automated trains operate every 2½-8 mins, depending on the time of day, between 0600 and 2400.

Fare stages are posted in station concourses, and tickets dispensed, with change, from vending machines. Fares are 90¢-S$2.10.

Taxi
Taxis are the fastest and easiest way to get around the island in comfort. However, with the continued erection of ERP gantries they are losing their competitive edge. Nevertheless, compared with the UK they are excellent value. There are more than 24,000 taxis, all of them metered and a/c, which ply the island's roads completing almost 600,000 road trips daily. Taxis can only be hailed at specified points; it's best to go to a taxi stand or about 50 m from traffic lights. The taxis' bells are an alarm warning cabbies they've exceeded the 80 kph expressway speed limit, but drivers rarely pay attention to this.

Fares start at S$2.80 for the first kilometre and rise 20¢ for every subsequent 385 m up to 10 km, after which they rise by 20¢ every 330 m. 20¢ is also added for every 30 seconds waiting time. There is a peak period surcharge of 35% added to the metered fare for trips commencing between 0700 and 0930 Mon-Fri and between 1700 and 2000 Mon-Sat. These surcharges do not apply on public holidays. A surcharge of S$3 is levied on all trips beginning from the Central Business District (CBD) between 1700 and 2400 on Mon-Sat. If there are more than 4 passengers there is a S$2 surcharge; luggage costs S$1 extra and there's a 50% 'midnight charge' from 2400 to 0600. There is also a S$3 (S$5 at peak times) surcharge for journeys starting from (but not going to) Changi International Airport or Seletar Airport. Trips paid for with credit cards incur a 10% surcharge on top of the fare and taxis hired between 1800 on the evening before a public holiday and 2400 on the day of the public holiday also get a S$1 surcharge. Passengers also need to reimburse the taxi driver for charges incurred by passing through ERP gantries in the centre. Charges for depend on location and time of day.

Even with this veritable extravaganza of surcharges, Singapore's taxis are fairly good value for money and are definitely the best way to get around. They provide a view of Singapore that is absent from the MRT (at least in the city centre) and are a great source of information. Drivers are usually polite and will even round down fares to the nearest dollar. Unlike most of the rest of Asia, language is not a barrier to communication.

For taxi services ring: **Comfort and City Cab** T6552 1111, **Premier Cab** T6363 6888, **Smart** T6485 7777, **SMRT** T6555 8888. Charges for advance telephone booking apply.

● Directory

Singapore *p70, map p74*
Embassies and consulates Australia (High Commission), 25 Napier Rd, T6836 4100, www.australia.org.sg. **Austria**, 600 North Bridge Rd, T6396 6350. **Belgium**, 8 Shenton Way, 1401 Temasek Tower, T6220 7677 www.diplomatie.be/Singapore. **Canada** (High Commission), 1 George St, 1101, T6854 5900. **Denmark**, 1301 United Sq, 101 Thomson Rd, T6355 5010. **France**, 101-103 Cluny Park Rd, T6880 7800, www.ambafrance-sg.org. **Germany**, 1200 Singapore Land Tower, 50 Raffles Pl, T6533 6002, www.sing.diplo.de. **Indonesia**, 7 Chatsworth Rd, T6737 7422, www.kbrisingapura.com. **Israel**, 24 Stevens Cl,

T6834 9200. **Italy**, 101 Thomson Rd, No 27-02 United Sq, T6250 6022. **Japan**, 16 Nassim Rd, T6235 8855. **Malaysia (High Commission)**, 301 Jervois Rd, T6235 0111. **Netherlands**, 1301 Liat Towers, 541 Orchard Rd, T6737 1155. **New Zealand** (High Commission), 391A Orchard Rd, T6235 9966. **Norway**, 1401 Hong Leong Building, 16 Raffles Quay, T6220 7122. **South Africa** (High Commission), 15th floor, Odeon Towers, 331 North Bridge Rd, T6339 3319. **Spain**, 3800 Suntec Tower One, 7 Temasek Blvd, T6725 9220. **Sweden**, 05-01 Singapore Power Building, 111 Somerset Rd, T6415 9720. **Thailand**, 370 Orchard Rd, T6737 2644. **UK (High Commission)**, 100 Tanglin Rd, T6424 4270, www.ukinsingapore. fco.gov.uk. **USA**, 27 Napier Rd, T6476 9100.

Internet There are internet cafés all over Singapore. In Little India, try **AJs Internet**, with several branches charging S$2 per hr. Those with Wi-Fi equipment should be able to log in at most cafés and hotels in Singapore. **Medical services** Alexandra, 378 Alexandra Rd, T6472 2000, www.alex hosp.com.sg. **East Shore**, 321 Joo Chiat Pl, T6735 5000. **Gleneagles**, 6A Napier Rd (at the end of Orchard Rd), T6470 5700, the best place to go in an emergency; large A&E. **Mount Elizabeth**, 3 Mount Elizabeth, T6731 2218, has a good reputation. **National University**, 5 Lower Kent Ridge Rd, T6772 5000. **Raffles Hospital**, 585 North Bridge Rd, T6311 1555, www.raffleshospital.com, pricey but professional private facility with specialist emergency and dental centres, among others. **Singapore General**, Outram Rd, T6321 4311. **Traveller's Health and Vaccination Clinic**, Tan Tock Seng Hospital Medical Centre, Level 1, 11 Jln Tan Tock Seng, T6357 8766, www.ttsh.com.sg, specialist advice and treatment for travel-related illnesses and a walk-in vaccination service, phone ahead to arrange consultation, Mon-Fri 0800-1700 and Sat 0800-1200.

Contents

Footprint features

Sarawak

★ Don't miss ...

1 Sarawak Museum, page 96.
2 Bako National Park, page 108.
3 Kuching waterfront, page 114.
4 Longhouse stay, page 124.
5 Sungai Rejang, page 130.
6 Niah National Park caves, page 143.
7 Mulu hike, page 162.
8 Kelabit Highlands, page 165.

N

40 km
40 miles

East Sea

BRUNEI

INDONESIA

KALIMANTAN

SARAWAK

To Luconia Island

Sapulut
Tomani
Tenom
Sipitang
Lawas
Long
Semado
Bario
Limbang
Telok Brunei
Gunung Mulu
(2376m)
Gunung Mulu
National Park
Kelabit Highlands
Loagan Bunut
National Park
Baram
Marudi
Miri
Long
Ayak
Long
Muma
Belaga
Bakun
Dam
Balui
Lambir Hills
National Park
Niah
National Park
Niah
Caves
Baleh
Sungai Rejang
Pelagus
Rapids
Kapit
Song
Balleh
Similajau
National Park
Bintulu
Tatua
Kemena
Kanowit
Rejang
Lanjak-Entiman
Wildlife Sanctuary
Batang Ai
National Park
Mukah
R Baling
Batang Ai
Reservoir
Sibu
Sarikei
Skrang
Betong
Bandar Sri
Aman
Batang Ai
Santubong
Bako
National Park
Kuching
Gunung
Penrissen
Bau Semonggoh
Orang Utan
Sanctuary
Batu Kawa
Kubah National Park
Gunung
Gading
National Park
Sematan
Tanjung Datu
National Park
Entikong

Introduction

Sarawak, the 'land of the hornbill', is the largest state in Malaysia, covering an area of nearly 125,000 sq km in northwest Borneo with a population of just over two million. Sarawak has a swampy coastal plain, a hinterland of undulating foothills and an interior of steep-sided, jungle-covered mountains. The lowlands and plains are dissected by a network of broad rivers which are the main arteries of communication and where the majority of the population is settled.

In the mid-19th century, Charles Darwin described Sarawak as "one great wild, untidy, luxuriant hothouse, made by nature for herself". Sarawak is Malaysia's great natural storehouse, where little more than half a century ago great swathes of forest were largely unexplored and where tribal groups, collectively known as the Dayaks, would venture downriver from the heartlands of the state to exchange forest products of hornbill ivory and precious woods.

Today the Dayaks have been gradually incorporated into the mainstream and the market economy has infiltrated the lives of the great majority of the population. But much remains unchanged. The forests, although much reduced by a rapacious logging industry, are still some of the most species-rich on the globe; more than two-thirds of Sarawak's land area, roughly equivalent to that of England and Scotland combined, is still covered in jungle, although this is diminishing.

Kuching and around

→ *Colour map 3, C1. Population: around 460,000.*

Due to Kuching's relative isolation and the fact that it was not bombed during the Second World War, Sarawak's state capital has retained much of its 19th-century dignity and charm, despite the increasing number of modern high-rise buildings. Chinese shophouses still line many of the narrow streets. Kuching is a great starting point to explore the state and there are many sights within its compact centre, including the renowned Sarawak Museum and the Petra Jaya State Mosque.

Within easy reach is the Semenggoh Orang-Utan Sanctuary and the national parks of Gunung Gading, Kubah and Tanjung Datu. North of Kuching is the Damai Peninsula, featuring the worthwhile Sarawak Cultural Village and Bako National Park on the Muara Tebas Peninsula.
▸▸ *For listings, see pages 110-121.*

Ins and outs

Getting there
The **airport** ⓘ *T082-457373*, is 10 km south of Kuching. At the time of research, the bus service to and from the airport was suspended due to lack of custom. To take a taxi to town, buy a fixed-price coupon (RM22) from the counter in arrivals. Or catch the Tune Hotel shuttle bus which departs every hour 0800-2000 (RM10). This service drops passengers off at the Tune Hotel on Jalan Borneo. ▸▸ *See Transport, page 119.*

Getting around
The central portion of the city, which is the most interesting, can be negotiated on foot. Sampans (*perahu tambang*) provide cross-river transport and operate as river taxis. There are two city bus companies that provide a cheap and fairly efficient service. Taxis are found outside many of the larger hotels and at designated taxi stands. There are several international as well as local self-drive car hire firms in Sarawak.

Best time to visit
Kuching is hot and humid year-round. While heavy showers can happen at any time, they are more likely during the rainy season (November to February), which could make trekking difficult. May and June are also the months for Gawai Dayak (see page 29), a kind of harvest festival and a time for feasting and partying. There's also the popular Rainforest Music Festival held every July at the Sarawak Cultural Village, see www.sarawaktourism.com for exact dates.

Tourist information
Sarawak Tourism Board ⓘ *Visitors' Information Centre, Jln Tun Abang Haji Openg, T082-410944, www.sarawaktourism.com, Mon-Fri 0800-1800, Sat-Sun 0900-1500*, is housed in the beautiful Old Courthouse Complex. It has a good stock of maps and pamphlets. The staff are very knowledgeable and friendly. The smaller branch office of the **Sarawak Tourism Association** ⓘ *Waterfront, Main Bazaar, T082-240620, F427151, Mon-Thu 0800-1245 and 1400-1645, Fri 0800-1130 and 1430-1645, Sat 0800-1245 (closed 1st and 3rd Sat of the month)*, has a good range of information. There is a desk at **Kuching International Airport** ⓘ *T082-450944*, which has information on bus routes, approved travel agents and itineraries. **Tourism Malaysia** ⓘ *Bangunan Rugayah, Jln Song Thian Cheok, T082-246575, F246442*, has information on Sarawak and Sabah and a good stock of

brochures. The state and national tourism organizations are both well informed and helpful; they can advise on itineraries and travel agents and have up-to-date information on national park facilities.

National parks information

For information and accommodation booking for the national parks of Bako, Gunung Gading and Kubah and Matang Wildlife Centre, contact the **National Parks and Wildlife Booking Office** ⓘ *Old Courthouse, Jln Tun Abang Hj Openg, T082-248088, Mon-Fri 0800-1700*; or see www.sarawakforestry.com, click on online services, and then booking of national park; also npbooking@sarawak.net.gov.my.

Background

Shortly after dawn on 15 August 1839, the British explorer James Brooke sailed around a bend in the Sarawak River and, from the deck of his schooner, *The Royalist*, had his first view of Kuching. According to the historian Robert Payne, he saw "...a very small town of brown huts and longhouses made of wood or the hard stems of the nipah palm, sitting in brown squalor on the edge of mudflats." The settlement, 32 km upriver from the sea, had been established less than a decade earlier by Brunei chiefs who had come to oversee the mining of antimony in the Sarawak River valley. The antimony – used as an alloy to harden other metals, particularly pewter – was exported to Singapore where the tin plate industry was developing.

By the time James Brooke had become rajah in 1841, the town had a population of local Malays, Dayaks and Cantonese, Hokkien and Teochew traders. Chinatown dominated the south side of the river while the Malay kampongs were strung out along the riverbanks to the west. A few Indian traders also set up in the bazaar among the Chinese shophouses. Under Charles Brooke, the second of the White Rajahs, Kuching began to flourish; he commissioned most of the town's main public buildings. Brooke's wife, Ranee Margaret, wrote: "The little town looked so neat and fresh and prosperous under the careful jurisdiction of the Rajah and his officers, that it reminded me of a box of painted toys kept scrupulously clean by a child."

Sarawak's capital is divided by the Sarawak River; the south is a commercial and residential area, dominated by Chinese, while the north shore is predominantly Malay in character with the old kampong houses lining the river. The **Astana**, **Fort Margherita** and the **Petra Jaya area**, with its modern government offices, are also on the north side of the river. The two parts of the city are very different in character and even have separate mayors. Kuching's cosmopolitan make-up is immediately evident from its religious architecture: Chinese and Hindu temples, the imposing state mosque and Protestant and Roman Catholic churches.

Of all the cities in Malaysia, Kuching has been the worst affected by the smog – euphemistically known as 'the haze' – that periodically engulfs large areas of Borneo and the Indonesian island of Sumatra, largely blamed on slash-and-burn deforestation in Kalimantan. This was most severe in mid-1997, but occurs to some extent every year. At the peak of the 'emergency' – for that is what it became – in late September 1997, Kuching came to a standstill. It was too dangerous to drive and, seemingly, too dangerous to breathe. People were urged to remain indoors. Schools, government offices and factories closed. The port and airport were also closed. Tourism traffic dropped to virtually zero and for 10 days the city stopped. At one point there was even discussion of evacuating the population of the State of Sarawak. People began to buy up necessities and the prices of some commodities rose 500%.

Sights

Sarawak Museum

ⓘ *Jln Tun Haji Openg, T082-244232, www.museum.sarawak.gov.my, daily 0900-1630, closed on first day of public holidays, free. There is a library and a bookshop attached to the museum as well as a gift shop, the Curio Shoppe, all proceeds of which go to charity. Permits to visit Niah's Painted Cave can be obtained, free of charge, from the curator's office.*

Kuching's biggest attraction is this internationally renowned museum, housed in two sections on both sides of Jalan Tun Haji Openg. The old building to the east of the main road is a copy of a Normandy town hall, designed by Charles Brooke's French valet. The Rajah was encouraged to build the museum by the naturalist Alfred Russel Wallace, who spent over two years in Sarawak, where he wrote his first paper on natural selection. The museum was opened in 1891, extended in 1911, and the 'new' wing built in 1983. Its best known curators have been naturalist Eric Mjoberg, who made the first ascent of Sarawak's highest peak – Gunung Murudi (see page 166) – in 1922, and ethnologist and explorer Tom Harrisson, whose archaeological work at Niah made world headlines in 1957. The museum overlooks pleasant botanical gardens and the Heroes Memorial, built to commemorate the dead of the Second World War, the Communist insurgency and the confrontation with Indonesia. Across the road, and linked by a footbridge, is the Dewan Tun Abdul Razak building, the newer extension of the museum.

The museum has a strong ethnographic section, although some of its displays have been superseded by the **Cultural Village** (see page 106), Sarawak's 'living museum'. New sections of the museum are being opened, including a contemporary art section, for Borneo's rapidly evolving culture, and a natural history section. The old museum's ethnographic section includes a full-scale model of an Iban longhouse, a reproduction of a Penan hut and a selection of Kayan and Kenyah woodcarvings. There is also an impressive collection of Iban war totems (*kenyalang*) and carved Melanau sickness images (*blum*) used in healing ceremonies. The museum's assortment of traditional daggers (*kris*) is the best in Malaysia. The Chinese and Islamic ceramics include 17th-20th century Chinese jars, which are treasured heirlooms in Sarawak (see page box, 101). Temporary exhibitions are held, often sponsored by major corporations, with a small entry fee (RM5).

The natural history collection, covering Sarawak's flora and fauna, is also noteworthy. The new Tun Abdul Razak ethnological and historical collection includes prehistoric artefacts from the Niah Caves, Asia's most important archaeological site (see page 143); there is even a replica of Niah's Painted Cave – without the smell of guano.

Sarawak Islamic Museum

ⓘ *Jln P Ramlee, T082-244232, Sat-Thu 0900-1630, free.*

Not far from the Sarawak Museum, this collection is housed in the restored Maderasah Melayu Building, an elegant, single-storey colonial edifice. As its name suggests, the museum is devoted to Islamic artefacts from all the ASEAN countries, with the collection of manuscripts, costumes, jewellery, weaponry, furniture, coinage, textiles and ceramics spread over seven galleries, each with a different theme, and set around a central courtyard.

Waterfront

Around Main Bazaar are some other important buildings dating from the Brooke era; most of them are closed to the public. The **Supreme Court** on Main Bazaar was built in 1874 as an administrative centre. State council meetings were held here from the 1870s

A town called Cat

There are a few explanations as to how Sarawak's capital acquired the name 'Cat'. (Kuching means 'cat' in Malay, although today it is more commonly spelt *kucing* as in modern Bahasa 'c' is pronounced 'ch'.)

Local legend has it that James Brooke, pointing towards the settlement across the river, enquired what it was called. Whoever he asked mistakenly thought he was pointing at a passing cat. If that seems a little far fetched, the Sarawak Museum offers a few more plausible alternatives. Kuching may have been named after the wild cats (*kucing hutan*) which, in the 19th century, were commonly seen along jungled banks of the Sarawak River. Another theory is that it was named after the fruit *buah mata kucing* ('cat's eyes'), which grows locally. Most likely, however, is the theory that the town may originally have been known as Cochin (port), a word commonly used across India and Indochina.

until 1973, when it was converted to law courts. In front of the grand entrance is a memorial to Rajah Charles Brooke (1924) and on each corner there is a bronze relief representing the four main ethnic groups in Sarawak – Iban, Orang Ulu, Malay and Chinese. The clocktower was built in 1883. The **Square Tower**, also on Main Bazaar, was built as an annexe to Fort Margherita in 1879 and was used as a prison. Later in the Brooke era it was used as a ballroom. The square tower marks one end of Kuching's waterfront esplanade which runs alongside the river for almost 900 m to the **Hilton**.

The **waterfront** has been transformed into a landscaped esplanade through restoration and a land-reclamation project. It has become a popular meeting place, with foodstalls, restaurants and entertainment facilities including an open-air theatre used for cultural performances. There is a restored Chinese pavilion, an observation tower, a tea terrace and musical fountains, as well as a number of modern sculptures. During the day, the waterfront offers excellent views of the Astana, Fort Margherita and the Malay kampongs that line the north bank of the river. At night, the area comes alive as younger members of Kuching's growing middle class make their way down here to relax.

A good way to see the Sarawak River is to take a 90-minute **cruise** ① *tickets from Layar Warisan, Level 9, Medan Pelita Lebuh Temple, T082-240366, info@sarawakrivercruise.com.my, or from tourist agencies, hotels or at the waterfront booths halfway along the esplanade, RM60, children RM30, with a minimum of 2 passengers,* during the day. There are three departures daily at 0900, 1200 and 1500, or in the early evening at 1730.

The **General Post Office**, with its majestic Corinthian columns, stands in the centre of town, on Jalan Tun Haji Openg. Dating back to 1931, it was one of the few edifices built by Vyner Brooke, the last Rajah. It has been renovated and there are long-term plans to make it the home of the Sarawak Art Museum.

The **Courthouse complex**, which now houses the Sarawak Tourism Board's Visitors' Centre, was built in 1871 as the seat of Sarawak's government and was used as such until 1973. It remains one of Kuching's grandest structures. The buildings have *belian* (ironwood) roofs and beautiful detailing inside and out, reflecting local art forms. It also continues to house the state's high court and magistrates' court as well as several other local government departments. The colonial-baroque **Clocktower** was added in 1883 and the **Charles Brooke Memorial** in 1924. The complex also includes the **Pavilion Building** which was built in 1907 as a hospital. During the Japanese occupation it was used as an information and propaganda centre and it is now undergoing renovation with a view to making it the home of a new Textile Museum. Opposite the Courthouse is the **Indian Mosque (Mesjid India)** on Lebuh India, originally had an *atap* roof and *kajang* (thatch) walls; in 1876 *belian* (ironwood) walls were erected. The mosque was built by South Indians and is in the middle of an Indian quarter where spices are sold along the Main Bazaar. When the mosque was first built only Muslims from South India were permitted to worship here; even Indian Muslims from other areas of the subcontinent were excluded. In time, as Kuching's Muslim population expanded and grew more diversified, so this rigid system was relaxed. It is hard to get to the mosque as it is surrounded by buildings. However a narrow passage leads from Lebuh India between shop numbers 37 and 39.

Kuching

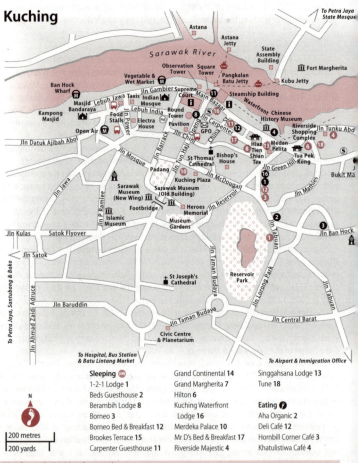

Sleeping	Grand Continental 14	Singgahsana Lodge 13
1-2-1 Lodge 1	Grand Margherita 7	Tune 18
Beds Guesthouse 2	Hilton 6	
Berambih Lodge 8	Kuching Waterfront	**Eating**
Borneo 3	Lodge 16	Aha Organic 2
Borneo Bed & Breakfast 12	Merdeka Palace 10	Deli Café 12
Brookes Terrace 15	Mr D's Bed & Breakfast 17	Hornbill Corner Café 3
Carpenter Guesthouse 11	Riverside Majestic 4	Khatulistiwa Café 4

The **Round Tower** on Jalan Tun Abang Haji Openg (formerly Rock Road) was originally planned as a fort in 1886, but was never completed. The whole area is undergoing restoration for future art galleries and cultural exhibits. The **Steamship Building** ⓘ *52 Main Bazaar*, was built in 1930 and was previously the offices and warehouse of the Sarawak Steamship Company. It has been extensively restored and now houses a restaurant, souvenir stalls, a handicrafts gallery and an exhibition area.

The **Bishop's House** ⓘ *off Jln McDougall, near the Anglican Cathedral of St Thomas*, is the oldest surviving residence in Sarawak. It was built in 1849, entirely of wood, for the first Anglican Bishop of Borneo, Dr McDougall. The first mission school was started in the attic – developed into St Thomas's and St Mary's School, which is now across the road on Jalan McDougall.

Chinatown

Kuching's Chinese population, part of the town's community since its foundation, live in the shophouses lining the narrow streets around **Main Bazaar**. This street opposite the waterfront is the oldest in the city, dating from 1864. The Chinese families who live here still pursue traditional occupations such as tinsmithing and woodworking. Kuching's highest concentration of antique and handicraft shops is to be found here. **Jalan Carpenter**, parallel to Main Bazaar, has a similar selection of small traders and coffee shops, as well as foodstalls and two small Chinese temples. Off **Lebuh China** (Upper China Street), there is a row of perfectly preserved 19th-century Chinese houses. The oldest Chinese temple in Kuching, **Tua Pek Kong** (also known as Siew San Teng), in the shadow of the **Hilton** on Jalan Tunku Abdul Rahman, was built in 1876, although it is now much modernized. There is evidence that the site has been in use since 1740 and a Chinese temple was certainly here as early as 1770. The first structure was erected by a group of Chinese immigrants thankful for their safe journey across the hazardous South China Sea. New immigrants still come here to give thanks for their safe arrival. The Wang Kang festival to commemorate the dead is also held here. Just to the east of here, **Jalan Padungan** has some of Kuching's finest Chinese shophouses. Most were built during the rubber boom of the 1920s and have been

restored. There are also some great coffee shops in this quarter of town. Further east still, the kitsch statue of the **Great Cat of Kuching** – the sort of thing to induce nightmares in the aesthetically inclined – mews at the junction of Jalan Padungan and Jalan Central.

The **Chinese History Museum** ① *T082-244232, daily 0900-1630, free,* stands on the waterfront opposite Tua Pek Kong temple. The museum documents the history of the Chinese in Sarawak, from the early traders of the 10th century to the waves of Chinese immigrants in the 19th century. The exhibits are now a little worse for wear. The building itself is simple, with a flat roof, and shows English colonial influences. It was completed in 1912 and became the court for the Chinese population of Kuching. The Third Rajah was keen that the Chinese, like other ethnic groups, should settle disputes within their community in their own way and he encouraged its establishment. From 1912 until 1921, when the Chinese court was dissolved, all cases pertaining to the Chinese were heard here in front of six judges elected from the local Chinese population. In 1993 it was handed over to the Sarawak Museum and was turned into the museum.

Hian Tien Shian Tee (Hong San) temple, at the junction of Jalan Carpenter and Jalan Wayang, was built in 1897.

The Moorish, gilt-domed **Masjid Bandaraya** (Old State Mosque) is near the market, on the west side of town; it was built in 1968 on the site of an old wooden mosque dating from 1852.

Civic Centre and Planetarium
① *Jln Taman Budaya, Mon-Thu 0915-1730, Sat 0915-1800, viewing platform 0900-1700. Planetarium shows, RM2 (6 shows daily); see www.planetarium-sarawak.org. Take bus No 14A, 14B or14C from Chim Lan Long Bus Station on Jln Masjid.*
On the south side of the river the extraordinary-looking Civic Centre is Kuching's stab at the avant garde. As well as the viewing platform for panoramas of Kuching, the Civic Centre complex houses an art gallery with temporary exhibits (mainly of Sarawakian art), a restaurant and a pub-cum-karaoke bar one floor down, together with a public library. Malaysia's first planetarium is also within the complex. **Sultan Iskandar Planetarium** has a 15-m dome and a 170-seat auditorium.

Astana
① *Take a sampan across the river from the Pangkalan Batu jetty next to Square Tower on the waterfront to the Astana and fort, around RM0.30 with other passengers one way. The boats can also be hired privately for around RM30 per hr.*
Apart from the Sarawak Museum, the White Rajahs bequeathed several other architectural monuments to Kuching. The Astana, a variant of the usual spelling *istana* (palace), was built in 1870, two years after Charles Brooke took over from his uncle. It stands on the north bank of the river almost opposite the market on Jalan Gambier. The Astana was hurriedly completed for the arrival of Charles' new bride (and cousin), Margaret. It was originally three colonial-style bungalows, with wooden shingle roofs, the largest being the central bungalow with the reception room, dining and drawing rooms. The crenellated tower on the east end was added in the 1880s at her request. Charles Brooke is said to have cultivated betel nut in a small plantation behind the Astana, so that he could offer fresh betel nut to visiting Dayak chiefs. Today, it's the official residence of the governor of Sarawak and is only open to the public on Hari Raya Puasa, a day of prayer and celebration to mark the end of Ramadan (see page 28). To the west of the Astana, in the traditionally Malay area, are many old wooden kampong houses.

A ceramic inheritance

Family wealth and status in Sarawak was traditionally measured in ceramics. In the tribal longhouses upriver, treasured heirlooms include ancient glass beads, brass gongs and cannons and Chinese ceramic pots and beads (such as those displayed in the Sarawak Museum). They were often used as currency and dowries. Spencer St John, the British consul in Brunei, mentions using beads as currency on his 1858 expedition to Gunung Mulu. Jars (*pesaka*) had more practical applications; they were (and still are) used for storing rice, brewing *tuak* (rice wine) or for keeping medicines.

Their value was dependent on their rarity: brown jars, emblazoned with dragon motifs, are more recent and quite common while olive-glazed dusun jars, dating from the 15th-17th centuries, are rare. The Kelabit people, who live in the highlands around Bario, in particular treasure the dragon jars. Although some of the more valuable antique jars have found their way to the Sarawak Museum, many magnificent jars remain in the Ian and other tribal longhouses along the Skrang, Rejang and Baram rivers. Many are covered by decoratively carved wooden lids.

Chinese contact and trade with the north coast of Borneo has gone on for at least a millennium, possibly two. Chinese Han pottery fragments and coins have been discovered near the estuary of the Sarawak River and, from the seventh century, China is known to have been importing birds' nests and jungle produce from Brunei (which then encompassed all of north Borneo), in exchange for ceramic wares. Chinese traders arrived in the Nanyang (South Seas) in force from the 11th century, particularly during the Sung and Yuan dynasties. Some Chinese pottery and porcelain even bore Arabic and Koranic inscriptions – the earliest such dish is thought to have been produced in the mid-14th century. In the 1500s, as China's trade with the Middle East grew, many such Islamic wares were traded and the Chinese emperors presented them as gifts to seal friendships with the Muslim world, including Malay and Indonesian kingdoms.

Fort Margherita

ⓘ *Jln Sapi; to get to the fort, see Astana, above.*

Not far away from the Astana, past the Kubu jetty, is this fort. It was also built by Rajah Charles Brooke in 1879 and named after Ranee Margaret, although there was a fort on the site from 1841 when James Brooke became Rajah. It commanded the river approach to Kuching, but was never used defensively, although its construction was prompted by a near-disastrous river-borne attack on Kuching by the Ibans of the Rejang in 1878. Even so, until the Second World War a sentry was always stationed on the lookout post on top of the fort; his job was to pace up and down all night and shout 'All's well' on the hour every hour until 0800. The news that nothing was awry was heard at the Astana and the government offices.

After 1946, Fort Margherita was first occupied by the Sarawak Rangers and was finally converted into a police museum in 1971. However, in 2008 this museum was closed and the exhibits moved back into police custody. Visitors can't enter the fort, but can have a look at the exterior.

Towering above Fort Margherita is Sarawak's new **State Assembly** building (Dewan Undangan Negeri). In a break from the norm, this huge structure resembles a cross between Brunei's Bolkiah Mosque and an Apollo moon lander. Borneo's take on avant garde, it's a fitting tribute to the rapid modernization of East Malaysia.

The **Malay kampongs** along the riverside next to Fort Margherita are seldom visited by tourists, despite their beautiful examples of traditional and modern Malay architecture.

Petra Jaya

The new **State Mosque** is situated north of the river at Petra Jaya and was completed in 1968. It stands on the site of an older mosque dating from the mid-19th century and boasts an interior of Italian marble.

Kuching's architectural heritage did not end with the White Rajahs; the town's modern buildings are often based on local styles. The new administration centre is in Petra Jaya: the **Bapak** (father) **Malaysia** building is named after the first prime minister of Malaysia and houses government offices; the **Dewan Undangan Negeri** (State Legislative Assembly of Sarawak) next door, is based on the Minangkabau style. Kuching's latest building is the ostentatious **Masjid Jamek**. Also in Petra Jaya, like a space launch overlooking the road to Damai Peninsula, is the **Cat Museum** ⓘ *daily 0900-1700 (closed public holidays), free, camera RM3, take Petra Jaya Transport No 2C or 2D – tell the driver where you want to go, as the museum is a 15-min walk from the nearest bus stop*, which houses everything you ever wanted to know about cats.

Nearby, the **Timber Museum** ⓘ *Wisma Sumber Alam (next to the stadium), Mon-Thu 0800-1300 and 1400-1700, Fri 0830-1140 and 1400-1700, closed public holidays, take a taxi, RM15 as there is no bus*, is meant to look like a log. It was built in the mid-1980s to try to engender a better understanding of Sarawak's timber industry. The museum, which has many excellent exhibits and displays, toes the official line about forest management and presents facts and figures on the timber trade, along with a detailed history of its development in Sarawak. The exhibition provides an insight into all the different forest types. It has information on and examples of important commercial tree species, jungle produce and many traditional wooden implements. The final touch is an air-conditioned forest and wildlife diorama, complete with leaf litter; all the trees come from the Rejang River area. A research library is attached to the museum. While it sidesteps the more delicate moral issues involved in the modern logging business, its detractors might do worse than to brush up on some of the less emotive aspects of Sarawak's most important industry.

Around Kuching → *Colour map 3, C1.*

Semenggoh Orang-Utan Sanctuary

ⓘ *Daily 0800-1245, 1400-1615, RM3. The bus service to the sanctuary has been reduced to 2 services a day, departing in front of the Kuching Waterfront Lodge at 0730 and 1330 (one way RM2.60). However, return times are highly erratic and visitors often have to hire a taxi to get back. A good alternative to the public bus is the efficient shuttle service that departs from the waterfront in front of the Old Courthouse at 0800 (returns 1020) and 1400 (returns 1620). RM25 including admission to the sanctuary. A taxi to the sanctuary costs RM45 one way plus RM10 per hour of waiting time. Feeding times 0900-1000 and 1500-1600.*

Semenggoh, 32 km from Kuching, on the road to Serian, became the first forest reserve in Sarawak when the 800 ha of jungle were set aside by Rajah Vyner Brooke in 1920. They were turned into a wildlife rehabilitation centre for monkeys, orang-utans, honey bears and hornbills in 1975. All were either orphaned as a result of logging or were confiscated, having been kept illegally as pets. The aim has been to reintroduce as many of the animals as possible to their natural habitat. In late 1998 many of the functions which previously attracted visitors to Semenggoh were transferred to the Matang Wildlife Centre (see page 105). However, there are a few trails around the park including a plankwalk and a botanical research centre, dedicated to jungle plants with medicinal applications and orang-utans still visit the centre for food handouts. Even when Semenggoh was operating as an orang-utan rehabilitation centre, it did not compare with Sepilok in Sabah, which is an altogether more sophisticated affair.

Gunung Penrissen → *Altitude: 1329 m.*

This is the highest peak in the mountain range south of Kuching running along the Kalimantan border. The mountain was visited by naturalist Alfred Wallace in 1855. Just over 100 years later the mountain assumed a strategic role in Malaysia's *Konfrontasi* with Indonesia (see page 174) – there is a Malaysian military post on the summit. Gunung Penrissen is accessible from Kampong Padawan; it lies a few kilometres south of Anna Rais, right on the border with Kalimantan. It is a difficult mountain to climb requiring two long days, but affords views over Kalimantan to the south and Kuching and the South China Sea to the north. Prospective climbers are advised to see the detailed trail guide in John Briggs' *Mountains of Malaysia*. The book is usually available in Sarawak Museum bookshop. It's 100 km from Kuching to Anna Rais. There are no buses and visitors need to charter a taxi.

Around Kuching

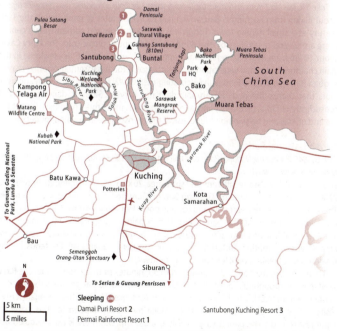

Sleeping
Damai Puri Resort **2**
Permai Rainforest Resort **1**
Santubong Kuching Resort **3**

Gunung Gading National Park

① T082-735144, RM10. The park is 5 mins' drive from Lundu; taxis charge around RM10. From Kuching take STC (Green) Bus Nos EP7 (RM10) to Lundu from the Regional Bus Terminal (3rd mile).

This park was constituted in 1983 and covers 4104 ha either side of Sungai Lundu, 65 km northwest of Kuching. There are some marked trails, the shortest of which takes about two hours and leads to a series of waterfalls on the Sungai Lundu. Gunung Gading and Gunung Perigi summit treks take seven to eight hours; it is possible to camp at the summit. The park is made up of a complex of mountains with several dominant peaks including Gunung Gading (906 m). The rafflesia, the world's largest flower (see box, page 214), is found here but if you're keen to see one in bloom, phone the Park HQ first, since it has a very short flowering period.

Lundu and Sematan

① To get there, bus 2 goes from Kuching to Bau from where there are buses to Lundu (2 hrs). STC Bus No EP7 goes directly to Lundu from the Regional Express Terminal (3rd mile) in Kuching.

These villages have beautiful, lonely beaches and there is a collection of deserted islands off Sematan. One of the islands, **Talang Talang**, is a turtle sanctuary and permission to visit it must be obtained from the **Forest Department** *① Wisma Sumba Alam, Jln Stadium, Petra Jaya, Kuching, T082-442180, www.sarawakforestry.com.*

Bau

① Take STC bus No 2 from Jln Masjid; the journey takes 1 hr. Tour companies also organize trips.

About 60 km from Kuching is **Bau**, which had its five minutes of fame during the 19th century as a small mining town. Today, it is a market town and administrative centre. There are several caves close by; the **Wind Cave** is a popular picnic spot. The **Fairy Cave**, about 10 km from Bau, is larger and more impressive, with a small Chinese shrine in the main chamber and varied vegetation at the entrance. A torch is essential. Another reason to go to Bau is to see the Bindayuh celebrating their Gawai Padi, a festival with animistic roots that thanks the gods for an abundant rice harvest. Singing, dancing, massive consumption of *tuak* (rice wine) and colourful shamans make this a highlight. It's held at the end of May and beginning of June. Ask at the tourist office in Kuching for details.

Kubah National Park

① T082-845033, but the National Parks and Wildlife Booking Office in Kuching, see page 95, is likely to be more helpful; RM10.

This is a mainly sandstone, siltstone and shale area, 20 km west of Kuching, covering some 2230 ha with three mountains: **Gunung Serapi**, **Gunung Selang** and **Gunung Sendok**. There are at least seven waterfalls and bathing pools. Flora include mixed dipterocarp and *kerangas* (heath) forest; the park is also rich in palms (93 species) and wild orchids. Wildlife includes bearded pig, mouse deer, hornbills and numerous species of amphibians and reptiles. Unfortunately for visitors here, Kubah's wildlife tends to stay hidden; it's not really a park for 'wildlife encounters'.

There are four marked trails, ranging from 30 minutes to three hours; one, the **Rayu Trail**, passes through rainforest that contains a number of bintangor trees (believed to contain two chemicals which have showed some evidence of being effective against HIV). Visitors may be able to see some trees which have been tapped for this potential rainforest remedy. The park is easy to visit as a day trip, but there is no scheduled bus service. Visitors will need to charter a taxi (one-way RM45) or minivan from Kuching. Travel agents also arrange tours.

The **Matang Wildlife Centre** ① *T082-225012; animal feeding times vary. Animals to see at the feedings include orang-utans, sambar deer, and crocodiles*, is part of the Kubah National Park. It houses endangered wildlife in spacious enclosures which are purposefully placed in the rainforest. The key attraction are the orang-utans, which are rehabilitated for release back into the wild. Other animals include sambar deer, sun bears, civets and bear cats. There is an information centre and education programmes, which enable visitors to learn more about the conservation of Sarawak's wildlife. The centre has also established a series of trails.

Pulau Satang Besar
① *Ask at the Visitor Information Centre, overlooking the Padang, Kuching, T082-410942, for departures from Santubong or Kampong Telaga Air.*
North of Kampong Telaga Air, Pulau Satang Besar has been designated a **Turtle Sanctuary** to protect the green turtles that come ashore here to lay their eggs. It's an excellent spot for snorkelling.

Tanjung Datu National Park
This is the newest and smallest park in Sarawak, first gazetted in 1994, at the westernmost tip, 100 km from Kuching. It is covered with mixed dipterocarp forest, rich flora and fauna, and beautiful beaches with crystal clear seas and coral reefs. To get there, take a bus to Lundu (see Gunung Gading National Park, page 104) and on to Sematan. At the jetty in Sematan, hire a boat (40 minutes, RM100 to hire the whole boat; there is no scheduled service). The seas are too rough for the journey between October and February. The boat will drop you off at the Park HQ's jetty. You can also jump in a boat to Teluk Melano (more regular) from Sematan (about 40 minutes), and then hire a 10-minute boat trip to the park.

Damai Peninsula → *Colour map 3, C1.*

The Peninsula, 35 km north of Kuching, is located at the west mouth of the Santubong River and extends northwards as far as **Mount Santubong**, a majestic peak of 810 m. Its attractions include the **Sarawak Cultural Village**, trekking up Mount Santubong, sandy beaches, a golf course, adventure camp and three resorts which are particularly good value off season when promotional rates are available.

From Kuching, it's a 40-minute bus ride north to **Buntal**. Take bus No 26 from the Petra Jaya terminal. Buses depart every 40 minutes throughout the day. From here, they wind through the foothills to Santubong.

Santubong and Buntal
The village of Santubong itself, located at the mouth of the Santubong River, is small and quiet. Formerly a fishing village, most of the villagers now work in one of the nearby resorts. However, some fishing still goes on, and the daily catch is still sold every morning at the quayside. Nearby are two or three Chinese-run grocery stores and a coffee shop. The rest of the village is made up of small houses strung out along the road, built in the Malay tradition on stilts – many are wooden and painted in bright colours. Another village here is Buntal, which is just off the Kuching-Santubong road and is popular with local Kuchingites, who come to visit at the weekends for the seafood restaurants.

Sarawak Cultural Village

ⓘ *T082-846108, www.scv.com.sg. Daily 0900-1730, cultural shows at 1130 and 1600 (45 mins). RM60, children (6-12 years) RM30.00, prices include cultural show.*

The Sarawak Cultural Village (Kampong Budaya Sarawak), 35 km north of Kuching, was the brainchild of the **Sarawak Development Corporation** which built Sarawak's 'living museum' at a cost of RM9.5 million to promote and preserve Sarawak's cultural heritage, opening it in 1990. With increasing numbers of young tribal people being tempted from their longhouses into the modern sectors of the economy, many of Sarawak's traditional crafts have begun to die out. The Cultural Village set out to teach the old arts and crafts to new generations. For the State Development Corporation, the concept had the added appeal of creating a money-spinning 'Instant Sarawak' for the benefit of tourists lacking the time or inclination to head into the jungle. While it is rather contrived, the Cultural Village has been a great success and contains some superb examples of traditional architecture. It should be on the sightseeing agenda of every visitor to Kuching, if only to provide an introduction to the cultural traditions of all the main ethnic groups in Sarawak.

Each tribal group is represented by craftsmen and women who produce handicrafts and practise traditional skills in houses built to carefully researched design specifications. Many authentic everyday articles have been collected from longhouses all over Sarawak. In one case the village has served to preserve a culture – pickled – that is already effectively dead: today the Melanau people all live in Malay-style kampongs, but a magnificent traditional wooden Melanau house has been built at the Cultural Village and is now the only such building in Sarawak. Alongside it there is a demonstration of traditional sago processing. A resident Melanau craftsman makes sickness images (*blum*), each representing the spirit of an illness, which were floated downriver in tiny boats as part of the healing ritual.

There are also Bidayuh, Iban and Orang Ulu longhouses, depicting the lifestyles of each group. In each there are textile or basket weavers, woodcarvers or swordmakers. There are exhibits of beadwork, bark clothing, and *tuak* (rice wine) brewing. At the Penan hut there is a demonstration of blowpipe making and visitors are invited to test their hunting skills. There is a Malay house and even a Chinese farmhouse with a pepper garden alongside. The tour of the houses, seven in all (you can collect a stamp from each one for your passport) is capped by an Andrew Lloyd Webber-style cultural show which is expertly choreographed, if rather ersatz. It is held in the air-conditioned onsite theatre.

Special application must be made to attend heritage centre workshops where courses can be requested in various crafts such as woodcarving, mat weaving or batik painting; they also run intensive one-day and three- to four-day courses. There is a restaurant and craft shop, **Sarakraf**, at the village.

A regular shuttle bus service operates from the **Grand Margherita** in Kuching to resort hotels and the Cultural Village (RM12 each way – return RM20; sometimes it's cheaper to buy both the entrance ticket and bus tickets from tour agencies or the Grand Margherita where they often have special offers). These run from 0730 to 2200; the last bus back from Damai is at 2100.

The Cultural Village is also the venue for the fabulous annual **Rainforest Music Festival** ⓘ *www.rainforestmusic-borneo.com*, which takes place sometime between June and August. There are foodstalls and jamming sessions are held in the different sections, culminating in a great evening show.

The Cultural Village employs 140 people, including dancers, who earn around RM400 a month and take home the profits from handicraft and *tuak* sales.

The Penan: museum pieces for the 21st century?

Economic progress has altered many Sarawakians' lifestyles in recent years; the oil and natural gas sector now offers many employment prospects and upriver tribespeople have been drawn into the logging industry. But it is logging that has directly threatened the 9000-strong Penan tribe's traditional way of life.

Sarawak's nomadic hunter-gatherers emerged as 'the noble savages' of the late 20th century, as their blockades of logging roads drew world attention to their plight. In 1990, Prince Charles's remarks about Malaysia's "collective genocide" against the Penan prompted an angry letter of protest from former Prime Minister Dr Mahathir Mohamad. He is particularly irked by western environmentalists – especially Bruno Manser, who lived with the Penan in the late 1980s. "We don't need any more Europeans who think they have a white man's burden to shoulder", Dr Mahathir said.

Malaysia wants to integrate the Penan into mainstream society, on the grounds that it is morally wrong to condemn them to a life expectancy of 40 years, when the average Malaysian lives to well over 60. "There is nothing romantic about these helpless, half-starved, disease-ridden people", Dr Mahathir said. The government has launched resettlement programmes to transform the Penan from hunters into fishermen and farmers. One of these new longhouses can be visited in Mulu (see page 161). It has failed to engender much enthusiasm from the Penan, although 4000 to 5000 Penan have now been resettled. Environmentalists countered that the Penan should be given the choice, but, the government asks, what choice do they have if they have only lived in the jungle?

The Sarawak Cultural Village, opened by Dr Mahathir, offered a compromise of sorts – but the Penan had the last laugh. One tribal elder, Apau Madang, and his grandson were paid to parade in loincloths and make blowpipes at the Penan hut while tourists took their snapshots. The arrangement did not last long as they did not like posing as artefacts in Sarawak's 'living museum'. They soon complained of boredom and within months had wandered back to the jungle where they could at least wear jeans and T-shirts. Today, the Penan hut is staffed by other Orang Ulu. There are thought to be only 400 Penan still following their traditional nomadic way of life.

Gunung Santubong → Altitude: 810 m.

Situated on the Santubong Peninsula, Gunung Santubong's precipitous southwestern side provides a moody backdrop to Damai Beach. The distinctive mountain is most accessible from the east side, where there is a clear ridge trail to the top. There are two trails to the summit; one begins opposite the **Palm Beach Seafood Restaurant and Resort**, about 2.5 km before the **Holiday Inn Damai Beach**. The conical peak – from which there are spectacular views – can be reached in seven to nine hours (the last stretch is a tough scramble). Take your own food and water supplies. Guides are not necessary (but can be provided); check with hotel recreation counters or at the **Santubong Mountain Trek Canteen** ⓘ *T082-846153*. The official Damai guide provides a more detailed description of the trek.

There is a bus to Damai Beach. Alternatively take a minivan from the open-air market on Jalan Masjid, RM5; these only depart when full. A taxi to Damai should cost around RM45 one way.

Kuching Wetlands National Park

Designated in 2002 this relatively small national park encompasses 6610 ha of dense mangrove and heath forest where the Sibu and Salak Rivers meet the South China Sea. The area is rich in wildlife and an important site for a range of water birds, crocodiles and primates, including the proboscis monkey. One of park's truly distinctive inhabitants is the irrawaddy dolphin, a small slow swimming mammal that lives in shallow seas – and often far up major rivers into freshwater areas – throughout Southeast Asia. The dolphin is rare almost everywhere, but the Kuching wetlands is one of the best places to see them in Malaysia.

Several Kuching tour agencies offer dolphin and wildlife spotting boat tours of the park's waterways. These also run in the evening, when it's easier to spot crocodiles and fireflies. Most tours depart from Santubong Boat Club or Damai Beach; from here it's only a 20-30 minute boat ride to the park. A recommended tour operator is **CPH Travel Agency** ① *70 Jln Padungan, Kuching, T082-243708, www.cphtravel.com.my*.

Bako National Park → *Colour map 3, C1.*

Bako is situated on the beautiful Muara Tebas Peninsula, a former river delta which has been thrust above sea level. Its sandstone cliffs, which are patterned and streaked with iron deposits, have been eroded to produce a dramatic coastline with secluded coves and beaches and rocky headlands. Millions of years of erosion by the sea has resulted in the formation of wave-cut platforms, honeycomb weathering, solution pans, arches and sea stacks. Bako's most distinctive feature is the westernmost headland – **Tanjung Sapi** – a 100-m-high sandstone plateau, which is unique in Borneo. Established in 1957, Bako was Sarawak's first national park. It is very small (2742 ha) but it has an exceptional variety of flora and guaranteed wildlife spotting. Its beaches and accessible trails make it a wonderful place to relax for a few days.

Ins and outs

Getting there Bako lies 37 km north of Kuching, an hour's bus journey (RM2.50) from Petra Jaya terminal. Take the orange bus No 6 that leaves every hour between 0700 and 1800 from just below Electra House on Lebuh Market to Kampong Bako. The bus continues just beyond to the Bako NP boat jetty where the driver turns around and heads back to Kuching. There are also minibuses (no fixed schedule) from Lebuh Market, RM4. The last buses returning to **Kuching** depart around 1700 – ask the driver on your way to Bako to confirm the day's last bus. From Kampong Bako, charter a private boat to Sungai Assam (30 mins), which is a short walk from the Park HQ, RM47 per boat each way – ask price before boarding (up to 5 people). Travelling by car, the drive from Kuching takes about 40 minutes. Parking is safe at Kampong Bako and the park offices, from where you rent a boat (see above).

Getting around It also is possible to hire boats around the park: speed boats (for up to six) charge a negotiable rate, usually around RM300 per day, good for exploring the park's beaches and the island of Pulau Lakei.

Tourist information On arrival visitors are required to register at the Park HQ; the information centre next door has a small exhibition on geology and flora and fauna within the park. Visitors can ask to see a 40-minute introductory video to the park. The Park HQ has a canteen.

To obtain the necessary permits, contact the the **National Parks and Wildlife Booking Office** ① *Tourist Information Centre, the Old Courthouse, Jln Tun Abang Hj Openg,*

Flora and fauna

There are seven separate types of vegetation in Bako. These include mangroves (*bakau* is the most common stilt-rooted mangrove species), swamp forest and heath forest, known as *kerangas*, an Iban word meaning 'land on which rice cannot grow'. Pitcher plants (*Nepenthes ampullaria*) do however grow in profusion on the sandy soil. There is also mixed dipterocarp rainforest (the most widespread forest type in Sarawak, characterized by its 30- to 40-m-high canopy), beach forest, and *padang* vegetation, comprising scrub and bare rock from which there are magnificent views of the coast. The rare *daun payang* (umbrella palm) is also found in Bako Park; it is a litter-trapping plant as its large fronds catch falling leaves from the trees above and funnel them downwards where they eventually form a thick organic mulch enabling the plant to survive on otherwise infertile soil. There are also wild durian trees in the forest, which can take up to 60 years to bear fruit.

Bako is one of the few areas in Sarawak inhabited by the rare proboscis monkey (*Nasalis larvatus*), known by Malays as Orang Belanda (Dutchmen) or even Pinocchio of the Jungle, because of their long noses (see page 377). Bako is home to approximately 150 proboscis monkeys. They are most often seen in the early morning or at dusk in the Teluk Assam and Teluk Delima areas (at the far west side of the park, closest to the headquarters) or around Teluk Paku (a 45-minute walk from the Park HQ). Another good place to spot them is on the beach when the tide is out and they come down, so you can see them up close.

The park also has resident populations of squirrels, mouse deer, sambar deer, wild pigs, long-tailed macaques, flying lemur, silver leaf monkeys and palm civet cats. Teluk Assam,

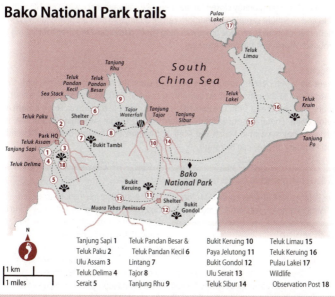

Bako National Park trails

Pulau Lakei

South China Sea

Tanjung Rhu

Teluk Limau

Teluk Pandan Kecil *Teluk Pandan Besar*

Sea Stack

Teluk Lakei

Teluk Kruin

Teluk Paku

Shelter

Tajor Waterfall

Tanjung Tajor *Tanjung Sibur*

Park HQ *Teluk Assam*

Bukit Tambi

Tanjung Po

Tanjung Sapi

Teluk Delima

Bako National Park

Bukit Keruing

Muara Tebas Peninsula

Shelter *Bukit Gondol*

N

1 km
1 miles

Tanjung Sapi 1	Teluk Pandan Besar &	Bukit Keruing 10	Teluk Limau 15
Teluk Paku 2	Teluk Pandan Kecil 6	Paya Jelutong 11	Teluk Keruing 16
Ulu Assam 3	Lintang 7	Bukit Gondol 12	Pulau Lakei 17
Teluk Delima 4	Tajor 8	Ulu Serait 13	Wildlife
Serait 5	Tanjung Rhu 9	Teluk Sibur 14	Observation Post 18

in the area around the Park HQ, is one of the best places for birdwatching: over 150 species have been recorded in the park, including pied and black hornbills. Large numbers of migratory birds come to Bako between September and November. Other inhabitants of the park are the blue fiddler crab, which has one big claw and is forever challenging others to a fight, and mudskippers, evolutionary throwbacks (resembling half-fish, half-frog), which are common in mangrove areas.

Also in the park there are two species of otter: the oriental small clawed otter and the hairy nosed otter (the best area to see them is at Teluk Assam). The Bornean bearded pig is the largest mammal found Bako and is usually seen snuffling around the Park HQ. There are many lizards too, the largest being the water monitor which is often found near the accommodation. Snakes occasionally seen include the poisonous bright green Wagler's pit viper and sometimes pythons and tree snakes on night walks. Nocturnal animals include flying lemur, pangolin, mouse deer, bats, tarsier, slow loris and palm civet (the beach by the Park HQ is a great place for a night-time stroll).

Treks

There's a good range of well-marked trails throughout the park – over 30 km in total; all paths are colour coded, corresponding to the map available from Park HQ. The shortest trek is the steep climb to the top of **Tanjung Sapi**, overlooking Telok Assam, with good views of Gunung Santubong, on the opposite Peninsula, across Tanjung Sipang, to the west. The 3.5-km trek to Tajor Waterfall is among the most popular, with varied walking (including some steep climbs), spectacular views and a chance of a refreshing swim at the waterfall. A few meters further on you reach a secluded beach.

The longest trek is to Telok Limau; a five- to seven-hour walk through a variety of terrain. You can arrange with Park HQ to lay on a boat to bring you back (around RM200). Some trails are temporarily closed for maintenance – always check with Park HQ. Full day treks and overnight camping expeditions can be arranged. There are plankwalkways with shelters at intervals to provide quiet watching spots, particularly required for viewing the proboscis monkey in the early morning.

Beaches

There are seven beaches around the park, but some are rather inaccessible, with steep paths down to the cliffs. The best swimming beach is at **Telok Pandan Kecil**, about 1½ hours' walk, northeast from the Park HQ. It is also possible to swim at **Telok Assam** and **Telok Paku**. Enquire about jellyfish at the Park HQ before swimming in the sea; it is advisable not to swim in March and April. In the monsoon season, between November and February, the sea can be rough.

◉ Kuching and around listings

For Sleeping and Eating price codes and other relevant information, see Essentials pages 23-27.

● Sleeping

Kuching *p94, map p98*

It is possible to negotiate over room rates and many of the hotels offer special deals. There is a good choice of international-standard hotels in Kuching. For an additional listing of hotels and resorts with websites see the Sarawak Tourism Board site, www.sarawaktourism.com.

Recent years have seen unprecedented growth in mid- to budget-priced accommodation and Kuching now has the best selection of guesthouses in Malaysia. With so many options to choose from, finding a bed is rarely a problem. However, guesthouses are booked solid for the annual Rainforest Music Festival and finding somewhere to sleep could be problematic.

For an alternative to the usual hotels and guesthouses, you could try a **Homestay programme**, see page 113.

L-AL Hilton, Jln Tunku Abdul Rahman, T082-248200, www.hilton.com. Minimalistic but very stylish accommodation and the best hotel facilities in town, with many restaurants, gym, tennis courts and pool. Some major discounts make this great value. Good for a treat after a tough jungle trek!

L-AL Riverside Majestic, Jln Tunku Abdul Rahman, T082-247777, www.riversidemajestic.com. Despite a slightly dated feel, this business hotel has spacious rooms and suites. Views blocked by luxury suites on the lower floors. Located in a shopping centre with a cinema.

AL-A Grand Continental, Jln Ban Hock, T082-230399, www.ghihotels.com. Small pool and business centre. Rooms have TV, IDD, minibar and tea- and coffee-making facilities.

AL-A Grand Margherita, Jln Tunku Abdul Rahman, T082-423111, contact@gmh.my. Standard business fare with weekend discounts. More expensive rooms have good river views. Rooms are comfortable, with a faux bamboo theme and have bathroom with bathtub, cable TV, safety box and fridge. There is a pool at the back of the hotel and a bar with live music, popular with expats at the weekend.

AL-A Merdeka Palace, Jln Tun Haji Openg, T082-258000, www.merdekapalace.com. Central location overlooking playing field. Pool, health club and business facilities, and broadband in every room. The 214 rooms have minibar and satellite TV. 6 bars and restaurants onsite. Great value. Recommended.

A-B Borneo, 30 Jln Tabuan, T082-244122, F254848. Large and cheerless place, more popular with domestic travellers than with foreign visitors. Rooms are a little musty, and

those with a view (not spectacular by any means) are more expensive. Rooms have a/c, TV and bathroom with bathtub. The hotel is located a good 10-min walk from the centre.

B Brookes Terrace, 231 Jln Abell, T082-427008, www.brookesterrace.org. Run by the friendly font of local knowledge, Seamus, this boutique guesthouse has a relaxed atmosphere, a good mix of local and eccentric international decor. Rooms are comfortable, spacious, and have LCD TV, Wi-Fi and attached bathroom. Highly recommended.

B Tune, Jln Borneo, T082-238221, www.tunehotels.com. Chain based on budget airline model; the earlier you book, the cheaper the room. Rooms are spotless, a little sterile, but comfortable. A/c, towels and Wi-Fi are all chargeable add-ons.

B-C Kuching Waterfront Lodge, Main Bazaar, T082-231111, www.kuchingwaterfront lodge.com. Located along the bustling main bazaar, this hotel is filled with artefacts from around the region with beautifully carved tables and tribal door frames, a stay here will not be short on atmosphere. The dorms are a little dark, as are some of the double rooms on the top floor. Slightly overpriced.

B-D 1-2-1 Lodge, Lot 121, 33 Section KTLD, Jln Tabuan, T082-428 121, www.lodge121. com. Calm and colourful guesthouse with popular TV room, communal dining area and the cheapest laundry in town. Rooms are simple and comfortable, although some lack natural light. All rooms have clean shared bathrooms and toilets and there are numerous washbasins scattered around to prevent lengthy morning queues. Wi-Fi throughout. Owner Henry Lim is a good source of local knowledge. Recommended.

B-D Beds Guesthouse, Lot 91, Section 50, Jln Padungan, T082-424229, www.bedsguest house.com. This small and friendly place has a stylish and comfortable social area, a dining room at the back which is a popular spot for a glass of longhouse *tuak* in the evenings, and free internet and Wi-Fi access throughout. Rooms are comfortable and stylish and kept spotlessly clean. Free breakfast. Highly recommended.

B-D Berambih Lodge, 104 Jln Ewe Hai, T082-231589, www.berambih.com. With its faux longhouse interior and relaxed communal area, this guesthouse is a relaxed option in the heart of town. Rooms are simple and all have a/c, but could do with a good clean. Breakfast included in the price and free Wi-Fi throughout.

B-D Mr D's Bed and Breakfast, 26 Jln Carpenter, T082-248852, www.misterd bnb.com. Functional place with simple, somewhat dark rooms and dorms with shared bathroom. There is free Wi-Fi throughout and free breakfast as well as free tea and coffee.

B-D Singgahsana Lodge, 1 Lebuh Temple, T082-429277, www.singgahsana.com. Well-established guesthouse owned by Donald and Marina Tan whose travel photos from around the world adorn the corridors. Staff here are efficient and the hotel is a well-run and cheerful place with funky decor, a rooftop bar open until the wee hours and free internet and Wi-Fi access. There is a selection of rooms, from large dorms to the stylish and sensual honeymoon suites with attached bathroom. The double rooms on the ground floor have an interesting mezzanine level, although suffer from a lack of natural light.

C-D Borneo Bed & Breakfast, Jln Tabuan (next to **Borneo Hotel**), T082-231200, borneobedbreakfast@yahoo.com. One of the cheapest options in town, with run-down rooms and plenty of dark nooks and crannies. The family can offer fair value trips to their ancestral longhouse.

Gunung Penrissen *p103*

L-AL Hornbill Golf & Jungle Club, Borneo Highlands Resort, Jln Borneo Heights, Padawan, T082-578980, www.borneo highlands.com.my. As its name suggests, this is a mountain hideaway for golf fanatics. There are luxurious chalets and suites beautifully furnished with golfing touches like paintings of greens. The resort lies at 1000 m and so the weather is cooler and more spring-like. Golf, jungle treks and longhouse tours, a rabbit farm, spas and flower gardens.

Gunung Gading National Park *p104*

A-E National park accommodation. Bookings taken through the **National Parks and Wildlife Parks Booking Office**, the Old Courthouse, Jln Tun Abang Hj Openg, T082-248088, www.sarawakforestry.com. 2- and 3-bedroom chalets (around RM150 per chalet) and a hostel (RM15 per person). Camping for RM5 per head, although visitors need to bring their own equipment.

Lundu and Sematan *p104*

A Ocean Resort, 176 Siar Beach, Jln Pandan, Sematan, T082-452245 (Kuching office) or T011-225001 (resort). Some rooms in hostel, also 2-bedroom chalets with attached kitchen. The plushest place to stay in Sematan.

C Lundu Gadung, Lot 174 Lundu Town District, T082-735199. A/c, shared bathroom.

Kubah National Park *p104*

A-F National park accommodation. Bookable through the **National Parks and Wildlife Booking Office** in Kuching, Old Courthouse, T082-248088 or www.sarawak forestry.com. There are fan chalets (RM150), an 8-room hostel (RM15.75) and 5 huge bungalows at the Park HQ with full kitchen facilities, 4 beds (2 rooms), a/c, hot water, TV and veranda (RM225 for the whole chalet). Bring your own food.

Damai Peninsula *p105, map p103*

AL-A Damai Puri Resort, Damai Beach, T082-846900, www.damaipuriresort.com. Just below a mansion belonging to the Sultan of Brunei, this upmarket hotel has 207 elegant rooms offering stunning views either of the rainforest and Gunung Santubong on one side or the sea on the other. Facilities include a pool, tennis courts and full spa centre. Discounts available.

A Permai Rainforest Resort, Pantai Damai Santubong, PO Box B91, Satok Post Office, T082-846487, www.permairainforest.com. At the foot of Mount Santubong, this resort markets itself as a low impact eco-resort, and offers lots of green and healthy activities from jungle trekking, night mangrove cruises to sea kayaking. There are comfy a/c treehouses, built on stilts 6 m above ground and attached hot water bathroom, or for those with less cash to splash, there are 23 comfortable a/c cabins a little closer to the earth. Camping is also available at RM12 per person. Cafeteria and tents and camping equipment for hire.

A Santubong Kuching Resort, Jln Pantai Damai, Santubong, PO Box 2364, T082-846888, www.santubongresort.com. Surrounded by the Damai golf course, 380 a/c rooms, restaurant, large pool surrounded by greenery, chalets with jacuzzis, tennis, basketball, volleyball, gym, mountain biking, etc. Nestling beneath Mount Santubong, this low-rise resort is particularly popular with golfers who come to hit a few rounds on the Arnold Palmer-designed golf course.

Bako National Park *p108, map p109*

All bookings to be made at the National Parks and Wildlife Booking Office, Kuching, T082-248088 (see page 95). **Hostels** have mattresses, kerosene stoves and cutlery; **lodges** offer electricity and fridges. Both have fans. Accommodation is always booked up, so you should reserve as early as possible before you want to go. Bako can be visited on a day trip, although this gives almost no opportunity to explore the parks trails – an overnight or 2 night, 3 days would be preferable. **Lodge**, RM157 per house, RM105 per room. **Hostel**, RM55 per room, RM15.75 per person, checkout time 1200.

Camping

Unless you are intending to trek to the other side of the park, it is not worth camping as monkeys steal anything left lying around and macaques can be aggressive. In addition, the smallest amount of rain turns the campsite into a swimming pool. It is, however, necessary to camp if you go to the beaches on the Northeast Peninsula. Tents can be hired for RM8 (sleeps 4); campsite RM5.

Homestays

It's worth checking with the Sarawak Tourist Board for their latest recommendations and advice on homestay programmes. In Kuching, the tourist offices recommend **Abas Homestay** in the Malay Kampong on the north side of the river. Accommodation is simple and clean and the homestay offers a great way to get a feel for local life. Contact Mr Hj Mahmud Hj Sabli, T019-857 1774, eduquest@streamyx.com.

In Kampung Santubong, there is the Santubong Village Homestay, T082-422495, www.santubonghomestay.com.my. This homestay offers a chance to learn about local cuisine, games and can help organize trips to local attractions. Prices include all meals.

🍴 Eating

Kuching *p94, map p98*

Kuching, with all its old buildings and godowns along the river, seems made for open-air restaurants and cafés – but good ones are notably absent or have quite a high turnover. However, the town is not short of hawker centres. Local dishes worth looking out for include *umai* – a spicy salad of raw marinated fish with limes and shallots and *laksa* (spicy noodles – a Malaysia-wide dish, but especially good here). Other distinctive Sarawakian ingredients are *midin* and *paku* – jungle fern shoots. See also Food glossary, page 385.

All the major hotels have Chinese restaurants; most open for lunch and dinner, closing in between. There are several cheap Indian Muslim restaurants along Lebuh India.

There is excellent seafood here. On Kampong Buntal are several seafood restaurants on stilts over the sea, 25 km north of Kuching, popular with Kuchingites. ₩₩₩ **Serapi**, **Holiday Inn**, Jln Tunku Abdul Rahman. Specializes in North Indian tandoori, good vegetable dishes, excellent selection of grills and seafood, imported steak, elegant surroundings. Recommended.

♥♥ **Tom's**, 82 Jln Padungan, T082-247672. Tue-Sun 1130-2300. Excellent Western dishes including steaks and salads in a slick modern setting. There's a good beer garden out the back, ideal for a pre-dinner tipple.

♥ **Aha Organic**, No 38, Lot 36, Section 47, Jln Tabuan, T082-420808. Mon-Sat 0830-1830. Smart place with a selection of tasty organic dishes including pastas, salads and excellent soups – the chicken ginseng soup is excellent. There is also a range of juices.

♥♥ **James Brooke Bistro and Café**, on the waterfront, Main Bazaar, T082-412120. Facing the river near the Chinese museum. Open-air restaurant in fine Casablanca style, especially the mirrored bar. Fairly expensive but fine food from Malaysian curries to colonial favourites.

♥♥ **The Junk**, 80 Jln Wayang, T082-259450. Closed Tue. Intimate little gem of a restaurant filled with antiques like old cash registers and lit by lanterns. Serves good but not fantastic pasta, steaks and other Western and Asian dishes. Recommended.

♥♥ **Khatulistiwa Café**, Waterfront. In a circular pavilion-style building. Great views from this 24-hr café serving Malay and international dishes. There's an R&B music café on the 2nd floor open at 2300. Good breakfast.

♥♥ **Little Lebanon**, The Old Courthouse, Jln Barrack, T082-233523. Small place with outdoor seating, *sheesha* pipes with a range of flavoured tobacco and a long menu of Lebanese favourites including kebabs, tabbouleh and hummus.

♥♥ **The Living Room**, 23 Jln Tabuan, T082-426608. Stylish and sophisticated restaurant divided into several distinct sections, one of which is a tranquil Japanese garden - a good spot to unwind. A wide range of cuisine is offered, the fish is excellent and the venue can also order food from **Blah, Blah, Blah** next door, giving you almost infinite choice – just don't expect it to be cheap!

♥♥ **Lyn's Tandoori**, Lot 62, 10G Lg 4, Jln Nanas. A worthwhile taxi ride from the centre for genuine North Indian tandoori cuisine, excellent naan. Recommended by locals. Closed Sun evenings.

♥♥ **Meisan**, Grand Margherita, Jln Tunku Abdul Rahman. Dim sum, set lunch; Sun all-you-can-eat dim sum special, also Sichuan cuisine. Recommended.

♥♥ **Orchid Garden**, Grand Margherita, Jln Tunku Abdul Rahman. Good breakfast and evening buffets, international and local cuisine. Recommended.

♥♥ **See Good**, Jln Bukit Mata Kuching, behind MAS office. Closed 4th and 18th of every month. Extensive range of seafood. Strong-flavoured sauces, lots of herbs, extensive and exotic menu, unlimited free bananas. Recommended by locals.

♥♥ **Waterfront**, Hilton Hotel, Jln Tunku Abdul Rahman. Reasonably priced for the venue. The best pizzas, and a family brunch buffet on Sun which is very popular.

♥ **Lok Thian**, 1st floor, Bangunan Beesan, Jln Padungan, T082-331310. Good food, pleasant surroundings and excellent service. Booking advisable, especially at weekends.

♥ **Minsion Canteen**, end of Jln Chan Chin Ann, on right. Speciality is *daud special* (noodles in herbal soup with chunks of chicken).

♥ **Waterfront Café**, 2nd floor, Lot 10531, Blk 16, Jln Tun Tugah, T082-458311. Pleasant, clean eatery on the waterfront offering a range of Malay and Chinese dishes. Try local dishes such as *laksa Sarawak, umai* and *mee kolok*. Wi-Fi available.

Coffee shops

There are several Malay/Indian coffee shops on Lebuh India including **Madinah Café**, **Jubilee** and **Malaysia Restaurant**. Many Chinese coffee shops serve excellent *laksa* (breakfast) of curried coconut milk with a side plate of *sambal belacan* (chillied prawn paste). **Deli Café**, 88 Main Bazaar, T082-232788. Atmospheric Western-style café, fair sandwiches, snacks and pastries, good coffee. Try the excellent carrot cake. Free internet and plenty of magazines to read.

Foodstalls and food centres

There are great open-air informal places along the waterfront selling everything from kebabs to *ais cream goreng* (fried ice cream) that start opening towards the evening. It makes a great place for an evening meal. Most of the foodstalls are clustered around the **Hilton** end of the promenade selling Malay dishes and fruit juices (no alcohol). There are beautiful views of the river, accompanied by popular Malay-love songs.

Some of the best food centres are located in the suburbs; a taxi is essential.

Batu Lintang open-air market, Jln Rock (to the south of town, past the hospital).

Chinese Food Centre, Jln Carpenter (opposite temple). Chinese foodstalls offering hot and sour soups, fish balls and more.

Hock Hong Garden, Jln Ban Hock, opposite Grand Continental. Finest hawker stall food in Kuching, little English spoken but definitely worth trying to be understood.

King's Centre, Jln Simpang Tiga (bus No 11 to get there). Large range of foodstalls, busy and not many tourists.

Kubah Ria Hawker stalls, Jln Tunku Abdul Rahman (on the road out of town towards Damai Beach, next to Satok Suspension Bridge). Specialities include *sop kambling* (mutton soup).

Petanak Central Market, Jln Petanak, above Kuching's early morning wet market. Light snacks, full seafood selection, good atmosphere, especially early in the morning.

Song Thieng Hai Food Centre, between Jln Padungan and Jln Ban Hock. Every type of noodle available.

The Spring Food Bazaar, Spring Mall, Jln Simpang Tiga. A clean and comfortable setting to eat with a selection of Asian favourites, from Japanese teppanyaki to Sarawak *laksa*.

Top Spot Food Court, Jln Bukit Mata Kuching, top floor of a car park. Range of stalls, popular.

Damai Peninsula *p105, map p103*

New Dolphin Seafood, Kampong Buntal, T082-846441. Great position on the coast, about 5 km east of Santubon, good food, above-average prices.

Santubong Mountain Trek Canteen, 5 mins' walk from hotels, T082-846153. Rice and noodle dishes, in nearby Buntal village there are excellent seafood restaurants.

Bako National Park *p108, map p109*

The canteen is open 0700-2100. It serves local food at reasonable prices and sells tinned foods and drinks. No need to take food, there is a good seafood restaurant near the jetty.

Bars and clubs

Kuching *p94, map p98*

There are enough clubs, pubs and bars to keep most people reasonably happy. Clubs and discos usually have a cover charge, although there is often a drink or two thrown in with the price. Expect to pay RM10-15 for a beer and RM20-25 for spirits.

Most places have happy hours and 2-for-1 offers. Bars tend to close around 0100-0200, a little later in hotels. Most bars are along **Bukit Mata** off Jln Pandungan and along Jln Borneo next to the **Hilton**.

The main centres of evening entertainment are along **Jln Tunku Abdul Rahman, Jln Mendu, Jln Padungan** and **Jln Petanakin**, an area known locally as Travillion.

Cat City, Jln Chan Chin Ann (turn left at Pizza Hut). Open late. Happy hour 2030-2215, followed by live bands (usually Filipino) playing a mixture of Western rock covers and Malay and Chinese ballads.

Fire, Jln Petanak. New and friendly spot with a long happy hour and a crowd that grooves to Chinese dance music.

Grappa, 58 Jln Padungan. Stylish place popular with the young crowd. Music is famously loud and the beer some of the cheapest in town.

Marina Dangdut, Jln Ban Hock. Fri, Sat and evenings of public holidays. Top 40 hits and plenty of hip-shaking Indonesian and Malay *dangdut* to *joged* to.

Mojo@Denise, on the junction of Jln Padungan and Jln Abell. Wine and cocktail bar with themed evenings including poetry nights and live music.

Music Café, 100 Jln Petanak, 1800-0200. Good spot to meet locals with live music, DJs and big jugs of beer.

Monsoon, Riverside Complex, Jln Tunku Abdul Rahman. Balcony jutting out over the river. Good mix of locals and tourists.

Rajang Lobby Lounge, Grand Margherita. Small but popular and with plenty of good drinks promotions.

Ruaikitai Tribal Café and Restaurant, 3 Jln Green Hill, T019-8056107, peter@pegari.com.my. Iban local Peter Jaban runs this cool café/bar. Good decor, rockin' music and tasty food make this a good evening venue. There's sometimes a free welcome *tuak* (fiery local stuff) for patrons. Peter also runs tours to longhouses, including the Skrang river, and aims to keep trips as authentic and rugged as possible.

Senso, Hilton Hotel. The best cocktails and good live music, but drinks are pricey.

Tribes, downstairs at **Grand Margherita**. Open 1600-0100. Ethnic food, tribal decor and a variety of live music.

Damai Peninsula *p105, map p103*
Gecko at Damai Puri Inn, Damai Beach.Lovely tropical-style bar with plenty of comfy seats and a good selection of drinks. Simple Asian and Western snacks served.

⊕ Entertainment

Kuching *p94, map p98*
Cinemas
Riverside Cineplex, Riverside Complex, Jln Tunku Abdul Rahman, in the basement of **Riverside Majestic**, T082-427061. Check local press for programme details.

Star Cineplex, Level 9, Medan Pelita, top floor of car park on Temple St.

Cultural shows
Cultural Village, Damai Beach. Daily 1130 and 1600. Cultural shows, with stylized and expertly choreographed tribal dance routines.

⊛ Festivals and events

Bau *p104*
May-Jun The Bindayuh celebrate **gawai padi**, a festival with animistic roots that thanks the gods for an abundant rice harvest. Ask at the tourist office in Kuching for exact details.

⦿ Shopping

Kuching *p94, map p98*
When it comes to choice, Kuching is the best place in Malaysia to buy tribal handicrafts, textiles and other artefacts, but they are not cheap. In some of Sarawak's smaller coastal and upriver towns, you are more likely to find a better bargain, although the selection is not as good. If buying several items, it's a good idea to find a shop that sells the lot, as good discounts can be negotiated. It is essential to shop around: the best-stocked handicraft and antique shops in and near the big hotels are usually the most pricey. It is possible to bargain everywhere. Most shops are closed Sun.

It is illegal to export any antiquity without a licence from the curator of the Sarawak Museum. An antiquity is defined as any object made before 1850. Most things sold as antiquities are not; some very convincing weathering and ageing processes are used.

Antiques, art and handicrafts
Most handicraft and antique shops are along **Main Bazaar**, **Lebuh Temple** and **Lebuh Wayang**, with a few in the Padungan area. There is a **Sun market** (which starts on Sat afternoon) on Jln Satok, to the southwest of town, with a few handicraft stalls. Sat evening or early Sun morning are the best times to visit. There are rows of pottery stalls along **Jln Penrissen**, out of town, take a bus (No 3, 3A, 9A or 9B) or taxi to Ng Hua Seng Pottery bus stop. Antique shops sell this pottery too. **Artrageously Ramsay Ong**, 94 Main Bazaar, T082-424346, www.artrageouslyasia.com. Art gallery of Sarawak artiste extraordinaire **Ramsay Ong** who made fame with his tree

bark works. Now showing an eclectic collection of contemporary Malaysian art including some beautiful pieces by celebrated Bidayuh artist Narong Daun. Recommended.
Borneo Art Gallery, Sarawak Plaza, Jln Tunku Abdul Rahman.
Fabriko, Main Bazaar. Set in a beautifully restored Chinese shophouse, interesting souvenirs and gallery.
Galleri M, Hilton lobby, 26 Main Bazaar. Exclusive jewellery, bead necklaces and antiques, best available Iban hornbill carvings. Also paintings from Sarawakian artists.
Karyaneka (handicrafts) Centre, Cawangan Kuching, Lot 324 Bangunan Bina, Jln Satok.
Sarakraf, Upper ground floor, Sarawak Plaza Shopping Complex, sarakraf@tm.net.my. Wide range of souvenirs and handicrafts with outlets in major hotels in Kuching, Damai, Sarawak Cultural Village and Miri airport (chain set up by the Sarawak Economic Development Corporation).
Sarawak Batik Art Shop, 1 Lebuh Temple.
Sarawak House, 67 Main Bazaar. More expensive but better quality crafts, carvings, fabrics and pots.
Thian Seng, 48 Main Bazaar. Good for *pua kumbu*.

Books and maps
Berita Book Centre, Jln Haji Taha, has a good selection of English language books.
HN Mohd Yahia & Sons, Holiday Inn, Jln Tunku Abdul Rahman, and in the basement of the Sarawak Shopping Plaza. Sells a 1:500,000 map of Sarawak.
Times Books, 1st floor, Riverside Shopping Complex, Jln Tunku Abdul Rahman. Biggest and best place for foreign language books.

Markets
Vegetable and wet markets are on the riverside on Jln Gambier; further up is the **Ban Hock Wharf market**, now full of cheap imported clothes. The **Sunday Market** on Jln Satok sells jungle produce, fruit and vegetables (there are a few handicraft stalls) and all sorts of intriguing merchandise;

it starts on Sat night and runs through to Sun morning and is well worth visiting. There is a jungle produce market, **Pasar Tani**, on Fri and Sat at Kampong Pinang Jawa in Petra Jaya.

Shopping malls
Riverside Shopping Complex, next to **Riverside Majestic**. Has **Parkson Department Store** and good supermarket in basement.
Sarawak Plaza, next to the **Holiday Inn**, Jln Tunku Abdul Rahman.
The Spring, Jln Simpang Tiga (on the way to the airport). Kuching's newest shopping mall with a range of high street shops and a good food court.

▲ Activities and tours

Kuching *p94, map p98*
Climbing
Batman Wall, rock climbing at the Fairy Caves outside Bau. 20 routes and rises to 40 m.

Diving
Southern Sarawak has yet to open up as a popular diving centre. Visibility is generally poor most of the year, perhaps due in part to the vast amounts of silt being carried down the major rivers. But the marine life (if you can see it) is rich and relatively undisturbed, so there's a lot of potential for exploration. Apr-Sep are considered the best diving months.
Kuching Scuba Centre, 159 Jln Chan Chin Ann, T082-428842, www.kuchingscuba.com. One possible option.

Fishing
Fui Lip Marketing, 15 ground floor, Wisma Phoenix, Jln Song Thian Cheok. Offshore from Santubong or deep-sea game fishing at Tanjung Datu (near Indonesian border). Contact Mr Johnson.

Golf
Damai Golf & Country Club, see page 118.
Hornbill Golf & Jungle Club, Borneo Highlands Resort, Padawan, T082-790800,

www.borneohighlands.com.my. 18-hole golf course at 1000 m.
Kelab Golf Course, Petra Jaya, T082-440966. An 18-hole course.
Sarawak Golf and Country Club, Petra Jaya, T082-440966.

Mountain biking
Good trails from **Kamppung Singgai**, about 30 mins from Kuching (across the Batu Kawa bridge). Beginners to intermediate: good trail near **Kampong Apar**. Advanced trail: **Batang Ai**. Alternatively, hire a bike from Kuching and tour the Malay villages adjacent to the Astana and Fort Margherita. Cross the Sarawak River by sampan (around RM1 for you and your bike) and then follow the small road that runs parallel to the river.
Borneo Adventure, see under Tour operators. Rents mountain bikes and can arrange specialized tours.

Spectator sports
Football See Malaysia Cup football matches in the **Stadium Negeri Sarawak**, Petra Jaya.
Horse racing The Kuching Turf Club, Serian Rd, is the biggest in Borneo (see newspapers for details of meetings).

Swimming
Kuching Municipal Pool, next to Kuching Turf Club, Serian Rd. Open mornings only.

Water sports
Permai Rainforest Resort, see page 112. Aimed at families with many activities on offer, including kayaking, windsurfing, sailing and rafting. Also offers trekking.

Tour operators
Most tour companies offer city tours as well as trips around Sarawak to **Semenggoh**, Bako, Niah, **Lambir Hills**, Miri, **Mulu** and **Bario**. There are also competitively priced packages to longhouses (mostly up the Skrang River, see page 122). It is cheaper and easier to take organized tours to Mulu, but arrange these in Miri (see page 155) as they are much more

expensive if arranged from Kuching. Other areas are easy to get to independently.
Borneo Adventure, No 55 Main Bazaar, T082-245175, www.borneoadventure.com. Known for its environmentally friendly approach to tourism. Offers tours all over Sarawak. Recommended.
Borneo Exploration, 76 Jln Wayang, T082-252137, www.borneoexplorer.com.my. Organizes a variety of longhouse tours, a city tour and trips to the national parks.
Borneo Fairyland, 18 Main Bazaar, T082-420194, www.borneofairyland.tripod.com. Aimed at backpackers with good-value tours around Sarwak. A 4-day/3-night trip to a longhouse costs RM750.
Borneo Interland Travel, 63 Main Bazaar, T082-413595, www.bitravel.com.my. Helpful staff. The only agency licensed to sell bus and boat tickets in town.
Borneo Trek and Kayak Adventure, T082-240571, www.rainforestkayaking.com. Highly regarded outfit that offers kayaking trips combined with other cultural activities. Day trips from RM188 per person. Recommended.
CPH Travel Agency, 70 Jln Padungan, T082-243708, www.cphtravel.com.my. Longhouse trips, national park tours, day trips to the Kuching wetlands. Recommended.
Ibanika Expeditions, Lot 435, ground floor, Jln Ang Cheng Ho, T082-424022, ibanika@po. jaring.my. Long-established company offering longhouse and more general tours, also has French- and German-speaking guides.
Interworld, 1st floor, 161/162 Jln Temple, T082-252344, 424515. Can arrange packages to the Rainforest Music Festival.
Pan Asia Travel, 2nd floor, Unit 217-218, Sarawak Plaza, Jln Tunku Abdul Rahman, T082-419754. Half-day trips from Kuching.
Ruaikitai Tribal Café and Restaurant, see page 116. Peter John Jaban runs rough 'n' ready but interesting longhouse trips.

Damai Peninsula *p105, map p103*
Golf
Damai Golf & Country Club, Jln Santubong, PO Box 400, T082-846088, www.damaigolf.com.

International-standard, 18-hole golf course designed by Arnold Palmer, laid out over approximately 6.5 km, 10-bay driving range right on the sea. A very long 18 holes, with electric buggies to stop you expiring through perspiring. Caddies, clubs and shoes for hire, spacious clubhouse, restaurant, bar, pro shop, tennis, squash and pool are also available. Due to its popularity, bookings should be made 3 days in advance.

Mountain biking
Damai Cross-Country Track. Close to the Permai Rainforest Resort, this is a purpose-built track where visitors can get very hot, sweaty and dirty as they career around the 3.5-km track; bikes can be hired from hotels.

Water sports
Damai Puri Resort, see page 112. A range of water sports from jet skiing to sailing. Snorkelling trips also arranged.
Permai Rainforest Resort, see page 112. A slightly more limited range of watersports.

⊖ Transport

Kuching *p94, map p98*
Air
For details of transport from the airport to Kuching centre, see Getting there, page 94.

Regular connections with **KL** (8-10 flights daily), **Kota Kinabalu (KK)** and **Brunei**. AirAsia flies to KL, KK, **JB**, **Miri**, **Bintulu**, **Penang**, **Macau**, **Jakarta** and **Singapore**; book online for the best rates. **Jet Star Asia** and **Tiger Airways** both offer regular connections with Singapore. **Batavia Air** flies 3 times a week (Tue, Thu, Sun) to **Pontianak** in West Kalimantan (from RM246) at 1255 and then on to Jakarta.

Malaysian Airlines subsidiary **MASwings** has a fleet of Twin Otters, Fokker F50s and ATR 72-500s to smaller destinations in Sabah and Sarawak. Tickets can be purchased online. Destinations include Bintulu, **Mukah**, **Tanjung Manis**, **Gunung Mulu National**

Park via **Miri** and **Sibu**. There are connections to KK via Sibu and Bintulu.

Airline offices AirAsia, Wisma Ho Ho Lim, ground floor, 291 Jln Abell, T082-283222. **Batavia Air**, T082-626299. MAS, Lot 215, Jln Song Thian Cheok, T082- 246622. **Royal Brunei**, 1st floor, Rugayah Building, Jln Song Thian Cheok, T082-243344. **Sin Hwa Travel Service**, 8 Lebuh Temple, T082-246688.

Boat
Sampans cross the Sarawak River from next to the Square Tower on Main Bazaar to **Fort Margherita** and the **Astana** on the north bank for around RM0.30. Small boats and some express boats connect with outlying kampongs on the river. Sampans can also be hired by the hour (RM40) for a tour up and down the river.

Express boats leave from the Sin Kheng Hong Wharf, 6 km out of town. Take a taxi (RM18). Tickets for **Kuching-Sibu** are only for sale at 2 places in town: Borneo Interland, 63 Main Bazaar, T082-413595, and **Lim Magazine bookshop**, 19 Ban Hock Lane, T082-410076. Otherwise turn up at the ferry 30 mins before departure to get a ticket. 1 daily departure for **Sibu** via Sarakei at 0830 (5 hrs, RM45).

Bus
Local 2 bus companies operate here. Blue and white **Chin Lian Long** buses serve the city and its suburbs; major bus stops are at Jln Masjid and opposite the post office. The green and yellow **Sarawak Transport Company** (STC) buses leave from the end of Lebuh Jawa, next to Ban Hock Wharf and the market.

Buses depart from the **Regional Express Bus Terminal** on Jln Penrissen at Mile 3.5 (a taxi ride costs around RM10). You either have to buy tickets at the bus station itself a few kilometres outside of the centre, or from Borneo Interland, 63 Main Bazaar, T082-413595, closed Sun. Buses to **Sibu** (7 hrs, RM40, first departure 0645, last 2200) **Bintulu** (RM60) and **Miri** (15 hrs, RM80, first 0100 last 2100). Biaramas has an office on Jln Wayang,

T012-883 3410 and sells bus tickets to major cities in Sarawak and to Pontianak.
International connections There are express bus departures to **Pontianak** in Kalimantan, Indonesia, (0730-2300, 10 hrs, RM45, a comfy VIP bus goes daily at 1100, RM75).

Since November 2008, the border crossing at Entikong has been given VOA (Visa On Arrival) status, meaning tourists can get a 30-day visa (US$25) on arrival. However, the visa situation in Indonesia is extremely volatile, and it is imperative that travellers contact the consulate in Kuching for the latest updates (see below). Buses leave from the **Regional Express Bus Terminal**. There are several departures daily from Kuching via Miri and Kuala Belait to **Bandar Seri Begawan** (Brunei, RM130).

Interior towns are sometimes difficult to access by road.

Car
It is possible to enter Sarawak from Kalimantan driving a private vehicle (including rental vehicles) as long as it has international insurance cover.
Car hire Flexi Car Rental, Lot 7050, 2nd floor, Jln Sekama, T082-335282, www.flexicarrental.com. Also at the airport.
Golden System Car Rental & Tours, 58-1B, 1st floor, Block G, Pearl Commercial Centre, Jln Tun Razak, T082-333609, www.goldencr.com.my. Also has a desk at the airport. A wide range of cars, vans and 4WDs. Free pick-up and delivery in the Kuching area.
Pronto Car Rental, 1st floor, 98 Jln Padungan, T/F082-236889.
Wah Tung Travel Service, 7 Jln Ban Hock, T082-248888, www.wahtunggroup.com.my.

Taxi
Local taxis congregate at the taxi stand on Jln Market, or outside the big hotels; they don't use meters, so agree a price before setting off. 24-hr radio taxi service, T082-343343 or T082-342255. Short distances around town should cost RM10.

Damai Peninsula *p105, map p103*
Bus
There are shuttle buses from the **Grand Margherita** in **Kuching** (RM12 each way, RM5 children, 40 mins, first bus at 0730 from Kuching, last return bus at 2200) or take the public bus No 2B, operated by **Petra Jaya Transport** (yellow buses with black and red stripes) to **Santubong** at a fraction of the price (RM3.30) from the market place at the end of Jln Gambier. Tour companies offer packages for various prices including transport, entry to the Sarawak Cultural Village and lunch.

Taxi
From **Kuching** is negotiable and costs between RM40 and RM45 depending on bargaining skills.

Bako National Park *p108, map p109*
For details on transport to and from Kuching, see page 108.

ℹ Directory

Kuching *p94, map p98*
Banks
Money changers in the main shopping complexes usually give a much better rate for cash than the banks, although for TCs the rates are much the same. ATMs are everywhere. Note that the 1st and 3rd Sat of every month is a bank holiday. **American Express**, 70 Jln Padungan (assistance with Amex TCs), T082-252600; **HSBC**, Bangunan Binamas (near Cat Statue) on Jln Padungan; **Majid & Sons Money Changer**, 45 Jln India; **Mohamed Yahia & Sons** (money changer), GF3, Sarawak Plaza, some of the best rates in Kuching; **Standard Chartered**, Wisma Bukit Mata Kuching (opposite Grand Margherita), Jln Tunku Abdul Rahman. **Embassies and consulates** Australian Honorary Consul, T082-233350; British Honorary Representative, T012-322 0011; French Honorary Consul, Telang Usan Hotel, T082-415588; Indonesian Consulate, 111 Jln Tun

Haji Openg, T082-241734; **New Zealand Honorary Consul**, T082-482177.
Immigration 1st floor, Bangunan Sultan Iskandar (Federal Complex) Jln Simpang Tiga, T082-245661. **Internet** Most guesthouses offer free internet access. Also try **Cyber City**, Taman Sri Sarawak (opposite the Hilton, open 1000-2200, RM4 per hr; **Dot.com**, Wayang St (next to Ting & Ting supermarket and Borneo Hotel), open 0900-2100, RM2 per hr. **Waterfront Cyber Café**, Steamship Building, open 0900-2100, RM4 per hr. International calls can be made from most public cardphones. Major hotels all have cardphones in their lobbies. **Medical services** Abdul Rahman Yakub, T082-440055, private hospital with good reputation; **Doctor's Clinic**, Main Bazaar, opposite Chinese History Museum, said to be excellent and is used to treating travellers' more minor ailments (between RM20 and RM30 for consultation); **Normah Medical Centre**, across the river on Jln Tun Datuk Patinggi, T082-440055; **Sarawak General Hospital**, Jln Tan Sri Ong Kee Hui, off Jln Tun Haji Openg, T082-276666, consultation from RM50; **Timberland Medical Centre**, Rock Rd, T082-234991. Recommended. **Pharmacies: Apex Pharmacy**, 125 1st floor, Sarawak Plaza, open 1000-2100; **UMH**, Ban Hock Rd, Mon-Fri 0900-2030, Sat 0900-1800; **YK Farmasi**, 22 Main Bazaar, 0830-1700. **Police** Tourist Police, Kuching Waterfront, T082-250522. **Post office** General Post Office, Jln Tun Haji Openg, Mon-Sat 0800-1800, Sun 1000-1300. Operates a poste restante service.

Bandar Sri Aman and around

→ *Colour map 3, C2.*
Previously called Simmanggang, Bandar Sri Aman lies on the Batang Lupar, a three- to four-hour journey from Kuching, and is the administrative capital of the Second Division. The river is famous for its tidal bore; several times a year, a wall of water rushes upstream wreaking havoc with boats and divides into several tributaries: the Skrang River is one of these. It is possible to spend the night in longhouse homestays on the river. The Batang Ai National Park is home to hornbills, orang-utans and gibbons. ◆◆ *For listings, see pages 125-126.*

Ins and outs
Bandar Sri Aman is accessible from Kuching and Sibu by bus. To reach Skrang longhouses, buses and then chartered boats must be arranged. There is one hotel in Batang Ai National Park. It arranges transport for its guests. Trips to longhouses and the national park can be organized through **Borneo Adventure Travel Company**, see page 125.

Sights
The major sight in Bandar is the defensive Fort Alice. Most tourists do not stop in Bandar but pass through on day trips from Kuching to visit traditional Iban longhouses sited along the Skrang River. The route to Bandar goes through pepper plantations and many 'new' villages. During Communist guerrilla activity in the 1960s (see page 174), whole settlements were uprooted in this area and placed in guarded camps.

Fort Alice was constructed in 1864. It has small turrets, a central courtyard, a medieval-looking drawbridge and is surrounded by a fence of iron spikes. Rajah Charles Brooke lived in the Batang Lupar district for about 10 years, using this fort – and another downriver at Lingga – as bases for his punitive expeditions against pirates and Ibans in the interior. The fort is the only one of its type in Sarawak and was built commanding this stretch of the Batang Lupar River as protection against Iban raids. The original fort here was built in 1849 and named Fort James; the current fort was constructed using much of the original material. It was renamed Alice in honour of Ranee Margaret Brooke (it was her second name). It is said that every evening, until the practice was ended in 1964, a policeman would call from the fort (in Iban): "Oh ha! Oh ha! The time is now eight o'clock. The steps have been drawn up. The door is closed. People from upriver, people from downriver, are not allowed to come to the fort anymore." (It probably sounded better in Iban.)

Skrang longhouses → *Colour map 3, C3.*

The Skrang River was one of the first areas settled by Iban immigrants in the 16th to 18th centuries. The slash-and-burn agriculturalists originally came from the Kapual River basin in Kalimantan. They later joined forces with Malay chiefs in the coastal areas and terrorized the Borneo coasts; the first Europeans to encounter these pirates called them Sea Dayaks (see page 176). The Ibans took many heads. Blackened skulls – which local headmen say date back to those days – hang in some of the Skrang longhouses. In 1849 more than 800 Iban pirates from the Batang Lupar and Skrang River were massacred by Rajah James Brooke's forces in the notorious Battle of Beting Marau. Four years later the Sultan of Brunei agreed to cede these troublesome districts to Brooke; they became the Second Division of Sarawak.

There are many traditional Iban longhouses along the Skrang River, although those closer to **Pias** and **Lamanak** (the embarkation points on the Skrang) tend to be very touristy – they are visited by tour groups almost every day. **Long Mujang**, the first Iban longhouse, is an hour upriver. Pias and Lamanak are within five hours' drive of Kuching. Jungle trekking is available (approximately two hours). The guide provides an educational tour of the flora and fauna.

Batang Ai and Batang Ai National Park

The Batang Ai River, a tributary of the Batang Lupar, has been dammed to form Sarawak's first hydroelectric plant, which came into service in 1985; it provides 60% of Sarawak's electricity supply, transmitting as far as Limbang. The area was slowly flooded over a period of six months to give animals and wildlife a chance to escape, but it has affected no fewer than 29 longhouses, 10 of which are now completely submerged. The rehousing of the longhouse community has been the topic of fierce controversial debate. The communities were moved into modern longhouses and given work opportunities in local palmeries. However, it now seems that the housing loans that were initially given are not commensurate with local wages and will be very difficult for the longhouse communities to pay off. In addition, modern longhouses were not provided with farmland, so many local people have returned to settle on the banks of the reservoir. Near the dam there is a freshwater fish nursery. These fish are exported to South Korea, Japan and Europe. Those families displaced by the flooding of the dam largely work here and many of the longhouses surrounding the dam depend upon this fishery for their own fish supply.

The Batang Ai dam has created a vast and picturesque man-made lake covering some 90 sq km, stretching up the Engkari and Ai rivers. Beyond the lake, more than an hour's boat ride upriver from the dam, it is possible to see beautiful lowland mixed dipterocarp forest.

The **Batang Ai National Park**, 250 km from Kuching and two hours from the jetty by boat, covers an area of over 24,040 ha and was inaugurated in 1991. It protects the much-endangered orang-utan and is home to a wide variety of other wildlife, including

The longhouse: prime location apartments

Most longhouses are built on stilts, high on the riverbank, on prime real estate. They are 'prestigious properties' with 'lots of character', and with 'commanding views of the river', they are the condominiums of the jungle. They are long-rise rather than high-rise, however, and the average longhouse has 20-25 'doors' (although there can be as many as 60). Each represents one family. The word 'long' in a settlement's name – as in Long Liput or Long Terawan – means 'confluence' (the equivalent of *kuala* in Malay), and does not refer to the length of the longhouse.

Behind each of the doors – which even today, are rarely locked – is a *bilik* (apartment), which includes the family living room and a loft, where paddy and tools are stored. In Kenyah and Kayan longhouses, paddy (which can be stored for years until it is milled) is kept in elaborate barns, built on stilts away from the longhouse, in case of fire. In traditional longhouses, the living rooms are simple with *atap*-roofs and bamboo floors; in modern longhouses, designed on the same principles, living rooms have sofas, lino floors, TV and en suite bathroom.

At the front of the *bilik* is the *dapur*, where the cooking takes place. All *biliks* face out onto the *ruai* (gallery), which is the focus of communal life and is where visitors are usually entertained. The width of the wall which faces onto the *ruai* indicates the status of that family. Attached to the *ruai* there is usually a *tanju* (open veranda) running the full length of the house – where rice and other agricultural products are dried. Long ladders – notched hardwood trunks – lead up to the *tanju*; they can get very slippery and do not always come with handrails.

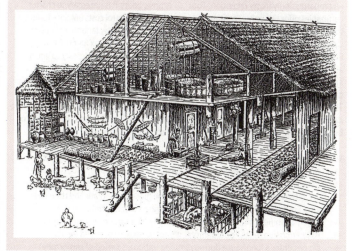

hornbills and gibbons. As yet there are no visitor facilities, but five walking trails have been created, one of which takes in an ancient burial ground. Trips to one of the 29 longhouses surrounding the dam and to Batang Ai National Park are organized by the **Borneo Adventure Travel Company**, see Activities and tours, below.

Visiting longhouses: house rules

There are more than 1500 longhouses in Sarawak. They are usually located along the big rivers and their tributaries, notably the Skrang (see page 122), the Rejang (see page 126) and the Baram (see page 146). The Iban, who are characteristically extrovert and hospitable to visitors, live on the lower reaches of the rivers. The Orang Ulu tribes – mainly Kayan and Kenyah – live further upriver and are generally less outgoing than the Iban. The Bidayuh live mainly around Bau and Serian, near Kuching. Their longhouses are usually more modern than those of the Iban and Orang Ulu, and are visited less often for that reason. The Kelabit people live on the remote plateau country near the Kalimantan border around Bario (see page 166).

The most important ground rule is not to visit a longhouse without an invitation. People who arrive unannounced may get an embarrassingly frosty reception. Tour companies offer the only exception to this rule, as most have tribal connections. Upriver, particularly at Kapit, on the Rejang (see page 126), such 'invitations' are not hard to come by; it is good to ensure your host actually comes from the longhouse you are being invited to. The best time to visit Iban longhouses is during the gawai harvest festival at the beginning of June, when communities throw an open house and everyone is invited to join the festivities.

On arrival, visitors should pay an immediate courtesy call on the headman (the *tuai rumah* in Iban longhouses). It is normal to bring him gifts; those staying overnight should offer the headman around RM20 per person. The money is kept in a central fund and saved for use by the whole community during festivals. Small gifts such as beer, coffee, biscuits, whisky, batik and food (especially rice or chicken) go down well. It is best to arrive at a longhouse during late afternoon after people have returned from the fields. Visitors who have time to stay the night generally have a much more enjoyable experience than those who pay fleeting visits. They can share the evening meal and have time to talk and drink.

If you go beyond the limits of the express boats, it is necessary to charter a longboat. Petrol costs RM2.50-5 a litre, depending on how far upriver you are. Guides charge approx RM60-100 a day and sometimes it is necessary to hire a boatman or frontman as well. Prices increase in the dry season when boats have to be lifted over shallow rapids. Permits are required for most upriver areas; these can be obtained at the residents' or district office in the nearest town.

Visitors should note the following:

→ On entering a longhouse, take off your shoes.
→ Accept food and drink with both hands. If you do not want to eat or drink, the accepted custom is to touch the brim of the glass or the plate and then touch your lips as a symbolic gesture. Sit cross-legged when eating.
→ When washing in the river, women should wear a sarong and men, shorts.
→ Ask permission to take photographs. It's not unusual to be asked for a small fee.
→ Do not enter a longhouse during *pantang* (taboo), a period of misfortune usually following a death. There is normally a white (leaf) flag hanging near the longhouse as a warning to visitors. During this period (normally one week) there is no singing, dancing or music, and no jewellery is worn.
→ Bow your head when walking past people older than you.

For Sleeping and Eating price codes and other relevant information, see Essentials pages 23-27.

● Sleeping

Bandar Sri Aman and around *p121*

B Bukit Saban Resort, on the rarely visited Paku River, just north of the Skrang and Lemnak rivers, about 4½ hrs from Kuching, T082-477145, F477103 (Kuching sales office), T083-648949 (at the resort). 50 rooms in longhouse style with traditional sago palm thatch, restaurant, a/c, TV, hot water.
B Champion, 1248 Main Bazaar, T082-320140. A small but central establishment.

Skrang longhouses *p122*

All longhouses along the Skrang River are controlled by the Ministry of Tourism so rates are the same – RM40 inclusive of all meals. Resthouses at most of the longhouses can accommodate 20-40 people; mattresses and mosquito nets are provided in a communal sleeping area with few partitions. Basic, with flush toilet, shower, local food, phone and a clinic nearby. If the stay is 3 days/2 nights, on the 2nd night it's possible to camp in the jungle and then get a return boat ride to the longhouse.

Batang Ai and Batang Ai National Park *p122*

Tour companies provide accommodation in longhouses here, in a much more central location within the park than the **Hilton**.
A Hilton International Batang Ai Longhouse Resort, T083-584388, www.hilton.com. On the eastern shore of the lake. Opened in 1995, the resort is made up of 11 longhouses, built of the local *belian* (ironwood) to traditional designs. Despite its lakeside location there are no views, except from the walkways, as longhouses are built, for purposes of defence, to face landwards – in this case, over the buggy track. However, there are compromises to modern comforts: all 100 rooms have a/c, fan, TV, shower room, minibar. Other facilities

include a pool and paddling pool, restaurant, 18-km jogging track, shuttle from **Kuching Hilton International** tour desk. The hotel arranges transport. If the **Hilton** is not your style, there is, unfortunately, not much else.

● Eating

Bandar Sri Aman and around *p121*

ﾟ **Alison Café & Restaurant**, 4 Jln Council. Chinese cuisine.
ﾟ **Chuan Hong**, 1 Jln Council. Chinese coffee shop, also serves Muslim food.
ﾟ **Melody**, 432 Jln Hospital. Chinese and Muslim food.

▲ Activities and tours

Bandar Sri Aman and around *p121*

Many of the restaurant staff in the resort are locals and discreet enquiries may get you a trip to a longhouse and/or Batang Ai National Park for considerably less than the **Borneo Adventure Travel Company** charge.
Borneo Adventure Travel Company, 55 Main Bazaar, Kuching, T082-410569, www.borneoadventure.com, and at the Hilton Batang Ai Longhouse Resort.

● Transport

Bandar Sri Aman and around *p121*
Bus
Regular connections with **Kuching**, RM15 (135 km) and **Sibu** (via Sarikei).

Skrang longhouses *p122*
Bus
Buses No 14 and 19 to **Pias** and bus No 9 to **Lemanak**. Self-drive car rental (return) or minibus (8-10 people, return) from **Kuching** to **Entaban**. From these points it is necessary to charter a boat to reach the nearest

longhouses. Many of the Kuching-based tour agencies offer cut-price deals for 1- to 2-day excursions to Skrang and Lemanak river longhouses (see page 118). Unless you are already part of a small group, these tours work out cheaper because of the boat costs.

Sibu, Kapit and Belaga

The third largest town in Sarawak, Sibu is sited at the confluence of the Rejang and the Igan rivers 60 km upstream from the sea. It is the starting point for trips up the Rejang to the Kapit and Belaga. The Rejang is an important thoroughfare and Malaysia's longest river at 563 km. Tours to upriver longhouses can be organized from Sibu or more cheaply from Kapit and Belaga.

▶▶ *For listings, see pages 134-140.*

Sibu

Sleeping 🛏	Phoenix 10	Eating 🍴
Bahagia 13	Premier 11	Ark Galley & Café 1
Eden Inn 1	RH 4	Blue Splendour 4
Garden 5	River Park 8	Café Café 3
Kingwood 6	Tanahmas 15	Kasturi 5
Li Hua 7	Victoria Inn 2	Mama Café 7

Sibu

Ins and outs

Getting there and around The airport is 25 km from Sibu and there are flights to KL, Kuching and KK; ⓘ **Sibu airport information centre** *T084-307755*. To get from the airport by taxi you need to buy a taxi coupon (RM32). Or take Lanang Bus No 3A, which leaves every two hours between 0630 and 1600.

The new long-distance bus station is about 3 km out of town. Take a taxi, RM15, or a Lorong Road bus (no number) or Sungei Merah bus No 12 or 17 to the local bus station near the ferry terminal. There are daily connections with Bintulu and Miri, and Kuching via Sarikei. Boats for Kuching and Sarikei dock at two wharves close to the town centre.

Although this is Sarawak's third largest town, it's still possible to see most of Sibu's sights on foot. ▸▸ *See also Transport, page 139.*

Rex Food Court **6**
Sri Menanti **2**
Sri Menanti
  Chicken Rice **8**

Tourist information

The **Visitors' Information Centre** ⓘ *ground floor, 32 Jln Tukang Besi (around the corner from the Methodist Church), T084-340980, www.sarawaktourism.com, Mon-Fri 0800-1700 (closed on public holidays)*, is very friendly and helpful. As well as information on Sibu they can advise for trips onwards to Kapit and Belaga. A visit here is highly recommended. For the latest information on riverboats leaving Sibu, phone the **Sarawak Riverboat Information Line** ⓘ *T084-339936.*

Background

Thanks to the discovery of the Kuala Paloh channel in 1961, Sibu is accessible to boats with a sizeable draft. Sibu is a busy Chinese trading town – the majority of the population came originally from China's Fujian Province – and is the main port on the Rejang (also spelt Rajang). In 1899, Rajah Charles Brooke agreed with Wong Nai Siong, a Chinese scholar from Fujian, to allow settlers to Sibu. Brooke had reportedly been impressed with the industriousness of the Chinese: he saw the women toiling in the paddy fields from dawn to dusk and commented: "If the women work like that, what on earth must the men be like?"

The Kuching administration provided these early agricultural pioneers with temporary housing on arrival, a steamer between Sibu and Kuching, rice rations for the first year and tuition in Malay and Iban. The town grew rapidly (its expansion is documented in a photographic exhibition in the Civic Centre) but was razed to the ground in the great fire of 1828. The first shophouses to be constructed after the fire are the three-storey ones still standing on Jalan Channel. At the beginning of the 20th century, Sibu became the springboard for Foochow migration to the rest of Sarawak. Today it is an industrial and trading centre for timber, pepper and rubber, and home to some of Sarawak's wealthiest families, mostly timber *towkays* (merchants).

Sights

The old trading port has now been graced with a pagoda, a couple of big hotels and a smart esplanade. The 1929 **shophouses** along the river are virtually all that remains of the old town. The seven-storey **pagoda**, adjacent to **Tua Pek Kong Temple**, cost RM1.5 million to build; there are good views over the town from the top, you'll need to ask for the key. The pagoda and temple are well worth visiting for the caretaker, Tan Teck Chiang, alone. Chiang speaks great English and gives impromptu animated lectures filled with unique interpretations and humour on the temple, Chinese culture and Taoism. Just turn up and ask for Chiang. In the **Sibu Civic Centre** ① *2.5 km out of town on Jln Tun Abang Haji Openg, Tue-Sun 0800-1700; take Sungei Merah bus No 4 from the bus terminal and ask for the Civic Centre*, there is an exhibition of old photographs of Sibu and a mediocre tribal display. This serves as Sibu's municipal museum. Five aerial photographs of the town, taken since 1947, chart the town's explosive growth.

There are a couple of interesting Chinese temples out of town. The **Taoist Tiger Temple** is unique in that it is the only temple in Malaysia dedicated to the seven tiger deities. The temple has the tigers in various fierce poses dressed in human clothes. The myth goes back to the mountains of rural China, where after years of being attacked and killed by the local human population, seven tiger brothers took their revenge and went on a violent killing spree until they were caught and imprisoned by Kuan Keng, a Chinese general from the Three Kingdoms period. The tigers were released after 400 years of captivity, by which time they had become half human and had vowed to become strict vegetarians. Each of the statues in the temple represents the qualities of a different deity; the tiger nearest the entrance is in charge of the environment, and next to him is Tsai Shen, the fifth tiger deity and God of Wealth. The tigers receive vegetarian offerings from the local Chinese population. To get there, take a taxi to Jalan Trusan, off Jalan Teku (RM12). Recently completed, the Sibu **Yu Lung San Tian Ensi** ① *T019-892 8128*, is the largest Chinese temple in Southeast Asia. It's the temple that turns heads on the road from Bintulu with its enormous size, sweeping gables and multicoloured buildings. To get there, take Lanang bus No 2 (hourly from 0515, RM3) from Jalan Maju. A taxi costs RM30.

Kapit → *Population: 100,000.*

Kapit, which means 'twin' in local dialect, is the capital of Sarawak's Seventh Division, through which flows the **Rejang River** and its main tributaries, the Batang Baleh, Batang Katibas, Batang Balui and Sungai Belaga. In a treaty with the Sultan of Brunei, Rajah James Brooke acquired the Rejang Basin for Sarawak in 1853. Kapit is the last big town on the Rejang and styles itself as the gateway to 'the heart of Borneo', after Redmond O'Hanlon's *Into the Heart of Borneo*, which describes his adventure up the Batang Baleh in the 1980s. Kapit is full of people who claim to be characters in this book.

The main sights are Fort Sylvia and the Kapit Museum but, like O'Hanlon and his journalist companion James Fenton, most visitors simply use the town as a pit stop before continuing their adventures into the interior to explore the upper Rejang and its tributaries, where there are many Iban and Orang Ulu longhouses. Maps of the Kapit Division and other parts of Sarawak are available from the **Land Survey Department** ⓘ *Jln Beletik on Jln Airport*. Permits for upriver trips are available from the **government administration centre** ⓘ *Resident Office, Kapit Division, 96800 Kapit, T084-796445*, which is outside town near the old airport. Take one of the local buses heading 'downstream' from Kapit town centre for around RM2. Tourists going up the Balleh River or Upper Rejang must sign a form saying they understand they are travelling at their own risk.

Background

There are only a few tens of kilometres of surfaced road in and around Kapit, but the small town has a disproportionate number of cars. It is a trading centre for the tribespeople upriver and has grown enormously in recent years with the expansion of the logging industry upstream. Logs come in two varieties: floaters and sinkers. Floaters are pulled downstream by tugs in huge chevron formations. Sinkers – like *belian* (ironwood) – are transported in the Chinese-owned dry bulk carriers that line up along the wharves at Kapit. When the river is high these timber ships are able to go upstream, past the Pelagus Rapids. The Rejang at Kapit is normally 500 m wide and, in the dry season, the riverbank slopes steeply down to the water. When it floods, however, the water level rises more than 10 m, as is testified by the high-water marks on Fort Sylvia.

Sights

Fort Sylvia near the wharves was built of *belian* by Rajah Charles Brooke in 1880, and is now occupied by the Kapit Museum. It was originally called Kapit Fort but was renamed in

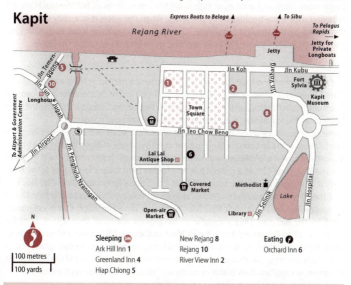

Kapit

Express Boats to Belaga ▲   ▲ To Sibu

To Pelagus
Rapids

Rejang River

Jetty for
Private
Longboats

Jetty

Jln Koh

Jln Yohang

Jln Kubu

Fort
Sylvia

Kapit
Museum

Longhouse

Town
Square

Jln Teo Chow Beng

Lai Lai
Antique Shop

Covered
Market

Methodist

Lake

Jln Hospital

Open-air
Market

Library

Jln Selinik

Jln Airport

Jln Penghulu Nyanggan

Jln Temenggong

To Airport & Government
Administration Centre

N

100 metres
100 yards

Sleeping
Ark Hill Inn **1**
Greenland Inn **4**
Hiap Chiong **5**

New Rejang **8**
Rejang **10**
River View Inn **2**

Eating
Orchard Inn **6**

1925 after Rajah Vyner Brooke's wife. Most of the forts built during this time were designed to prevent the Orang Ulu going downriver; Fort Sylvia was built to stop the belligerent Iban headhunters from attacking Kenyah and Kayan settlements upstream.

Kapit Museum ① *Tue-Sun, 1000-1200 and 1400-1700, free (if closed at these times search for the curator to open it)*, was enlarged in the 1990s and moved to Fort Sylvia. It has exhibits (all labelled in English) on Rejang tribes and the local economy. Set up by the Sarawak Museum in Kuching, it includes a section of an Iban longhouse and several Iban artefacts including a wooden hornbill. The Orang Ulu section has a reconstruction of a longhouse and a mural painted by local tribespeople. An Orang Ulu *salong* (burial hut), totem pole and other woodcarvings are also on display. The museum has representative exhibits from the small Malay community and the Chinese. Hokkien traders settled at Kapit and Belaga and traded salt, sugar and ceramics for pepper, rotan and rubber; they were followed by traders from Fujian. The Chinese exhibit is a shop. In addition, there are also displays on the natural history of the upper Rejang and modern industries such as mining, logging and tourism.

Kapit has a particularly colourful daily **market** in the centre of town. Tribeswomen bring in fruit, vegetables and animals to sell; it is quite normal to see everything from turtles, frogs, birds and catfish to monkeys, wild boar and even pangolin and pythons. **Note** If you do see animals such as monkeys, pangolins, wild cats or birds, please remember that most of them are protected species and in serious danger of extinction, due to the wildlife 'pet' trade and the rising demand for 'traditional' medicines like ground bone and body parts such as monkey gall bladders. Please do not buy them or in any way encourage this business.

Pelagus Rapids

Forty-five minutes upstream from Kapit on the Rejang River, this 2.5-km-long series of cataracts and whirlpools is the result of a sudden drop in the riverbed, caused by a geological fault line. Express boats can make it up the Pelagus to Belaga in the wet season (September-April) and at times of high water the rest of the year, but the rapids are still regarded with some trepidation by the pilots. When the water is low, they can only be negotiated by the smallest longboats. There are seven rapids in total, each with local names such as The Python, The Knife and one, more ominously, called The Grave.

Longhouses

① *To go upriver beyond Kapit it is necessary to get a permit (no charge) from the offices in the State Government Complex; the permit is valid for travel up the Rejang as far as Belaga and for an unspecified distance up the Baleh. For upriver trips beyond Belaga another permit must be obtained there; however, these trips tend to be expensive and dangerous.*

Some longhouses are accessible by road and several others are within an hour's longboat ride from town. In Kapit you are likely to be invited to visit one of these. Visitors are strongly advised not to visit a longhouse without an invitation, ideally from someone who lives in it; see also box, page 124. As a general rule, the further from town a longhouse is, the more likely it is to conform with the image of what a traditional longhouse should be like. That said, there are some beautiful traditional longhouses nearby, which are mainly Iban. One of the most accessible is **Rumah Seligi**, about 30 minutes' drive from Kapit. Cars or vans can be hired by the half day. Only a handful of longhouses are more than 500 m from the riverbanks of the Rejang and its tributaries. Most longhouses still practise shifting cultivation; rice is the main crop but under government aid programmes many are now growing cash crops such as cocoa. Longhouses are also referred to as *Uma* (*Sumah*) and the name of the headman, ie Long Segaham is known locally as *Uma Lasah* (Lasah being the chief).

Longhouses between Kapit and Belaga on the upper Rejang river are accessible by the normal passenger boats, but these express boats travel a limited distance on the Baleh River (2½ hours). To go further upriver it is necessary to take a tour or organize your own guides and boatmen. The sort of trip taken by Redmond O'Hanlon and James Fenton (as described in O'Hanlon's book *Into the Heart of Borneo*) would cost more than RM1800 a head. Large-scale logging operations are currently underway on the Baleh River and although this may increase boat traffic and the opportunities to access this part of Sarawak, brace yourself for a very different experience from that described in *Into the Heart of Borneo*. ➤➤ *See Activities and tours, page 138.*

The vast majority of the population, about 68%, in Sarawak's Seventh Division is Iban. They inhabit the Rejang up to and a little beyond Kapit, as well as the lower reaches of the Balleh and its tributaries. The Iban people are traditionally the most hospitable to visitors but, as a result, their longhouses are the most frequently visited by tourists. Malays and Chinese account for 3.4% and 7% of the population respectively. The Orang Ulu live further upriver; the main tribes are the Kayan and the Kenyah (12%) and a long list of sub-groups such as the Kejaman, Beketan, Sekapan, Lahanan, Seping and Tanjong. In addition there are the nomadic and semi-nomadic Penan, Punan and Ukit. Many tribal people are employed in the logging industry and, with their paid jobs, have brought the trappings of modernity to even the most remote longhouses.

Rumah Tuan Lepong Balleh Only enter this longhouse with the local policeman, Selvat Anu, who lives there; ask for him at Kapit police station. During the day Selvat and some members of the longhouse can take visitors on various adventure tours: river trips, visiting longhouses, jungle treks, fishing, pig hunting, camping in the jungle, trips up to logging areas, swimming in rivers and mountain trekking. Selvat is very knowledgeable and has good relations with longhouse communities. Visitors can eat with the family and occasionally have the chance to experience a traditional Iban ceremony.

Belaga → *Colour map 3, C4.*

This is the archetypal sleepy little town, most people while away the time in coffee shops. They are the best places to watch life go by and there are always interesting visitors in town, from itinerant wild honey collectors from Kalimantan to Orang Ulu who have brought their jungle produce downriver to the Belaga bazaar or those who are heading to the metropolis of Kapit for medical treatment. At night, when the neon lights flicker on, coffee shops are invaded by thousands of cicadas, beetles and moths.

A few Chinese traders set up shop in Belaga in the early 1900s and traded with the tribespeople upriver, supplying essentials such as kerosene and cooking oil. The Orang Ulu brought their beadwork and mats as well as jungle produce such as beeswax, ebony, *gutta-percha* (rubbery tree gum) and, most prized of all, bezoar stones. These are gall-stones found in certain monkeys (the wah-wahs, jelu-merahs and jelu-jankits) and porcupines. To the Chinese, they have much the same properties as rhinoceros horn and, even today, they are exported from Sarawak to Singapore, where they fetch S$300 per kilogram.

Belaga serves as a small government administration centre for the remoter parts of the Seventh Division as it is the last settlement of any size up the Rejang.

It's also a major centre for the illegal logging business, with many locals having been paid off handsomely to say nothing negative regarding the huge scale logging operations close to the Kalimantan border. For such a small village Belaga boasts a large number of expensive cars and 4WDs, and the money's not from ecotourism.

Belaga is also a good place to arrange visits to the Kayan and Kenyah longhouses on the Linnau River. There is a very pretty **Malay kampong** (Kampong Bharu) along the esplanade downriver from the Belaga Bazaar. The **Kejaman burial pole** on display outside the Sarawak Museum in Kuching was brought from the Belaga area in 1902.

The **District Office** (for upriver permits) is on the far side of the basketball courts.

Upriver from Belaga

ⓘ *To go upriver beyond Belaga it is technically necessary to obtain a permit from the Residents' Office, T084-321963, and permission from the police station. The situation 'on the ground' is usually a lot more relaxed, with local guides and boat owners able to travel with the minimum of paperwork; ask in Belaga hotels and coffee shops on arrival.*

When the river is high, express boats go upstream as far as the vast **Bakun Dam** (see box opposite). From the dam a paved road connects to Bintulu on the coast, around four hours away, providing the main artery of supply for the Bakun project. Several basic shops and even a couple of 'motels' have been set up in the area to provide for the needs of the workers employed here. Beyond the Bakun dam itself logging roads continue further into the interior and it's sometimes possible to hire a driver and 4WD to explore.

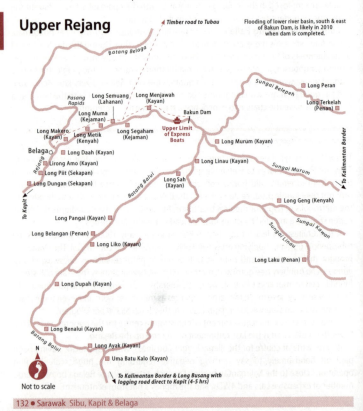

Upper Rejang

Not to scale

Build and be dammed: an ecological time bomb

The Bakun Dam Scheme, upriver from Belaga on the upper Rejang and 400 km east of Kuching, has had more twists and turns than the river on which it is being built.

The RM9.12 billion project, one of the largest in Southeast Asia, will flood a tract of virgin rainforest that supports at least 43 species of endangered mammals and birds. In preparation for the flooding, 9000 longhouse-dwelling tribespeople have been displaced from their ancestral homeland.

The dam is going to be twice the height of the Aswan Dam in Egypt and will flood 69,000 ha – an area bigger than Singapore. Environmentalists say it will be an ecological time bomb in the heart of Borneo.

The project has been on and off the books countless times. In 1990 it was scrapped for environmental reasons, but was back on again in 1993. Again, in late 1997, in the midst of Malaysia's economic crisis, when money was scarce, it was shelved only to be restarted in 2001. In 2004, with the government struggling to find buyers for the dam's electricity, it was rumoured that the project would again be scrapped or postponed. Government figures are determined to see the project through, although its original completion date of 2003 was pushed back to late 2007 and then onto 2010. Even during the hiatus preparations for the eventual flooding went on. Thousands of locals were moved from their villages and jungle longhouses and rehoused elsewhere.

The plan is for Bakun to generate 2400 MW of electricity. The power will be consumed within Sabah and Sarawak, and possibly Brunei and Kalimantan, and will involve the construction of 800 km of high-voltage power lines. Plans for an undersea cable more than 600 km long have been revived with a possible completion date of 2015 at a cost of around RM9 billion. The cable is to carry power to Peninsular Malaysia where energy needs are increasing, unlike Borneo where there does not seem to be the growth in demand to warrant the dam's construction. It is also possible that the cable will be used to carry power to other ASEAN members.

Roads need to be carved through dense jungle to bring building materials and engineering equipment to the remote site above the Bakun Rapids. Malaysian lobby groups such as the Environmental Protection Society predict the project will cause severe soil erosion in an area already suffering from the effects of logging. In the early 1990s the river water was clear and fish were abundant; now the river is a muddy brown and water levels fluctuate wildly. Nor is the project a long-term one: even the government admits its productive life is likely to be in the region of 25 years before it silts up. Friends of the Earth Malaysia say: "This project is going to have a tremendous effect on the lives of natives, plants and animals and on the biodiversity of the pristine forests where it is going to be built".

The local tribespeople, mainly Kayan and Kenyah whose ancestors battled for decades against the White Rajahs, have, it seems, finally met their match in Malaysia's relentless thrust towards modernity. Some 9000 of them have been pushed off their ancestral homelands and moved to longhouse settlements in Sungai Asap. Activists claim that many tribespeople were promised jobs on the dam that never materialized. As money concerns have crept in, many of these once proud subsistence farmers have turned to the bottle for comfort.

Many lowlying areas are to be flooded on completion of the dam and boat transport may again be more organized further upriver. Indigenous communities above the Bakun Dam have been resettled in the Sungai Asap area some 40 km away on the Bintulu road. It's possible to stop at Asap when heading back to Bintulu on the coast.

Although these communities have been given compensation, land and housing it seems they had little choice once the dam scheme was finalized. No financial compensation or land was given to upriver longhouses beyond the direct area of flooding in the Bakun Basin – for example, the Kayan Longhouses of Long Benalui, Long Ayak and Uma Batu Kalo. These communities still reside in their original homes. It's possible to stop at the Asap resettlement area when heading back to Bintulu on the coast.

The biggest impact of this project seems to have been felt by the nomadic and semi-nomadic Penan people. Due to their non-agricultural way of life little or no land rights or compensation have been provided, despite having lived in the area for hundreds, perhaps thousands, of years. Logging – and its associated disturbance of the forest – means nomadic people are finding it increasingly difficult to find enough food and make a living in the Upper Rejang basin.

Many of the longhouses around Belaga are quite modern, although several of the Kenyah and Kayan settlements have beautifully carved wooden *salongs* (tombstones) nearby. All the longhouses beyond Belaga are Orang Ulu, upriver tribal groups. Even longhouses which seem to be very remote (such as Long Busang) are now connected by logging roads from Kapit, only four hours' drive away. To get well off the beaten track, into Penan country, it is possible to organize treks from Belaga towards the Kalimantan border, staying in longhouses en route.

About 2 km up the Batang Belaga from Belaga are the **Pasang Rapids** (hire a boat from Belaga), the biggest in Sarawak. No one has deliberately tried to shoot them as they are too dangerous. Boats can get reasonably close, however, and in the dry season it is possible to climb up to a picnic area overlooking the white water.

◉ Sibu, Kapit and Belaga listings

For Sleeping and Eating price codes and other relevant information, see Essentials pages 23-27.

● Sleeping

Sibu p127, map p126

Cheaper hotels tend to be around the night market in Chinatown, but there's also a selection within walking distance of the jetty.
AL-A RH, Jln Kampung Nyabor, T084-365888, www.rhhotels.com.my. Huge, sparkling, new hotel overlooking Wisma Sanyan shopping complex and Sibu's spacious new town square. Styling itself as Sibu's No 1 business hotel, this place boasts plenty of luxurious suites (more expensive) with excellent park views and crisp, modern decor. It has a pool and steam bath, and

rooms have Wi-Fi, cable TV and safety deposit boxes. The **Oriental Bistro** serves good coffee and international dishes. Huge discounts often available. Good.
AL-A Tanahmas, Jln Kampong Nyabor, T084-333188, www.tanahmas.com.my. Tall building in the heart of town offering modern, well-furnished rooms with Wi-Fi and good views over the rooftops. There's a pool, karaoke lounge and good restaurant.
A Kingwood, 12 Lorong Lanang 4, T084-335888, kingwood.sibu@yahoo.com.my. Fairly unexciting hotel primarily targeting business visitors. Rooms are comfortable and have cable TV and Wi-Fi. Some have town views and the more expensive ones have good river views. There is a top Chinese restaurant, **Mingziang**, and pool and fitness centre.

A Premier, Jln Kampong Nyabor, T084-323222, www.premierh.com.my. Good restaurant and café with Wi-Fi, clean rooms with a/c, TV, own bath, some with river view. Helpful staff, adjoins **Sarawak House Shopping Centre and Cinema**, discounts often available. Recommended.

B Garden, 1 Jln Huo Ping, T084-317888, gardenhotel_sbw@yahoo.com. This hotel has a flash lobby with a bewildering array of mirrors next to the coffee shop. Rooms are comfortable, but furnishings are a little tatty and old. Renovations are promised in the near future. Staff are friendly and there is Wi-Fi access throughout. Decent buffet breakfast included in the price.

C Li Hua, 18 Lorong 2, Jln Lanang, T084-324000, F326272. Run by one of the local Chinese associations, and often packed with visiting ethnic Chinese, this friendly place has simple, large rooms with TV and attached bathroom. Many rooms offer sweeping views over the Rejang and the dense forest beyond. Highly recommended.

C Phoenix, 1 & 3 Jln Kai Peng (off Jln Kampong Nyabor), T084-313877, F320392. Spotless, slightly old hotel with a selection of clean a/c rooms with attached bathroom and TV. Good value.

C Victoria Inn, 80 Jln Market, T084-320099, F320055. New place with clean rooms, some windowless in the heart of town. Rooms are well furnished and good value.

C-D Eden Inn, 1 Jln Lanang, T084-337277. Next to the 60s-style Sacred Heart Church, this well-run place is owned by a local Catholic association and has a selection of large, spotless a/c rooms with TV and attached bathroom. Excellent value. Recommended.

C-D River Park, 51-53 Jln Maju, T084-316688, F316689. Close to the action on the esplanade, this functional hotel has clean rooms, more expensive with river views.

D Bahagia, 21 Jln Wong Nai Siong, T084-331131, F320536. Small place off a busy street with friendly management and clean rooms with TV, Wi-Fi access and attached bathroom. There's a good restaurant downstairs.

Kapit *p128, map p129*

All are within walking distance of the wharf.

B Greenland Inn, 463 Jln Teo Chow Beng, T084-796388, F797989. This clean place offers 19 well-maintained spacious rooms with a/c, TV and attached bathroom. Often full at weekends. A little expensive given the competition in town.

B-C Ark Hill Inn, Lot 451, Jln Penghulu Gerining (off the Town Square), T084-796168, arkhill@streamyx.com. Fair value place with 20 a/c rooms with attached bath and TV. The single rooms here are small, but doubles offer greater value. Although clean, the walls could do with a lick of paint. Wi-Fi access available.

B-C River View Inn, 10 Jln Tan Sit Leong. Largely uninspiring place with a selection of spacious, clean a/c rooms with Wi-Fi access and TV. Many of the rooms are windowless.

C New Rejang Inn, 28 Jln Temenggong Jugah, T084-796600, F799600. Friendly hotel with 4 flights of steep steps and spotless a/c rooms with TV (1 cable channel), powerful showers and liberally scattered bibles. Room 401 has a good partial view of the murky Rejang. Recommended.

D Hiap Chiong, 33 Jln Temenggong Jugah, T084-796314. This place has a strangely institutional feel but looks like it has survived the test of time. Rooms, though old, are good value with small TV, attached bathroom and TV. Room 307 is huge and offers the finest river views of any hotel in town.

D Rejang, 28 New Bazaar, T084-796709. Archaic place with furniture made before you were born. The TVs and fridges are similarly old, but rooms, though not particularly cheerful, are cheap. The **Hiap Chong** is better value in this price range.

Pelagus Rapids *p130*

A-B Pelagus Resort, set on the banks of the Rejang overlooking the rapids, T084-799051, www.theregencyhotel.com.my. 40 longhouse-style rooms, with restaurant, pool, bar and sun deck, de luxe rooms have a/c, otherwise fans. Trips organized from resort to longhouses, nature treks and river safaris, whitewater rafting on the rapids. Express boats pass through rapids upstream.

Longhouses *p130*
D Rumah Tuan Lepong Balleh, see page 131. Stay in this longhouse, RM30 inclusive of meals, generator until 2300, basic. It's about 1 hr from Kapit; take a minibus and ask for **Selvat and Friends Traditional Hostel and Longhouse**.

Belaga *p131*
C-D Belaga Hotel, 14 Belaga Bazaar, T086-461244. Some a/c, restaurant, no hot water, friendly proprietor, good coffee shop, in-house video and cicadas. Best option.
D B&B, 4 Belaga Bazaar (upstairs from **Worldwide Exploration Travel and Tour** office), T086-461512. Run by the Mr Hasbee of Hasbee Enterprises, this mellow place has a dorm and a double room with fan and a/c on offer. This is a good place to source local information and guides.
D Bee Lian, 11 Belaga Bazaar, T086- 461439. A/c, 9 rooms, all reasonable.
D Sing Soon Huat, 26-27 New Bazaar. T086-461413, F461346. Smart, friendly, pleasant living area with TV, movies, etc. A good choice.
D-E Sing Soon Hing, 15 New Bazaar. Same owners and contact details as **Sing Soon Huat**. Much cheaper resthouse kind of affair, a little gloomy, but clean, rooms with private shower. Good for those on a tight budget.

🍴 Eating

Sibu *p127, map p126*
With such a large Chinese population, it's no surprise that the many coffee shops and hawker centres are packed with Chinese eateries. One Sibu speciality is *kampua mee*, a fatty dish of noodles and pork lard served with roasted pork or pork balls with soup.
🍴🍴 **Ark Café and Gallery**, Jln Maju, T084 313 445. Open 1000-2300. Uber-stylish place on the riverfront with elevated seating and river views. The restaurant is set around a banyan

tree with plenty of water features and has a menu of international and local favourites.
🍴🍴 **Blue Splendour** 3rd floor, Wisma Sanyan Shopping Complex. Good Shanghainese, Cantonese and Hokkien cuisine including *nestum* prawns, *kampua mee* and steamed fish dishes. Held in high regard by locals.
🍴🍴 **Café Café**, 10 Jln Chew Geok Lin, T084 328 101. Open 1200-1600 and 1800-2300. Friendly and stylish eatery with Nyonya, Thai and Western dishes. Good value.
🍴🍴 **Golden Palace**, Tanahmas hotel, Jln Kampong Nyabor. Cantonese and Sichuan.
🍴🍴 **Mama Café**, 4th floor, Wisma Sanyan Shopping Complex. Relaxed place with large glass windows looking over the eastern side of town. The menu has lots of coffees, mocktails and Korean dishes. Their signature is the Korean steamboat.
🍴🍴 **Peppers Café**, Tanahmas Hotel, Jln Kampong Nyabor. A favourite with visiting foreigners, this hotel eatery has a good selection of Western and local food. Popular.
🍴🍴 **Sri Meranti**, 1A Jln Hardin. Friendly staff, good seafood, nice sitting-out area with cold beer and tablecloths.
🍴 **Kasturi**, 18 Jln Tunku Osman. One of the town's most celebrated Malay places with great curries and seafood. Also a selection of Melanau dishes and including *tebaloi* and *umai* (raw fish salad – delicious)
🍴 **Mr and Mrs Yeo's Stall**, Lorong Tiong Hua (mornings only). This friendly local spot dishes up a local speciality, *konpia*, a fresh bread roll served with pork broth and slices of pork.
🍴 **Rafis Café**, Jln Kampong Datu. Open 0700-2300. Very popular place with a great *nasi campur* selection. Recommended by locals.
🍴 **Sri Menanti Chicken Rice**, 26 Jln Mission, T084-316 904. Open 0830-2100. Functional a/c restaurant offering chicken rice in every conceivable form with good Chinese vegetable dishes in sauces including *sambal belacan*.

Foodstalls
Jln Market Food Court, Jln Market, near Premier Hotel. Good selection of Chinese and Malay stalls.

Sibu Central Market, 1st floor. Over 30 stalls serving mainly Chinese dishes, but with a few interesting local offerings.
Rex Food Court, 28 Jln Cross. New and clean.

Kapit *p128, map p129*

There is nothing very exciting about dining in Kapit. Most of the locals are content with eating and relaxing in the town's many coffee shops. Food to look out for includes fresh river fish (including the very expensive *emparau*, Borneo masheer), and Rejang prawns.

🍴 **Orchard Inn**, Jln Teo Chow Beng, T084-796325. A/c restaurant with a simple menu of Chinese seafood and meat dishes. Not a bad choice for a meal and beer. Popular with the local Chinese.

🍴 **Ah Kau**, Jln Berjaya. Good spot for local seafood dishes.

🍴 **Chun Cheng**, Jln Pedral. Held in high regard among the locals, this place offers mainly Chinese and some halal Malay dishes.

🍴 **MAS Islamic Café**, Jln Pedral. Good choice for well-made Malay specialities.

🍴 **MI**, Jln Pedral. Good selection of Malay staples including *ayam bakar, laksa Sarawak* and a good *nasi campur* spread, all in a/c comfort.

Bakeries and coffee shops

Chuong Hin, opposite the Sibu wharf. Best-stocked coffee shop in town.
Ung Tong Bakery, opposite the market. Very friendly family-run bakery offering sweet treats, simple breakfasts and Asian-style (soft and sweet) fresh bread. Big selection of rolls and good coffee, fresh bread baked daily (1500). Recommended.

Foodstalls

Gelanggang Kenyalang, opposite the Orchard Inn. Look for the brightly painted exterior of this covered food court. It's usually the first place recommended by locals and has a range of Chinese and Malay stalls. Here you can find a Kapit speciality, the heart- stoppingly unhealthy, but fiendishly tasty, deep-fried *roti canai*, found at the Malay stall on the 1st floor.

Belaga *p131*

Several small, cheap coffee shops along Belaga Bazaar and Main Bazaar.

O Shopping

Sibu *p127, map p126*
Handicrafts

Stalls along express boat wharves at Jln Channel, mainly selling basketware.
Chop Kion Huat, Jln Market, just behind the tourist information office. Sarawak handicrafts: batik, basketware, T-shirts and carvings.

Markets

Native market (Lembangan market), Lembangan River between Jln Mission and Jln Channel. Sells jungle produce.
Pasar Malam (night market), High St, Jln Market and Lembangan Lane, Chinatown.

Pottery
2 potteries at Km 7 and 12 Ulu Oya Rd.

Supermarket
Sarawak House Shopping Complex, Jln Kampong Nyabor, has **Premier Department Store**. There's a good minimarket opposite **Chop Kion Huat** handicraft shop on Jln Market with fruit juice, wine, spirits and Marmite, and is a good place to stock up on shampoo and shower gel. There's a book and magazine shop on the ground floor of Sarawak House Complex that sells English magazines.

Kapit *p128, map p129*
Handicrafts

Din Chu Café, next to Methodist Guesthouse. Sells antiques and handicrafts.
Lai Lai Antique Shop, the second floor of the Gelanggang Kenyalang complex. Small range of woven rugs/sarongs, prices are high but similar to the starting prices at longhouses.

Belaga p131
Handicrafts
Chop Teck Hua, Belaga Bazaar. An intriguing selection of tribal jewellery, old coins, beads, feathers, woodcarvings, blowpipes, parangs, tattoo boards and other curios buried under cobwebs and gecko droppings at the back of the shop; the owner is noticeably uninformed about the objects he sells.

▲▲ Activities and tours

Sibu p127, map p126
Golf
Sibu Golf Club, Km 17, Ulu Oya Rd.

Tour operators
Most companies run city tours plus tours of longhouses, Mulu National Park and Niah Caves. It is cheaper to organize upriver trips from Kapit or Belaga than from Sibu.
Greatown Travel, No 6 1st floor, Lorong Chew Siik Hiong 1A, T084-211243, www.rajangtourism.blogspot.com. Currently the leading operator offering longhouse tours and rainforest treks. Highly recommended.
Sazhong Trading & Travel, 4 Jln Central, T084-336017, www.geocities.com/sazhong. Director Frankie Ting can arrange budget stays for groups in a longhouse in Kapit and beyond.
Travel Consortium, 14 Jln Central, T084-334455, F330589. Good for air ticketing.

Kapit p128, map p129
Tour operators
There has been a number of recent complaints made by tourists who feel they have been overcharged for unsatisfactory tours. Often the guides are young local guys with a fair command of English but limited experience guiding foreigners who are paying handsomely for the experience. The Sarawak Tourist Information Office in Sibu and the Kapit Resident's Office recommend using guides from **Alice Tours and Travel**,

Lorong 6 Jln Airport (a good 25-min walk from town in a residential area past the overgrown airport), T019-859 3126, atta_kpt@yahoo.com. Day trips to visit the longhouse at Bundong start at RM198, and an overnight trip including a stay at the longhouse starts at RM285. Owner Alice Chua recommends booking tours at least a week in advance. Local expert **Joshua Muda**, T084-796600, joshuamuda@hotmail.com, arranges sensitive and authentic longhouse trips. Some hotels will help organize trips, or ask at the police station.

Belaga p131
Tour operators
Belaga Hotel will contact guides for upriver trips and the district office can also recommend a handful of experienced guides. In this part of Sarawak, guides are particularly expensive – sometimes up to RM80 a day, mainly because there are not enough tourists to justify full-time work. It is necessary to hire experienced boatmen too, because of the numerous rapids. Guides recommended by Sarawak Tourism include **John Belakirk**, T086-461512, johneddie1@hotmail.com; **Hamdani Louis**, T086-461039, hamdani@hotmail.com; **Andreas Bato**, T019-3722972, niestabato@yahoo.com, an Orang Ulu guide with perfect English; **Councilor Daniel Levoh**, No.34, Lot 1051, Jln Bato Luhat, New Bazaar, H/P 013-8486351, T086-461176, daniellevoh@hotmail.com. This guide often seems busy picking up clients for upriver trips, with his family contacts throughout the area, and much of Belaga's tourism business is under his control. While it's true Daniel is good at the arranging and bureaucracy side, he falls pretty short with the guiding itself, spending most his time snoozing away the day.

Prices for longhouse trips upriver vary according to distance and water level, but are similar to those in Kapit. English is not widely spoken upriver so basic Bahasa comes in handy.

⊖ Transport

Sibu *p127, map p126*
Air

The airport is 25 km north of town. Regular connections with **Kuching** on MAS, MASwings and AirAsia (around 7 flights a day), **Bintulu** (on MASwings, 2 flights daily), **Miri** on MASwings (3 flights daily), **KK** (2 direct flights daily with MASwings and AirAsia, 2 daily flights via Bintulu) and **KL** (MAS flies daily and AirAsia, has 3 daily flights).

Airline offices MAS, 61 Jln Tunku Osman, T084-326166. AirAsia, Jln Kai Peng.

Boat

All boats leave from the wharf. The time of the next departure is shown by big clock faces on whiteboards; just buy the ticket at the jetty. There is 1 express boat daily between Sibu and **Kuching** (5 hrs RM45). Ekspress Bahagia (T084-319228) leaves at 1130. This boat stops off at **Sarekei** (RM10). There are regular express boats to **Kapit**, every 30 mins from 0545 until 1500, 2-3 hrs RM20 economy/RM25 second class/RM30 first class, and in the wet season, when the river is high enough, they continue to **Belaga**, 5-6 hrs. It is not possible to travel up river to Belaga in a day, as you need a permit from the Resident's Office in Kapit. However, in case the situation changes, there is a daily boat from Sibu to Belaga (RM40) at 0530 when the water is high enough. This service doesn't usually run in the dry season (Jul-Sep). Some Sibu – Kapit boats stop off at **Kanowit** and **Song** on their way upriver.

Bus

Local Buses leave from Jln Khoo Peng Loong. **Long distance** Buses leave from the long-distance bus terminal at Jln Pahlawan. To get there take a taxi (a negotiable RM15), or bus No 12 or No 17 from the local bus station. There are 3 main long-distance bus companies: **Biaramas Express**, **Borneo Highway Express** and **Suria Express** which all have routes from Sibu to **Bintulu**, **Miri** and

Kuching. Regular connections with **Bintulu**, 4 hrs RM20, and Miri 6-7 hrs RM40, along a surfaced road. First bus leaves around 0630, and last bus at 0100, departures every hour or so. Best to purchase tickets the day before departure – there are ticket offices for the different companies around the jetty or else buy from the bus station. Early morning buses to Bintulu connect with the buses direct to **Batu Niah** (see page 156). There are also daily connections with **Kuching** via **Sarikei** (8 hrs to Kuching, RM40, 2 hrs to Sarikei, RM10). There are around 10 daily departures 0700-2400.

International connections There are evening departures to **Pontianak**, Kalimantan (RM80, 16 hrs).

Kapit *p128, map p129*
Boat

All 3 wharves are close together. A new Kapit/Sibu Express Boat Terminal opened in late 2009. Regular connections with **Sibu**, 0630-1500, RM20-30 depending on class, 2-3 hrs. **Belaga** is not accessible by large express boats during the dry season (Jul-Sep). There is a daily express boat to Belaga at 0930, RM35. In the dry season smaller speed boats sometimes go upriver (RM60-100 per person).

Belaga *p131*
Air

At the time of research flights between Belaga and Bintulu had been suspended. Check www.maswings.com.my for updates.

Airline offices MAS, c/o Lau Chun Kiat, Main Bazaar.

Boat

There is a daily boat from **Kapit** leaving at 0930, RM35, only in the wet season; the journey takes around 5 hrs. In the dry season speedboats leave from Kapit, from RM60 per person. When the river is very low the only option is to drive to Belaga from **Bintulu**.

To **Tubau** and on to **Bintulu**: it is possible to hire a boat from Belaga to Kestima Kem (logging camp) near Rumah Lahanan Laseh

(RM60 per person in a group or RM260 for 2-3 people); from there logging trucks go to Tabau on the Kemena River. Logging trucks leave irregularly and you can get stuck in logging camps. It is a 3-hr drive to Tabau; this trip is not possible in the wet season. There are regular express boats from Tabau to Bintulu (RM12). This is the fastest and cheapest route to Bintulu, but not the most reliable. It is necessary to obtain permission from the Residents' Office and the police station in Belaga to take this route.

Car

At the moment Belaga is comparatively isolated and overland links are poor. During the dry season it is possible to travel by 4WD overland to **Bintulu** (see below), but it is drawn out and expensive. It is likely that road links will keep improving, particularly with the controversial Bakun Dam project still under construction. The Bakun to Bintulu road has been gradually upgraded and is now surfaced along almost its full length. To charter a 4WD for the whole journey to Bintulu costs RM300-400 for 5 people and the journey takes 5 hrs. **Hasbee Enterprises**, 4 Belaga Bazaar, can help with a 4WD or try **Hap Kiat Transport**, T013-807 5598. They have a Toyota Landcruiser that leaves Belaga daily at 0730 and returns from Bintulu at 1330 (RM60). Those wishing to travel overland from Bintulu must report to the Bintulu Resident's Office and the Belaga Resident's Office. For more information phone the Kapit Resident's Office, T084-796445. Keep a close eye on people's driving abilities in this area – many drive while drunk and large logging trucks speeding round the sharp bends can be a significant danger.

ⓘ Directory

Sibu *p127, map p126*
Banks Standard Chartered, 25 Jln Tukang Besi HSBC, Bangunan Grand Merlin, 131 Jln Nyabor. Apart from the banks, cash can be exchanged at good rates at goldsmiths around town. **Internet** There are a number of good places in the Wisma Sanyan Shopping Complex. **Police** Jln Kampong Nyabor, T084-322222. **Post office** General Post Office, Jln Kampong Nyabor 0800-1800. **Residents' Office** T084-321963.

Kapit *p128, map p129*
Banks There are 2 banks which will accept TCs, one in the New Bazaar and the other on Jln Airport, but it is easier to change money in Sibu. **Libraries** On the other side of the road from 1st floor State Government Complex. Good selection of books on history and natural history of Borneo. There's also internet access. Mon-Sat 1615-2030, Sun 0900-1115, 1400-1630.

Belaga *p131*
Internet Hasbee Enterprises, 4 Belaga Bazaar (RM6 per hr), 0700-1900. Painfully slow connection. **Post office** In the District Office.

North coast

The north coast of Sarawak is fairly remote, with Bintulu, Miri and Marudi being the only significant towns. Close to Bintulu is Similajau National Park where green turtles lay their eggs. Niah National Park boasts famous limestone caves and is home to jungle birds and primates. Miri is the launch pad for river trips into the interior and Marudi is an upriver trading post and the start of a cross-border trek. Bintulu is accessible by air, boat from Tubau in the interior and bus. Miri is accessible by air and bus and Marudi by air and boat. » *For listings, see pages 150-158.*

Bintulu → *Colour map 3, B4.*

On the Kemena River, Bintulu is in the heart of Melinau country and was a fishing and farming centre until the largest natural gas reserve in Malaysia was discovered offshore in the late 1970s, making Bintulu a boom town overnight. **Shell**, **Petronas** and **Mitsubishi** then moved into the town in force. Modern Bintulu has a frontier town atmosphere, with muddy 4WDs ploughing streets lined with an inordinate number of short-time hotels and sleazy *dangdut* and karaoke lounges popular with stimulation-starved oil men on boozy weekend escapades.

Few tourists stay long in Bintulu, despite it being the jumping-off point for the Similajau National Park and the Niah Caves. The longhouses on the Kemena River are accessible, but tend not to be as interesting as those further up the Rejang and Baram rivers. The Penan and Kayan tribes are very hospitable and eager to show off their longhouses and traditions to tourists.

The word Bintulu is believed to be a corruption of Mentu Ulau, which translates as 'the place for gathering heads'.

There is no government tourist information office in Bintulu; for enquiries contact the **Bintulu Development Authority** ⓘ *T086-332011*. The **Sarawak Forestry Department** ⓘ *www.sarawak. forestry.gov.my*, provides information on the national parks around Bintulu. Visitors can also contact the **National Parks Booking Office** ⓘ *T086-331117, ext 50, F331923*.

Background

The remnants of the old fishing village at Kampong Jepak are on the opposite bank of the Kemena River. During the Brooke era the town was a small administrative centre. The **clocktower** commemorates the meeting of five members of the Brooke government and 16 local chieftains, creating Council Negeri, the state legislative body.

The first project to break ground in Bintulu was the RM100-million crude oil terminal at Tanjong Kidurong from which 45,000 barrels of petroleum are exported

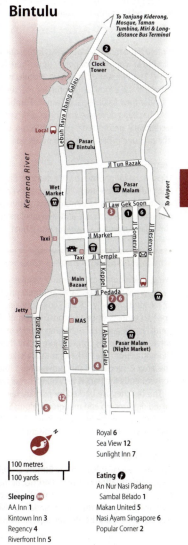

Bintulu

100 metres
100 yards

Sleeping
AA Inn **1**
Kintown Inn **3**
Regency **4**
Riverfront Inn **5**
Royal **6**
Sea View **12**
Sunlight Inn **7**

Eating
An Nur Nasi Padang
 Sambal Belado **1**
Makan United **5**
Nasi Ayam Singapore **6**
Popular Corner **2**

daily. A deep-water port was built and the liquefied natural gas (LNG) plant started operating in 1982. The abundant supply of natural gas also created investment in related downstream projects. The main industrial area at Tanjong Kidurong is 20 km from Bintulu. The **viewing tower** at Tanjong Kidurong gives a panoramic view of the new-look Bintulu and out to the timber ships on the horizon. They anchor 15 km offshore to avoid port duties and the timber is taken out on barges.

Sights

Bintulu has a modern Moorish-style mosque called the **Masjid Assyakirin**; visitors may be allowed in when it is not prayer time. There is a colourful, centrally located Chinese temple called **Tua Pek Kong**. The **Pasar Bintulu** is an impressive building in the centre of town, built to house a local jungle produce market, foodstalls and some limited handicrafts stalls. A landscaped wildlife park, **Taman Tumbina** ① *www.tumbina.com.my, daily 0800-1800, RM2*, has been developed on the outskirts of town, on the way to Tanjong Batu. It is a local recreational area and contains a small zoo, including a hornbill collection, a botanic garden (the only one in Sarawak) and a newly opened **Butterfly World**.

Longhouses

Trips to the longhouses on the Kemena River (which are rarely visited) can be organized from Bintulu. More than 20 Kemena River longhouses can be reached by road or river within 30 minutes of Bintulu. Iban longhouses are the closest; further upriver are the more traditional Kayan and Kenyah longhouses. Overpriced tours are organized by **Similajau Adventure Tours**; or hire a boat from the wharf.

Similajau National Park → *Colour map 3, B4.*

Lying 20 km northeast of Bintulu, Similajau is a coastal park with sandy beaches, broken by rocky headlands. It is Sarawak's most unusually shaped national park, being more than 32 km long and only 1.5 km wide. Similajau was demarcated in 1978, but has only been open to tourists since the construction of decent facilities in 1991. **Pasir Mas** (Golden Sands) is a beautiful 3.5-km-long stretch of coarse beach, to the north of the Likau River, where green turtles come ashore to lay their eggs between July and September. A few kilometres from the Park HQ at **Kuala Likau** is a small coral reef, known as **Batu Mandi**. The area is renowned for birdwatching. Bintulu is not on the main tourist route and consequently the park is very quiet. Its seclusion makes it a perfect escape.

The beaches are backed by primary rainforest: peat swamp, *kerangas* (heath forest), mixed dipterocarp and mangrove (along Sungai Likau and Sungai Sebubong). There are small rapids on the Sebulong River. Sadly, the rivers, particularly the beautiful **Sungai Likau**, have been polluted by indiscriminate logging activities upstream.

Ins and outs

Permits are available from the **Bintulu Development Authority** ① *T086-332011.* There's also an **information centre** ① *Park HQ, at the mouth of Sungai Likau, across the river from the park.* A boat is needed to cross the 5 m of crocodile-infested river. Because the park facilities are outside the park boundaries, visitors do not need a permit to stay there. This has led to the 'park' becoming popular with Bintulites at the weekend.

Niah's guano collectors: scraping the bottom

Eight bat species live in the Niah Caves. Some are quite common, such as the horseshoe bat and fruit bats, while other, more exotic, varieties include the bearded tomb bat, Cantor's roundleaf horseshoe bat and the lesser bent-winged bat.

The ammonia-stench of bat guano permeates the humid air. People began collecting guano in 1929 and it is used as a fertilizer and to prevent pepper vines from rotting. Guano collectors pay a licence fee for the privilege of sweeping up *tahi sapu* (fresh guano) and digging up *tahi timbang* (mature guano), which they sell to the Bat Guano Cooperative at the end of the plankwalk.

Flora and fauna

On arrival at Kuala Likau there is a prominent sign advising against swimming in the river and to watch your feet around the Park HQ area; Similajau is well known for its saltwater crocodiles (*Crocodylus perosus*). It also has 24 resident species of mammal (including gibbons, Hose's langurs, banded langurs, long-tailed macaques, civets, wild boar, porcupines and squirrels) and 185 species of birds (including many migratory species). There are some good coral reefs to the north and marine life includes dolphins, porpoises and turtles. Pitcher plants grow in the *kerangas* forest and along the beach.

Treks

Several longish but not-too-difficult trails have been cut from the Park HQ by park rangers. One path follows undulating terrain, parallel to the coast. It is possible to cut to the left, through the jungle, to the coast, and walk back to Kuala Likau along the beach. The main trail to **Golden Beach** is a 3-4-hour walk crossing several streams and rivers where estuarine crocodiles are reputed to lurk. Most of these crossings are on 'bridges', which are usually just felled trees with no attempt made to assist walkers; a good sense of balance is required. Another enjoyable walk is the trail to **Selansur Rapids**, around 2½ hours in total. Follow the trail to Golden Beach; after about an hour a marked trail leads off into the forest. The walk ends at the rapids where it is possible to take a dip and cool off.

Niah National Park → *Colour map 3, A5.*

Niah's famous caves, tucked into a limestone massif called Gunung Subis (394 m), made world headlines in 1958, when they were confirmed as the most important archaeological site in Asia. The park is one of the most popular tourist attractions in Sarawak and more than 15,000 visitors come here every year. The caves were declared a national historic monument in 1958, but it was not until 1974 that the 30 sq km of jungle surrounding the caves were turned into a national park to protect the area from logging.

The park primarily comprises alluvial or peat swamp and mixed dipterocarp forest. Long-tailed macaques, hornbills, squirrels, flying lizards and crocodiles have all been recorded here. There are also bat hawks, which provide an impressive spectacle when they home in on one of the millions of bats which pour out of the caves at dusk.

Ins and outs

Getting there The nearest town to the park is Batu Niah. There are regular bus connections with Miri (just under two hours), Bintulu (two hours) and Sibu. From Batu

Niah it is around 3 km to the Park HQ and the caves. Either walk through the forest (45 minutes), take a longboat, or take a taxi. ▸▸ *See Transport, page 157.*

Getting around From Park HQ there are well-marked trails to the caves. Longboats can be chartered for upriver trips.

Tourist information Park HQ ⓘ *Pangkalan Lubang next to Sungai Niah, park daily 0800-1700, caves daily 0800-1630, RM10, children RM5 (camera RM5, video RM10, professional photography RM200); for more information on the park, contact the Deputy Park Warden, Niah National Park, PO Box 81, Miri Post Office, Batu Niah, T085-737454 or T085-737 450.* Guides are not essential but they provide information and can relate legends about the paintings. Even with a guide, visitors cannot cross the barrier 3 m in front of the cave wall. Guides charge RM40 for groups of up to 20 and can be hired from the Park HQ. Longboats can be hired from Park HQ for upriver trips (maximum of eight people per boat). Bring a powerful torch for the caves. Walking boots are advisable during the wet season as the plankwalk can get very slippery.

History

About 40,000 years ago, when the Gulf of Thailand and the Sunda Shelf were still dry ground and a land bridge linked the Philippines and Borneo, Niah was home to *Homo sapiens*. It was the most exciting archaeological discovery since Java man (*Homo erectus*).

   Scientist and explorer A Hart Everett led expeditions to Niah Caves in 1873 and 1879, after which he pronounced that they justified no further work. Some 79 years later, Tom Harrisson, ethnologist, explorer, conservationist and curator of the Sarawak Museum, confirmed the most important archaeological find at that time in Southeast Asia at Niah. He unearthed fragments of a 37,000-year-old human skull – the earliest evidence of *Homo sapiens* in the region – at the west mouth of the Niah Great Cave itself. The skull was buried under 2.4 m of guano. His find debunked and prompted a radical reappraisal of

Niah National Park

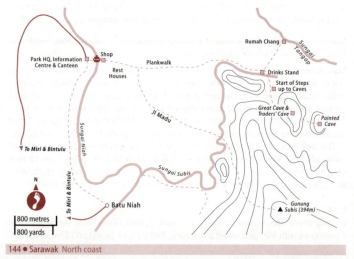

How to make a swift buck

The Malay name for the Painted Cave is Kain Hitam (black cloth), because the profitable rights to the birds' nests were historically exchanged for bolts of black cloth.

The Chinese have had a taste for swiftlets' nests for well over 1000 years, and the business of collecting them from 60 m up in the cavernous chamber of the Great Cave is as lucrative – and as hazardous – a profession now as it was then. The nests are used to prepare birds' nest soup – blended with chicken stock and rock salt – which is a famous Chinese delicacy, prized as an aphrodisiac and for its supposed remedial properties for asthma and rheumatism.

Birds' nests are one of the most expensive foods in the world: they sell for up to US$500 per kg in Hong Kong, where about 100 tonnes of them (worth US$40 million) are consumed annually. The Chinese communities of North America import 30 tonnes of birds' nests a year. Locally, they fetch RM150-600 per kg, depending on the grade.

Hundreds of thousands – possibly millions – of swiftlets (of the Collocalia swift family) live in the caves. Unlike other parts of Southeast Asia, where collectors use rotan ladders to reach the nests (see Gomantong Caves, Sabah, page 248), Niah's collectors scale *belian* (ironwood) poles to heights of more than 60 m. They use bamboo sticks with a scraper attached to one end (called *penyulok*) to pick the nests off the cave roof. The nests are harvested three times each season (the seasons run from August to December and January to March). On the first two occasions, the nests are removed before the eggs are laid and a third are left until the nestlings are fledged. Nest collectors are now all supposed to have licences but, in reality, no one does. Although the birds' nests are supposed to be protected by the national park in the off-season, wardens turn a blind eye to illegal harvesting; the collectors also know many secret entrances to the caves. Officially, people caught harvesting out of season can be fined RM2000 or sent to jail for a year, but no one's ever caught.

Despite being a dangerous operation (there are usually several fatal accidents at Niah each year), collecting has become so popular that harvesters have to reserve their spot with a lamp. Nest collecting is run on a first-come, first-served basis. Nests of the white-nest swiftlets and the black-nest swiftlets are collected – the nests of the mossy-nest and white-bellied swiftlets require too much effort to clean. The nests are built by the male swiftlets using a glutinous substance produced by the salivary glands under the tongue which is regurgitated in long threads; the saliva sets like cement producing a rounded cup which sticks to the cave wall. In the swifts' nest market, price is dictated by colour: the best are the white nests which are without any plant material or feathers. Most of the uncleaned nests are bought up by middle-men, agents of traders in Kuching, but locals at Batu Niah also do some of the cleaning. The nests are first soaked in water for about three hours and, when softened, feathers and dirt are laboriously removed with tweezers. The 'cakes' of nests are dried over-night: if left in the sun they turn yellow.

popular theories about where modern man's ancestors had sprung from. A wide range of palaeolithic and neolithic tools, pottery, ornaments and beads was also found at the site. Anthropologists believe Niah's caves may have been permanently inhabited until around AD 1400. Harrisson's excavation site, office and house have been left intact in the mouth of the Great Cave. A total of 166 burial sites have been excavated, 38 of which are Mesolithic (up to 20,000 years ago) and the remainder neolithic (4000 years ago). Some of the finds are now in the Sarawak Museum in Kuching.

Park Information Centre
ⓘ *Mon-Fri 0800-1230 and 1400-1615, Sat 0800-1245, Sun 0800-1200.*
At the Park HQ is this centre, with displays on birds' nests and flora and fauna. The exhibition includes the 37,000-year-old human skull which drew world attention to Niah in 1958. Also on display are 35,000-year-old oyster shells and palaeolithic pig bones, monkey bones, turtle shells and crabs, found littering the cave floor. There are also burial vessels dating from 1600 BC and carved seashell jewellery from 400 BC.

The caves
To reach the caves, take a longboat across the river from Park HQ at Pangkalan Lubang to the start of the 4-km **belian** (ironwood) plankwalk to the entrance of the **Great Cave**. Take the right fork 1 km from the entrance. The remains of a small kampong, formerly inhabited by birds' nest collectors (see below) and guano collectors, is just before the entrance, in the shelter of overhanging rocks. It is known as **Traders' Cave**. Beware of voracious insects; wear long trousers and plenty of repellent. There are no lights in the Great Cave, so torches are needed.

The **Painted Cave** is beyond the Great Cave. Prehistoric wall paintings – the only ones in Borneo – stretch for about 32 m along the cave wall. Most of the drawings are of dancing human figures and boats, thought to be associated with a death ritual. On the floor of the cave, several 'death-ships' were found with some Chinese stoneware, shell ornaments and ancient glass beads. These death-ships served as coffins and have been carbon-dated to between AD 1 and AD 780. By around AD 700 there is thought to have been a flourishing community based in the caves, trading hornbill ivory and birds' nests with the Chinese in exchange for porcelain and beads. But then it seems the caves were suddenly deserted in about 1400. In Penan folklore there are references to 'the ancestors who lived in the big caves' and tribal elders are said to be able to recall funeral rites using death boats similar to those found at Niah.

Treks
A lowland trail called **Jalan Madu** (Honey Road), traverses the peat swamp forest and ascends Gunung Subis; it is not well marked. Return trips need a full day. The trail leads off the plankwalk to the right, about 1 km from Pangkalan Lubang (Park HQ). The left fork on the plankwalk, before the gate to the caves, goes to an Iban longhouse, Rumah Chang (40 minutes' walk), where cold drinks can be bought.

Miri and the Baram River → *Colour map 3, A5.*

Miri is the starting point for adventurous trips up the Baran River to Marudi, Bario and the Kelabit Highlands. Also accessible from Miri and Marudi is the incomparable Gunung Mulu National Park with the biggest limestone cave system in the world and one of the richest assemblages of plants and animals. The capital of Sarawak's Fourth Division is a prosperous, predominantly Chinese town with one of Malaysia's best selections of restaurants and back streets filled with karaoke lounges and ladies of the night. While there isn't a great deal to do in the town itself, many visitors find Miri a good place to recuperate after the rigours of the road and often spend a couple of days enjoying the bustling streets and bountiful food on offer. The waterfront development on the north side of town has a marina; there is a pleasant walk on the Peninsula here across the Miri River, and some good fishing.

Ins and outs

Getting there The **airport** ① *T085-615433*, is close to the centre of town. Taxi coupon from the airport into town costs RM22. Bus No 28 (RM2.20) goes almost hourly to the airport 0700-1830. Buses from the airport run almost hourly from 0720-1850 and drop passengers at the local bus terminal near the Tourist Information Centre. The new bus terminal at Pujuk Padang Kerbau, Jln Padang, is around 4 km from the town centre. A taxi to the terminal costs RM15. Or take bus No 33 from outside the tourist centre.

Tourist information The **Tourist Information Centre** ① *Jln Malay (next to bus station and just across from the Park Hotel), T085-434181, www.sarawaktourism.com, Mon-Fri 0800-1800 and Sat, Sun and public holidays 0900-1500,* can offer maps and tourist information, but contrary to popular belief, they do not assist with accommodation booking.

Permits These are now only required for travel to Bario. Apply at the **Residents' Office** ① *Jln Kwantung, T085-433202/03*, with a passport photocopy. For further information visitors can also contact the **National Parks and Wildlife Office** ① *Jln Puchong, T085-436 637, F431975.* Book national park accommodation through the relevant national park office: for **Gunung Mulu** ① *T085-792300 or T085-432561*; for the **Lambir Hills** ① *T085-491030*; for **Loagan Bunut** ① *T085-779410*; for **Niah** ① *T085-737454*, and for **Similajau** ① *T085-391284.*

A **visa extension** this can be obtained at the **immigration office**, see page 158.

Background

In the latter years of the 19th century, a small trading company set up in Sarawak to import kerosene and export polished shells and pepper. In 1910, when 'earth oil' was first struck on the hill overlooking Miri, the small trading company took the plunge and diversified into the new commodity – making, in the process, Sarawak's first oil town. The company's name was **Shell**. Together with the Malaysian national oil company, **Petronas**, Shell has been responsible for discovering, producing and refining Sarawak's offshore oil deposits. Oil is a key contributor to Malaysia's export earnings and Miri has been a beneficiary of the boom. There is a big refinery at Lutong to the north, which is connected by pipeline with Seria in Brunei. Lutong is the next town on the Miri River and the main headquarters for Shell.

The oil boom in this area began on Canada Hill, behind the town (incidentally, this limestone ridge provides excellent views). **Oil Well No 1** was built by Shell and was the first oil well in Malaysia, spudded on 10 August 1910. The well was still yielding oil 62 years later, but its productivity began to slump. It is estimated that a total of 600,000 barrels were extracted from Well No 1 during its operational life. It was shut off in 1972. There are now 624 oil wells in the Miri Field, producing 80 million barrels of oil a year.

Sights

Juxtaposed against Miri's modern boom-town image is **Tamu Muhibba** ① *open 24 hrs*, the native jungle produce market, which is opposite the **Park Hotel** in a purpose-built concrete structure with pointed roofs on the roundabout connecting Jalan Malay and Jalan Padang. The Orang Ulu come downriver to sell their produce and a walk around the market provides an illuminating lesson in jungle nutrition. Colourful characters run

Miri

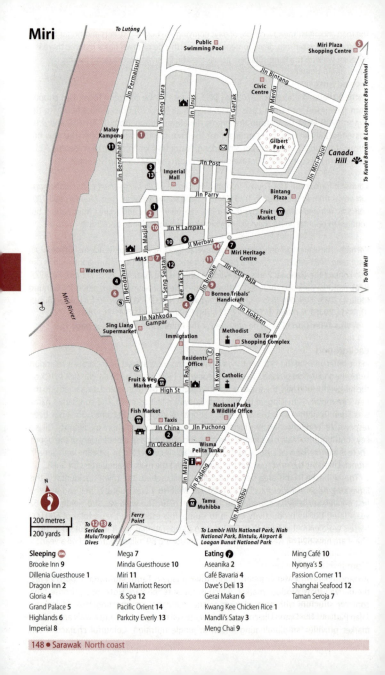

To Lutong

Public Swimming Pool

Miri Plaza Shopping Centre

Jln Permaisuri

Jln Bintang

Civic Centre

Jln Meru

Miri-Puut Long-distance Bus Terminal

Jln Yu Seng Utara

Jln Unus

Jln Gartak

Gilbert Park

Canada Hill

To Kuala Baram & Bintulu

Malay Kampong

Jln Bendahara

Imperial Mall

Jln Post

Jln Parry

Bintang Plaza

Fruit Market

To Oil Well

Jln Masjid

Jln H Lampan

Jln Merbau

Miri Heritage Centre

MAS

Jln Yu Seng Selatan

Lee Tak St

Jln Brooke

Jln Setia Raja

Waterfront

Borneo Tribals' Handicraft

Jln Hokkien

Jln Nahkoda Gampar

Sing Liang Supermarket

Immigration

Methodist

Oil Town Shopping Complex

Residents' Office

Jln Kwantung

Catholic

Jln Raja

Fruit & Veg Market

High St

National Parks & Wildlife Office

Fish Market

Taxis

Jln China

Jln Puchong

Jln Oleander

Wisma Pelita Tunku

Jln Malay

Jln Padang

Tamu Muhibba

Jln Muhibbu

Miri River

N

200 metres

200 yards

To Seridan Mulu/Tropical Dives

Ferry Point

To Lambir Hills National Park, Niah National Park, Bintulu, Airport & Loagan Bunut National Park

Sleeping	Mega 7	**Eating**	Ming Café 10
Brooke Inn 9	Minda Guesthouse 10	Aseanika 2	Nyonya's 5
Dillenia Guesthouse 1	Miri 11	Café Bavaria 4	Passion Corner 11
Dragon Inn 2	Miri Marriott Resort	Dave's Deli 13	Shanghai Seafood 12
Gloria 4	& Spa 12	Gerai Makan 6	Taman Seroja 7
Grand Palace 5	Pacific Orient 14	Kwang Kee Chicken Rice 1	
Highlands 6	Parkcity Everly 13	Mandli's Satay 3	
Imperial 8		Meng Chai 9	

148 ● Sarawak North coast

impromptu stalls from rattan mats, selling yellow cucumbers that look like mangoes, mangoes that look like turnips, huge crimson durians, tiny loofah sponges, sackfuls of fragrant Bario rice (brown and white), every shape, size and hue of banana, *tuak* (rice wine) in old Heineken bottles and a menagerie of jungle fauna – including mouse deer, falcons, pangolins and the apparently delicious long-snouted *tupai* (jungle squirrel). There are handicrafts and a large selection of dried and fresh seafood: fish and *bubok* (tiny prawns) and big buckets boiling with catfish or stacked with turtles.

Taman Bulatan is a scenic, centrally located park with foodstalls and boats for hire on the man-made lake.

Around Miri

Hawaii Beach is a pristine, palm-fringed beach, popular for picnics and barbecues. It's privately owned and visitors are asked to pay RM12 to enter. To get there, it's a 15-minute taxi ride from Miri (RM20) or take bus No 13 (RM2). There are a couple of other beaches closer to Miri including Luak Bay and Taman Selera. Bus No 11 (RM1) runs to both these spots. Don't expect anything akin to Mauritius here; these places are mellow city escapes.

Lambir Hills National Park ⓘ *T085-491030, RM10, children RM5, photography RM5, video camera RM10, professional camera RM200; to get there, take Bintulu or Bakong bus from Park Hotel (40 mins RM3) or go by taxi (30 mins RM60)*, mainly consists of a chain of sandstone hills bounded by rugged cliffs, 19 km south of Miri and just visible from the town; the main attractions are the beautiful waterfalls. *Kerangas* (heath forest) covers the higher ridges and hills while the lowland areas are mixed dipterocarp forest. Bornean gibbons, bearded pigs, barking deer and over 100 species of bird have been recorded in the park. There is only one path across a rickety suspension bridge at present, but there are numerous waterfalls, tree towers for birdwatching, and several trails which lead to enticing pools for swimming. The park attracts hordes of day trippers from Miri at weekends. It's possible to stay overnight, see Sleeping, page 153. The Park HQ is close to the Miri – Niah road and contains an audiovisual room.

Loagan Bunut National Park ⓘ *T085-779410, take a local bus from Miri to Lapok Bridge and then hire a car/taxi for the remaining 10 km to the park*, is located in the upper reaches of the Sungai Bunut and contains Sarawak's largest natural lake covering approximately 650 ha. The water level in the lake is totally dependent on the water level of the rivers Bunut, Tinjar and Baram. The level is at its lowest in the months of February, May and June and sometimes, for a period of about two to three weeks, the lake becomes an expanse of dry, cracked mud. The lake's main cultural attraction is the traditional method of fishing (*selambau*), which has been retained by the Berawan fishermen. The surrounding area is covered with peat swamp forest. Common larger birds found here are darters, egrets, herons, bittern, hornbill and kites. Gibbons are also common.

Although visibility might not be comparable to more well known sites, such as Sipadan off the east coast of Sabah, the extensive **coastal reefs of Miri** are an area of rich marine life and unexploited hard and soft coral gardens. With patch reefs, steep drop-offs descending into the depths and diverse wreck sites, there's something to interest divers of any level of experience. Combine that with world-beating biodiversity and divers are in for a little known adventure. So, why isn't this one of the world's most popular diving areas? The answer is that visibility is often low, at many sites 10 m or less, with bad weather sometimes making diving impossible. Miri's sites are fairly easy to access and the Miri-Sibuti area has recently been declared a conservation zone. Some of the more distant regions offshore seem to have become more difficult to access.

Luconia Shoals, more than a day's sail from Miri, is a good example of this with few boats (liveaboards required) prepared to sail out to this area, charging prohibitive fees. A few years ago, some in the diving world claimed that Luconia was one of Malaysia's greatest diving sites, and while that may still be the case, several sources suggest that illegal dynamite fishing has inflicted a heavy price recently. For more detailed and up-to-the-minute information, contact Mr Voo Heng Kong, Miri's own godfather of diving, at **Seridan Mulu/Tropical Dives**, see page 156. The shop is located in a small commercial centre just before the **Park City Everly Hotel**, a RM1 bus or a short taxi ride out of town towards the town's very own Brighton Beach – a good spot for a sunset stroll or a seafood snack.

Marudi → Colour map 3, A5.

Four major tribal groups – Iban, Kelabit, Kayan and Penan – come to Marudi to do business with Chinese, Indian and Malay merchants. Marudi is the furthest upriver trading post on the Baram and services all the longhouses in the Tutoh, Tinjar and Baram river basins. Most tourists only stop long enough in Marudi to down a cold drink before catching the next express boat upriver; as the trip to Mulu National Park can now be done in a day, not many have to spend the night here. Because it is a major trading post, however, there are a lot of hotels, and the standards are reasonably good.

Fort Hose was built in 1901, when Marudi was still called Claudetown, and has good views of the river. It is named after the last of the Rajah's residents, the anthropologist, geographer and natural historian Dr Charles Hose. The fort is now used as administrative offices. Also of note is the intricately carved **Thaw Peh Kong Chinese Temple** (diagonally opposite the express boat jetty), also known as Siew San Teen. The temple was shipped from China and erected in in the early 1900s, although it was probably already 100 years old by the time it began life in its new location.

The **Marudi Kampong Teraja log walk** is normally done from the Brunei end, as the return trek, across the Sarawak/Brunei border, takes a full day, from dawn to dusk. It is, however, possible to reach an Iban longhouse inside Brunei without going the whole distance to Kampong Teraja. The longhouse is on the Sungai Ridan, about 2½ hours down the jungle trail. The trail starts 3 km from Marudi, on the airport road. There's no customs post on the border; the trail is not an official route into Brunei. Trekkers are advised to take their passports in the unlikely event of being stopped by police, who will probably turn a blind eye. Kampong Teraja in Brunei is the furthest accessible point that can be reached by road from Labi.

Three **longhouses** – Long Seleban, Long Moh and Leo Mato – are accessible by 4WD from Marudi.

◉ North coast listings

For Sleeping and Eating price codes and other relevant information, see Essentials pages 23-27.

⬤ Sleeping

Bintulu *p140, map p141*
There aren't any places specifically geared towards budget foreign travellers here, and there are plenty of seedy short-time hotels that are worth avoiding.

AL-A The Regency, 116 Taman Sri Dagang, Jln Abang Galau, T086-335111, rihbtu@ tm.net.my. A hotel with upmarket pretensions and a fair number of empty rooms. This place has a decent restaurant, bar with occasional live music, and Wi-Fi access in the lobby. Rooms are comfortable, with all mod cons, including a bathroom with bathtub.
B Riverfront Inn, 256 Taman Sri Dagang, T086-339 577, riverf@tm.net.my. One of the

town's more upmarket offerings and popular with foreign oil workers. Rooms are modern and clean, and ones at the front have good views over the river. However, there is a lingering odour of cigarette smoke throughout the hotel which is off-putting. Wi-Fi available in the lobby.

B-C AA Inn, 107 Taman Sri Dagang, T086-313237, F331237. Good-value new hotel with sleek modern bathrooms, comfortable bedrooms with tiny TVs and Wi-Fi access throughout. Recommended.

B-C Kintown Inn, 93 Jln Keppel, T086-333666. Large orange building offering a selection of carpeted a/c rooms with TV and attached bathroom. Wi-Fi. Fair value.

B-C Royal, 12 Jln Pedada, T086-315888, F334028. Fair-value mid-range hotel offering carpeted a/c rooms with attached bathroom and cable TV. Wi-Fi access throughout.

C Sea View, 254 Jln Masjid, T086-339118. Offers a/c, shower and TV in spacious rooms with views over the river.

C Sunlight Inn, 7 Jln Pedada, T086-332577 F334075. Slightly worn a/c rooms with cable TV and attached bathroom. Staff here are friendly, and despite the wear and tear, the hotel is generally clean and rooms are good value. Wi-Fi access available. Recommended.

Similajau National Park p142
To book accommodation, contact Similajau National Park, T086-391284.

B-C National park accommodation. 2 chalets, and 2 'forest' hostels with bargain-basement dorm beds (RM15). The hostels have attractive polished hardwood decor. It can get block booked. The more expensive accommodation is in the chalets, which have 8 beds to a room, settees and a sea view. 24-hr electricity. The canteen at Park HQ serves basic food and there are picnic shelters at Park HQ. You can camp for RM5 a night.

Niah National Park p143, map p144
It's advisable to book accommodation at least 2-3 days in advance, through the National Parks Booking Office, not the tourist information office. **Niah National Park**, T085-737454 or T085- 737450; **National Parks Booking Office**, T085- 434184, www.forestry.sarawak.gov.my. Also npbooking@ sarawak.net.gov.my. All places have 24-hr electricity and treated water.

There's a **Family chalet**, similar to a hostel but with cooker and a/c, 2 rooms with 4 beds in each, RM150 per room or RM225 per chalet. There is a slightly cheaper chalet with fan for RM100 per room or RM150 per house. **Hostels**, 5 hostels each with 4 rooms of 4 beds each, all rooms have private bathrooms, clean, and Western-style with shower, toilet, electric fans, fridges, large sitting area and kitchen. No cooking facilities, but kettle, crockery and cutlery provided on request. RM40 for 1 room, 4 beds, or RM15 for 1 bed. There is a campsite with space for 30, RM5 per night.

C Niah Caves, T085-737726. Some a/c, shared facilities, 6 rooms (singles, doubles and triples available). Basic, but light and clean, next to the river.

C Niah Caves Inn, T085-737333, F737332. With a/c, TV, shower and spacious, fully carpeted rooms. Reasonable value.

There are also 4 small hotels in Batu Niah (4 km from Park HQ).

Camping
Tents can be hired from Park HQ (RM8) or from the site (RM5).

Miri and the Baram River p146, map p148
Most people going to Mulu will have to spend at least a night in Miri. The town has a fair selection of dreary mid-range accommodation and a couple of excellent new budget options, which are good value. Many mid-range hotels are around Jln Yu Seng Selatan. Being an oil town, and close to Brunei, Miri has a booming prostitution industry and the warblings from the karaoke bars go on late into the night.

AL-A Miri Marriott Resort & Spa, Jln Temenggong Datuk Oyong Lawai, T085-421121, www.marriotthotels.com. Luxurious resort-style hotel overlooking the sea a short taxi ride from Miri. 5-star comforts, 220 a/c rooms, all with minibar, TV and internet access. International restaurant, expensive, but excellent coffee house with highly recommended cakes. There's also the largest pool in the Miri area, tennis, a 24-hr gym and a health centre. Balinese-style spa and massage parlour. Good deals are available but watch for pricey extras. **Wildlife Expeditions** arrange tours from their office in the lobby.

A Grand Palace, 2 km Jln Miri-Pujut, **Pelita Commercial Centre**, T085-428888, www.grandpalacehotel.com.my. Imposing peach and pastel building on town outskirts next to **Miri Plaza Shopping Centre**. 125 comfortable rooms with dreary carpet and intense burgundy curtains and decor. Rooms have cable TV, a/c and smart attached bathroom. There is Wi-Fi access in the lobby. There's a pool and a couple of good restaurants with occasional theme buffets.

A Imperial, Jln Post, T085-431133, www.imperialhotel.com.my. Set in a towering block to the east of the town centre, this hotel offers comfortable, modern rooms with cable TV and internet access. The suites here are massive and come with full settees. Lovely poolside area with café offering excellent views over the city, particularly at sunset. Part of the **Imperial Shopping Mall**. Serviced rooms or rental apartments. Apartments feature internet, hi-fi, fully equipped kitchen, and, in some cases, a washing machine. The hotel has some excellent dining options.

A Mega, Jln Merbau, T085-432432, www.megahotel.com.my. Another beast of a building, towering over the town with 293 rooms and good promotional rates. Rooms are comfortable and functional though not particularly inspiring, and have the usual range of facilities for this class. There is an oddly shaped pool with a jacuzzi and lounge chairs, bar and karaoke lounge and good Chinese restaurant. Free Wi-Fi throughout. There is a shopping mall below the hotel.

A Parkcity Everly, Jln Temenggong Datuk Oyong Lawai, T085-440288, www.vhhotels.com. 2 km from town centre, at the mouth of the Miri River, this modern hotel curves around the South China Sea. 168 a/c rooms with cable TV, bathroom, minibar and balcony. You can watch sunsets over sea and colourful but noisy river traffic. There's a palm-lined free-form pool with swim-up bar and a jacuzzi. The beach is too near town to be clean and the sea is not safe for swimming but is good for sunset strolls. Also coffee house, Chinese restaurant, bar, bakery/deli, fitness centre, sauna. Good rates if booked in advance online. Recommended.

B Dragon Inn, Lot 355, Jln Masjid, T085-422266, www.dragoninnmiri.com. A new place with an outrageous psychedelic carpet and flowery wallpaper clash in the corridors, which is quite disturbing after a few hours in the sun. Thankfully, decor in the rooms is toned down, with comfy beds, flatscreen TV, kettle, fridge and free Wi-Fi access. Good value. Recommended.

B Gloria, 27 Jln Brooke, T085-416699, F418866. Selection of bright carpeted a/c rooms with cable TV and attached bathroom with bathtub. Free Wi-Fi in lobby and good Chinese restaurant downstairs. Gets busy at weekends. Rooms here are fair value, but nothing special. Some of the cheaper rooms are windowless.

B Miri, 47 Jln Brooke, T085-421212, F412002. Fair value mid-range option with musty but clean rooms with free Wi-Fi access, TV and attched bathroom. A couple of cafés downstairs serve Western and Chinese fare.

B Pacific Orient, 49 Jln Brooke, T085-413333, pohotel@streamyx.com. Prices have risen considerably here over the years and this place is no longer the great bargain that it once was. Aiming for domestic business travellers, rooms are comfortable, plain and have a/c, TV and attached bathroom. Free Wi-Fi in the lobby and a cheap food court on the ground floor offering local delights.

B-D Dillenia Guesthouse, Lot 846, 1st floor, Jln Sida, T085-434204, dillenia.guesthouse@gmail.com. Superb new guesthouse that gets unanimously good reviews from guests for its homely atmosphere, simple but spotless rooms, excellent free breakfasts and Wi-Fi access throughout. This place is easily the best of the bunch. Highly recommended.

C Brooke Inn, 14 Jln Brooke, T085-412881, brookeinn@hotmail.com. Unpretentious place with clean, basic rooms with TV and a/c. You get what you pay for here.

C Highlands, Lot 1271, Block 9, Jln Sri Dagang (off Jln Bendahara), Miri Waterfront, T085-422327, highlan@streamyx.net. Well-established backpacker haunt on the top floor of a shophouse with spartan, functional double rooms and dorms with shared bathroom. Joanne, who runs the place enthusiastically, is a good source of travel information.

C Minda Guesthouse, Lot 607, 1st floor, Jln Yu Seng Utara, T085-411422, www.minda guesthouse.com. Another new offering which is well set up for budget travellers, with clean dorms and a couple of doubles. Free Wi-Fi access, breakfast and a good travellers' noticeboard. The roof terrace is a little bare, but is a fine spot for a sunset beer. Recommended.

Around Miri p149
Book accommodation through the **National Parks Booking Office**, T085-491030 for Lambir Hills.

A-B Lambir Hills, there's plenty of choice here, from 3-room a/c chalets at RM150 per chalet or RM100 per room and fan chalets for RM75 per chalet or RM50 per room (2 beds in a room). Camping at RM5 per person.

D Loagan Bunut National Park accommodation. To book, call the **National Parks Booking Office**, T085-779410. There is 1 forest hostel with 4 rooms each with 7 double bunk beds with fan and own toilet. RM15 per bed. The park has a canteen. Electricity available from 0600-0200.

Marudi p150
B-C Grand, Lot 350 Backlane, T085-755711, F775293. Large but good hotel close to jetty. With restaurant, 30 clean rooms with cable TV and some a/c. Information on upriver trips. Wi-Fi.

B-C Mount Mulu, Lot 80 & Lot 90, Marudi Town District, T085-756671, F756670. A/c; discounts available which make this place excellent value. Internet access.

C Mayland, 347 Mayland Building, T085-755106, F755333. With a/c and 41 rooms. Slightly run down but a good range of accommodation

C Victoria, Lot 961-963 Jln Merdeka, T085-756067. All 21 rooms have cable TV and attached bathroom.

❼ Eating

Bintulu p140, map p141
Umai, raw fish pickled with lime or the fruit of wild palms (*assam*) and mixed with salted vegetables, onions and chillies, is a Melanau speciality. Bintulu is famed for its *belacan* – prawn paste – and in the local dialect, prawns are *urang*, not *udang*.

❦ An Nur Nasi Padang Sambal Belado, Jln Somerville. It's worth getting here early when there is still a good selection of tasty Indonesian-style curries and vegetable dishes.

❦ Makan United, Jln Abang Galau (below Sunlight Inn). Cheap and cheerful place with English menu knocking out plates of fried rice, noodles and soups.

❦ Nasi Ayam Singapore, Jln Somerville. Large place offering up plates of steamed and roast Hainan chicken rice. Good spot for lunch.

❦ Popular Corner, opposite hospital. This place is definitely one of the better places to eat in Bintulu with a range of good fresh seafood dishes, dim sum at lunchtime and refreshing juices. Recommended.

Foodstalls
Chinese stalls behind the Chinese temple on Jln Temple. Stalls at both markets.
Pantai Ria, near Tanjong Batu. Mainly seafood, open evenings only. Recommended.

Niah National Park 143, map p144
Emergency rations recommended.
The **Guano Collectors' Cooperative** shop at

the beginning of the plankwalk sells basic food and cold drinks and camera film. There is another basic **shop/restaurant** just outside the park gates. There is a **canteen** at Park HQ, which serves good local food and full Western breakfast, good value, barbecue site provided, the canteen is supposed to be open 0700-2300 but is a little erratic.

Miri and the Baram River p146, map p148

Locals take their food pretty seriously in Miri and there are more than enough good places to choose from. A walk after dark along Jln Yu Seng will reveal an array of eateries, from simple Malay stalls to top-notch seafood joints. Below is a selection of the better ones.

¶¶ **Café Bavaria**, Miri Waterfront, T085-429 4959. Pricey halal German dishes, cheaper Malay food. Run by Monikka from Germany, this place is a quaint slice of Bavaria pasted into Miri. Despite being close to the river, there are no views. But it's open-walled, making it a pleasant place for an iced coffee.

¶¶ **Dave's Deli**, Jln Yu Seng Utara. Open 0900-2300. The Peninsula has **Kenny Rogers** and Miri has **Dave's** to satisfy the local craving for roast chicken and mash. An interesting menu of American-themed Western food including the mighty 1-ft-long sausage. Ice cream, creamy soups and plenty of cholesterol.

¶¶ **Meng Chai**, Jln Merbau. Open from 1700. Members of the local Chinese community rave about this place, with a variety of types of fish and shellfish cooked myriad ways. Recommended.

¶¶ **Passion Corner**, 856 Jln Permaisuri, T085-423213. Small and clean family-run eatery offering MSG-free mini-steamboats, light Chinese and Korean meals and a range of Chinese teas.

¶¶ **Shanghai Seafood**, Jln Yu Seng Selatan. Open for lunch and dinner. Another popular seafood place where customers happily get stuck into treats such as prawns cooked in Chinese wine and steamed seafish. Recommended.

¶ **Aseanika**, Jln Yu Seng Selatan. Serves good Indian and Indonesian food.

¶ **Kwang Kee Chicken Rice**, Jln Yu Seng Utara. Plates of delicious fresh chicken rice. Busy at lunchtimes.

¶ **Mandli's Satay**, Jln Yu Seng Utara. This is the town's top satay joint with delicious beef and chicken satay sold alongside Malay curries and *murtabak*. It's justifiably very popular with locals. Recommended.

¶ **Ming Café**, on the corner of Jln Merbau and Jln Yu Seng Utara. Open 0800-2400. Collection of different hawker stalls offering some good Indian fare, Chinese beef noodles and *asam pedas*. This place is popular with tourists and locals and gets a bit boozy in the evenings with its numerous drinks promotions and loud, but inoffensive music. Recommended.

¶ **Nyonya's**, 21 Jln Brooke. This place has changed hands recently, although the name plate has stayed the same. Serves cheap and filling Javanese staples doled out to Indonesian workers. The menu includes *ayam penyet, ikan lalapan* and the vegetarian delight of *gado-gado*. Good, cheap lunches.

Foodstalls

Gerai Makan, near Chinese temple at end of Jln Oleander. Malay food.
Taman Seroja, Jln Brooke. Malay food, best in the evenings.
Tamu Muhibba (Native Market), opposite Park Hotel on roundabout connecting Jln Malay and Jln Padang. Best during the day.
Tanjong seafood stalls, Tanjung Lobung (south of Miri). Best in the evenings.

Marudi p150

There are several coffee shops in town.
Rose Garden, opposite **Alisan Hotel**. A/c coffee shop serving mainly Chinese dishes.

✲ Festivals and events

Miri International Jazz Festival is held each year in May at the Park City Everly Hotel with bands from around the world playing their own brands of jazz. Tickets cost around RM60 for a day. See www.mirijazzfestival.com.

O Shopping

Bintulu *p140, map p141*
Handicrafts
Dyang Enterprise, Plaza Hotel, lobby floor, Jln Abang Galau. Rather overpriced because of the Plaza's more upmarket clientele.
Li Hua Plaza, near the Plaza Hotel. The best place for handicrafts.

Miri and the Baram River *p146, map p148*
Books
Parksons Department Store, Bintang Plaza.
Pelita Book Centre, 1st floor, Wisma Pelita Tunku department store.

Handicrafts
Borneo Arts, Jln Yu Seng Selatan (next to Cosy Inn). Daily 0900-2100. T-shirts, pottery, handicrafts, wood carvings, batik, Iban textiles, Chinese porcelain, kris daggers, Dayak warrior swords and shields.
Miri Handicrafts Centre, Jln Brooke (about 15 mins' walk from the local bus station). Stalls with local artists' batik, beads, basketry, musical instruments and some tourist tack, café. Worth checking out.
Olly Dress Making, 2nd floor, Wisma Pelita Tunku, Jln Puchong, T019-875 1854. Traditional tailored women's dresses and local handicrafts.
Rong Reng Heritage, Borneo Tribals' Handicraft, 14 Jln Brooke, next to Brooke Inn, T013-833 2406. Straightforward locals George and Eva run this well-stocked craft centre with a diverse range of crafts, from woven mats to beads and T-shirts. George and Eva will tell you the product origins. Inexpensive.

Shopping complexes
Boulevard (BSC), Jln Pujut Lutong. Miri's biggest shopping complex, food court, supermarket, department store and boutiques.
Imperial Mall, part of the Imperial hotel complex. Money changers, a department store and supermarket in the basement.
Soon Hup Tower, next to Mega Hotel. With Parkwell's supermarket and department store.

Supermarkets
Ngiukee, moving from Pelita to Imperial Mall; **Parkson Grand**, Bintang Plaza; **Pelita**, ground floor, **Sing Liang Supermarket** on Jln Nakhoda Gampar, Chinese store; **Wisma Pelita Tunku**, useful for supplies for upriver expeditions.

▲ Activities and tours

Bintulu *p140, map p141*
Golf
Tanjong Kidurong, north of town, by the sea (regular buses from town), 18-hole course.

Sports complex
Swimming pool (RM2), tennis, football. To get there, fork right from the Miri road at the Chinese temple, 1 km from town centre.

Tour operators
Deluxe Travel, 30 Jln Law Gek Soon, T086-331293, F334995; **Hunda Travel Services**, 8 Jln Somerville, T086-331339, F330445; **Similajau Adventure Tours**, Sublot 5, 4359 Medan Jaya Commercial Centre, T086-331 552, F330 097, offers tours around the city, and to Niah caves, longhouses and Similajau National Park.

Miri and the Baram River *p146, map p148*
Golf
Eastwood Valley Golf and Country Club, Lot 1379, Block 17, KBLD, T085-421010, www.eastwoodvalley.com. Located out near the Miri bypass, this lovely new place has good facilities. A round of 18 holes starts at RM175.

Swimming
Public pool off Jln Bintang, close to the Civic Centre, RM1.

Tour operators
Although most tour companies specialize in trips up the Baram River to Mulu National Park, some are much better than others – in terms of facilities and services offered. Every agency in Miri has a Mulu National Park itinerary covering the caves, pinnacles and

summits. It is also possible to trek to Bario and Mount Murud as well as to Limbang from Mulu. Most agencies employ experienced guides who will be able to advise on longer, more ambitious treks. The Mulu National Park is one destination where it is usually cheaper to go through a tour company than to try to do it independently. Costs vary considerably according to the number of people in a group. For a 3-day Mulu trip, a single tourist can expect to pay at least RM500 with all accommodation, food, travel and guide costs included. An 8-day tour of Ulu Baram longhouses would cost RM2000 for 1 person and RM1400 per person in a group of 10. A 20-day trek will cost 2 people (minimum number) around RM2300 each, and a group of 6-10, RM1500 a head. For remote longhouses, tour companies present by far the best option. Tour fees cover 'gifts' and all payments to longhouse headmen for food, accommodation and entertainment. **Borneo Mainland**, Jln Merpati, T085-433511, www.borneomainland.com; **JJ Tour Travel**, Lot 231, Jln Maju Taman, Jade Centre, T085-418690, F413308, ticketing agents; **KKM Travel & Tours**, 236 Jln Maju, T085-417899, F414629; **Limbang Travel Service**, 1G Park Arcade (near Park Hotel), T085-413228, efficient ticket service.
Seridan Mulu/Tropical Dives, Lot 273, ground floor, Brighton Centre, Jln Temen- ggong Datuk Oyong Lawai, T085-415582, www.seridanmulu. com. Runs tailor-made land trips in the region. Manager Mr Voo Heng Kong also stands out from others in the area for being Miri's only dive operator, running dives on all local reefs or in more remote locations on request. Superb knowledge of Miri's diving possibilities. Tours for land lubbers also organized.
Tropical Adventure Tours and Travel, ground floor, **Mega Hotel**, Lot 907, Jln Merbau, T085-419337, www.borneotropical adventure.com. Professional and with lots of experience. Tailor-made trips in Malaysia or Indonesia. Boss Richard Hii has an excellent working knowledge of Kalimantan and its more remote corners – it's worth checking

their website for the latest special deals. There are some excellent offers for those with residence permits in Singapore, Malaysia or Brunei. At the time of writing, they offer the cheapest all-inclusive tours to Mulu, starting at RM399 for 2 days/1 night. Recommended.

⊖ Transport

Bintulu p140, map p141
Air
AirAsia and MAS have regular connections with **Kuala Lumpur** and **Kuching**. MAS flies to **Miri**, **Sibu** and **Kota Kinabalu**.
Airline offices MAS and MASwings, Jln Masjid, T086-331554.

Boat
Enquire at the wharf for times and prices. Regular connections with **Tubau**, last boat at 1400 (2½-3 hrs RM22). Connections with **Belaga**, via logging road, see page 139; this route is popular with people in Belaga as it is much cheaper than going from Sibu. However, tourists need a permit to get to Belaga, and there is no accommodation in Tubau for those who get stuck. If you really want to do this, call Mr Hasbee in Belaga (T013-842 9767) and see if any drivers are making the return trip to Belaga from Bintulu (RM60); alternatively, try **Hup Kiat Transport** in Belaga (T013-807 5598), as they have Toyota Landcruisers leaving Bintulu at 1330 daily for Belaga (RM60). If travelling overland from Bintulu, report to the Bintulu Resident's Office and the Belaga Resident's Office. For more information, call the Kapit Resident's Office, T084-796445.

Bus
There are 2 stations in town. The local bus terminal is in the centre. The long-distance Medan Jaya station is 10 mins by taxi from the centre, on the road towards Miri (RM15). Regular connections with **Miri** (RM20), **Sarikei Batu Niah** (RM12) and **Sibu** (RM20) and **Kuching** (RM60). There are at least 10 bus companies, and buses leave frequently

all day. One of the more organized companies ploughing the bumpy roads is Biaramas, T086-314 999, www.busasia.net.

Taxi
For **Miri** and **Sibu**, taxis leave from Jln Masjid. Because of the regular bus services and the poor state of the roads, most taxis are for local use only and chartering them is pricey.

Similaju National Park *p142*
There is no regular bus service to the park. Take a taxi (30 mins, RM50 Bintulu – Similaju trip, RM100 for a return trip). Bintulu taxi station, T086-332009. Boats can be chartered from the wharf at Bintulu, from RM200.

Niah National Park *p143, map p144*
Boat
From Batu Niah (near the market) to Park HQ at Pangkalan Lubang, Niah National Park by boat (RM15 per person or if more than 5 people, RM3 per person) or 45 mins' walk.

Bus
Every 2 hrs for a connection with **Miri** (2 hrs RM12); 6 buses a day to **Bintulu (RM12)** and Sibu via Bintulu to **Batu Niah**.

Taxi
From **Miri** to Park HQ, will only leave when there are 4 passengers. Most visitors jump on a bus from Miri to Bintulu or Sibu and get off at Batu Niah (2 hrs) and then take a taxi for 20 mins (RM20) to get to the park HQ. From **Bintulu** to Batu Niah (RM10). A taxi to Park HQ costs RM20 from the bus station at Batu Niah but the riverboat is far more scenic (see Boat, above).

Miri and the Baram River *p146, map p148*
Air
For details of the airport, see page 147. Take a bus No 28 (RM2.20) to the airport, but ask the driver to drop you off outside, otherwise you will be dropped off on the highway, a 10-min trek from the terminal.

AirAsia and MAS fly to **Kuching**, **Kota Kinabalu** and **Kuala Lumpur**. AirAsia also

flies to **JB**. Miri is a hub for MASwings with flights to **Ba'kelalan**, **Bario**, **Bintulu**, **Lawas**, **Limbang**, **Long Akah**, **Long Banga**, **Long Lellang**, **Long Seridan**, **Marudi**, **Mukah**, **Mulu**, **Sibu** and **Labuan**. Sarawak-based airline **Hornbill Skyways** flies to rural parts of Sarawak including Mukah, **Tanjung Manis** (via Mukah), Kuching (via Mukah or Tanjung Manis), and Mulu.

Note that it is crucial to book the excellent-value flights to Bario and Mulu in advance. Travellers hoping to show up and get on a flight will probably be disappointed. There are no flights between Miri and **Brunei**.

Airline offices AirAsia, Jln Asmaram, T085-438022. Hornbill Skyways, T085-611066. MAS and MASwings, 239 Halaman Kabor, off Jln Yu Seng Selatan, T085-414144.

Bus
Regular connections from early morning to early/mid-afternoon with **Batu Niah** (2 hrs, RM12), **Bintulu** (4 hrs, RM20), **Sibu** (7 hrs, RM40) and **Kuching** (13 hrs, RM80).

Regular bus connections with **Kuala Baram** and the express boat upriver to **Marudi**. There are also taxis to Kuala Baram, either private or shared (RM35 or more). Express boats upriver to **Marudi** from Kuala Baram, 3 hrs. Roughly 1 boat every 2 hrs from 0800. Last boat 1500 (RM20). This is the first leg of the journey to Mulu and the interior.

Several departures a day to **Kuala Belait** in **Brunei** and these leave from Miri's central bus station near the Park Hotel and Tourist Information Centre (2 hrs, RM13), via Sungai Tujuh checkpoint, with onward connections to **Bandar Seri Begawan**. These buses are run by the **Miri Belait Transport Co**. From the checkpoint you need to change buses at Kuala Belait for Seria (B$1) and then onwards to Bandar Seri Begawan (B$6). You can use Singapore dollars in Brunei. Note the last bus from Seria leaves at 1520, which means you need to catch a morning bus from Miri (0700 or 1000) to make the connection, or you will need to stay the night in Kuala Belait or Seria. Travelling by your own means of transport from Miri, it is necessary to take the ferry across the Belait River. This crossing is just served by a small passenger boat, with another bus waiting on the far side – check on the car ferry status before driving across the border. At weekends and public holidays there are long queues for the ferries/boats as well as at immigration. Be warned also that the ferry across the Belait River takes an unscheduled 1-hr break for lunch. The distance itself is nothing – the ferry crossings take no more than 10 mins and Miri to Kuala Belait is just 27 km. Bus passengers sometimes bypass the queues because they board the ferry as foot passengers and then hop on another bus the other side of the river. From Kuala Belait regular connections with Seria, (45 mins B$1), and from Seria regular buses with Bandar Seri Begawan (1-2 hrs B$6). It takes at least 5 hrs to reach Bandar Seri Begawan.

Alternatively, there is now a service offered by Mr Foo and his son with a 7-seater Toyota departing Miri daily around 0900 and arriving in BSB around noon. The fare is RM60. Seats can be booked via the Dillenia Guesthouse (see page 152) or by calling Mr Foo, T013-833 2231. **Highlands** (see page 153) offers a similar service for the same price. It's a slightly less adventurous way of arriving in BSB, but can shave hours off travel time.

There is a daily bus service to Kota Kinabalu leaving the long-distance bus terminal at 0800 (RM93). This travels via Limbang and Lawas and takes 9-10 hrs. There is also a bus to Pontianak departing daily at 0730 which travels via Kuching. Both services are run by **Bintang Jaya Bus Co** (T085-432178) from the long-distance terminal.

Car
Car hire Avis, Permaisuri Rd, T085-430222; Lee Brothers, 17 River Rd, T085-410606; Kong Tek, Counter 2, Ground Floor, Public Concourse Terminal Building, T085-617 767. Decent range of cars starting at RM128 a day. Also, driver services offered for trips to longhouses and the interior.

Marudi p150
Air
The airport is 5 km from town. Connections with **Miri** (3 daily), **Bario** and **Long Lellang** with MASwings.

Boat
These leave opposite the Chinese temple. Connections with **Kuala Baram**, 5 boats a day from 0700-1500 (RM20); **Tutoh**, for longboats to Long Terawan, 1 boat daily at 1200 (RM25); **Long Lama**, for longboats to **Bario**, 1 boat every hour 0730-1400. From Long Terawan the longboat journey takes up to 2 hrs (RM55 each for group of 5 or more). From Miri to Kuala Baram take bus No 1 (RM3, 1st bus 0530) or a shared taxi (RM35).

Directory

Bintulu p140, map p141
Banks HSBC and Standard Chartered, both on Jln Keppel. **Post office** GPO (Pos Laju) far side of the airport near the Residents' Office, 2 km from centre.

Miri and the Baram River p146, map p148
Banks All major banks here.
Immigration Pajabat Imigresen, 2nd floor Tingkat 2&3, Yu Lan Plaza, T085-442118. New office in huge skyscraper at Jln Brooke/Jln Raja. For an extension to your entry stamp or visa. **Internet** There are internet cafés in the Imperial Plaza and Soon Hup Shopping Complex. Most of the popular lodgings offer internet access. **Medical services** Hospital, on the edge of town on Jlln Cahaya, T085-420033. **Police** Police station, Jln Kingsway, T085-433730. **Post office** General Post Office, on Jln Post behind the Imperial Mall. **Telephone** Telecom Office, Jln Gartak, daily 0730-2200.

Marudi p150
Banks There are 2 local banks with foreign exchange. **Police** Police station, Airport Rd. **Post office** Post Office, Airport Rd.

Northern Sarawak

The impressive peak of Gunung Mulu is the centrepiece of the eponymous national park. The luscious jungle, home to orchids and hornbills, also boasts the largest limestone cave system on the planet. The cooler climes of the Kelabit Highlands provide good walking opportunities around Bario. Limbang is frontier country and the start of a cross-border trek. ▶▶ *For listings, see pages 167-169.*

Gunung Mulu National Park → *Colour map 3, A6.*

Tucked in behind Brunei, this 529 sq km park lays claim to **Gunung Mulu**, which at 2376 m is the second highest mountain in Sarawak, and the biggest limestone cave system in the world. Mulu is basically a huge hollow mountain range, covered in 180-million-year-old rainforest. Its primary jungle contains an astonishing biological diversity. The park was awarded UNESCO World Heritage status in 2000.

Just outside the national park boundary on the Tutoh River there are rapids which it is possible to shoot; this can be arranged through tour agencies.

Ins and outs
Park essentials RM10, children RM5, camera RM5, video RM10, professional filming RM200.

Equipment A small store at the Park HQ sells basic necessities; there is also a small shop just outside the park boundary, at Long Pala. A sleeping bag is essential for Gunung Mulu trips; other useful items include a good insect repellent, wet weather gear and a powerful torch.

Guides No visitors are permitted to enter the caves without an authorized guide; guides can be arranged from Park HQ or booked in advance from the national parks office in Miri, see page 147. There are some treks around the park that can be done without a guide. Most of the Mulu Park guides are very well informed about flora and fauna, geology and tribal customs. Tour agencies organize guides as part of their fee. Guide fees: from RM20 per cave (or per day) and an extra RM10 per night. Mulu summit trips, RM1000 for a group of up to five (four days, three nights) and Melinau Gorge and Pinnacles, minimum RM400 for five people (three days, two nights). Ornithological guides cost an additional RM10 a day. Porterage: maximum 10 kg and RM30 per day, RM1 for each extra kilogramme. Mulu summit, minimum RM90; Melinau Gorge (Camp 5), minimum RM65. It is usual to tip guides and porters.

Tourist information For up-to-date information on Mulu, see www.mulupark.com. For cavers wishing to explore caves not open to the public (those open to visitors are known as 'show' caves), there are designated 'adventure caves' within an hour of Park HQ. Experienced cave guides can be organized from headquarters. The most accessible adventure cave is the one-hour trek following the river course through **Clearwater Cave**. Cavers should bring their own equipment. Tougher caves such as the Sarawak Chamber can only be visited by advanced cavers who have some experience. The Park Manager needs to approve this trip.

Best time to visit It is best to avoid visiting the park during school and public holidays. In December the park is closed to locals, but remains open to tourists.

Gunung Mulu National Park

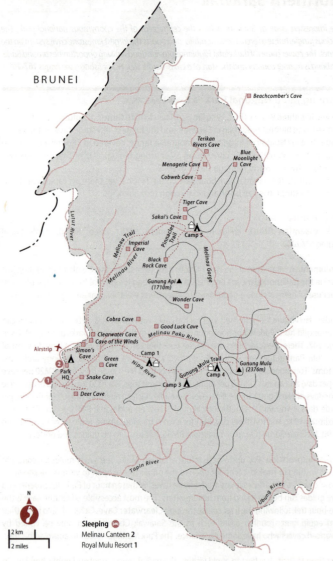

BRUNEI

Beachcomber's Cave

Terikan
Rivers Cave

Blue
Moonlight
Cave

Menagerie Cave

Cobweb Cave

Tiger Cave

Sakai's Cave

Camp 5

Lutut River

Melinau Trail

Imperial
Cave

Pinnacles Trail

Melinau River

Black
Rock Cave

Melinau Gorge

Gunung Api
(1710m)

Wonder Cave

Cobra Cave

Good Luck Cave

Clearwater Cave

Melinau Paku River

Cave of the Winds

Airstrip

Camp 1

Simon's
Cave

Green
Cave

Nipa River

Gunung Mulu Trail

Camp 4

Gunung Mulu
(2376m)

Park
HQ

Snake Cave

Camp 3

Deer Cave

Tapin River

Ubung River

N

2 km
2 miles

Sleeping
Melinau Canteen **2**
Royal Mulu Resort **1**

Background

In Robin Hanbury-Tenison's book *The Rain Forest*, he says of Mulu: "All sense of time and direction is lost." Every scientific expedition that has visited Mulu's forests has encountered plant and animal species unknown to science. In 1990, five years after it was officially opened to the public, the park was handling an average of 400 visitors a month. Numbers have increased markedly since then – the area is now attracting more than 12,000 tourists a year – and as the eco-tourism industry has extended its foothold, local tribespeople have been drawn into confrontation with the authorities. In the early 1990s, a series of sabotage incidents was blamed on the Berawan tribe, who claim the caves and the surrounding jungle are a sacred site.

In 1974, three years after Mulu was gazetted as a national park, the first of a succession of joint expeditions led by the British Royal Geographical Society (RGS) and the Sarawak government began to make the discoveries that put Mulu on the map. In 1980 a cave passage over 50 km long was surveyed for the first time. Since then, a further 137 km of passages have been discovered. Altogether 27 major caves have now been found speleologists believe they may represent a tiny fraction of what is actually there. The world's biggest cave, the **Sarawak Chamber**, was not discovered until 1984.

The first attempt on Gunung Mulu was made by Spencer St John, the British consul in Brunei, in 1856 (see also his attempts on Gunung Kinabalu, page 232). His efforts were thwarted by "limestone cliffs, dense jungle and sharp pinnacles of rock". Dr Charles Hose, Resident of Marudi, led a 25-day expedition to Gunung Mulu in 1893, but also found his path blocked by 600-m-high cliffs. Nearly 50 years later, in 1932, a Berawan rhinoceros hunter called Tama Nilong guided Edward Shackleton's Oxford University expedition to the summit. One of the young Oxford undergraduates on that expedition was Tom Harrisson, who later made the Niah archaeological discoveries, see page 144. Tama Nilong, the hunter from Long Terawan, had previously reached the main southwest ridge of Mulu while tracking a rhinoceros.

The cliffs of the Melinau Gorge rise a sheer 600 m, and are the highest limestone rock faces between north Thailand and Papua New Guinea. The limestone massifs of Gunung Api and Gunung Benarat were originally at the same elevation as Gunung Mulu, but their limestone outcrops were more prone to erosion than the Mulu's sandstone. Northwest of the gorge lies a large, undisturbed alluvial plain which is rich in flora and fauna. Penan tribespeople (see page 107) are permitted to maintain their lifestyle of fishing, hunting and gathering in the park. At no small expense, the Malaysian government has encouraged them to settle at a purpose-built longhouse at **Batu Bungan**, just a few minutes upriver from the Park HQ, but its efforts have met with limited success because of the desire of many Penan to maintain their travelling lifestyle. Penan shelters can often be found by riverbanks.

Reeling from international criticism, the Sarawak state government set aside 66,000 ha of rainforest as what it called 'biosphere', a reserve where indigenous people could practise their traditional lifestyle. Part of this lies within the park. In Baram and Limbang districts, the remaining 300 Penan will have a reserve in which they can continue their nomadic way of life. A further 23,000 ha has reportedly been set aside for 'semi-nomadic' Penan.

In 1961 geologist Dr G Wilford first surveyed Deer Cave and parts of the Cave of the Winds. But Mulu's biggest subterranean secrets were not revealed until the 1980s.

Flora and fauna

In the 1960s and 1970s, botanical expeditions were beginning to shed more light on the Mulu area's flora and fauna: 100 new plant species were discovered between 1960 and

1973 alone. Mulu Park encompasses an area of diverse altitudes and soil types – it includes all the forest types found in Borneo except mangrove. About 20,000 animal species have been recorded in Mulu Park, as well as 3500 plant species and 8000 varieties of fungi (more than 100 of these are endemic to the Mulu area). Mulu's ecological statistics are astounding: it is home to 1500 species of flowering plant, 170 species of orchid and 109 varieties of palm. More than 280 butterfly species have been recorded. Within the park boundaries, 262 species of bird (including all eight varieties of hornbill), 67 mammalian species, 50 species of reptile and 75 amphibian species have been recorded.

Mulu's caves contain an unusual array of flora and fauna too. There are three species of swiftlet, 12 species of bat and nine species of fish, including the cave flying fish (*Nemaaramis everetti*) and blind catfish (*Silurus furnessi*). Cave scorpions (*Chaerilus chapmani*) – which are poisonous but not deadly – are not uncommon. Other subterranean species include albino crabs, huntsman spiders, cave crickets, centipedes and snakes (which dine on swiftlets and bats). These creatures have been described as "living fossils... [which are] isolated survivors of ancient groups long since disappeared from Southeast Asia."

Gunung Mulu

The minimum time to allow for the climb is four days, three nights; tents are not required if you stay at Camps 1 and 2. The main summit route starts from the plankwalk at Park HQ heading towards Deer Cave. The Mulu walkway forks left after about 1 km. From the headquarters it is an easy four- to five-hour trek to Camp 1 at 150 m, where there is a shelter, built by the RGS/Sarawak government expedition in 1978. The second day is a long uphill slog (eight to 10 hours) to Camp 4 (1800 m), where there is also a shelter. Past Camp 3, the trail climbs steeply up Bukit Tumau, which affords good views over the park, and above which the last wild rhinoceros in Sarawak was shot in the mid-1940s. There are many pitcher plants (*Nepenthes lowii*) along this stretch of trail. From Camp 4, known as 'The Summit Camp', the path passes the helicopter pad, from where there are magnificent views of Gunung Benarat, the Melinau Gorge and Gunung Api. The final haul to the summit is steep; there are fixed ropes. Around the summit area, the *Nepenthes muluensis* pitcher plant is common – it is endemic to Mulu. From Camp 4 it takes 1½ hours to reach the summit, and a further seven hours back down the mountain to Camp 1.

Equipment Camps 1, 3 and 4 have water (providing the tank has been filled by rain water). Water should be boiled before drinking. It is necessary to bring your own food; in the rainy season it is wise to bring a gas cooking stove. A sleeping bag and waterproofs are also necessary and spare clothes, wrapped in a plastic bag, are a good idea.

Treks from Camp 5

For a three-day trip, a longboat will cost about RM370. It takes two to three hours, depending on the river level, from Park HQ to Kuala Berar; it is then a two- to three-hour trek (8 km) to Camp 5. Visitors to the Camp 5 area are also advised to plan their itinerary carefully as it is necessary to calculate how much food will be required and to carry it up there. There is a fairly well-equipped shelter with kitchen, bathrooms with shower and communal sleeping space which can house a maximum of 50 people. The camp is next to the Melinau River; river water should be boiled before drinking. There is a solar power generator to power radios, pump river water and for low lighting after dark.

Camp 5 is located in the Melinau Gorge, facing Gunung Benarat, about four to six hours upstream from the Park HQ. From the camp it is possible to trek up the gorge as well as to the Pinnacles on Gunung Api. It is advisable to hire a longboat for the duration of your time at and around Camp 5. The boat has to be abandoned at Kuala Berar, at the confluence of the Melinau and Berar rivers. It is only used for the first and last hours of the trip, but in the event of an emergency, there are no trails leading back to the Park HQ and there are stories of fever-stricken people being stuck in the jungle.

Melinau Gorge

Camp 5 nestles at the end of the gorge, across a fast-flowing section of the Melinau River and opposite the unclimbed 1580-m Gunung Benarat's stark, sheer limestone cliffs. The steep limestone ridges, which lead eventually to Gunung Api, comprise the east wall of the gorge. Heading out from Camp 5, the trail fizzles out after a few minutes. It takes an arduous two to three hours of endless river crossings and scrambles to reach a narrow chute of whitewater, under which is a large, deep and clear jungle pool with a convenient sandbank and plenty of large boulders to perch on. Alfred Russel Wallace's *Troides brookiana* – the majestic Rajah Brooke's birdwing – is particularly common at this little oasis, deep in undisturbed jungle. The walk involves criss-crossing through waist-deep, fast-flowing water and over stones that have been smoothed to a high polish over centuries: strong shoes are recommended as is a walking stick. Only occasionally in the walk upstream is it possible to glimpse the towering 600 m cliffs. Mulu can also be climbed from the south ridge of Melinau Gorge; it is three hours to Camp 1, five hours to Camp 3, a steep four- to five-hour climb to Camp 4, and finally two hours to the top.

The Pinnacles

The Pinnacles are a forest of sharp limestone needles three-quarters of the way up Gunung Api. Some of the pinnacles rise above treetops to heights of 45 m. The trail leaves from Camp 5, at the base of the Melinau Gorge. It is a very steep climb all the way and a maximum time of three to four hours is allowed to reach the pinnacles (1200 m); otherwise you must return. There is no source of water en route. It is not possible to reach Gunung Api from the Pinnacles. It is strongly recommended that climbers wear gloves as well as long-sleeved shirts, trousers and strong boots to protect themselves against cuts from the razor-sharp rocks. Explorers on Spenser St John's expedition to Mulu in 1856 were cut to shreds on the Pinnacles: "three of our men had already been sent back with severe wounds, whilst several of those left were much injured," he wrote, concluding that it was "the world's most nightmarish surface to travel over".

Gunung Api (Fire Mountain)

The vegetation is so dry at the summit that it is often set ablaze by lightning in the dry season. The story goes that the fires were so big that locals once thought the mountains were volcanoes. Some of the fires could be seen as far away as the Brunei coast. The summit trek takes a minimum of three days. At 1710 m, it is the tallest limestone outcrop in Borneo and, other than Gunung Benarat (on the other side of the gorge), it is probably the most difficult mountain to climb in Borneo. Many attempts to climb it ended in failure; two Berawans from Long Terawan finally made it to the top in 1978, one of them the grandson of Tama Nilong, the rhinoceros-hunter who had climbed Gunung Mulu in 1932. It is impossible to proceed upwards beyond the Pinnacles.

From Camp 5, cross the Melinau River and head down the **Limbang Trail** towards Lubang Cina. Less than 30 minutes down the trail, fork left along a new trail which leads along a ridge to the south of Gunung Benarat. Climbing higher, after about 40 minutes, the trail passes into an area of leached sandy soils called *kerangas* (heath) forest. This little patch of thinner jungle is a tangle of many varieties of pitcher plants.

It is possible to trek from Camp 5 to **Limbang**, although it is easier to do it the other way (see page 166).

Clearwater Cave

This part of the Clearwater System, on a small tributary of the Melinau River, is 107 km long. The cave passage – 75 km of which has been explored – links Clearwater Cave (Gua Ayer Jernih) with the **Cave of the Winds** (Lubang Angin), to the south. It was discovered in 1988. Clearwater is named after the jungle pool at the foot of the steps leading up to the cave mouth, where the longboats moor. Two species of monophytes – single-leafed plants – grow in the sunlight at the mouth of the cave. They only grow on limestone. A lighting system has been installed down the path to **Young Lady's Cave**, which ends in a 60-m-deep pothole.

On the cave walls are some helictites – coral-like lateral formations – and, even more dramatic, are the photokarsts, tiny needles of rock, all pointing towards the light. These are formed in much the same way as their monstrous cousins, the Pinnacles (see above), by vegetation (in this case algae), eating into and eroding the softer rock, leaving sharp points of harder rock which 'grow' at about 0.5 mm a year. Inside Clearwater you can hire a rowing boat for RM10 and follow the river for 1.5 km upstream, although the current is strong.

Clearwater can be reached by a 30-minute longboat ride from the Park HQ (RM27 per person). Individual travellers must charter a boat for a return trip. Tour agents build the cost of this trip into their package, which works out considerably cheaper. There are daily scheduled guided tours of the cave at 0945 or 1030 (RM10)

Deer Cave

ⓘ *An hour's trek along a plankwalk from Park HQ.*

This is another of Mulu's record breakers: it has the world's biggest cave mouth and the biggest cave passage, which is 2.2 km long and 220 m high at its highest point. Before its inclusion in the park, the cave had been a well-known hunting ground for deer attracted to the pools of salty water running off the guano. The silhouettes of some of the cave's limestone formations have been creatively interpreted; notably the profile of Abraham Lincoln. Adam's and Eve's Showers, at the east end of the cave, are hollow stalactites; water pressure increases when it rains. This darker section at the west end of Deer Cave is the preferred habitat of the naked bat. Albino earwigs live on the bats' oily skin and regularly drop off. The cave's east entrance opens onto 'The Garden of Eden' – a luxuriant patch of jungle, which was once part of the cave system until the roof collapsed. This separated Deer Cave and Green Cave, which lies adjacent to the east mouth; it's open only to caving expeditions.

The west end of the cave is home to several million wrinkle-lipped and horseshoe bats. Hundreds of thousands of these bats pour out of the cave at dusk. Bat hawks can often be seen swooping in for spectacular kills. The helipad, about 500 m south of the cave mouth, provides excellent vantage points. VIPs' helicopters, arriving for the show, are said to have disturbed the bats in recent years. From the analysis of the tonnes of saline bat guano, scientists conclude that they make an 80-km dash to the coast for meals of insects washed down with seawater. Cave cockroaches eat the guano, ensuring that the cavern does not become choked with what locals call 'black snow'.

Lang's Cave

Part of the same hollow mountain as Deer Cave, Lang's Cave is less well known but its formations are more beautiful and it contains impressive curtain stalactites and intricate coral-like helictites. The cave is well lit and protected by bus-stop-style plastic tunnels.

The Sarawak Chamber

Discovered in 1984, this chamber is 600 m long, 450 m wide and 100 m high – big enough, it is said, to accommodate 40 jumbo jets wing-tip to wing-tip and eight nose-to-tail. It is the largest natural chamber in the world. It is now possible for cavers with some experience to visit the cave, with the approval of the Park Manager. It is a three-hour trek to the cave following the summit trail. Access to the cave is through Gua Nasib Bagus, following a river trail bordered by 50-m-high sheer rock faces on both sides for 800 m. After a further scramble, cavers reach the dark mouth of the chamber. It is not permitted to enter any further as it is considered too dangerous. Guide fees are RM500 for a group of up to five.

Bario and the Kelabit Highlands → *Colour map 4, C2.*

Bario (Bareo) lies in the Kelabit Highlands, a plateau 1000 m above sea level close to the Kalimantan border in Indonesia. The undulating Bario valley is surrounded by mountains and fed by countless small streams that in turn feed into a maze of irrigation canals.

Ins and outs

Bario is only accessible by air or via a seven-day trek from Marudi. For information on Bario and the Kelabits, see www.kelabit.net. The best time to visit the area is between March and October.

Background

The local Kelabits' skill in harnessing water has allowed them to practise wet rice cultivation rather than the more common slash-and-burn hill rice techniques. Fragrant Bario rice is prized in Sarawak and commands a premium in the coastal markets. The more temperate climate of the Kelabit Highlands also allows the cultivation of a wide range of fruit and vegetables.

The plateau's near-impregnable ring of mountains effectively cut the Kelabit off from the outside world; it is the only area in Borneo which was never penetrated by Islam. In 1911 the Resident of Baram mounted an expedition which ventured into the mountains to ask the Kelabit to stop raiding the Brooke Government's subjects. It took the expedition 17 days to cross the Tamu Abu mountain range, to the west of Bario. The Kelabit were then brought under the control of the Sarawak government.

The most impressive mountain in the Bario area is the distinctive twin peak of the sheer-faced 2043 m **Bukit Batu Lawi** to the northwest of Bario. The Kelabit traditionally believed the mountain had an evil spirit and so never went near it. Today such superstitions are a thing of the past since locals are mostly evangelical Christians.

In 1945, the plateau was selected as the only possible parachute drop zone in North Borneo not captured by the Japanese. The Allied Special Forces that parachuted into Bario were led by Tom Harrisson, who later became curator of the Sarawak Museum and made the famous archaeological discoveries at Niah Caves (see page 146). His expedition formed an irregular tribal army against the Japanese, which gained control over large areas of North Borneo in the following months.

Treks around Bario

Because of the rugged terrain surrounding the plateau, the area mainly attracts serious mountaineers. There are many trails to the longhouses around the plateau area, however. Treks to Bario can be organized through travel agents in Miri, see page 155. Guides can also be hired in Bario and surrounding longhouses for RM30-40 per day. It is best to go through the Penghulu, Ngiap Ayu, the Kelabit chief. He goes around visiting many of the longhouses in the area once a month. It is recommended that visitors to Bario come with sleeping bags and camping equipment. There are no formal facilities for tourists and provisions should be brought from Miri or Marudi. There are no banks or money changers in Bario.

Several of the surrounding mountains can be climbed from Bario, but they are, without exception, difficult climbs. Even on walks just around the Bario area, guides are essential as trails are poorly marked. The lower 'female' peak of **Bukit Batu Lawi** can be climbed without equipment, but the sheer-sided 'male' peak requires proper rock climbing equipment; it was first scaled in 1986. **Gunung Murudi** (2423 m) is the highest mountain in Sarawak and it is a very tough climb.

Limbang → *Colour map 4, B2.*

Limbang is the administrative centre for the Fifth Division and was ceded to the Brooke government by the Sultan of Brunei in 1890. The Trusan Valley, to the east of the wedge of Brunei, had been ceded to Sarawak in 1884. Very few tourists reach Limbang or Lawas but they are good stopping-off points for more adventurous routes to **Sabah** and **Brunei**. Limbang is the finger of Sarawak territory which splits Brunei in two. To contact the **Residents' Office** ① *T085-21960*.

Sights

Limbang's **Old Fort** was built in 1897, renovated in 1966, and was used as the administrative centre. During the Brooke era, half the ground floor was used as a jail. It is now a centre of religious instruction, Majlis Islam. Limbang is famous for its **Pasar Tamu** every Friday, where jungle and native produce is sold. Limbang also has an attractive small museum, **Muzium Wilayah** ① *400 m south of the centre along Jln Kubu, Tue-Sun 0900-1800*. Housed in a wooden beige and white villa, the museum has a collection of ethnic artefacts from the region, including basketry, musical instruments and weapons. To the right of the museum, a small road climbs the hill to a park with a man-made lake.

To trek to the **Gunung Mulu National Park** (see page 159), take a car south to Medamit; from there hire a longboat upriver to Mulu Madang, an Iban longhouse (three hours, depending on water level). Alternatively, go further upriver to Kuala Terikan (six to seven hours when the water's low, four hours when it's high) where there is a simple zinc-roofed camp. From there take a longboat one hour up the Terikan River to Lubang China, which is the start of a two-hour trek along a well-used trail to Camp 5. There is a park rangers' camp about 20 minutes out of Kuala Terikan where it is possible to obtain permits and arrange for a guide to meet you at Camp 5. The longboats are cheaper to hire in the wet season.

Lawas

Lawas District was ceded to Sarawak in 1905. The Limbang River, which cuts through the town, is the main transport route. It is possible to travel from Miri to Bandar Seri Begawan (Brunei) by road, then on to Limbang and Lawas. From Lawas there are direct buses to Kota Kinabalu in Sabah.

For Sleeping and Eating price codes and other relevant information, see Essentials pages 23-27.

⊜ Sleeping

Gunung Mulu National Park *p159, map p160*

Park chalets must be booked in advance at the **National Parks and Wildlife Office Forest Department** in Miri (T085-792300 or T085-792301, enquiries@mulupark.com), www.mulupark.com. Booking fee is RM20 per party (maximum 10 people). Bookings must be confirmed 5 days before visit.

AL-A Royal Mulu Resort, Sungai Melinau, Muku, Miri, a 20-min (RM5) boat ride downstream from Park HQ, T085-790100, www.royal muluresort.com. This resort has 188 well-designed rooms with cable TV and a/c. There is also a pool, a gym, a spa and restaurants. Travellers who are desperate to visit the park and find that all the other accommodation is booked can usually find a (pricey) bed here. It has sparked much resentment among local tribespeople. The Berawan claim the resort's land as theirs by customary right.

A-E Park HQ. The park also offers its own accommodation. Top of the range are the **de luxe longhouses** (**A**) which have attached bathroom, a/c, and 4 single beds, or a twin share. For 4 people sharing, it works out at RM41 each and breakfast is included. **Rainforest Rooms** (**B**) sleep up to 4 and have fans and attached bathroom, at just over RM25 per person. There is also a **hostel** (**C**) with 21 dorm beds, fan and shared bathrooms for RM37 per person. At Camp 5 is a **simple hostel** (**D**) with kitchen for self-catering, mats for sleeping and shared bathrooms. There are also simple wooden shelters on the summit trail (**E**). For both of these, bring your own sleeping bag.

D Melinau Canteen, T085-657884. One of several hostels just outside the park. Privately owned, with dorm beds, about 5 mins' walk downstream from the Park HQ on the other bank of the river.

Camping

E Camping is only allowed at the campsite at Park HQ (RM10). Bring your own sleeping bag.

Bario and the Kelabit Highlands *p165*

C Bariew Lodge, T085-791038, bariew lodge@yahoo.com. Popular backpacker option with simple rooms and a pleasant lounge area. All meals are included, as are airport transfers. Guide service offered for RM65 per half day. Recommended.

C-D De Plateau Lodge, munney_bala@kelabit.net. 2 km from the airport, this wooden house has plenty of funky native decor and offers simple rooms with meals included. There's a pleasant communal area, and guide services for treks and walks, as well as birdwatching trips around the highlands at RM65 per half day.

D Tarawe. A well-run place to stay with a good source of information. Simple rooms and a veranda overlooking a fish pond. Cable TV and electricity after dark. Recommended.

Limbang *p166*

Limbang has become a sex stop for Bruneians, whose government takes a more hardline attitude to such moral transgressions, and consequently many hotels and guesthouses have a fair share of short-time guests.

B Centre Point Hotel, T085-212922. Newish place, with a/c and restaurant, tops Limbang's limited bill of hotels.

B-C Metro, Lot 781, Jln Bangkita, T085-211133, F211051. A fairly new addition to Limbang's mid-range places, with less than 30 small but clean rooms, all with a/c, TV, fridge, good quality beds. Recommended.

B-C Muhibbah, Lot T790, Bank St, T085-213705, F212153. Located in town centre, this place has seen better days, but rooms are fairly clean with a/c, TV and bathroom.

B-C National Inn, 62a Jln Buangsiol, T085-212922, F212282. Probably the best of the 3 hotels along the river, comfortable a/c rooms with TV, minibar. Higher rates for river view.

Lawas p166

A-B Country Park Hotel, Lot 235, Jln Trusan, T085-85522. A/c and restaurant.
C Lawas Federal, 8 Jln Masjid Baru, T085-85115. A/c and restaurant.
D Hup Guan Lodging House, T085-85362. Some a/c, can be noisy, but the rooms are clean and spacious and reasonable value for money.

🍴 Eating

Gunung Mulu National Park p159, map p160

There are stoves and cooking utensils available and the small store at Park HQ also sells basic supplies. The **Café Mulu** at Park HQ (0730-2100) has a range of simple Asian and Western dishes. Alcohol is not available but guests are allowed to bring their own. As an alternative, cross the suspension bridge and walk alongside the road to the first house on the left; down the bank from here is the **Mulu Canteen**, which fronts onto the river. There is also the **Melinau Canteen**, just downriver from the Park HQ. There is a small shop with basic supplies at Long Pala. All tour companies with their own accommodation offer food.

Limbang p166

🍴 **Tong Lok**. A/c Chinese restaurant next to **National Inn**, gruesome pink tablecloths and fluorescent lighting, but good Chinese food.
🍴 **Hai Hong**, 1 block south of **Maggie's**. Simple coffee shop – good for breakfast with fried egg and chips on the menu.
🍴 **Maggie's Café** on the riverside near **National Inn**. Chinese coffee shop, pleasant location, tables outside next to river in the evening. Braziers set up in evening for good grilled fish on banana leaf. Recommended.

🎊 Festivals and events

Limbang p166

May The (movable) Buffalo Racing Festival marks the end of the harvesting season.

▲▲ Activities and tours

Gunung Mulu National Park p159, map p160

Visitors are recommended to go through one of the Miri-based travel agents (see page 155). The average cost of a Mulu package (per person) is RM750 (4 days/ 3 nights) or RM850 (6 days/5 nights). Independent travellers will find it more expensive arranging the trip on their own.

Limbang p166

Sitt Travel, T085-420567. Specializes in treks in this area and is the ticketing agent for Miri tour operators.

⊖ Transport

Gunung Mulu National Park p159, map p160

Longboats can be chartered privately from Park HQ (maximum 10 people per boat). The cost is calculated on a rather complicated system which includes a rate for the boat, a charge for the engine based on its horsepower, a separate payment for the driver and frontman, and then fuel. Total costs can be over RM100. How far these boats can get upriver depends on the season. They often have to be hauled over rapids whatever the time of year.

Air

Daily flights from **Miri** to Mulu, 20 mins. The airstrip is just downriver from Park HQ. **MASwings** currently has 2 flights daily from Miri (book well in advance). The price of a flight is only marginally more expensive than taking the bus and boat from Miri and is much faster. The airline operates thrice-weekly flights to **Kuching** and daily flights to **Kota Kinabalu** via Miri.

Bus/boat/taxi

Bus or taxi from **Miri** to **Marudi** express boat jetty near **Kuala Baram** at mouth of the Baram River (see page 157). Regular express boats from **Kuala Baram** to **Marudi** (3 hrs RM20) from 0800 until about 1500. One express boat per day (leaves at 1200) from Marudi to **Long Terawan** on the Tutoh River, via **Long Apoh** (RM25). During the dry season express boats cannot reach Long Terawan and terminate at Long Panai on the Tutoh River, where longboats continue to Long Terawan (RM25). Longboats leave Long Terawan for Mulu Park HQ: this used to be regular and relatively cheap; now that most people travel to Mulu by air, longboats need to be privately chartered – an expensive business at RM350 a pop. Mulu Park HQ is 1½ hrs up the Melinau River, a tributary of the Tutoh. As you approach the park from Long Terawan the Tutoh River narrows and becomes shallower; there are 14 rapids before the Melinau River, which forms the park boundary. When the water is low, the trip can be very slow and involve pulling the boat over the shallows; this accounts for high charter rates. The first jetty on the Melinau River is **Long Pala**, where most of the tour companies have accommodation. The Park HQ is another 15 mins upriver. Longboats returning to Long Terawan leave the headquarters at dawn each day, calling at jetties en route.

Bario and the Kelabit Highlands *p165*
Air
The only access to Bario is by air on MASwings. Bario's airstrip is very small and because of its position, flights are often cancelled due to mist. Flights are always booked up. There is at least 1 flight a day

(2 flights on Tue, Thu, Fri, Sun) on MASwings. There is also one connection a day to **Marudi**.

Walking
It is a 7-day trek from **Marudi** to Bario, sleeping in longhouses en route. This trip should be organized through a Miri travel agent (see page 155).

Limbang *p166*
Air
There are 2 daily connections with **Miri** with MASwings. The airport is 5 km from town and taxis ferry passengers in.

Boat
Regular connections with **Lawas**, depart early in the morning (2 hrs, RM20). There is also an early-morning express departure to **Labuan**. Regular boat connections with **Bandar Seri Begawan**, Brunei (30 mins, RM20).

Lawas *p166*
Air
Frequent connections with **Miri** and a twice-weekly flight to **Ba'kelalan** with MASwings.

Boat
Regular connections to **Limbang**, 2 hrs. Daily morning boat departures for **Brunei**.

Bus
Connections with **Merapok** on the Sarawak/Sabah border (RM8). From here there are connections to **Beaufort** in Sabah. Twice-daily connections with **KK** (4 hrs RM26).

Background

History
Sarawak earned its place in the archaeological textbooks when a 37,000-year-old human skull belonging to a boy of about 15 was unearthed in the Niah Caves in 1958 (see page 144), predating the earliest relics found on the Malay Peninsula by about 30,000 years. The caves were continuously inhabited for tens of thousands of years and many shards of palaeolithic and neolithic pottery, tools and jewellery as well as carved burial boats have been excavated at the site. There are also prehistoric cave paintings. In the first

millennium AD, the Niah Caves were home to a prosperous community, which traded birds' nests, hornbill ivory, bezoar stones, rhinoceros horns and other jungle produce with Chinese traders in exchange for porcelain and beads.

Some of Sarawak's tribes may be descended from these cave people, although others, notably the Iban shifting cultivators, migrated from Kalimantan's Kapuas River valley from the 16th to 19th centuries. Malay Orang Laut, sea people, migrated to Sarawak's coasts and made a living from fishing, trading and piracy. At the height of Sumatra's Srivijayan Empire in the 11th and 12th centuries, many Sumatran Malays migrated to north Borneo. Chinese traders were active along the Sarawak coast from as early as the seventh century: Chinese coins and Han pottery have been discovered at the mouth of the Sarawak River.

From the 14th century right up to the 20th century, Sarawak's history was inextricably intertwined with that of the neighbouring Sultanate of Brunei, which, until the arrival of the White Rajahs of Sarawak, held sway over the coastal areas of north Borneo. For a more detailed account of how Sarawak's White Rajahs came to whittle away the sultan's territory and expand into the vacuum of his receding empire, see Robert Payne's *The White Rajahs of Sarawak*.

Enter James Brooke

As the Sultanate of Brunei began to decline around the beginning of the 18th century, the Malays of coastal Sarawak attempted to break free from their tributary overlord. They claimed an independent ancestry from Brunei and exercised firm control over the Dayak tribes inland and upriver. But in the early 19th century Brunei started to reassert its power over them, dispatching Pangiran Mahkota from the Brunei court in 1827 to govern Sarawak and supervise the mining of high-grade antimony ore, exported to Singapore to be used in medicine and as an alloy. The name 'Sarawak' is from the Malay word *serawak (antimony)*.

Mahkota founded Kuching, but relations with the local Malays became strained and Mahkota's problems were compounded by the marauding Ibans of the Saribas and Skrang rivers who raided coastal communities. In 1836 the local Malay chiefs, led by Datu Patinggi Ali, rebelled against Governor Mahkota, prompting the Sultan of Brunei to send his uncle, Rajah Muda Hashim to suppress the uprising. But Hashim failed to quell the disturbances and the situation deteriorated when the rebels approached the Sultan of Sambas, now in northwest Kalimantan, for help from the Dutch. Then, in 1839, James Brooke sailed up the Sarawak River to Kuching.

Hashim was desperate to regain control and Brooke, in the knowledge that the British would support any action that countered the threat of Dutch influence, struck a deal with him. He pressed Hashim to grant him the governorship of Sarawak in exchange for suppressing the rebellion, which he duly did. In 1842 Brooke became Rajah of Sarawak. Pangiran Mahkota – the now disenfranchised former governor of Sarawak – formed an alliance with an Iban pirate chief on the Skrang River, while another Brunei prince, Pangiran Usop, joined Illanun pirates. Malaysian historian J Kathirithamby-Wells wrote: "… piracy and politics became irrevocably linked and Brooke's battle against his political opponents became advertised as a morally justified war against the pirate communities of the coast."

The suppression of piracy in the 19th century became a full-time job for the Sarawak and Brunei rulers, although the court of Brunei was well known to have derived a large chunk of its income from piracy. Rajah James Brooke believed that as long as pirates were free to pillage the coast, commerce wouldn't grow and his kingdom would never develop; ridding Sarawak's estuaries of pirates – both Iban (Sea Dayaks) and Illanun – became an act of political survival. In *The White Rajahs of Sarawak*, Robert Payne wrote:

"Nearly every day people came to Kuching with tales about the pirates: how they had landed in a small creek, made their way to a village, looted everything in sight, murdered everyone they could lay their hands on, and then vanished as swiftly as they came. The Sultan of Brunei was begging for help against them."

Anti-piracy missions afforded James Brooke an excuse to extend his kingdom, as he worked his way up the coasts, 'pacifying' the Sea Dayak pirates. Brooke declared war on them and with the help of Royal Naval Captain Henry Keppel (of latter-day Singapore's Keppel Shipyard fame), he led a number of punitive raids against the Iban Sea Dayaks in 1833, 1834 and 1849. "The assaults", wrote DJM Tate in *Rajah Brooke's Borneo*, "largely achieved their purpose and were applauded in the Straits, but the appalling loss of life incurred upset many drawing room humanitarians in Britain." There were an estimated 25,000 pirates living along the North Borneo coast when Brooke became Rajah. He led many expeditions against them, culminating in his notorious battle against the Saribas pirate fleet in 1849.

In that incident, Brooke ambushed and killed hundreds of Saribas Dayaks at Batang Maru. The barbarity of the ambush (which was reported in the *Illustrated London News*) outraged public opinion in Britain and in Singapore; a commission in Singapore acquitted Brooke, but badly damaged his prestige. In the British parliament, he was cast as a 'mad despot' who had to be prevented from committing further massacres. But the action led the Sultan of Brunei to grant him the Saribas and Skrang districts (now Sarawak's Second Division) in 1853, marking the beginning of the Brooke dynasty's relentless expansionist drive. Eight years later, James Brooke persuaded the sultan to give him what became Sarawak's Third Division, after he drove out the Illanun pirates who disrupted the sago trade from Mukah and Oya, around Bintulu.

In 1857, James Brooke ran into more trouble. Chinese Hakka goldminers, who had been in Bau (further up the Sarawak River) longer than he had been in Kuching, had grown resentful of his attempts to stamp out the opium trade and their secret societies. They attacked Kuching, set the Malay kampongs ablaze and killed several European officials; Brooke escaped by swimming across the river from his astana. His nephew, Charles, led a group of Skrang Dayaks in pursuit of the Hakka invaders, who fled across the border into Dutch Borneo; about 1000 were killed by the Ibans on the way; 2500 survived. Robert Payne writes: "The fighting lasted for more than a month. From time to time Dayaks would return with strings of heads, which they cleaned and smoked over slow fires, especially happy when they could do this in full view of the Chinese in the bazaars who sometimes recognized people they had known." Payne says Brooke was plagued by guilt over how he handled the Chinese rebellion, for so many deaths could not easily be explained away. Neither James nor Charles ever fully trusted the Chinese again, although the Teochew, Cantonese and Hokkien merchants in Kuching never caused them any trouble.

The second generation: Rajah Charles Brooke

Charles Johnson (who changed his name to Brooke after his elder brother, Brooke Johnson, had been disinherited by James for insubordination) became the second Rajah of Sarawak in 1863. He ruled for nearly 50 years. Charles did not have James Brooke's forceful personality, and was much more reclusive – probably as a result of working in remote jungle outposts for 10 years in government service. Robert Payne noted that "in James Brooke there was something of the knight errant at the mercy of his dream. Charles was the pure professional, a stern soldier who thought dreaming was the occupation of fools. There was no nonsense about him." Despite this he engendered great loyalty in his administrators, who worked hard for little reward.

Charles maintained his uncle's consultative system of government and formed a Council Negeri, or national council, of his top government officials, Malay leaders and tribal headmen, which met every few years to hammer out policy changes. His frugal financial management meant that by 1877 Sarawak was no longer in debt and the economy gradually expanded. But it was not wealthy, and had few natural resources; its soils proved unsuitable for agriculture. In the 1880s, Charles's faith in the Chinese community was sufficiently restored to allow Chinese immigration, and the government subsidized the new settlers. By using 'friendly' downriver Dayak groups to subdue belligerent tribes upriver, Charles managed to pacify the interior by 1880.

When Charles took over from his ailing uncle in 1863 he proved to be even more of an expansionist. In 1868 he tried to take control of the Baram River valley, but London did not approve secession of the territory until 1882, when it became the Fourth Division. In 1884, Charles acquired the Trusan Valley from the Sultan of Brunei, and in 1890, he annexed Limbang ending a six-year rebellion by local chiefs against the sultan. The two territories were united to form the Fifth Division, after which Sarawak completely surrounded Brunei. In 1905, the British North Borneo Chartered Company gave up the Lawas Valley to Sarawak too. "By 1890," writes Robert Payne, "Charles was ruling over a country as large as England and Scotland with the help of about 20 European officers." When the First World War broke out in 1914, Charles was in England and he ruled Sarawak from Cirencester.

The third generation: Charles Vyner Brooke

In 1916, at the age of 86, Charles handed power to his eldest son, Charles Vyner Brooke, and he died the following year. Vyner was 42 when he became Rajah and had already served his father's government for nearly 20 years. "Vyner was a man of peace, who took no delight in bloodshed and ruled with humanity and compassion," wrote Robert Payne. He was a delegator by nature, and under him the old paternalistic style of government gave way to a more professional bureaucracy. On the centenary of the Brooke administration in September 1941, Vyner promulgated a written constitution, and renounced his autocratic powers in favour of working in cooperation with a Supreme Council. This was opposed by his nephew and heir, Anthony Brooke, who saw it as a move to undermine his succession. To protest against this, and his uncle's decision to appoint a mentally deranged Muslim Englishman as his Chief Secretary, Anthony left for Singapore. The Rajah dismissed him from the service in September 1941. Three months later the Japanese Imperial Army invaded; Vyner Brooke was in Australia at the time, and his younger brother, Bertram, was ill in London.

Japanese troops took Kuching on Christmas Day 1941 having captured the Miri oilfield a few days earlier. European administrators were interned and many later died. A Kuching-born Chinese, Albert Kwok, led an armed resistance against the Japanese in neighbouring British North Borneo (Sabah) – see page 274 – but in Sarawak, there was no organized guerrilla movement. Iban tribespeople instilled fear into the occupying forces, however, by roaming the jungle taking Japanese heads, which were proudly added to much older longhouse head galleries. Despite the Brooke regime's century-long effort to stamp out headhunting, the practice was encouraged by Tom Harrisson (see box page 173) who parachuted into the Kelabit Highlands towards the end of the Second World War and put together an irregular army of upriver tribesmen to fight the Japanese. He offered them 'ten-bob-a-nob' for Japanese heads. Australian forces liberated Kuching on 11 September 1945 and Sarawak was placed under Australian military administration for seven months.

After the war, the Colonial Office in London decided the time had come to bring Sarawak into the modern era, replacing the anachronistic White Rajahs, introducing an

Tom Harrisson: life in the fast lane

Reputed to be one of the most important figures in the development of archaeology in Southeast Asia, Tom Harrisson, the charismatic 'egomaniac', put Borneo and Sarawak on the map.

Tom Harrisson loved Sarawak and, it would seem, Sarawak loved him. He first visited Sarawak in 1932 as part of a Royal Geographical Expedition sent, along with around 150 kg of Cadbury's chocolate, to collect flora and fauna from one of the world's great natural treasure stores. Instead Harrisson found himself entranced by the territory's human populations and so the love affair began.

By all accounts, Harrisson was a difficult fellow – the sort that imperial Britain produced in very large numbers indeed. He was a womaniser with a particular penchant for other people's spouses, he could be horribly abusive to his fellow workers and he apparently revelled in putting down uppity academics. But he was also instrumental in putting Sarawak, and Borneo on the map and in raising awareness of the ways in which economic and social change was impacting on Sarawak's tribal peoples.

Before taking up the curatorship of the Sarawak Museum in 1947 Harrisson also distinguished himself as a war hero, parachuting into the jungle and organizing around 1000 headhunters to terrorize the Japanese. All in all, Tom Harrisson led life in the fast lane.

Those wanting to read a good biography of Harrisson should get hold of *The Most Offending Soul Alive* by Judith M Heimann, Honolulu, Hawaii University Press, 1998.

---

education system and building a rudimentary infrastructure. The Brookes had become an embarrassment to the British government as they continued to squabble among themselves. Anthony Brooke desperately wanted to claim what he felt was his, while the Colonial Office wanted Sarawak to become a crown colony or revert to Malay rule. No one was sure whether Sarawak wanted the Brookes back or not.

The end of empire

In February 1946 the ageing Vyner shocked his brother Bertram and his nephew Anthony, the Rajah Muda (or heir apparent), by issuing a proclamation urging the people of Sarawak to accept the King of England as their ruler. In doing so he effectively handed the country over to Britain. Vyner thought the continued existence of Sarawak as the private domain of the Brooke family an anachronism; but Anthony thought it a betrayal. The British government sent a commission to Sarawak to ascertain what the people wanted. In May 1946, the Council Negeri agreed – by a 19-16 majority – to transfer power to Britain, provoking protests and demonstrations and resulting in the assassination of the British governor by a Malay in Sibu in 1949. He and three other anti-cessionists were sentenced to death. Two years later, Anthony Brooke, who remained deeply resentful about the demise of the Brooke Dynasty, abandoned his claim and urged his supporters to end their campaign.

As a British colony, Sarawak's economy expanded and oil and timber production increased, which funded the much-needed expansion of education and health services. As with British North Borneo (Sabah), Britain was keen to give Sarawak political independence and, following Malaysian independence in 1957, saw the best means to this end as being through the proposal of Malaysian Prime Minister Tunku Abdul Rahman. The prime minister suggested the formation of a federation to include Singapore, Sarawak, Sabah and

Brunei as well as the Peninsula. In the end, Brunei opted out, Singapore left after two years, but Sarawak and Sabah joined the federation, having accepted the recommendations of the British government. Indonesia's President Sukarno denounced the move, claiming it was all part of a neo-colonialist conspiracy. He declared a policy of confrontation – **Konfrontasi**. A United Nations commission which was sent to ensure that the people of Sabah and Sarawak wanted to be part of Malaysia reported that Indonesia's objections were unfounded.

Communists had been active in Sarawak since the 1930s. The Konfrontasi afforded the Sarawak Communist Organization (SCO) Jakarta's support against the Malaysian government. The SCO joined forces with the North Kalimantan Communist Party (NKCP) and were trained and equipped by Indonesia's President Sukarno. But following Jakarta's brutal suppression of the Indonesian Communists, the Partai Komunis Indonesia (PKI), in the wake of the attempted coup in 1965, Sarawak's Communists fled back across the Indonesian border, along with their Kalimantan comrades. There they continued to wage guerrilla war against the Malaysian government throughout the 1970s. The Sarawak state government offered amnesties to guerrillas wanting to come out of hiding. In 1973 the NKCP leader surrendered along with 482 other guerrillas. A handful remained in the jungle, most of them in the hills around Kuching. The last surrendered in 1990.

Politics and modern Sarawak

In 1957 Kuala Lumpur was keen to have Sarawak and Sabah in the Federation of Malaysia and offered the two states a degree of autonomy, allowing their local governments control over state finances, agriculture and forestry. Sarawak's racial mix was reflected in its chaotic state politics. The Ibans dominated the Sarawak National Party (SNAP), which provided the first chief minister, Datuk Stephen Kalong Ningkan. He raised a storm over Kuala Lumpur's introduction of Bahasa Malaysia in schools and complained bitterly about the federal government's policy of filling the Sarawakian civil service with Malays from the Peninsula. An 'us' and 'them' mentality developed: in Sarawak, the Malay word *semenanjung* (Peninsula) was used to label the newcomers. To many, *semenanjung* was Malaysia, Sarawak was Sarawak.

In 1966 the federal government ousted the SNAP, and a new Muslim-dominated government led by the Sarawak Alliance took over in Kuching. But there was still strong political opposition to federal encroachment. Throughout the 1970s, as in Sabah, Sarawak's strongly Muslim government drew the state closer and closer to the Peninsula: it supported *Rukunegara* – the policy of Islamization – and promoted the use of Bahasa Malaysia. Muslims make up less than one-third of the population of Sarawak. The Malays, Melanaus and Chinese communities grew rich from the timber industry; the Ibans and the Orang Ulu (the upriver tribespeople) saw little in the way of development. They did not reap the benefits of the expansion of education and social services, they were unable to get public sector jobs and, to make matters worse, logging firms were encroaching on their native lands and threatening their traditional lifestyles.

It has only been in more recent years that the tribespeoples' political voice has been heard at all. In 1983, Iban members of SNAP – which was a part of former Prime Minister Dr Mahathir Mohamad's ruling Barisan Nasional (National Front) coalition – split to form the Party Bansa Dayak Sarawak (PBDS), which, although it initially remained in the coalition, became more outspoken on native affairs. At about the same time, international outrage was sparked over the exploitation of Sarawak's tribespeople by politicians and businessmen involved in the logging industry. The plight of the Penan hunter-gatherers came to world attention due to their blockades of logging roads and the resulting publicity highlighted the rampant corruption and greed that characterized modern Sarawak's political economy.

The National Front remain firmly in control in Sarawak. But unlike neighbouring Sabah, Sarawak's politicians are not dominated by the centre. The chief minister of Sarawak is Abduly Taib Mahmud, a Melanau, and his Parti Pesaka Bumiputra Bersatu is a member of the UMNO-dominated (United Malays National Organisation) National Front. But in Sarawak itself UMNO wields little power.

The ruling National Front easily won the 1999 election in Sarawak, successfully playing on voters' local concerns and grievances. The problem for the opposition is that local people think it is the state legislature that can help, not the federal parliament in KL, which seems distant and ineffective. So UMNO does not have a presence and it is the Parti Pesaka Bumiputra Bersatu which represents Sarawak in the National Front.

The challenge of getting the voters out in the most remote areas of the country was clearly shown in Long Lidom. There it cost the government RM65,000 to provide a helicopter to poll just seven Punan Busang in a longhouse on the Upper Kajang, close to the border with Indonesia. Datuk Omar of the Election Commission said that mounting the general election in Sarawak, with its 28 parliamentary seats, was a "logistical nightmare". Along with a small air force of helicopters, the Commission used 1032 long boats, 15 speed boats and 3054 land cruisers. The Commission's workforce numbered a cool 13,788 workers in a state with a population of just two million.

The 2006 state elections in Sarawak was won convincingly by the Barisan Nasional, winning 62 out of the 71 contested seats.

Today there are many in Sarawak as well as in Sabah who wish their governments had opted out of the Federation, as did Brunei. Sarawak is of great economic importance to Malaysia, thanks to its oil, gas and timber. The state now accounts for more than one-third of Malaysia's petroleum production (worth more than US$800 million per year) and more than half of its natural gas. As with neighbouring Sabah however, 95% of Sarawak's oil and gas revenues go directly into federal coffers.

Culture

People

About a third of the population is made up of Iban tribespeople who live in longhouses on the lower reaches of the rivers. Chinese immigrants, whose forebears arrived during the 19th century, make up another third. A fifth of the population is Malay; most are native Sarawakians, but some came from the Peninsula after the state joined the Malaysian Federation in 1963. The rest of Sarawak's inhabitants are indigenous tribal groups, of which the main ones are the Melanau, the Bidayuh and upriver Orang Ulu such as the Kenyah, Kayan and Kelabits; the Penan are among Southeast Asia's few remaining hunter-gatherers. The population of the state is almost 2.2 million. The people of the interior are classified as Proto-Malays and Deutero-Malays and are divided into at least 12 distinct tribal groups including Iban, Murut (see page 281), Melanau, Bidayuh, Kenyah, Kayan, Kelabit and Penan.

Bidayuh In the 19th century, Sarawak's European community called the Bidayuh Land Dayaks, mainly to distinguish them from the Iban Sea Dayak pirates. The Bidayuh make up 8.4% of the population and are concentrated to the west of the Kuching area, towards the Kalimantan border. There are also related groups living in west Kalimantan. They were virtually saved from extinction by the White Rajahs, because the Bidayuh were quiet, mild-mannered people, they

The Iban in Borneo

The Iban are an outgoing people and usually extend a warm welcome to visitors. Iban women are skilled weavers; even today a girl is not considered eligible until she has proven her skills at the loom by weaving a ceremonial textile, the *pua kumbu* (see page 184). The Ibans love to party and, during the harvest festival in June, visitors are welcome to drink copious amounts of *tuak* (rice wine) and dance through the night.

Probably because they were shifting cultivators, the Iban remained in closely bonded family groups and were a classless society. Historian Mary Turnbull said: "they retained their pioneer social organization of nuclear family groups living together in long-houses and did not evolve more sophisticated political institutions. Long-settled families acquired prestige, but the Ibans did not merge into tribes and had neither chiefs, rakyat class, nor slaves".

The Iban have a very easygoing attitude to love and sex, which is best explained in Redmond O'Hanlon's book *Into the Heart of Borneo*. Free love is the general rule among Iban communities that have not become evangelical Christians although, once married, the Iban divorce rate is low and they are monogamous.

were at the mercy of the Iban headhunters and the Brunei Malays who taxed and enslaved them. The Brookes afforded them protection from both groups.

Most live in modern longhouses and are dry rice farmers. Their traditional long-houses are exactly like Iban ones, but without the tanju veranda. The Bidayuh tribe comprises five sub-groups: the Jagoi, Biatah, Bukar-Sadong, Selakau and Lara, all of whom live in far west Sarawak. They are the state's best traditional plumbers and are known for their ingenious gravity-fed bamboo water systems. They are bamboo specialists, making it into everything from cooking pots to finely carved musical instruments (see page 184). Among other tribal groups, the Bidayuh are renowned for their rice wine and sugarcane toddy. Henry Keppel, who with Rajah James Brooke fought the Bidayuh's dreaded enemies, the Sea Dayaks, described an evening spent with the Land Dayaks thus: "They ate and drank, and asked for everything, but stole nothing."

Chinese Hakka goldminers had already settled at Bau, upriver from Kuching, long before James Brooke arrived in 1839. Cantonese, Teochew and Hokkien merchants also set up in Kuching, but the Brookes did not warm to the Chinese community, believing the traders would exploit the Dayak communities if they were allowed to venture upriver. In the 1880s, however, Rajah Charles Brooke allowed the immigration of large numbers of Chinese – mainly Foochow – who settled in coastal towns like Sibu. Many became farmers and ran rubber smallholdings. The Sarawak government subsidized the immigrants for the first year. During the Brooke era, the only government-funded schools were for Malays and few tribal people ever received a formal education. The Chinese, however, set up and funded their own private schools and many attended Christian missionary schools, leading to the formation of a relatively prosperous, educated elite. Today the Chinese comprise nearly a third of the state's population and are almost as numerous as the Iban; they are the middle-men, traders, shopkeepers, timber towkays (magnates) and express boat owners.

Iban Sarawak's best-known erstwhile headhunters make up nearly a third of the state's population and while some have moved to coastal towns for work, many remain in their

Skulls in the longhouse

Although headhunting has been largely stamped out in Borneo, there is still the odd reported case once every few years. But until the early 20th century, headhunting was commonplace among many Dayak tribes and the Iban were the most fearsome of all.

Following a headhunting trip, the freshly taken heads were skinned, placed in rattan nets and smoked over a fire, or sometimes boiled. The skulls were then hung from the rafters of the longhouse and they possessed the most powerful form of magic.

The skulls were considered trophies of manhood (they increased a young bachelor's eligibility) and symbols of bravery. They also testified to the unity of a longhouse. The longhouse had to hold festivals – or *gawai* – to appease the spirits of the skulls. Once placated, the heads were believed to bring great blessing – they could ward off evil spirits, save villages from epidemics, produce rain and increase the yield of rice harvests. Heads that were insulted or ignored were

capable of wreaking havoc in the form of bad dreams, plagues, floods and fires. To keep the spirits of the skulls happy, they would be offered food and cigarettes and made to feel welcome in their new home. As the magical powers of a skull faded with time, fresh heads were always in demand. Tribes without heads were seen as spiritually weak.

Today, young Dayak men no longer have to take heads to gain respect. They are, however, expected to go on long journeys (the equivalent of the Australian aborigines' Walkabout), or *bejalai* in Iban. The one unspoken rule is that they should come back with plenty of good stories, and, these days, as most *bejalai* expeditions translate into stints at timber camps or on oil rigs, they are expected to come home bearing video recorders, TVs and motorbikes.

Many Dayak tribes continue to celebrate their headhunting ceremonies. In Kalimantan, for example, the Adat Ngayau ceremony uses coconut shells, wrapped in leaves, as substitutes for freshly cut heads.

traditional longhouses. But with Iban men now earning good money in the timber and oil industries, it is increasingly common to see longhouses bristling with TV aerials, equipped with fridges and flush toilets and Land Cruisers in the car park. Even modern longhouses retain the traditional features of gallery, veranda and doors. ►► *See also box opposite.*

The Iban are shifting cultivators who originated in the Kapuas River basin of west Kalimantan and migrated into Sarawak's Second Division in the early 16th century, settling along the Batang Lupar, Skrang and Saribas rivers. By the 1800s, they had begun to spill into the Rejang River valley. It was this growing pressure on land as more migrants settled in the river valleys that led to fighting and headhunting (see box above).

The Iban joined local Malay chiefs and turned to piracy, which is how Europeans first came into contact with them. They were dubbed Sea Dayaks as a result, which is really a misnomer as they are an inland people. The name stuck, however, and in the eyes of Westerners, it distinguished them from Land Dayaks, who were Bidayuh people from the Sarawak River area (see page 175). While Rajah James Brooke only won the Iban's loyalty after he had crushed them in battle (see page 171), he had great admiration for them and they bore no bitterness. He described them as "good-looking a set of men, or devils ... Their wiry and supple limbs might have been compared to the troops of wild horses that followed Mazeppa in his perilous flight."

The Kelabit in Borneo

The Kelabit, who live in the highlands at the headwaters of the Baram River, are closely related to the Murut (see page 281) and the Lun Dayeh and Lun Bawang of interior Kalimantan.

They are skilled hill-rice farmers. The hill climate also allows vegetable cultivation.

Kelabit parties are also famed as boisterous occasions, and large quantities of *borak* (rice beer) are consumed, despite the fact that the majority of Kelabit has converted to Christianity. They are also regarded as among the most hospitable people in Borneo.

Kelabit Tom Harrisson parachuted into Kelabit territory with the Allied Special Forces towards the end of the Second World War. The Kelabit Highlands around Bario were chosen because they were so remote. Of all the tribes in Sarawak, the Kelabit have the sturdiest, strongest builds, which is usually ascribed to the cool and invigorating mountain climate. Their fragrant Bario rice is prized throughout Sarawak. ▸▸ *See also box above.*

Kenyah and Kayan These probably originally migrated into Sarawak from the Apo Kayan district in East Kalimantan. Kenyah and Kayan raids on downriver people were greatly feared, but their power was broken by Charles Brooke, just before he became the second White Rajah, in 1863. The Kayan had retreated upstream above the Pelagus Rapids on the Rejang River (see page 130), to an area they considered out of reach of their Iban enemies. In 1862 they killed two government officers at Kanowit and went on a killing spree. Charles Brooke led 15,000 Iban past the Pelagus Rapids, beyond Belaga and attacked the Kayan in their heartland. Many hundreds were killed. In November 1924, Rajah Vyner Brooke presided over a peace-making ceremony between the Orang Ulu and the Iban in Kapit (there is a photograph of the ceremony on display in the Kapit Museum). ▸▸ *See also box opposite.*

The Kenyah and Kayan in Sarawak live in pleasant upriver valleys and are settled rice farmers. Subgroups include the Kejaman, Skapan, Berawan and Sebop.

Malay About half of Sarawak's 300,000-strong Malay community lives around the state capital; most of the other half lives in the Limbang Division, near Brunei. The Malays traditionally live near the coast, although today there are small communities far upriver. There are some old wooden Malay houses with carved façades in the kampongs along the banks of the Sarawak River in Kuching. In all Malay communities, the mosque is the centre of the village, but while their faith is important to them, the strictures of Islam are generally less rigorously enforced in Sarawak than on the Peninsula. During the days of the White Rajahs, the Malays were recruited into government service, as they were on the Malay Peninsula. They were renowned as good administrators and the men were mostly literate in Jawi script. Over the years there has been much intermarriage between the Malay and Melanau communities. Traditionally, the Malays were fishermen and farmers.

Melanau The Melanau are a relaxed and humorous people. Rajah James Brooke, like generations of men before and after him, thought the Melanau girls particularly pretty. He said that they had "agreeable countenances, with the dark, rolling, open eye of the Italians, and nearly as fair as most of that race". The Melanau live along the coast between the Baram and Rejang rivers; originally they lived in magnificent communal houses built high off the ground, like the one that has been reconstructed at the Sarawak Cultural Village in

The Kenyah and Kayan in Borneo

These two closely related groups now live mainly in Sarawak and Kalimantan. They were the traditional rivals of the Iban and were notorious for their warlike ways. Historian Robert Payne, in his history *The White Rajahs of Sarawak*, described the Kayan of the upper Rejang as "a treacherous tribe, [who] like nothing better than putting out the eyes and cutting the throats of prisoners, or burning them alive".

They are very different from other tribal groups, have a completely different language (which has ancient Malayo-Polynesian roots) and are class conscious, with a well-defined social hierarchy. Traditionally their society was composed of aristocrats, nobles, commoners and slaves (who were snatched during raids on other tribes). One of the few things they have in common with other Dayak groups is the fact that they live in longhouses, although even these are of a different design, and are much more carefully constructed, in ironwood. Many have now been converted to Christianity (most are Protestant).

In contrast to their belligerent history, the Kenyahs and Kayans are much more introverted than the Ibans; they are slow and deliberate in their ways and are very artistic and musical. They are also renowned for their parties; visitors recovering from drinking *borak* rice beer have their faces covered in soot before being thrown in the river. This is to test the strength of the newly forged friendship with visitors, who are ill-advised to lose their sense of humour on such occasions.

Their artwork is made from wood, antlers, metal and beads. They use a lot of wooden statues and masks to scare evil spirits at the entrances to their homes.

Kuching, but these have long since disappeared. The houses were designed to afford protection from incessant pirate raids (see page 170), for the Melanau were easy pickings, being coastal people. Their stilt-houses were often up to 12 m off the ground. Today most Melanau live in Malay-style pile-houses facing the river. Hedda Morrison, in her classic 1957 book *Sarawak*, wrote: "As a result of living along the rivers in swamp country, the Melanaus are an exceptionally amphibious people. The children learn to swim almost before they can walk. Nearly all progress is by canoe, sometimes even to visit the house next door."

The traditional Melanau fishing boat is called a *barong*. Melanau fishermen employed a unique fishing technique. They would anchor palm leaves at sea as they discovered that shoals of fish would seek refuge under them. After rowing out to the leaves, one fisherman would dive off his *barong* and chase the fish into the nets which his colleague hung over the side. The Melanaus were also noted for their production of sago, which they ate instead of rice. At Kuching's Cultural Village there is a demonstration of traditional sago production, showing how the starch-bearing pith is removed, mashed, dried and ground into flour. Most Melanau are now Muslim and have assimilated with the Malays through intermarriage. Originally, however, they were animists (animist Melanau are called Likaus) and were particularly famed for their elaborately carved 'sickness images', which represented the form of spirits which caused specific illnesses (see page 183).

Orang Ulu The jungle, or upriver, people comprise a range of different small tribal groups. Orang Ulu longhouses are usually made of *belian* (ironwood) and are built to last. They are well-known swordsmiths, forging lethal parangs from any piece of scrap metal they find. They are also very artistic people – skilled carvers and painters and famed for their

Tribal tattoos

Tattooing is practised by many indigenous groups in Borneo, but the most intricate designs are those of the upriver Orang Ulu tribes.

Designs vary from group to group and for different parts of the body. Circular designs are mostly used for the shoulder, chest or wrists, while stylized dragon-dogs (*aso*), scorpions and dragons are used on the thigh and, for the Iban, on the throat.

Tattoos can mean different things; for the man it is a symbol of bravery and for women, a good tattoo is a beauty feature. More elaborate designs often denote high social status in Orang Ulu communities –

the Kayan, for example, reserved the *aso* design for the upper classes and slaves were barred from tattooing. In these Orang Ulu groups, the women have the most impressive tattoos; the headman's daughter has her hands, arms and legs completely covered in a finely patterned tattoo.

Designs are first carved on a block of wood, which is then smeared with ink. The design is printed on the body and then punctured into the skin with needles dipped in ink, usually made from a mixture of sugar, water and soot. Rice is smeared over the inflamed area to prevent infection, but it usually swells up for some time.

beadwork – taking great care decorating even simple household utensils. Most Orang Ulu are decorated with traditional tattoos (see box above).

Penan Perhaps Southeast Asia's only remaining true hunter-gatherers live mainly in the upper Rejang area and Limbang. They are nomads and are related, linguistically at least, to the Punan, former nomadic forest dwellers who are now settled in longhouses along the upper Rejang. The Malaysian government has long wanted the Penan to settle too, but has had limited success in attracting them to expensive new longhouses. Groups of Penan hunter-gatherers still wander hunt wild pigs, birds and monkeys and search for sago palms to make their staple food, sago flour. The Penan are considered to be the jungle experts by all the other inland tribes. As they live in the shade of the forest, their skin is relatively fair. They have a great affection for the coolness of the forest and until the 1960s were rarely seen by the outside world. For them sunlight is extremely unpleasant. They are broad and more stocky than other river people and are extremely shy, having had little contact with the outside world. Most trade is conducted with remote Kayan, Kenyah and Kelabit longhouse communities on the edge of the forest.
➤ *See also box, page 107.*

In the eyes of the West, the Penan have emerged as the 'noble savages' of the late 20th century for their spirited defence of their lands against encroachment by logging companies. This spirited defence continues today. But it is not just recently that they have been cheated: they have long been the victims of other upriver tribes. A Penan, bringing baskets full of rotan to a Kenyah or Kayan longhouse to sell, may end up exchanging his produce for one bullet or shotgun cartridge. In his way of thinking, a bullet will kill one wild boar which will last his family 10 days. In turn, the buyer knows he can sell the same rotan downstream for RM50-100. Penan still use the blowpipe for small game, but shotguns for wild pig. If they buy the shotgun cartridges for themselves, they have to exchange empties first. Some of the Penan's shotguns date back to the Second World War, when the British supplied them to upriver tribespeople to fight the Japanese. During the Brooke era, a large annual market would be held which both Chinese traders and

The palang

One of the more exotic features of upriver sexuality is the *palang* (penis pin), which is the versatile jungle version of the French tickler.

Traditionally, women suffer heavy weights being attached to their ear lobes to enhance their sex appeal. In turn, men are expected to enhance their physical attributes and entertain their womenfolk by drilling a hole in their organs, into which they insert a range of items, aimed at heightening their partner's pleasure.

Tom Harrisson, a former curator of the Sarawak Museum, was intrigued by the *palang*; some suspect his authority on the subject stemmed from first-hand experience. He wrote: "When the device is put into use, the owner adds whatever he prefers to elaborate and accentuate its intention. A lively range of objects can so be employed – from pigs' bristles and bamboo shavings to pieces of metal, seeds, beads and broken glass. The effect, of course, is to enlarge the diameter of the male organ inside the female."

It is said that many Dayak men, even today, have the tattoo man drill a hole in them. As the practice is now centuries old, one can only assume that its continued popularity proves it is worth the agony.

Orang Ulu (including Penan) used to attend; the district officer would have to act as judge to ensure the Penan did not get cheated.

Those wishing to learn more about the Penan should refer to Denis Lau's *The Vanishing Nomads of Borneo* (Interstate Publishing, 1987). Lau has lived among the Penan and has photographed them for many years; his photographs appear in *Malaysia – Heart of Southeast Asia* (Archipelago Press, 1991).

Dance

Dayak tribes are renowned for their singing and dancing, most famously for the hornbill dance. In her book *Sarawak*, Hedda Morrison wrote: "The Kayans are probably the originators of the stylized war dance now common among the Ibans but the girls are also extremely talented and graceful dancers. One of their most delightful dances is the hornbill dance, when they tie hornbill feathers to the ends of their fingers which accentuate their slow and graceful movements. For party purposes everyone in the longhouse joins in and parades up and down the communal room led by one or two musicians and a group of girls who sing." On these occasions, drink flows freely. With the Ibans, it is *tuak* (rice wine), with the Kayan and Kenyah it is *borak*, a bitter rice beer. After being entertained by dancers, a visitor must drink a large glassful, before bursting into song and doing a dance routine themselves. The best guideline for visitors on how to handle such occasions is provided by Redmond O'Hanlon in his book *Into the Heart of Borneo*. The general rule of thumb is to be prepared to make an absolute fool of yourself. This will immediately endear you to your hosts.

The following are the most common dances in Sarawak. **Kanjet Ngeleput** (Orang Ulu) dance is performed in full warrior regalia, traditionally celebrating the return of a hunter or headhunters. **Mengarang Menyak** (Melanau) dance depicts the processing of sago from the cutting of the tree to the production of the sago pearls or pellets. **Ngajat Bebunuh** (Iban) war dance is performed in full battledress, armed with sword and shield. **Ngajat Induk** (Iban) is performed as a welcome dance for those visiting longhouses. Ngajat Lesong (Iban) dance of the *lesong* or mortar is performed during gawai. **Tarian Kris**

(Malay) dance is of the *kris*, the Malay dagger, which symbolizes power, courage and strength. **Tarian Rajang Beuh** (Bidayuh) dance is performed after the harvesting season as entertainment for guests to the longhouse. **Tarian Saga Lupa** (Orang Ulu) is performed by women to welcome guests to the longhouse, accompanied by the *sape* (see Music below). **Ule Nugan** (Orang Ulu) dance is to the sound of the *kerebo bulo*, or bamboo slates. The music is designed to inspire the spirit of the paddy seeds to flourish. The male dancers hold a dibbling stick used in the planting of hill rice.

Music

Gongs range from the single large gong, the *tawak*, to the *engkerumong*, a set of small gongs, arranged on a horizontal rack, with five players. An *engkerumong* ensemble usually involves five to seven drums, which include two suspended gongs (*tawak* and *bendai*) and five hour-glass drums (*ketebong*). They are used to celebrate victory in battle or to welcome home a successful headhunting expedition. Sarawak's Bidayuh also make a bamboo gong called a *pirunchong*. The *jatang uton* is a wooden xylophone which can be rolled up like a rope ladder; the keys are struck with hardwood sticks.

The Bidayuh, Sarawak's bamboo specialists, make two main stringed instruments: a three-stringed cylindrical bamboo harp called a *tinton* and the *rabup*, a rotan-stringed fiddle with a bamboo cup. The Orang Ulu (Kenyah and Kayan tribes) play a four-stringed guitar called a *sape*, which is also common on the Kalimantan side of the border. It is the most common and popular lute-type instrument, whose body, neck and board are cut from one piece of softwood. It is used in Orang Ulu dances and by witch doctors. It is usually played by two musicians, one keeping the rhythm, the other the melody. Traditional *sapes* had rotan strings; today they use wire guitar strings and electric pick-ups. Another stringed instrument, more usually found in Kalimantan, or deep in Sarawak's interior, is the *satang*, a bamboo tube with strings around the outside, cut from the bamboo and tightened with pegs.

One of the best-known instruments is the *engkerurai* (or *keluri*), the bagpipes of Borneo, which is usually linked with the Kenyah and Kayan, but is also found in Sabah (where it is called a *sompoton*). It is a hand-held organ in which four bamboo panpipes of different lengths are fixed to a gourd, which acts as the wind chamber. Simple *engkerurai* can only play one chord; more sophisticated ones allow the player to use two pipes for the melody, while the others provide a harmonic drone. The Bidayuh are specialists in bamboo instruments and make flutes of various sizes; big thick ones are called *branchi*, long ones with five holes are *kroto* and small ones are called *nchiyo*.

Arts and crafts

Bamboo carving The Bidayuh (Land Dayaks) are best known for their bamboo carving. The bamboo is usually carved in shallow relief and then stained with dye, which leaves a pattern in the areas which have been scraped out. The Bidayuh carve utilitarian objects as well as ceremonial shields, musical instruments and spirit images used to guard the longhouse. The Cultural Village (Kampong Budaya) in Kuching is one of the best places to see demonstrations of Bidayuh carving.

Basketry A wide variety of household items are woven from rotan, bamboo, bemban reed as well as nipah and pandanus palms. Malaysia supplies 30% of the world's demand for *manau rotan* (rattan). Basketry is practised by nearly all the ethnic groups in Sarawak and they are among the most popular handicrafts in Sarawak. A variety of baskets are made for harvesting, storing and winnowing paddy as well as for collecting and storing other items. The Penan are reputed to produce the finest rattan sleeping mats – closely plaited and pliable – as well as the *ajat* and *ambong* baskets (all-purpose jungle rucksacks, also produced by the Kayan and Kenyah). Many of the native patterns used in basketry are derived from Chinese patterns and take the form of geometrical shapes and stylized birds. The Bidayuh also make baskets from either rotan or sago bark strips. The most common Bidayuh basket is the *tambok*, which is simply patterned and has bands of colour; it also has thin wooden supports on each side.

Beadwork Among many Kenyah, Kayan, Bidayuh, and Kelabit groups, beads have long been symbols of status and wealth; necklaces, skullcaps and girdles are handed down from generation to generation. Smaller glass or plastic beads, usually imported from Europe, are used to decorate baby carriers, baskets, headbands, jackets, hats, sheaths for knives, tobacco boxes and handbags. Beaded baby carriers are mainly used by the Kelabit, Kenyah and Kayan and often have shells and animals' teeth attached, which make a rattling sound to frighten away evil spirits. Rounded patterns require more skill than geometric ones; the quality of the pattern is used to reflect the status of the owner. Only upper classes are permitted to have beadwork depicting 'high-class' motifs such as human faces or figures. Early beads were made from clay, metal, glass, bone or shell (the earliest found in Niah Caves). Later on, many of the beads that found their way upriver were from Venice, Greece, India and China – even Roman and Alexandrian beads have made their way into Borneo's jungle. Orang Ulu traded them for jungle produce. Tribes attach different values to particular types of beads.

Blowpipes These are made by several Orang Ulu tribes in Sarawak and are usually carved from hardwood – normally *belian* (ironwood). The first step is to make a rough cylinder about 10 cm wide and 2.5 m long. This is tied to a platform, from which a hole is bored through the rod. The bore is skilfully chiselled by an iron rod with a pointed end. The rod is then sanded down to about 5 cm in diameter. Traditionally, the sanding was done using the rough underside of macaranga leaves. The darts are made from the nibong and wild sago palms and the poison itself is the sap of the upas (Ipoh) tree (*Antiaris toxicari*) into which the point is dipped.

Hats The Melanau people living around Bintulu make a big colourful conical hat from nipah leaves called a *terindak*. Orang Ulu hats are wide-brimmed and are often decorated with beadwork or cloth appliqué. Kelabit and Lun Bawan women wear skullcaps made entirely of beads, which are heavy and extremely valuable.

Pottery Malaysia's most distinctive ceramic designs are found in Sarawak where Iban potters reproduce shapes and patterns of Chinese porcelain which was originally brought to Borneo by traders centuries ago (see page 101). Copies of these old Chinese jars are mostly used for brewing *tuak* (rice wine).

Sickness images The coastal Melanau, who have now converted to Islam but used to be animists, have a tradition of carving sickness images (*blum*), usually from sago or other softwoods. The image is believed to take the form of the evil spirit causing a specific illness. They are carved in different forms according to the ailment. The Melanau developed elaborate healing ceremonies; if someone was struck down by a serious illness, the spirit medium would perform the *berayun* ceremony, using the *blum* to extract the illness from the victim's body. Usually, the image is in a half-seated position, with the hands crossed over the part of the body which is affected. During the ceremony, the medium tries to draw the spirit from the sick person into the image, after which it is set adrift on a river in a tiny purpose-made boat or hidden in the jungle. These images are roughly carved and can, from time to time, be found in antique shops.

Textiles The weaving of cotton *pua kumbu*, literally 'blanket' or 'cover', is one of the oldest Iban traditions. Iban legend recounts that 24 generations ago the God of War, Singalang Burong, taught his son how to weave the most precious of all *pua*, the *lebor api*. Dyed deep red, this cloth was traditionally used to wrap heads taken in battle.

The weaving of *pua kumbu* is done by the women and is a vital skill for a would-be bride to acquire. There are two main methods employed in making and decorating *pua kumbu*: the more common is the ikat tie-dyeing technique, known as *ngebat* by the Iban. The other method is the *pileh*, or floating weft. The Iban use a warp-beam loom which is tied to two posts, to which the threads are attached. There is a breast-beam at the weaving end, secured by a back strap to the weaver. A pedal, beneath the threads, lowers and raises the alternate threads which are separated by rods. The woven material is tightly packed by a beater. The material is tie-dyed in the warp.

Because the *pua kumbu* is made by the warp-tie-dyeing method, the number of colours is limited. The most common are a rich browny-brick-red colour and black, as well as the undyed white sections; blues and greens are used in more modern materials. Traditionally, *pua kumbu* were hung in longhouses during ceremonies and were used to cover images during rituals. Designs and patterns are representations of deities which figure in Iban myths and are believed to protect individuals from harm; they are passed down from generation to generation. Such designs, with deep spiritual significance, can only be woven by wives and daughters of chiefs. Other designs and patterns are representations of birds and animals, including hornbills, crocodiles, monitor lizards and shrimps, which are either associated with worship or are sources of food. Symbolic representations of trees, plants and fruits are also included. A typical example is the zigzag pattern which represents the act of crossing a river – the zigzag course is explained by the canoe's attempts to avoid strong currents. Many of the symbolic representations are highly stylized and can be difficult to pick out.

Malay women in Sarawak are traditionally renowned for their *kain songket*, sarongs woven with silver and gold thread.

Woodcarvings Many tribal groups are skilled carvers, producing everything from huge burial poles (like the Kejaman pole outside the Sarawak Museum in Kuching) to small statues and masks. Kenyah's traditional masks, used during festivals, are elaborately carved and often have large protruding eyes. Eyes are always emphasized, as they frighten the enemy. Other typical items include spoons, stools, doors, walking sticks, *sapes* (guitars), shields, tattoo plaques and the hilts of *parang ilang* (ceremonial knives). The most popular Iban motif is the hornbill, which holds an honoured place in Iban folklore (see page 378), as the messenger for the sacred Brahminy kite, the ancestor of the Iban. Another famous carving is the sacred measuring stick, the *tuntun peti*, used to trap deer; it is carved to represent a forest spirit. The Kayan and Kenyah's most common motif is the *aso*, a dragon-like dog with a long snout. The Kenyah and Kayan carve huge burial structures (*salong*), as well as small ear pendants made of hornbill ivory. The elaborately carved masks used for their harvest ceremony are unique.

Footprint Mini Atlas
Borneo

Kota Kinabalu
Sandakan
BANDAR SERI BENGAWAN
BRUNEI
SABAH
Tawau
Bintulu
Tanjungselor
Sibu
SARAWAK
Kuching
KALTIM
Sangkulirang
Singkawang
KALIMANTAN
KALBAR
Samarinda
KALTENG
Balikpapan
Palangkaraya
Pangkalanbun
Sampit
KALSEL

N

100 km
100 miles

National highway
Main road
Minor road
Track

Altitude in metres
2000
1000
500
200
0

Neighbouring country

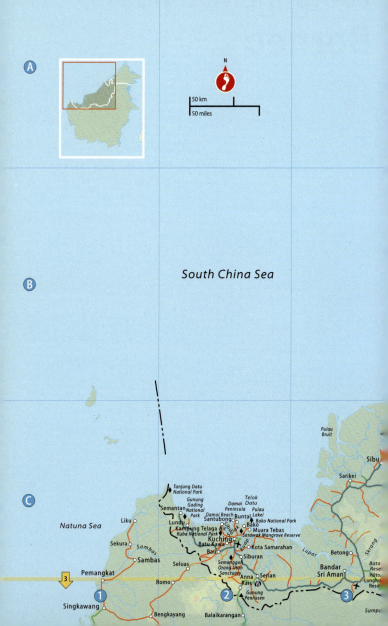

Map 1

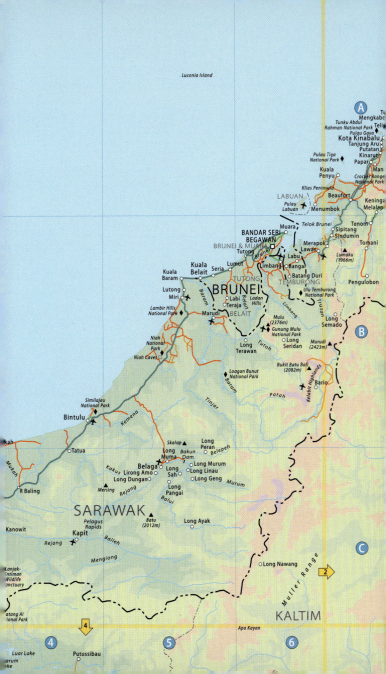

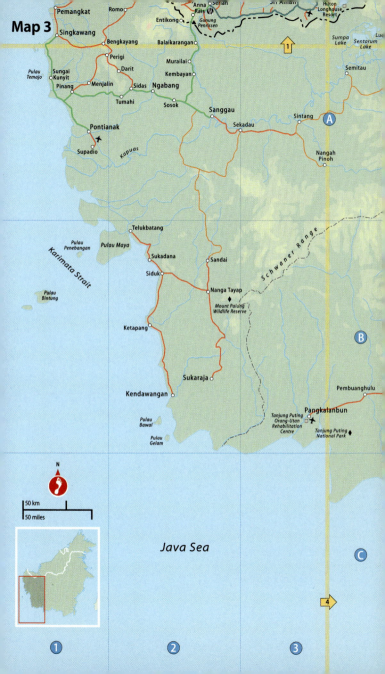

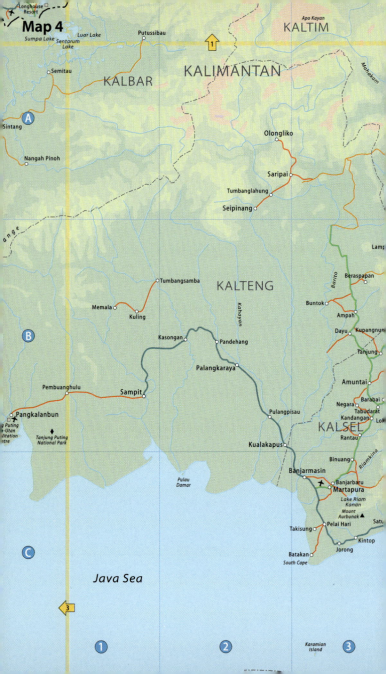

Map symbols

- ▢ Capital city
- ○ Other city, town
- ⇉ International border
- ⇉ Regional border
- ⊖ Customs
- ⬭ Contours (approx)
- ▲ Mountain, volcano
- ⇁ Mountain pass
- ⏟ Escarpment
- ◡ Glacier
- ▦ Salt flat
- ⬭ Rocks
- ⚘ Seasonal marshland
- ▦ Beach, sandbank
- ⦚ Waterfall
- ⌐ Reef
- ━━ National highway
- ━ Paved road
- ─ Unpaved or *ripio* (gravel) road
- ╌╌╌ Track
- ⋯⋯ Footpath
- ── Railway
- ⊢━ Railway with station
- ✈ Airport
- 🚌 Bus station
- Ⓜ Metro station
- ---- Cable car
- ++++ Funicular
- ⛴ Ferry
- ▦ Pedestrianized street
- Σ ⊏ Tunnel
- → One way-street
- ▥ Steps
- ⋈ Bridge
- ▰▰ Fortified wall
- ▦ Park, garden, stadium
- ● Sleeping
- ⓔ Eating
- ⓝ Bars & clubs

- ▦ Building
- ▪ Sight
- ⛪ Cathedral, church
- ☎ Chinese temple
- ⚑ Hindu temple
- ⚘ Meru
- ☪ Mosque
- ⌂ Stupa
- ✡ Synagogue
- ℹ Tourist office
- 🏛 Museum
- ⊠ Post office
- ⓟ Police
- Ⓢ Bank
- @ Internet
- ♪ Telephone
- ☎ Market
- ➕ Medical services
- 🅿 Parking
- ⛽ Petrol
- ⛳ Golf
- ⁂ Archaeological site
- ◆ National park, wildlife reserve
- ✿ Viewing point
- ▲ Campsite
- ⌂ Refuge, lodge
- ▣ Castle, fort
- ⚑ Diving
- ♣ Deciduous, coniferous, palm trees
- ✿ Mangrove
- ⌂ Hide
- ♬ Vineyard, winery
- ⚗ Distillery
- ⚓ Shipwreck
- ✕ Historic battlefield
- ➡ Related map

Contents

Footprint features

★ Don't miss ...
1 Crocker Range whitewater rafting or kayaking, page 205.
2 Manukan Island, page 209.
3 Murut villages, page 216.
4 Gunung Kinabalu, page 234.
5 Sungai Kinabatangan, page 249.
6 Tabin Wildlife Reserve, page 250.
7 Sipadan, page 254.

Sulu Sea

Celebes Sea

East Sea

Tunku Abdul Rahman National Park

Pulau Tiga National Park

Klias Peninsula

To Layang Layang

SABAH
MALAYSIA

KALIMANTAN
INDONESIA

SARAWAK

BRUNEI

LABUAN

Introduction

Sabah may not have the colourful history of neighbouring Sarawak, but there is still a great deal to entice the visitor. It is the second largest Malaysian state after Sarawak, covering 72,500 sq km, making it about the size of Ireland. Occupying the northeast corner of Borneo, it is shaped like a dog's head, the jaws reaching out in the Sulu and Celebes seas, and the back of the head facing onto the South China Sea.

The highlights of Sabah are natural and cultural, from caves, reefs, forests and mountains to tribal peoples. The Gunung Kinabulu National Park is named after Sabah's (and Malaysia's) highest peak and is one of the state's most visited destinations. Also popular is the Sepilok Orang-Utan Rehabilitation Sanctuary outside Sandakan. Marine sights include the Turtle Islands National Park and Sipadan Island, one of Asia's finest dive sites.

While Sabah's indigenous tribes were not cherished as they were in Sarawak by the White Rajahs, areas around towns such as Kudat, Tenom, Keningau and Kota Belud still provide memorable insights into the peoples of the region.

Kota Kinabalu

→ *Colour map 4, A3. Population: 354,000.*

KK is most people's introduction to Sabah for the simple reason that it is the only town with extensive air links to other parts of the country as well as a handful of regional destinations. KK is a modern state capital with little that can be dated back more than 50 years. Highlights include the State Museum and the town's markets. Out of town, within a day's excursion, are beaches such as Tanjung Aru and those near Tuaran, as well as a number of Kadazan and Bajau districts, with their distinctive markets. While it is necessary to go further afield to get a real view of tribal life, this is better than nothing.

The city is strung out along the coast, with jungle-clad hills as a backdrop. Two-thirds of the town is built on land reclaimed from the shallow Gaya Bay and at spring tides it is possible to walk across to Gaya Island. Jalan Pantai, or Beach Road, is now in the centre of town. Successive land reclamation projects have meant that many of the original stilt villages, such as Kampong Ayer, have been cut off from the sea and some now stand in stinking, stagnant lagoons. The government is cleaning up and quickly reclaiming these areas and the inhabitants of the water villages are being rehoused. ▸▸ *For listings, see pages 197-207.*

Ins and outs

Getting there
KK's **airport** ① *T088-238555*, the second busiest in Malaysia, is 6 km south of town. For buses into town, there is a bus stop five minutes' walk from the airport (RM1.50 to the city centre). Taxis from the airport cost RM20 to the city centre; buy coupons in advance from the booths outside the arrivals hall. ▸▸ *See Transport, page 206.*

Getting around
City buses and minibuses provide a service around town and to nearby destinations. Red taxis are unmetered, dark blue taxis metered. There are plenty of car hire firms.

Best time to visit
Sabah's equatorial climate means that temperatures rarely exceed 32°C or fall below 21°C, making it fairly pleasant all year. However, October to March is the rainy season, which spoils plans for the beach and makes climbing Mount Kinabalu or trekking in Sabah's national parks an unpleasant and slippery experience. For spotting turtles on the east coast islands, your best chance is between May and September. **Sabah Fest**, a big carnival of dancing, music and cow races, takes place in May, when the Kadazun/ Dusun celebrate their harvest festival. ▸▸ *See Festivals and events, page 28.*

Tourist information
Sabah Tourism Board ① *51 Jln Gaya, T088-212121, www.sabahtourism.com, Mon-Fri 0800-1700, Sat-Sun 0900-1600*, is a great first point for help when arriving in KK. It is well stocked with leaflets and information and has courteous and helpful staff. **Tourism Malaysia** ① *ground floor, Uni Asia Building, 1 Jln Sagunting, T088-211732, mtpbki@tourism. gov.my*, is not as useful for Sabah, but still does its best. A great tourist website for Sabah is www.sabahtravelguide.com.

Tours that are widely available include: Kota Belud *tamu* (Sunday market), Gunung Kinabalu Park (including Poring Hot Springs), Sandakan's Sepilok Orang- Utan

Rehabilitation Centre, train trips to Tenom through the Padas Gorge and tours of the islands in the Tunku Abdul Rahman National Park. Several companies specialize in scuba-diving tours. ▸▸ *See Tour operators, page 204.*

Parks offices All accommodation and trekking at **Mount Kinabalu** and **Poring Hot Springs** is organized through **Sutera Sanctuary Lodges** ⓘ *ground floor, Wisma Sabah, KK, T088-243629, www.suterasanctuarylodges.com, Mon-Fri 0900-1830, Sat 0900-1630, Sun 0900-1500.*

For **Danum Valley** and **Maliau Basin**, contact **Borneo Nature Tours** (connected to the **Sabah Foundation**, see below) ⓘ *Block D, Lot 10, ground floor, Sadong Jaya Complex, T088-267637, www.borneonaturetours.com,* which deal with the majority of tourism-related activity in Danum Valley and Maliau Basin and are perhaps the easiest first point of contact. You can also contact **Sabah Parks** ⓘ *Lot 3, Block K, Sinsuran Complex, T088-211881, www.sabahparks.org.my.* The official body that regulates the parks is the **Sabah Foundation (Yayasan Sabah Group)** ⓘ *12th floor, Menara Tun Mustapha, KK, T088-326300, www.borneoforest heritage.org.my; see Likas Bay, page 193,* for details.

1 Kota Kinabalu

South China Sea

Gaya Island

Tunku Abdul Rahman Marine Park

Sabah Port / To Sabah Foundation, Bird Sanctuary & 3

Likas Stadium

Jl Tuaran

Jl Damai

Sutera Harbour Golf & Country Club

Sutera Harbour

Jl Kolam

Masjid Sabah

Sabah State Museum & Science Museum

Sabah Golf & Country Club

Queen Elizabeth

Jl Mat Balleh

Jl Bundai Ulam Raya

Kota Kinabalu maps
1 Kota Kinabalu, page 189
2 Kota Kinabalu centre, page 190
3 Around Kota Kinabalu, page 195

Tanjung Aru Marina

Jl Penampang

TANJUNG ARU

Jl Putatan

Tanjung Aru Beach

N

To Monsopiad Cultural Village

800 metres
800 yards

Sleeping
Farida's Bed & Breakfast 3
Magellan Sutera 1

Pacific Sutera 2
Shangri-La Tanjung Aru
Resort 6

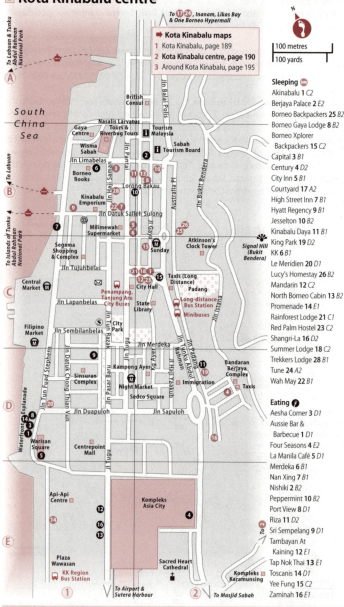

To 17 24, Inanam, Likas Bay
& One Borneo Hypermall

➡ **Kota Kinabalu maps**
1 Kota Kinabalu, page 189
2 **Kota Kinabalu centre, page 190**
3 Around Kota Kinabalu, page 195

100 metres
100 yards

British
Consul

Jln Balai Polis

*South
China
Sea*

To Labuan & Tunku
Abdul Rahman
National Park

A

Gaya
Centre

Nasalis Larvatus
Tours &
Riverbug Tours

Tourism
Malaysia

i

Sabah
Tourism Board

i

Wisma
Sabah

Jln Limabelas

Jln Pantai

To Labuan

Borneo
Books

6

Jln Haji Saman

Jln Bukit Bendera

Australia Pl

Kinabalu
Emporium

11

13

10

Lorong Bakau

10

B

To Islands of Tunku
Abdul Rahman
National Park

9

22

7

@

Milimewah
Supermarket

Jln Datuk Salleh Sulong

Jln Gaya

26

25

7

6

5

Atkinson's
Clock Tower

Signal Hill
(Bukit
Bendera)

Segama
Shopping
& Complex

Jln Tujuhbelas

15

Sunday

Central
Market

M

Jln Lapanbelas

21

23

1

City Hall

15

Taxis (Long
Distance)

Padang

Penampang,
Tanjung Aru
City Buses

12

State
Library

Long-distance
Bus Station

Minibuses

C

Filipino
Market

M

Jln Sembilanbelas

$

City
Park

Jln Tun Razak

Jln Merdeka

Jln Padang

Jln Istana

9

Jln Datuk Chong Thian Vun

Jln Tun Fuad Stephens

Jln Pasar Baru

Kampong Ayer

Kg Ayer

Jln Tunku Abdul Rahman

Jln Haji Yaakub

Bandaran
Berjaya
Complex

Sinsuran
Complex

Night Market

11

19

Immigration

Taxis

Sedco Square

4

Jln Duapuloh

Jln Sapuloh

20

Waterfront Esplanade

8

3

1

Warisan
Square

5

Centrepoint
Mall

Jln Tugu

16

Api-Api
Centre

14

12

16

13

Kompleks
Asia City

4

Plaza
Wawasan

KK Region
Bus Station

Sacred Heart
Cathedral

Kompleks
Karamunsing

To 2

1

To Airport &
Sutera Harbour

2

To Masjid Sabah

Sleeping 😴
Akinabalu **1** *C2*
Berjaya Palace **2** *E2*
Borneo Backpackers **25** *B2*
Borneo Gaya Lodge **8** *B2*
Borneo Xplorer
  Backpackers **15** *C2*
Capital **3** *B1*
Century **4** *D2*
City Inn **5** *B1*
Courtyard **17** *A2*
High Street Inn **7** *B1*
Hyatt Regency **9** *B1*
Jesselton **10** *B2*
Kinabalu Daya **11** *B1*
King Park **19** *D2*
KK **6** *B1*
Le Meridien **20** *D1*
Lucy's Homestay **26** *B2*
Mandarin **12** *B1*
North Borneo Cabin **13** *B2*
Promenade **14** *E1*
Rainforest Lodge **21** *C1*
Red Palm Hostel **23** *C2*
Shangri-La **16** *D2*
Summer Lodge **18** *C2*
Trekkers Lodge **28** *B1*
Tune **24** *A2*
Wah May **22** *B1*

Eating 🍴
Aesha Corner **3** *D1*
Aussie Bar &
  Barbecue **1** *D1*
Four Seasons **4** *E2*
La Manila Café **5** *D1*
Merdeka **6** *B1*
Nan Xing **7** *B1*
Nishiki **2** *B2*
Peppermint **10** *B2*
Port View **8** *D1*
Riza **11** *D2*
Sri Sempelang **9** *D1*
Tambayan At
  Kaining **12** *E1*
Tap Nok Thai **13** *E1*
Toscanis **14** *E1*
Yee Fung **15** *C2*
Zaminah **16** *E1*

Background

Kota Kinabalu started life as a trading post, established in 1881 by the **British North Borneo Chartered Company** under the directorship of William C Cowie (see page 241); not on the mainland, but on Gaya Island, opposite the present town, where a Filipino shanty town is today. On 9 July 1897 rebel leader Mat Salleh (see page 192), who engaged in a series of hit-and-run raids against the British North Borneo Chartered Company's administration, landed on Pulau Gaya. His men looted and sacked the settlement and Gaya township was abandoned.

Two years later the Europeans established another township but this time located on the mainland, opposite Pulau Gaya, adjacent to a Bajau stilt village. The kampong was called 'Api Api' ('Fire! Fire!') because it had been repeatedly torched by pirates over the years. After the Gaya experience, it was an inauspicious name. The Chartered Company rechristened it Jesselton, after Sir Charles Jessel, one of the company directors. However, for years, only the Europeans called it Jesselton; locals preferred the old name, and even today Sabahans sometimes refer to their state capital as Api.

Jesselton owed its raison d'être to a plan that backfired. William C Cowie, a former gun-runner for the Sultan of Sulu, became managing director of the Chartered Company in 1894. He wanted to build a trans-Borneo railway and the narrow strip of land just north of Tanjung Aru and opposite Pulau Gaya, with its sheltered anchorage, was chosen as a terminus.

Photographs in the Sabah State Museum chart the town's development from 1899, when work on the North Borneo Railway terminus began in earnest. By 1905, Jesselton was linked to Beaufort by a 92-km narrow gauge track. By 1911 it had a population of 2686, half of whom were Chinese and the remainder Kadazans and Dusuns; there were 33 European residents. Jesselton was of little importance in comparison to Sandakan, the capital of north Borneo.

When the Japanese Imperial Army invaded Borneo in 1942, Jesselton's harbour gave the town strategic significance and it was consequently completely flattened by the Allies during the Second World War. Jesselton followed Kudat and Sandakan as the administrative centre of north Borneo at the end of the Second World War, and the city was rebuilt from scratch. In September 1967 Jesselton was renamed Kota Kinabalu after the mountain; its name is usually shortened to KK.

Sights

Only three buildings remain of the old town: the old **General Post Office** on Jalan Gaya, **Atkinson's Clocktower** (built in 1905 and named after Jesselton's first district officer) and the old red-roofed **Lands and Surveys building**. The renovated post office now houses the **Sabah Tourism Board**.

Masjid Sabah and Sabah State Museum

ⓘ *To get to Masjid Sabah and the Sabah State Museum complex there are minibuses that stop near Wisma Kewangan on the Kota Kinabalu to Tanjung Aru road, and near Queen Elizabeth Hospital on the Kota Kinabalu to Penampang road.*

The golden dome of **Masjid Sabah** ⓘ *Jln Tunku Abdul Rahman*, is visible from most areas, although it is actually about 3 km out of town. Regular minibuses connect it with the town centre. Completed in 1975, it is the second biggest mosque in Malaysia and, like the Federal Mosque in Kuala Lumpur, a fine example of contemporary Islamic architecture. It can accommodate 5000 worshippers.

Mat Salleh: fort builder and folk hero

Mat Salleh was a Bajau, and son of a Sulu chief, born in the court of the Sultan of Sulu. He was the only native leader to stand up against the increasingly autocratic whims of the North Borneo government as it sequestrated land traditionally belonging to tribal chiefs. Under the **British North Borneo Chartered Company** and the subsequent colonial administration, generations of schoolchildren were taught that Mat Salleh was a rabble-rouser and troublemaker. Now Sabahans regard him as a nationalist hero.

In the *British North Borneo Herald* of 16 February 1899, it was reported that when he spoke, flames leapt from his mouth; lightning flashed with each stroke of his *parang* (cutlass) and when he scattered rice, the grains became wasps. He was said to have been endowed with 'special knowledge' by the spirits of his ancestors and was also reported to have been able to throw a buffalo by its horns.

In 1897 Mat Salleh raided and set fire to the first British settlement on Pulau Gaya (off modern day Kota Kinabalu). For this, and other acts of sabotage, he was declared an outlaw by the governor. A price tag of 700 Straits dollars was put on his head and an administrative officer, Raffles Flint, was assigned the unenviable task of tracking him down. Flint failed to catch him and Mat Salleh gained a reputation as a military genius.

Finally, the managing director of the Chartered Company, Scottish adventurer and former gunrunner, William C Cowie, struck a deal with Mat Salleh and promised that his people would be allowed to settle peacefully in Tambunan, which at that time was not under Chartered Company control.

Half the North Borneo administration resigned as they considered Cowie's concessions outrageous. With it looking increasingly unlikely that the terms of his agreement with Cowie would be respected, Mat Salleh retreated to Tambunan where he started building his fort; he had already gained a fearsome reputation for these stockades. West coast resident G Hewett described it as "the most extraordinary place and without [our] guns it would have been absolutely impregnable". Rifle fire could not penetrate it and Hewett blasted 200 shells into the fort with no noticeable effect. The stone walls were 2.5 m thick and were surrounded by three bamboo fences, the ground in front of which was studded with row upon row of sharpened bamboo spikes. Hewett's party retreated, having suffered four dead and nine wounded.

Mat Salleh had built similar forts all over Sabah and the hearts of the protectorate's administrators must have sunk when they heard he was building one at Tambunan. A government expedition arrived in the Tambunan Valley on the last day of 1899. There was intensive fighting throughout January, with the government taking village after village, until at last the North Borneo Constabulary came within 50 m of Mat Salleh's fort. Its water supply had been cut off and the fort had been shelled incessantly for 10 days. Mat Salleh was trapped. On 31 January 1900 he was killed by a stray bullet which hit him in the left temple.

Perched on a small hill overlooking the mosque is the relatively new purpose-built **Sabah State Museum** (and State Archives) ⓘ *Jln Mat Salleh/Bukit Istana Lama (Old Palace Hill), www.mzm.sabah.gov.my, daily 0900-1700, RM15, also guided tours*, which is designed like a Rungus longhouse. It is divided into ethnography, natural history, ceramics, history and archaeology. The ethnographic section includes an excellent display on the uses of bamboo. There is also tribal brassware, silverware, musical instruments, basketry and pottery, as well as a collection of costumes and artefacts from Sabah tribes such as the Kadazan/Dusun, Bajau, Murut and Rungus.

One of the most interesting items in this collection is a *sininggazanak*, a sort of totem pole. If a Kadazan man died without an heir, it was the custom to erect a *sininggazanak* – a wooden statue supposedly resembling the deceased – on his land. There is also a collection of human skulls (*bangkaran*), which before the tribe's wholesale conversion to Christianity, would have been suspended from the rafters of Kadazan longhouses. Every five years a *magang* feast was held to appease the spirits of the skulls.

The museum's archaeological section contains a magnificently carved coffin found in a limestone cave in the Madai area. Upstairs, the natural history section provides a good introduction to Sabah's flora and fauna. Next door is a collection of jars, called *pusaka*, which are tribal heirlooms. They were originally exchanged by the Chinese for jungle produce, such as beeswax, camphor and birds' nests.

Next door to the State Museum is the **Science Museum**, containing an exhibition on Shell's offshore activities. The **Art Gallery and Multivision Theatre**, within the same complex, is also worth a browse. The art gallery is small and mainly exhibits works by local artists; among the more interesting items on display are those of Suzie Mojikol, a Kadazan artist, Bakri Dani, who adapts Bajau designs, and Philip Biji, who specializes in burning Murut designs onto chunks of wood with a soldering iron. The ethnobotanical gardens are on the hillside below the museum. There is a cafeteria in the main building.

Sabah has a large Christian population and the **Sacred Heart Cathedral** has a striking pyramidal roof that is clearly visible from the Sabah State Museum complex.

Viewpoints

Further into town nearer the coast are a series of water villages, including **Kampong Ayer**, although it has shrunk dramatically in recent years. **Signal Hill** (Bukit Bendera), just southeast of the central area, gives a panoramic view of the town and islands. In the past, the hill was used as a vantage point for signalling to ships approaching the harbour.

Likas Bay

There is an even better view of the coastline from the top of the **Sabah Foundation (Yayasan Sabah) Complex** ① *4 km northeast of town, overlooking Likas Bay*. This surreal glass sculpture houses the chief minister's office. The Sabah Foundation was set up in 1966 to help improve Sabahans' quality of life. The foundation has a 972,800 ha timber concession, which it claims to manage on a sustainable-yield basis (achievement of a high-level annual output without impairing the long-term productivity of the land). More than two-thirds of this concession has already been logged. Profits from the timber go towards loans and scholarships for Sabahan students, funding the construction of hospitals and schools and supplying milk, textbooks and uniforms to school children. The Foundation also operates a 24-hour flying ambulance service to remote parts of the interior. In recent years the Foundation has begun to invest more directly in conservation, seeing potential financial returns from ecotourism and rainforest-derived medicines amongst others. The major pristine areas that haven't been logged within the concession are Danum Valley, the Maliau Basin Conservation area and the Imbak Canyon.

Between the Yayasan Sabah and the city centre is one of Borneo's largest squatter communities, visibly demonstrating that not all share equally in the timber boom.

Over in Likas Bay is **Kota Kinabalu City Bird Sanctuary** ⓘ *Tue-Sun 0800-1800, RM10, children RM5*, a 24 ha spread of mangrove forest with a 1.5 km boardwalk that snakes inside. Possible sightings include egrets, kingfishers, green pigeons, purple herons, plover and redshanks. A pair of binoculars is recommended.

Markets

Gaya street market ⓘ *Sun 0600-1300*, sells a vast range of goods from jungle produce and handicrafts to pots and pans. The market almost opposite the main minibus station on Jalan Tun Fuad Stephens is known as the **Filipino market** (Pasar Kraftangan) as most of the stalls are run by Filipino immigrants. Filipino and local handicrafts are sold in the hundreds of cramped stalls along winding alleyways that are strung with low-slung curtains of shells, baskets and bags. The Filipino market is a good place to buy cultured pearls (RM5 each) and has everything from fake gems to camagong-wood salad bowls, fibre shirts and traditional Indonesian medicines. Further into town, on the waterfront, is the **central market** selling mainly fish, fruit and vegetables. The daily fishing catch is unloaded on the wharf near the market. There is a lively **evening market** selling cheap T-shirts and jewellery in front of the City Park.

Tanjung Aru Beach

This is the best beach near KK, after those in Tunku Abdul Rahman National Park, and is close to **Shangri-La Tanjung Aru Resort**, 5 km south of KK (see page 200). It is particularly popular at weekends and there is a good open-air food court that looks onto the beach. To get there take the Tanjung Aru (beach) bus from the station in front of City Hall.

Around Kota Kinabalu

Penampang

The old town of Donggongon, 13 km southeast of KK, was demolished in the early 1980s and the new township built in 1982. The population is mainly Kadazan or Sino-Kadazan and about 90% Christian. The oldest church in Sabah, **St Michael's** Roman Catholic church, is on a steep hill on the far side of the new town. Turn left just before the bridge – and after the turn-off to the new town – through the kampong and turn left again after the school. It's a 20-minute walk. A granite building with a red roof, it was originally built in 1897 but is not dramatic to look at and has been renovated over the years. Services are in Kadazan but are fascinating, and visitors are warmly welcomed; hymns are sung in Kadazan and Malay. The social focus of the week is the Sunday **market**. To get to Penampang, take a green and white **Union Transport** bus from just in front of City Hall.

There are many **megaliths** in the Penampang area that are thought to be associated with property claims, particularly when a landowner died without a direct heir. Some solitary stones standing in the middle of paddy fields are more than 2 m tall. The age of the megaliths has not been determined. Wooden figures called *sininggazanak* can also be seen in rice fields (see page 193). **Yun Chuan**, Penampang New Town (also known as Donggongon Township), specializes in Kadazan dishes such as *hinava* (raw fish), the Kadazan equivalent of sushi. *Tapai* chicken is also recommended.

Monsopiad Cultural Village

ⓘ *www.monsopiad.com, daily 0900-1700, cultural shows at 1100, 1400 and 1600, RM65*. This is in Kampong Monsopiad – named after a fearsome Kadazan warrior-cum-headhunter, Siou do Mohoing, the so-called Hercules of Sabah – just outside Penampang. There are 42 fragile human skulls, some of which are said to be 300 years old and possess spiritual powers. They are laced together with leaves of the hisad palm, representing the victims' hair. For those who have already visited longhouses in Sarawak, this collection of skulls, in the rafters of an ordinary little kampong house overlooking the village and the Penampang River, is a bit of an anticlimax. But Dousia Moujing and his son Wennedy are very hospitable and know much about local history and culture. They preside over their ancestor's dreaded sword (although Wennedy reckons it's not the original, even though there are strands of human hair hanging off it). A three-day, three-night feast is held in May, in the run-up to the harvest festival. Visitors should remove footwear and not touch the skulls or disturb the rituals or ceremonies in progress. A reconstruction of the original Monsopiad main house gives an insight into the life and times of the warrior and his

3 Around Kota Kinabalu

Kota Kinabalu maps
1 Kota Kinabalu, page 189
2 Kota Kinabalu centre, page 190
3 Around Kota Kinabalu, page 195

Sleeping
Layang Layang Island Resort **4**
Mimpian Jadi Resort **1**
Nexus Golf Resort Karambunai **2**
Rasa Ria Resort **3**

descendants. There is a good restaurant serving traditional dishes; the *kadazandusun hinara* is recommended. It consists of fresh sliced raw fish marinated in lime juice, mixed with chilli, garlic and shallots.

For more information, contact **Borneo Legends and Myths** ⓘ *5 km Ramaya-Putaton Rd, Penampang, T088-761336, www.monosopiad.com*, who manage the village. The house is hard to find; from the new town take the main road east past the Shell station and turn right at sign to Jabatan Air; past St Aloysus Church, the house is on the left about 1.5 km from the turn-off. Minibuses run from Donggongon Township, 10 km south of KK, to Kampong Monsopiad. Take a bus to Donggongon Town and then change to a bus for Monsopiad Cultural Village. A taxi from KK costs RM40. For RM80 you can catch a shuttle bus from the Sutera Magellan and back and get entrance to the village. Buses leave for the village from Sutera Magellan on Monday, Wednesday, Friday and Sunday at 0930 and 1400, and on Tuesday, Thursday and Saturday at 0900 and 1400.

Tamparuli
This popular stop for tour buses is 32 km north of KK at the junction of the roads north and east. It has a suspension bridge straddling the Tuaran River, which was built by the British Army in 1922. There is a good handicraft shopping centre here. Buses marked Tamparuli leave from the long-distance bus station at the bottom of Signal Hill.

Mengkabong Water Village and Tuaran
This Bajau (sea gypsy) fishing stilt village is within easy reach of KK and is likened to an Asian Venice. The village is particularly photogenic in the early morning, before Mount Kinabalu – which serves as a dramatic backdrop – is obscured by cloud. The fishermen leave Mengkabong at high tide and arrive back with their catch at the next high tide. They use sampan canoes, hollowed out of a single tree trunk, which are crafted in huts around the village. Some of the waterways and fields around Mengkabong are choked by water hyacinth, an ornamental plant that was originally introduced by Chinese farmers as pig fodder from South America.

For visitors wanting to escape the popular beaches close to KK, **Tuaran**, 45 minutes north of KK, offers a quieter alternative and is a good access point for several different destinations including Mengkabong. To get there, take a Tuaran bus from the long-distance bus station at the foot of Signal Hill, then change to a local minibus to Mengkabong Water Village. Taxis charge about RM45, or you can take a tour.

The nearby **Karambunai Beach** has a good picnic area, clean beach and sea. Close by is the **Mimpian Jadi Resort**, see page 200.

Karambunai Peninsula
This scenic Peninsula 30 km north of KK has been transformed by a sprawling multimillion-dollar golf and beach complex, **Nexus Golf Resort**, see page 199.

Layang Layang
Some 300 km northwest of KK in the South China Sea, Layang Layang (Swallow Reef) is a man-made atoll originally built for the Malaysian navy. It has become a famous, albeit expensive, dive site. There is one resort on the island that caters solely to divers. You need to book a flight through the resort; there are usually at least four flights a week to the island, but details need to be confirmed in advance, with plenty of notice. See also page 16.

For Sleeping and Eating price codes and other relevant information, see Essentials pages 23-27.

⊜ Sleeping

Kota Kinabalu *p188,*
maps p189, p190 and p195

Well-heeled tourists will seek the more refined out-of-town resorts; but in KK itself, mid-range hotels have improved immeasurably in recent years. The increased number of budget airlines flying into KK has prompted the opening of a number of budget guesthouses, and those on a fairly modest budget are well catered for in KK.

AL Hyatt Regency, Jln Datuk Salleh Sulong, T088-221234, www.kinabalu.regency. hyatt.com. With a/c, 288 rooms and 3 restaurants. Three's also a pool and kids' pool. It's in a central location. Rooms vary in standard. There's live entertainment (**Shenanigan's Fun Pub**) and Club Olympus, a popular spa and massage centre with views over the bay from the treadmills. Tours and treks organized. Good value.

AL Le Meridien, Jln Tun Fuad Stephens, Sinsuran, T088-322222, www.lemeridien.com/ kota kinabalu. Popular hotel with the well-heeled with 306 smart, modern rooms, some with superb views over the bay. There's a pool, gym and excellent restaurant and club. For the best prices, book online well in advance.

AL Promenade, 4 Lorong Api-Api 3, Api-Api Centre, T088-265555, www.promenade.com.my. 4-star hotel along the seafront, popular with domestic business travellers. Sea view rooms are only a fraction more expensive than the city view rooms and worth every ringgit for the sunset. There are 4 dining outlets, a large pool and gym. Wi-Fi available in room for a steep RM30 per 24 hrs.

AL Sutera Harbour Resort,1 Sutera Harbour Blvd, T088-318888, www.suteraharbour.com. South of the city centre, this resort was created from reclaimed land covering 156 ha that was previously the South China Sea. The **Harbour** is

2 hotels (1000 rooms in total): the **Magellan Sutera**, and the **Pacific Sutera**. The **Magellan Sutera** is the more relaxed, with many sports activities, including 27 holes of golf and a spa. The **Pacific Sutera** is more a business hotel, with superb conference facilities.

A Berjaya Palace, 1 Jln Tangki, Karamunsing, T088-211911, www.berjayaresorts.com.my. This distinctive, castellated hotel stands on a hill south of KK. 160 rooms, pool, sauna and gym, conference rooms. The proprietor James Sheng has a small resort with chalets on Pulau Gaya, at Maluham Bay, east of Police Bay, enquire at hotel.

A Capital, 23 Jln Haji Saman, T088-231999, capitalh@streamyx.com. 102 a/c rooms that are looking a little dated, TV, coffee shop, central position. Overpriced, given the competition in town.

A Jesselton, 69 Jln Gaya, T088-223333, www.jesseltonhotel.com. The first to open in KK, this classic hotel dates from 1954. With just 32 rooms, it was upgraded in the mid-1990s and is now considered KK's premier boutique-style hotel. It's an old establishment, with everything from a shiny red London cab to shoe shining at your service. There's an Italian restaurant on the ground floor and all rooms have Wi-Fi.

A Shangri-La, 75 Bandaran Berjaya, T088-212800, kkshang@po.jaring.my. Not part of the international **Shangri-La** group, and popular with business visitors. The rooms are a/c and comfortable but vastly overpriced.

A-B Courtyard, Unit G–800, One Borneo Hypermall, Jln Sulaiman, T088-528228, www.courtyardhotel1borneo.com. Super-slick rooms with gargantuan LCD TV, the same model of bed that was used by athletes in the Sydney Olympics and free access to their Elusion lounge. Wi-Fi in bar and lobby. The room rates are excellent value, but the compulsory breakfast at RM50 a room hikes prices up unnecessarily.

B Century, Jln Masjid Lama, T088-242222, www.firstcenturyhotel.com. Chinese hotel at the edge of town, backing on to a hill with a lobby area overlooking a verdant patch of greenery. Rooms are functional, clean and have TV and Wi-Fi. Fair value for this price range.

B Kinabalu Daya, 9 Jln Pantai, T088-240000, www.bestwestern.com. Owned by the Best Western chain, the 68 rooms are comfortable and modern with cable TV and a/c. Rooms on the top floor have good views over the city. Hunter's Bar downstairs is a popular watering hole with live music at weekends. Breakfast and daily paper included.

B King Park, Jln Masjid Lama, T088-270500, www.kingparkhotel.com.my. Newish place in a bright yellow tower block overlooking town. Rooms are a bit on the small side, but are clean, modern and elegant. Good value.

B Mandarin, 138 Jln Gaya, T088-225222, F225481. Functional place with gleaming marble floors, clean rooms with TV (local channels only), minifridge and attached bathroom with hot water. The de luxe and super-de luxe rooms are particularly spacious. The 6th-floor rooms have good views over town. Fair value.

B-C Wah May, 36 Jln Haji Saman, T088-266118, wahmayhtl.com.my. Modern, typical Chinese hotel with 24 functional and clean rooms with a/c, cable TV, Wi-Fi, minifridge and attached bathroom with hot water. Tight security with CCTV in operation.

B-D Rainforest Lodge, 48 Jln Pantai, T088-258228, www.rainforestlodgekk.com. Excellent new addition to the lodgings scene. Smart en suite rooms have spacious balconies overlooking the town and eatery below, cable TV, a/c and Wi-Fi. The comfortable a/c dorm room is fair value at RM30. Breakfast is included. Good promotional rates. Recommended.

C City Inn, 41 Jln Pantai, T088-218933, F218937. A/c, bathroom and TV. Good value, often full.

C High Street Inn, 38 Jln Pantai, T088-218111, F219111. Rooms with a/c, TV and hot water are soulless but functional and comfortable. Very typical of hotels in this price range.

C Red Palm Hostel, Jln Gaya, T088-211130, www.redpalmkk.com. With rooms built around a friendly common area, this new

place is a cosy spot to relax. Rooms have a/c and Wi-Fi with shared bathroom facilities. TV and free internet available in the lounge. They can help with tours around the region.

C Tune, Unit G 803, One Borneo Hypermall, Jln Sulaiman, T03-7962 5888, www.tune hotels.com. New place at One Borneo 7 km from the city and run using the same model – book early, pay less – as budget airlines. This chain is the latest venture of AirAsia supreme Tony Fernandez. Rooms are comfortable and have attached bath but are plastered with advertisements. Pay extra for TV, a/c and Wi-Fi.

C-D North Borneo Cabin, 1st and 2nd floor, 74 Jln Gaya, T088-272800, F272900, www.northborneocabin.com. A collection of spacious, spartan rooms and dorms (RM23) with shared bathroom, free breakfast and Wi-Fi access. Friendly staff.

C-D Summer Lodge, 2nd/3rd and 4th floor, Lot 120 Gaya St, T088-244499, www.summer lodge.com.my. Spacious and popular hotel in the centre near a few good eating and drinking options. Rooms are simple, cleanish and have high ceilings and a/c. There's a rooftop garden for the smokers on the 4th floor and plenty of bathrooms scattered about the place, although more expensive rooms are en suite. There are often DVDs playing in the reception, and Beach St market kicks off in a colourful style on weekends. The friendly staff offer a range of tours and the reception is home to a few bounding kittens – strays adopted by the guesthouse – which further add to the cheery mood. Dorms (RM25) and Wi-Fi available.

C-E Akinabalu, Lot 133, Jln Gaya, T088-272188, www.akinabaluyh.com. Popular backpacker haunt with massive communal space and free internet access. Rooms are a bit gloomy, with windows onto a corridor only. Good spot to meet other travellers.

C-E Borneo Gaya Lodge, 78 Jln Gaya, T088-242477, www.borneogayalodge.com. Another new offering, this quiet and relaxed hotel has a selection of clean and comfortable a/c rooms and an a/c dorm. Rooms have TV with cable, Wi-Fi and breakfast is included. Many rooms are windowless. Tour information available.

C-E Borneo Xplorer Backpackers, 1st floor, 106 Jln Gaya, T088-538780, www.xplobackpackers.com. Run by a couple of friendly local guys, this guesthouse is spread over 2 wings. Rooms in the newer wing are the best bet, recently renovated and with a common balcony. Dorms are not too squashed and some sleep 4. Free breakfast and Wi-Fi access. Guests get a 10% discount at nearby **Gaya Reflexology**, see page 204.

C-E Farida's Bed & Breakfast, 413 Jln Saga, Mile 4.5 Jln Tuaran, Likas, T088-428733, www.homeaway.com.my/farida.htm. Friendly, whitewashed lodge with 12 rooms, from dorms to doubles with attached bathroom. Internet, kitchen, laundry and free breakfast. It's a 10-min drive north of KK in Inananam and handy for early morning bus departures to Sandakan and Tawau. They may be able to offer free pickup; phone in advance, or take a Likas bus from Plaza Wawasan and get off before the mosque. It's a 5-min walk from there. Run by tour company **Home Away from Home**.

C-E Trekkers Lodge, 30 Jln Haji Saman, T088-252263, www.trekkerslodge.com. Very busy place, so book ahead by several days to get a/c or fan double room. En suite rooms (**B**) are not good value. Well set up for travellers, with helpful staff, sitting-out area, library, tour information (good deals with **Borneo Divers**). Due to its popularity, however, it feels cramped and can get a bit grubby, particularly the dorms.

D Borneo Backpackers, 24 Lorong Dewan, at the foot of Signal Hill on the corner with the roundabout, T088-234009, www.borneo backpackers.com. In a renovated 1950s printing works. 50 beds, internet, laundry, lounge, roof garden, and tourist information. The ground floor houses a post-war era coffee shop stacked with wartime photos and antique-style furniture. A variety of rooms, plus dorms with fan (RM20 per person) or a/c (RM25 per person).

D KK, 46 Jln Pantai, 1st floor, T088-248587. Just 2 floors down from **Beach Lodge**, this place has cheap doubles with shared bathroom, but is not geared towards travellers. No travel information or communal lounge, simply a cheap, basic place to stay if all the other guesthouses are full.

D-E Lucy's Homestay (Backpacker Lodge), Australia Pl, 25 Lorong Dewan (by the Atkinson Clock Tower), T088-261495, welcome.to/ backpackerkk. Owned by the genial Lucy, who gets rave reviews from her guests, this sociable spot is one of the better budget options in town, although when lots of guests are staying, it can feel a bit cramped. Accommodation is mainly in dorms, although there are also 3 private rooms. Simple kitchen, excellent library and small balcony. Due to its popularity it's a good idea to book some days in advance. Free breakfast with a large pot of Marmite providing solace to the homesick. Recommended.

Homestays

Homestays in Sabah are now organized through **Nature Heritage Travel and Tours**, ground floor, Wisma Sabah, T088-318747, nhtt@nature-heritage.com.

Around Kota Kinabalu *p194, map p195*

L-A Nexus Golf Resort Karambunai, Menggatal, Karambunai Peninsula, T088-411222, www.nexusresort.com. Built on 13.5 sq km sprawling along the coast, with 490 ocean-view rooms and a full range of facilities including 18-hole golf course, 3 pools and sports activities. Popular with business guests and for conferences.

AL Layang Layang Island Resort, T088-709121, www.layanglayang.com. Or book through the reservation office in KL: Block A, ground floor, A-0-3, Megan Av 11, 12 Jln Yap Kwan Seng, 50450, KL, T03-2162 2877. This 3-star resort has 76 rather plain rooms and 10 suites, movie room, pool, restaurant and bar. Apart from the resort the atoll is rather bleak with only an airstrip. Most reservations are included in an all-inclusive diving package. In 2007 this was US$1260 for 6 days/5 nights with 3 dives a day, plus a flight costing US$256 per person. You have to enjoy your diving to make the visit worthwhile, but the underwater world is spectacular.

AL Rasa Ria Resort, overlooking Pantai Dalit Beach, near Tuaran (take a local bus to Tuaran), T088-792888, www.shangri-la.com. Top-class Shangri-La resort with 330 rooms, a free-form pool, water sports, an 18-hole golf course, a driving range, spacious gardens, conference facilities, horse riding, cultural events, several restaurants including an Italian and a seafood beachfront one and 30 ha of forest nature reserve with semi-tame orang-utans. There have been some complaints about the integrity of an orang-utan fostering programme run by the resort and the cleanliness of the surrounding beach away from the resort. Recommended.

A-B Mimpian Jadi Resort, No 1 Kuala Matinggi, Kampong Pulau, Simpangan, Karambunai Beach, T088-787799, F787775. Chalets, private beach, water sports, fishing, mini zoo, karaoke bar, horse riding, volleyball, children's playground, Malay/Chinese and Western food. To get there, take a bus to Menggatal, then a bus to Karambunai. **Surusup** is 10-15 mins beyond Tuaran. Ask at the store in Surusup for Haji Abdul Saman, who will take visitors by boat to the lesser-known Bajau fishing village, Kampong Penambawan, also likened to an Asian Venice, on the north bank of the river. Nearby there is a suspension bridge and rapids where it is possible to swim.

Tanjung Aru Beach *p194*
AL Shangri-La Tanjung Aru Resort, 20 Jln Aru, T088- 225800, www.shangri-la.com. With a/c, 500 rooms and a pool, this is one of the best hotels in Sabah, along with its sister hotel, the **Rasa Ria** at Tuaran. Tanjung Aru is a public beach 5 km from KK and frequented by kiteflyers, swimmers, joggers and lovers; the hotel is noticeably on the honeymoon circuit for Europeans. Recommended.

🍴 Eating

Kota Kinabalu *p188, maps p189, p190 and p195*
The waterfront has a range of restaurants with outdoor seating facing the South China Sea. Seafood is seasonally prone to toxic red tide. Locals will know when it's prevalent. Avoid all shellfish if there's any suspicion.

🍴 **Aussie Bar and Barbecue**, Waterfront Esplanade, Jln Tun Fuad Stephens. Simple no-frills Australian bar-cum-steakhouse, with a bright green and yellow frontage. This is a good spot for carnivores on the hunt for steaks, but it also has fusion dishes and salads.

🍴 **Chinese Restaurant**, Hyatt Hotel, Jln Datuk Salleh Sulong. Broad menu of good Chinese cuisine including Shanghainese, Sichuan and Cantonese, although its signature dish, the delicious Peking duck, hails from the north. Recommended.

🍴 **Four Seasons**, Kompleks Asia City, Jln Tugu. Tucked away at the back of this shopping centre is this Cantonese place with excellent dim sum and steamboats. Good value.

🍴 **Gardenia Grill Room**, Jesselton hotel, 69 Jln Gaya, T088-223333. Elegant dining.

🍴 **Little Italy**, ground floor, **Hotel Capital**, 23 Jln Haji Saman, T088-232231. Open for lunch and dinner. Award-winning pizza and pasta place with Italian chef. Recommended.

🍴 **Nagisa**, Hyatt Hotel, see page 197. Fancy Japanese place with tables facing the South China Sea. Open kitchen, sushi bar, teppanyaki counters and a private tatami room for the wealthy.

🍴 **Nishiki**, Jln Gaya (opposite Wing On Life Building). Japanese. Friendly staff and good-sized portions.

🍴 **Port View**, the Waterfront, T088-221753. Garish Chinese seafood palace with a gigantic bank of aquariums featuring the catch of the day including lobster, grouper, crab and more. The chilli crab is renowned. Very popular at weekends. Recommended.

🍴 **Seri Selera Kampung Air**, Sedco Sq, Kampung Air, T088-210400. Open 1500-0200. Fun tourist-orientated place with 7 different seafood eateries, street stalls and nightly cultural shows.

🍴 **Sri Melaka**, 9 Jln Laiman Diki, Kampong Ayer (Sedco Complex, near **Shiraz**). Popular with the fashionable KK set, serves great Malay and Nyonya food.

Tap Nok Thai, Unit 6, G/F Api Api Centre, T088-258328. Open 1130-1430 and 1800-2230. Authentic Thai restaurant with simple wooden decor and good soups, seafood and salads.

Toscanis, Lot 14, Waterfront Esplanade, Jln Tun Fuad Stephens. Small but popular Mediterranean eatery that draws locals and expats alike with Italian and Spanish seafood dishes, pasta, tapas and delicious desserts.

Aesha Corner, Anjung Perdana (the Waterfront). Cheap Malay canteen facing the sea.

Golf Field Seafood, 0858 Jln Ranca-Ranca. Better known by taxi drivers as **Ahban's Place**. Excellent marine cuisine. A local favourite.

Korean, Jln Bandaran Berjaya, next to **Asia Hotel**. Large selection, barbecues a speciality.

La Manila Fish & Co, ground floor, Blk D, Warisan Sq, Jln Tun Fuad Stephens, T088-488996. Open 1000-2200. Strange name for a restaurant specializing in Penang and Nyonya cuisine, but let the food do the talking. Well-priced dishes including Penang *char kway teow*, *asam laksa*, curry *mee* and Penang prawn *mee*.

Nan Xing, Jln Datuk Salleh Sulong, opposite the **Hyatt** and **Emporium**. Dim sum and Cantonese specialities.

Peppermint, Lot 25, G/F, Jln Pantai. Hugely popular lunchtime draw with local workers, arrive after 12 noon and you'll have to join the queue. Simple, short but effective menu of *pho* (noodle soup), beef stew, spicy chicken rice and spring rolls. Recommended.

Restoran Islam, Segama Complex, opposite **Hyatt Hotel**. Best in a string of coffee shops, all of which are good value for money and curries with a decidedly Indonesian flavour.

Riza, next to the **King Park Hotel** on Jln Masjid Lama. This Malay canteen has big servings of tasty grub in a clean and friendly environment.

Shiraz, Lot 5, Block B, Sedco Sq, Kampong Ayer. Indian. Recommended.

Sri Sempelang, Sinsuran 2 (on the corner with Jln Pasar Baru). Great Malay canteen with enormous fruit juices and tables outside. Locals recommend it.

Tambayan At Kaining, G/F Api Api Centre, T016-818 5311. Outrageously authentic Filipino restaurant with lots of rattan furniture and leafy plants. Popular with overseas Filipinos, the menu includes *sinagang*, garlic rice, and *calderata*. Recommended.

Yee Fung, 127 Jln Gaya. Open 0630-1700. Local Chinese residents rave about this simple eatery, which gets packed out at lunch with hungry punters wanting their signature *yee fung laksa*, fragrant claypot chicken rice and, for those with a stomach for organs, the *ngau chap* should satisfy the craving. Recommended.

Zaminah, Api-Api Centre. Open 1000-2200. Fairly standard Malaysian Indian Muslim restaurant with the usual rotis and curries.

Foodstalls

There are stalls above central market. **Sedco Square**, Kampong Ayer, is a large square filled with stalls, with a great atmosphere in the evenings, ubiquitous *ikan panggang* and satay. Night market on **Jln Tugu**, on the waterfront at the **Sinsuran Food Centre** and at **Merdeka Foodstall Centre**, Wisma Merdeka.

Tanjung Aru Beach *p194*

There are mainly seafood foodstalls in Tanjung Aru Beach – recommended for *ikan panggang* – and satay stalls. It's very busy at weekends, but on weekdays it is rather quiet, with only a few stalls to choose from.

Garden Terrace, Tanjung Aru Resort, T088-225800. Open 0600-2300. Asian and Western buffet (dim sum available) and à la carte, with tables facing pretty gardens.

Peppino, Tanjung Aru Resort, T088-225800. Tasty but expensive Italian, good Filipino cover band.

Seafood Market, Tanjung Aru Beach, T088-238313. Pick your own fresh seafood and get advice on how to have it cooked.

Bars and clubs

Kota Kinabulu *p188, maps p189, p190 and p195*

Bars

Many popular bars are along the **Waterfront Esplanade**. Notable drinking venues along

this stretch include the **Cock and Bull**, an English-style pub; **Shamrock's Irish Bar**, with Kilkenny and Guiness; and **Aussie Bar and Barbecue**. All are in a strip and make a colourful short pub crawl. Bars and restaurants, all with outdoor seating, are strung along **Beach St**, a pedestrianized lane between Jln Pantai and Jln Gaya.
BB Café, Beach St. Closes 2400. Live music, Kenny G and cheap beer pulls in the punters.
Café Upperstar, Segama Complex (opposite **Hotel Hyatt**). Sandwiches and fried food. Jugs of Long Island iced tea for RM45.

Clubs
Bed, at the end of Waterfront Esplanade. Popular late-night club with a big dance floor, live music and lounge area. It gets a little wild and is a great place to blow off some steam.
Shenanigan's at the Hyatt and **Rumba** at Le Meridien are also good late-night venues.

In Tanjung Aru is **Blue Note**, with chilled grooves at the Tanjung Aru Resort, and **Tiffiny**, opposite the Sacred Heart Church.

Karaoke is very popular in KK; found in Damai, Foh Sang and KK centre.

🌐 Entertainment

Kota Kinabalu *p188, maps p189, p190 and p195*
Cinemas
Cinema in Centrepoint Mall and at Golden Screen Cinema and Mega Pavilion on Jln Sepuluh. There's a large **Cineplex** at One Borneo on Jln Sulaiman.

Cultural shows
Cultural Palace Theatre Restaurant, Jln Tanjung Lipat, T088-251844. Dance shows by Kadazan-Dusun, Bajau and Murut. Dinner and show RM42 (from 1845, closed Mon). You'll need a taxi to get there.
Kadazan-Dusun Cultural Centre (Hongkod Koisaan), KDCA Bldg, Mile 4.5, Jln Penampang. Restaurant open all year, but in late May, during the harvest festival, the cultural

association comes into its own, with dances, feasts and shows and lots of *tapai* (RM15).
Kampong Nelayan also has dance shows during dinner.

🌸 Festivals and events

Kota Kinabalu *p188, maps p189, p190 and p195*
May Magavau (see page 28), a post-harvest celebration, is carried out at Hongkod Koisaan (cultural centre), Mile 4.5, Jln Penampang. To get there, take a green and white bus from the MPKK Building, next to the state library.

🛍 Shopping

Kota Kinabalu *p188, maps p189, p190 and p195*
Antiques
Good antiques shop at the bottom of the Chun Eng Bldg on Jln Tun Razak, and a couple on Jln Gaya. **Merdeka Complex** and **Wisma Wawasan 2020** hold a number of antiques shops. You need an export licence from Sabah State Museum to export rare antiques.

Books
Borneo Books/ Borneo Books 2, Wisma Merdeka ground and 2nd floor, T088-538077, www.borneobooks.com. Eco-friendly books on Borneo, plus a travellers' book exchange and large collection of classic National Geographic magazines. **Times Books**, Warisan Square. The best selection of books in town, with fiction, magazines, and local interest.
Zenithway, 29 Jln Pantai. English books and magazines, also Penguin books.

Clothes
Centrepoint Mall. Branded clothing.
House of Borneo Vou'tique, Lot 12A, 1st floor, Lorong Bernam 3, Taman Saon Kiong, Jln Kolam, T088-268398. For that ethnic, exotic and exclusive look for men and women; souvenirs, tablecloths, cushion covers, etc.

Electronic goods

VCDs, DVDs and stereo equipment are considered the cheapest in the country here. Try **Karamunsing Kompleks** and **Centrepoint**.

Handicrafts

Mainly baskets, mats, tribal clothing, beadwork and pottery. **Api Tours**, Lot 49, Bandaran Berjaya, has a small selection of handicrafts. **Borneo Gifts**, ground floor, Wisma Sabah. **Borneo Handicraft**, 1st floor, Wisma Merdeka, local pottery and material made up into clothes. **Elegance Souvenir**, 1st floor, Wisma Merdeka, lots of beads of local interest (another branch on ground floor of Centrepoint). **Kampong Ayer Night Market**, mainly Filipino handicrafts. **Kraftangan Kompleks/Filipino Market**, Jln Tun Fuad Stephens (see page 194). **Malaysian Handicraft**, Cawangan Sabah, No 1, Lorong 14, Kg Sembulau, T088-234471, Mon-Sat 0815-1230, Fri 0815-1600. **Sabah Art and Handicraft Centre**, 1st floor, Block B, Segama Complex (opposite New Sabah Hotel). **Sabah Handicraft Centre**, Lot 49 Bandaran Berjaya (next to **Shangri-La**), good selection (also has branches at the museum and the airport). **The Crafts**, Lot AG10, ground floor, Wisma Merdeka, T088-252413. There is also a handicraft shop at the **airport**.

Jewellery

Most shops in Wisma Merdeka.

Shopping complexes

Kinabalu Emporium, Wisma Yakim, Jln Daruk Salleh Sulong. The main department store. **Likas Square**, Likas. Pink monstrosity with 2 floors of shopping malls, foodstalls and restaurants. Cultural shows in central lobby. **One Borneo Hypermall**, Jln Sulaiman (7 km outside the city, free shuttle buses from Warisan Square every hr), www.1borneo.net. The largest shopping mall in Borneo, this gargantuan mall has it all – designer boutiques, a handicraft centre, bowling lanes, hotels, a cineplex and some good eateries – making it ideal for people who want a day of hedonistic consumerism. East

Malaysia's largest aquarium, **Aquatica KK** is currently being constructed here. Check www.aquaticakk.org for updates. **Segama**, Jln Tun Fuad Stephens, and **Sinsuran**. **Warisan Square**. New complex with eateries, boutiques and swimwear outlets.

Tanjung Aru Beach *p194*

Kaandaman Handicraft Centre, below Seafood Market Restaurant in Tanjung Aru Beach. **Tanjung Aru Resort**, a few handicraft shops in the arcade.

▲ Activities and tours

Kota Kinabalu *p188, maps p189, p190 and p195*

The sports complex at Likas is open to the general public. It has volleyball, tennis, basketball, gym, badminton, squash, aerobics and a pool. To get there take a Likas-bound minibus from Plaza Wawasan. **Likas Square** (see above), the pink shopping complex north of Likas Sports Complex, has a recreation club with tennis, squash, jogging, golf, driving range, pool and children's playground.

Bowling

Centrepoint, Jln Lebuh Raya Pantai Baru and at **One Borneo**, Jln Sulaiman.

Diving

Do not believe dive shops if they tell you that you must book through their offices in KK – it's often cheaper to book through local offices in the area where you want to dive. One exception to this rule is Sipadan Island. Only limited numbers of divers are allowed to dive in the area per day due to conservation concerns. Diver limits only apply to Sipadan; Mabul and other islands have yet to impose restrictions. To obtain permits in advance, contact Sipadan tour operators, page 269.

Golf

Green fees are considerably higher over the weekend, up to double the weekday rate.

Fees range from RM200 plus to RM450. Prices drop considerably for night golf after 1700. **Golf Booking Centre Malaysia**, nbtt@tm.net.my, provides escorted golf tours. **Sabah Golf and Country Club**, Bukit Padang, T088-247533 www.sgccsabah.com. The oldest course in the state, this 18-hole championship course affords magnificent views of Mt Kinabalu. **Sutera Harbour Golf and Country Club**, www.suteraharbour.com, on reclaimed land just to south of the city. A 27-hole layout with great views across to the islands of Tunku Abdul Rahman Park.

Sailing and water sports
Tanjung Aru Marina. Snorkelling RM35 per day, waterskiing RM250 per hr, fishing RM75 per day, sailing RM80 per hr. **Yacht club**, Tanjung Aru, next to the hotel.

Spas
The big name hotels have their own spas. **Gaya Reflexology**, 114 Jln Gaya. Offers good-value massage and other treatments, helpful to those who have stiff legs after a Kinabalu climb. A full body massage starts at RM60.

Tour operators
The Sabah Tourism Board has a full list of tour agents. See also www.sabahtourism.com. **Api Tours** Lorong Kacang, Jln Kolombong, Inanam, T088-424 156, www.apitours.com. Wide variety of tours, treks in the Crocker Range, homestays and overnight stays in longhouses. Recommended. **Borneo Divers**, ground floor, Wisma Sabag, T088-222227, www.borneodivers.info. Operates exotic scuba-diving trips all over Borneo including Sipadan, accommodation on Mamutik Island (Tunku Abdul Rahman); they also have an office in Tawau, T089-761214. Dive trips are well organized but expensive, it's possible to bargain. **Trekker's Lodge** can sometimes help with good deals with this dive shop. **Borneo Eco Tours**, Lot 1, Pusat Perindustrian, Kolombong Jaya, 88450, T088-438300, www.borneoecotours.com. Award-winning operator that specializes in environmentally aware tours. Their **Sukau Rainforest Lodge** (www.sukau.com) on the Kinabatangan River is highly recommended. **Borneo Nature Tours**, ground floor, Lot 10, Block D, Sadong Jaya Complex, T088- 267637, www.borneonaturetours.com. Official agent operating within the excellent Danum Valley Conservation Area (including **Borneo Rainforest Lodge**), see page 251, and the Maliau Basin, page 257. **Borneo Sea Adventures**, 1st floor, 8a Karamunsing Warehouse, T088-230000, www.bornsea.com. Scuba-diving courses and diving and fishing trips around Sabah (see page 254). They run **Mantanani Island Resort** on this island, see page 227. **Borneo Ultimate**, ground floor, Wisma Sabah, www.borneoultimate.com.my. Adventure

---

BORNEO RAINFOREST LODGE, DANUM VALLEY

The award-winning Borneo Rainforest Lodge is nestled in a magnificent setting alongside the Danum River flowing through Sabah's largest protected Lowland Rainforest – Danum Valley Conservation Area – 43,8000 Hectres of pristine and undisturbed tropical flora and fauna in the Eastern part of Sabah.

The lodge has only 31 individual Chalets with fans and en-suite bathrooms, accommodating up to only 60 guests on any one day and on a full board basis. Each chalet provides the comfort within the wilderness and tranquillity of the most pristine rainforest in Sabah's largest protected lowland rainforest.

Beside the Day trekking, Safari Night drives and Night Treks is also included as part of the Activities Package.

Borneo Nature Tours Sdn Bhd, (208366-X KP/LN:3219), Block D, Lot D, Sadong Jaya Complex.88100 Kota Kinabalu, Sabah, MALAYSIA
Reservation: T : +60 88 267 637, F : +60 88 251 636,
Email: infor@borneonaturetours.com

tours including whitewater rafting, mountain biking, jungle trekking, and sea kayaking.

Borneo Wildlife Adventures, Lot F, 1st floor, General Post Office building, T088-213668, www.borneo-wildlife.com. Specializing in nature tours, wildlife and cultural activities.

Diethelm Borneo Expeditions, Suite 303, 2nd floor, EON-CMG Life Building, 1 Jln Sagunting, T088-222271, dbex@tm.net.my.

Discovery Tours, ground floor, Wisma Sabah, Jln Haji Saman, T088-221244, www.infosabah.com.my/discovery/. Run by experienced tour operator Albert Wong. Packages include trips to longhouses, whitewater rafting and wildlife trips. Recommended.

Down Below Marine and Adventures, KK Times Square, 3rd floor, Lot 12, Block B, T088-488997, www.divedownbelow.com. Run by a friendly British couple, this outfit has received plaudits from readers for their dive and snorkel trips out to Pulau Gaya (where they have a Five-Star PADI Dive Station), Pulau Tiga and the Usukan Bay Second World War wrecks. They can also arrange land tours to Kinabatangan and Gomantong. Recommended.

Exotic Borneo, Likas Post Office, Likas, T088-245920, www.exborneo.com. Runs well-run theme tours including culture, adventure and nature, at a price.

Intra Travel Service, Lot No A-1-7, Block A, 1st floor, Tanjung Aru Plaza, Jln Mat Salleh, T088-261558, www.intra-travel.com.my. Best place to book trips in the excellent Tabin Wildlife reserve, see page 250.

KK Tours & Travel, J-60-5, Signature Office, KK Times Square, Off Coastal Highway, T088-868818, www.kktours.com. Good operator with a wide range of tours, from golfing to island hopping around Pilau's Tiga and Mantanani and luxury helicopter rides in the mountains. Also have own tours and accommodation in the Klias Wetlands, see page 213.

Mountain Torq, Unit 3-49, 3rd floor, Asia City Complex, Jln Asia City, T088-268126, www.mountaintorq.com. Organizes Via Ferrata treks on the north face of Gunung Kinabalu.

Nasalis Larvatus Tours, contact General Manager Alexander Yee (friendly and genuinely interested in conservation), Lot 226, 2nd floor, Wisma Sabah, Jln Tun Abdul Razak, T088-230534, www.nasalislarvatus tours.com. For **Nature Lodge Kinabatangan**, www.naturelodgekinabatangan.com, excellent mid-range lodge about 1 hr upriver from Sukau. More luxurious accommodation is in the process of being built, recent upgrades include hot showers. Currently a fairly quiet part of the river with a wide range of activities including kayaking, nature walks and river boat trips. At least 2-3 nights needed to get the most from the area. Great wildlife viewing, with elephants, many bird species, crocodiles, orang-utans and many primates often spotted.

Pan Borneo Tours & Travel, 1st floor, Lot 127, Wisma Sabah, T088-221221, www.panborneo.com. Sightseeing, diving and wildlife.

Riverbug/Traverse Tours, White Water Rafting Specialist, Lot 227-229, 2nd floor, Wisma Sabah, Jln Tun Fuad Stephen, T088-260501, www.traversetours.com. Well-organized 1-day rafting trips on the Padas (grade III-IV) river run from KK. Good guides, transport and safety equipment, plus a post-river barbecue. Good facilities. Not terrifying rapids for hardcore paddlers, but big waves, warm water and the spectacular scenery of the Crocker Range make this a fun day out for everyone. The smaller Kiulu River (grades II-III) is just as picturesque, but with smaller rapids and occasional slow moving sections interspersed with deep pools, good for learning basic kayaking skills or for a first white water descent. They also run a probosis monkey wetland tour, climbing Mount Trusmadi and trekking, biking and camping tours across Sabah.

Scuba Paradise, Lot G28, ground floor, Jln Tun Razak Wisma Sabah, T088-266695, www.scubaparadiseborneo.com.my. Reliable local dive operator offering both open water courses and fun dives around Tunku Abdul

Rahman National Park, Mantanani Island and Sipadan/Mabul islands. Recommended for day dives in the TARP area and Mantanani. **Tanjung Aru Tours**, The Marina, **Tanjung Aru Resort**, T088-214215, F240966. Fishing and island tours – particularly to Tunku Abdul Rahman National Park.

Whitewater rafting
Papar River (grades I and II), Kadamaian River (grades II and III), Padas River (grade IV). Usually requires a minimum of 3 people. Main operators include **Api Tours**, **Diethelm Borneo Expeditions**, **Traverse Tours/ Riverbug** and **Discovery Tours** (see above).

● Transport

Kota Kinabulu *p188, maps p189, p190 and p195*
Air
Air is the most widely used form of transportation between major towns in Sabah. MASwings connect KK with **Sandakan**, **Tawau** and **Lahad Datu** and it's cheap. Regular connections with **KL**. There are also connections from KK with **Bintulu**, **Johor Bahru**, **Kuching**, **Labuan**, **Miri** and **Sibu**. International connections are to **Singapore**, **Brunei**, **Hong Kong**, **Manila** (with Cebu Pacific), **Cebu**, **Seoul**, **Jakarta**, and various cities in China including **Shenzhen**, **Guangzhou** and **Kaohsiung** (Taiwan). Singapore is now well connected to KK with budget airlines **Tiger Airways**, **AirAsia** and **Jet Star Asia** offering frequent connections. AirAsia plans to make KK its hub for China flights, with connections to **Guilin** and **Xiamen** expected by the time this guide is published.

Airline offices AirAsia, Jln Gaya, T088-438222. Asiana, Suite 7-7E, 7th floor, Menara MAA, 6 Lorong Api Api, T088- 268677. **Cebu Pacific**, c/o Skyzone Tours, Suite G-02, Menara MAA, 6 Lorong Api Api, T088-448871. **Dragonair**, Lot CG, G/F, Block C, Kompleks Kuwasa, T088-254733. **Korean Air**, Lot 2B, Airport, T088-251152. **Malaysia Airlines** (for MAS and MASwings), PO Box 10194, T088-239111. **Royal Brunei**, Lot BG, 3B, G/F Kompleks Kuwasa, T088-242193. **Silk Air**, Tg Aru Plaza, 1st floor, Block B, Jln Mat Salleh, T088-265771.

Boat
Getting from Brunei overland takes 6 hrs including 2 ferries from Muara to Labuan and then on to Kota Kinabalu, or a 45-min flight.

There is a ferry service between KK and **Labuan** with departures at 0800 (daily), 1330 (Mon-Thu) and 1500 (Fri-Sun), the journey takes 3 hrs (RM31 one way). There are 6 daily ferries to **Serasa Muara** (**Brunei**) from the Labuan jetty between 0900 and 1630 (1 hr, RM30). For travellers heading through to Muara from KK, there is a package including both ferry tickets for RM53. This does not include the RM10 departure tax payable in Labuan. For travellers heading to Brunei, it's essential to catch the first departure of the day. From Muara's Serasa Ferry Terminal, minibuses run to Bandar Seri Begawan (45 mins, B$2).

Bus
There's no central bus station in KK. Buses further afield but still in the KK region leave from next to Plaza Wawasan. Destinations include **Sipitang**, **Beaufort** and **Lawas**.

Buses into the interior wait in the scruffy car park at the base of Signal Hill; destinations include **Tenom**, **Ranau**, **Kota Belud**, **Papan**, **Sipitang**, **Lawas**, **Tambunan** and **Keningan**.

City minibuses leave from the station on Jln Tun Razak, next to the City Park. Long-distance buses to **Sandakan**, **Semporna**, **Lahad Datau** and **Tawau** leave from the terminal in Inanam, 10 km from the centre. To get there, hop on local bus No 3, or take a taxi (RM15). Buses around the state are cheaper than minibuses but not as regular or efficient. The large buses go mainly to destinations in and around KK itself.

There are lots of bus companies and when you arrive at the bus station touts will try to get you to use their company. All the prices should be the same, and it's advisable to buy your ticket the day before. The time on the ticket is a rough guide only. Get there 10 mins before to guarantee your seat, but you may have to wait until the bus is full. Buses to **Tenom** (0800, 1200, 1600, 3 hrs RM17), **Keningau** (8 departures daily, 2½ hrs RM13), **Beaufort** (more than 10 every day, 2 hrs RM10), **Tawau** (0730, 0745, 1400, 2000, 9 hrs RM71.40), **Sandakan** (0730, 0800, 0930, 1130, 1200, 1400, 6 hrs RM71.40), **Semporna** (0730, 0830, 0900, 2000, 9 hrs RM75), **Lahud Datu** (0700, 0830, 0900, 2000, 8 hrs RM52).

Daily buses leave at 0800 from the Wawasan Plaza Terminal for **Bandar Seri Begawan** (7 hrs RM100) and **Miri** (10 hrs RM90).

Minibus
All minibuses have their destinations on the windscreen, most rides in town cost RM1-RM2 and leave when full. You can get off wherever you like.

Car
Not all roads in the interior of Sabah are paved and a 4WD vehicle is advisable for some journeys. Car hire is expensive (RM30-80 per hr) and rates often increase for use outside a 50-km radius of KK. All vehicles have to be returned to KK as there are no agency offices outside KK, although local car hire is usually available. Drivers must be between the ages of 22 and 60 and possess an international driving licence. **ABAN-D Rent a Car**, Lot 22, 1st floor, Taman Victory, Mile 4.5, Jln Penampang, T088-722300, F721959. **Adaras Rent-a-Car**, Lot G03, ground floor, Wisma Sabah, T088-2166671, F216010. **Hertz**, Level 1, Lot 39, Kota Kinabalu airport, T088-317740. **Kinabalu Rent-a-Car**, Lot 3.61, 3rd floor, Karamunsing Kompleks, T088-232602, www.kinabalurac.com/. **Samzain Rent a Car**, Lot 10, Tingkat 2 Putatan Point, Penampang, T088-765805.

Taxis
There are taxi stands outside most of the bigger hotels and outside the General Post Office, the Segama complex, the Sinsuran complex, next to the DPKK building, the Milemewah supermarket, the Capitol cinema and in front of the clocktower (for taxis to **Ranau**, **Keningau** and **Kudat**). Approximate fares from town: RM15 to **Tanjung Aru Resort**, RM15 to **Sabah Foundation**, RM12 to the museum, RM15-20 to the airport. See also minibus, above.

Train
The station is 5 km out of town in Tanjung Aru. There is only 1 train line in Sabah, and rolling stock dates from the colonial era. At the time of writing no services were operating due to an upgrade. Services are expected to resume in late 2010.

❶ Directory

Kota Kinabulu *p188, maps p189, p190 and p195*
Banks There are money changers in main shopping complexes: **HSBC**, 56 Jln Gaya; **Maybank**, Jln Kemajuan/Jln Pantai; **Sabah Bank**, Wisma Tun Fuad Stephens, Jln Tuaran; **Standard Chartered**, 20 Jln Haji Saman. **Embassies and consulates** British Consul, Hong Kong Bank Building, 56 Jln Gaya; **Indonesian Consulate**, Lorong Kemajuan, Karimunsing, T088-218600, indocon@indocon.po.my; **Japanese Consulate**, Wisma Yakim, T088-428169. **Immigration** 4th floor, Government Building, Jln Haji Yaakub, visas can be renewed at this office, without having to leave the country. **Internet** Web access is easily available and cheap. Many of the more jazzy coffee shops (including Western chains like **Starbucks**) and many hotels and guesthouses offer free Wi-Fi for customers with their own laptops. Local internet cafés are often noisy and crammed with game-playing locals. Expect to pay RM3 per hr. **Post office** General Post Office, Jln Tun Razak, Segama Quarter (poste restante facilities). **Telephone** Telekom, Block C, Kompleks Kuwaus, Jln Tunku Abdul Rahma. International and local calls, fax service.

Off the coast and south of Kota Kinabalu

West of KK is the Tunku Abdul Rahman Park, a reef and coral marine park. Travelling south from KK, the route crosses the Crocker Range to Tambunan. Continuing south the road passes through the logging town of Keningau and on to Tenom, where the North Borneo railway used to run (which should be back in action late 2010), snaking down the Padas Gorge to Beaufort. The Padas River is the best place to go whitewater rafting in Sabah. Few towns are worth staying in for long on this route, but it is a scenic journey.

Pulau Tiga National Park is a forest reserve where the pied hornbill can be spotted and Pulau Labuan is a tax-free haven off the coast. ►► *For listings, see pages 217-224.*

Tunku Abdul Rahman National Park → *Colour map 4, A3.*

The five islands in Gaya Bay, which make up Tunku Abdul Rahman Park (TAR), lie 3-8 km offshore. Coral reefs fringe all the islands in the park. The best reefs are between **Pulau Sapi** and **Pulau Gaya**, although there is also reasonable coral around **Manukan**, **Mamutik** and **Sulug**. Named after Malaysia's first prime minister, they became Sabah's first national park in 1923 and were gazetted in 1974 in an effort to protect their coral reefs and sandy beaches. Geologically, the islands are part of the Crocker Range formation, but as sea levels rose after the last ice age, they became isolated from the massif. The islands can be visited all year round.

Ins and outs

Getting there Boats for the park leave from Jesselton Point Ferry Terminal, 10 minutes' walk north of the town and cost RM23 return. There are frequent departures and the last boat back is at 1700. Ferries to Labuan leave from here too. There are also frequent boats from the Sutera Harbour Resort. ►► *See Transport, page 223.*

Tourist information Park HQ is on Pulau Manukan; there are ranger stations on Gaya, Sapi and Mamutik.

Flora and fauna

Some of the only undisturbed coastal dipterocarp forest left in Sabah is on Pulau Gaya. On the other islands most of the original vegetation has been destroyed and established secondary vegetation predominates, such as ferns, orchids, palms, casuarina, coconut trees and tropical fruit trees. Mangrove forests can be found at two locations on Pulau Gaya. Animal and birdlife includes long-tailed macaques, bearded pig and pangolin (on Pulau Gaya), white-bellied sea eagle, pied hornbill, green heron, sandpipers, flycatchers and sunbirds.

There is a magnificent range of marine life because of the variety of the reefs surrounding the islands. The coral reefs are teeming with exotica such as butterfly fish, Moorish idols, parrot fish, bat fish, razor fish, lion fish and stone fish, in stark contrast to the areas that have been depth-charged by Gaya's notorious dynamite fishermen.

The islands

By far the largest island, **Pulau Gaya** was the site of the first British North Borneo Chartered Company settlement in the area in 1881; the settlement lasted only 15 years before being destroyed in a pirate attack. There is still a large community on the island on the promontory facing KK, but today it is a shanty town, populated mainly by Filipino immigrants. On Pulau Gaya there are 20 km of marked trails including a plankwalk across a mangrove swamp and many beautiful little secluded bays. Police Bay is a popular, shaded beach. **Gayana Island EcoResort** is a big chalet development on the island with its own ferry from the KK jetty. **Pulau Sapi**, the most popular of the islands for weekenders, also has good beaches and trails. It is connected to Pulau Gaya at low tide by a sandbar. There are good day-use facilities but no accommodation except camping.

Pulau Mamutik, closer to the mainland, is the smallest island but has a well-preserved reef off the northeast tip. **Pulau Manukan** is the site of the Park HQ and most of the park accommodation. It has good snorkelling to the south and east and a particularly good beach on the east tip. It is probably the best of all the islands but is heavily frequented by day trippers and rubbish is sometimes a problem. There is accommodation here; book through **Sutera Sanctuary Lodges**, see page 189. Marine sports facilities stretch to the hire of mask, snorkel and fins (RM15, plus RM50 deposit for the day), and diving equipment. There's a swimming pool, water sports centre for sailing, banana boat and windsurfing. Glass-bottom boat trips are available. Fish feeding off the jetty attracts large shoals of fish, making it a good place for snorkelling. The best reefs are off **Pulau Sulug**, which is less developed as it is a bit further away. This small island has a sand spit, making it good for swimming. There are dive facilities and a restaurant. You can also camp here.

Pulau Tiga National Park → *Colour map 4, B2.*

This park is 48 km south of KK. Declared a forest reserve in 1933, the 15,864 ha park is made up of three islands: Pulau Tiga, Kalampunian Damit and Kalampunian Besar.

Ins and outs
Getting there and around Drive 140 km to Kuala Penyu at the tip of the Klias Peninsula (two hours, RM18), and then take a 30-minute boat ride (scheduled departures at 1000, 1030 and 1500 from Kuala Penyu – price usually included in resort packages – book in advance). Alternatively charter a speedboat from KK; contact **Sipadan Dive Centre** ⓘ *11th floor, Wisma Merdeka, Jln Tun Razak, KK, T088-240584, www.pulau-tiga.com*, who run the island's resort, to organize transport to the island. **Sabah Parks Office** can also help arrange the boat trip. Speedboats cost RM350 for 10 people, but it's possible to bargain down to RM250 for the boat if there are fewer people.

Tourist information The Park HQ, on the south side of Pulau Tiga, is mainly used as a botanical and marine research centre and tourism is not vigorously promoted; as a result there are no special facilities for tourists. The best time to visit is between February and April, when it is slightly drier and the seas are calmer.

National park
Pulau Tiga achieved notoriety as the location for the reality TV series *Survivor*, chosen for its unspoilt natural landscape. Pulau Tiga's three low hills were all formed by mud volcanoes. The last big eruption, in 1941, was heard 160 km away and covered the island in a layer of boiling mud. The bubbling mud pools that remain at three points across the island are a slightly bizarre but interesting bathing experience and something that distinguishes the island from others in the area. The dipterocarp forests on the islands are virtually untouched and they contain species not found on other west coast islands, such

as a poisonous amphibious sea snake (*Laticauda colubrina*), also known as the banded sea krait, which comes ashore on Pulau Kalampunian Damit to lay its eggs. Rare birds such as the pied hornbill (*Anthracoceros convexus*) and the megapode (*Megapodus freycinet*) are found here, as well as flying foxes, monitor lizards, wild fruit trees and mangrove forest. A network of trails, marked at 50-m intervals, leads to various points of interest.

Underwater the island offers good diving at a diverse range of sites. There's excellent coral growth mid-channel and plenty of smaller marine life and fish making this a colourful spot. It's variable after storms and strong winds. The small offshore house reef is good, with lots of anemones, clown fish and the occasional turtle. As long as you're not expecting the vast underwater cliffs and crystal-clear conditions of the Sipadan area, Pulau Tiga has plenty to keep you entertained on the marine front.

Pulau Labuan → *Colour map 4, B2.*

Labuan is one of the historically stranger pieces of the Bornean jigsaw. Originally part of the Sultanate of Brunei, the 92-sq-km island, 8 km off the coast of Sabah, was ceded in 1846 to the British who were enticed to take it on by the discovery of rich coal deposits. It joined the Malaysian Federation in 1963, along with Sabah and Sarawak. In 1984 it was declared a tax-free haven – or an 'International offshore financial centre' – and hence this small tropical island with just 80,000-odd inhabitants has a plethora of name-plate banks and investment companies. For the casual visitor – rather than someone wanting to salt away

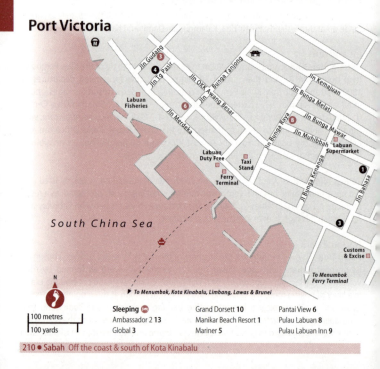

Port Victoria

South China Sea

Labuan Fisheries

Labuan Duty Free

Labuan Supermarket

Taxi Stand

Ferry Terminal

Jln Gudang
Jln Tg Pasir
Jln OKK Awang Besar
Jln Bunga Tanjong
Jln Merdeka
Jln Kemajuan
Jln Bunga Melati
Jln Bunga Raya
Jln Bunga Mawar
Jln Muhibbah
Jln Bunga Kenanga
Jln Bahasa

Customs & Excise

To Menumbok Ferry Terminal

To Menumbok, Kota Kinabalu, Limbang, Lawas & Brunei

N

100 metres
100 yards

Sleeping
Ambassador 2 **13**
Global **3**

Grand Dorsett **10**
Manikar Beach Resort **1**
Mariner **5**

Pantai View **6**
Pulau Labuan **8**
Pulau Labuan Inn **9**

their million – it offers some attractions, but not many. There are good hotels, lots of duty-free shopping, a golf course, sport fishing and diving, plus a handful of historic and cultural sights.

Ins and outs

Getting there and around The airport is 5 km from town. There is a reasonable island bus network, a few car hire firms and a small number of taxis. ▸▸ *See Transport, page 223.*

Tourist information **Tourist Information Office** ① *Lot 4260, Jln Dewan/Jln Berjaya, T087-423445.* See also www.labuantourism.com.my.

Background

With a superb deep-water harbour, Labuan promised an excellent location from which the British could engage the pirates who were terrorizing the northwest Borneo coast. Labuan also had coal, which could be used to service steamships. Sarawak's Rajah James Brooke became the island's first governor in 1846 and two years later it was declared a free port. It also became a penal colony: long-sentence convicts from Hong Kong were put to work on the coal face and in the jungle, clearing roads. The island was little more than a malarial swamp and its inept colonial administration was perpetually plagued by fever and liver disorders. Its nine drunken civil servants provided a gold mine of eccentricity for novelists Joseph Conrad and Somerset Maugham. In *The Outstation*, Maugham describes the desperate attempt by Resident Mr Warburton to keep a grip on civilization in the wilds of

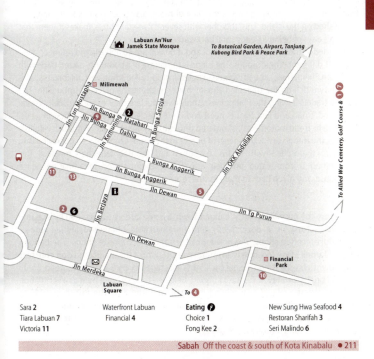

Sleeping		Eating 🍴	
Sara **2**	Waterfront Labuan	**Eating 🍴**	New Sung Hwa Seafood **4**
Tiara Labuan **7**	Financial **4**	Choice **1**	Restoran Sharifah **3**
Victoria **11**		Fong Kee **2**	Seri Malindo **6**

Malaysia: "The only concession he made to the climate was to wear a white dinner jacket; but otherwise, in a boiled shirt and high collar, silk socks and patent leather shoes, he dressed as formally as though he was dining at his club in Pall Mall..."

By the 1880s ships were already bypassing the island and the tiny colony began to disintegrate. In 1881 William Hood Treacher moved the capital of the new territory of British North Borneo from Labuan to Kudat and eight years later the Chartered Company was asked to take over the administration of the island. In 1907 it became part of the Straits Settlements, along with Singapore, Malacca (Melaka) and Penang.

Modern Labuan

In 1946 Labuan became a part of British North Borneo and was later incorporated into Sabah as part of the Federation of Malaysia in 1963. Datuk Harris is thought to own half the island (including the **Hotel Labuan**). As chief minister, he offered the island as a gift to the federal government in 1984 in exchange for a government undertaking to bail out his industrial projects and build up the island's flagging economy. The election of a Christian government in Sabah in 1986, making it Malaysia's only non-Muslim-ruled state, proved an embarrassment to the then prime minister Doctor Mahathir Mohamad. Labuan has strategic importance as a federal territory, wedged between Sabah and Sarawak. It is used by garrisons of the Malaysian army, navy and air force.

In declaring Labuan a tax haven the Malaysian government set out its vision of Labuan becoming the Bermuda of the Asia-Pacific for the 21st century; 4065 offshore firms had set up on the island by the end of 2003, and in 2000, the **Labuan International Financial Exchange** (LFX), a wholly owned subsidiary of the Kuala Lumpur Stock Exchange, was established on the island. This, together with several five-star hotels, makes it seem that Labuan's days of being a sleepy rural backwater are over.

Included in the island's population of about 80,000 are 10,000 Filipino refugees, with about 21 different ethnic groups. The island is the centre of a booming 'barter' trade with the South Philippines; Labuan is home to a clutch of so-called string vest millionaires, who have grown rich on the trade. In Labuan, 'barter' is the name given to smuggling. The Filipino traders leaving the Philippines simply over-declare their exports (usually copra, hardwood, rotan and San Miguel beer) and under-declare the imports (Shogun jeeps, Japanese hi-fi and motorbikes), all ordered through duty-free Labuan. With such valuable cargoes, the traders are at the mercy of pirates in the South China Sea. To get round this, they arm themselves with M-16s, bazookas and shoulder-launched missiles. This ammunition is confiscated on their arrival in Labuan, stored in a marine police warehouse, and given back to them for the return trip.

Sights

Away from the busy barter jetty, Labuan Town, a name largely superseded by its name of **Port Victoria**, is a dozy, seedy and unremarkable Chinese-Malaysian mix of shophouses, coffee shops, sleazy karaoke bars and cheap booze shops. The **Labuan An'Nur Jamek State Mosque** is an impressive site, whilst the manicured **golf course** is popular with businessmen. Illegal cockfights are staged every Sunday afternoon. There is an old brick **chimney** at Tanjung Kubong, believed to have been built as a ventilation shaft for the short-lived coal mining industry established by the British in 1947 to provide fuel for their steamships on the Far Eastern trade route. Remnants of the industry, which had petered out by 1911, are to be found in a maze of **tunnels** in this area. Near Tanjung Kubong is a **Bird Park**.

On the west coast there are pleasant beaches, mostly lined with kampongs. There is a large **Japanese war memorial** on the east coast and a vast, well-tended, **Allied war cemetery** between the town and the airport with over 3000 graves, most of which are unknown soldiers. The **Peace Park** at Layang Layangan marks the Japanese surrender point on 9 September 1945, which brought the Second World War to an end in Borneo.

Boat trips can be made to the small islands around Labuan, although only by chartering a fishing vessel. The main islands are **Pulau Papan** (an uninspiring island between Labuan and the mainland), **Pulau Kuraman**, **Pulau Rusukan Kecil** (known locally as the floating lady) and **Pulau Rusukan Besar** (floating man). These last three have good beaches and coral reefs but none have any facilities.

Off the south coast of the island is the **Marine Park**; a great place to dive, especially as there are four shipwrecks scattered in these waters. The park has 20 dive sites. ▶▶ *See Activities and tours, page 222.*

South of Kota Kinabalu

Papar → *Colour map 4, B3.*
Formerly a sleepy Kadazan village, 38 km south of KK, Papar is developing fast. In *bandar lama* (the old town) there are rows of quaint wooden shophouses, painted blue and set along spacious boulevards lined with palms. There is a large market in the centre. The Papar area is famous for its fruit and there is a good *tamu* every Sunday.

There is a scenic drive between Papar and KK, with paddy fields and jungle lining the roadside. Nearby, **Pantai Manis**, a 3-km stretch of golden sand with a deep lagoon good for swimming, can be reached easily from Papar. It is also possible to make boat trips up the Papar River, which offers gentle rapids for less energetic whitewater rafters. Rafting trips can be organized through tour agents in KK (see page 204).

The **Klias Wetlands** is a new destination promoted by **Sabah Tourism**, popular with visitors who do not have time to visit the east coast of Sabah. Boat trips operate through a mangrove swamp and the Klias River, with the chance to spot proboscis monkeys, long-tailed macaques, silver langur monkeys and an abundance of birdlife. The Klias Peninsula lies 120 km south of KK; trips down the Klias River depart from the Kota Klias jetty. Booking via a tour operator is recommended. Contact tour operators in KK such **Diethelm Borneo Expeditions** and **KK Tours & Travel**, see page 204.

Tambunan → *Colour map 4, B3. Population: 28,000.*
The twisting mountain road that cuts across the **Crocker Range National Park** (see page 215) and over the Sinsuran Pass at 1649 m is very beautiful. There are dramatic views down over Kota Kinabalu and the islands beyond and glimpses of Mount Kinabalu to the northeast. The road itself, from KK to Tambunan, was the old bridleway that linked the west coast to the interior. Inland communities traded their tobacco, rattan and other jungle produce for salt and iron at the coastal markets. The road passes through Penampang. Scattered farming communities grow hill rice, pineapples, bananas, mushrooms and other vegetables that are sold at roadside stalls, where wild and cultivated orchids can also be found. After descending from the hills the road enters the sprawling flood plain of Tambunan – the Pegalam River runs through the plain – which, at the height of the paddy season, is a magnificent patchwork of greens.

The Tambunan area is largely Kadazan/Dusun, Sabah's largest ethnic group, and the whole area explodes into life each May during the harvest festival when copious

Rafflesia: the world's largest flower

The rafflesia (*Rafflesia arnoldi*), named after Stamford Raffles, the founder of modern Singapore, is the largest flower in the world. The Swedish naturalist Eric Mjoberg wrote in 1930 on seeing the flower: "The whole phenomenon seems so amazing, so unfamiliar, so fantastic, that we are tempted to explain: such flowers cannot be real!"

Stamford Raffles, who discovered the flower for Western science 100 years earlier during his first sojourn at Bengkulu on the west coast of Sumatra, noted that it was "a full yard across, weighs 15 pounds, and contains in the nectary no less than eight pints [of nectar]...".

The problem is that the rafflesia does not flower for very long – only for a couple of weeks, usually between August and December. At other times of the year there is usually nothing to see. The plant is in fact parasitic, so appropriately its scent is more akin to rotting meat than any perfume. Its natural habitat is moist, shaded areas.

quantities of *lihing*, the famed local rice wine, are consumed and *Bobolians* (high priestesses) still conduct various rituals (see box page 280). There is a *lihing* brewery inside the Tambunan Village Resort Centre. The Tambunan District covers an area of 134,540 ha. At 650 m to 900 m, it enjoys a spring-like climate during much of the year.

Tambunan (Valley of the Bamboo), so-called as there are at least 12 varieties of bamboo to be found here, also lays claim to the Kitingan family. Joseph was Sabah's first Christian chief minister until he was deposed in March 1994. His brother, Jeffrey, was formerly head of the Sabah Foundation. He entered politics in 1994 on his release from detention on the Malaysian Peninsula. He had been charged under Malaysia's internal security act of being a secessionist conspirator.

A concrete structure at Tibabar, just outside Tambunan, situated amongst the rice fields and surrounded by peaceful kampong houses, commemorates the site of **Mat Salleh's fort** ⓘ *daily 0900-1700, free*, and the place of his death. Mat Salleh, now a nationalist folk hero, led a rebellion for six years against the **Chartered Company** administration until he was killed in 1900 (see box, page 192). The memorial has been set up by the Sabah State Museum and houses some exhibits including weapons, Salleh paraphernalia and a photo of the man himself.

The Rafflesia Information Centre ⓘ *daily 0800-1500, T087-774691*, is located at the roadside on the edge of a forest reserve that has been set aside to conserve this remarkable flower (see box above). The information centre has a comprehensive and attractive display on the rafflesia and its habitat and information on flowers in bloom. If trail maps are temporarily unavailable, ask the ranger to point out the sites where blooms can be seen on the large relief model of the forest reserve at the back of the information centre. The blooming period of the flower is very short so, to avoid disappointment, it's worth phoning the centre first. Ranger guides are available at the centre and cost RM100 for a group of six or less.

Ahir Terjan Sensuron is a waterfall 4 km from the Rafflesia Information Centre on the Tambunan – KK road (heading towards KK). From the road, it is a 45-minute walk to the waterfall. Every Thursday morning a large market is held here, selling tobacco, local musical instruments, clothing, strange edible jungle ferns and yeast used to make fermented rice wine. There are also bundles of a fragrant herb known as *tuhau*, a member of the ginger family that is made into a spicy condiment or sambal redolent of the jungle. A smaller market is held on Sunday in Kampong Toboh, north of Tambunan.

Crocker Range National Park ⓘ *no visitors' facilities have yet been developed*, incorporates 139,919 ha of hill and montane forest, which includes many species endemic to Borneo. It is the largest single totally protected area in Sabah. Private development is taking place along the narrow strips of land each side of the KK – Tambunan road, which were unfortunately overlooked when the park was gazetted. To get there, see Transport, page 224 (as for Tambunan).

The **Mawah Waterfall** is reached by following the road north towards Ranau to Kampong Patau, where a sign beside the school on the left indicates a gravel road leading almost to the waterfall (Mawah Airterjun). It is 15 minutes down the road by car and between five and 10 minutes' walk along the trail.

Gunung Trusmadi, 2642 m, 70 km southeast of Kota Kinabalu, is the second highest mountain in Malaysia, but very few people climb it: the route is difficult and facilities, compared with Gunung Kinabalu, are few. There are two main routes to the top: the north route, which takes four days to the summit (and three days down) and the south route, which is harder but shorter; two days to the summit. Trusmadi is famous for its huge, and very rare, pitcher plant *Nepethes trusmadiensis*, found only on one spot on the summit ridge. It is also known for its fantastic view north, towards Gunung Kinabalu, which rises above the Tambunan Valley. There is a wide variety of vegetation on the mountain as it rises from dipterocarp primary jungle through oak montane forest with mossy forest near the summit and heath-like vegetation on top. An expedition to Trusmadi requires careful planning and should not be undertaken casually. A more detailed account of the two routes is in *Mountains of Malaysia – A Practical Guide and Manual*, by John Briggs.

Keningau → *Colour map 4, B3.*

The Japanese built fortifications around their base in Keningau during the Second World War. It is now rather a depressing, shabby lumber town, smothered in smoke from the sawmills. The timber business in this area turned Keningau into a boom town in the 1980s and the population virtually doubled within a decade. The felling continues, but there is not much primary forest left these days. There are huge logging camps all around the town and the hills to the west. Logging roads lead into these hills off the Keningau – Tenom road, which are accessible by 4WD vehicles. It is just possible to drive across them to Papar, which is a magnificent route. If you do attempt the drive, steer well clear of log-laden trucks on their way down the mountain. There is an interesting weekly *tamu* held here on Sunday mornings, principally noted for its Kadazan handicrafts.

Sapulut is deep in Murut country and is accessible from Keningau by a rough road via Kampong Nabawan (4WD required). At Sapulut, follow the river of the same name east through Bigor and Kampong Labang to Kampong Batu Punggul at the confluence of Sungai Palangan, a 2½-hour journey. **Batu Punggul** is a limestone outcrop protruding 200 m above the surrounding forest, about 30 minutes' walk from the kampong; it can be climbed without any equipment, but with care. It is quite a dangerous climb, but there are plenty of handholds and the view of the surrounding forest from the top is spectacular. Both the forest and the caves in and around Batu Punggul are worth exploring. Nearby is the less impressive limestone outcrop, **Batu Tinahas**, with huge caves and many unexplored passages. It is thought to have at least three levels of caves and tunnels. Some tour operators in KK offer trips here.

There is a short stretch of road leading from Sapulut to Agis, just a four-hour boat ride from the Kalimantan border. There is even an immigration checkpoint at Pegalungan, which is a settlement en route. (**Note** It's not possible to cross into Indonesia from here.)

There are many rivers and longhouses worth exploring here. One particular longhouse is **Kampong Selungai**, only 30 minutes from Pegalungan. Here it is possible to see traditional boatbuilders at work, as well as weaving, mat making and beadwork. Given the luxury of time, it is a fascinating area where traditional lifestyles have not changed much. It is possible to charter a minibus along the Nabawan road to Sapulut, where you can hire boats upriver. At Sapulut, ask for Lantir (the headman, or *kepala*). He will arrange the trip upriver, which could take up to two days, with accommodation in Murut longhouses, through the gloriously named **Sapulut Adventurism Tourism Travel Company**, which he runs. As in neighbouring Sarawak, these long upriver trips can be prohibitively expensive unless you are in a decent-sized group.

Tenom → *Colour map 4, B3.*

Situated at the end of the North Borneo Railway, southwest of Keningau on the banks of the Sungei Lapas, Tenom is a hilly inland town, with a population of about 46,000, predominantly Chinese. Although it was the centre of an administrative district under the Chartered Company from the turn of the century, known as Fort Birch, most of the modern town was built during the Japanese occupation in the Second World War. It is in the heart of Murut country, but don't expect to see longhouses and Murut in traditional costume; many Murut have moved into individual houses, except in the remoter parts of the interior and their modernized bamboo homes are often well equipped.

The surrounding area is very fertile and the main crops are soya beans, maize and a variety of vegetables. Cocoa is also widely grown. The cocoa trees are often obscured under shade trees called *pokok belindujan*, with bright pink flowers. The durians from Tenom (and Beaufort) are thought to be the best in Sabah. *Tamu* (market) is on Sunday.

There are many **Murut villages** surrounding Tenom, all with their own churches. In some villages there is also an oversized mosque or *surau*. The **Murut Cultural Centre** ① *T088-734506*, is 10 km out of town. Run by the Sabah Museum, it displays the material culture of the Murut people including basketry, cloth and the famous Murut trampolines of *lansaran*. The *Pesta Kalimaran* is held for two days each year at the centre at the start of April and showcases the culture of the Murut through music, dance and art. It's very touristy but well worth a visit. The best longhouses are along the Padas River towards Sarawak at Kampong Marais and Kampong Kalibatang where blowpipes are still made. At **Kemabong**, 25 km south of Tenom, the Murut, who are keen dancers, have a *lansaran* dancing trampoline; a wooden platform sprung with bamboo which can support 10 Murut doing a jig.

Sabah Agricultural Park ① *T088-258529, www.sabah.net.my/agripark, 15 km northeast of Tenom, Tue-Sun 0900-1630, RM25, children RM10*, is a research initiative developed by the Sabah State Government. This is also the site of Tenom's **orchid farm**, which has been developed into an agro-tourism park. One of the more celebrated aspects of the park is the Bee Centre, highlighted in a Sir David Attenborough BBC documentary. Almost half of the world's bee species can be seen here.

Beaufort → *Colour map 4, B3.*

This small, sleepy, unexciting town is named after British Governor P Beaufort of the North Borneo Company, who was a lawyer and was appointed to the post despite having no experience of the East or of administration. He was savaged by Sabahan historian KG Tregonning as "the most impotent governor North Borneo ever acquired and who, in the manner of nonentities, had a town named after him." Beaufort is a quaint town, with riverside houses built on stilts to escape the constant flooding of the Padas River. The *tamu* (market) is on Saturday.

Sipitang → *Colour map 4, B2.*

Located on the coast, Sipitang is a sleepy town with little to offer the traveller apart from a supermarket and a few hotels (see page 220). Sipitang is south of Beaufort and the closest town in Sabah to the Sarawak border. It is possible to take minibuses from Beaufort to Sipitang and on to Sindumin, where you can connect with buses bound for Lawas in Sarawak by walking across the border to Merapok. There is an immigration checkpoint here and month-long permits are given for visitors to Sarawak.

◉ Off the coast and south of Kota Kinabalu listings

For Sleeping and Eating price codes and other relevant information, see Essentials pages 23-27.

● Sleeping

Tunku Abdul Rahman National Park
p208

There are significant discounts Mon-Fri.
AL Chalets, Pulau Manukan, contact **Sutera Sanctuary Lodges**, ground floor, Wisma Sabah, T088-243629, www.suterasanctuary lodges.com, for bookings on Manukan. Delightful wooden chalets, some 2 storey, with cable TV and jungle-themed bathrooms. There's a pool, restaurant, tennis and squash courts, football field, 1500-m jogging track and dive centre. Slightly overpriced.
A Gayana Island EcoResort, Lot 16, ground floor, Wisma Sabah, Jln Tun Razak, Pulau Gaya, T088-245158, www.gayana-ecoresort. com. Set on the east coast of the island, 44 a/c chalets, good service but slightly run down, restaurant serving Asian and Western dishes, private beach, reef rehabilitation research centre with some interactive programmes available for interested visitors. Activities include diving, snorkelling, fishing windsurfing, jungle trekking and yachting. Dank smelling mangroves and some reports of dirty water around the resort from the nearby shanty town.

Camping

It's possible to camp on any island. Obtain permission from the **Sabah Parks Office** in KK,

Lot 3, Block K, Sinsuran Complex, T088-211881, www.sabahparks.org.my. The island gets packed with tourists during the day, but if you camp you can enjoy a near-deserted island after 1700 when the rabble departs. Beware of leaving your clothing unattended at the edge of the forest, as monkeys have been known to run off with it!

Pulau Tiga National Park *p209*
AL-A Pulau Tiga Resort, T088-240584, www.pulau-tiga.com. Owned by **Sipadan Dive Centre** and with standard chalets, a/c superior rooms with comfortable kingsize beds and drink-making facilities. Budget triples in a longhouse. All rooms have sea views. The resort also organizes water sports, treks and trips to nearby islands. There is a Survivor package where visitors take part in numerous gruelling activities including challenges and building a shelter. Games room, **Survivor Bar** and restaurant. Many packages include meals, making it good value, especially for those staying in the cheaper rooms.

There is also a **hostel** that can hold up to 32 people. Book in advance through the Sabah Parks Office in KK, see above; there is also an attached canteen. It is possible to camp.

Pulau Labuan *p 210, map p211*
Hotels in Labuan are generally poor value compared to towns in Sabah and Sarawak. Prices at more expensive places drop during the week. There is little for budget travellers.

AL Grand Dorsett, 462 Jln Merdeka, T087-422000, www.dorsetthotels.com/labuan. This is Labuan's most upmarket offering, with a huge sparkling lobby, pool, fitness centre and an array of food and beverage outlets including **Victoria's Brasserie** with superb seafood and daily themed buffet dinners. The **Fun Pub** has live music and nightly drinks specials. Rooms are opulent and some have excellent views over the port. Wi-Fi access throughout. Staff are professional and offer top service with a smile. Recommended.

A Manikar Beach Resort, Jln Batu Manikar, T087-418700, manikar@tm.net.my. On the northwest tip of Labuan, 20 mins from town centre by free shuttle. A stylish resort built with polished wood (the owner is a timber tycoon), set in 15 ha of gardens dotted with tall palms which reach down to the beach. The 250 rooms, all sea facing with generous balconies, are very spacious, tastefully furnished, with a/c, minibar, TV, in-house video. Large pool at sea level with swim-up bar, separate children's pool, fitness centre, tennis, playroom, business centre, duty-free shop. The beach is regularly cleaned and sprayed so sandflies are not a problem, but the sea is not recommended for swimming due to jellyfish. Restaurant with excellent food and good value theme buffet nights.

A Tiara Labuan, Jln Tanjung Batu, T087-414300, F410195. On the west coast next to the golf course, 5-min taxi ride from town centre. Beautiful hotel and serviced apartments surrounding a large lotus pond and deep blue pool complete with jacuzzi. Built onto Adnan Kashoggi's old mansion, it has an Italian feel with terracotta tiles, putty pink stone, a glorious gilt fountain and long shady arcades. The original mansion now has the reception, restaurant (food mediocre) and acres of opulent lounge including an Arab section with low sofas, hubbly bubbly pipes and a marble fountain. All 25 rooms, and also the 48 serviced apartments (1 or 2 bedroom) have a/c, TV, minibar, electric hob, sink and a living room. Tanjung Batu beach across the road is rather muddy, but good for walks

when the tide is out. **Labuan Beach Restaurant** is here too. Holidaymakers, especially families, opt for the larger hotels as the **Tiara** has no organized activities or kiddy pool, but this is partly what makes it a haven of tranquillity. Recommended.

A Waterfront Labuan Financial, 1 Jln Wawasan, T087-418111, F413468. Overlooking the yacht marina (and also an industrial seascape), this place has a marina-look combined with the atmosphere of being on a luxury cruise. Over 200 rooms, all with a/c, minibar, TV and opulent fittings. The main restaurant, the **Clipper**, serves Western and local food. There is also a bar, the **Anchorage**, with live entertainment nearly every evening. Pool, tennis and health centre. The hotel manages the 50-berth marina with internationally rated facilities. The harbourmaster also organizes yacht charters and luxury cruises. Recommended.

B Ambassador 2, Lot 2 Jln Bunga Kesuma, T087-411711, F411337. Chinese-run hotel with a range of clean rooms, unfortunately reeking of cigarettes. The small single rooms are tiny and an extra RM10 will get a much more spacious 'superior' room. All rooms with TV and a/c and attached bath

B Global, U0017, Jln OKK Awang Besar (near market), T087-425201, www.skynary.com/globalhotel. Smallish rooms with cable TV, tatty carpet and attached hot water bathroom. Many rooms are windowless. The staff are friendly enough, but this place is overpriced.

B Mariner, Jln Tg Purun (on crossroads opposite police HQ), T087-418822, mhlabuan@streamyx.net. Spic and span place with 60 clean a/c rooms with attached bathroom and TV with in-house movies. Staff are on the ball here. Fair value.

B Pantai View, Lot U0068, Jln OKK Awang Besar, T087-411339, hpv2009@hotmail.com. Recently renovated, this place is one of the better hotels in town with simple clean rooms, friendly staff and spacious rooms with Wi-Fi, cable TV, marble floor and attached hot water bathroom. There are a couple of good Indian restaurants downstairs for late-night snacks. Free tea, coffee and mineral water. Recommended.

B Pulau Labuan, 27-28 Jln Muhibbah, T087-416288, F416255. Fair value hotel with limited character but clean a/c rooms with TV and attached bathroom. A coffee shop downstairs serves Western food and cold beer.

B Pulau Labuan Inn, Lot 8, Jln Bunga Dahlia, T087-416833, F441750. Downmarket sister of the **Pulau Labuan**, spotlessly clean but small a/c rooms.

B Sara, Jln Dewan, T087-417811, saratel@ tm.net.my. Smart hotel popular with families and business folk without the seedy undertones of many other city hotels. Rooms have cable TV and attached bathroom and there is Wi-Fi on the 1st floor and lobby. Excellent Malay eatery (**Seri Malindo**).

B Victoria, U0360 Jln Tun Mustapha, T087-412411, F412550. The oldest hotel in town with an archaic lift with a concertina door. The carpets in the rooms are tatty and stained and the furniture is ancient. However, prices here are lower than most other places in town and rooms have TV, a/c and attached bathroom with lukewarm water. Seedy massage parlour leads off the lobby.

Homestays

The local government offers a variety of homestay packages with local families in traditional Malay kampongs, a great way to see the island and learn about Malay life. On offer is a stay at the water village opposite Port Victoria, a night at Sungai Labu village on the coast 12 km from the town and a 2-night stay at Bukit Kuda. Various activities are offered from joining a *gotong royong* (communal clean-up), cooking lessons, fishing trips and Kedayan cultural performances. Prices start at RM65 a night including all meals. Highly recommended. Contact **Labuan Tourism Action Council**, Labuan Sea Port Complex, T087-422622, www.labuantourism.com.my.

Papar *p213*

A Beringgis Beach Resort, Km 26, Jln Papar, Kampong Beringgis, Kinarut, T088-752333, www.beringgis.com. Sprawling resort on the beach with spotless, stylish a/c rooms with TV, minibar and hot water bathroom. There is a pool, restaurant, lots of Asian games such as *carom* and *congkak* and Wi-Fi access in the lobby. Very family-friendly place.

A Langkah Syabas Beach Resort, Jln Papar Baru, Kinarut, T088-752000, www.langkah syabas.com.my. 21 km south of KK. 18 chalets of varying size with spacious verandas set around the pool. A/c, fans, TV, tennis and riding centre close by, attractive tropical garden. 100 m to the beach.

B-D Seaside Travellers Inn, Km 20 Papar-KK Highway, Kinarut, T088-750555, www.infosabah.com.my/seaside. Fairly unexciting place with a/c rooms and a dorm set in a pleasant location off the beach. Tennis court, pool. Horse riding and tours can be organized.

C Mai Aman Country Rest House, Km 35, off Old Papar Rd, Kinarut, T088-914486, maiamanresort@hotmail.com. 6-room country resthouse and 12-room bush hostel. Fishing onsite in spacious grounds with an orchard and a nightclub with karaoke for those in a masochistic frame of mind.

Tambunan *p213*

The area is renowned for its rice wine (*lihing*); see it being brewed at the TVRC factory.

B-C Borneo Heritage Village Resort (also known as **TVRC**, or Tambunan Village Resort Centre), signposted off main road before town, on both sides of the Pegalam River, T088-774076, F774205. Chalets and a 'longhouse' dorm made of split bamboo. Restaurant, motel and entertainment centre (with karaoke and slot machines), hall and sports field. There are also a couple of retreat centres located about 10 mins' walk away.

C-E Gunung Emas Highlands Resort, Km 52 (about 7 km from the **Rafflesia Centre**), T013- 868 9830. Dorms, basic tree houses, a fresh climate and good views. Mini zoo and restaurant serving local food. To get there take the Rabunan or the Keningau minibus and then bus from Tambunan.

Keningau p215
A-L Juta, T087-337888,
www.sabah.com.my/juta. The swankiest pad
in town. Marble-lobbied business tower,
de luxe rooms have minibar and circular
beds. Attractive wooden theme. Bar with
live crooners, café and restaurant. Business
centre with internet access
A Perkasa, Jln Kampong Keningau,
T088- 331045, www.perkasahotel.com.my.
Business hotel with comfortable a/c rooms
on the edge of town. There's a Chinese
restaurant, coffee house and health centre.
B-C Hillview Garden Resort, 1 Jln Menawo,
T087-333678, hillview@alfons.com.
New place with 25 rooms. Good option.
C Kristal, Pegalan Shopping Complex,
T087- 338888, F330562. Reasonable but a
bit characterless. A relatively cheap option
in a town lacking decent budget places.

Tenom p216
Orchid and Sri Jaya are both within walking
distance of the bus stop.
B Perkasa, top of the hill above town,
T087-735811, www.perkasahotel.com.my.
A large, modern business hotel with superb
views over Tenom and countryside. Rooms
are spacious and attractively furnished, with
TV, a/c and en suite bathroom. As guests are
few and far between, the restaurant, **Tenom
Perkasa**, has a limited but well-priced range
of Chinese and Western dishes. Staff are
friendly and helpful in arranging sightseeing.
Excellent value. Recommended.
C Orchid, Block K, Jln Tun Mustapha, T087-
737600, excelng@tm.net.my. Small but
friendly with clean, well-maintained rooms.
**C-D Rumah Rehat Lagud Sebren
(Agricultural Research Station Resthouse)**,
agripark@sabah.net.my. Located in the heart
of the agricultural park. Dorms and camping
(RM10 per person). Dorms are packed during
the school holidays, so book in advance.
C-D Sri Perdana, Lot 71, Jln Tun Mustapha,
T087-734001. Cheap, standard rooms.
Fair value.

D Sri Jaya, PO Box 47, T087-735007. The
cheapest option in town, with 12 a/c rooms,
shared bathroom, basic but clean.

Beaufort p216
A poor selection of hotels, all roughly the
same and slightly overpriced. Rooms have
a/c and bathrooms.
C Beaufort, Lot 19-20, Lochung Park, T087-
211911, F212590. Central, a/c, 25 rooms.
C Mandarin Inn, Lot 38, Jln Beaufort Jaya,
T087-212800. A/c rooms. It garners better
reviews than the Beaufort.

Sipitang p217
A-B SFI Motel, SFI Housing Complex,
10 Jln Jeti, T087-802097. Clean place with
a selection of a/c rooms with attached hot
water bathroom.
B-C Asanol, T087-821506. Good-value rooms
with bathrooms.
B-C Shangsan, T088-821800. Comfortable
rooms with a/c and TV. There is the
ubiquitous coffee shop in the same street.

🍴 Eating

Tunku Abdul Rahman National Park
p208
Excellent restaurant on Pulau Manukan. Pulau
Mamutik and Pulau Sapi each have a small
shop selling limited and expensive food and
drink and Sapi has some hawker-style food.
For Pulau Sulug, Sapi and Mamutik take all the
water you need – there is no drinkable water
supply here – shower and toilet water is only
provided if there has been sufficient rain.

Pulau Labuan p210, map p211
Several basic Chinese places to be found
along Jln Merdeka and Jln OKK Awang Besar.
🍴 **Clipper**, Waterfront Labuan Financial
Hotel. 24-hr upmarket coffee shop with local
and Western cuisine. Recommended.
🍴 **Fisherman's Wharf**, next to the Sara hotel
on Jln Dewan Pusat Bandar. Open for lunch
and dinner. This a/c place offers great

Cantonese-style seafood dishes and steamboats. Recommended.

Fong Kee, Lot 5 and 6, Jln Kemuning. While this place certainly won't win any awards for cleanliness, it's buzzing at lunchtimes as punters get stuck into generous plates of chicken rice, steaming bowls of delicious prawn mee and a daily dim sum selection.

Labuan Beach, Jln Tanjung Batu, T087-415611. International and local cuisine, breezy location on seashore, food not special but ambience makes up for it, as does well chilled draft Carlsberg.

Pulau Labuan, Lot 27-28, Jln Muhibbah. Smart a/c interior with chandeliers. Fish sold by weight; good tiger prawns. Recommended.

Victoria's Brasserie, Grand Dorsett. Changing daily theme buffet selection that includes Penang street food, barbecue nights and, perhaps in celebration of the town's colonial past, English night. The steamboat buffet is the one to look out for though, with fresh seafood in chicken or *tom yam* broth. Recommended.

Choice, Jln Bahasa. Great selection of north and south Indian dishes from dosai to naan, and biryani to tender tandoori. The fish biryani is particularly good. Recommended.

New Sung Hwa Seafood, Jln Ujong Pasir, PCK Building. Amongst the best-value seafood restaurants in Malaysia, chilli prawns, superb grilled stingray steak, no menu. Recommended.

Restoran Sharifah, Jln Merdeka. Just opposite the ferry terminal, this busy place has a good choice of Malay and Indian Muslim dishes. The *roti prata* here fly out the kitchen at an alarming rate.

Seri Malindo, next to Sara hotel. Spotless a/c restaurant offering good *nasi campur*.

Foodstalls
Above wet market and at other end of town, along the beach next to the **Island Club**. Stalls on Jln Muhibbah opposite the end of Jln Bahasa, west of the cinema, and a few hawker stalls behind **Hotel Pulau Labuan**.

Papar *p213*
There are several run-of-the-mill coffee shops and restaurants in the old town.

Seri Takis, New Town (below the lodging house). Padang food.

Sugar Buns Bakery, Old Town. Sweet bread and thick coffee.

Keningau *p215*
Seri Wah Coffee Shop, on the corner of the central square and near some foodstalls.

Tenom *p216*
Curry Emas. Specializes in monitor lizard claypot curries, dog meat and wild cat.

Jolly, near the station. Serves Western food (including lamb chops), karaoke.

Restoran Chi Hin. Chinese coffee shop.

Sabah, Jln Datuk Yaseen. Muslim Indian food, clean and friendly.

Sapong, Perkasa hotel. Local and Western.

Y&L (Young & Lovely) Food & Entertainment, Jln Sapong (2 km out of town). Noisy, but easily the best restaurant in Tenom. Mainly Chinese food: freshwater fish (steamed *sun hok*, also known as *ikan hantu*) and venison; washed down with the local version of *air limau* (or *kitchai*) which comes with dried plums. Giant TV screen. Recommended.

Yong Lee. Coffee shop serving cheap Chinese fare in town centre.

Beaufort *p216*
Beaufort Bakery, behind **Beaufort** hotel, 'freshness with every bite'.

Ching Chin Restaurant. Chinese coffee shop in town centre.

Jin Jin Restaurant, behind **Beaufort** hotel. Chinese, popular with locals.

O Shopping

Pulau Labuan *p210, map p211*
Duty free
If you plan to take duty-free goods into Sabah or Sarawak, you have to stay on Labuan for a

Sabah's markets and trade fairs

In Sabah, an open trade fair is called a *tamu*. Locals gather to buy and sell jungle produce, handicrafts and traditional wares. *Tamu* comes from the Malay word *tetamu*, to meet, and the biggest and most famous is held at Kota Belud, north of Kota Kinabalu in Bajau country.

Tamus were fostered by the pre-war **British North Borneo Chartered Company**, when district officers would encourage villagers from miles around to trade among themselves. It was also a convenient opportunity for officials to meet with village headmen. They used

to be strictly Kadazan affairs, but today *tamus* are multicultural events. Sometimes public auctions of water buffalo and cattle are held. Some of the biggest *tamus* around the state are:

Monday: Tandek
Tuesday: Kiulu, Topokan
Wednesday: Tampuruli
Thursday: Keningau, Tambunan, Sipitang, Telipok, Simpangan
Friday: Sinsuran, Weston
Saturday: Penampang, Beaufort, Sindumin, Matunggong, Kinarut
Sunday: Tambunan, Tenom, Kota Belud, Papar, Gaya Street (KK)

---

minimum of 72 hrs. **Labuan Duty Free**, Bangunan Terminal, Jln Merdeka, T087-411573. Opened in Oct 1990, 142 years after Rajah James Brooke first declared Labuan a free port. The island's original duty-free concession did not include alcohol or cigarettes, but the new shop was given special dispensation to sell them. 2 months later the government extended the privilege to all shops on the island, which explains the absurd existence of a duty-free shop on a duty-free island. The shop claims to be the cheapest duty free in the world; however, you will find competitively priced shops in town too. **Monegain**, for example, can undercut most other outlets on the island due to the volume of merchandise it turns over: worth more than RM1 million a month. The shop owes its success to Filipino 'barter traders' who place bulk purchase orders for electronic goods or cigarettes. These are smuggled back to Zamboanga and Jolo and find their way onto Manila's streets within a week. Brunei's alcohol-free citizens also keep the shop in business; they brought liquor worth nearly RM2 million from Labuan into Brunei within the first 3 months of trading.

Handicrafts

Behind Jln Merdeka and before the fish market, there is a congregation of tin-roofed shacks housing a Filipino handicrafts and textile market and an interesting wet market.

Supermarkets

Financial Park, Jln Merdeka. Shopping complex with Milimewah supermarket. **Labuan Supermarket**, Jln Bunga Kenanga, centre of town. **Milimewah**, Lot 22-27, Lazenda Commercial Centre, Phase II, Jln Tun Mustapha, department store with supermarket on ground floor. **Thye Ann Supermarket**, central position below Sri Mutiara.

Tambunan *p213*
Handicrafts

There is a *tamu* (market) on Thu. The **Handicraft Centre**, just before the Shell petrol station, sells traditional local weaving and basketry.

▲ Activities and tours

Pulau Labuan *p210, map p211*
Diving

There are at least 10 popular dive sites around the TAR islands, with reef depths from

3-21 m, providing a variety of experiences. It's possible to dive all year with an average visibility of about 12 m. The water is cooler Nov-Feb, when visibility is not as good. For extensive information on the various coral/fish/dive sites, contact **Borneo Divers**. **Borneo Divers**, 1 Jln Wawasan, **Waterfront Labuan Financial** hotel, T087-415867, www.borneodivers.info. Specializes in 2-day packages diving on shipwrecks off Labuan for certified scuba-divers. There are 4 wrecks in total and each wreck costs about RM100.

Fishing
Fishing with a hook and line is permitted but the use of spearguns and nets is not. Permits are not necessary.

Golf
Kelab Golf, Jln Tanjung Batu, T087-421810. Magnificent 9-hole golf course. You may be asked for proof of handicap or a membership card from your own club. Also tennis and a pool.

Horse riding
Labuan Horse Riding Centre, T087-466828. For a different way to go sightseeing. It offers beach and paddock rides plus lessons.

Snorkelling
Snorkel, mask and fins can be rented from boatmen at the KK jetty (although snorkelling equipment is for hire on Sapi and Manukan).

Sipitang *p217*
Tour operators
Sipitang Tours & Services, Lot 5, Tingkat 1, Kedai SEDCO, T013-869 1570.

⊖ Transport

Tunku Abdul Rahman National Park *p208*
Air
There are flights to **KK** and **KL** (MAS and AirAsia) and to **Miri** with MASwings.

Boat
All boats leave from the main jetty 10 mins' walk north of town.

There are regular speedboats to **KK** and **Menumbok** (used by those who want to take their car onto Labuan, 1 hr's drive from KK) and several daily boat connections with **Lawas** and **Limbang** (Sarawak) and **Sipitang**. There's also a regular ferry service with **Kota Kinabalu** and with **Muara** in **Brunei**.

Small boats carry 6 people and will leave for any of the islands (RM15 per person fixed price) when full, but everyone needs to agree a destination and a return time. It will cost an extra RM50 if you want to return the next day. There's a regular service for **Gayana** between 0800 and 2300, roughly every 2 hrs (RM23 return), 38 km. For 2 island hops it costs RM33 and for 3 hops, RM43. It's possible to charter a boat for tours, from RM350 for a 3-island tour or RM600 for a 5-island tour, for 12 passengers. It's possible to negotiate trips with local fishermen. Boats also leave from **Tanjung Aru Beach Hotel**. There is a RM3 park fee payable for entry to the park.

Pulau Labuan *p210, map p211*
Air
The airport is 5 km from town. Regular connections with **KK**, **Kuala Lumpur**, and **Miri**.
Airline offices AirAsia, c/o HMD Tours & Travel, T087-416117. **MAS**, airport, T087-412263.

Boat
From Bangunan Terminal Feri Penumpang next to the duty-free shop on Jln Merdeka. All times are subject to change, tickets are sold at arrival points at the ferry terminal, but can be bought in town at **Duta Muhibbah Agency**, T087-413827. 2 connections a day with **Menumbok** (RM10, the nearest mainland point) by speedboat (30 mins) or car ferry. It's a 2-hr bus ride from here to **KK**. Currently there are 2 boats a day to **Kota Kinabalu** (2½ hrs, RM31, 0830-1500). There are 2 daily boats to **Limbang** at 1230 and

1400 (1½ hrs, RM20) and one to **Lawas** (both Sarawak), at 1230 (1½ hrs, RM20). **To Brunei** On weekends and public holidays in Brunei the ferries are packed and it's a scramble to get a ticket. You can reserve tickets to Brunei at the ticket office at the ferry terminal. 6 boats leave Labuan for Brunei (**Serasa Muara**) daily, 0830-1630, (1½ hrs, RM35).

Bus
Local buses around the island leave from Jln Bunga Raya.

Car
Adaras Rent-a-Car, T087-421590. Travel Rent-a-Car, T087-423600.

Taxi
Old Singapore NTUC cabs are not abundant, but are easy enough to get at the airport and around hotels. It is impossible to get a taxi after 1900 but minibuses abound.

Papar *p213*
Minibus
These leaves from the Bandar Lama area. There are regular connections with **KK**, 1 hr and **Beaufort**, 1 hr.

Tambunan *p213*
Minibus
Buses marked Tambunan go from the long-distance bus station at the bottom of Signal Hill in **KK** (1½ hrs).

Taxi
To **KK** for RM120.

Keningau *p215*
Minibus
These leave from the centre, by the market. Regular buses to **KK** and **Tenom**.

Taxi
KK costs around RM200

Tenom *p216*
Minibus
Minibuses leave from centre of town on Jln Padas. Regular connections with **Keningau** (45 mins(and **KK** (3 hrs).

Taxi
To **KK** costs around RM220 or shared taxis are available for a fraction of the price; they leave from the main street (Jln Padas).

Beaufort *p216*
Minibus
Minibuses leave from centre of town. Regular connections with **KK** (2 hrs RM10).

Sipitang *p217*
There is a line of minibuses and taxis along the waterfront. The jetty for ferries to **Labuan** (daily departures) is a 10-min walk from the centre.

ⓘ Directory

Pulau Labuan *p210, map p211*
Banks HSBC, Jln Merdeka; **Standard Chartered**, Jln Tanjung Kubang (next to Victoria Hotel); **Syarikat K Abdul Kader**, money changer. **Post office** General Post Office Jln Merdeka.

Beaufort *p216*
Banks HSBC and Standard Chartered in centre of town. **Post office** General Post Office & Telekom, next to Hong Kong Bank.

North of Kota Kinabalu

From KK, the route heads north to the sleepy Bajau town of Kota Belud which wakes up on Sunday for its colourful tamu (market). Near the northernmost tip of the state is Kudat, the former state capital. The region north of KK is more interesting, with Gunung Kinabalu always in sight. From Kota Belud, the mountain looks completely different. It is possible to see its tail, sweeping away to the east, and its western flanks, which rise out of the rolling coastal lowlands. ▸▸ *For listings, see pages 228-229.*

Kota Belud → *Colour map 4, A3.*

This busy little town is in a beautiful location, nestling in the foothills of Mount Kinabalu on the banks of the Tempasuk River, but is of little interest except for its market. It is the heart of Bajau country, the so-called 'cowboys of the East', which is also lacking in sights.

The first Bajau to migrate to Sabah were pushed into the interior, around Kota Belud. They were originally a seafaring people but then settled as farmers in this area. The famed Bajau horsemen wear jewelled costumes, carry spears and ride bareback on ceremonial occasions. The ceremonial headdresses worn by the horsemen, called *dastars*, are woven on backstrap looms by the womenfolk of Kota Belud. Each piece takes four to six weeks to complete. Traditionally, the points of the headdress were stiffened using wax; these days, strips of cardboard are inserted into the points.

Sabah's largest **market** (*tamu*) is held every Sunday in Kota Belud behind the mosque, starting at 0600. A mix of people – Bajau, Kadazan/Dusun, Rungus, Chinese, Indian and Malay – come to sell their goods and it is a social occasion as much as a market. Aside from the wide variety of food and fresh produce on sale, there is a weekly water buffalo auction at the entrance. Visitors are strongly recommended to get there early, but don't expect to find souvenirs at these markets. However, the *tamu besar* (big market) held in November has cultural performances and handicrafts on sale.

This is an account of the market by a civil servant, posted to the KB district office in 1915: "The *tamu* itself is a babel and buzz of excitement; in little groups the natives sit and spread their wares out on the ground before them; bananas, langsats, pines and bread-fruit; and, in season, that much beloved but foul-smelling fruit, the durian. Mats and straw-hats and ropes; fowls, goats and buffaloes; pepper, gambia sirih and vegetables; rice (*padi*), sweet potatoes and *ubi kayu*; *dastars* and handkerchiefs, silver and brassware. In little booths, made of wood, with open sides and floors of split bamboos and roofs of *atap* (sago palm-leaf) squat the Chinese traders along one side of the *tamu*. For cash or barter they will sell; and many a wrangle, haggle and bargain is driven and fought before the goods change hands, or money parted with."

Tempasuk River has a wide variety of migrating birds and is a proposed conservation area. More than 127 species of bird have been recorded along this area of the coastal plain and over 500,000 birds flock here every year, many migrating from northern latitudes in winter. These include 300,000 swallows, 50,000 yellow longtails and 5000 water birds. The best period for birdwatching is October to March. Between Kota Belud and the sea are mangrove swamps with colonies of proboscis monkeys. You can hire small fishing boats in town to go down the Tempasuk River (RM20 per hour).

Tamus (markets) in Kota Belud District

Monday and Saturday: Kota Belud. Market time is 0600-1200. All *tamus* provide many places to eat.

Tuesday: Pandasan (along the Kota Belud to Kudat road).

Wednesday: Keelawat (along the Kota Belud to KK road).

Thursday: Pekan Nabalu (along the Kota Belud to Ranau road).

Friday: Taginambur (along the Kota Belud to Ranau road, 16 km from Kota Belud).

Kudat → Colour map 4, A4.

Kudat town, surrounded by coconut groves, is right on the northern tip of Sabah, 160 km from KK. The local people here are the Rungus, members of the Kadazan tribe. Gentle, warm and friendly, Rungus have clung to their traditions more than other Sabahan tribes and some still live in longhouses, although many are now building their own houses. Rungus longhouses are built in a distinctive style with outward-leaning walls; the Sabah State Museum incorporates many of the design features of a Rungus longhouse. The Rungus used to wear coils of copper and brass round their arms and legs and today the older generation still dress in black. They are renowned for their fine beadwork and weaving. A handful of Rungus longhouses are dotted around the Peninsula, away from Kudat town.

The East India Company first realized the potential of the Kudat Peninsula and set up a trading station on Balambanganan Island, to the north of Kudat. The settlement was finally abandoned after countless pirate raids. Kudat became the first administrative capital of Sabah in 1881, when it was founded by a Briton, AH Everett. William Hood Fletcher, the protectorate's first governor, first tried to administer the territory from Labuan, which proved impossible, so he moved to the newly founded town of Kudat which was nothing more than a handful of *atap* houses built out into the sea on stilts. It was a promising location, however, situated on an inlet of Marudu Bay, and it had a good harbour. Kudat's glory years were shortlived; it was displaced as the capital of North Borneo by Sandakan in 1883.

Today it is a busy town dominated by Chinese and Filipino traders (legal and illegal) on the coast and prostitutes trading downtown. Kudat was one of the main centres of Chinese and European migration in the late 19th century. Most of the Chinese who came to Kudat were Christian Hakka vegetable farmers: 96 of them arrived in April 1883 and they were followed by others, given free passages by the Chartered Company. More Europeans, especially the British, began to arrive on Kudat's shores with the discovery of oil in 1880. Frequent pirate attacks and an inadequate supply of drinking water forced the British to move their main administrative offices to Sandakan in 1883.

Sights

Kudat is dotted with family farms cultivating coconut trees, maize and groundnuts and keeping bees. Being by the sea, seafood is also a staple element in the diet and fisheries an important industry. Kudat is inhabited by many other ethnic groups: Bonggi, Bajau, Bugis, Kadazandusun, Obian, Orang Sungai and Suluk. The market is on Mondays.

There are some beautiful unspoilt white sand beaches north of town; the best known is **Bak-Bak**, 11 km north of Kudat. This beach, however, can get crowded at weekends and there are plans to transform it into a resort. It is signposted off the Kota Belud – Kudat road. You can take a minibus, but they are irregular; the best option is a taxi, but this is expensive.

Sikuati, 23 km west of Kudat on the northwest side of the Kudat Peninsula, has a good beach. Every Sunday, at 0800, the Rungus come to the market in this village. Local handicrafts are sold. You can get there by minibus.

Between Kota Belud and Kudat there is a marsh and coastal area with an abundance of birds. Costumed Bajau horsemen can sometimes be seen here.

The **Longhouse Experience** is possibly the most memorable thing to do in Kudat. A stay at a longhouse enables visitors to observe, enjoy and take part in the Rungus' unique lifestyle. There are two Baranggaxo longhouses with 10 units. Nearby are the village's only modern amenities, toilets and showers. During the day, the longhouse corridor is busy with Rungus womenfolk at work stringing elaborate beadworks and weaving baskets and their traditional cloth. Visitors can experience and participate in these activities. Longhouse meals are homegrown; fish and seafood come from nearby fishing villages, drinks are young coconuts and local rice wine. Evening festivities consist of the playing of gongs with dancers dressed in traditional Rungus costume. Tour companies organize trips. See box, page 124, for advice on visiting longhouses; for more details, contact **Sabah Tourism**, T088-212121, www.sabahtourism.com.

Matunggong is a less touristy area found on the road south of Kudat best known for its longhouses, though they are rather dilapidated now.

At **Kampong Gombizau**, visitors get to see bee keeping and the harvesting of beeswax, honey and royal jelly, while at **Kampong Sumangkap**, an enterprising little village, you can learn about traditional gong- and handicraft-making.

Mantanani Island → *Colour map 4, A3.*

One hour by speedboat from Kota Belud off Sabah's northwestern coast is Pulau Mantanani. The island and its surrounding islets offer a more rugged, unrestrained vibe than the sanitized upmarket resorts around Sabah's coastline. **Mantanani Island Resort** is run by **Borneo Sea**, a family business, offering a good chance to relax and get away from it all – just don't expect the island to be manicured exclusively for all your needs. While admiring another magnificent sunset, don't be surprised if all of a sudden a mother dairy cow and her calf wander up – just another resident of an island that boasts a couple of local fishing communities in addition to a diverse range of wildlife.

Mantanani also offers some more specific attractions. Surrounding waters can't be always be described as crystal clear, but they're renowned in the scuba community for their muck diving opportunities, nude branches and diverse underwater life, plus several interesting wrecks. Until recently, the waters were well known for the charming presence of Nick, a local and distinctive dugong (*Dugong dugon*) or sea cow with a small, unique indent or 'nick' – hence the name – in his tail. However, as of 2007 Nick and his friends seem to have migrated north to the southern Philippines.

Mantanani's remaining highlight has everything to do with location. Get yourself out of bed just before sunrise on a clear day and you'll be treated with a breathtakingly vast silhouette of Mount Kinabalu rising more than 4 km into the morning sky, framed in golden light as the sun rises behind it. Whilst daylight has already reached most of Sabah, a huge triangular shadow, tens of kilometres across, holds Mantanani and the nearby coast in darkness for a just a few minutes longer – a truly spectacular way to begin your day on the island. On the not uncommon overcast days, dark storm clouds laced with lightning around the mountains summit can also be quite beautiful.

☉ North of Kota Kinabalu listings

For Sleeping and Eating price codes and other relevant information, see Essentials pages 23-27.

⊜ Sleeping

Kota Belud *p225*
B-C Impian Siu Motel, Kg Sempirai, Jln Kuala Abai, T088-976617. Just 10 rooms in this reasonable place.
B-C Kota Belud Travellers Lodge, Lot 6, Plaza Kong Guan, T088-977228. Simple place with a variety of clean rooms.

Homestays
There's no limit to your length of stay. Live with and be treated as part of the family, getting invited to celebrations such as weddings. Activities include buffalo riding, jungle trekking, river swimming, cultural dancing, visits to local *tamus*, padi planting. Contact **Nature Heritage Travel and Tours**, ground floor, Wisma Sabah, KK, T088-318747, nhtt@nature-heritage.com, or **Taginambur Homestay**, T088-976595, taginambur@gmail.com. Very affordable for young travellers and an excellent way to learn the language and gain an in-depth knowledge of the culture.

Kudat *p226*
The **Sunrise** and **Oriental** hotels are within walking distance of the bus stop.
A Kudat Golf & Marina Resort, off Jln Urus Setia, T088-611211, www.kudatgolf marinaresort.com. A spanking-new orange monster next to a marina. Main attraction is the 18-hole championship golf course.
C Greenland, Lot 9/10, Block E, Sedco Shophouse (new town), T088-613211, F611854. A/c, standard rooms, shared bath.
C Kinabalu, Kudat Old Town, Jln Melor, T088-613888, F615388. A/c, clean, average value.
D Southern, Kudat Old Town, T088-613133. 10 rooms, but quite cheap and reasonable value compared with others in this category.

Mantanani Island *p227*
Book through **KK Tours & Travel**, page 205, or directly through **Borneo Sea Adventures**, page 204.

KK-based dive operation **Scuba Paradise**, see page 205, also runs day trips diving (RM560 per person) and snorkelling (RM380 per person) around Mantanani.
L-AL Mantanani Resort, book at Borneo Sea Adventures www.bornsea.com/mantanani. A bit rough round the edges, but the hexagonal en suite chalets are surprisingly elegant inside, and the home cooking is fresh and supplied in vast quantities. Prices are per person and usually sold in packages inclusive of food and activities: kayaking, snorkelling, up to 3 boat dives and unlimited shore dives per day. Good value if you use the island's facilities. Published rates are RM1900 (US$550) for a 3-day/2-night package (including transport to and from KK). Discounts for non-divers and children sharing with adults. Drinks and equipment hire are extra.

☉ Eating

Kota Belud *p225*
There are several Indian coffee shops around the main square.

♟ **Bismillah Restoran**, 35 Jln Keruak (main square). Excellent *roti telur*.
♟ **Indonesia Restoran**, next to the car park behind the **Kota Belud Hotel**.

☸ Festivals and events

Kota Belud *p225*
Nov The annual **Tamu Besar** includes a parade and equestrian games by the Bajau horsemen, a very colourful event. Contact Sabah Tourism for some more information.

O Shopping

Kota Belud *p225*
Daily market in main square, fish market south of the main market. Large *tamu* every Sun and an annual *tamu besar* with a wide variety of local handicrafts.

O Transport

Kota Belud *p225*
Minibus
From main square. Regular connections with **KK**, **Kudat** and **Ranau**. It takes 90 mins for **KK** to **Kudat** and Kota Belud could be a stop along the way, as connections are easy.

Kudat *p226*
Minibus
Minibuses leave from Jln Lo Thien Hock. Regular connections with **KK**, 4 hrs.

O Directory

Kota Belud *p225*
Banks Bank Pertanian, Jln Kudat; Public Bank Berhad, Jln Kota Kinabalu; Sabah Finance, Jln Ranau.

Kudat *p226*
Banks Standard Chartered Bank, Jln Lo Thien Hock.

Gunung Kinabalu National Park

→ *Colour map 4, A3.*
Gunung Kinabalu is the pride of Sabah, the focal point of the national park and probably the most magnificent sight in Borneo. In recognition of this, the park was declared a World Heritage Site by UNESCO in 2000 – a first for Malaysia. Although Gunung Kinabalu has foothills, its dramatic rockfaces, with cloud swirling around them, loom starkly out of the jungle. The view from the top is unsurpassed and on a clear day you can see the shadow of the mountain in the South China Sea, over 50 km away – Mantanani Island, page 227, is a great spot to see the mountain and its shadow from a different perspective. Even if you're not planning on climbing Gunung Kinabalu itself, it's well worth spending a few days exploring the park, one of the most biodiverse areas in Borneo.
▸▸ For listings, see pages 237-239.

Best time to visit

The average rainfall is 400 cm a year, with an average temperature of 20°C at Park HQ but at Panar Laban it can drop below freezing at night. With the wind chill factor on the summit, it feels very cold. The best time to climb Gunung Kinabalu is in the dry season between March and April when views are clearest. The worst time has traditionally been November to December during the monsoon, although wet or dry periods can occur at any time of the year. Avoid weekends, school and public holidays if possible.

The park is occasionally closed to climbers. Contact the **Sutera Sanctuary Lodges**, see below, to check the mountain is open for climbing when you visit.

Note The climb has become extremely popular in the last few years and it is worth booking a slot as early as possible.

Permits, entrance fees and accommodation

It costs RM100 per person (RM40 per child) to climb Gunung Kinabalu; a RM15 entry fee must be paid on arrival by all park visitors and compulsory insurance costs RM7. The park is run by **Sutera Sanctuary Lodges** ① *ground floor of Wisma Sabah, Kota Kinabalu, T088-243629, www.suterasanctuarylodges,com, Mon-Fri 0900-1830, Sat 0900-1630, Sun 0900-1500.* All accommodation in the park must be booked in advance through its office. ➤ *See also Sleeping, page 237.*

Equipment

A thick jacket is recommended, but at the very least you should have a light waterproof or windcheater to beat the wind chill on the summit. You can hire jackets from Laban Rata but you need to book ahead as there are limited numbers. Carry a dry sweater and socks in your backpack and change just before you get to the peak – if it's raining the damp chill is worse than the actual cold. There are small shops at Park HQ and Laban Rata that sell gloves, hats, raincoats, torches and food for the climb (but it's cheaper if you stock up in KK). It is also best to bring a sweater or thick shirts; the shops in Wisma Merdeka sell cheap woollies. Walking boots are recommended, but not essential; many people climb the mountain in trainers. Stock up on food, chocolate and drinking water in KK the day before. Essential items include a torch, toilet paper, water bottle, plasters, headache pills and suntan lotion. A hat is good for guarding against the sun and the cold. Lockers are available, RM1 per item, at the Park HQ reception office. Sleeping bags are provided free of charge in the **Laban Rata Resthouse**; essential for a good night's sleep. The resthouse also has hot water showers, but soap and towels are not provided. Some of the rooms are well heated, cheaper ones leave you to freeze.

Guides

Hiring a guide is compulsory: RM70 for the round trip (one to three people), RM80 for the Mesilau trail. Porters are available for between RM40 and RM62 (for 10 kg carried). Guides and porters should be reserved at least a day in advance at the Park HQ or at **Sutera Sanctuary Lodges**. On the morning of your climb, go to the HQ and a guide will be assigned to you. While a tour will cost around RM750 each (often excluding the RM100 climbing permit fee), a group of you can hire a taxi, book dorm accommodation and share a guide for the climb for slightly less per person than a tour, including all the fees. If you are doing it by yourselves it is best to get to the park a day in advance, and stay at Park HQ to get up early for the first part of the climb to Laban Rata. Alternatively, you can get up at 0600 in KK and try and arrive at the Park HQ before 0900 to be sure of finding a guide.

If you are desperate to go, short of time and have been informed that there is no accommodation available on the mountain in the next few days (as can happen during busy periods such as school holidays), it might still be worth turning up in person to enquire, but be aware that some hardy enthusiasts have spent nights sleeping on cold floors waiting for a spot. A shuttle bus to the park leaves from the Sutera Harbour in KK at 0715, and will drop you outside Park HQ around 0930; arrive no later if you are hoping to climb the mountain that day. You may still be able to pick up a guide if you are there before 1000, although you will be unlikely to find anyone else to share with; the climb should begin around 1100, allowing enough time to reach Laban Rata. Reports suggest that beds/mattresses up the mountain can sometimes be found if someone turns up in person. This method should be an absolute last resort, and it is by no means guaranteed to work. If things don't work out, accommodation will probably be available at Park HQ, or there are a number of good places within 2 km of the park.

Park HQ

These located a short walk from the main Ranau – KK road, and all the accommodation and restaurants are within 15 minutes' walk from the main compound. There is a shop next to the Park HQ that has good books on the mountain and its flora and fauna. Slide and film shows are held in the mini-theatre in the administration building at 1400 during

Gunung Kinabalu Trail

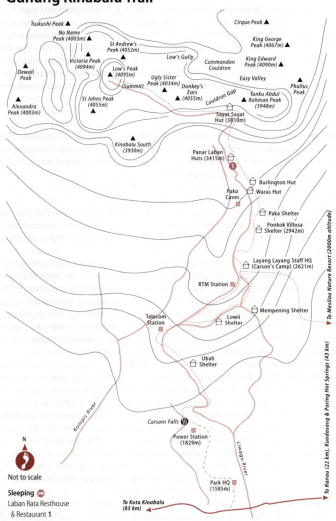

Tsukushi Peak ▲

No Name Peak (4003m) ▲

St Andrew's Peak (4052m) ▲

Victoria Peak (4094m) ▲

Dewall Peak ▲

Low's Peak (4095m) ▲ (Summit)

Ugly Sister Peak (4034m) ▲

St Johns Peak (4055m) ▲

Alexandra Peak (4003m) ▲

Cirque Peak ▲

King George Peak (4067m) ▲

Low's Gully

Commandon Couldron

King Edward Peak (4090m) ▲

Easy Valley

Donkey's Ears ▲ (4055m)

Couldron Gap

Tunku Abdul Rahman Peak (3948m) ▲

Phallus Peak ▲

Sayat Sayat Hut (3810m)

Kinabalu South (3930m)

Panar Laban Huts (3415m) 🏠 **1**

Burlington Hut 🏠

Paka Caves

Waras Hut 🏠

Paka Shelter 🏠

Ponkok Villosa Shelter (2942m) 🏠

Layang Layang Staff HQ (Carson's Camp) (2621m) 🏠

RTM Station 🏠

Mempening Shelter 🏠

Telecom Station 🏠

Lowii Shelter 🏠

Ubah Shelter 🏠

Carsons Falls ♨

Power Station (1829m)

Kolopis River

Liwogu River

Park HQ (1585m)

To Mesilau Nature Resort (2000m altitude) ▶

To Ranau (22 km), Kundasang & Poring Hot Springs (43 km) ▶

N

Not to scale

Sleeping

Laban Rata Resthouse & Restaurant **1**

To Kota Kinabalu (85 km) ◀

the week and at 1930 on weekends and public holidays (RM2), while naturalists give escorted trail walks every morning at 1100 (RM3). The museum displays information on local flora and fauna, beetles and foot-long stick insects.

Treks

A small colour pamphlet, *Mount Kinabalu/A Guide to the Summit Trail*, published by Sabah Parks, are a good guide to the wildlife and the trail itself. Most treks are well used and are easy walks, but the **Liwagu Trail** is a good three- to four-hour trek up to where it joins the summit trail and is very steep and slippery in places; not advised as a solo trip. There is a daily guided trail walk at 1100 from the park administration building. This is a gentle walk with a knowledgeable guide, although the number of participants tends to be large. The climb to the summit of Mount Kinabalu is not something that should be undertaken lightly. It can be perishingly cold on the summit and altitude sickness is a problem. Some points of the trail are steep and require adequate footware. Changeable weather conditions add to the hazards.

Background

In the first written mention of the mountain, in 1769, Captain Alexander Dalrymple of the East India Company, wrote from his ship in the South China Sea: "Though perhaps not the highest mountain in the world, it is of immense height." During the Second World War Kinabalu was used as a navigational aid by Allied bombers – one of whom was quoted as saying "That thing must be near as high as Mount Everest". It's not, but at 4095 m, Gunung Kinabalu is the highest peak between the Himalayas and New Guinea. It is not the highest mountain in Southeast Asia: peaks in Northern Myanmar (Hkakabo Razi) and the Indonesian province of Papua (Puncak Jaya, Gunung Trikora and Gunung Mandala) are all higher, placing Kinabalu fifth on the list – a fact rarely reflected in the Malaysian school geography syllabus.

There are a number of theories about the derivation of its name. The most convincing is the corruption of the Kadazan Aki Nabulu, 'the revered place of the spirits'. For the Kadazan, the mountain is sacred as they consider it to be the last resting place of the dead and the summit was believed to be inhabited by their ghosts. In the past the Kadazan are said to have carried out human sacrifices on Mount Kinabalu, carrying their captives to the summit in bamboo cages, where they would be speared to death. The Kadazan guides still perform an annual sacrifice to appease the spirits. Today they make do with chickens, eggs, cigars, betel nuts and rice on the rock plateau below the Panar Laban rockface.

The Chinese also lay claim to a theory. According to this legend, a Chinese prince arrived on the shores of northern Borneo and went in search of a huge pearl on the top of the mountain, which was guarded by a dragon. He duly slew the dragon, grabbed the pearl and married a beautiful Kadazan girl. After a while he grew homesick and took the boat back to China, promising his wife that he would return. She climbed the mountain every day for years on end to watch for her husband's boat. He never came and in desperation and depression, she lay down and died and was turned to stone. The mountain was then christened China Balu, or Chinaman's widow.

In 1851, Sir Hugh Low, the British colonial secretary in Labuan, made the first unsuccessful attempt at the summit. Seven years later he returned with Spencer St John, the British consul in Brunei. Low's feet were in bad shape after the long walk to the base of the mountain, so St John went on without him, with a handful of reluctant Kadazan porters. He made it to the top of the conical southern peak, but was "mortified to find that the most westerly [peak] and another to the east appeared higher than where I sat." He retreated and returned three months later with Low, but again failed to reach the summit, now called Low's Peak (standing at 4095 m above sea level). It remained unconquered for another 30 years. The first to reach the summit was John Whitehead, a zoologist, in 1888. Whitehead spent several months on the mountain collecting birds and mammals and many of the more spectacular species bear either Low's or Whitehead's name. More scientists followed and then a trickle of tourists, but it was not until 1964, when Kinabalu Park (encompassing 75,000 ha) was gazetted, that the 8.5-km trail to the summit was opened. Today the mountain attracts 200,000 visitors a year. Although the majority are day visitors who do not climb the peak, the number of climbers is steadily increasing, with at least 30,000 making the attempt each year.

In plan, the top of the mountain is U-shaped, with bare rock plateaux. Several peaks stand proud of these plateaux, around the edge of the U; the space between the western and eastern arms is the spectacular gully known as Low's Gully. No one has ever scaled its precipitous walls, nor has anyone climbed the Northern Ridge (an extension of the eastern arm) from the back of the mountain. From Low's Peak, the eastern peaks, just 1.5 km away, look within easy reach. As John Briggs points out in his book *Mountains of Malaysia*, "It seems so close, yet it is one of the most difficult places to get to in the whole of Borneo".

Flora and fauna

The range of climatic zones on the mountain has led to the incredible diversity of plant and animal life. Kinabalu Park is the meeting point of plants from Asia and Australasia. There are thought to be more than 1200 species of orchid alone and this does not include the innumerable mosses, ferns and fungi. These flowering plants of Kinabalu are said to represent more than half the families of flowering plants in the world. Within the space of 3 km, the vegetation changes from lowland tropical rainforest to alpine meadow and cloud forest. The jungle reaches up to 1300 m; above that, to a height of 1800 m, is the lower montane zone, dominated by 60 species of oak and chestnut; above 2000 m is the upper montane zone with true cloud forest, orchids, rhododendrons and pitcher plants. Above 2600 m, growing among the crags and crevices of the summit rock plateau are gnarled tea trees (*Leptospermums*) and stunted rhododendrons. Above 3300 m, the soil disappears, leaving only club mosses, sedges and Low's buttercups (*Ranunculus lowii*), which are alpine meadow flowers.

Among the most unusual of Kinabalu's flora is the world's largest flower, the rust-coloured rafflesia (see box, page 214). It can usually only be found in the section of the park closest to Poring Hot Springs. Rafflesia are hard to find as they only flower for a couple of weeks between August and December.

Kinabalu is also famous for the carnivorous pitcher plants, which grow to varying sizes on the mountain. A detailed guide to the pitcher plants of Kinabalu can be bought in the shop at Park HQ. Nine different species have been recorded on Kinabalu. The largest is the giant Rajah Brooke's pitcher plant; Spencer St John claimed to have found one of these containing a drowned rat floating in four litres of water. Insects are attracted by the scent and, when they settle on the lip of the plant, they cannot maintain a foothold on the waxy, ribbed surface. At the base of the pitcher is an enzymic fluid which digests the 'catch'.

Rhododendrons line the trail throughout the mossy forest (there are 29 species in the park), especially above the Paka Cave area. One of the most beautiful is the copper-leafed rhododendron, with orange flowers and leaves with coppery scales underneath. There are an estimated 1000 species of orchid in the park, along with 621 species of fern and 52 palm species.

It is difficult to see wildlife on the climb to the summit as the trail is well used, although tree shrews and squirrels are common on the lower trails. There are, however, more than 100 species of mammal living in the park. The Kinabalu summit rats, which are always on cue to welcome climbers to Low's Peak at dawn, and nocturnal ferret badgers are the only true montane mammals in Sabah. As the trees thin with altitude, it is often possible to see tree shrews and squirrels, of which there are more than 28 species in the park. Large mammals, such as flying lemurs, red-leaf monkeys, wild pigs, orang-utan and deer, are lowland forest dwellers. Nocturnal species include the slow loris (*Nycticebus coucang*) and the mischievous-looking bug-eyed tarsier (*Tarsius bancanus*). If heading to Kinabalu specifically to spot wildlife, then the longer, less visited Mesilau Trail is almost certainly a more productive option.

More than half of Borneo's 518 species of bird have also been recorded in Kinabalu Park, but the variety of species decreases with height. Two of the species living above 2500 m are endemic to the mountain: the Kinabalu friendly warbler and the Kinabalu mountain blackbird.

More than 61 species of frog and toad and 100 species of reptile live here. Perhaps the most interesting frog in residence is the horned frog, which can be impossible to spot thanks to its mastery of camouflage. The giant toad is common at lower altitudes; it's covered with warts, which are poisonous glands. When disturbed, these squirt a stinking, toxic liquid. Other frogs found in the park include the big-headed leaf-litter frog, whose head is bigger than the rest of its body, and the green stream shrub frog, who has a magnificent metallic green body, but is deadly if swallowed by any predator.

The famous flying tree snake has been seen in the park. It spreads its skin flaps, which act as a parachute when the snake leaps blindly from one tree to another.

There are nearly 30 species of fish in the park's rivers, including the unusual Borneo sucker fish (*Gastomyzon borneensis*), which attaches itself to rocks in fast- flowing streams. One Sabah Parks publication likens them to 'underwater cows', grazing on algae as they move slowly over the rocks.

Walkers and climbers are more likely to come across the park's abundant insect life than anything else. Examples include pill millipedes, rhinoceros beetles, the emerald green and turquoise jewel beetles, stick insects, 'flying peapods', cicadas, and a vast array of moths (including the giant atlas moth) and butterflies (including the magnificent emerald green and black Rajah Brooke's birdwing).

Gunung Kinabalu

The climb to the summit and back should take two days; four to six hours from Park HQ at 1585 m to the **Laban Rata Resthouse** (3550 m) on the first day. It is three hours to the summit for dawn on the second day, returning to the Park HQ at around 1200 hours on the second day.

Note There is a slightly tougher walk starting from Mesilau which takes two to three hours longer to get to Laban Rata, but which has far less tourists; the guide fee is slightly higher on this route at RM84 per person and porter fees to Laban Rata from Mesilau are RM88 per person.

Asia's first **Via Ferrata** (iron road) ⓘ *www.mountaintorq.com*, opened in 2007 and is also the world's highest. It is still relatively quiet with three possible routes taking between two to five hours to complete. The trail uses fixed rungs, rails, cables and stemples wrapped around the north face of the mountain. This slightly hair-raising adventure provides an experience akin to mountain climbing and a chance to see parts of the mountain usually never experienced by most visitors. The trail starts at Panar Laban Rock Face (3300 m) and reaches its highest point at 3800 m.

Gurkha soldiers and others have made it to the summit and back in well under three hours. For the really keen, or foolhardy, depending on your perspective, there is also the annual Kinabalu Climbathon (www.climbathon.sabahtourism.com) held in early October. Having said that the climb to the top requires no special skills, the death of a British teenage girl on the mountain in 2001 highlights the hazards of climbing an unfamiliar mountain where changes in the weather can be sudden and dramatic. Keep to the trails and keep your group together.

A minibus for 12 people can take groups from headquarters to the power station at 1829 m where the trail starts (RM5 per person). It is a 25-minute walk from the power station to the first shelter. The trail splits in two soon afterwards, the left goes to the radio station and the helipad and the right towards the summit. The next stop is **Layang Layang staff headquarters** (with drinking water, cooking facilities and accommodation), also known as **Carson's Camp** (2621 m). There is one more shelter, **Ponkok Villosa** at 2942 m, about 45 minutes from Carson's Camp, before the stop at the path to **Paka Caves**, which is really just an overhanging rock by a stream. Paka is a 10-minute detour to the left, where Low and St John made their camps.

From the cave/fifth shelter the vegetation thins out and it is a steep climb to **Panar Laban huts** – which includes the well-equipped **Laban Rata Resthouse** – affording magnificent views at sunset and in the early morning. The name Panar Laban is derived from Kadazan words meaning Place of Sacrifice: early explorers had to make a sacrifice here to appease the spirits and this ritual is still performed by the Kadazan once a year. **Sayat Sayat** (3810 m) hut – named after the ubiquitous shrubby tea tree – is an hour further on, above the Panar Laban rockface. Most climbers reach Panar Laban (or the other huts) in the early afternoon in order to rest up for a 0300 start the next morning to reach the summit by sunrise. This second part of the trail – 3 km long – is more demanding technically, but the trail is well laid out with regular resting points every 500 m. Ladders, handrails and ropes are provided for the steeper parts (essential in the wet, as the granite slabs can be very slippery). The final 1 km has no hand rails or ropes but is less steep. The first two hours after dawn are the most likely to be cloud free. For enthusiasts interested in alternative routes to the summit, John Briggs's *Mountains of Malaysia* provides a detailed guide to the climb.

Mountain Garden
ⓘ *Tours leave at 0900, 1200, 1500; the garden is closed at other times, RM5.*
Situated behind the park administration building, this landscaped garden has species from the mid-levels of the mountain, which have been planted in natural surroundings.

Mesilau Nature Resort
This rainforest resort nestles at the foot of Mount Kinabalu at 2000 m. The main attractions are the cool climate and the superb views up the mountain and across the plains toward Ranau and the sea. It is possible to scale the peaks of the mountain using the resort as a base, providing an alternative route to Low's Peak. Taking this new trail, one would join the main trail at Layang Layang. Alternatively, there are a number of walks to be made around the reserve in this secluded location.

Poring → *Colour map 2, A1.*

ⓘ *T088-878801, if you've already paid the entrance fee to the national park, keep your ticket for entrance to the hot springs; if staying at Poring there is no charge and the baths can be used all night; permits are not necessary.*

Poring lies 43 km from Gunung Kinabalu Park HQ and is part of the national park. The **hot sulphur baths** ⓘ *RM15 per hr; sulphur bath and jacuzzi, RM20 per hr*, were installed during the Japanese occupation of the Second World War for the jungle-weary Japanese troops. There are individual concrete pools that can fit two people, with taps for hot- and cold-spring mineral water; once in your bath you are in complete privacy. However, many visitors now complain that the water is no longer hot, more like lukewarm. The springs are on the other side of the Mamut River from the entrance, over a suspension bridge. They are a fantastic antidote to tiredness after a tough climb up Gunung Kinabalu. There is also a cold water rock pool. The pools are in a beautiful garden setting of hibiscus and other tropical flowers, trees and thousands of butterflies. There are some quite luxurious private cabin baths available and also large baths which hold up to eight people. The de luxe cabins have lounge areas and jacuzzis. The Kadazans named the area Poring after the towering bamboos of that name nearby.

The **jungle canopy walk** ⓘ *daily 0900-1600, RM5, camera RM5, video RM30, guides available*, at Poring is a rope walkway 35 m above the ground, which provides a monkey's-eye view of the jungle; springy but quite safe. The entrance is five minutes' walk from the hot springs and the canopy walkway is 15 minutes' walk from the entrance. The canopy walkway at Danum Valley is far more exciting. If the weather is clear at Ranau, it is generally safe to assume that the canopy walk will also be clear.

Kipungit Falls are only about 10 minutes' walk from Poring and swimming is possible here. Follow the trail further up the hill and after 15 minutes you come to bat caves; a large overhanging boulder provides shelter and a home for the bats.

The **Langanan Waterfall** trail takes 90 minutes one way, is uphill, but worth it. There is another hard, 90-minute trail to **Bat Cave** (inhabited by what seems to be a truly stupendous number of bats) and a waterfall. The **Butterfly Farm** ⓘ *daily 0900-1600, RM4*, was established close to the springs by a Japanese-backed firm in 1992 and is very educational in the descriptions of butterflies and other insects.

There is also an information centre, a rafflesia centre, orchid centre, aviary and tropical garden at Poring. It is better not to visit the hot springs at the weekend or on public holidays if you want to relax in a peaceful atmosphere. Minibuses to the springs leave Park HQ at 0900, 1300, 1600; alternatively, flag down a bus/minibus to Ranau on the main road a two-minute walk from HQ and take a taxi from there to Poring.

Ranau and Kundasang → *Colour map 2, A1.*

The Ranau plateau, surrounding the Kinabalu massif, is one of the richest farming areas in Sabah and much of the forest not in the park has now been devastated by market gardeners. Even within the national park's boundaries, on the lower slopes of Mount Kinabalu itself, shifting cultivators have clear-felled tracts of jungle and planted their patches. More than 1000 ha are now planted out with spinach, cabbage, cauliflower, asparagus, broccoli and tomatoes, supplying much of Borneo.

Kundasang and Ranau are unremarkable towns a few kilometres apart; the latter is bigger. The **war memorial**, behind Kundasang, which unfortunately looks like Colditz, is in memory of those who died in the death march in the Second World War (see page 275). The walled gardens represent the national gardens of Borneo, Australia and the UK.

Mentapok and Monkobo are southwest of Ranau. Both are rarely climbed. Mentapok, 1581 m, can be reached in 1½ days from Kampong Mireru, a village at the base of the mountain. A logging track provides easy access halfway up the south side of the mountain. Monkobo is most easily climbed from the northwest, a logging track from Telupid goes up to 900 m and from here it is a two-hour trek to the top. It is advisable to take guides, organized from Ranau or one of the nearby villages.

Some 17 km on the road to Sandakan is the **Sabah Tea Garden** ⓘ *Km 17, Ranau – Sandakan Rd, Kampung Nalapak, T088-440882, www.sabahtea.net,* the only organic tea farm in Borneo and offering a range of activities other than just sitting back with a cuppa and admiring the views. They offer a variety of packages including a rainforest adventure, where tourists sleep in a bamboo forest and swim in the Sapayon River before learning some survival cooking techniques. More genteel activities include tea tree planting and a factory visit. There is also some good accommodation available here.

◉ Gunung Kinabalu National Park listings

For Sleeping and Eating price codes and other relevant information, see Essentials pages 23-27.

◉ Sleeping

Gunung Kinabalu Park *p229, map p231*
Management of the park is privatized. It is managed by **Sutera Sanctuary Lodges**, all accommodation in the park must be booked in advance through its office: ground floor, Wisma Sabah, KK, T088-243629, www.sutera sanctuarylodges.com, Mon-Fri 0900-1830, Sat 0900-1630, Sun 0900-1500. Prices have shot up dramatically recently, putting what was quite reasonably priced accommodation out of the reach of many visitors.

Park HQ *p231*
Each cabin has a fireplace, kitchen, shower, gas cooker, fridge, and cooking and eating utensils. Electricity, water and firewood are provided free of charge. The rates quoted below are reduced on weekdays. The most expensive option at the Park HQ is the **Rajah Lodge**, sleeping 6 people, RM8000 for the whole lodge with all meals and a personal butler; very comfortable. **Kinabalu Lodge**, 6 people, RM3500 per night, all meals, cable TV, also very comfortable. The **Summit Lodge**, 4 people, RM2275 per night, and the **Garden Lodge**, 4 people, RM2275 per night, are both very comfortable and meals are included; also

cable TV; nice and toasty inside. **Nepenthes Lodge**, 4 people, RM760 per night. **Peak Lodge**, 4 people, RM660 per night. **Ligawu Suite**, 2 people, RM490 per night, cable TV, breakfast and hot showers. **Hill Lodge**, 2 people, RM390 per night. **Rock Twin Share**, 2 people, RM350 per night, has a shared bathroom and common area with fireplace. **Grace Hostel**, unheated dorms with shared bathroom for RM120 per bed, includes breakfast. The **Rock Hostel** offers much of the same for the same price.

The following are close to Park HQ.
A Haleluyah Retreat Centre, Jln Linouh, Km 61, Tuaran-Ranau Highway, T088-423993, kandiu@tm.net.my. This Christian centre is open to all, located at 1500 m close to the foot of Mount Kinabalu. It makes a good stop-off point before climbing the mountain. Set amidst natural jungle and approximately 15 mins' walk from the Park HQ, it is isolated but safe, clean, friendly and with a relaxing atmosphere. Cooking and washing facilities, camping area, multi-purpose hall and meeting rooms make it a suitable venue for seminars, meetings, youth camps or family holidays. Reasonably priced food in the canteen, dorm beds also available.
A-C Sonny's Cottage, T088-750555. 6 rooms with spectacular views.
A-D D'Villa Lodge (Rina Ria Lodge), Batu 36, Jln Tinompok, Ranau, T088-889282,

www.dvillalodge.com. About 1 km from the Kinabalu National Park, rooms have attached kitchen and basic bathroom, armchairs and beautiful views. There's also a shop. Prices increase at weekends. Dorms also available (RM30). Breakfast included.

B Kinabalu Rose Cabin, Km18, Ranau-Kinasaraban Rd, Kundasang, T088-889233, www.kinabalurosecabin.8m.com. A/c, restaurant, 2 km from the park, towards golf course (30% discount to golfers); range of rooms, suites all with mountain views, attached bathroom with hot water and TV. There's also a restaurant and internet access.

C Mountain View Motel, 5 km east of Kinabalu National Park on the Ranau-Tamparuli Highway, T088-875389, bbmt kinabalu@hotmail.com. Breakfast included, hot water, restaurant, laundry facilitites, local tours, climbing gear available for hire. The corrugated iron roof can be loud when it rains.

E Mountain Resthouse and Restaurant, T088-771109. Located just outside the park, this has small 4-person dorms that are cheaper, newer, cleaner and warmer than the park dorms. Spectacular views. Arguably preferable to the park accommodation.

Gunung Kinabalu *p234*

Laban Rata Resthouse, Panar Laban. 54 rooms (space is often made for extra people by laying out matresses on the restaurant floor), a good-quality though pricey canteen (but sometimes rather limited food – it all has to be walked up the mountain) and hot water showers, plus electricity and heated rooms; bedding provided. Most expensive rooms are the heated de luxe Buttercup rooms at RM765 per night, beds in the heated dorms go for a pricey RM395 per bed. Rates include all meals and a packed lunch.

Mesilau Nature Resort *p235*

L-A Mesilau Nature Resort, managed by Sutera Sanctuary Lodges, T088-871733, www.suterasanctuarylodges.com. A range of tasteful wooden chalets that blend neatly into their surroundings, housing up to 4

people (RM2275 per unit) with all meals, personal butler, cable TV, heater and hot water bathroom. More budget accommodation provided in dorms in the hostel (RM120 per bed). Laundry, gift shop and regular educational talks. The nature reserve is situated close to the **Mount Kinabalu Golf Club**, a few mins' drive away.

Poring *p236*

Booking recommended. Camping RM6. The following are all **E Serindit Hostel**, dorms with space for 20 people, RM120 per person; **Serindit twin share**, 2 people, RM350 per chalet, shared bathroom; **Jungle Lodge**, 2 people, huge rooms, jungle shower, living room with cable TV, RM420 per unit; **River Lodge**, 4 people, RM740 per unit, comfortable, **Palm Villa** RM3500, 6 people, personal butler. All meals.

Ranau and Kundasang *p236*

L-A Zen Garden Resorts, Km 2, Jln Mohimboyan Kibas, T088-889242, www.zengarden resort.com/index.cfm. 3/4-room lodges with equipped kitchen, living room with TV and bedroom. Also, rooms with TV and some with fridge for considerably less. Very pleasant environment with some wonderful views of the mountains. The biggest resort in the area.

AL-A Mount Kinabalu Heritage Resort and Spa, visible on the hill above Kundasang (a further 1 km down the road from Kinabalu Pine), T088-889511, www.perkasahotel. com.my. Recently revamped with some lovely but pricey accommodation available in stilted chalets with excellent views. Other rooms in the main block are less impressive. Very professional spa centre on the 6th floor offering rejeuvnating therapies to tired walkers.

B Kinabalu Pine Resort, Kampong Kundasang, T088-889388, www.kinabalupine resort.com. A/c rooms with TV constructed from selangan batu hardwood and with great mountain views in this attractive but isolated area, 6 km from the national park. Good value.

B-D Sabah Tea House, KM 17 Ranau–Sandakan Rd, Kampung Nalapak, T088-

889330, www.sabahtea.com. Good selection of accommodation including clean chalets, funky Rungus longhouse with shared bathroom and a campsite with space for 100.

🍴 Eating

Gunung Kinabalu Park *p229, map p231*
The best places to stay are at Park HQ but the restaurants are rather spread out, requiring a walk between buffet and bed.

🍴 **Liwagu**. Open 1100-2130. Beer, chips, curries and other international treats.
🍴 **Balsam Cafeteria**. Open 0630-2130. The cheaper option for filling Malay staples. Breakfast is included in the price of all accommodation.

There are cooking facilities at the hostels plus good quality meals are provided for guests at **Rajah Lodge**, **Summit Lodge**, **Garden Lodge** and **Kinabalu Lodge**.

Mesilau Nature Resort *p235*
🍴 **Renanthera Terrace**. Open 0700-2200. Provides the 3 main meals.
🍴 **Renanthera Café**. Open 0700-2200. Has a stunning veranda offering great views of the mountain.

Poring *p236*
🍴 **Rainforest**. Open 0700-2200. Comfortable place to kick back and get stuck into Malay, Chinese and international fare.
🍴 **Restaurant**. Quite good Chinese and Malay food at the springs and stalls outside the park.

Ranau and Kundasang *p236*
There are several restaurants along the roads serving simple food in Kundasang. Open 0600-2100.
🍴 **Tinompok**, at the Mount Kinabalu Heritage Resort and Spa, Kundasang. Local and Western dishes, good service, excellent food.
🍴 **Five Star Seafood**, Ranau. Chinese, opposite the market.
🍴 **Sin Mui Mui**, top side of the square near the market. Closed Fri afternoons.

🛍 Shopping

Ranau and Kundasang *p236*
Cheap sweaters and waterproofs for the climb from **Kedai Kien Hin**, Ranau. A *tamu* (market) is held near Ranau on the 1st of each month and every Sat. Kundasang *tamu* is held on the 20th of every month and also every Fri.

🏔 Activities and tours

Ranau and Kundasang *p236*
Kundasang Golf Course, 3 km behind Kundasang. Club hire from the **Perkasa Hotel**, Kundasang. The **Mount Kinabalu Heritage Resort and Spa** offers golfing packages which include golf fees, accommodation, breakfast and lunch, and transfer from hotel to course.

🚌 Transport

Gunung Kinabalu Park *p229, map p231*
Bus
All buses heading to **Sandakan** and **Ranau** will drop you off at the turn-off to the park.

Minibus
Regular connections from **KK** to **Ranau**, ask to be dropped at the park, 2 hrs. Return minibus (roughly every hour) must be waved down from the main road.

Taxi
RM160 negotiable, taxi from outside the Padang Merdeka in **KK**.

Poring *p236*
Minibuses can be shared from **Ranau** for RM5. Buses running between **KK** and **Sandakan** stop in town on Jln Kibarambang. Taxis are also available.

Ranau and Kundasang *p236*
Minibuses leave from the market place. Regular connections to **Park HQ**, **KK** and **Sandakan** (4 hrs).

East coast

From Ranau it is possible to reach Sandakan by road. Several key sights are within reach of Sandakan: the Turtle Islands National Park, 40 km north in the Sulu Sea; Sepilok Orang-Utan Rehabilitation Centre; and the Kinabatangan Basin, to the southeast. From Sandakan, the route continues south to the wilds of Lahad Datu and Danum Valley and on to Semporna, the jumping off point for Pulau Sipadan, an island that has achieved legendary status among snorkellers and scuba-divers. Tawau Hills State Park has some unusual natural features that draw visitors at weekends. ▶▶ *For listings, see pages 260-272.*

Sandakan → *Colour map 4, B5.*

Sandakan is at the neck of a bay on the northeast coast of Sabah and looks out to the Sulu Sea. It is a postwar town, much of it rebuilt on reclaimed land, and is Malaysia's biggest fishing port; it even exports some of its catch to Singapore. Sandakan is often dubbed 'mini Hong Kong' because of its Cantonese influence; its occupants are well-heeled and the town sustains many prosperous businesses, despite being rather scruffy as a whole. It is now also home to a large Filipino community, mostly traders from Mindanao and the Sulu Islands. Manila still officially claims Sabah in its entirety – Sandakan is only 28 km from Philippines' territorial waters. Large numbers of illegal Indonesian workers have made Sandakan their home in recent years, further adding to the town's cosmopolitan atmosphere.

New developments are slowly encircling the generally charmless heart of the town, with bright, cheery blocks on the outskirts and the new Sandakan Harbour Square on the waterfront with a few fancy shops, a gleaming new hotel and smart promenade pointing the way to a more attractive future for the city.

Ins and outs
Getting there The airport is 10 km north of town. There are daily connections with KL, KK and several lesser destinations in Sabah. Minibuses travel from the airport to the station at the southern end of Jalan Pelabuhan. From the long-distance bus terminal 5 km to the west of town, there are connections with KK, Tawau, Ranau, Lahad Datu, Semporna and several other destinations. Boats from Zamboanga in the Philippines call into Sandakan twice a week. ▶▶ *See also Transport, page 270.*

Getting around Sandakan is not a large town and it is easy enough to explore the central area on foot, although it does stretch some way along the coast. Minibuses provide links with out-of-town places of interest.

Tourist information The privately run **Tourist Information Centre** ① *next to the municipal council building opposite Lebuh Empat, T089-229751, Mon-Fri 0800-1600*, should be the first port of call for any visitor to Sandakan. Despite limited resources, Elvina Ong is an absolute goldmine of information about Sandakan and its environs. She is extremely well organized and can help tourists arrange tours. It was opened by the owner of the **Sepilok Jungle Resort**, but it provides impartial advice.

Background

The Sandakan area was an important source of beeswax for the Sulu traders and came under the sway of the Sultans of Sulu. William Clarke Cowie, a Scotsman with a carefully waxed handlebar moustache who ran guns for the Sultan of Sulu across the Spanish blockade of Sulu (later becoming the managing director of the North Borneo Chartered Company), first set up camp in Sandakan Bay in the early 1870s. He called his camp, which was on Pulau Timbang, 'Sandakan', the Sulu name for the area for 200 years, but it became known as Kampong German as there were several German traders living there and early gunrunners tended to be German. The power of the Sulu sultanate was already waning when Cowie set up. In its early trading days, Europeans, Africans, Arabs, Chinese, Indians, Javanese, Dusun and Japanese all lived here. It was an important gateway to the interior and used to be a trading centre for forest produce like rhinoceros horn, beeswax and hornbill ivory, along with marine products like pearls and sea cucumbers (*tripang*, valued for their medicinal properties). In 1812, English visitor John Hunt estimated that the Sandakan/Kinabatangan area produced an astonishing 37,000 kg of wild beeswax and 23,000 kg of birds' nests each year.

The modern town of Sandakan was founded by an Englishman, William Pryer, in 1879. Baron von Overbeck, the Austrian consul from Hong Kong who founded the Chartered Company with businessman Alfred Dent, had signed a leasing agreement for the territory with the Sultan of Brunei, only to discover that large tracts on the east side of modern day Sabah actually belonged to the Sultan of Sulu. Overbeck sailed to Sulu in January 1878 and on obtaining the cession rights from the Sultan, dropped William Pryer off at Kampong German to make the British presence felt. Pryer's wife Ada later described the scene: "He had with him a West Indian black named Anderson, a half-caste Hindoo named Abdul, a couple of China boys. For food they had a barrel of flour and 17 fowls and the artillery was half a dozen sinder rifles." Pryer set about organizing the three existing villages in the area, cultivating friendly relations with the local tribespeople and fending off pirates. He raised the Union Jack on 11 February 1878.

Cowie tried to do a deal with the Sultan of Sulu to wrest control of Sandakan back from Pryer, but Dent and Overbeck finally bought him off. A few months later Cowie's Kampong German burned to the ground, so Pryer went in search of a new site, which he found at Buli Sim Sim. He called his new settlement Elopura, meaning 'beautiful city', but the name did not catch on. By the mid-1880s it was renamed Sandakan and, in 1884, became the capital of North Borneo when the title was transferred from Kudat. In 1891 the town had 20 Chinese-run brothels and 71 Japanese prostitutes; according to the 1891 census there were three men for every one woman. The town quickly established itself as the source of birds' nests harvested from the caves at Gomantong and shipped directly to Hong Kong, as they are today.

Timber was first exported from this area in 1885 and was used to construct Beijing's Temple of Heaven. Sandakan was, until the 1980s, the main east-coast port for timber and it became a wealthy town. In its heyday, the town is said to have boasted one of the greatest concentrations of millionaires in the world. The timber-boom days are over: the primary jungle has gone, and so has the big money. In the mid-1990s the state government adopted a strict policy restricting the export of raw, unprocessed timber. The hinterland is now dominated by vast plantations of cocoa and oil palm.

Following the Japanese invasion in 1942, Sandakan was devastated by Allied bombing. In 1946 North Borneo became a British colony and the new colonial government moved the capital to Jesselton (later to become Kota Kinabalu).

Sights

Sandakan is strung out along the coast but in the centre of town is the riotous **daily fish market**, which is the biggest and best in Sabah. The best time to visit is at 0600 when the boats unload their catch. The **Central Market** along the waterfront, near the local bus station, sells fruit, vegetables, sarongs, seashells, spices and sticky rice cakes.

The **Australian war memorial** ⓘ *take Labuk bus service Nos 8, 12 and 14 and stop at the Esso petrol station*, near the government building at Mile Seven on Labuk Rd, between Sandakan and Sepilok, stands on the site of a Japanese prison camp and commemorates Allied soldiers who lost their lives during the Japanese occupation. Each year on ANZAC day (24 April) crowds of former servicemen and their families come to the memorial park to commemorate the lives of those that died In the bloody conflict in Sabah. The Japanese invaded North Borneo in 1942 and many Japanese also died in the area. In 1989 a new **Japanese war memorial** ⓘ *walk 20 mins up Red Hill (Bukit Berenda)*, was built in the Japanese cemetery, financed by the families of the deceased soldiers.

St Michael's Anglican church is one of the very few stone churches in Sabah and is an attractive building, designed by a New Zealander in 1893. Most of Sandakan's stone churches were levelled in the war and, indeed, St Michael's is one of the few colonial-era buildings still standing. It is just off Jalan Singapura, on the hill at the south end of town. In

Sandakan

To Goddess of Mercy Temple · To Trig Hill & ⑧

St Michael's

Jln Utara

Sam Sing Kung Temple

Three Saints Temple

Jln Puncak

BUKIT ELTON

Jln Tokong

To Tanah Merah Town, Pertubuhan Ugama Buddhist & ⑤⑪❸❼

Jln Singapura

Padang

Night

Jln Leila

Tun Razak Park

Community Centre

Minibuses

Lebuh Tiga (3rd Av)

Jln Dua (2nd Av)

Jln Europa

Minibuses

Centre Point Plaza

Local Bus Station

Fisherma

N

100 metres
100 yards

Sleeping
City View **1**
Hsiang Garden **5**
London **3**
Mayfair **4**

Nak **2**
Sabah **8**
Sanbay **11**
Sandakan **6**
Sandakan Backpackers **7**

Sunset Harbour Botik Hostel **9**
Swiss Inn **10**
Winho Lodge **12**

1988 a big **mosque** was built for the burgeoning Muslim population at the mouth of Sandakan Bay. The main Filipino settlements are in this area of town. The mosque is outside Sandakan, on Jalan Buli Sim Sim where the town began in 1879, just after the jetty for Turtle Islands National Park, and is an imposing landmark. There is also a large water village here.

There are a couple of other notable Chinese temples in Sandakan. The oldest one, the **Goddess of Mercy Temple** is just off Jalan Singapura, on the hillside. Originally built in the early 1880s, it has been expanded over the years. Nearby is **Sam Sing Kung Temple**, which becomes a particular focus of devotion during exam periods since one of its deities is reputed to assist those attempting examinations. The **Three Saints Temple**, further down the hill at the end of the padang, was completed in 1887. The three saints are Kwan Woon Cheung, a Kwan clan ancestor, the goddess Tien Hou (or Tin Hau, worshipped by seafarers) and the Min Cheong Emperor.

Sabah's only **Crocodile Farm** ⓘ *daily 0800-1730, RM5, children RM2, weekday crocodile shows at 1145 and 1600 and snake and crocodile shows at 1145, 1400 and 1600 at weekends, feeding times are throughout the day*, is a commercial licensed enterprise, set up in 1982 when the government made the estuarine crocodile a protected species. The original stock was drawn from a population of wild crocodiles found in the Kinabatangan River. Visitors can see around 2000 crocs at all stages of maturity waiting in concrete pools for the day when their skins are turned into bags and wallets and their meat is sold to local butchers. There are numerous other animals to see here at their mini zoo including snakes, civets and sun bears. The farm, at Mile 8, Labuk Road, has about 200 residents. To get there take the Labuk Road bus.

The **Forest Headquarters** (Ibu Pejabat Jabatan Perhutanan) ⓘ *Mile 6 Labuk Rd, T089-660811*, next to the Sandakan Golf Course, contain an exhibition centre and a well-laid out and interesting mini-museum showing past and present forestry practice.

The **Sandakan Heritage Trail** is a loop which supposedly takes in the historical gems of this scruffy town including a good lookout point; the walk should take a leisurely 90 minutes. The tourist office has trail maps. It starts off at the town mosque and nips up the 'stairs with 100 steps', a nice shady climb with good views from the top where young local couples gather to whisper sweet nothings to each other and smoke clandestine cigarettes. It's rather dark here at night, so lone travellers are advised to climb in the day. A couple of tourists were mugged here in 2004.

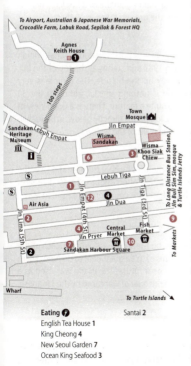

To Airport, Australian & Japanese War Memorials, Crocodile Farm, Labuk Road, Sepilok & Forest HQ

Agnes Keith House 1

100 steps

Town Mosque

Jln Empat

Sandakan Heritage Museum

Lebuh Empat

Wisma Sandakan 6

Wisma Khoo Siak Chiew 3

Lebuh Tiga

Jln Tiga (3rd St)

Air Asia

Jln Empat (4th St)

Jln Dua

To Long Distance Bus Station, Jln Buli Sim Sim, mosque & Turtle Islands Jetty

Jln Lima (5th St)

Central Market

Jln Pryer

Fish Market

Sandakan Harbour Square

Wharf

To Markets

To Turtle Islands

Eating ⓘ
English Tea House 1
King Cheong 4
New Seoul Garden 7
Ocean King Seafood 3

Santai 2

Agnes Keith's house

American authoress Agnes Keith lived with her English husband in Sandakan from 1934 to 1952. He was the conservator of forests in North Borneo and she wrote three books about her time in the colony.

The Land Below the Wind tells stories of dinner parties and tiffins in pre-war days. *Three Came Home* is about her three years in a Japanese internment camp during the war on Pulau Berhala, off Sandakan, and in Kuching, and was made into a film. *White Man Returns* tells the story of their time in British North Borneo. The Keiths' rambling wooden house on the hill above the town was destroyed during the war, but was rebuilt by the government to exactly the same design when Harry Keith returned to his job when the war ended.

From here the trail passes through **Agnes Keith's house** ① *daily 0900-1700, RM15 discounts for children*, see box above, the restored British colonial government quarters built on the site of her home. Inside the grounds, there's an **English Tea House** serving scones and pastries on manicured lawns. From here, the trail takes in the Goddess of Mercy Temple, St Michael's Anglican Church and ends up at the **Sandakan Heritage Museum** ① *next to the tourist office, daily 0900-1700, free*, a rather slipshod affair with some early photos of the town and an unexplained mannequin dressed in a kilt. There is, however, a good wall photo of Sandakan razed to the ground taken in 1945.

Tanah Merah

Pertubuhan Ugama Buddhist (Puu Jih Shih Buddhist temple) overlooks Tanah Merah town. The US$2 million temple was completed in 1987 and stands at the top of the hill, accessible by a twisting road that hairpins its way up the hillside. The temple is very gaudy, contains three large Buddha images and is nothing special, although the 34 teakwood supporting pillars, made in Macau, are quite a feature. There is a good view of Sandakan from the top, with Tanah Merah and the log ponds directly below, in Sandakan Bay. The names of local donors are inscribed on the walls of the walkway.

Pulau Lankayan

This dive resort is on a near uninhabited island, 90 minutes by boat from Sandakan in the Sulu Sea. **Lankayan Island Dive Resort**, see page 260, offers more than 40 dive sites including a couple of wrecks. Sightings of whale sharks are common from April to May.

Pulau Berhala

① *To get to the beach charter a boat from the fish market.*

Famed for its 200-m rust-coloured sandstone cliffs on the south end, with a beach at the foot, this island is within easy reach by boat, but there isn't a great deal to do here. There are plans to develop the island for tourism in the near future. The island was used as a leper colony before the Second World War and as a prisoner of war camp by the Japanese. Agnes Keith was interned here during the war, see box above.

Turtle Islands National Park → *Colour map 4, A5.*

Located 40 km north of Sandakan, Turtle Islands are at the south entrance to Labuk Bay. The park is separated from the Philippine island of Bakkungan Kecil by a narrow stretch of water. These eight tiny islands in the Sulu Sea are among the most important turtle-breeding spots in Southeast Asia. The turtle sanctuary is made up of three tiny islands (**Pulau Selingan**, **Pulau Bakkungan Kecil** and **Pulau Gulisan**) and also encompasses the surrounding coral reefs and sea, covering 1700 ha. On Pulau Bakkungan Kecil there is a small mud volcano.

Ins and outs

Best time to visit The driest months and the calmest seas are between March and July. The egg laying season is July to October. Seas are rough October to February.

Tourist information The number of visitors is restricted to 50 per night in an effort to protect the female turtles, that are easily alarmed by noise and light when laying. Visitors are asked not to build campfires, shine bright torches or make noise at night on the beach. The turtles should be watched from a distance to avoid upsetting the nesting process. The park is managed by **Sabah Parks** ⓘ *Sabah Parks Office Room 906, 9th floor, Wisma Khoo, Lebuh Tiga, T089-273453, entrance fee RM10, plus a camera fee of RM10 (no flash photography permitted)*. All accommodation must be booked through **Crystal Quest** (see page 269). This is booked up weeks, sometimes months, in advance.

The islands

The islands are famous for their green turtles (*Chelonia mydas*), which make up 80% of the turtles in the park, and hawksbill turtles (*Eretmochelys imbricata*), known locally as *sisik*. There were four reported landings of Olive Ridley turtle (*Lepidochelys Olivacea*) between 1996 and 1988, but none since. Most green turtles lay their eggs on Pulau Selingan. The green turtles copulate 50-200 m off Pulau Selingan and can be seen during the day, their heads popping up like submarine periscopes. Hawksbills prefer to nest on Pulau Gulisan.

Both species come ashore, year-round, to lay their eggs, although the peak season is between July and October. Even during the off-season between four and 10 turtles come up the beach each night to lay their eggs. Pulau Bakkungan Kecil and Pulau Gulisan can only be visited during the day but visitors can stay overnight on Pulau Selingan to watch the green turtles.

Only the females come ashore; the male waits in the sea nearby for his mate. The females cautiously crawl up to nest after 2000 or with the high tide. The nesting site is above the high-tide mark and is cleared by the female's front and hind flippers to

Sandakan Bay

The tough life of a turtle

Historically, green and hawksbill turtles have been hunted for their meat, shells and their edible eggs (a Chinese delicacy). They were a favourite food of British and Spanish mariners for centuries. Japanese soldiers slaughtered thousands of turtles for food during the Second World War. Dynamite fishermen are also thought to have killed off many turtles in Indonesian, Malaysian and Philippines waters in recent years.

Malaysia, Hong Kong, Japan and the Philippines, where green turtle meat and eggs are in demand, are all signatories of the Convention in International Trade in Endangered Species (CITES) and trading in sea turtles has been banned under the Convention since 1981.

In his book *Forest Life and Adventures in the Malay Archipelago*, the Swedish adventurer and wildlife enthusiast Eric Mjoberg documents turtle egghunting and shell collecting in Borneo in the

1920s. He tells of how the Bajau would lie in wait for hawksbills, grab them and put them on the fire so their horny shields could be removed.

"The poor beasts are put straight on the fire so that their shield may be more readily removed, and suffer the tortures of the damned. They are then allowed to go alive, or perhaps half-dead into the sea, only to come back again after a few years and undergo the same cruel process."

The Bajau, he says, used an "ingenious contrivance" to hunt their prey. They would press pieces of common glass against their eyes "in a watertight fashion" and would lie face-down on a piece of floating wood, dipping their faces into the water, watching for hawksbills feeding on seaweed. They would then dive in, armed with a small harpoon, and catch them, knocking them out with a blow to the head.

make a 'body pit', just under a metre deep. She then digs an egg chamber with her powerful rear flippers after which she proceeds to lay her eggs. The clutch size can be anything between 40 and 200; batches of 50-80 are most common.

When all the eggs have been laid, she covers them with sand and laboriously fills the body pit to conceal the site of the nest, after which the exhausted turtle struggles back to the sea, leaving her Range Rover-like tracks in the sand. The egg-laying process can take about an hour or two to complete. Some say the temperature of the sand affects the sex of the young: if it is warm the batch will be mostly female and if cold, mostly male. After laying her eggs, a tag reading "If found, return to Turtle Island Park, Sabah, East Malaysia" is attached to each turtle by the rangers, who are stationed on each island. Over 27,000 have been tagged since 1970; the measurements of each turtle are recorded and the clutches of eggs removed and transplanted to the hatchery where they are protected from natural predators, like monitor lizards, birds and snakes.

The golf ball-sized eggs are placed by hand into 80 cm-deep pits, covered in sand and surrounded by wire. They take up to 60 days to hatch. The hatchlings mostly emerge at night when the temperature is cooler, breaking their shells with their one sharp tooth. There are hatcheries on all three islands and nearly every night a batch is released into the sea. Millions of hatchlings have been released since 1977. They are released at different points on the island to protect them from predators: they are a favoured snack for white-bellied gulls and sadly only about 1% survive to become teenage turtles.

Sepilok Orang-Utan Sanctuary and Rehabilitation Centre → *Colour map 4, B5.*

Sepilok, a reserve of 43 sq km of lowland primary rainforest and mangrove, was set up in 1964 to protect the orang-utan (*Pongo pygmaeus*) from extinction. It is the first and largest of only four orang-utan sanctuaries in the world and now has 40,000 visitors a year. Logging has seriously threatened Sabah's population of wild orang-utan, as has their capture for zoos and as pets. The orang-utan lives on the islands of Borneo and Sumatra and there are estimated to be as few as 10,000 still in the wild. In Sabah there are populations of orang-utan in the Kinabatangan basin region (see page 249), Danum Valley Conservation Area and a few other isolated tracts of jungle.

Ins and outs

Getting there There are several buses a day from Sandakan.

Park information Sepilok Orang-Utan Sanctuary ⓘ *T089-5311180, soutan@po.jaring.my, Sat-Thu 0900-1230 and 1400-1600, Fri 0900-1100 and 1400-1600, RM30 (children RM5), camera RM10.* It is worth getting to the park early. The **Information Centre** ⓘ *video viewing times at 0830, 1100, 1200, 1410 and 1530*, next to the Park HQ, runs a nature education exhibition with replicas of jungle mammals and videos. If you want to do the walks, arrive at the centre in the morning so you can get a permit. The pass is valid all day so you can see both feeds if you arrive early. Feeding times: Platform A, 1000 and 1500. For more details contact the coordinator, Sepilok Orang-Utan Rehabilitation Centre, Sabah Wildlife Department, T089-531180, F531189. **Note** The morning feed is packed with tour groups; the afternoon feed is generally quieter.

The sanctuary

Sepilok is an old forest reserve that was gazetted as a forestry experimentation centre as long ago as 1931, and by 1957 logging had been phased out. Orphaned or captured orang-utans that have become too dependent on humans through captivity are rehabilitated and protected under the Fauna Conservation Ordinance and eventually returned to their natural home. Many, for example, may have been captured by the oil-palm planters because they eat the young oil palm trees. Initially, the animals at the centre and in the surrounding area are fed every day but, as they acclimatize, they are sent further and further away or are re-released into the Tabin Wildlife Reserve near Lahad Datu. In 1996, researchers placed microchip collars on the orang-utans enabling them to be tracked over a distance of up to 150 km so that a better understanding of their migratory habits and other behaviour could be acquired.

After an initial period of quarantine at Sepilok, newly arrived orang-utans are moved to Platform A and taught survival skills by rangers. At the age of seven they are moved deeper into the forest to Platform B, about 30 minutes' walk from Platform A and not open to the public. At Platform B, they are encouraged to forage for themselves. Other animals brought here include Malay sun bears, wild cats and baby elephants.

Sepilok also has a rare Sumatran rhinoceros (*Didermoceros sumatrensis*), the Asian two-horned rhinoceros, see box page 252. This enclosure is sometimes closed to the public.

The **Mangrove Forest Trail** takes two to three hours one way and passes transitional forest, some pristine lowland rainforest, a boardwalk into a mangrove forest, water holes and a wildlife track. The visitors' reception centre provides other information.

Rainforest Discovery Centre

ⓘ *Jln Sepilok, T089-533780, www.forest.sabah.gov.my/rdc, daily 0800-1700, RM10, children RM5. A free booklet is available; for more details contact the Forest Research Centre, PO Box 14-07, T089-531522.*

This centre located within the Kabili-Sepilok Forest Reserve is 2 km from the Orang-utan Rehabilitation Centre and provides detailed displays about the vegetation in the area. It is run by the **Forest Research Centre**, also found on this road. Emphasis is on participation, with questionnaires, games and so on; it offers a wide range of information about all aspects of tropical rainforests and the need for conservation. It is situated in the Forest Research Centre's arboretum and there is an 800-m rainforest walk around the lake. There also a 150-m canopy walkway offering the opportunity to walk over the forest canopy and spot wildlife. Keep your eyes peeled for hornbills, kingfishers and the Bornean bristlehead.

Gomantong Caves

The Gomantong Caves are 32 km south of Sandakan Bay, between the road to Sukau and the Kinabatangan River, or 110 km overland on the Sandakan – Sukau road. The name Gomantong means 'tie it up tightly' in the local language and the caves are the largest system in Sabah. They are located in the 3924 ha Gomantong Forest Reserve.

Ins and outs

At the Park HQ there is an information centre, a small cafeteria where drinks and simple dishes are sold and a pit latrine. Good walking shoes are essential, as is a torch. If you're squeamish about cockroaches give this cave a miss. If you arrive independently then one of the nest workers, a person from the information centre or a ranger will show you around. The bats can be seen exiting from the caves between 1800 and 1830; to request to see this it is necessary to ask at the **Gomantong Wildlife Department** ⓘ *T011-817529*, at the information centre.

The caves and reserve

ⓘ *Daily 0800-1600, RM30.*

There are sometimes orang-utan, mouse deer, wild boar and wild buffalo in the reserve, which was logged in the 1950s. There are several cave chambers. The main limestone cave is Simud Hitam (Black Cave). This cave, with its ceiling soaring up to 90 m overhead, is just a five-minute walk from the registration centre and picnic area. The smaller and more complex Simud Putih (White Cave) is above. It is quite dangerous climbing up as there is no ladder to reach the caves and the rocks are slippery. Between 200,000 and 300,000 bats of two different species are thought to live in the caves; at sunset they swarm out to feed. Sixty-four species of bat have been recorded in Sabah; most in these caves are fruit- and wrinkled-lipped bats whose guano is a breeding ground for cockroaches. The squirming larvae make the floor of the cave seethe. The guano can cause an itchy skin irritation. The bats are preyed upon by birds like the bat hawk, peregrine falcon and buffy fish owl.

There are also an estimated one million swiftlets that swarm into the cave to roost at sunset, the birds of bird's nest soup fame (see box, page 145). The swiftlets of Gomantong have been a focus of commercial enterprise for 400 or 500 years. However, it was not until 1870 that harvesting birds' nests became a serious industry here. The caves are divided into five pitches and each is allocated to a team of 10-15 people. Harvesting periods last 10 days and there are two each year (February-April and July-September). Collecting nests from hundreds of feet above the ground is a dangerous business and deaths are not uncommon. Before each harvesting period a chicken or goat is sacrificed to the cave spirit; it is thought that deaths are not caused by human error, but by an angry spirit. Birdlife around the caves is rich, with crested serpent eagles, kingfishers, Asian fairy bluebirds and leafbirds often sighted. Large groups of richly coloured butterflies are also often seen drinking from pools along the track leading from the forest into the caves.

Sungai Kinabatangan

At 560 km, this river is Sabah's longest. Much of the lower basin is gazetted under the Kinabatangan Wildlife Sanctuary and meanders through a flood plain, creating numerous oxbow lakes and an ideal environment for some of Borneo's best wildlife.

Ins and outs
Visitors who prefer an in-depth look at the area's wildlife can stay overnight at Sukau, two hours by road from Sandakan, where accommodation is provided by local tour operators. Tour operators take visitors by boat in the late afternoon through freshwater swamp forest to see proboscis monkeys and other wildlife. There are also walks through the jungle. Those who wish to visit for a day can charter a cab from Sandakan for around RM300.

Kinabatangan Riverine Forest area
One of the principal reasons why the Kinabatangan has remained relatively unscathed by Sabah's rapacious logging is because much of the land is permanently waterlogged and the forest contains only a small number of commercially valuable trees. Just some of the animals include: tree snake, crocodile, civet cat, otter, monitor lizard, long-tailed and pig-tailed macaque, silver-, red- and grey-leaf monkey and proboscis monkey. It is the most accessible area in Sabah to see proboscis monkeys, which are best viewed from a boat in the late afternoon, when they converge on treetops by the river banks to settle for the night. Sumatran rhinoceros have also been spotted (see box, page 252) and herds of wild elephant often pass through the park. The birdlife is particularly good and includes oriental darter, egret, storm's stork, osprey, coucal owl, frogmouth, bulbul, spiderhunter, oriole, flowerpecker and several species of hornbill. The night trip is well worth doing as you can get close to the sleeping birds and they look very colouful.

Because of the diversity of its wildlife, the Kinabatangan Riverine Forest area is becoming a wildlife reserve; however, there's some debate as to whether enough land is being set aside for the protection of the region's fauna. In addition, there has been little disturbance from human settlements: the Kinabatangan basin has always been sparsely inhabited because of flooding and the threat posed by pirates. The inhabitants of the Kinabatangan region are mostly Orang Sungai or people of mixed ancestry including Tambanua, Idahan, Dusun, Suluk, Bugis, Brunei and Chinese. A good destination for a jungle river safari is not on the Kinabatangan itself, but on the narrow, winding Sungai Menanggol tributary, about 6 km from Sukau. The Kinabatangan estuary, largely mangrove, is also rich in wildlife and is a haven for migratory birds. Boats can be chartered from Sandakan to Abai (at the river mouth).

Batu Tulug, also known as Batu Putih (white stone), on the Kinabatangan River 100 km upstream from Sukau, is a cave containing wooden coffins dating back several hundred years. Some of the better examples have been removed to the Sabah State Museum in KK. The caves are about 1 km north of the Kinabatangan Bridge, on the east side of the Sandakan – Lahad Datu road.

Lahad Datu and around → *Colour map 4, B5.*

Lahad Datu is Malaysia's 'wild East' at its wildest and its recent history testifies to its reputation as the capital of cowboy country. The population is an intriguing mixture of Filipinos, Sulu islanders, Kalimantan migrants, Orang Bugis, Timorese and a few Malays. Most came to work on the palm oil plantations. Nowadays there are so many migrants few can find employment in this grubby and uninteresting town. There are reckoned to be more illegal Filipino immigrants in Lahad Datu than the whole population put together. Piracy in the Sulu Sea and the offshore islands in Kennedy Bay is rife; local fishermen live in terror. In October 2003, a band of Abu Sayyaf rebels kidnapped six Filipino and Indonesian workers from **Borneo Paradise Resort** near Kunak. Eight months later, four hostages were freed. It is thought a Malaysian businessman paid a ransom.

During the Second World War, the Japanese made Lahad Datu their naval headquarters for east Borneo. After the war, the timber companies moved in and the **British Kennedy Bay Timber Company** built Lahad Datu's first plywood mill in the early 1950s. Oil palm plantations grew up in the hinterland after the timber boom finished in the 1970s. As for the town, what it lacks in aesthetic appeal is made up for by its colourful recent history.

Kampong Panji is a water village with a small market at the end of Jalan Teratai, where many of the poorer immigrant families live.

The only good beaches are on the road to Tungku; Pantai Perkapi and Pantai Tungku. They can be reached by minibus from Lahad Datu or by boat from the old wharf. It is possible to get to the nearby islands from the old wharf behind the Mido Hotel, but because of lawlessness in the area, particularly at sea, a trip is not advisable. In April 2000, the Philippines-based radical Islamic group Abu Sayyaf kidnapped 21 people from Sipadan (see page 254).

Madai Caves are about 2 km off the Tawau – Lahad Datu road, near Kunak. The caves are an important archaeological site; there is evidence they were inhabited over 15,500 years ago. Birds' nests are harvested from the caves three times a year by local Idahan people whose lean-to kampong goes right up to the cave mouth. Your own transport is required for this trip as it's not catered for by tour operators.

Another 15 km west of Madai is **Baturong**, another limestone massif and cave system in the middle of what was originally Tingkayu Lake. The route is not obvious so it is advisable to take a local guide. Stone tools, wooden coffins and rock paintings have been found there. Evidence of humans dating from 16,000 years ago, after the lake drained away, can be found at the huge rock overhang (take a torch; it is possible to camp here). To get to Baturong, take a minibus from Lahad Datu.

At **Gunung Silam**, 8 km from Lahad Datu on the Tawau road, a track leads up the mountain to a Telekom station at 620 m and from there, a jungle trail to the summit. There are good views over the bay, when it isn't misty, and out to the islands beyond. It is advisable to take a guide. You can stay at **Silam Lodge** (see page 263).

Tabin Wildlife Reserve → *Colour map 4, B6.*

ⓘ *Book at Lot 11-1, Blk A, Damai Point, Jln Damai, KK, T088-267266, www.tabinwildlife.com.my.*
Gazetted in 1984 as a protected forest area, Tabin is one of Sabah's largest and most important wildlife reserves and, according to the WWF, one of the last refuges of the critically endangered Sumatran rhino, see box page 252. Since the opening of **Tabin Jungle Resort** in 2002, around 50 km or one hour's drive from Lahad Datu, it's also one one of the easiest and most comfortable to visit. In addition, it's in one of the most

exciting settings, close to a large mud-volcano – favoured as a mineral lick by mammals. The reserve offers a wide variety of trails and various wildlife habitats. There are several huge bubbling mud volcanoes an easy trek from the resort.

Since the reserve consists of large areas of previously logged and now recovering forest and also due to its considerable size, covering 120,500 ha, it's particularly good for observing Bornean mammals. Pygmy elephants (see box, page 253), wild pigs, civets and macaques are often seen on evening safaris close to palm oil plantations; otters make their homes in the river below the jungle resort; and by staking out the mud volcano for a night even a close encounter is possible with a sun bear; see box, page 258. There are occasional sightings of the Sumatran Rhinoceros as Tabin is one of their last natural breeding spots. It is estimated that only 300 of these animals are left in the wild.

There are various packages available to visit the reserve, including day trips that start at RM285 per person (minimum two people) and include transfers from Lahad Datu.

Danum Valley Conservation Area → *Colour map 4, B5.*

Danum Valley's 438 sq km of virgin jungle is the largest expanse of undisturbed lowland dipterocarp forest in Sabah. Segama River runs through the area and past the field centre. Danum River is a tributary of the Segama joining it 9 km downstream of the field centre. Gunung Danum (1093 m) is the highest peak, 13 km southwest of the field centre. Within the area is a tightly controlled Yayasan Sabah timber concession.

Ins and outs

The field centre, 65 km west of Lahad Datu and 40 km from the nearest habitation, was set up by the Sabah Foundation (Yayasan) in 1985 for forest research, nature education and recreation; the centre is only open to visiting scientists and researchers. If you are a biologist or an educator you may be able to get permission to visit the centre; contact the **Sabah Foundation** ① *Likas Bay, T088-326327, www.ysnet.org.my,* for permission. Guides charge RM5 per hour. Tourists are allowed to visit only through the **Borneo Rainforest Lodge**, see Sleeping and Transport, pages 260 and 270 respectively.

The valley

This area has never been inhabited, although there is evidence of a burial site that is thought to have been for the Dusun people who lived here about 300 years ago. There is also growing evidence of prehistoric cave dwellers in the Segama River area. Not far downstream from the field centre, in a riverside cave, two wooden coffins have been found, together with a copper bracelet and a *tapai* jar, all of uncertain date. There is evidence of some settlement during the Japanese occupation; townspeople came upstream to escape from the Japanese troops. The area was first recommended as a national park by the WWF's Malaysia Expedition in 1975 and designated a conservation area in 1981. The field centre was officially opened in 1986.

The main aims of this large area are to research the impact of logging on flora and fauna and to try and improve forest management, to understand processes that maintain tropical rainforest and to provide wildlife management and training opportunities for Sabahans. Many are collaborative projects between Malaysian and foreign scientists.

The Sumatran rhinoceros

Although not as rare as its Javan brother, the Sumatran, or Asian two-horned rhinoceros (*Didermoceros sumatrensis*) is severely endangered. The species has suffered from the destruction of its natural habitat and the price placed on its head by the value that the Chinese attach to its grated horn as a cure-all. Should the Sumatran rhino disappear so, too, it is thought, will a number of plants whose seeds will only germinate after passing through the animal's intestines.

It was once widespread through mainland and island Southeast Asia but there are now only around 300 in the wild, mostly in the most remote forests of Sumatra but with small populations in Borneo (including Sepilok Orang-Utan Sanctuary, page 247, and Tabin Wildlife Reserve, page 250), Peninsular Malaysia and Vietnam. It is now a protected species. Only on Sumatra does it seem to have a chance of surviving.

The situation has become so serious that naturalists established a captive breeding programme as a precaution against extinction in the wild. Unfortunately this has been spectacularly unsuccessful. Around a third of animals have died during capture or shortly thereafter and, according to naturalists Tony and Jane Whitten, the only recorded birth in captivity was in Calcutta in 1872.

In a startlingly similar Darwinesque manner to Borneo's bears and elephants, these rhinos have evolved dwarf characteristics, a feature that has helped them to survive in dense undergrowth. The Sumatran rhino is the smallest of all the family, only growing to 600-900 kg. It is a shy, retiring creature, inhabiting thick forest. Tracks have been discovered as high as 3300 m in Mount Leuser National Park, Sumatra. It lacks the armoured skin of other species and has a soft, hairy hide. It also has an acute sense of smell and hearing, but poor eyesight.

Until recently the rhino's destiny continued looking bleak, but there has been recent evidence in Sabah that rhinos are breeding and in early 2007 some of the first wild footage of a Sumatran rhino was captured in Sabah with a WWF camera trap, giving hope that the rhino might be on the rebound from extinction.

However, much more help is still needed if that dream is going to become reality. Find out more at www.panda.org, www.sosrhino.com or www.tabinwildlife.com.my. Programmes are run by various organizations for fit and enthusiastic volunteers to make a contribution. For accommodation, activites and tours in the Tabin Wildlife Reserve, see www.tabinwildlife.com.my.

Flora and fauna

Due to its size and remoteness, Danum Valley is home to some of Sabah's rarest animals and plants. The dipterocarp forest is some of the oldest, tallest and most diverse in the world, with 200 species of tree per hectare; there are over 300 labelled trees. The conservation area is teeming with wildlife: Sumatran rhinoceros have been recorded, as have elephant, clouded leopards, orang-utans, proboscis monkeys, crimson langur, pig-tailed macaques, sambar deer, bearded pigs, Western tarsier, sun bears (see page 258) and 275 species of bird including hornbills, rufous picolet, flowerpeckers and kingfishers. A species of monkey, which looks like an albino version of the red-leaf monkey, was first seen on the road to Danum in 1988 and appears to be unique to this area. There are guided nature walks on an extensive trail system. Features include a

The gentler beast of Borneo

It was dung that eventually solved the mystery surrounding Borneo's rare elephants. For a long time scientists couldn't decide whether the animals were native to the island or introduced by human settlers. One argument suggested that the British East India Company gave the beasts as gifts to the Sultan of Sulu in the 17th century.

Using evidence gleaned from DNA analysis of the mucus which sticks to elephant droppings, scientists from Columbia University in the US discovered the pachyderm is indeed indigenous. From genetic data they concluded the Borneo variety is a distinct sub-species of Asian elephant, having been isolated from its cousins 300,000 years ago. In recognition of its new status, the animal was rechristened the Borneo pygmy elephant in 2003.

The animals are smaller than the Asian elephant, with larger ears, longer tails and straighter tusks. They are also said to be gentler in temper. Scientists believe elephants trooped across swampy land joining Borneo with Sumatra when sea levels were lower during the ice ages.

Conservation groups estimate there are only around 2000 of the endangered elephants left, which are threatened by ivory poachers and loss of habitat.

canopy walkway, a heart-stoppingly springy platform 107 m long and 27 m above the ground, ancient Dusun burial site, waterfalls and a self-guided trail.

Semporna → Colour map 4, B6.

Semporna is a small fishing Bajau town at the end of the Peninsula and is the main departure point for Sipadan Island. It has a lively and very photogenic market, spilling out onto piers over the water, and is known for its seafood. There are scores of small fishing boats, many with outriggers and square sails. There is a regatta of these traditional boats every March. The town is built on an old coral reef, said to be 35,000 years old, which was exposed by the uplift of the seabed. Many illegal Filipino immigrants pass through Semporna as it is only two hours from the nearest Philippine island, which gives the place quite a different feel from that of other Malaysian towns. The town is grubby and charmless with street corners populated by gangs of lingering youths. However, it's a friendly enough place with some good seafood on offer.

The islands off Semporna stand along the edge of the continental shelf, which drops away to a depth of 200 m to the south and east of Pulau Ligitan, the outermost island in the group. Darvel Bay and the adjacent waters are dotted with small, mainly volcanic, islands, which are all part of the 9300-ha **Semporna Marine Park**. The bigger ones are Pulau Mabul, Pulau Kapalai, Pulau Si Amil, Pulau Danawan and Pulau Sipadan. The attractive hilly island that can be seen on the horizon is affectionately termed the island of the sleeping beauty. With a little imagination, the island has the profile of a rather busty lady lying down. The reefs surrounding these islands have around 70 genera of coral, placing them, in terms of their diversity, on a par with Australia's Great Barrier Reef. More than 200 species of fish have also been recorded in these waters.

Locals live in traditional boats called *lipa-lipa* or in pilehouses at the water's edge and survive by fishing. In the shallow channels off Semporna there are three fishing villages built on stilts: Kampong Potok Satu, Kampong Potok Dua and Kampong Larus. There are many more islands than are marked on the map; most are hilly, uninhabited and have beautiful white sandy beaches.

Reefs in Semporna Marine Park include Sibuan Ulaiga, Tetugan, Mantabuan Bodgaya, Sibuan, Maigu, Selakan, Sebangkat and Bohey Dulang. The latter is a volcanic island with a Japanese-run pearl culture station. Visitors can only visit if there is a boat from the pearl culture station going out. The **Kaya Pearl Company** leases part of the lagoon and Japanese pearl oysters are artificially implanted with a core material to induce pearl growth. The oysters are attached to rafts moored in the lagoon. The pearls are harvested and exported direct to Japan. Some islands, like Sibuan, Sebangkat, Maigu and Selakan, can be reached by local fishing boats from the main jetty by the market.

Sipadan Island Marine Reserve → *Colour map 4, C6.*

The venerable French marine biologist Jacques Cousteau 'discovered' Sipadan in 1989 and, after spending three months diving around the island from his research vessel, *Calypso* said: "I have seen other places like Sipadan 45 years ago, but now no more. Now we have found an untouched piece of art." Since then Sipadan has become a sub-aqua shangri-la for serious divers. It is regularly voted one of the top dive destinations in the world by leading scuba magazines. The reef is without parallel in Malaysia. But Sipadan Island is not just for scuba-divers: it is a magnificent, tiny tropical island with pristine beaches and crystal-clear water and its coral can be enjoyed by even the most amateur of snorkellers.

Ins and outs

The island's tourist facilities are run by a handful of tour companies, who control everything (see Activities and tours, page 203). In 2004, after much legal wrangling, the tour operators agreed to close all resort facilities on the island to protect the environment; although dive boats can still take visitors around the island, numbers are limited to 120 tourist permits per day. Park permits cost RM40 per day to visit Sipidan. Tourists can still stay on Mabul, Kapalai and Mataking, and these islands are likely to be developed further.

Best time to visit The best diving season is from mid-February to mid-December when visibility is greater (20-60 m); most of the dives involve drift diving; the night diving is said to be absolutely spectacular.

Note Due to the issuing of a limited number of permits per day, visitors are advised to book a trip at least two to three weeks in advance. Those showing up without a booking are unlikely to find a slot.

Background

While Sipadan may win lots of points from dive enthusiasts, it has also been in the news for less savoury reasons. In April 2000 Abu Sayyaf, a separatist group in the Philippines, kidnapped 21 people including 10 foreign tourists from the island. Abu Sayyaf, linked to Osama bin Laden's al-Qaeda, spirited the hostages to the Philippine island of Jolo. Here they remained under guard and threat of execution while the armed forces of the Philippines tried, sometimes incompetently, to rescue them. The hostages were freed in dribs and drabs with the final batch being released in September 2000, but it wasn't the sort of publicity that Sipadan was looking for. There is a heavy Malaysian navy presence on the island and around Semporna.

The island is disputed by the Indonesian and Malaysian governments. Indonesia has asked Malaysia to stop developing marine tourism facilities on Sipadan. Malaysia's claim to the island rests on historical documents signed by the British and Dutch colonial administrations. Periodically the two sides get around the negotiating table, but neither is prepared to make a big issue of Sipadan. Occasionally guests on the island see Indonesian or Malaysian warships just offshore. A third party also contests ownership of Sipadan: a Malaysian who claims his grandfather, Abdul Hamid Haji, was given the island by the Sultan of Sulu. He has the customary rights to collect turtles eggs on the island, although the Malaysian government disputes this.

Pulau Sipadan

Pulau Sipadan is the only oceanic island in Malaysia; it is not attached to the continental shelf and stands on a limestone and coral stalk, rising 600 m from the bed of the Celebes Sea. The limestone pinnacle mushrooms out near the surface, but a few metres offshore drops off in a sheer underwater cliff to the seabed. The reef comes right into the island's small pier, allowing snorkellers to swim along the edge of the coral cliff, while remaining close to the coral-sand beach. The edge is much further out around the rest of the island. The tiny island has a cool, forested interior and it is common to see flying foxes and monitor lizards. It is also a stopover point for migratory birds, and was originally declared a bird sanctuary in 1933. It has been a marine reserve since 1981 and a large wildlife department and anti-poaching group is now permanently stationed on the island. In addition, the island is a breeding ground for the green turtle; August and September are the main egg laying months. With the exception of the beach close to the jetty, beaches now also have restricted access in order to protect turtle nesting sites.

Sipadan is known for its underwater overhangs and caverns, funnels and ledges, all of which are covered in coral. A cavern, known as the Turtle Cave, is located on the drop-off in front of the island's accommodation area. The cave originally acquired its fame due to turtles being encountered deep within the cave's depths – some of these turtles had become disorientated and died in the caves and, with the deaths of a few panicked divers, venturing far into the caverns is now reserved for experienced divers only. The island's geography and location focus nutrient-rich upwellings towards the island, and in areas such as the South and Barracuda Points, large pelagic (open sea) species such as grey reef sharks and sometimes even hammerheads are spotted.

Mabul Island

Located between Semporna and Sipadan, this island of 21 ha is considerably larger than Sipadan and is partly home to Bajau fishermen who live in traditional palm-thatched houses. In contrast to Sipadan's untouched forest, the island is predominantly planted with coconut trees. Diving has been the most recent discovery; an Australian diver claims it is "one of the richest single destinations for exotic small marine life anywhere in the world". It has already become known as the world's best muck diving, so called because of the silt-filled waters and poor visibility (usually around 12 m, which is quite reasonable compared with many other places in the area). The island is surrounded by gentle sloping reefs with depths from 3-35 m and a wall housing numerous species of hard corals. Since the closure of Sipadan's luxury resorts, several companies have moved their accommodation to Mabul, only 20 minutes away by fast boat. Places to stay at affordable backpacker budget places are available with island homestays or Semporna tour operators; see page 269. Depending on your bargaining skills, RM100 should get you a return boat trip to the island. Bajau culture remains fairly traditional on the island and while visitors will be stared at, especially women in Western dress, people are friendly, albeit in an intense manner.

Mataking and Kapalai

Mataking has only been open as a dive resort for a few years, but with the closure of Sipadan its popularity is almost guaranteed to rocket. There are about 30 good dive sites around the island including various reefs (plenty of good shallow ones making it an ideal spot for beginner divers), a sea fan garden, a 100-m crevice called Alice Channel that runs to Pulau Sipadan and Sweet Lips rock, a good night-diving spot. Accommodation is at the upmarket **Mataking Island Reef Dive Resort**, see page 265.

Kapalai is a sandbar, heavily eroded and set on top of Ligitan Reefs between Sipadan and Mabul. Semporna tour operators take people diving in Sipadan and in the shallow waters around Kapalai. **Bohedulang** is a volcanic, mountainous island east of Semporna, reminiscent of many Thai islands in the Andaman Sea. You pass its thickly forested slopes if heading for dive sites or resorts at Mataking, Bohayan or Mantabuan. The area is exceptionally beautiful above and below the waves.

Tawau → Colour map 4, C5.

Tawau is a timber port in Sabah's southeastern corner. It is a busy commercial centre and the main entry point of Indonesian workers into Sabah. A great contrast to the newly built hotel and business area, the waterfront has plenty of colourful markets and foodstalls and some picturesque views across the bay, including to Kalimantan.

The town was developed in the early 19th century by the British who planted hemp. The British also developed the logging industry in Sabah using elephants from Burma. The **Bombay Burma Timber Company** became the **North Borneo Timber Company** in 1950, a joint British and Sabah government venture.

In the last few years Tawau has began to develop rapidly as a regional hub of transport and commerce. Tawau centre has been cleaned up and has a few decent hotels and restaurants. The town has wide, clean streets and an air of prosperity not seen in many other Sabahan towns. Many travellers heading for Semporna now fly directly to Tawau, with its daily air connections to KL. With a couple of days' notice you can obtain a 60-day Indonesian visa and cross into eastern Kalimantan. As with many sections of Indonesian Borneo, transport is poor and very few westerners make this journey; of those that do, a large proportion head for pre-booked and exclusive diving operations off the coast. Although mud logging tracks exist on the Indonesian side of Sebuku Bay, most people usually find boat transport to the Indonesian towns of Nunukan and Tarakan further south much more comfortable and efficient.

With the development of a new road cutting across the south of Sabah towards KK nearing completion (passing just to the south of Maliau Basin), Tawau is set to receive more foreign visitors.

Tawau is surrounded by plantations and smallholdings of rubber, copra, cocoa and palm oil. The local soils are volcanic and very fertile and palm oil has recently taken over from cocoa as the predominant crop. Malaysian cocoa prices dropped when its quality proved to be 20% poorer than cocoa produced in Nigeria and the Ivory Coast and this, coupled with disease outbreaks in the crop, caused many of the cocoa growers to emigrate to the Ivory Coast. KL is now an established research centre for palm oil where there are studies on using palm oil as a fuel.

Now that the Sandakan area has been almost completely logged, Tawau has taken over as the main logging centre on the east coast. The forest is disappearing fast but there are some reforestation programmes. At **Kalabakan**, west of Tawau, there is a well-established, large-scale reforestation project with experiments on fast-growing trees such as *Albizzia falcataria*, said to grow 30 m in five years. There are now large plantation areas. The tree is processed into, among other things, paper for making money.

Tawau Hills State Park

ⓘ *Contact Ranger Office, Tawau Hills Park, T089-810676, F011-884917, RM2.*

This park, 24 km northwest of Tawau, protects Tawau's water catchment area. The Tawau River flows through the middle of the 27,972 ha park and forms a natural deep-water pool, at Table Waterfall, which is good for swimming. There is a trail from there to hot springs and another to the top of Bombalai Hill, an extinct volcano. Most of the forest in the park below 500 m has been logged; only the forest on the central hills and ridges is untouched. The park is popular with locals at weekends. Camping is possible but bring your own equipment. Access to the park is via a maze of rough roads through the **Borneo Abaca Limited** agricultural estates. It is advisable to hire a taxi.

Maliau Basin Conservation Area → *Colour map 4, B3.*

ⓘ *Conservation and Environmental Management Division, Yayasan Sabah Group, PO Box 11622, T088-326300, www.borneoforestheritage.org.my. Obtain permission in advance. Entry permits (RM50) are sold at the Shell Maliau Basin Reception and Information Building.*

In the rugged forest-clad hills in Sabah's heart lies an area known as Sabah's Lost World. Covering an area of 390 km², the Maliau Basin is one of the state's last areas of primary rainforest largely unaffected by agriculture or large-scale logging. It has remained undisturbed partly due to the difficulty of access and the geography of the basin. From the air, it looks like a vast meteor crater, measuring up to 25 km in diameter and surrounded by steep cliffs up to 1700 m in height on all but the southern and southeastern sides. Scientists believe that the crater was made through sedimentary forces over 15 million years ago, combined with major geological shifts, creating more than 30 spectacular waterfalls in the valley. The conservation area covers 588 sq km.

Granted government protection in the late 1990s and subject to growing scientific interest, Maliau is finally opening its doors to the public with its state-of- the-art visitors' centre completed in 2007. A major logging road cutting across the south of Sabah, from Tawau to Keningau and the west coast, is close to completion as a major paved highway. This will improve access to the zone, but will also increase threats to wildlife.

Flora and fauna

Maliau Basin is an area of incredible biodiversity featuring areas of lowland rainforest, heath forests and oak conifer, with cloud forests on the higher elevations. With over 1800 species of plant being recorded here, including 80 species of orchid, it is also only one of two sites in Sabah to have the rare rafflesia.

For wildlife watchers the park contains the full range of Bornean mammals, with animals such as the sun bear (see box, page 258), clouded leopard, Bornean gibbon, proboscis monkey and orange-utan being recorded in the park. These and other wildlife like the rare banteng (Asian wild cattle), elephant and pangolin are sometimes spotted on night safaris. However, it's unlikely you'll ever be lucky enough to spot the rarest resident,

It's a bear's life

The least studied and understood of all the bears, the sun or honey bear has differing names in the scientific community. The largest potentially carnivorous mammal in Borneo, sun bears are nevertheless the smallest of the world's eight bear species. A male sun bear weighs up to 65 kg, the female up to 50 kg, and bears are covered in short black fur, except for a yellow chest patch, unique to each bear in shape. It roams the dense forests of Southeast Asia, from Assam in India to Southern China and the lush islands of Sumatra and Borneo.

Using outsized claws tailored for an arboreal lifestyle, sun bears are excellent climbers, sometimes reaching up to 50 m in the forest canopy in search of food as diverse as palm hearts, termites, birds, small mammals, eggs and wild honey, which they love, lapping it up with long tongues. Bears often use their long claws like safety hooks to sleep high in the branches. Rare to see on the forest floor, sun bears are quite aggressive if cornered or startled, and with poor eyesight, they have been known to charge. If you're lucky enough to find a bear in the forest, it would be advisable to back away quietly while facing the bear, keeping as calm as possible. Remember, this is the bear's territory, not yours.

Massive forest destruction in Southern Asia means that the habitat of sun bears is under threat. Bears are widely hunted for their body parts, for use in traditional medicines; claws, gall bladders and other bones are found in markets throughout China and Southeast Asia.

Bears also face competition from other predators – pythons and crocodiles in Borneo sometimes hunt bears and in mainland Asia they share a shrinking habitat with tigers and leopards, plus Asian black bears and sloth bears in Eastern India.

To protect bears, follow these rules:
→ Never buy bear products in markets. In many countries (including Malaysia) this is illegal. If you see these products, report them to the local authorities.
→ Support projects to protect the rainforest and its habitat. WWF's Heart of Borneo programme aims to protect and conserve national parks and Borneo's most valuable forest areas. See www.panda.org for more information.
→ Support environmentally sustainable ecotourism projects by visiting and perhaps volunteering to protect or replant forest areas.
→ Encourage local people to become involved in ecotourism or forest-friendly industries. Hiring local and especially indigenous guides such as those from Kelabit, Penan and Iban tribal groups helps both the people and the forest.
→ If you have to buy wooden products, choose sustainably produced forest products such as those certified by the FSC (Forest Stewardship Council).
→ The US-based Rainforest Action Network, www.ran.org, is another good source of information.

the secretive Sumatran rhino, which is on the verge of extinction (see box, page 252). There are also nearly 300 species of birds. After the rains this area becomes packed with leeches, so specialized leech socks are worth considering.

Trekking

A network of trails linking a series of comfortable but basic scientific camps provides some of the best, and toughest, trekking in Northern Borneo. The treks pass numerous spectacular waterfalls, including the famous multi-tiered Maliau Falls and Takob Akob Falls, over 38 m high. If you're lucky with the weather you should get some panoramic views of the conservation area from the ridge tops.

It's a long drive back to Tawau or Semporna; however, the roads are improving all the time. Make sure you budget for trekking costs, including the entry fee, food of RM80 per day (if you arrange it through the park), accommodation and guide fees. Porters are also available. Each trip has to be individually organized to match trekkers' needs.

To make the most of the conservation area's facilities, a trek of a minimum five days and four nights is recommended (see the sample itinerary below). For truly serious trekkers and those with lots of time (and money) it may be possible to arrange a two-week expedition to Strike Ridge Camp in the north of the basin. As well as trek-based activities there's also a canopy walkway at Belian Camp and an observation platform, 30m high up a huge primary forest tree close to Camel Trophy Camp. This is a suggested basic five-day itinerary, covering 30 km:

Day 1: Many visitors arrive at Agathis Camp after driving from the well-organized (and interestingly Shell-sponsored) reception and information centre, which sells entry permits. Keep your eyes open for wildlife along the road and get some rest for a tough trek the next day.

Day 2: There's a tough climb uphill for a few hours through magnificent primary forest to the ridge top bordering Maliau's southern edge. Gibbons are often heard calling in forest here, a beautiful, emotional sound that encapsulates the spirit of the jungle. The 7-km-long trail leads to the basic Camel Trophy Camp. Behind is the 33-m-high observation tower in an Agathis tree. Additional trails lead to the spectacular Takob Akob Falls, two hours' walk away, and the nearer Giluk Falls. Don't underestimate the hikes after the initial six hours. This is a wildlife-rich area worthy of time and exploration. **Note** Watch out for poisonous red centipedes.

Day 3: A big day. You hike over highlands, mist-clad montane forest and stunted heathlands. These areas are crammed with orchids and pitcher plants, a botanist's dream. A five-hour walk takes you to Lobah Camp. From here, you can get to Maliau Falls, another few hours' return hike to the spectacular multi-level cascade.

Day 4: Take a break to enjoy the forest and the falls. A couple of hours' walk to Ginseng Camp.

Day 5: Another six- to eight-hour hike brings you back to your starting point, Agathis Camp, a good spot for a night hike or a drive to spot some wildlife. Civets, pangolins, small cats and deer are often spotted. You can even get a certificate to state that you've completed the circuit.

For Sleeping and Eating price codes and other relevant information, see Essentials pages 23-27.

● Sleeping

Sandakan *p240, map p242*

AL-B Swiss Inn, Sandakan Harbour Square, T089-240888, www.swissgarden.com. New hotel on the waterfront. Rooms are elegant, bright and modern with large flatscreen TV, Wi-Fi access and minibar. The more expensive ones have expansive sea views. Good café and bar downstairs. Decent promotion rates available. Recommended.

A Sabah, Km 1, Jln Utara, T089-213299, www.sabahhotel.com.my. Surrounded by forest, and with some tremendous views over the treetops, this smart 4-star hotel has modern, comfortable rooms with a/c, cable TV and marble bathrooms. Facilities include gym, pool, tennis court, spa and its own nature trail.

A Sanbay, Mile 1.25, Jln Leila, T089-275000, www.sanbay.com.my. 3-star hotel with bright and spacious en suite rooms with piped music and cable TV.

A Sandakan, 4th Av, T089-221122, www.hotelsandakan.com.my. Despite the old-fashioned carpets and heavy decor, rooms here are comfortable and good value. De luxe rooms are spacious and have views over the rooftops of Sandakan and down to the Sulu Sea. Good Cantonese restaurant and bar. This hotel is efficiently run and has some excellent promotional rates. Recommended.

B-C City View, Lot 1, Block 23, 3rd Av, T089-271122, www.citystar.com.my. Hotel with functional, comfortable rooms with a/c, cable TV, Wi-Fi and attached bathroom in the heart of town. Popular restaurant downstairs. Fair value, given the cost of backpacker accommodation in town. Recommended.

B Hsiang Garden, Km 1, T089-273122, F273127. A/c, restaurant, good bar.

B-D Nak, Jln Pelabuhan Lama, T089-272988, www.nakhotel.com. Recently upgraded hotel with tasteful Chinese decor and spacious rooms with slightly old, but clean bathrooms. Rooms have cable TV and Wi-Fi. Stylish rooftop café with excellent views. A/c dorm.

C London, Lot D1, Block 10, Jln Empat, T089-216372, www.hlondon.com.my. Excellent mid-range place offering a/c spotless, light rooms with cable TV with HBO movies, Wi-Fi and attached bathroom. There's a pleasant rooftop garden. Newly refurbished in classical style. Recommended.

C-D Mayfair, 24 Jln Pryer, T089-219855. Rooms with a/c, shower and TV. Owner has a vast collection of DVDs free to watch. As there's little to do in Sandakan after 2100, this hotel offers some welcome entertainment. Arranges transport to the airport and Sepilok for reasonable prices. The decor isn't great but it has a friendly atmosphere and a central location.

C-D Sandakan Backpackers, Lot 108, Sandakan Harbour Square, T089-221104, www.sandakanbackpackers.com. Miles ahead of the pack in this price range, this hostel has spacious bright rooms with Wi-Fi access and a/c, friendly common area with a pool table and rooftop garden. Can arrange tours to local attractions. Highly recommended.

C-D Winho Lodge, Lot 8, Jln Dua, T089-212310, www.winholodge.com. Large, old-school hostel with functional rooms, free Wi-Fi and internet access and 4-bed a/c dorms. Lacking in charm but reasonable value.

C-E Sunset Harbour Botik Hostel, Lot 125 Harbour Square, T089-229875, www.sunsethostels.com.Clean and friendly Malay-run place with a range of a/c rooms and a 10-bed dorm. There's also a kitchen. Internet access available. Fair value.

Pulau Lankayan *p244*

AL Lankayan Island Dive Resort, run by Pulau Sipadan Resort & Tours, 1st floor, Bandar Sabindo, Tawau, T089-765200, www.lankayan-island.com. The resort offers quiet chalets with electricity and attached bathroom by the beach and more than 40 dive sites including a couple of wrecks. Sightings of whale sharks are said to be common here Apr-May. There is an open-air café for meals and a TV room where dive fanatics gather to watch footage of the day's diving trip.

Turtle Islands National Park p244
The number of visitors to the islands is restricted, even in peak season. 3 chalets (one with 2 doubles, 2 with 6 doubles) on Pulau Selingan (RM260-370 per person, minimum 2 people). Book well in advance through **Crystal Quest**, page 269. Tour agencies can also organize trips to the island.

Sepilok Orang-Utan Sanctuary and Rehabilitation Centre p247
A-D Sepilok Jungle Resort (and Wildlife Lodge), Km 22 Labuk Rd, Sepilok Orang-Utan Sanctuary, 100 m behind the government resthouse, T089-533031, www.sepilokjungle resort.com This resort is the realization of a dream for John and Judy Lim, who have gradually purchased all the land on the edge of the forest and landscaped the area surrounding 3 man-made lakes. They've planted many flowering and fruiting trees, attracting butterflies and birds. The resort offers dorms with shared hot water bathrooms; double rooms with fan, a/c and hot water bathrooms; comfortable a/c double and family rooms; and more luxurious rooms, with cable TV, a/c, large balcony and tasteful tropical flourishes, surrounded by forest. Pleasant restaurant and in a great setting. This place is clean and comfortable. Boats for fishing available. Campsite (see below). The resort also has a large pool, gym and jacuzzi (RM5 a day). The owners are actively involved in Sandakan tourism and opened the tourist information office in town. Recommended.

The same team have opened **Bilit Adventure Lodge**, offering mid-range rooms along the Kinabatangan River. Rooms, with either a/c or fan, are usually offered in combination with tour packages.
B-D Sepilok B&B, Jln Arboreum, off Jln Sepilok, Mile 14, PO Box 155, T089-534050, www.sepilokbednbreakfast.com. Comfortable and bright rooms with polished wooden floors and a variety of rooms from a dorm to a de luxe room with TV and private balcony. All have attached bathroom with hot water. Wi-Fi, free breakfast and campsite under construction at the time of writing. Around 1 km from the sanctuary. Fair value.
B-D Sepilok Resthouse, Mile 14 Labuk Rd, T089-534900. Octagonal wooden house next to the orang-utan sanctuary. Government owned and now privately run. Big rooms, with bathtub and balcony. It's mostly occupied by long-term residents (young foreigners volunteering at the sanctuary), so it can be a bit noisy.
C Sepilok Country Restouse, 22KM, Labuk Rd, Jln Sepilok, T089-535784, www.sepilok countryresthouse.com. It's a fair old trek to the sanctuary from here and the place is a little sterile, but if things are full elsewhere this place offers clean rooms, café, a communal area with pool table and a 22 ft-deep fish pond.
C Uncle Tan Bed and Breakfast, Jln Sepilok, Lot 1, Mile 14, T089-531639, www.uncletan.com. Recently moved from Sandakan, this bed and breakfast has dorm-only accommodation and the price includes 3 meals a day. Double rooms should be ready by the time you read this. The staff here have a wealth of knowledge and can help organize trips to their famed Wildlife Camp in Kinabatangan. Recommended.
C-D Sepilok Forest Edge Resort, Jln Rambutan off Jln Sepilok, Mile 14, T089-533245, www.sepilokforestedge.com. A 10-min walk from the bus stop on Jln Sepilok. Chalets here are new, with attached bathroom and fan. There's also a dorm and a jacuzzi (RM6). Good communal area and jungle trail. They also have their own small farm, and a large pond. One of the owners, Robert Chong, is a birdwatching guide and can arrange tailored trips for birders.

Camping
E There's a campsite at **Sepilok Jungle Resort**, but you must bring your own gear.

Sungai Kinabatangan *p249*

Most companies running tours to the Kinabatangan put their guests up in Sukau or in camps along the river. See also **Sepilok Jungle Resort** above.

A Sukau Rainforest Lodge, Borneo Eco-Tours, 2nd floor, Lorong Bernam, Taman Soon Kiong, KK, T088-234009, www.sukau.com. Award-winning operator with a large selection of packages. This resort is accessible by boat from Sukau, and is run with eco-friendly ideals. There's accommodation for 40 in traditional Malaysian-style chalets on stilts. All 20 rooms with solar-powered fans, twin beds, mosquito netting, and attached tiled bathroom with hot water. Excellent restaurant and two boardwalks, including the 1500ft Hornbill boardwalk. Pleasant garden and sundeck overlooking the rainforest, and gift shop. Internet and satellite phone available. Friendly, efficient service. A shining example of ecotourism at its best. It must be good – past visitors include the Prince of Denmark and S Club 7! Shoe-string package available for budget travellers – contact Borneo Ecotours for more information. Highly recommended.

B Bilit Rainforest Lodge, contact **Tropical Gateway Tours**, 117 Ground Floor, Sandakan Harbour, T089-202311, www.tropicalg.com. New operation offering excellent value accommodation in spacious wooden a/c chalets with attached bathroom and hot water. They also run the more basic **Bilit Safari Camp (D)**, an option for budget travellers with dorms and highly competitive rates.

B Nature Lodge Kinabatangan, usually booked via **Nasalis Larvatus Tours**, Lot 226, 2nd floor, Wisma Sabah, Jln Tun Adbul Razak, KK, T088-863 6263, www.naturelodge kinabatangan.com/index.php. Excellent wildlife viewing lodge on a quiet section of the river about 1 hr by boat from Sukau. Accommodation is in simple Orang Sungei huts with electricity. The posher Agamind chalets have attached bathrooms with hot water. Good night walks and knowledgeable

and professional guides. Variety of packages offered, including transfers from Sandakan and entrance to the Sepilok Orang-utan Sanctuary.

C Proboscis Lodge, run by **Sipadan Dive Centre**, 10th floor, Wisma Merdeka, KK, T088-240584,www.proboscislodge.com. A more upmarket Kinabatangan experience, near Sukau, not in the heart of the jungle like the jungle camps. Chalets with hot-water showers, a/c and 24-hr electricity. Lovely large airy main building for meals and socializing and sun deck for observing riverine happenings. Visitors are limited to a maximum of 47 at a time, so it never feels too hectic. Various packages available.

D Uncle Tan Wildlife Adventures, Jln Sepilok, Lot 1, Mile 14, T089-531639, www.uncletan.com. A long-established budget option for exploring the lower Kinabatangan Valley. The camp recently relocated to its present site on the Lokam river, upriver from their previous camp. Accommodation is in simple huts with no doors or window and lino flooring. Guests are provided a clean sheet, a thin mattress and a mosquito net and all rooms are shared. There is a bathouse with water pumped from the river for bathing and visitors are reminded not to leap in the river as several large crocodiles have been lingering. All meals are provided and vegetarians catered for. This is a great way to get back to nature. A 3-day, 2-night package including van transport to the river from the B&B on Jln Sepilok, several river cruises including an amazing night cruise, jungle treks and all meals (simple but hearty) costs RM380 (extra nights for RM80 each). Prepare to get very muddy; wellies are available. Bring raincoat and torch. The camp is very remote and in the middle of the jungle. It is run by enthusiastic young locals who speak pretty good English, love to mix with guests and, while not expert naturalists, are knowledgeable about the wildlife. Some have been working here for years. The camp was started by Uncle Tan, who began taking tourists out to the jungle in 1988. A colourful character, he fought stridently for conservation issues in the region.

He died in 2002 and the running of the resort has been taken over by his brother, based in Singapore. This place is deservedly popular, so book ahead. It's common to see proboscis monkeys and wild orang-utan sightings are not rare. Perhaps your best chance of seeing Sabah's wildlife. Recommended.

Lahad Datu and around *p250*

Lahad Datu is not a popular tourist spot and accommodation is poor and expensive. Avoid **Perdana** and **Venus** hotels on Jln Seroja.
A **Tabin Jungle Resort**, Tabin Wildlife Reserve, book at Lot 11-1, Blk A, Damai Point, Jln Damai, KK, T088-267266, www.tabinwildlife.com.my. Great for serious wildlife enthusiasts or anyone on a romantic weekend or escaping to nature for a few days. Beautifully designed wooden cabins with balconies overlooking the Lipad river in Tabin Wildlife Reserve. All cabins with ceiling fan and hot showers. Variety of packages available. Recommended.
B **Silam Lodge**, Gunung Silam, T088-243245, F254227. Owned by **Borneo Rainforest Lodge** and mostly used by people in transit to the Danum Valley. Minibuses from Lahad Datu.
B-C **Jagokota**, Jln Kampong Panji, T089-882000, F881526. A well-furnished place.
C **Permaisaba**, Block 1, Lot 3, 1/4 Jln Tengah Nipah, T089-883800, F883681. Five mins' drive from the airport and town. Seafood restaurant, Malaysian and Indian food, conference hall, free transfers to/from the airport and town. Large rooms with attached bathroom and hot water, information on the Danum Valley, characterless but convenient.

Danum Valley Conservation Area *p251*

AL **Borneo Rainforest Lodge**, c/o Borneo Nature Tours, Block 3, ground floor, Fajar Centre, Lahad Datu, T089-880207, F885051. KK office: Block D, Lot 10, 3rd floor, Sadong Jaya Complex, T088-243245, www.borneorainforestlodge.com. One of the finest tourism developments in Sabah. 18 bungalows in a magnificent setting beside the river, built on stilts from *belian* (ironwood) and based on traditional Kadazan design with connecting wooden walkways. 28 rooms with private bathroom and balcony overlooking the Danum River, good restaurant, jacuzzi (solar-heated water). Designed by naturalists, the centre aims to combine a wildlife experience in a remote primary rainforest with comfort and privacy and provide high-quality natural history information. There is a conference hall, excellent guides; visits to a centre for forest management, a library of resource books, after-dinner slide shows and a gift shop. Rafting is available and night drives can be organized. Mountain bikes, fishing rods and river tubes can be hired. Electricity is available all day. Expensive but well worth it. Price includes meals and guided jungle trips. If you get permission to stay at the centre, the **Sabah Foundation** has dorms for RM45 per night, or RM80 for a single room.

Semporna *p253*

AL-B **Seafest**, Jln Kastam, T089-782333, www.seafesthotel.com. A high-rise building on the waterfront, somewhat out of character with the rest of the town but a lack of business has forced them into offering very good walk-in promotional rates. Rooms are comfortable but characterless. There's a restaurant and a new pool. Wi-Fi is available up to the 6th storey. Front-facing rooms have great views of the bay.
A-B **Sipadan Inn**, Block D, Lot No19-24, seafront, T089-782766, www.sipidan-inn.com. Newish place near the main jetty, popular with people on dive courses. It has huge well-furnished de luxe rooms with massive TV, attached bathroom and lounge area. The smaller a/c standards are a bit of a squeeze, but comfortable and clean. Wi-Fi.
B-C **City Inn**, Lot 2, Block K, Bangunan, Hing Loong, close to the Dyana Express bus office, T089-784733, www.cityinn-semporna.com. This well-run place has spotless, slightly old rooms with TV, attached bathroom and a/c in the busy commercial heart of the town – it's a

good 5-min walk to the jetty, but handy for the bus station. Wi-Fi and internet access in the lobby. Recommended.

B-D Borneo Global Backpackers, Bangunan Seafest, Jln Causeway, T089-785088, www.bgbackpackers.com. New place right on the waterfront with large a/c dorms with attached bathroom and spacious family rooms. Rooms at the front have excellent views over the bay. Very clean and well-managed. Arranges trips to Sipidan and Mabul.

B-D Dragon Inn, Jln (next to the jetty), T089-781088, F781099, www.dragoninnfloating com.my. All rooms are built in wooden longhouses over the sea. Unfortunately much of the sea here is filled with the detritus of urban coastal life, which detracts from the charm. Some very large, well-furnished doubles and smaller twins with a/c, TV and attached bathroom. Cavernous dorms are excellent value with over 20 beds that are often empty. Great experience to have a shower and see the green ocean through the wooden slatted floor. Recommended.

C Lee's Resthouse and Café, Pekau Baru, T/F089-784491. Clean guesthouse with pokey rooms with a/c, TV and attached bathroom. Some rooms are windowless. Slighty overpriced, but staff are very friendly and there is a superb restaurant next door.

C-D Damai Traveller's Lodge, TL 89, 3rd floor, town centre, T089-782011, F781525. Particularly unexciting place in the town centre. Rooms have a/c, attached bathroom and TV but many are windowless. Can arrange tours and trips to islands. Some rooms have sea views. Average value.

C-E Scuba Junkie Backpacker, PO Box 458, Block B Lot 36, seafront, T089-785372, www.scuba-junkie.com. Opposite **Scuba Junkie**'s dive shop and with a bar/restaurant attached. Good location with a variety of rooms from dorms to en suites. Excellent value with breakfast and internet included and discounts for SJ's divers and snorkellers. Some private rooms are a little cave-like with no windows and not always perfectly clean. Book ahead as this place is often rammed.

Mabul *p255*

With the closure of all Sipadan resorts Mabul Island is a convenient place to stay. There are several resorts here, plus some cheaper options. Food is often included in the price.

L Mabul Water Bungalows, book via **Explore Asia Tours**, Lot A-1-G, Block A, Signature Office, KK Times Square, off Coastal Highway, T088-486389, www.mabul waterbungalows.com. A pricey and luxurious resort built on stilts above the Mabul reef. Dive packages and facilities including nitrox and cave diving are available. A good choice for people who want all their home comforts, with cable TV, minibar, a/c and business centre with internet access.

L Sipadan Mabul Resort, at the southern tip of the island overlooking Sipadan and a pleasant beach, the same company, contact address, website and phone number as **Mabul Water Bungalows** above. 25 newly refurbished beach chalets with a/c, hot-water showers, balcony, pool and jacuzzi, restaurant serving Chinese and Western buffet food, all-inclusive price, PADI diving courses, snorkelling, windsurfing, deep-sea fishing, volleyball, diving boats.

L Sipadan Water Village, reservations: PO Box 62156, T089-751777, www.sipadan-village.com.my. Stunning resort constructed on several wharves in Bajau, water-villagestyle on ironwood stilts over the water. 45 chalets with private balconies, hot-water showers, restaurant serving good range of cuisine, well-organized dive shop and centre, deep-sea fishing tours. Relaxing, tranquil place, with no TV or unnecessary noise. 3 daily boat dives are usually included in packages and there's quite a bit of marine life on the house reef directly below the resort. Reserve in advance for Sipadan Island dives/licenses.

A Borneo Divers Mabul Resort, Head Office, 9th floor, Menara Jubili, 53 Jln Gaya, Kota Kinabalu, T088-222226, www.borneo divers.info. Small office just outside the entrance to **Dragon Inn** next to **Uncle Chang's**. One of the few mid-range places on the island, prices include food. Pool. Not particularly stylish, but decent value facing the beach and the **Seaventures** platform. All diving facilities.

A Seaventures Dive Resort, run by Sea Ventures Dives, 4th floor 422-423, Wisma Sabah, Kota Kinabalu, T088-261669, www.seaventuresdive.com. Just offshore is the strange site of a refurbished oil rig. A true diver's spot, it offers boat dives to Sipadan and other nearby islands and is locally famous for its excellent muck diving directly beneath the platform. Good value and an exciting location for divers who enjoy macrolife and underwater photography.

C per person. **The Longhouse** book through Scuba Junkie, Semporna, see page 270, price includes food if diving with **Scuba Junkie**. Very basic but superb value. Interesting location in Bajau village house. 6 new rooms constructed and a bar on the way. RM40 each way for transfer to the island if you're not diving.

C per person. **Uncle Chang's**, book through Uncle Chang's dive shop, see Dragon Inn, Semporna, see opposite. Another good backpacker option, located in the Bajau village on the far side of Mabul island. Rates include food and Uncle Chang has all the diving kit, plus years of experience above and below the waves in the region. He is currently trying to open a place on Maita island. Recommended.

Mataking and Kapalai *p256*
L Mataking Island Reef Dive Resort, book through Jln Bunga, Tawau, T089-770022, or ground floor, Wisma Sabah, KK, T088-318022, www.mataking.com. It also has a counter in Semporna at the jetty on Jln Kastam. The resort has 3 speedboats daily from Semporna jetty and the journey takes 45 mins. The resort has a/c chalets and de luxe rooms, some with sea view and balcony. Facilities at the resort include a *jammu* (native medicinal) spa, satellite TV, internet, bar and restaurant. In 2006 the resort sank an old cargo boat and renamed it the Mataking 1, with the hopes

that this will encourage a new reef to grow. The wreck is home to Malaysia's only underwater post office – now that's a postbox with a difference!

AL Sipadan-Kapalai Dive Resort, run by Pulau Sipadan Resort & Tours, 1st floor, Bandar Sabindo, Tawau, T089-765200, www.sipadan-kapalai.com. This resort straddles Kapalai's sandback on stilts. The resort, modelled as a water village, has 40 twin-sharing wooden chalets, with attached bathrooms, balconies and amazing sea views all round, linked by a network of wooden platforms. Dive centre, internet access.

Tawau *p256*
Rock-bottom places in Tawau are grim and visitors are advised to spend a few more ringgit to get somewhere safe and clean. There aren't any guesthouses to speak of, but a number of good value mid-range places aimed at local business travellers. Hotels are concentrated around the intersection of Jln Bunga and Jln Haji Karim.

A Belmont Marco Polo, Jln Abaca/Jln Clinic, T089-777988, F763739. Smart upmarket hotel primarily aimed at business travellers, but offering great walk-in promotional rates. Rooms are clean and feature cable TV, Wi-Fi access, and rather stiff, formal furnishings. Bathrooms have bathtubs. There's also a health centre, café and good Chinese restaurant.

A-B De Choice, Jln Masjid, T089-776655. Sterile business hotel with a selection of spacious clean rooms all with a/c, Wi-Fi access and attached bathroom. Fair value.

A-B Heritage, Jln Bunga, Fajar Complex, T089-766222, www.heritagehotel.com.my. Well-managed hotel with stylish, modern rooms. All rooms have sofas and complimentary daily newspapers. More expensive rooms have bathtubs, free Wi-Fi access and jacuzzi. Recommended.

B King Park, 30 Jln Haji Karim, T089-766699, kingpark@streamyx.com. Good mid-range option with 100 clean rooms in a mint green tower block overlooking the city. Rooms at the front have views of the sea in the distance. All

rooms have cable TV, a/c, attached bathroom and Wi-Fi access. Good promotional rates.
B MB, Jln Masjid, T089-701333, www.mavblossomhotel.com. New hotel with spotless, modern rooms. Limited in character but with all the facilities needed for a comfortable stay. Good promotional rates. Recommended.

B-C Monaco, 214 Jln Haji Karim (on the corner of Jln Bunga), T089-769912, F769922. The best value lodgings in town with carpeted a/c rooms (some windowless) with Wi-Fi access, cable TV and attached bathroom. Staff are friendly and rooms on the corner have good views over the rooftops to the hills surrounding Tawau. Recommended. This hotel is run by the same groups that runs the **Monaco Dynasty Hotel** (**B-C**) and **Istana Monaco Hotel** (**B-C**), opposite on Jln Bunga. All 3 hotels have similar facilities, but the **Istana** has the newest rooms. Rooms at the **Dynasty** are looking a little tatty and are mostly windowless.

C First, 208 Jln Bunga, T089-778989, F761296. Popular with domestic travellers, this place is looking a little rough round the edges but has clean rooms with a/c and attached bathroom. There are better value options along the street.

C Grace, 4263 Jln Chester, T089-751555. Handy for the port for boats to Indonesia and in the bustling centre, this place has passable a/c rooms with TV and attached bathroom.

Maliau Basin *p257*
E per person. **Maliau Basin camps**. Basic dorms, beds must be booked in advance due to limited availability. Camps have 20-40 beds, apart from Camel Trophy Camp with only 8 places available.

● Eating

Sandakan *p240, map p242*
Sandakan is justifiably renowned for its inexpensive and delicious seafood; try the semi-outdoor restaurants situated at the top of Trig (Trigonometry) Hill.

¶ English Tea House & Restaurant, Agnes Keith House, T089-222544, www.englishtea house.org. Step back in time at this wonderful place with shady outdoor garden seating overlooking the bay, an immaculate croquet lawn and jugs of Pimms. An afternoon here could easily be mistaken for a freakishly hot day in Devon circa 1930. Scones, clotted cream and pots of tea are proffered alongside excellent fusion cuisine that makes this one of Malaysia's most charming eateries. Highly recommended.

¶ New Seoul Garden, Hsiang Garden Estate, Mile 1.5, Leila Rd. Korean food.

¶ Ocean King Seafood, Mile 2.5, Jln Batu Sapi, T089-618111. Great seafood place built on stilts over the water. Big, over-the-top statues of lobster and marine life Disney-up the place. But unbeatable for a relaxing sunset meal, great views.

¶ Palm Garden, Hotel Sandakan. Open for lunch and dinner. Well known for its steamboats and dim sum buffets, this place is a good spot to sample Sandakan's Cantonese cuisine. There's an international buffet every Friday in the **Palm Café** downstairs.

¶ Pesah Putih Baru, on the coast, nearly at the end of Sandakan Bay, about 5 km from the port. Great views of Sandakan and good food. Recommended.

¶ Trig Hill Ming, Sabah Hotel, Km 1, Jln Utara, T089-213299. Cantonese and Sichuan cuisine, renowned for dim sum (breakfast).

¶ Balin Rooftop Garden, Nak Hotel, Jln Pelabuhan Lama. Open 1630-2400. Lovely rooftop garden serving simple Western fare and cold beers, making this an ideal spot for a sundowner. Recommended.

¶ Fairwood, Jln Dua. A cheap, a/c fast-food place with all the local favourites, situated in the centre of town.

¶ Fat Cat, 206 Wisma Sandakan, 18 Jln Haji Saman. Several branches around town, breakfasts recommended.

¶ Hawaii, City View Hotel, Lot 1, Block 23, 3rd Av. Pseudo Western and local food, busy at 1200 as workers come for the cheap set lunch.

¶ Kedai Makanan King Cheong, Jln Dua. Open for breakfast and lunch. The quality of this great place is testified to by the lunchtime crowds that ram in daily. Trolleys of dim sum weave between tables of punters getting stuck into simple Cantonese fare and some interesting oddities: Marmite fans will want try the *nasi ayam marmite*.

🍴 **Restoran Hikmah**, Jln Batu Empat, Mile 4. Reputed to be the best spot in town for Malay food, with good seafood dishes and some *asam pedas*.

🍴 **Santai**, Waterfront, Sandakan Harbour Sq. Cheap seafood dishes, including superb noodles and fried rice, this popular spot is right on the waterfront offering a relaxing view of the fishing boats on the horizon. Busy in the evenings. Recommended.

🍴 **ZL Vegetarian Restaurant**, Lot 6, Block 1, Bandar Pasar Raya, Batu Empat. Great value selection of Chinese vegetarian dishes on the edge of town.

Foodstalls

Next to minibus station, just before the community centre on the road to Ramai Ramai, also at summit of Trig Hill.

Sepilok Orang-Utan Sanctuary and Rehabilitation Centre *p247*

By far the best place to eat is the veranda restaurant at the **Sepilok Jungle Resort**, which serves international and Malaysian food. The food is OK but the setting is lovely.

Lahad Datu and around *p250*

🍴🍴 **Melawar**, 2nd floor, Block 47, off Jln Teratai (around the corner from the **Mido Hotel**). Seafood restaurant, popular with locals.

🍴🍴 **Ping Foong**, 1.5 km out of Lahad Datu, on Sandakan Rd. Open-air seafood restaurant, highly recommended by locals.

🍴 **Ali**, opposite **Hotel New Sabah**. Indian, good roti.

🍴 **Evergreen Snack Bar and Pub**, on 2nd floor, Jln Teratai, opposite Hap Seng Building. A/c, excellent fish and chips and best known for its tuna steaks. Recommended.

🍴 **Golden Key**, on stilts over the sea opposite the end of Jln Teratai. Just a tumbledown wooden coffee shop, but well known for its seafood.

🍴 **Good View**, just over 500 m out of town on Tengku Rd. Recommended by locals.

🍴 **Seng Kee**, Block 39, opposite **Mido Hotel** and next to **Standard Chartered Bank**. Cheap and good.

Foodstalls

Pasar Malam, behind **Mido Hotel** on Jln Kastam Lama. Spicy barbecued fish (*ikan panggang*) and skewered chicken wings recommended.

The new market has foodstalls upstairs with attractive views out to sea.

Semporna *p253*

This grubby little town is no diner's fantasy, but there is some good seafood on offer and plenty of little eateries offering Malay curries. Don't leave it too late for dinner in the evening as Semporna goes to bed early.

🍴🍴 **Pearl City Restaurant**, attached to **Dragon Inn**. Chinese-style seafood in a wooden restaurant over the sea. Verify prices before ordering. Great setting. Recommended.

🍴🍴 **Seafest**, next to the **Seafest Inn**. Mainly Malay food with some excellent fish dishes. Good standard for very reasonable prices.

🍴 **Anjung Paghalian**, next to police station near bridge to jetty. Simple outdoor place with good, cheap seafood and giant iced avocado juices. Recommended.

🍴 **Lee's Café**, next to **Lee's Hotel**. This place is the best eatery in town with excellent Chinese dishes at very good prices. The prawns here are plump, the beer cold and the staff friendly. Simple Western breakfasts are available from 0700 onwards. Recommended.

🍴 **Mabul Café** (a few shops down from Scuba Junkie). Mainly a Chinese restaurant but with plenty of pseudo-Western dishes such as king prawn wrapped in a kraft cheddar slice, steaks, fries and all the usual suspects. The Asian dishes are the better choice here. Plenty of beer available.

🍴 **Sinar Harapan**, next to **Mabul Café**. Simple Malay place with curries, noodles and *tom* yam. Friendly spot to neck a plate of *pisang goreng* on a listless tropical afternoon.

Tawau *p256*
Foodstalls along the seafront.

🍴 **CJs Bistro**, Jln Bunga (next to Heritage Hotel). Good pizza, coffee, naughty desserts and Western dishes in a convivial, clean restaurant with Wi-Fi access. Recommended.

🍴 **Kam Ling Seafood**, Sabindo Square. Delicious fresh seafood including crab and huge prawns. The fresh lime juice here is excellent. Very popular.

🍴 **Kublai Khan**, Marco Polo Hotel, Jln Clinic. Open for lunch and dinner. Large, traditionally furnished Chinese eating hall specialising in Cantonese food, with a good value weekly steamboat buffet (Sat, 1900). There is also the **Venice Coffee House** here serving a range of fair international cuisine and huge weekend brunches.

🍴 **May Garden**, 1 km outside town on road to Semporna. Outside seating.

🍴 **Asnur**, 325B, Block 41, Fajar Complex. Thai and Malay, large choice.

🍴 **Dragon Court**, 1st floor, Lot 15, Block 37 Jln Haji Karim. Chinese, popular with locals, lots of seafood.

🍴 **Olive**, 1878 Jln Haji Karim. Open 1100-1430 and 1800-2230. Cheap eatery serving glasses of red wine, cold beer and a menu of pizza, tapas and pasta dishes. Don't expect the real deal with these prices, but not a bad spot nevertheless.

🍴 **Yasmin**, Jln Chester. Excellent selection of *nasi campur* dishes served with an interesting cinnamon-infused chicken soup.

🍴 **Yassin Curry House**, Sabindo Square (near the minibus terminal). Biryani, tandoori chicken, kebabs and outrageously sweet lassis, 10 mins' walk from the town centre. There is a/c seating.

🍴 **Yun Lo**, Jln Abaca (below the Hotel Loong). Good Malay and Chinese. A popular spot with locals, good atmosphere. Recommended.

🎭 Entertainment

Sandakan *p240, map p242*
There is a karaoke parlour on just about every street. **Tiffany Discotheatre and Karaoke**, Block C, 7-10, Jln Leila, Bandar Ramai-Ramai.

Tawau *p256*
Cinema, Jln Stephen Tan, next to central market. There are **karaoke** bars on every street corner. Several hotels have nightclubs and bars.

🛍 Shopping

Sandakan *p240, map p242*
Almost everything in Sandakan is imported. There are some inexpensive batik shops and some good tailors. **Centre Point**, near the bus station, is even more down at heel than Wisma Sandakan. **Handicrafts Sabakraf**, opposite Hotel Sandakan, has basketry, pearls and souvenirs. **Wisma Sandakan**, next to the town mosque, has 3 floors of dimly lit shopping.

Lahad Datu and around *p250*
The central market is on Jln Bungaraya and there is a spice market off Jln Teratai where Indonesian smugglers tout Gudang Garam cigarettes and itinerant dentists and *bumohs* (witch doctors) draw large crowds.

Semporna *p253*
Cultured pearls are sold by traders in town. Filipino handicrafts.

Tawau *p256*
General and fish market at the west end of Jln Dunlop, near the customs wharf.

🔺 Activities and tours

Sandakan *p240, map p242*
Bowling
Champion Bowl, Jln Leila, Bandar Ramai Ramai. Jln Leila is the main road that heads

out of Sandakan, Champion Bowl is just out of town at Mile 1¼, T089-211396.

Golf
Sandakan Golf Club, Jln Kolam, Bukit Padang, T088-247533, 10 km out of town. Open to non-members.

Social clubs
Sepilok Recreation Club, Bandar Ramai Ramai. Snooker, sauna, darts and karaoke.

Tour operators
Many tour operators have their offices in Wisma Khoo Siak Chiew.
Borneo Ecotours, c/o Hotel Hsiang Garden, PO Box 82, Jln Leila, T089-220210, F213614.
Capac Travel Service, ground floor, Rural District Building, Jln Tiga, T089-217288. Ticketing, tour and hotel services.
Crystal Quest, Sabah Park Jetty, Jln Buli Sim Sim, T089-212711, cquest@tm.net.my or cq1996@streamyx.net. The only company running accommodation on Pulau Selingan, Turtle Islands National Park.
SI Tours, 1st floor, Wisma Khoo Siak Chiew, T089-213501, www.sitours.com.my. Well-established company running tours to Gomantong Caves, Kinabatangan and Turtle Islands National Park. Recommended.
Tropical G, 117, Block 12, Sandakan Harbour Square, T089-202333, www.tropicalg.com. Offers Sabah-wide packages including trips to Kinabatangan, Gomontong caves and Selingan turtle islands, Danum Valley and Maliau Basin.
Wildlife Expeditions, Room 903, 9th floor, Wisma Khoo Siak Chiew, Lebuh Tiga, Jln Buli Sim-Sim, T089-219616, F214570 (in **Sabah Hotel**). The most expensive, but the most efficient, with the best facilities and guides.

Turtle Islands National Park *p244*
The average cost of a 1-night tour including accommodation and boat transfer is RM350 or more. An expedition to the islands needs to be well planned; the vagaries, such as bad weather, which can prevent you from leaving the islands as planned, can mess up itineraries. Most visitors book trips well in advance.

Gomantong Caves *p248*
It is easiest to visit the caves on a tour, see Sandakan above. They are accessible by an old logging road, which can be reached by bus from the main Sandakan-Sukau Rd. The timing of the bus is inconvenient for those wishing to visit the caves. Alternatively take a taxi (around RM150 from Sandakan). It is a good idea to visit the caves on the way to Sukau, where you can stay overnight.

Sungai Kinabatangan *p249*
Tour operators will transport guests to the lodge or camp as part of the package, some offer tours of Gomantong and/or Sepilok en route. **Uncle Tan's** picks up from its base in Sepilok. Others have transport from Sandakan, Tawau, Danum Valley and Semporna. Book trips at tour operators in Sandakan, see above, or KK, page 204.

Lahad Datu and around *p250*
Tour operators
Borneo Nature Tours, Block 3, Fajar Centre, T089-880207, F885051.

Semporna *p253*
Tour operators
Today Travel Services, No 90, Lot 2, Tingkat Bawah, T089-781112. Sells **AirAsia** and **MAS** flights to KK and KL from Tawau, the nearest airport.

Sipadan Island Marine Reserve *p254*
Tour operators
Most dive centres here offer PADI courses. Each operator arranges permits, rents out equipment (RM50-75 per day) and provides all food and accommodation. Pre-arranged packages operated by the companies sometimes include air transfer to and from Kota Kinabalu. Walk-in rates are cheaper. Book trips to Sipidan well in advance as only 120 permits are issued daily.

Borneo Divers, Rooms 401-412, 4th floor, Wisma Sabah, KK, T088-222226, www.borneodivers.info. A major Sipadan player; it organizes trips from KK to Sipadan with accommodation on Mabul. However, some complain it has gone downhill. 3-day package with 10 dives and stay on Mabul around RM1200.

Pulau Sipadan Resort, 484, Block P, Bandar Sabindo, Tawau, T089-765200, www.sipadan-resort.com. Organizes dive tours, food and lodging and diving instruction, snorkelling equipment is also available, maximum of 30 divers at any one time. It also runs accommodation on Pulau Kapalai.

Scuba Junkie, Blk B, Lot 36, Semporna seafront, T089-785372, www.scuba-junkie.com. Well-run outfit that offers a variety of courses and trips to Mataking, Sipidan, Kapalai and Mabul. Accommodation on Mabul available. 2-dive trip to Sipidan (RM330), snorkelling to outer islands and night dives arranged.

Sipadan Dive Centre, A1103, 11th floor, Wisma Merdeka, Jln Tun Razak, KK, T088-240584, www.sipidandivers.com. Packages (all-in) approximately US$740 (5 days/4 nights). Recommended.

Uncle Chang's, entrance to **Dragon Inn**, Semporna, T089-781002. Uncle Chang, entrepreneur extraordinaire, offers the budget traveller everything. He can get discount bus tickets, offers shuttle service to the airport, gets discounts for the **Dragon Inn**, has an efficient laundry service and runs some great dive trips out to Sipadan including courses. 3 boat dives including all equipment hire and lunch for RM360 Snorkelling day trips to Sipidan (RM225) and Mabul (RM115), plus night diving at Mabul. Excellent value accommodation on Mabul. Recommended.

Tawau *p256*
Diving
Borneo Divers, 46, 1st floor, Jln Dunlop, T089-762259, F761691.

Pulau Sipadan Resort & Tours, 1st floor, Bandar Sabindo, Tawau, T089-765200, F763563.

Reef Dive Resort and Tours, Jln Bunga, T089-770022, www.mataking.com. Arranges packages to the upmarket **Reef Dive Resort** on Mataking.

Golf
9-hole golf course, modest green fees, even cheaper during the week.

Tour operators
GSU, T089-772531. This is the booking agent for Kalimantan.

⊖ Transport

Sandakan *p240, map p242*
Air
The airport is 10 km north of the town centre (RM20 by taxi into town). Early morning flights from **KK** to Sandakan allow breathtaking close-up views of Mt Kinabalu as the sun rises. **AirAsia** and **MAS** have daily connections with **KL** and KK. **MASwings** flies daily to **Tawau** and KK.

Airline offices MAS, ground floor, Sabah Bldg, Jln Pelabuhan, T089-273966; AirAsia, Jln Dua.

Boat
The MV Kristle Jane 3 sails to **Zamboanga** in the southern **Philippines**. The journey takes 12-16 hrs and leaves at 1700 every Tue and Fri from Sandakan (RM280 for a suite). Contact **Aleson Shipping Lines** (T089-212063 or T089-224009) for ticketing.

Bus and minibus
Local minibuses from the bus stop between the Esso and Shell stations on Jln Pryer.

Sandakan's a/c long-distance buses leave from the bus station at Mile 2.5. Some buses and all minibuses don't leave until they are full, so be prepared for a long wait. Regular connections with most towns in Sabah including **Kota Kinabalu**, (6 hrs RM42), **Ranau**, (4 hrs RM27), **Lahad Datu** (3-4 hrs RM20). Buses start at 0715, and then several departures until 1100. After this you will have to take a Tawau bus, get off at Simpang Assam and take a minibus into Lahad Datu (RM1). **Tawau** (6 hrs RM40), buses from 0630, every 30 mins until 1100. 1 bus at 1400. **Semporna** (6 hrs RM40), departs 0800.

Turtle Islands National Park *p244*
Tour operators have their own boats and the fee is included with the package price, so times will vary.

Sepilok Orang-Utan Sanctuary and Rehabilitation Centre *p247*
Bus
There are 5 daily public buses from **Sandakan**, from the central minibus terminal in front of Nak Hotel from 0900-1400 (40 mins RM4). Ask for the Sepilok Batu 14 line. From the airport, the most convenient way to reach Sepilok is by taxi. Sepilok is 1.9 km from the main road. A taxi should cost around RM35 into Sandakan. You can charter a car for RM40 into Sandakan from **Sepilok Jungle Resort**. There are 6 buses to Sandakan from 0700-1600 (40 mins RM4).

Lahad Datu and around *p250*
Air
Connections with **KK**.
   Airline offices MAS, ground floor, Mido Hotel, Jln Main, T089-881707.

Boat
Fishing boats take paying passengers from the old wharf (end of Jln Kastam Lama) to **Tawau** and **Semporna**, although time-wise (and, more to the point, safety-wise) it makes much more sense to go by road or air.

Minibus
Minibuses and what are locally known as wagons (7-seater, 4WD Mitsubishis) leave from the bus station on Jln Bunga Raya (behind Bangunan Hap Seng at the mosque end of Jln Teratai) and from opposite the Shell station. Regular connections with **Tawau** (2½ hrs), **Semporna**, **Sandakan** and **Madai**.

Danum Valley Conservation Area *p251*
From Lahad Datu, turn left along the logging road at Km 15 on the Lahad Datu – Tawau road to Taliwas and then left again to field centre, 85 km west of Lahad Datu. **Borneo Rainforest Lodge** is 97 km (not an easy trip) from **Lahad Datu**; it provides a transfer service (2 hrs); phone the lodge for details.

Semporna *p253*
Bus and Minibus
Minibus station in front of USNO HQ. Regular connections with **Tawau** (1½ hrs RM13) and **Lahad Datu**. Most departures are in the morning. Minibus to **Tawau airport**. 1 daily bus to Sandakan (6 hrs RM40). 2 daily buses to **KK** (0730, 1930, 11 hrs RM75). The mid-morning AirAsia flight from Tawau is a better option. Prices start at RM70.

Mataking and Kapalai *p256*
Air and boat
Flight to **Tawau**, minibus, taxi or resort van to Semporna (1½ hrs), from where speed boats depart for the islands (30-60 mins). Boats to the islands are taken either with dive companies or as a transfer to a resort. Lots of boats leave daily but generally only in the morning at around 0730, for day trips (RM100).

Tawau *p256*
Air
The airport is 2 km from town centre. Regular connections with **MAS** and **AirAsia** to KK and KL and **MASwings** to Sandakan.
   Flights to Tarakan and elsewhere in Indonesia have been suspended. Those travelling to Kalimantan will have to take a boat to Nunukan.
   Airline offices AirAsia office at the airport and on Jln Bunga opposite the Heritage Hotel. MAS, Lot 1A, Wisma SASCO, Fajar Complex, T089-765533.

Boat
Packed boats leave Tawau's customs wharf (behind Pasar Ikan) twice daily at 1100 and 1600 for **Pulau Nunukan Timur, Kalimantan**

(1 hr RM75). More convenient is the boat to **Indonesia**'s **Tarakan** (daily at 1130 except Sun, 4 hrs RM140). There is limited transport available from Nunukan, and travellers will need to travel to Tarakan for more transport options (there are 2 daily **Kal Star** flights from Nunukan to Tarakan at 1330 and 1400, Rp 250,000). Nunukan is connected to Pare Pare, **Pantoloan**, by PELNI ferry. Tarakan is connected to **Balikpapan** and **Surabaya** by air and with Toli Toli Surabaya, and **Jakarta** with PELNI ferry. All visitors need to get a visa before arriving in Indonesia. Tickets available from offices near the Pasar Ikan (fish market). Agents include **Saumdera Indah**, T089- 753320.

Note PELNI ferries in Indonesia generally call in every 2 weeks. Travellers wishing to catch a ferry should time their arrival in Nunukan or Tarakan to meet the ferry. Schedules are available at www.pelni.co.id.

Bus

Station on Jln Wing Lock (west end of town). Minibus station on Jln Dunlop (centre of town). Direct service from Tawau to **Kota Kinabalu** leaving at 2000 to arrive 0500 in KK (RM75). It's a better option to take the mid-morning flight to KK on **AirAsia**, from RM70. Minibuses to **Semporna** leave when full from the Sabindo Complex (1½ hrs RM13).

It's possible to drive from **Sapulut** (south of **Keningau**) across the interior to Tawau on logging roads (4WD vehicle is required).

Maliau Basin *p257*

There isn't much public transport to Maliau; however, due to road improvements this may change in the near future. If you don't have your own transport you can arrange to hire a 4WD and driver through the Maliau Basin Conservation Area organization, see page 257. Vehicles can carry up 5 people and their gear. The return 4-5 hr trip to the Basin from either Tawau or Keningau (on the west coast) will cost RM600-700 per vehicle.

Directory

Sandakan *p240, map p242*

Banks Most are situated on Lebuh Tiga and Jln Pelabuhan. HSBC, Lebuh Tiga/Jln Pelabuhan; Standard Chartered, Jln Pelabuhan. **Immigration** Federal Bldg, Jln Leila. **Internet** Sandakan Cybercafé, 2nd floor, Wisma Sandakan; also in Centre Point mall. **Parks Office** Sabah Parks Office, Room 906, 9th floor, Wisma Khoo, Lebuh Tiga, T089-273453. Bookings for Turtle Islands National Park. **Post office** General Post Office, Jln Leila, to the west of town; parcel post off Lebuh Tiga.

Telephone Telecom Office, 6th floor, Wisma Khoo Siak Chiew, Jln Buli Sim-Sim.

Lahad Datu and around *p250*

Banks Standard Chartered, in front of Mido Hotel. **Post office** Post office, Jln Kenanga, next to the Lacin cinema.

Semporna *p253*

Bank Maybank (near the mosque). The queues for the ATM here are horrendous on a daily basis. Visitors are recommended to bring enough cash with them or face a long wait to get on the machine.

Internet Cyber Planet (opposite Damai), 1st floor, 0800-2200, RM3 per hr; Zanna Computer, next to Maybank, 1st floor; @DCCN opposite bus station, RM2 per hr (often closed). **Post office** General Post Office next to minibus station.

Tawau *p256*

Banks Bumiputra, Jln Nusantor, on seafront; HSBC, 210 Jln Utara, opposite the padang; Standard Chartered, 518 Jln Habib Husein (behind HSBC); exchange kiosk at wharf. **Embassies and consulates** Indonesian Consulate, Jln Apas, Mile 1.5. **Immigration** Office on Jln Stephen. **Post office** Post Office off Jln Nusantor, behind the fish market.

Background

The name Sabah is probably from the Arabic *Zir-e Bad* (the land below the wind). This is appropriate, as the state lies just south of the typhoon belt. Officially, the territory has only been called Sabah since 1963, when it joined the Malay federation, but the name appears to have been in use long before that. When Baron Gustav Von Overbeck was awarded the cession rights to North Borneo by the Sultan of Brunei in 1877, one of the titles conferred on him was Maharajah of Sabah. In the *Handbook of British North Borneo*, published in 1890, it says: "In Darvel Bay there are the remnants of a tribe which seems to have been much more plentiful in bygone days – the Sabahans". From the founding of the Chartered Company until 1963, Sabah was British North Borneo.

Sabah has a population of just over 2.5 million plus a good number of illegal immigrants on top of that. Sabah's inhabitants can be divided into four main groups: the Kadazan Dusun, the Bajau, the Chinese and the Murut, as well as a small Malay population. These groups are subdivided into several different tribes (see page 278).

History

Prehistoric stone tools have been found in eastern Sabah, suggesting that people were living in limestone caves in the Madai area 17,000-20,000 years ago. The caves were periodically settled from then on; pottery dating from the late neolithic period has been found, and by the early years of the first millennium AD, Madai's inhabitants were making iron spears and decorated pottery. The Madai and Baturong caves were lived in continuously until about the 16th century and several carved stone coffins and burial jars have been discovered in the jungle caves, one of which is exhibited in the Sabah State Museum. The caves were also known for their birds' nests; Chinese traders were buying the nests from Borneo as far back as AD 700. In addition, they exported camphor wood, pepper and other forest products to Imperial China.

There are very few archaeological records indicating Sabah's early history, although there is documentary evidence of links between a long-lost kingdom, based in the area of the Kinabatangan River, and the Sultanate of Brunei, whose suzerainty was once most of North Borneo. By the early 18th century, Brunei's power had begun to wane in the face of European expansionism. To counter the economic decline, it is thought the sultan increased taxation, which led to civil unrest. In 1704 the Sultan of Brunei had to ask the Sultan of Sulu's help in putting down a rebellion in Sabah and, in return, the Sultan of Sulu received most of what is now Sabah.

The would-be White Rajahs of Sabah

It was not until 1846 that the British entered into a treaty with the Sultan of Brunei and took possession of the island of Labuan, in part to counter the growing influence of the Rajah of Sarawak, James Brooke. The British were also wary of the Americans; the US Navy signed a trade treaty with the Sultan of Brunei in 1845 and in 1860 Claude Lee Moses was appointed American consul-general in Brunei Town. However, he was only interested in making a personal fortune and quickly persuaded the sultan to cede him land in Sabah. He sold these rights to two Hong Kong-based American businessmen who formed the American Trading Company of Borneo. They styled themselves as rajahs and set up a base at Kimanis, just south of Papar. It was a disaster. One of them died of malaria, the Chinese labourers they imported from Hong Kong began to starve and the settlement was abandoned in 1866.

The idea of a trading colony on the North Borneo coast interested the Austrian consul in Hong Kong, Baron Gustav von Overbeck, who, in turn, sold the concept to Alfred Dent, a wealthy English businessman also based in Hong Kong. With Dent's money, Overbeck bought the Americans' cession from the Sultan of Brunei and extended the territory to cover most of modern-day Sabah. The deal was clinched on 29 December 1877, and Overbeck agreed to pay the sultan 15,000 Straits dollars a year. A few days later Overbeck discovered that the entire area had already been ceded to the Sultan of Sulu 173 years earlier, so he immediately sailed to Sulu and offered the sultan an annual payment of 5000 Straits dollars for the territory. On his return, he dropped three Englishmen off along the coast to set up trading posts; one of them was William Pryer, who founded Sandakan (see page 241). Three years later, Queen Victoria granted Dent a royal charter and, to the chagrin of the Dutch, the Spanish and the Americans, the British North Borneo Company was formed. London insisted that it was to be a British-only enterprise however, and Overbeck was forced to sell out. The first managing director of the company was the Scottish adventurer and former gunrunner William C Cowie. He was in charge of the day-to-day operations of the territory, while the British government supplied a governor.

The new chartered company, with its headquarters in the City of London, was given sovereignty over Sabah and a free hand to develop it. The British administrators soon began to collect taxes from local people and quickly clashed with members of the Brunei nobility. John Whitehead, a British administrator, wrote: "I must say, it seemed rather hard on these people that they should be allowed to surrender up their goods and chattels to swell even indirectly the revenue of the company". The administration levied poll tax, boat tax, land tax, fishing tax, rice tax, *tapai* (rice wine) tax and a 10% tax on proceeds from the sale of birds' nests. Resentment against these taxes sparked the six-year Mat Salleh rebellion (see box page 192) and the Rundum Rebellion, which peaked in 1915, during which hundreds of Muruts were killed by the British.

Relations were not helped by colonial attitudes towards the local Malays and tribal people. One particularly arrogant district officer, Charles Bruce, wrote: "The mind of the average native is equivalent to that of a child of four. So long as one remembers that the native is essentially a child and treats him accordingly he is really tractable." Most recruits to the chartered company administration were fresh-faced graduates from British universities, mainly Oxford and Cambridge. For much of the time there were only 40-50 officials running the country. Besides the government officials, there were planters and businessmen: tobacco, rubber and timber became the most important exports. There were also Anglican and Roman Catholic missionaries. British North Borneo was never much of a money-spinner – the economy suffered whenever commodity prices slumped – but it mostly managed to pay for itself until the Second World War.

The Japanese interregnum

Sabah became part of Dai Nippon, or Greater Japan, on New Year's Day 1942, when the Japanese took Labuan. On the mainland, the Japanese Imperial Army and Kempetai (military police) were faced with the might of the North Borneo Armed Constabulary, about 650 men. Jesselton (Kota Kinabalu) was occupied on 9 January and Sandakan 10 days later. All Europeans were interned and when Singapore fell in 1942, 2740 prisoners of war were moved to Sandakan, most of whom were Australian, where they were forced to build an airstrip. On its completion, the POWs were ordered to march to Ranau, 240 km

The Borneo Death March

The four years of Japanese occupation ended when the Australian ninth division liberated British North Borneo. Sandakan was chosen by the Japanese as a regional centre for holding Allied prisoners. In 1942 the Japanese shipped 2750 prisoners of war (2000 of whom were Australian and 750 British) to Sandakan from Changi Prison, Singapore. A further 800 British and 500 Australian POWs arrived in 1944. They were ordered to build an airfield (on the site of the present airport) and were forced to work from dawn to dusk.

Many died, but in September 1944 2400 POWs were force-marched to Ranau, a 240-km trek through the jungle which only six Australians survived. This 'Death March', although not widely reported in Second World War literature, claimed more Australian lives than any other single event during the war in Asia, including the building of the notorious Burma-Siam railway.

For more information on the march, including details of sensitive tours and walks take a look at www.sandakan-deathmarch.com.

through the jungle. This became known as the Borneo Death March and only six men survived (see box above).

The Japanese were hated in Sabah and the Chinese mounted a resistance movement which was led by the Kuching-born Albert Kwok Hing Nam. He also recruited Bajaus and Sulus to join his guerrilla force which launched the Double Tenth Rebellion (the attacks took place on 10 October 1943). The guerrillas took Tuaran, Jesselton and Kota Belud, killing many Japanese and sending others fleeing into the jungle. But the following day the Japanese bombed the towns and troops quickly retook them and captured the rebels. A mass execution followed in which 175 rebels were decapitated. On 10 June 1945 Australian forces landed at Labuan, under the command of American General MacArthur. Allied planes bombed the main towns and virtually obliterated Jesselton and Sandakan. Sabah was liberated on 9 September and thousands of the remaining 21,000 Japanese troops were killed in retaliation, many by Muruts.

A British military administration governed Sabah in the aftermath of the war and the cash-strapped chartered company sold the territory to the British crown for £1.4 million in 1946. The new crown colony was modelled on the chartered company's administration and rebuilt the main towns and war-shattered infrastructure. In May 1961, following Malaysian independence, Prime Minister Tunku Abdul Rahman proposed the formation of a federation incorporating Malaya (ie Peninsular Malaysia), Singapore, Brunei, Sabah and Sarawak. Later that same year, Tun Fuad Stephens, a timber magnate and newspaper publisher formed Sabah's first-ever political party, the United National Kadazan Organization (UNKO). Two other parties were founded soon afterwards: the Sabah Chinese Association and the United Sabah National Organization (USNO). The British were keen to leave the colony and the Sabahan parties debated the pros and cons of joining the proposed federation. Elections were held in late 1962 in which a UNKO-USNO alliance (the Sabah Alliance) swept to power and the following August Sabah became an independent country ... for 16 days. Like Singapore and Sarawak, Sabah opted to join the federation to the indignation of the Philippines and Indonesia who both had claims on the territory. Jakarta's objections resulted in the Konfrontasi, an undeclared war with Malaysia (see page 174) that was not settled until 1966.

Modern Sabah

Politics

Sabah's political scene has always been lively and never more so than in 1994 when the then Malaysian prime minister, Doctor Mahathir Mohamad, pulled off what commentators described as a democratic coup d'état. With great political dexterity, he out-manoeuvered his rebellious rivals and managed to dislodge the opposition state government, despite the fact that it had just won a state election.

Following Sabah's first state election in 1967, the Sabah Alliance ruled until 1975 when the newly formed multi-racial party, Berjaya, swept the polls. Berjaya had been set up with the financial backing of the United Malays National Organization (UMNO), the mainstay of the ruling Barisan Nasional (National Front) coalition on the Peninsula. Over the following decade that corrupt administration crumbled and in 1985 the opposition Sabah United Party (PBS), led by the Christian Kadazan Datuk Joseph Pairin Kitingan, won a landslide victory and became the only state government in Malaysia that did not belong to the UMNO-led coalition. It became an obvious embarrassment to then Prime Minister Doctor Mahathir Mohamad to have a rebel Christian state in his predominantly Muslim federation. Nonetheless, the PBS eventually joined Barisan Nasional, believing its partnership in the coalition would help iron things out. It did not.

When the PBS came to power, the federal government and Sabahan opposition parties openly courted Filipino and Indonesian immigrants in the state, almost all of whom are Muslim, and secured identity cards for many of them, enabling them to vote. Doctor Mahathir has made no secret of his preference for a Muslim government in Sabah. Nothing, however, was able to dislodge the PBS, which was resoundingly returned to power in 1990. The federal government had long been suspicious of Sabahan politicians, particularly following the PBS's defection from Doctor Mahathir's coalition in the run-up to the 1990 general election, a move which bolstered the opposition alliance. Doctor Mahathir described this as "a stab in the back", and referred to Sabah as "a thorn in the flesh of the Malaysian federation". But in the event, the prime minister won the national election convincingly without PBS help, prompting fears of political retaliation. Those fears proved justified in the wake of the election.

Sabah paid heavily for its 'disloyalty'; prominent Sabahans were arrested as secessionist conspirators under Malaysia's Internal Security Act, which provides for indefinite detention without trial. Among them was Jeffrey Kitingan, brother of the chief minister and head of the Yayasan Sabah, or Sabah Foundation (see page 193). At the same time, Joseph Pairin Kitingan was charged with corruption. The feeling in Sabah was that the men were bearing the brunt of Doctor Mahathir's personal political vendetta.

As the political feud worsened, the federal government added to the fray by failing to promote Sabah to foreign investors. As investment money dried up, so did federal development funds; big road and housing projects were left unfinished for years. Many in Sabah felt their state was being short-changed by the federal government. The political instability had a detrimental effect on the state economy and the business community felt that continued feuding would be economic lunacy. Politicians in the Christian-led PBS, however, continued to claim that Sabah wasn't getting its fair share of Malaysia's economic boom. They said that the agreement which enshrined a measure of autonomy for Sabah when it joined the Malaysian federation had been eroded.

The main bone of contention was the state's oil revenues, worth around US$852 million a year, of which 95% disappeared into federal coffers. There were many other causes of dissatisfaction, too, and as the list of grievances grew longer, the state government exploited them to the full. By 1994, anti-federal feelings were running high. The PBS continued to promote the idea of 'Sabah for Sabahans', a defiant slogan in a country where the federal government was working to centralize power. Because Doctor Mahathir likes to be in control, the idea of granting greater autonomy to a distant, opposition-held state was not on his agenda. A showdown was inevitable.

It began in January 1994. As Datuk Pairin's corruption trial drew to a close, he dissolved the state assembly, paving the way for fresh elections. He did this to cover the eventuality of his being disqualified from office through a 'guilty' verdict: he wanted to have his own team in place to take over from him. He was convicted of corruption but the fine imposed on him was just under the disqualifying threshold and, to the prime minister's fury, he led the PBS into the election. Doctor Mahathir put his newly appointed deputy, Anwar Ibrahim, in charge of the National Front alliance campaign.

Datuk Pairin won the election, but by a much narrower margin than before. He alleged vote buying and ballot rigging. He accused Doctor Mahathir's allies of whipping up the issue of religion. He spoke of financial inducements being offered to Sabah's Muslim voters, some of whom are Malay, but most of whom are Bajau tribespeople and Filipino immigrants. His swearing-in ceremony was delayed for 36 hours; the governor said he was sick; Datuk Parin said his political enemies were trying to woo defectors from the ranks of the PBS to overturn his small majority. He was proved right.

Three weeks later, he was forced to resign; his fractious party had virtually collapsed in disarray and a stream of defections robbed him of his majority. Datuk Parin's protestations that his assemblymen had been bribed to switch sides were ignored. The local leader of Doctor Mahathir's ruling party, Tan Sri Sakaran Dandai, was swiftly sworn in as the new chief minister.

In the 1995 general election the PBS did remarkably well, holding onto eight seats and defeating a number of Front candidates who had defected from the PBS the previous year. Sabah was one area, along with the east coast state of Kelantan, which resisted the Mahathir/BN electoral steamroller.

The March 1999 state elections pitted UMNO against Pairin's PBS. Again the issues were local autonomy, vote rigging, the role of national politics and political parties in state elections, and money. A new element was the role that Anwar Ibrahim's trial might play in the campaign but otherwise it was old wine in old bottles.

The outcome was a convincing win for Mahathir and the ruling National Front who gathered 31 of the 48 state assembly seats – three more than the prime minister forecast. Mahathir once again used the lure of development funds from KL to convince local Sabahans where their best interests might lie. "We are not being unfair" Mahathir said. "We are more than fair, but we cannot be generous to the opposition. We can be generous to a National Front government in Sabah. That I can promise."

But, worryingly for the National Front, the opposition Parti Bersatu Sabah (PBS) still managed to garner the great bulk of the Kadazan vote and in so doing won 17 seats. As in Sarawak, the election, in the end, was more about local politics than about the economic crisis and the Anwar trial.

However, in the 2004 state and federal elections, the PBS rejoined the National Front and, faced only with the disunity of opposition parties, the BN-PBS coalition won resounding victories in both polls. A legitimate alternative to KL's ruling steamroller has all but died. The BN gave itself half the seats, one third to non-Malays, and distributed the rest between Chinese representatives. The message is that Sabahans accept dominance by the Malay minority from KL in return for money and development. The Sabah state elections were held simultaneously with the federal elections in 2008. and were again won comfortably by the BN-PBS coalition with only one of the 60 contested seats going to another party, the Democratic Action Party.

Culture

People

According to Malaysia's 2000 Population and Housing Census (next one due 2010), the main ethnic group in Sabah is Kadazan Dusun (18.4%), followed by Bajau (17.3%) and Chinese (13.2%). The Kadazan mostly live on the west coast, the Murut inhabit the southern interior and the Bajau are mainly settled around Gunung Kinabalu. There are more than 30 tribes, more than 50 different languages and about 100 dialects. Sabah also has a large Chinese population and many illegal Filipino immigrants.

Bajau The Bajau, the famous cowboys of the Wild East, came from the south Philippines during the 18th and 19th centuries and settled in the coastal area around Kota Belud, Papar and Kudat, where they made a handsome living from piracy. The Bajau who came to Sabah joined forces with the notorious Illanun and Balinini pirates. They are natural seafarers and were dubbed sea gypsies; today, they form the second largest indigenous group in Sabah and are divided into subgroups, notably the Binadan, Suluk and Obian. They call themselves 'Samah'; it was the Brunei Malays who first called them Bajau. They are strict Muslims and the famous Sabahan folk hero, Mat Salleh, who led a rebellion in the 1890s against British Chartered Company rule, was a Bajau (see box, page 192). Despite their seafaring credentials, they are also renowned horsemen and (very occasionally) still put in an appearance at Kota Belud's *tamu* (see page 225). Bajau women are known for their brightly coloured basketry – *tudong saji*. The Bajau build their *atap* houses on stilts over the water and these are interconnected by a network of narrow wooden planks. The price of a Bajau bride was traditionally assessed in stilts, shaped from the trunks of bakau mangrove trees. A father erected one under his house on the day a daughter was born and replaced it whenever it wore out. The longer the daughter remained at home, the more stilts he got through and the more water buffalo he demanded from a prospective husband.

Chinese The Chinese accounted for nearly a third of Sabah's population in 1960; today they make up just over a tenth. Unlike Sarawak, however, where the Chinese were a well-established community in the early 1800s, Sabah's Chinese came as a result of the British North Borneo Chartered Company's immigration policy, designed to ease a labour shortage. About 70% of Sabah's Chinese are Christian Hakka, who first began arriving at the end of the 19th century, under the supervision of the company. They were given free passage from China and most settled in the Jesselton and Kudat areas; today most Hakka are farmers. There are also large Teochew and Hokkien communities in Tawau, Kota Kinabalu and Labuan while Sandakan is mainly Cantonese, originating from Hong Kong.

Filipinos Immigration from the Philippines started in the 1950s and refugees began flooding into Sabah when the separatist war erupted in Mindanao in the 1970s. Today there are believed to be upwards of 700,000 illegal Filipino immigrants in Sabah (although their migration has been undocumented for so long that no one is certain) and the state government fears they could soon outnumber locals. There are many in Kota Kinabalu, the

The Kadazan in Borneo

Formerly known as Dusuns (peasants or orchard people), a name given to them by outsiders and picked up by the British, the Kadazan live in Sabah and East Kalimantan.

The Kadazans traditionally traded their agricultural produce at large markets, held at meeting points, called *tamus* (see box, page 222).

They used to be animists and were said to live in great fear of evil spirits; most of their ceremonies were rituals aimed at driving out these spirits. The job of communicating with the spirits of the dead, the *tombiivo*, was done by priestesses, called *bobohizan*. They are the only ones who can speak the ancient Kadazan language, using a completely different vocabulary from modern Kadazan. Most converted to Christianity, mainly Roman Catholicism, during the 1930s, although there are also some Muslim Kadazan.

The big cultural event in the Kadazan year is the harvest festival that takes place in May. The ceremony, known as the Magavau ritual, is officiated by a high priestess. These elderly women, who wear black costumes and colourful headgear with feathers and beads, are now rarely seen. The ceremony ends with offerings to the *Bambaazon* (rice spirit). After the ceremonies Catholic, Muslim and animist Kadazan all come together to play traditional sports such as wrestling and buffalo racing. This is about the only occasion when visitors are likely to see Kadazan in their traditional costumes. Belts of silver coins (*himpogot*) and brass rings are worn round the waist; a colourful sash is also worn. Men dress in a black, long-sleeved jacket over black trousers; they also wear a *siga*, colourful woven headgear. These costumes have become more decorative in recent years, with colourful embroidery.

state capital, and a large community – mainly women and children – in Labuan, but the bulk of the Filipino population is in Semporna, Lahad Datu, Tawau and Kunak (on the east coast) where they already outnumber locals by a majority of three to one. One Sabah government minister, referring to the long-running territorial dispute between Malaysia and the Philippines, was quoted as saying "We do not require a strong military presence at the border any more: the aliens have already landed".

Although the federal government has talked of its intention to deport illegal aliens, it is mindful of the political reality: the majority of the Filipinos are Muslim, and making them legal Malaysian citizens could ruin Sabah's predominantly Christian, Kadazan-led state government. The Filipino community is also a thorn in Sabah's flesh because of the crime wave associated with their arrival: the Sabah police claim 65% of crime is committed by Filipinos. The police do not ask questions when dealing with Filipino criminal suspects; about 40 to 50 are shot every year. Another local politician was quoted as saying: "The immigrants take away our jobs, cause political instability and pose a health hazard because of the appalling conditions in which some of them live".

There are six different Filipino groups in Sabah: the Visayas and Ilocano are Christian as are the Ilongo (Ilo Ilo), from Zamboanga. The Suluks are Muslim; they come from south Mindanao and have the advantage of speaking a dialect of Bahasa Malaysia. Many Filipinos were born in Sabah and all second-generation immigrants are fluent in Bahasa. Migration first accelerated in the 1950s during the logging boom and continued when the oil palm plantation economy took off. Many migrants have settled along the

The Murut in Borneo

The Murut live in the southwest of Sabah, in the Trusan Valley, North Sarawak and in Northeast Kalimantan. Some of those in more remote jungle areas retain their traditional longhouse way of life, but many Murut have opted for detached kampong-style houses.

Murut means hill people and is not the term used by the people themselves. They refer to themselves by individual tribal names.

The Nabai, Bokan and Timogun Murut live in the lowlands and are wet-rice farmers, while the Peluan, Bokan and Tagul Murut live in the hills and are mainly shifting cultivators. They are thought to be related to Sarawak's Kelabit and Kalimantan's Lun Dayeh people, although some of the tribes in the south Philippines have similar characteristics. The Murut staples are rice and tapioca; they are known for their weaving and basketry and have a penchant for drinking *tapai* (rice wine; see box opposite). They are also enthusiastic dancers and devised the *lansaran*, a sprung dance floor like a trampoline. The Murut are a mixture of animists, Christians and Muslims and were the last tribe in Sabah to give up headhunting, a practice stopped by the British North Borneo Chartered Company.

roadsides on the way to the Danum Valley; it is easy to claim land since all they have to do is simply clear a plot and plant a few fruit trees.

Kadazan The Kadazan are the largest ethnic group in Sabah and are a peaceful agrarian people with a strong cultural identity. Until Sabah joined the Malaysian Federation in 1963, they were known as Dusuns. It became, in effect, a residual category including all those people who were not Muslim or Chinese. Kadazan identity is therefore not particularly straightforward. In Malaysia's 2000 census, they were called Kadazan Dusun. The 1991 census, however, lists both Kadazan (110,866) and Dusun (229,194). The 1970 census listed all as Kadazan, while the 1960 census listed all as Dusun. In 1995 the Malaysian government agreed to add the common language of these people to the national repertoire to be taught in schools. This they named Kadazandusun. The others are Malay, Chinese, Tamil and Iban.

Most Kadazans call themselves after their tribal names. They can be divided into several tribes including the Lotud of Tuaran, the Rungus of the Kudat and Bengkoka Peninsulas, the Tempasuk, the Tambanuo, the Kimarangan and the Sanayo. Minokok and Tengara Kadazans live in the upper Kinabatangan River basin, while those living near other big rivers are just known as Orang Sungai (river people).

The majority of Kadazans used to live in longhouses; these are virtually all gone now. The greatest chance of coming across a longhouse in Sabah is in the Rungus area of the Kudat Peninsula; even there, former longhouse residents are moving into detached, kampong-style houses while one or two stay for the use of tourists.

All the Kadazan groups used to have similar customs and modes of dress (see below). Up to the Second World War, many Kadazan men wore the *chawat* loin cloth. The Kadazans used to hunt with blowpipes and in the 19th century were still headhunting. Today, however, they are known for their gentleness and honesty; their produce can often be seen sitting unattended at roadside stalls and passing motorists are expected to pay what they think fair. The Kadazan are farmers, and the main rice producers of Sabah.

Tapai: Sabah's rice wine

Tapai, the fiery Sabahan rice wine, is much loved by the Kadazan and the Murut people of Borneo. It was even more popular before the two tribal groups converted to Christianity in the 1930s. Writer Hedda Morrison noted in 1957 that "The squalor and wretchedness arising from [their] continual drunkenness made the Murut a particularly useful object of missionary endeavour."

In the Sabah State Museum there is a recipe for tapai, which reads: "Boil 12 lbs of the best glutinous rice until well done. In a wide-mouthed jar, lay the rice in layers of no more than two fingers deep, and between layers, place about 20½-oz yeast cakes. Add two cups of water, tinctured with the juice of six beetroots. Cover jar with muslin and leave to ferment. Each day, uncover it and remove dew which forms on the muslin. On the fifth day, stir the mixture vigorously and

leave for four weeks. Store for one year, after which it shall be full of virtue and potence and smooth upon the palate."

Oscar Cook, a former district officer in the North Borneo civil service, noted in his 1923 book *Borneo: the Stealer of Hearts*: "As an alternative occupation to headhunting, the Murut possess a fondness for getting drunk, indulged in on every possible occasion…Births, marriages, deaths, sowing, harvesting and any occasion that comes to mind is made the excuse for a debauch. It is customary for Murut to show respect to the white man by producing their very best tapai, and pitting the oldest and ugliest women of the village against him in a drinking competition." Cook admits that all this proved too much for him and when he was transferred to Keningau, he had to employ an 'official drinker'. "The applicants to the post were many," he noted.

For the May harvest festival, villages send the finalists of local beauty contests to the grand final of the Unduk Ngadau harvest festival queen competition in Penampang, near Kota Kinabalu. It is the Kadazans who dominate the Pasti Bersatu Sabah (PBS), the critical piece in Sabah's political jigsaw.

Murut The Murut live around Tenom and Pensiangan in the lowland and hilly parts of the interior. They were the last tribe in Sabah to give up headhunting, a practice stopped by the British North Borneo Chartered Company. ▸▸ *See also box opposite.*

Arts and crafts

Compared with neighbouring Sarawak and Kalimantan, Sabah's handicraft industry is rather impoverished. Sabah's tribal groups were less protected from Western influences than Sarawak's and traditional skills quickly began to die out as the state modernized and the economy grew. In Kota Kinabalu today, the markets are full of Filipino handicrafts and shell products; local arts and crafts are largely confined to basketry, mats, hats, beadwork, musical instruments and pottery.

The elongated Kadazan backpack baskets found around Mount Kinabalu National Park are called *wakids* and are made from bamboo, rattan and bark. Woven food covers, or *tudong saji*, are often mistaken for hats, and are made by the Bajau of Kota Belud. Hats, made from nipah palm or rattan, and whose shape varies markedly from place to place, are decorated with traditional motifs. One of the most common motifs is the *nantuapan* (meeting), which represents four people all drinking out of the same *tapai* (rice wine) jar. The Rungus people from the Kudat Peninsula also make linago basketware from a strong wild grass; it is tightly woven and not decorated. At *tamus*, Sabah's big open-air markets (see box on page 222), there are usually some handicrafts for sale. The Kota Belud *tamu* is the best place to find the Bajau horseman's embroidered turban, the *destar*. Traditionally, the Rungus people, who live on the Kudat Peninsula, were renowned as fine weavers and detailed patterns were woven into their ceremonial skirts (*tinugupan*). These patterns all had different names but, like the ingredients of the traditional dyes, many have now been forgotten.

Contents

Footprint features

Brunei

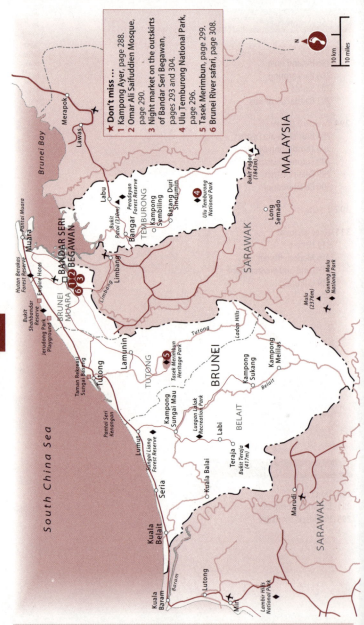

N

10 km
10 miles

Brunei Bay

Merapok

Lawas

MALAYSIA

South China Sea

Muara

Pantai Muara

Hutan Berakas
Forest Reserve

Empire Hotel

BRUNEI
MUARA

**BANDAR SERI
BEGAWAN**

6 1 2
3

Bukit
Shahbandar
Reserve

Jerudong Park
Playground

Labu

Limbang

*Bukit
Patoi (310m)*

Peradayan
Forest Reserve

Bangar

TEMBURONG

Kampong
Sembiling

Batang Duri
Sindumin

4
*Ulu Temburong
National Park*

*Bukit Pagod
(1843m)*

Long
Semado

SARAWAK

Limbang

Taman Rekreasi
Sungai Basong

Lamunin

TUTONG

5
*Tasek Merimbun
Heritage Park*

BRUNEI

Tutong

Ladab Hills

Mulu
(2376m)

Gunung Mulu
National Park

Tutong

*Pantai Seri
Kenangan*

Kampong
Sungai Mau

Kampong
Sukang

Kampong
Melilas

Lumut

*Sungai Liang
Forest Reserve*

Luagan Lalak
Recreation Park

Labi

Belait

BELAIT

Seria

Teraja
*Bukit Teraja
(417m)*

Kuala Balai

Kuala
Belait

Marudi

SARAWAK

Kuala
Baram

Baram

Lutong

Miri

Lambir Hills
National Park

Brunei is a one-off; a tiny oil-rich sultanate on the north coast of Borneo, cornered and split in two by the Malaysian state of Sarawak. Less than 400,000 Bruneians are ruled over by one of the world's wealthiest men – the living link in a dynasty of sultans stretching back 600 years. At one time, Brunei was the driving seat of Borneo, but its territories were whittled away piece by piece, first by the Sulu kings, then by the British. Today, Brunei is a peculiar mix of material wealth and Malay tradition. Affluence has numbed Sultan Bolkiah's subjects into submission to the political system – a monarchical autocracy, to all intents and purposes (albeit a benevolent one). Bruneians see no reason to complain: they pay no taxes and the purchase of cars and houses is heavily subsidized. Healthcare and education are free and trips to Mecca are a snip. Politics, it seems, is not their business. This climate of benign affluence, combined with the prohibition of alcohol and the complete lack of nightlife, makes Brunei's tagline – 'The Abode of Peace' – ring perfectly true.

Still, change is in the air. For the first time since Independence, Brunei is turning its back on the introspection that has kept it largely hidden from the world. The Asian financial crisis of 1997 hit Brunei hard, almost halving GDP, and, with oil reserves expected to dry up in 25 years and gas reserves in 40, the economy needs to diversify. The sultan's latest plan is to transform his realm into an offshore tax haven. But Brunei holds another trump card for the future: ecotourism. One of the happy consequences of its dependence on oil is the amount of rainforest left intact. With three-quarters of its landmass covered by virgin rainforest, Brunei can claim the highest proportion of primary forest of any country in the world. Brunei is the easy way in to Borneo. You get kampong culture, pristine jungle, endangered wildlife and all the creature comforts you could hope for. Just don't expect to rough it.

Bandar Seri Begawan

→ Colour map 1, B6.

Bandar Seri Begawan, more commonly referred to simply as Bandar (city in Malay), is the capital of Brunei and the only place of any real size. Even so, Bandar's population is barely 80,000, and with most people living in the suburbs or among the stilted homes of the water village, downtown Bandar feels extraordinarily sleepy. This is no bad thing for the visitor; traffic and crowds are restricted to the suburbs, where most of the shops are located, leaving the centre in relative peace and quiet. The streets are clean and spacious, and the only persistent noise is the whirr of outboards, as water taxis (tambang) ferry people to and from the water village.

Bandar sits on a bend of the Sungai Brunei, with the stilted homes of Kampong Ayer (water village) reaching out across the river from the opposite bank. Back on dry land, the dominant feature is the impressive Omar Ali Saifuddien Mosque – though the primary point of reference nowadays seems to be the Yayasan Complex, a smart shopping mall whose two wings are aligned to provide a colonnaded vista of both the mosque and the river. ▶▶ For listings, see pages 302-310.

Ins and outs

Getting there

Brunei International Airport is situated 11 km south of Bandar Seri Begawan. Between 0630-1800, there are regular buses from the airport to the bus station on Jalan Cator, in downtown Bandar. Buses from Sarawak and other parts of Brunei also terminate here. A taxi from the airport costs about B$25, or B$30 after 1800. ▶▶ See Transport, page 309.

Getting around

Downtown Bandar is tiny and easy to negotiate on foot. Water taxis are the major form of public transport here, with hundreds flying back and forth across the river, ferrying people to and from their stilted homes in Kampong Ayer. A short hop should cost no more than about B$2, while a 45-minute tour of the water village will cost about B$20 (less if you barter hard). The Brunei Museum, the Malay Technology Museum and the suburb of Gadong are all accessible on Central Line buses (daily 0630-1800), which pass through the bus station on Jalan Cator. Metered taxis operate in Bandar and its suburbs: B$3 for the first kilometre (B$4.50 2100-0600) and B$1 for every subsequent kilometre.

Tourist information

There is a government-run **Tourist Information Centre** ⓘ *in the arrivals area of the airport,* which offers the useful *Explore Brunei* visitors' guide with a detailed map of the local bus routes. There is also the out-of-town headquarters of **Brunei Tourism** ⓘ *Ministry of Industry and Primary Resources, Jln Menteri Besar, T238 2803, www.bruneitourism.travel.* In Bandar, **Mona Flora Fauna Tours** ⓘ *1st floor, Kiaw Lian Building, 209 Jln Pemancha, T223 0761,* acts as a de facto tourist office and has a few useful brochures.

Background

Bandar Seri Begawan's history can be traced back as far as the seventh century, by which time a water village was already well established on the banks of the Sungai Brunei. The original site of the village was Kota Batu, several kilometres to the east of today's capital (close to the Brunei Museum). Brunei's history is bound closely to the development of Kampong Ayer, which moved to its present-day location sometime before the 15th century.

By the time Portuguese explorer Ferdinand Magellan passed by on his round-the-world voyage in 1521, Kampong Ayer had developed from a small trading base and fishing settlement into a powerful entrepôt. The Spanish crew were astounded to find a sprawling water village of some 100,000 people – much larger than today's capital – complete with the trappings of great wealth. The settlement flourished as a collecting point for much-coveted jungle products such as sandalwood, beeswax, birds' nests, turtle shells, sago and camphor. Along with the trade in commodities came the blending of cultures and ideologies, with Islam first establishing a foothold in the late 14th century. Kampong Ayer went on to become the centre of a small empire whose sphere of influence extended across much of Borneo and the Philippines.

Bandar Seri Begawan – known as Brunei Town until 1970 – only established itself as a land-based settlement under the influence of the British. It was in 1904 that Stewart McArthur, the first British Resident, encouraged inhabitants to move onto reclaimed land beside the water village. One of the first buildings to appear was the British Residency, set in the wooden building known now as Bubongan Dua Belas (see page 292). The sultan himself followed in 1909, moving the *istana* (palace) onto land for the first time in 500 years.

It was not until the discovery of oil in 1929 that Brunei Town really began to develop, with the first grid of shophouses appearing and a new set of government buildings. The capital's modern landmarks – the Omar Ali Saifuddien Mosque and the Istana Nurul Iman – were built in the 1950s, after exports of oil and natural gas had begun to take off. But the capital never expanded beyond the dimensions of a small town. The centre of Bandar has remained a quiet, almost sleepy, place with development limited mainly to the suburbs. Kampong Ayer, meanwhile, is gradually dwindling in size, thanks to government initiatives to encourage its inhabitants to move inland. The water village, it seems, doesn't fit with the sultan's progressive vision of a modern Brunei.

Sights

The main entry point to Bandar is via Jalan Tutong, which crosses the Sungai Kedayan tributary at Edinburgh Bridge, providing the first views of Kampong Ayer and the golden dome of the mosque. The road becomes Jalan Sultan, which cuts past a handful of museums and a small grid of shophouses, before hitting the waterfront. The city centre is bordered to the west by Sungai Kedayan, and, barely 500 m to the east, by the narrow Sungai Kianggeh tributary. Along its banks is the Tamu Kianggeh, an open-air market.

A number of the city's more interesting sights are located along the picturesque road which follows the course of the river east out of town. Jalan Residency runs past the Arts and Handicrafts Centre and the old British Residency itself, before becoming Jalan Kota Batu and bypassing the tombs of two sultans, the Brunei Museum and the Malay Technology Museum.

The suburbs of Kampong Kiarong and Gadong lie several kilometres to the northwest of the city centre. The former is a residential quarter, home to the enormous Kiarong Mosque, while Gadong is the main commercial centre, full of department stores and restaurants, and home, too, to an excellent *pasar malam* (night market). North of town, near the airport, are the government offices and the impressive but ghostly quiet National Stadium.

Kampong Ayer

When people think of Bandar Seri Begawan, they think of Kampong Ayer, the stretch of stilted homes extending over 3 km along the banks of Sungai Brunei. Officially, Kampong Ayer isn't part of the Bandar municipality; a reflection, perhaps, of the government's long-term aim to rehouse the villagers on dry land. It is merely a suburb. Not long ago, however, Kampong Ayer

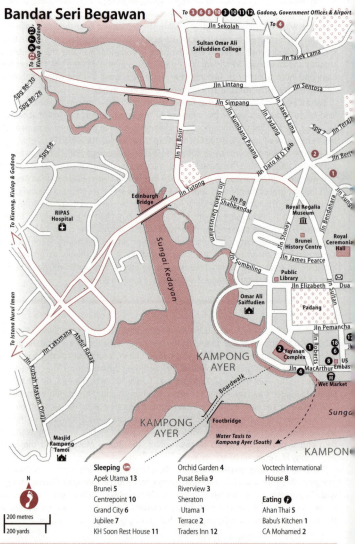

Bandar Seri Begawan

To ③ ⑥ ⑧ ⑩ ❸ ❿ ⓫ ⓬, Gadong, Government Offices & Airport

Jln Sekolah

To ④

Sultan Omar Ali Saifuddien College

Jln Tasek Lama

To ⓬ ⑨ ⑦ ⑬, Kiulap & Gadong

Jln Lintang

Jln Sentosa

Spg 86-30

Jln Simpang

Spg 86-26

Spg 7

Jln Teraja

Spg 69

Jln Padang

②

Jln Beri

Jln H Basir

Jln Kumbang Pasang

Jln Tutong

Jln Dato M D Taib

①

RIPAS Hospital

Edinburgh Bridge

Jln Pg Shahbandar

Jln Istana Darussalam

Royal Regalia Museum

Jln Stoney

Jln Bendahara

Jln Sungai

To Kiarong, Kiulap & Gadong

Sungai Kedayan

Brunei History Centre

Royal Ceremonial Hall

Jln Sumbiling

Jln James Pearce

Public Library

Jln Elizabeth Dua

Omar Ali Saiffudien

Padang

Jln Sultan

To Istana Nurul Iman

Jln Laksmana

Jln Pemancha

KAMPONG AYER

Jln Roberts

② Yayasan Complex

①

⑱ ⑥

Jln Kubah Makam Diraja

Abdul Razak

⑧

US Embassy

Jln MacArthur

④

KAMPONG AYER

Boardwalk

Wet Market

Footbridge

Sunga

Masjid Kampong Tamoi

Water Taxis to Kampong Ayer (South) ▲

KAMPONG

N

Sleeping
Apek Utama **13**
Brunei **5**
Centrepoint **10**
Grand City **6**
Jubilee **7**
KH Soon Rest House **11**

Orchid Garden **4**
Pusat Belia **9**
Riverview **3**
Sheraton
Utama **1**
Terrace **2**
Traders Inn **12**

Voctech International House **8**

Eating
Ahan Thai **5**
Babu's Kitchen **1**
CA Mohamed **2**

200 metres
200 yards

was all there was of Bandar; it was the British who began to develop the town on land, starting with construction of the Residency in 1906 (see Bubongan Dua Belas, page 292).

With its wonky walkways and ramshackle appearance, Kampong Ayer may look like a bit of a slum. Adventurer James Brooke got this false impression when he visited Brunei in the 1840s; he described Kampong Ayer as a "Venice of hovels, fit only for frogs". Antonio Pigafetta, the diarist on board the Magellan voyage of 1521, saw the village from a different perspective, describing it as the "Venice of the East".

The truth is that the architecture of Kampong Ayer is perfectly suited to the tropical environment, making use of local materials and allowing for excellent ventilation. The oldest houses stand on mangrove and ironwood posts, with walls of woven nipa palm. The modern buildings stand on reinforced concrete piles, which allow for double-storey structures to be built. Many of the houses are painted in a profusion of colours, with pot plants and bougainvillea spilling from covered verandas. It may look primitive, but take a closer look and you notice the trappings of wealth: all houses have electricity and a piped water supply; many have satellite dishes and internet.

Records of Kampong Ayer go back 14 centuries. In its 16th-century heyday, the 'village' had a population of 100,000 and was the centre of an empire stretching across most of Borneo, Mindanao and the Sulu archipelago. Though it still claims to be the world's largest water village, today's population is a mere 25,000-30,000. The village is separated into 42 different units, each governed by a *tua kampong* (headman). These units are grouped into *mukims* (wards). The community is self sufficient, with mosques, shops, schools, clinics and the odd karaoke lounge, even fire stations and floating petrol stations.

The future of Kampong Ayer looks somewhat uncertain. Many villagers have taken up the government's offer of free plots of land and subsidized housing and have moved on land. Meanwhile, the traditional cottage industries associated with each of the village units are giving way

Tasek
Recreational Park

Jln Kampong Barangan

Spg 39

Spg 67

Spg 75

9

Jln Kampong Kianggeh

To 13 Bubongan Dua Belas, Brunei Museum & Malay Technology Museum

7 5

Tamu
Kianggeh

Bukit Subok
Recreational Park

Sungai Kianggeh

or

Brunei

15

Jln Residency

Temburong
Jetty

Arts &
Handicraft
Centre

AYER

De Royalle Café **18**	Lee Loi Fatt Foodstall **7**
Dream Cones **3**	Pondok Sari Wangi **12**
Escapade Sushi **11**	Pureland Vegetarian **9**
Foodstalls **15**	RMS Portview Seafood **4**
Fratini's **10**	Saffron **13**
Fun Toast **6**	Seri Indah **8**
Isma Jaya **17**	Zaika **2**

to new professions (today's young Bruneians aspire to become lawyers or computer programmers rather than blacksmiths or boat builders). Still, there are plenty of artisans left, and some will open their doors to passing visitors.

To visit Kampong Ayer, jump aboard any of the water taxis (*tambang*) which race back and forth across the river. The main pick-up point is just south of the Yayasan Complex. The boatmen will compete raucously for your attention, then haggle with you over a price. The going rate is about B$20 for a very worthwhile one-hour tour. Most boatmen are happy to pass by the Istana (the best views are from the river); you may want to combine the tour with a trip downriver to spot proboscis monkeys (for an additional B$10); see box, page 295. **Note** Be extra careful when boarding a *tambang* at low tide as the steps can be very slippery.

It is also possible to access part of the water village by foot: set off along the boardwalk that runs along west from the Yayasan Complex and you soon come to a bridge across the Sungai Kedayan tributary. From here there are good views across the maze of stilted homes as far as the copper-domed Masjid Kampong Tamoi, an elegant new mosque built on the water's edge.

Omar Ali Saifuddien Mosque

ⓘ *The compound is open daily 0800-2030; visiting hours for non-Muslims: Sat-Wed 0800-1730 (except prayer times); visitors must leave shoes outside and dress conservatively. Sometimes the lift that runs to the top of the 44-m minaret is in operation.*

This mosque, built by and named after the 28th sultan (1950-1967), has become the symbol of Brunei, the nation's definitive monument. It is certainly one of Asia's finest-looking mosques, elegant and somehow modest, despite its great golden dome, its setting beside an artificial lake and its nightly illumination in unearthly green light.

Built in 1958 in classical Islamic style, the architecture is not overstated, although along with the sultan's hugely extravagant palace, the mosque was one of the first obvious signs of Brunei's oil wealth. When flakes of gold began falling from the central dome, due to contraction and expansion in the searing heat, the mosque quickly became something of a wonder to the villagers of Kampong Ayer (whose boardwalks run tight up to the edge of the mosque). Novelist Anthony Burgess' arrival as a teacher in Brunei coincided with the ceremonial opening of the mosque, and in his autobiography he recounts how this falling gold was "taken by the fisherfolk to be a gift from Allah".

The materials used to build and furnish the mosque came from right across the globe: carpets from Belgium and Arabia; chandeliers and stained glass from England; marble from Italy; granite from Shanghai; and, topping the central onion dome, a mosaic of more than three million pieces of gold-leafed Venetian glass. In the middle of the lake, which envelops the mosque on three sides, is a replica of a 16th-century *mahligai* (royal barge), used on special occasions and for Koran recital competitions.

Brunei Museum

ⓘ *About 4 km east of downtown Bandar along Jln Kota Batu, T224 4545, Sat-Thu 0930-1700, Fri 0900-1130 and 1430-1700, free.*

Brunei's national museum holds a mixed bag of galleries, although it's certainly worth a visit. If you have limited time, head straight for the **Islamic Gallery**, an outstanding collection of artwork and artefacts from the sultan's personal collection. In pride of place on a marble pedestal in the centre of the gallery is a page of ornate calligraphy written by the sultan himself, in which he encourages his subjects to memorize the Koran. Around the pedestal, in rooms 1 and 2, are the real McCoy: Korans and beautifully preserved

Estranged brothers

Prince Jefri's playboy lifestyle and his embezzlement of government funds would cause a scandal in any country. In the context of Brunei's modesty, the prince's behaviour stands out as plain shocking. He is the thorn in the side of his more conservative brother, the Sultan of Brunei.

In 1997 – year of the Asian Economic Crisis – Prince Jefri's company, the **Amedeo Development Corporation**, collapsed under the weight of US$3.5 billion of debts. Its legacy is the area around Jerudong, where the prince built the world's most extravagant polo ground, the theme park and the **Empire Hotel & Country Club** (complete with a Jack Nicklaus golf course). The hotel alone was said to have cost an astonishing US$800 million.

Surprisingly, Bruneians seem to have a soft spot for Prince Jefri. Over the years, his ambitious projects have provided many jobs. But this doesn't hide his playboy tendencies and when you have billions to play with, the sky is the limit. The name of his 165-ft yacht? Tits. And its two tenders? Nipple 1 and Nipple 2. Why ever not? Prince Jefri has four wives, 17 (official) children and a penchant for Filipino and American beauty queens, who he used to fly in for his own pleasure – until one of them tried to sue him in the US, claiming she had been lured to Brunei to become a sex slave.

In 2001, the sultan himself sued his brother for embezzling some US$20 billion from the **Brunei Investment Agency**, for which the prince had served as chairman. The brothers eventually settled the case out of court. The greatest publicity surrounded the auction in August 2001 of Prince Jefri's personal items, removed from his palaces by Amedeo's liquidator to appease creditors, including a set of gold-plated toilet brushes and an F1 racing-car simulator.

The sultan subsequently brought a further cases against his brother, to try and force Prince Jefri to reveal his remaining sources of income and to get back some properties claimed by Prince Jefri as part of his lifestyle expenses. The BIA reopened litigation proceedings against Prince Jefri in 2006 using the High Court of England to freeze the Princes assets. In 2008 Prince Jefri was summoned to court in London for contempt of court, after it was claimed he had made a number of misstatements at a previous hearing. The prince declined to show his face at the hearing, and the judge issued a warrant for his arrest. It is rumoured that Prince Jefri has been back in Brunei since late 2009.

---

pieces of calligraphy dating from as early as the ninth century. Across one wall is a talismanic banner from 18th-century India, on which the whole Koran is transcribed in tiny script. Further rooms hold collections of pottery and ceramics from the Islamic world; gold and silver jewellery and coins dating back to AD 661; delicate perfume bottles alongside a collection of Indian and Ottoman sabres; and several oddities, such as a decorative wooden boot with compass, inlaid with mother-of-pearl.

Also on the ground floor is the mediocre **Natural History Gallery** – full of awkward-looking stuffed animals, birds and insects – and the obligatory **Petroleum Gallery**, which charts the discovery and extraction methods of Brunei's black gold. Upstairs, in Gallery 4, is the **Traditional Culture Gallery**, with examples of *keris* (ceremonial daggers), *bedok* (call-to-prayer drums), *gasing* (spinning tops), traditional dress, hand-crafted kites and board games such as *congkak* and *pasang*. Traditional customs are explained, too (after birth, a date is placed on the tongue of a newborn and the placenta is either hung from a tree, buried or floated downriver). Next door, the **Archaeology and History Gallery** (Gallery 5) provides a thorough introduction to the history of the region from neolithic times. Gallery 6 is for temporary exhibitions.

A staircase leads down the hill from the back of the Brunei Museum to the **Malay Technology Museum** ⓘ *same opening hours as the Brunei Museum*, where a series of dioramas explain the development of fishing techniques, boatmaking, stilt house construction, metalwork and *songkok* (hats worn by Muslim men) weaving. The top floor of the museum includes examples of indigenous dwellings (from the Murut, Kedayan and Dusun tribes of the interior), along with tools such as blowpipes and fishing traps.

Along the road, between the museum and the centre of town, look out for the tombs of two of Brunei's greatest sultans. **Sultan Syarif Ali** (1426-1432) was the founder of Islamic rule in Brunei, while **Sultan Bolkiah** (1485-1524) presided over the 'golden age' of Brunei, conquering Sulu and the Philippines.

To get there, Eastern Line bus No 39 runs every 30 minutes from the main bus terminal (or wait at the stop opposite the Arts and Handicraft Centre, see below).

Bubongan Dua Belas

ⓘ *Jln Residency, 1 km or so east of the town centre, Sat-Thu 0900-1630, Fri 0900-1130 and 1430-1630, free.*

Bubongan Dua Belas, which means Twelve Roofs, served as the British Residency until Brunei's Independence in 1984. It was built on the side of a hill overlooking Kampong Ayer in 1906 and is one of Brunei's oldest surviving buildings, with traditional wood shingle roofing and hardwood floors. The building now hosts a small Relationship Exhibition, celebrating the ties between Brunei and the UK. There are charts and maps of the Kampong Ayer area dating from the time of the first British contact in 1764. There is also a fascinating report on Brunei, penned by Acting Consul Stewart McArthur, which led to the appointment of the first British Resident in 1904. He describes the "strange and picturesque" ceremony of the *mengalei padi* harvest festival: "Everyone was feasting and I regret to say that, when I left, nearly everyone was overcome by *borak*, an extremely nauseous drink made locally from *padi* and of which I was forced to partake."

Arts and Handicraft Centre

ⓘ *Jln Residency, T224 0676, daily 0800-1700, free.*

The Arts and Handicraft Centre was established as a means of preserving traditional skills, such as weaving, brass casting and *keris* making. The centre is focused more on workshops for young Bruneians than attracting tourists, though there is a handicraft shop selling hand-crafted jewellery, basketry, *keris* (ceremonial daggers), *songket* (traditional fabric woven with gold thread), *songkok* (hats worn by Muslim men) and other gifts.

Round the other side of the handicraft centre, past one of the most enormous strangler figs you're ever likely to see, is a small **art gallery** ⓘ *Sat-Thu 0830-1630, Fri 0830-1130 and 1400-1630*, with exhibits by local artists.

Royal Regalia Museum

ⓘ *Jln Sultan, T223 8358, Sat-Thu 0900-1630, Fri 0900-1130, 1430-1630, free (shoes have to be removed before entering).*

Dedicated almost exclusively to the present sultan's life, this is (predictably) the flashiest of all Brunei's museums, set in an extravagant domed building in the centre of town.

Bring an extra top – the main galleries are air conditioned to fridge temperatures – and try not to take too much notice of the guards, who are armed to the hilt (literally), each with truncheon, dagger and gun.

The museum's opening in 1992 coincided with the sultan's Silver Jubilee celebrations, and many of the exhibits relate to this event. The Royal Chariot – an enormous gold-winged thing that looks like a movie prop – is the largest exhibit, while the strangest is probably the creepy golden hand and forearm, used to support the chin of the sultan during the coronation. There are hundreds of photos, too, and a mass of ceremonial costumes, armoury and other regalia items. The **Constitutional Gallery** charts Brunei's recent history.

Next door is the **Brunei History Centre** ① *Sat-Thu 0745-1215 and 1330-1630, free*, which serves as a centre of research for documenting the history and genealogy of the royal family. The centre is open to the public, but there's not much to see.

The enormous building across the road is the **Lapau Di Raja** (**Royal Ceremonial Hall**), site of the 1968 coronation ceremony. The hall is closed to the public.

Parks and green spaces

For the best vantage points above Bandar and Kampong Ayer, head for the **Bukit Subok Recreational Park**, which rises steeply off Jalan Residency. The entrance to the park is just before Bubongan Dua Belas (the old Residency building). A boardwalk loops through the forest between a series of viewing towers. The going is steep, so avoid visiting during the middle part of the day.

The **Tasek Recreational Park** is a more sedate option, with a picnic area, a small waterfall and a reservoir. It is situated about 1 km north of the centre. To get there, head north along Jalan Tasek Lama and turn right opposite the Sultan Omar Ali Saifuddien College. From the park gates, it's another 500 m or so to the waterfall.

Bandar's suburbs → *For listings, see pages 302-310.*

The increasingly busy suburbs of Bandar lie a few kilometres to the northwest of the centre, across Edinburgh Bridge. **Gadong** is the commercial centre and primary suburb of Bandar Seri Begawan. It's not pretty on the eyes in the way that Bandar is (Gadong is a traffic-clogged grid of modern shophouses and department stores), but this is the modern-day heart and soul of the capital. It is where Bruneians come to shop and to eat, either in local restaurants and international franchises or at the foodstalls of the excellent *pasar malam* (night market), which serves up (mainly) Malay food seven days a week. **Kiulap**, a little closer to the city centre, is really an extension of Gadong, with more shops and offices. These two places act as a foil to the strangely quiet city centre and offer a refreshing glimpse into modern Brunei.

Just south of Kiulap is Kampong Kiarong, home to the stunning **Kiarong Mosque** ① *Sat-Wed 0800-1200, 1400-1500, 1700-1800, shoes must be removed before entering; sometimes closed to the public on Sat*. Known officially as Masjid Jame'Asr Hassanal Bolkiah, the mosque was built in 1992 to commemorate the sultan's Silver Jubilee. Though it supplanted Masjid Omar Ali Saifuddien (see page 290) as Brunei's national mosque, there seem to be mixed opinions as to which is superior. The older mosque conforms more to classical convention and forms the focal point of Bandar itself. The Kiarong Mosque, meanwhile, is bigger and brasher, set in landscaped gardens and immense in size, with a quartet of intricate minarets and 29 gilded cupolas. Around 5 km north of the city centre are the government offices, scattered widely around a leafy grid of streets near Brunei International Airport.

Around Brunei

The capital, Bandar Seri Begawan, makes the ideal base for forays deeper into Brunei. Most of the following sights can be visited on day trips from the capital, either on guided tours or with a hire car. Of Brunei's four districts, Temburong is the least populated and, for many people, the most appealing, thanks to the Ulu Temburong National Park. Each of the remaining districts offers its own diversions, with the interior of Belait providing the most challenging itineraries.
▸▸ *For listings, see pages 302-310.*

Brunei Muara District → *For listings, see pages 302-310.*

Brunei Muara is the smallest of Brunei's four districts, with Bandar Seri Begawan at its heart. As well as several notable sights on the outskirts of Bandar, there are a few minor sights further afield, including sandy beaches, forest reserves and a theme park.

Official residence of the sultan, the **Istana Nurul Iman** is situated several kilometres upriver from the capital, its twin gold cupolas clearly visible from the river. It is the largest residential palace in the world and must surely count as one of the most extravagant, too. Beneath the curving Minangkabau-style roofs lie a staggering 1778 rooms (including 257 toilets), which makes the Istana bigger than the Vatican and on a par with Versailles. The banquet hall seats 5000 and there's an underground car park to house the sultan's extensive collection of cars (which runs into three figures). Needless to say, the palace is not open to the public. For the best views, catch a water taxi from Bandar Seri Begawan. You'll pass by the royal helipad and the royal jetty, where the sultan's guests (including Queen Elizabeth II on her last visit) are welcomed.

Alternatively, make your way to the **Taman Persiaran Damuan**, a kilometre-long park that runs along the riverside just beyond the palace. Within the park are sculptures from each of the six original ASEAN nations.

If you're lucky, and you visit the park at dusk, you may spot proboscis monkeys (see box opposite) on **Pulau Ranggu**, the small island opposite the park. Proboscis monkeys are an endangered species endemic to Borneo. To guarantee sightings, take a proboscis tour by *tambang* along the Sungai Damuan tributary; it's one of the highlights of a trip to Brunei for any nature enthusiast. Look out for monkeys crossing the river (they swim doggy style, their bulbous noses raised above the water like snorkels). ▸▸ *See Activities and tours, page 307.*

Jerudong Park Playground ⓘ *Kampong Jerudong (along the Muara–Tutong highway northwest of Bandar Seri Begawan), T261 1894, www.jerudong-park.com/jpp, Wed-Sun 1700-2400 (except Sat 1700-0200), shorter hours during Ramadan so check the website, B$5, children (under 1.4 m) B$3,* is a peculiar theme park that opened in 1994 to coincide with the sultan's 48th birthday. By Western standards, it's nothing special, the highlight being the excellent log flume. Today it has a slightly jaded feel and, thanks to Brunei's tiny population, it is probably the quietest theme park in the world; on some days you'll have the park more or less to yourself. Beware, many of the rides are often out of action (ask before handing over the entry fee) and in recent times, probably due to low admission numbers, a lot of the major rides have been sold off.

Just along the coast from Jerudong Park is the extravagant **Empire Hotel & Country Club** (see page 303), which is worth a look for its towering, gold-adorned atrium; at 80 m it is said to be the tallest in the world. Both hotel and theme park were built by Prince Jefri, brother to the sultan and an endless source of scandal (see box, page 291).

Proboscis monkeys

Proboscis monkeys are not pretty to look at. At least, they're an acquired taste. With their pendulous noses, pot bellies and hooded eyes, they look more like caricatures than bona fide monkeys. The Malays had a special name for them; not *orang-utan* (man of the forest), but *orang belanda*, meaning Dutchman (more a snipe at their would-be oppressors than a simian insult). In Kalimantan they also have other local names including *bekantan*, *bekara*, *kahau*, *rasong*, *pika* and *batangan*.

It is one of Brunei's great secrets that it holds the world's largest population of proboscis monkeys. With an estimated 10,000 of them living along the banks of Sungai Brunei, this is more than the rest of their scattered populations put together. The Kinabatangan Wetlands of Sabah are widely thought to be the best place to spot proboscis monkeys. Not so; just minutes from Brunei's capital, by *tambang*, plentiful troops of proboscis monkeys feed peacefully among the mangrove trees. Proboscis monkeys are unique to Borneo. They are the world's largest monkeys, with adult males often exceeding 25 kg. They are great swimmers, too, with their long noses serving well as snorkels. Scientists, however, point to sex rather than swimming as the reason for the unusual hooter. Having a big nose is a matter of pride for a male proboscis (who, incidentally, sports a permanent erection). It's all to do with Darwinian sexual selection: the bigger the nose, the bigger the harem (proboscis monkeys live in troops of 10-30 animals with a single adult male at the helm). In common with most of larger mammals in Borneo, the proboscis monkey is a seriously threatened species – though you might not think so from their numbers on the Brunei River. It is thought that no more than 20,000 proboscis monkeys survive in the wild. See also page 377.

Muara and around → *Colour map 1, B6.*

At Brunei's northeast tip is the port of Muara, a nondescript place with a single sleepy grid of shophouses and nothing much to draw visitors. There are several nearby beaches that are pleasant enough, if you can bear the heat. Pantai Muara is a 4-km stretch of sand north of Muara, with a kids' playground and picnic shelters among the casuarinas, while to the south, at the end of a road lined with mansions, is a sandy spit known as Pantai Serasa, home to a fleet of traditional fishing boats and the Serasa Watersports Complex.

Boats from Labuan, Malaysia, arrive at the port ar Serasa Muara, from where express bus No 33 and taxis wait to shuttle visitors into town.

There are two forest reserves worth visiting along the main Muara–Tutong highway, which runs beside Brunei's north-facing coastline. **Bukit Shahbandar Reserve** (just east of Kampong Jerudong) is a popular spot with joggers and walkers, with some fairly demanding trails running up and down seven hills. At the highest point, there's a wooden observation tower. The park was used for the mountain biking event when Brunei hosted the Southeast Asian Games and a network of tough tracks criss-cross the hilly forest. At the time of writing, there were no bikes for rent at the park. To get to the park take bus No 55, and alight at the bridge before Pantai Jerutong. From there it is a hairy 15-minute walk along the highway to the park entrance. The **Hutan Berakas Forest Reserve** (directly north of the airport) is wilder, with trails weaving through casuarina forests and *kerangas* (heath forest), the favoured habitat of carnivorous pitcher plants. There are paved trails here, a popular picnic area and a lovely long beach used by Bruneians for swimming.

Out in Brunei Bay itself is **Pulau Selirong**, an uninhabited island covered in mangrove forest. The island has recently been designated a forest reserve and 2 km of elevated walkways have been installed. Monitor lizards, crabs, mud skippers and wading birds can be viewed, along with the occasional mangrove snake and saltwater crocodile. Tours can be arranged with many of the Bandar-based tour operators (see page 308).

Temburong District → For listings, see pages 302-310. Colour map 1, B6.

Temburong is the forested finger of land set adrift from the rest of Brunei by the Malaysian district of Limbang, which was snatched from Brunei's control in 1890 by Raja Brooke of Sarawak. The population of Temburong is barely 10,000, with Malays living alongside a scattered population of Iban, Murut and Kadazan tribespeople. The whole district has something of a village atmosphere; wherever you go in Temburong, it seems that everybody knows one another.

Speedboats for Temburong leave regularly from the jetty on Jalan Residency in Bandar Seri Begawan. They roar downriver, passing briefly into Brunei Bay, before weaving through the mangrove channels as far as Bangar, Temburong's main town. The journey is an adventure in itself: look out for proboscis monkeys swimming doggy style across the narrow channels.

Bangar (not to be confused with Bandar) is a quiet place with a single row of shophouses and a sultry, sleepy air. There's a mosque, a few government offices, a resthouse and a few coffee shops, otherwise there's no particular reason to linger. Most people carry straight on in the direction of the Ulu Temburong National Park, the principal attraction for visitors to the district.

Ulu Temburong National Park
ⓘ *Entry fee B$5. Be sure to get hold of an entry permit in advance from the Forestry Department Ministry of Industry and Primary Resources, Bandar Seri Begawan BB3910, T238 1687, forestrybrunei@hotmail.com.*

The 50,000-ha Ulu Temburong National Park is the jewel in the crown of Brunei's ecotourism push. It sits in the remote southern portion of Temburong, in the heart of the **Batu Apoi Forest Reserve**. The region has never been settled or logged, so there are no roads, and access to the park is by *temuai* (traditional longboat). Getting there is half the fun; the journey begins at Bandar Seri Begawan with a ride in a 'flying coffin', a wooden speedboat so called because of its shape (though, when you see the speed with which these things hurtle through the mangroves, you may suspect the name is fitting for other reasons). The speedboat passes briefly into the Malaysian territory of Limbang, before turning into the mouth of Sungai Temburong and speeding upriver as far as Bangar. A short car journey follows, bypassing a series of picturesque kampongs and longhouses, before the final leg by longboat from Batang Duri to the park headquarters, with towering dipterocarps climbing the river banks.

Despite being relatively unknown, Ulu Temburong compares favourably with the jungle reserves of neighbouring Malaysia. Work carried out at the **Belalong Rainforest Field Studies Centre** confirms the unusual biodiversity of Ulu Temburong; many species new to science have been found here and one scientist was reported to have identified more than 400 separate species of beetle on a single tree. The main attraction for visitors, however, is the towering canopy walkway, which stands 50 m tall and provides unbeatable views of the surrounding forest.

The fact that few people visit is also part of the appeal – the park remains unscathed by tourism, despite being easily accessible. There can't be many places in the world where you can leave the city mid-morning, have a picnic lunch deep in pristine rainforest and be back at your hotel by late afternoon.

Though it is possible to visit Ulu Temburong independently, most people find it simpler to use one of the Bandar-based tour operators (see page 308); they'll make all travel arrangements for you and provide guides and entry permits (with everything paid upfront – a day trip costs around B$128). It is perfectly possible to visit the park as a day trip, though there is accommodation available for longer stays (see page 303).

The journey to Ulu Temburong involves two boat journeys and a taxi ride. Bangar-bound speedboats leave regularly from the jetty on Jalan Residency in Bandar Seri Begawan (daily every 30 minutes 0745-1600; 45 minutes journey time; B$15 return, visitors are advised to carry their passport). From the Bangar jetty, there are taxis to take visitors south along a sealed road to **Batang Duri** (literally, Spiky Hamlet), a small settlement on the banks of Sungai Temburong. From here, visitors need to charter a longboat for the final leg of the journey upriver to the park headquarters (90 minutes, B$50-60 per boat). During dry season (July and August) water levels can be low and passengers may have to get out and help push the boat.

At park headquarters, visitors need to sign a register and pay the entry fee before heading into the park proper. There's a small information centre here with displays, and a series of chalets and dormitories, linked by plankwalks.

Flora and fauna Borneo's rainforests are among the most biodiverse places on Earth and Ulu Temburong is no exception. More species of tree can be found in a single hectare here than in the entirety of North America. Animal life is abundant too, though hard to spot. Some of the more conspicuous creatures include flying lizards, Wallace's flying frog, pygmy squirrels, wild boar, mousedeer, gibbons (more often heard than seen), various species of hornbill (the biggest being the majestic rhinoceros hornbill, frequently seen gliding across the river) and of course myriad weird and wonderful insects, from the peculiar lantern beetle to the Rajah Brooke birdwing butterfly. The canopy walkway provides the opportunity to look directly down upon the jungle canopy, home to the greatest density of life. Notice the abundance of epiphytes, plants that survive at this height by clinging on to host trees. From the walkway, it is sometimes possible to see tiger orchids, one of the largest of their species.

Treks With 7 km of wooden walkways, few visitors stray off the main trail, though there is unlimited scope for serious trekking in the vicinity (either using park headquarters as a base, or camping out in the forest). The terrain is steep and rugged and not suited to those without a moderate level of fitness. Wherever you go, take plenty of water. Falling trees and landslides often lay waste to sections of the boardwalk, making it unlikely that the whole trail will be open at any one time.

The boardwalk begins at park headquarters and leads across the Sungai Temburong via a footbridge to the foot of a towering hill, upon which stands the canopy walkway. The climb is steep and sweaty, with almost 1000 steps. Once you've conquered the hill, reaching the canopy walkway itself is no easy matter either; the walkway is suspended in sections between 50-m-tall aluminium towers built around a seemingly endless series of step ladders. The views from the top are truly magnificent, though vertigo sufferers will find it living hell. Standing on the walkway, above the jungle canopy, on top of a hill, you can see for many miles around, with the confluence of Sungai Temburong and Sungai Belalong at your feet. Gaze for long enough and you'll probably spot the black and white backs of hornbills as they glide from tree to tree along the riverbank.

From the walkway, the trail continues for several kilometres along a steeply descending boardwalk in the direction of a second suspension bridge across Sungai Temburong. The boardwalk ends at Sungai Apan, a narrow stream. By following the course of the stream upriver, you soon come to a picturesque waterfall, with a plunge pool deep enough for swimming (outside dry season). A steep trail traverses the hillside with the aid of ropes to a second waterfall.

Most people make their way back to park headquarters by longboat from the confluence of Sungai Apan and Sungai Temburong (returning on foot would mean retracing your steps along the boardwalk). You may cross tracks with local Iban, who fish this stretch of the river with traps and nets. They'll probably wave you over and offer you a swig of grog – rice wine, or more likely, Bacardi rum.

Those looking for the chance to explore largely uncharted rainforest may be interested in tackling the strenuous week-long trek to the summit of **Bukit Pagon** (1843 m), which is situated near the border with Sarawak in the southernmost corner of Temburong. Contact the tourist office, or one of the Bandar-based tour operators, for help with arrangements.

Elsewhere in Temburong

If time is very limited, you may consider skipping Ulu Temburong and heading instead for the **Peradayan Forest Reserve**, which is just 20 minutes east of Bangar by road (taxis cost around B$15 one-way). Within the reserve is a small forest recreation park with picnic tables and trails, one of which climbs to the summit of **Bukit Patoi** (310 m), passing caves along the way. The summit of the hill is a bare patch of stone, allowing wide views across the forest north to Brunei Bay and east to Sarawak. A tougher and less distinct trail continues from here to the summit of **Bukit Peradayan** (410 m).

Though the majority of Temburong's indigenous inhabitants have taken the opportunity to move into detached homes, plenty still live in longhouses. In theory, unannounced visits are welcome at any longhouse, but a handful have established formal arrangements with tour operators for receiving guests. The largest is a 16-door Iban longhouse (home to 16 families) situated along the road to Batang Duri, at **Kampong Sembiling**. Various guides and tour operators will stop off here, allowing visitors to meet the inhabitants and try a glass or two of *tuak* (rice wine). If it's daytime, there won't be many people around, but you'll get a chance to see inside a modern Iban longhouse, complete with satellite TV and parking bays for cars. Another longhouse offering homestays is the curiously named five-door **Amo C**, located just north of **Batang Duri** itself. Overnight guests are set up with mattresses on the *ruai* (communal veranda) and guided treks along hunting trails can be arranged for a fee.

Tutong District → *For listings, see pages 302-310. Colour map 1, B5/6.*

The central district of Tutong is wedged between Belait District to the west and Limbang (Malaysia) to the east, following the flood plain of Sungai Tutong. Recent growth in agriculture has seen the introduction of small-scale plantations in areas of Tutong, though most of the district is sparsely populated and covered by rainforest.

The coastal highway passes by the district capital, **Tutong**, a small and pleasant town on the banks of the river. There's nothing much for the visitor to do here, other than stop by the small wet market or the nearby *tamu* (the regional open-air market, held every Thursday afternoon through to Friday morning). The *tamu* draws Tutong's indigenous inhabitants – Kedayan, Dusun and Iban tribespeople – who come down from the interior to sell their produce. It is mainly a food market, though there are handicrafts on sale, too. A kilometre to the north of Tutong is the **Taman Rekreasi Sungai Basong**, a small recreation park with a pond, a stream and picnic tables. Meanwhile, just west of town is **Pantai Seri Kenangan** (Unforgettable Beach), a largely forgettable spit of sand dividing Sungai Tutong from the sea. Still, the beach is kept clean and the sea here is calm. Every July a local festival is held on the beach, with Malay games such as top spinning and kite flying.

The road continues along the spit as far as **Kampong Kuala Tutong**, a sleepy place set among coconut palms. There's a small boatyard here called Marine Yard, where river trips can sometimes be organized. The arrangement is pretty informal, and you'll have to just turn up and hope there's someone around. The boat weaves upriver through mangrove-lined swampland, past Dusun and Malay kampongs. Look out for monkeys and estuarine crocodiles, which can sometimes be seen basking on the sandbanks. River tours along Sungai Tutong can be arranged through **Ilufah Leisure Tours** (see page 308).

Tasek Merimbun

There is no public transport to Tasek Merimbun, Brunei's largest lake. If you've rented a car, head west from Bandar Seri Begawan on the old Tutong Road (rather than the coastal highway). At Mile 18, take the left fork for Lamunin. Beyond Kampong Lamunin itself, follow signs for Tasek Merimbun. The journey takes up to 1½ hours.

Tasek Merimbun is a beautiful and remote spot rich in wildlife. The lake and its environs are home to Dusun tribespeople, who for many centuries took advantage of the abundance of fish and wildlife. Now that the lake has been set aside as a nature reserve only a handful of Dusun people remain. Merimbun is becoming increasingly popular as a weekend escape for well-heeled Bruneians. The setting is magnificent: an S-shaped, peat-black body of water surrounded by dense jungle. In the centre of the lake is tiny island, accessible by boardwalk. The **Tasek Merimbun Heritage Park** encompasses the lake, plus wetlands, peat-swamp forest and lowland dipterocarp rainforest. The area is home to a great diversity of wildlife, including crocodile and clouded leopard (Borneo's biggest cat). The most important scientific discovery has been the white-collared fruit bat, which appears to be unique to Tasek Merimbun.

On the banks of the lake is a small visitors' centre with a few fish tanks, plus chalets for accommodation. Local Dusun have kayaks for rent, too. Opposite the chalets is a 2-km botanical trail through the rainforest. Guides can be hired for longer treks in the area.

Belait District → *For listings, see pages 302-310. Colour map 1, B5/6.*

Belait wears two faces. On the one hand it is oil country, the driving force behind Brunei's economy and home to a large population of British and Dutch expats. On the other, it is the best example of 'old' Brunei – Brunei before oil.

When oil was first discovered at Seria in 1929, the whole region was largely uninhabited, the lowlands dominated by peat swamps, mangroves and rainforest, with indigenous Iban and Dusun tribespeople sticking largely to the valley of Sungai Belait. Though the coastal strip has developed beyond recognition, the interior remains largely unscathed.

Aside from Temburong, Belait District is the best place to explore Brunei's rainforest and visit indigenous longhouses. Most visitors are unaware of this: the tourism infrastructure here remains underdeveloped, so few people visit – apart from British Army recruits undergoing a round of brutal jungle training. Nevertheless, the interior of Belait is earmarked as an important ecotourism destination for the future, and tour operators are beginning to put together itineraries into the region.

Seria

Seria is a surreal place. Once open swampland, Seria is now dominated by level fields full of lawn-mowing tractors, egrets and nodding donkeys – small land-based oil wells that nod back and forth as they pump oil to the surface. There is no real centre of town to speak of; row upon row of neat bungalows line the roads – home, presumably to Chinese and expat oil workers, whose wives ride about town in land cruisers. It is a strange, functional place with an odd mix of inhabitants that includes indigenous tribespeople and a garrison of Gurkhas.

The town straggles along the coastal strip between Seria and Kuala Belait, which serves as the centre of Brunei's oil production. On the edge of Seria is the **Billionth Barrel Monument**, commemorating the obscene productivity of Brunei's first oil field. For those who want to delve deeper into the history and technicalities of oil production, there is the **Oil & Gas Discovery Centre (OGDC)** ⓘ *F20 Seria, T337 7200; Tue-Thu 0900-1700, Fri 1000-1200 and 1400-1800, Sat-Sun 1000-1800; B$5*, set in a building that resembles an oil drum. It's a fun place for kids, with a gyroscope, a bed of nails and a fish pond.

Kuala Belait

Though it all started at Seria, Kuala Belait (known locally as KB) is the district's principal town. It also serves as the border town with nearby Sarawak. Like Seria, Kuala Belait is a purely functional place that has developed over time to serve the needs of the oil workers. The centre of town comprises a large grid of streets with Chinese shophouses alongside multinational outlets such as the **Body Shop** and **KFC**.

Kuala Belait sits on the east bank of the Sungai Belait and it's possible to hire a boat upriver as far as Kuala Balai (see below). Boats leave from behind the market building on Jalan Pasar, at the southern end of Jalan McKerron (sometimes spelt Mackeron).

Belait Interior

Kuala Balai

Before the oil boom, the main settlement in this part of Brunei was the riverine village of Kuala Balai, situated about an hour upriver from Kuala Belait. Between 1930 and 1980 the population slowly dwindled, until the village virtually ceased to exist. Today just a handful of permanent inhabitants remain.

The people from these parts are known as the Belait Malays and they have a lot in common with the Melanau people of coastal Sarawak, including their Muslim faith, their traditional reliance on sago processing and their stilted longhouses. Despite the fact that Kuala Balai is now little more than a ghost town, it is still possible to get a sense of how things once looked; the old longhouse, which deteriorated many years ago, has been rebuilt as part of a Raleigh International project. And there are still one or two old sago processors around, though they use light machinery now, rather than trampling the sago scrapings underfoot, as was once the way. Just downriver from the longhouse is a small wooden box on stilts by the riverside. Inside are 20 human skulls, victims of headhunters from as long ago as the 17th century.

As elsewhere in Belait District, tourism hasn't yet taken off and few people visit the longhouse, but at the time of writing there were plans to market Kuala Balai more actively as a tourist destination.

Jalan Labi

The other route into the interior of Belait is via Jalan Labi, a decent road which turns south off the coastal highway at Kampong Lumut, near the border with Tutong District. A little way along the road is Brunei's oldest forest reserve, the **Sungai Liang Forest Reserve**, with ponds, picnic shelters and various well-maintained paths into the surrounding forest. One climbs a steep hill as far as a treehouse (closed for renovation at the time of writing). Close by is the **Forestry Department** building, set back from the road, with a small Palmetum leading up to the offices. There's a tiny forestry museum here, too – the **Muzium Perhutanan** ⓘ *Mon-Thu and Sat 0800-1215 and 1330-1630*, with two rooms of displays that aren't worth going out of your way for.

The Labi road continues south through undulating rainforest as far as the village of Kampong Labi itself, passing another forest reserve along the way, the **Labi Hills Forest Reserve**. Within its boundaries is the 270-ha **Luagan Lalak Recreation Park**, covering an area of alluvial swampland, which floods to become a lake during the monsoon. The lake (or swamp, depending on the season) is accessible via a 200-m-long boardwalk.

Kampong Labi, some 40 km south of the coastal highway, is a small settlement that has served for years as a base for speculative (and unsuccessful) oil drilling in the surrounding hills. Tropical fruits, such as rambutan, durian, cempedak and jackfruit, are grown in the area. Beyond Labi, the road turns into a dirt track which serves as an access route to a number of Iban longhouses. The largest of these is the 12-door **Rumah Panjang Mendaram Besar**, home to 100 or so people. Like most of the longhouses in Brunei, this one has piped water and electricity, with the men commuting to the towns to work for either Shell or the government. A nearby trail leads to the **Wasai Mendaram**, a large waterfall with plunge pool for bathing.

At the end of the 12-km track is **Rumah Panjang Teraja**. The inhabitants of this six-door longhouse cultivate paddy, rear pigs and chickens, and grow their own fruit and vegetables. From the longhouse, a well-marked trail leads to the summit of Bukit Teraja, from where there are magnificent views as far as Gunung Mulu (see page 159) in Sarawak. Walking the trail to the summit takes about 1½ hours. Reported wildlife sightings along the way include orang-utans, Borneo bearded pigs, barking deer, macaques and hornbills.

Ulu Belait

Further longhouses can be found deep in the interior, along the upper reaches of Sungai Belait. These are accessible by longboat from Kampong Sungai Mau, which is situated halfway along the Jalan Labi. Of course, it is possible to begin the journey in Kuala Belait, passing Kuala Balai along the way, but this route takes many hours.

The journey upriver into Ulu Belait (Upriver Belait) depends on the level of the river; in the dry season its upper reaches are barely navigable. Kampong Sukang, some two hours from Kampong Sungai Mau by longboat, is a community of Dusun and Punan tribespeople, with two longhouses and a hamlet of family homes. The Punan are nomadic hunter-gatherers by tradition, though the inhabitants of Kampong Sukang were persuaded to settle here back in the 1970s. They now farm paddy rather than relying on the old staple diet of wild sago, but they still hunt in the traditional manner using blowpipes and poison darts.

If you're feeling still more intrepid, there is another hamlet of longhouses at **Kampong Melilas**, located one to three hours – depending on the water level – upriver from Kampong Sukang. These are home to Iban people and, like the Labi longhouses, they are upgraded versions of the traditional longhouse, though this community supports a thriving cottage industry in traditional basketry and weaving. Beyond Kampong Melilas, there are hot springs and plenty of waterfalls; a guide can be arranged at the village.

For Sleeping and Eating price codes and other relevant information, see Essentials pages 23-27.

☉ Sleeping

Bandar Seri Begawan *p286, map p288*
Large discounts are often available if you book in advance through hotel websites.
L Sheraton Utama, Jln Tasek Lama, T224 4272, www.sheraton.com/utama. The city's best business hotel with over 140 spacious and comfortable rooms with cable TV and internet access. Rooms at the back face lush greenery. There are 2 notable restaurants, a pool and a fitness centre. The staff also hands out a good map for joggers with routes as far as Tasek Waterfall. A shuttle bus runs between the hotel and malls in the suburbs. The hotel is a 10-min walk from office blocks downtown. Good weekend discounts.
A Brunei, 95 Jln Pemancha, T242 3729, www.quanix.com/business/bruhotel. Located in the heart of town, this place has a somewhat stiff atmosphere. Rooms, though uninspiring, are spacious and comfortable and have cable TV and minibar. Wi-Fi access is available in the lobby. There is also a good café.
A Jubilee, Jubilee Plaza, Jln Kampong Kianggeh, T222 8070, www.jubileehotel brunei.com. Located down a side road, 10 mins' walk from the waterfront. Popular with Asian business people, this place has spacious carpeted rooms with cable TV and large bathroom. More expensive rooms have a kitchenette and lounge area. Airport transfers are included in the rate. There is a host of facilities in the plaza, including a popular gym, **Ahan Thai** restaurant and an internet café filled with schoolboys. Good promotional rates offered.
A-B Terrace, Jln Tasek Lama, T224 3554, www.terracebrunei.com. This solidly 1980s hotel has a lift with chunky buttons, dark corridors and rooms that are well past their prime. All rooms have TV, fridge and cable TV and are reasonable value. There's a small

pool, fitness centre and business centre offering internet access.
C KH Soon Rest House, 140 Jln Pemancha, T222 2052, www.khsoon-resthouse .tripod.com. Sprawling hostel with large, bright but somewhat dirty rooms in the city centre. All rooms have a/c and more expensive ones have attached bathroom (with broken toilets, electricity sockets next to the shower, etc). The friendly staff can arrange tours and can offer a fair amount of good local information.
D Pusat Belia, Jln Sungai Kianggeh, T222 2900, www.pusatbelia.hos-kitani.com. By far and away the best cheap place in the country with spotless 4- and 10-bed dorms and friendly, relaxed staff. It's not a busy place and chances are that you'll get an entire room. There is one room available for couples, with a double bed. Pool (B$1) and internet café. For those who want to explore the country in depth, it's worth enquiring to see if staff will arrange stays in Brunei's other youth hostels in Temburong and Tutong. Highly recommended.

Bandar's suburbs *p293*
L The Centrepoint, Abdul Razak Complex, Gadong BE3519, T243 0430, reservation@ thecentreponthotel.com. Large and opulent hotel with plenty of marble and Malay-style Islamic touches, this place has 216 rooms from the comfortable and pragmatic de luxe to the gargantuan Presidential Suite (a whopping B$1700 a night). There are a number of restaurants, a kitsch piano lounge, pool, gym, squash and tennis courts and ballroom. Wi-Fi access in lobby only.
AL Orchid Garden, Lot 31954, Simpang 9, Kampong Anggerek Desa, Jln Berakas BB3713, T233 5544, www.orchidgarden brunei.com. A 4-star hotel next to the National Stadium (between the airport and the government complex), a few kilometres from Bandar centre. Spacious and comfortable rooms with internet access, cable TV and bathroom with bathub. There

are a couple of good places to eat here including **Vanda** Chinese restaurant. Also has a pool, gym and spa. This is the closest hotel to the airport, so is handy for stopovers.

AL Riverview, Km 1, Jln Gadong, T223 8238, rivview@brunet.bn. Set on its own near the suburb of Gadong, halfway between downtown Bandar and the airport. This place may not lead the way in the style stakes, but has big comfortable rooms, a large pool, jacuzzi and sauna and is close to the eating delights offered in Gadong. Good promotional rates.

B Grand City, Lot 25115, Block G, Kampong Pengkalan Gadong, BE3719, T245 2188, grandcity@brunet.bn. A solid mid-range option, if you don't mind staying out of town (in Gadong suburb). Rooms here are comfortable and have a/c, TV and tea and coffee facilities. Price includes airport transfer and breakfast. A handy shuttle bus service runs to nearby commercial areas. Free Wi-Fi access in the lobby area.

B Traders Inn, about halfway between the airport and the centre of BSB, in the new Beribi Commercial Area and just off Jln Gadong, T244 28208. Excellent value hotel with 84 clean, comfortable a/c rooms with TV, attached bathroom and Wi-Fi access. Though it's within easy walking distance of eateries and shops in Gadong, it is a little far out for those who need to be in the city centre. Highly recommended.

C Apek Utama, Simpang 229I, Jln Kota Batu, T222 0808. Located 3 km to the east of town (take bus No 39), This place is a bit far from the action. Nevertheless, the fan and a/c rooms are clean and it's a quiet spot for those happy to spend their evenings even more quietly than anyone else in BSB.

C Voctech International House, Jln Pasar Baharu, Gadong BE1318, T244 7992, voctech@brunet.bn. Owned by the Ministry of Education and used by visiting international guests, this good-value place is close to the eateries of Gadong and its renowned *pasar malam*. Rooms are simple and clean and have private balcony, a/c attached bathroom and TV. There is also an airport shuttle service. Recommended.

Brunei Muara District *p294*
LL Empire Hotel & Country Club, Jerudong BG3122, T241 8888, www.theempirehotel.com. Brunei's only beach resort and a monument to the extravagance of the sultan's brother, Prince Jefri (see box, page 291). No expense was spared in the construction of this 6-star hotel, which centres around an 80 m-high, marble-pillared atrium. The 400-plus rooms all have large balconies and huge marble-clad bathrooms, with walk-in showers and vast bathtubs. The Presidential Suite covers more than 650 sq m and has its own lavish indoor pool, with attached sauna, steam room and jacuzzi. With the click of a button, a cinema screen descends from the ceiling above the pool. There are antiques aplenty and swathes of gold leaf. 18-hole Jack Nicklaus golf course, sports club, cinema and numerous pools, including a meandering 11,000-sq-m lagoon pool with fake, sandy beach (great for kids). Kids' club, 7 dining outlets, water sports including scuba-diving, sailing, jet skiing, kayaking and parasailing. Free shuttle in and out of Bandar Seri Begawan, 4 times daily. Check for special discounts; low occupancy means that rooms are often excellent value.

Temburong District *p296*
A Ulu Temburong Resort, PO Box 2612, BSB, T244 1791, www.uluuluresort.com for online bookings. Virtually everyone visits Ulu Temburong on an organized tour, with accommodation pre-arranged for longer stays. If you want to arrange the trip yourself, there is a wide range of simple yet comfortable accommodation available here, some with verandas with day beds, which are perfect for an afternoon nap. There are also some deckchairs laid out along the riverside and a delightful lounge built in traditional kampong style with lots of comfy chairs and a simple café offering good food. Recommended.

C Government Resthouse, Jln Batang Duri, Bangar, T522 1239. The only place to stay in Bangar, situated a short walk from the jetty

along the road to Batang Duri. Simple, functional rooms, plus a few chalets for B$80.
D Longhouses. Visitors to Temburong District can stay at various longhouses, either informally or as part of an organized tour. Those most commonly visited are **Amo C** and the main longhouse at **Kampong Sembiling**, both along the Batang Duri road. **Amo C** longhouse has an informal homestay arrangement with guests: for a small amount (no more than B$10), they will feed you and set you up with mattresses on the *ruai* (common veranda). Hospitality is an important part of indigenous culture and, in theory, any longhouse will put you up for the night. In practice, this is only the case with the more traditional or remote longhouses. If you turn up at a longhouse unannounced, be sure to follow the correct etiquette. Always ask the permission of the headman, or Tuai Rumah, before heading inside. Remove shoes before entering a family room (*bilik*), or an area of the *ruai* laid with mats. More often than not, shoes are not worn at all in a longhouse and are left at the entrance to the *ruai*.

Tutong District *p298*
B Halim Plaza, Lot No 9003, Kampong Petani, Tutong TA1141, T426 0688, www.halimplazabrunei.com. Located inside a small shopping mall, this place offers a range of comfortable rooms with TV and attached bathroom and is mainly patronized by Malaysians or Bruneians on business. Great value for those stopping over in Tutong.
C Researchers' Quarter, Tasek Merimbun Heritage Park, c/o Director of Brunei Museum, T222 2713, bmdir@bunet.bn. If available, the Researchers' Quarter (a new wooden chalet) at Tasek Merimbun can be used by the public. Contact Brunei Museum in advance.

Belait District *p299*
AL Riviera, Lot 106, Jln Sungai, Kuala Belait KA2331, T333 5252. The best hotel in Kuala Belait, on the riverfront in the town centre, with 30 comfortable and modern rooms and suites. All rooms have a minibar, cable TV and a large marble bathtub. Frequent promotions make this hotel good value. Good restaurant mainly offering Malay cuisine, and special promotions offered at the gym over the road.
A Brunei Sentosa, 92-93 Jln McKerron, PO Box 252, Kuala Belait KA1131, T333 4341, www.bruneisentosahotel.com. In the heart of town and handy for the bus station for connections to Seria or Miri. With oil workers pouring out during the day, and a fairly grim façade, this place is not the most elegant of places to stay, Nevertheless, rooms are fairly comfortable (though some could use a clean) and have cable TV, a/c and attached bathroom.

Eating

The night market (*pasar malam*) in the suburb of **Gadong** is probably the best place to sample local fare. Every evening from about 1700, hundreds of stalls turn out seemingly endless varieties of satay, curries, grilled meats and Malay coconut-based sweets. The same sort of food is available on a smaller scale at the **Tamu Kianggeh** (open-air market) in downtown Bandar.

Also worth trying are the foodstalls on the waterfront near the Temburong jetty for *nasi campur* and *teh tarik*. The **Padian Foodcourt** (1st floor, Yayasan Complex; daily 0900-2200) is great for cheap local food and drink, as well as Thai and Indonesian staples. There is a good food court on the 3rd floor of Wisma Setia, Jln Pemancha with lashings of good-value Thai food. There are also larger food courts in **Gadong**, including one on the top floor of The Mall, which serves the full range of Asian cuisines: try Malay *nasi lemak* and beef *rendang*.

You'll find yourself drinking vast amounts of fruit juice in Brunei (it's served in place of alcohol). Obviously, there is no bar scene here; the closest you get are the mocktail lounges in the top hotels. Still, if you have brought in your allowance of alcohol (and declared it at customs), top-end restaurants will often allow you to drink it with your meal.

Restaurants come and go with great frequency in Brunei. A selection of the current favourites is listed below.

Bandar Seri Begawan *p286, map p288*

Tasek Brasserie, Sheraton Utama, Jln Tasek, T224 4272. Open 0630-2400. Posh restaurant offering good Western dishes including ploughman's lunches, decent burgers and chunky sandwiches. Recommended.

Zaika, G24, Block C, Yayasan Complex, T223 0817. Daily 1130-1430 and 1800-2000. Excellent North Indian cuisine in pleasing wood-panelled surroundings (*zaika* means fine dining in Urdu). Try tandoori chicken or lamb (straight from an authentic oven) and Kashmiri *rogan josh*. Classical Indian lamps hang overhead, old Indian paintings adorn the walls, and gentle Indian music tinkles in the background. The menu is vast.

Ahan Thai, ground floor, Jubilee Plaza, Jln Kampong Kianggeh, T223 9599. Daily 1000-2345. Friendly place with a huge English menu of Thai dishes. Good seafood and some tasty Thai salads. The juices here are enormous. There's a huge TV and Wi-Fi access. Excellent value for money.

Babu's Kitchen, Jln Roberts. Daily 0600-1800. Spotless place doling out large plates of Chinese and Thai food to hungry office workers. Don't be put off by the Maggi noodles adverts on the windows outside.

De Royalle Café, Jln Sultan, 2nd floor, Wisma Setia, T222 0257. Open 24 hrs. This smart café offers simple Western meals, large filled baguettes and plenty of coffee and cakes. There's also outdoor seating with newspapers to browse and Wi-Fi access.

Mawar Coffee Garden, 95 Jln Pacancha, part of the **Brunei Hotel**. Solid and pleasant city coffee shop with Malay and Chinese cuisine and the standard selection of juices and snacks.

RMS Portview Seafood, Jln MacArthur (opposite Yayasan Complex), T223 1466. Daily 1000-2300. Set right on the riverfront. Cheaper café downstairs (Malay, Chinese and Western) and a more formal restaurant

upstairs serving Thai, Japanese and Chinese cuisine. Excellent steamboats.

CA Mohamed, Unit 202, Yayasan Complex, T223 2999. Daily 0700-2100. Speak to any native about their top city dining choices and this one invariably crops up everytime. Solid selection of *mamak* (Indian Muslim) dishes such as *mee mamak* and *murtabak*. Not good for the heart, but delightful for the belly.

Isma Jaya, 27 Jln Sultan, T222 0229. Daily 0700-2100. A great place for Indian Muslim food, such as *roti canai*, as well as good biryani and curries.

Fun Toast, Jln Sultan. Daily 0600-0700. Smart bakery with excellent set breakfasts with chunky toast. There is also a daily set lunch. Good place to fill up before heading out on a trip.

Seri Indah, Jln MacArthur, T224 3567. A simple *mamak* (Indian Muslim) restaurant serving delicious *roti kosong* and *teh tarik*. Situated opposite the waterfront wet market.

Bandar's suburbs *p293*

Fratini's, No 1, Centrepoint Foodcourt, Abdul Razak Complex, Gadong, T245 1300. Daily 1000-2300. Well-established Italian restaurant next door to the **Centrepoint Hotel**, with a big range of Italian dishes including lasagne, pizza and pasta dishes (gnocchi, too), along with steaks and seafood. Good weekday promotions make this place fair value.

Saffron, Unit 8, ground floor, Seri Kiulap Complex, T223 5888. Open 0830-2300. Take your wallet out for a thrashing at this place, which has a selection of heady flavours covering the east from the souqs of Lebanon to the humid climes of the Malay Archipelago. Very popular. Reservations necessary at weekends.

Escapade Sushi, Unit 4-5, Block C, Abdul Raza Complex (opposite **Centrepoint Hotel**), Gadong, T244 3012. Open 1100-1430 and 1800-2230. Popular Japanese eatery with sushi on a conveyer belt at very reasonable prices. There is another branch in the Q-Lap Complex.

Lee Loi Fatt Foodstall, 4 Bgn Haji Abdul Rahman, Kiulap, T223 6432. Open 1000-1800. Famed for its *laksa* and delicious *cucur udang* (fried prawns with battered yam served with peanut sauce) this place offers some intriguing Malay/Chinese fusion flavours.

Pondok Sari Wangi, Unit 12-13, Abdul Razak Complex, Gadong, T244 5045. Daily 1000-2200. Excellent spot for authentic Indonesian cuisine including delicious *ikan pannggang* and well known Javanese dishes such as *nasi timbel*. Recommended.

Dream Cones, ground floor, The Mall, Gadong. While not a restaurant, this ice-cream kiosk deserves a mention for its highly unusual flavours that anyone with a sweet tooth will want to try. This *gelateria* has durian, coconut and most interstingly, *teh tarik* flavours to try. Very popular.

Pureland Vegetarian, Unit 15, Bangunan Awang Ahmand bin Haji Hassan, Kiulap. Mon-Sat 0800-1400 and 1730-2100. Operating on a pay-what-you-want idea, customers can choose from a buffet of over 30 Chinese vegetarian dishes, drinks, soups and desserts. There is no cashier, only a donation box that diners put in what they feel the meal was worth. The food is tasty, healthy and the atmosphere highly convivial. Recommended.

Brunei Muara District *p294*

Li Gong, Empire Hotel & Country Club, Jerudong BG3122, T241 8888, ext 7329. Tue-Thu and Sun 1830-2230, Fri-Sat 1100-1500 and 1830-2230. Excellent Chinese cuisine, set in a pavilion surrounded by koi ponds. The menu covers specialities from every province in China. There's an all-you-can-eat buffet on Wed and steamboat on Thu.

Spaghettini, Empire Hotel & Country Club, Jerudong BG3122, T241 8888, ext 7368. Daily 1830-2300, also Mon and Wed 1130-1430. Mimics an Italian trattoria, with its own authentic, wood-fired oven and dough-flinging chefs. Perched at the top of the towering atrium at the **Empire Hotel**.

⊛ Festivals and events

Bandar Seri Begawan *p286, map p288*
Jan-Feb Chinese New Year. A 2-week celebration beginning with a family reunion dinner on New Year's Eve.
23 Feb National Day Celebrations. Celebration of Independence at the Hassanal Bolkiah National Stadium.
Mar-Apr The Prophet's Birthday. As well as religious functions, there's a procession through the streets of Bandar Seri Begawan.
31 May Royal Brunei Armed Forces Day. Celebrates the creation of the Royal Brunei Armed Forces, with military parades.
15 Jul The Sultan's Birthday. One of the biggest events in the national calendar and the only time when the grounds of the Istana Nural Iman are open to the public. Royal address and an investiture ceremony.
Aug-Sep Ramadan. The holy month, when Muslims abstain from eating and drinking between dawn and dusk. During fasting hours it is considered ill-mannered to eat, drink or smoke openly in public. The end of Ramadan is marked by the **Hari Raya Puasa** celebration, when families gather for a feast.

⊛ Entertainment

Brunei *p283, map p288*
Brunei is a dry country and Bandar Seri Begawan is virtually deserted in the evening, except for the suburb of Gadong with its lively *pasar malam*. This is open until late and is busy with Bruneians buying the local food on sale.

In the top hotels, you can sip mocktails in mock bars and listen to sedate local bands and twinkling pianos. The Jerudong theme park is about as lively as it gets when it comes to entertainment and even that is deadly quiet by Western standards.

Stumble across a remote longhouse, and you enter another world. Guests are entertained with gusto and will almost certainly be offered traditional rice wine (*tuak* in Iban), a drink so ingrained in indigenous heritage that the sultan has exempted it from the ban on alcohol. Certainly, in the towns of Brunei, entertainment is something that happens – if at all – behind closed doors.

Cinema

Like Singaporeans, the citizens of Brunei take their cinema pretty seriously. To catch the latest blockbuster head to **Seri Qlap Cineplex**, Level 2, Seri Q-Lap Mall, T223 2277, www.sqcbrunei.com or **The Mall Cineplex**, The Mall, Gadong, T242 2455. Francophiles will enjoy a visit to the Cine Club at the **Alliance Francaise**, 29, Simpang 130-15, Jln Telanai, T265 4245, every Thu, 2000.

O Shopping

Bandar Seri Begawan *p286, map p288*
Brunei's main shopping district is centred on the suburb of **Gadong**, 4 km from the centre of Bandar Seri Begawan. The principal shopping malls here are **Gadong Centrepoint** and **The Mall**, both on the main thoroughfare. In **Bandar** itself, shopping is focused on the elegant **Yayasan Complex**, which has everything from small boutiques and restaurants to a supermarket and an upmarket department store (**Hua Ho**).

Crafts

Traditional handicrafts include brassware, silverware, *keris* (ornate ceremonial daggers) and a type of *songket* known as *jong sarat* – a traditional cloth, hand woven with gold and silver thread. Bandar's **Arts and Handicraft Centre** (see page 292) sells all these, though the choice is limited. Each of the major shopping malls has one or two gift shops selling Southeast Asian crafts (again, prices are much higher than in Malaysia). The **Sheraton Utama** has upmarket gift and antiques shops.

Occasionally there are handicrafts for sale at the **Tamu Kianggeh** in Bandar Seri Begawan, though this is predominantly a food market. **Kampong Ayer** is another place where it is possible to find crafts and antiques (at one time, the water village thrived as a centre for cottage industries, with silversmiths, brass casters, blacksmiths, boat builders and *songket* weavers). You won't find anything on your own; ask the boatmen.

Markets

24-hr Weekend Market, Jln Sultan. This street comes alive at the weekends, with an evening market with stalls serving tasty food, clothes and accessories. It's a popular place for an evening stroll and a spot of people watching. Sat and Sun from 1800.
Rimba Horicultural Centre, Rimba. Daily 0800-1800. This is a popular spot for plant lovers, with a colourful array of indoor and outdoor plants and gardening equipment.
Tamu Gadong, in the Gadong shopping centre. The largest market in town selling fresh produce. This place really comes alive after dark. On Fri and Sun mornings between 0700 and 1200, plant fetishists descend to scoop up tropical plants for their verandas.
Tamu Kianggeh, right in the heart of town, on the bank of the Kianggeh River. This buzzing market sells handicrafts, medicinal herbs, cheap local fruit and vegetables and some interesting delicacies.

Tutong District *p298*

For indigenous handicrafts that are better priced than those in Bandar Seri Begawan, you could try the weekly *tamu* (open-air market) in Tutong, which starts Thu afternoon and finishes late morning on Fri.

▲ Activities and tours

Brunei *p283, map p288*
Jungle trekking

Jungle trekking is one of the main attractions for visitors. The best place is the **Ulu Temburong National Park** (see page 296), but there are plenty of other opportunities in each of Brunei's districts. The easiest (and often the cheapest) way of organizing a trip into the rainforest is through one of the Brunei-based tour operators (see below).

River trips
No trip to Brunei is complete without a *tambang* ride along the Brunei River (Sungai Brunei). These trips can combine tours of the water village with a water safari in search of proboscis monkeys. Any of the tour operators listed below can arrange a river trip and most operators guarantee sightings of proboscis monkeys. Once the location has been reached, the boatman will cut the engine and paddle quietly into the mangroves to allow for a close encounter with the monkeys. 2-hr monkey spotting trips start from B$65 (min 2 people) It is cheaper to head to the river and hire a boatman to take you down river to spot the monkeys. However, the boatmen won't guarantee a sighting. B$30 for a 1½-hr trip.

Sailing
The Royal Brunei Yacht Club, Serasa, T277 2011, www.therbyc.com. Offers sailing courses from their clubhouse in Serasa. There are also kayaks and canoes for rent. Visitors who are members of other sailing clubs can use the facilities here if their club has a reciprocal relationship. The clubhouse is a sociable spot to spend an evening and has a pool and restaurant.

Sports
There's a stunning 18-hole floodlit golf course, designed by Jack Nicklaus, at the **Empire Hotel & Country Club** (see page 303). The Country Club also has facilities for tennis, squash, badminton, 10-pin bowling and snooker. As far as leisure centres go, you won't beat the **Hassanal Bolkiah National Stadium**, built to Olympic specifications, with a track-and-field complex, a tennis centre, squash courts and a pool. As you might imagine, you'll have the place to yourself. The sports complex is situated close to the government offices, between the airport and the centre of Bandar Seri Begawan. There are also plenty of private sports clubs catering to the large expat population, but visitors are limited to hotel facilities.

Tour operators
Independent travel in Brunei is a little more complicated than it is in Malaysia. That's not to say that it is impossible – anyone can visit Ulu Temburong independently, for example, but it works out cheaper to go as part of an organized tour. Plus, it saves the hassle of applying for permits and organizing transport. Because Brunei is still in its infancy as a tourist destination, you're very unlikely to find yourself in a large tour group (more often than not, you'll have a guide to yourself; many of them are indigenous to the region and hugely knowledgeable). The major tour operators based in Brunei are listed below.
Century Travel Centre, first floor, Darussalam Complex, Jln Sultan, BSB, T222 1747, www.centurytravelcentre.com.
Freme Travel Services, Wisma Jaya, Jln Pemancha, BSB, T333 5025, www.freme.com. Recommended.
Ilufah Leisure Tours, 20A, Bangunan Awg. Hj Ahmad Awg. Hassan & Anak-Anak, Kiulap, Gadong, T223 3524, ilufah_aq@brudirect.com.
Intrepid Tours, PO Box 2234, T222 1685, tours@bruneibay.net. Largely specializing in adventure and wildlife trips.
Mas Sugara Travel Services, 1st floor, Complex Warisan, Mata Simpang 322, Jln Gadong, T242 3963, www.massugara.com.
Mona Florafauna Tours, Room 209, 1st floor, Kiaw Lian Building, Jln Pemancha, BSB, T223 0761, mft.brunei@gmail.com. Day trips to Temburong, monkey spotting and Selirong island mangrove park. Recommended.
Pan Bright Travel Services, Haji Ahmad Laksamana Building, 38-39 Jln Sultan, T224 0980, www.panbright.com.
Scuba-Tech International, Empire Hotel & Country Club (see page 303), T241 8888, www.scubatechintl.com.
Sunshine Borneo Tours, No 2, Simpang 146, Jln Kiarong, T244 6509, www.exploreborneo.com.

If you are looking for an independent guide, it is worth contacting the highly knowledgable and friendly **Danny Baldhead**, T880 1180, danny25174@yahoo.com. He takes tourists out on good-value trips to Kampong Air and beyond and has plenty of anecdotes and insight into life in Brunei.

Water sports
These aren't big in Brunei. Your best bet is to contact **Scuba-Tech International**, based at the Empire Hotel & County Club (see page 303). They can arrange parasailing, jet skiing, deep-sea fishing, sailing and scuba-diving (there are a number of wreck sites off Brunei's coast and around Labuan). Another company worth contacting is YBK Divers and Seasports, T872 2347, yeo-boonkiat@hotmail.com.

⊖ Transport

Bandar Seri Begawan *p286, map p288*
To explore Brunei in any depth, you really need to hire a car. Thanks to subsidized vehicles and cheap petrol, most Bruneians drive; as a result of this, the public transport system is far from comprehensive. There are no internal flights within Brunei (it's so small that flying would be impractical).

Air
AirAsia has daily flights to **Kota Kinabalu** and **KL**. Royal Brunei Airlines connects BSB with the following cities: Bangkok-Suvarnabhumi, Ho Chi Minh City, Hong Kong, Jakarta, Kota Kinabalu, Kuala Lumpur, Kuching, Manila, Singapore and Surabaya in Asia. Other airlines flying from BSB are MAS (**KL**, **KK**) and Silk Air and **Singapore Airlines** (both to **Singapore**).
   Airline offices Malaysia Airlines, Jln Sultan, T222 4141. **Royal Brunei Airlines**, PO Box 737, BS 8671, T221 2222, www.bruneiair.com. **Singapore Airlines**, Jln Sultan T224 4901. **Thai Airways**, T224 2991.

Boat
Boats, of course, are the main form of transport around **Kampong Ayer**. Small, speedy *tambang* depart from the jetty behind the **Yayasan Complex** from dawn until late at night. A short journey across to the water village should cost no more than B$2. Regular speedboats leave from the **Jln Residency** jetty in Bandar Seri Begawan to **Bangar**, the main town in Temburong District (hourly 0745-1630; B$15 return). Access upriver to the interior of Brunei is by indigenous longboat. Journeys need to be pre-arranged (best to speak to a tour operator, see page 308).
   To Malaysia There are 7 daily boats to **Labuan** sailing from Serasa Muara from 0730-1330 (B$16) with connecting departures to **Kota Kinabalu** (RM31). Travellers wishing to go all the way through to KK are advised to catch an early boat from Serasa Muara. Express bus No 33 runs from Jln Cator to Serasa Muara (30-45 mins, B$2), a taxi costs around B$40 for the trip. Speedboats also depart from the main jetty to **Labuan**, **Lawas** and **Limbang**.

Bus
Buses serve Bandar Seri Begawan and the surrounding Brunei Muara district fairly regularly during daylight hours. There are 6 bus routes: the Eastern, Western, Northern, Southern, Central and Circle Lines, each of which runs buses every 15-20 mins, 0630-1800. The handiest route is probably the Central Line, which links the main bus station in Bandar Seri Begawan (on Jln Cator) with **Gadong** and the Brunei Museum (B$1). Buses for **Muara** (B$3), **Tutong** (B$4), **Seria** (B$6) and **Kuala Belait** (B$7.50) leave less regularly from the Jln Cator bus station.
   International There are numerous overland international options from BSB: **To Indonesia** There is a daily bus departing for **Pontianak** at 0900 (at least 24 hrs, B$90). Enquire at the bus station on Jln Cator.

To Malaysia There is a daily bus to **KK** (8 hrs, B$40). Contact **Jesselton Express,** T718 3838. The bus goes via **Limbang**, **Lawas**, **Beaufort** and **Sipitang**.

If travelling to **Miri**, take one of the large blue or white buses to **Seria**. These leave every hour from Jln Cator (2 hrs, B$6). At Seria transfer to a Kuala Belait-bound minibus (30 mins, B$1). There are 5 daily buses to Miri via the somewhat convoluted border and river crossing from Kuala Belait (0730, 0930, 1100, 1330 and 1530, 2 hrs, B$10.20). Alternatively, there is now a service offered by Mr Foo and his son with a 7-seater Toyota departing BSB daily around 1500 and arriving in Miri around 1800. The fare is B$27. Seats can be booked through the **Dillenia Guesthouse** in Miri (see page 152) or by calling Mr Foo directly on T013-833 2231- Malaysian mobile number.

Car
To make the most of a trip to Brunei, it's best to hire a car. The major car hire firms operate out of the airport or Bandar Seri Begawan, and there are plenty of cheaper local firms to choose from, too.

Car hire Avis, Sheraton Utama Hotel (see sleeping, page 302), Jln Tasek, T222 7100; **Budget U Drive**, T234 5573 **Hertz,** Lot Q33, West Berakas Link, T239 0300 (airport T245 2244), www.hertz.com; **Qawi Enterprise**, PO Box 1322, Gadong, T234 0380.

Taxi
Metered taxis ferry people about Bandar and its suburbs, with fares set at B$3 for the first kilometre (B$4.50 2100-0600) and B$1 for every subsequent kilometre. For longer journeys, it makes more sense to hire a car. Taxis can be waved down. Otherwise call T222 2214 (**Bandar Seri Begawan**); T333 4581 (**Kuala Belait**); T322 2030 (**Seria**); T234 3671 (**airport**).

ⓘ Directory

Bandar Seri Begawan *p286, map p288*
Banks Banking hours are Mon-Fri 0900-1500, Sat 0900-1100. **Citibank NA**, Jln Sultan, T224 3983; **HSBC**, Jln Sultan, T224 2305; **Malaysian Banking Berhad**, 1 Jln MacArthur, T224 2494; **Overseas Union Bank**, RBA Plaza, Jln Sultan, T222 5477; **Standard Chartered Bank**, Jln Sultan, T224 2386. **Embassies and consulates** Australia, Dar Takaful IBB Utama, Jln Pemancha, T222 9435, austhicom.brunei@ dfat.gov.bn; **Canada**, 5th floor, 1 Jln McArthur, T222 0043, hicomcda@brunet.bn; Indonesia, Lot 4498, Simpang 528, Kg Sungai Hanching Baru, Jln Muara, T2330180, kbribsb@pso. brunet.bn; **Malaysia**, 61 Simpang 396, Kampong Sungai Akar, Jln Kebangsaan, T238 1095-9, mwbrunei@brunet.bn; **Singapore**, 8 Simpang 74, Jln Subok, T226 2741, singa@ brunet.bn; **UK**, Level 2, Block D, Yayasan Complex, T222 2231, brithc@brunet.bn; **USA**, 3rd floor, Teck Guan Plaza, Jln Sultan, T222 0384, amembbsb@brunet.bn. **Emergencies** Ambulance T991; **Police** T993; **Fire** T995. **Internet** Deltech Communications, Unit 5, ground floor, Bangunan Hj Mohm Salleh, Simpang 103, Jln Gadong, T245 3808, daily 0900-2300, B$5 per hr; **E-Mart Cyber Junction**, GP Properties Building, Jln Gadong, T242 6010, daily 0800-2300, B$3 per hr; **KASCO IT Centre**, ground floor, 5 Jln Ong Sum Ping, T222 3541; **LA Ling Cyber Café**, 2nd floor, Yayasan Complex, T223 2800, daily 0930-2130, B$3 per hr. **Laundry** Superkleen, 95 Jln Pemancha, T224 2372. **Medical services** Jerudong Park Medical Centre, Jerudong, T261 1433. RIPAS Hospital, Jln Putera Al-Muhtadee Billah, T224 2424. **Post office** General Post Office Building, corner of Jln Sultan and Jln Elizabeth Dua, Mon-Thu and Sat 0745-1630, Fri 0800-1100 and 1400-1600. **Telephone** Pre-paid phonecards called 'Hallo Kad' are widely available and can be used with any phone (including phone booths). Coin phones are operable with 10- and 20-cent coins. Directory enquiries: T113.

Background

History

Brunei's early history is obscure, but although precise dates have been muddied by time, there is no doubt that the sultanate's early prosperity was rooted in trade. As far back as the seventh century, China was importing birds' nests from Brunei, and Arab, Indian, Chinese and other Southeast Asian traders were regularly passing through. Links with Chinese merchants were strongest: they traded silk, metals, stoneware and porcelain for Brunei's jungle produce: bezoar stones, hornbill ivory, timber and birds' nests. Chinese coins dating from the eighth century have been unearthed at Kota Batu, 3 km from Bandar Seri Begawan. Large quantities of Chinese porcelain dating from the Tang, Sung and Ming dynasties have also been found. The sultanate was on the main trade route between China and the western reaches of the Malayan archipelago and by the 10th to the 13th centuries trade was booming. By the turn of the 15th century there was a sizeable Chinese population settled in Brunei.

It is thought that in around 1370 Sultan Mohammad became first Sultan. In the mid-1400s, Sultan Awang Alak ber Tabar married a Melakan princess and converted to Islam. Brunei already had trade links with Melaka and exported camphor, rice, gold and sago in exchange for Indian textiles. But it was not until an Arab, Sharif Ali, married Sultan Awang Alak's niece that Islam spread beyond the confines of the royal court. Sharif Ali – who is said to have descended from the Prophet Mohammad – became Sultan Berkat. He consolidated Islam, converted the townspeople, built mosques and set up a legal system based on Islamic Sharia law. Trade flourished and Brunei assumed the epithet Darussalam (the abode of peace).

The golden years

The coastal Melanaus quickly embraced the Muslim faith, but tribal groups in the interior were largely unaffected by the spread of Islam and retained their animist beliefs. As Islam spread along the coasts of North and West Borneo, the sultanate expanded its political and commercial sphere of influence. By the 16th century, communities all along the coasts of present-day Sabah and Sarawak were paying tribute to the Sultan. The sultanate became the centre of a minor empire whose influence stretched beyond the coasts of Borneo to many surrounding islands, including the Sulu archipelago and Mindanao in the Philippines. Even Manila had to pay tribute to the Sultan's court.

On 8 July 1521 Antonio Pigafetta, an Italian historian on Portuguese explorer Ferdinand Magellan's expedition, visited the Sultanate of Brunei and described it as a rich, hospitable and powerful kingdom with an established Islamic monarchy and strong regional influence. Pigafetta published his experiences in his book, *The First Voyage Around the World*. He writes about a sophisticated royal court and the lavishly decorated Sultan's palace. Brunei Town was reported to be a large, wealthy city of 25,000 households. The townspeople lived in houses built on stilts over the water.

In 1526 the Portuguese set up a trading post in Brunei and from there conducted trade with the Moluccas – the famed Spice Islands – via Brunei. At the same time, more Chinese traders immigrated to Brunei to service the booming trade between Melaka and Macau and to trade with Pattani on the South Thai isthmus.

But relations with the Spaniards were not so warm; the King of Spain and the Sultan of Brunei had mutually exclusive interests in the Philippines. In the 1570s Spaniards attacked several important Muslim centres and in March 1578, the captain-general of the Philippines,

Francesco de Sande, led a naval expedition to Brunei, demanding the Sultan pay tribute to Spain and allow Roman Catholic missionaries to proselytize. The Sultan would have none of it and a battle ensued off Muara, which the Spaniards won. They captured the city, but within days the victors were stopped in their tracks by a cholera epidemic and had to withdraw. In 1579 they returned and once again did battle off Muara, but this time they were defeated.

The sun sets on an empire

Portugal came under Spanish rule in 1580 and Brunei lost a valuable European ally: the sultanate was raided by the Spanish again in 1588 and 1645. But by then Brunei's golden age was history and the Sultan's grip on his further-flung dependencies had begun to slip.

In the 1660s civil war erupted in Brunei due to feuding between princes and, together with additional external pressures of European expansionism, the once-mighty sultanate all but collapsed. Only a handful of foreign merchants dealt with the sultanate and Chinese traders passed it by. Balanini pirates from Sulu and Illanun pirates from Mindanao posed a constant threat to the Sultan and any European traders or adventurers foolhardy enough to take them on. In return for protection from these sea-borne terrorists, the Sultan offered the British East India Company a base on the island of Labuan in Brunei Bay in the late 1600s, although the trading post failed to take off.

For 150 years, Brunei languished in obscurity. By the early 1800s, Brunei's territory did not extend much beyond the town boundaries, although the Sarawak River and the west coastal strip of North Borneo officially remained under the Sultan's sway.

James Brooke – the man who would be king

The collection of mini-river states that made up what was left of the Sultanate were ruled by the *pangeran*, the lesser nobles of the Brunei court. In the 1830s Brunei chiefs had gone to the Sarawak valley to organize the mining and trade in the high-grade antimony ore, which had been discovered there in 1824. They recruited Dayaks as workers and founded Kuching. But, with the support of local Malay chiefs, the Dayaks rebelled against one of the Brunei noblemen, the corrupt, Pangeran Makota, one of the Rajah's 14 brothers. By all accounts, Makota was a nasty piece of work, known for his exquisite charm and diabolical cunning.

It was into this troubled riverine mini-state, in armed rebellion against Makota, that the English adventurer James Brooke sailed in 1839. Robert Payne, in *The White Rajahs of Sarawak*, describes Makota as a "princely racketeer" and "a man of satanic gifts, who practised crimes for pleasure". Makota confided to Brooke: "I was brought up to plunder the Dayaks, and it makes me laugh to think that I have fleeced a tribe down to its cooking pots." With Brooke's arrival, Makota realized his days were numbered.

In 1837, the Sultan of Brunei, Omar Ali Saiffuddin, had dispatched his uncle, Pengiran Muda Hashim, to contain the rebellion. He failed, and turned to Brooke for help. In return for his services, Brooke demanded to be made governor of Sarawak.

After he had been formally installed in his new role by Sultan Omar, Brooke set about building his own empire. Brooke exploited rivalries between various aristocratic factions of Brunei's royal court which climaxed in the murder of Pengiran Muda Hashim and his family.

No longer required in Sarawak, Hashim had returned to Brunei to become chief minister and heir apparent. He was murdered – along with 11 other princes and their families – by Sultan Omar. The Sultan and his advisers had felt threatened by their presence, so they disposed of Hashim to prevent a coup. The massacre incensed Brooke. In June 1846 his British ally, Admiral Sir Thomas Cochrane, bombarded Brunei Town, set it ablaze and chased the Sultan into the jungle.

Cochrane wanted to proclaim Brooke the sultan of Brunei, but decided, in the end, to offer Sultan Omar protection if he cleaned up his act and demonstrated his loyalty to Queen Victoria. After several weeks, the humiliated Sultan emerged from the jungle and swore undying loyalty to the Queen. As penance, Sultan Omar formally ceded the island of Labuan to the British crown on 18 December 1846. Although Brunei forfeited more territory in handing Labuan to the British, the Sultan calculated that he would benefit from a direct relationship with Whitehall. It seemed that London was becoming almost as concerned as he was about Brooke's expansionist instincts. A Treaty of Friendship and Commerce was signed between Britain and Brunei in 1847 in which the Sultan agreed not to cede any more territory to any power, except with the consent of the British government.

The Sultan's shrinking shadow

The treaty did not stop Brooke. His mission, since arriving in Sarawak, had been the destruction of the pirates who specialized in terrorizing Borneo's coastal communities. Because he knew the Sultan of Brunei was powerless to contain them, he calculated that their liquidation would be his best bargaining chip with the Sultan, and would enable him to prise yet more territory from the Sultan's grasp. Over the years he engaged the dreaded Balanini and Illanun pirates from Sulu and Mindanao as well as the so-called Sea-Dayaks and Brunei Malays, who regularly attacked Chinese, Bugis and other Asian trading ships off the Borneo coast. As a result, Sultan Abdul Mumin of Brunei ceded to Brooke the Saribas and Skrang districts, which became the Second Division of Sarawak in 1853 and, eight years later, he handed over the region that was to became the Third Division of Sarawak.

But by now the Sultan was as worried about territorial encroachment by the British as he was about Brooke and as a counterweight to both, granted a 10-year concession to much of what is modern-day Sabah to the American consul in Brunei. This 72,500 sq km tract of North Borneo later became British North Borneo and is now the state of Sabah.

With the emergence of British North Borneo, the British reneged on their agreement with the Sultan of Brunei again and the following year approved Brooke's annexation of the Baram river basin by Sarawak, which became its Fourth Division. The Sarawak frontier was advancing ever northwards.

In 1884 a rebellion broke out in Limbang and Rajah Charles Brooke refused to help the Sultan restore order. Sultan Hashim Jalilul Alam Aqamaddin, who acceded to the throne in 1885, wrote to Queen Victoria complaining that the British had not kept their word. Sir Frederick Weld was dispatched to mediate and his visit resulted in the Protectorate Agreement of 1888 between Brunei and Britain, which gave London full control of the Sultanate's external affairs. When Brooke annexed Limbang in 1890 and united it with the Trusan Valley to form the Fifth Division of Sarawak, while the Queen's men looked on, the Sultan was reduced to a state of disbelief. His sultanate had now been completely surrounded by Brooke's Sarawak.

From sultanate to oilfield

In 1906 a British Resident was appointed to the Sultan's court to advise on all aspects of government except traditional customs and religion. In his book *By God's Will*, Lord Chalfont suggests that the British government's enthusiastic recommitment to the Sultanate through the treaty may have been motivated by Machiavellian desires. "More cynical observers have suggested that the new-found enthusiasm of the British government may not have been entirely unconnected with the discovery of oil ... around the turn of the century." Oil exploration started in 1899, although it was not until the discovery of the Seria oilfield in 1929 that it merited commercial exploitation. Historian

Mary Turnbull notes the quirk of destiny that ensured the survival of the micro-sultanate: "It was ironic that the small area left unswallowed by Sarawak and North Borneo should prove to be the most richly endowed part of the old sultanate."

The Brunei oilfield fell to the Japanese on 18 December 1942. Allied bombing and Japanese sabotage prior to the sultanate's liberation caused considerable damage to oil and port installations and urban areas, necessitating a long period of reconstruction in the late 1940s and early 1950s. Australian forces landed at Muara Beach on 10 July 1945. A British Military Administration ruled the country for a year, before Sultan Sir Ahmad Tajuddin took over.

In 1948 the governor of Sarawak, which was by then a British crown colony, was appointed high commissioner for Brunei, but the Sultanate remained what one commentator describes as "a constitutional anachronism". In September 1959 the UK resolved this by withdrawing the Resident and signing an agreement with the Sultan giving Whitehall responsibility for Brunei's defence and foreign affairs.

Because of his post-war influence on the development of Brunei, Sultan Omar was variously referred to as the father and the architect of modern Brunei. He shaped his sultanate into the anti-Communist, non-democratic state it is today and, being an Anglophile, held out against independence from Britain. By the early 1960s, Whitehall was enthusiastically promoting the idea of a North Borneo Federation, encompassing Sarawak, Brunei and British North Borneo. But Sultan Omar did not want anything to do with the neighbouring territories as he felt Brunei's interests were more in keeping with those of peninsular Malaysia. The proposed federation would have been heavily dependent on Brunei's oil wealth. Kuala Lumpur did not need much persuasion that Brunei's joining the Federation of Malaysia was an excellent idea.

Democrats versus autocrat

In Brunei's first general election in 1962, the left-wing Brunei People's Party (known by its Malay acronym, PRB) swept the polls. The party's election ticket had marked an end to the Sultan's autocratic rule, the formation of a democratic government and immediate independence. Aware that there was a lot at stake, the Sultan refused to let the PRB form a government. The Sultan's emergency powers, under which he banned the PRB, which were passed in 1962, remain in force, enabling him to rule by decree.

On 8 December 1962, the PRB – backed by the Communist North Kalimantan National Army, effectively its military wing – launched a revolt. The Sultan's insistence on British military protection paid off as the disorganized rebellion was quickly put down with the help of a Gurkha infantry brigade and other British troops. Within four days the British troops had pushed the rebels into Limbang, where the hard core holed up. By 12 December the revolt had been crushed and the vast majority of the rebels disappeared into the interior, pursued by the 7th Gurkha Rifles and Kelabit tribesmen.

Early in 1963, negotiations over Brunei joining the Malaysian Federation ran into trouble, to the disappointment of the British. The Malaysian prime minister, the late Tunku Abdul Rahman, wanted the Sultanate's oil and gas revenues to feed the federal treasury in Kuala Lumpur and made the mistake of making his intentions too obvious. The Tunku envisaged central government exercising absolute control over oil revenues – in the way it controls the oil wealth of Sabah and Sarawak today. Unhappy with this proposal and unwilling to become 'just another Malaysian sultan', Omar abandoned his intention to join the Federation.

Meanwhile, Indonesia's Sukarno was resolute in his objective of crushing the new Federation of Malaysia and launched his *Konfrontasi* between 1963 and 1966. Brunei offered itself as an operational base for the British army. But while Brunei supported

Malaysia against Indonesia, relations between them became very strained following the declaration of the Federation in September 1963.

In 1975 Kuala Lumpur sponsored the visit of a PRB delegation to the UN, to propose a resolution calling on Brunei to hold elections, abolish restrictions on political parties and allow political exiles to return. In 1976 Bruneian government supporters protested against Malaysian 'interference' in Bruneian affairs. Nonetheless, the resolution was adopted by the UN in November 1977, receiving 117 votes in favour and none against. Britain abstained. Relations with Malaysia warmed after the death of Prime Minister Tun Abdul Razak in 1976, leaving the PRB weak and isolated. The party still operates in exile, although it is a spent force. Throughout the difficult years, the Sultan had used his favourite sport to conduct what was dubbed 'polo diplomacy', fostering links with like-minded Malaysian royalty despite the tensions in official bilateral relations.

By 1967, Britain's Labour government was pushing Sultan Omar to introduce a democratic system of government. Instead, the Sultan opted to abdicate in favour of his 21-year-old son, Hassanal Bolkiah. In November 1971, a new treaty was signed with Britain. London retained its responsibility for Brunei's external affairs, but its advisory role applied only to defence. The Sultan was given full control of all internal matters. Under a separate agreement, a battalion of British Gurkhas was stationed in the Sultanate. As Bruneians grew richer, the likelihood of another revolt receded.

Independence

Britain was keen to disentangle itself from the 1971 agreement: maintaining the protectorate relationship was expensive and left London open to criticism that it was maintaining an anachronistic colonial relationship. Brunei did not particularly relish the prospect of independence as, without British protection, it would be at the mercy of its more powerful neighbours. But in January 1979, having secured Malaysian and Indonesian assurances that they would respect its independence, the government signed another agreement with London, allowing for the Sultanate to become independent from midnight on 31 December 1983 after 150 years of close involvement with Britain and 96 years as a protectorate.

Politics

In January 1984, Sultan Hassanal Bolkiah declared Brunei a 'democratic' monarchy. Three years later, he told his official biographer Lord Chalfont: "I do not believe that the time is ripe for elections ... When I see some genuine interest among the citizenry, we may move towards elections." Independence changed little: absolute power is still vested in the Sultan, who mostly relies on his close family for advice. Following Independence, the Sultan took up the offices of prime minister, finance minister and minister of home affairs. In 1986, he relinquished the latter two, but appointed himself defence minister. He also took over responsibility for finance on the resignation of his brother, Prince Jefri (see box, page 291).

In May 1985 the Brunei National Democratic Party (BNDP) was officially registered. Its aim was to introduce a parliamentary democracy under the Sultan. But just before the Malays-only party came into being, the government announced that its employees would not be allowed to join any other party. In one stroke, the BNDP's potential membership was halved. In early 1986, the Brunei United National Party, an offshoot of the BNDP, was formed. Unlike its parent, its manifesto was multi-racial. The Sultan allowed these parties to exist until 1988 when he proscribed all parties and imprisoned, without trial, two BNDP leaders.

In the early 1990s, the Sultan was reported to have become increasingly worried about internal security and about Brunei's image abroad. Eight long-term political detainees, in prison since the abortive 1962 coup, were released in 1990. The last political detainee, the former deputy leader of the Brunei People's Party (PRB), Zaini Ahmad, is said to have written to the Sultan from prison following the releases. He apparently apologized for the 1962 revolt and called for the democratically elected Legislative Council – as outlined in the 1959 constitution – to be reconvened. To coincide with the Sultan's 50th birthday in 1996, Zaini Ahmad was released from prison. The exiled PRB has been greatly weakened and increasingly isolated since Brunei's relations with Malaysia became more cordial following the sultanate's accession to the Association of Southeast Asian Nations (ASEAN) in 1984 and clearly the Sultan and his adviser no longer feel threatened by the party.

Foreign relations

Brunei joined ASEAN on Independence in 1984. Prince Mohammed, the foreign affairs minister, is said to be one of the brightest, more thoughtful members of the royal family, but in foreign policy, Brunei is timid and goes quietly along with its ASEAN partners. Relations with Malaysia are greatly improved, but the sultanate's closest ties in the region, especially in fiscal and economic matters, are with Singapore. Their relationship was initially founded on their mutual distrust of the Malaysian Federation, which Brunei never joined and Singapore left two years after its inception in 1965. Singapore provides assistance in the training of Brunei's public servants and their currencies are linked.

As an ASEAN member, on good terms with its neighbours, Brunei doesn't have many enemies. But if its Scorpion tanks, ground-to-air missiles and helicopter gunships seem a little redundant, consider the experience of another oil-rich Islamic mini-state: Kuwait.

Modern Brunei

The last years of the 20th century saw Brunei's waning fortunes come to a head. By 2001, the country's per capita GDP was down almost 50% on what it had been at the time of Brunei's Independence. The troubles began with the Asian economic crisis of 1997 and were further compounded by falling oil prices and by the collapse of the country's biggest non-oil company, Amedeo Development Corporation, which had run up debts of US$3.5 billion. Amedeo had been owned and run by the sultan's brother and finance minister, Prince Jefri, a man of excessive extravagance and little business acumen (see box, page 291). The prince resigned from his position as finance minister, and a national scandal followed, with the sultan eventually suing his brother for siphoning billions of dollars from the Brunei Investment Agency, for which the prince had served as chairman. The brothers eventually settled out of court, but the publicity has had lasting consequences, damaging Brunei's credibility with foreign investors. Brunei's shaken economy has now stabilized, but the whole episode has served to highlight just how overdependent Brunei is on oil (at present Brunei's economy relies almost exclusively on exports of oil and LNG – liquefied natural gas). As oil prices peak and trough, so do Brunei's fortunes. More worryingly, the nation's oil and gas reserves are expected to dry up in 2018 and 2033 respectively. This vulnerability has prompted the sultan to initiate reforms – both economic and political. Diversification of the economy has now become a priority and the sultan has curbed government spending while encouraging the growth of privatization.

One of his primary visions was to transform Brunei into an Offshore Financial Haven (in the vein of Bermuda or the Isle of Man) and the government has now achieved this. So-called Islamic Finance is also being targeted. In 2000, the BIFC (Brunei International Finance Centre) began trading successfully.

Ecotourism, meanwhile, is another of Brunei's trump cards for the future (more than 70% of the land mass remains cloaked in virgin rainforest). Still, many commentators point out that visitor figures are likely to remain low until the government eases laws on the prohibition of alcohol. Perhaps more significant has been the political fallout of Brunei's economic problems. The new-found desire to attract investors and tourists has forced the sultan to reconsider Brunei's international image. There has been a shift away from the Islamic conservatism of the 1990s – a fact underlined by the dismissal in 2005 of the education minister, a conservative Islamist whose introduction of a strict religious education had become increasingly unpopular. Prior to this, the first tentative move towards 21st-century democracy was instigated, with the appointment of a new legislative council. In September 2004, the country's parliament reopened for the first time since Independence. Though no political parties are allowed, a new 45-seat council was called for, with 15 elected members. To all intents and purposes, the sultan still retains authoritarian control over his kingdom – just as his ancestors have for 600 years. Nevertheless, the pending elections are being viewed as the first step towards a modern Brunei – a Brunei without oil, but with a new politics of consensus. This 45-seat council has been whittled down to a proposed 20 seats, including 15 elected members and the remainder chosen by the Sultan. However, as of 2010, no election has been called. In the well-planned comfort of Brunei, democracy doesn't seem to be something citizens are clamouring for.

Population

In the days of Charles Brooke, the sultanate had a population of about 20,000. It now stands at 388,190 (January 2009 estimate). The city-state of Singapore has more than 10 times as many people. Today 60% of the country's population lives in towns; more than half is aged under 20 and a third is under 14. At 2.2% a year, Brunei has one of the fastest growing populations in the region; it also has the region's lowest death rate and second lowest infant mortality rate after Singapore; Bruneians' average life expectancy is 75. About 67% of the population is Malay, 11% Chinese, 3% indigenous tribal groups and 19% other (see People, page 319); there are also some 100,000 expatriate workers – both professionals and labourers. The average density of population is low: about 66 people per sq km; most are concentrated along the narrow coastal belt.

Land and environment

Geography and geology

Brunei Darussalam lies about 400 km north of the equator, between four degrees and five degrees north, on the northwest coast of Borneo. The sultanate has a 160 km-long coastline, facing the South China Sea. The country is divided into four districts: Brunei/Muara, Tutong, Belait and Temburong.

Territorially, modern Brunei is the rump of what was once a sprawling empire. Today the sultanate has a land area of 5769 sq km, a pinprick on the map, about twice the size of Luxembourg. In 1981 the government bought a cattle ranch at Willeroo, in Australia's Northern Territory, which is larger than the whole of Brunei. As a country, it is a geographical absurdity; its two wedges of territory are separated by Limbang, ceded to the expansionist Charles Brooke, Rajah of Sarawak in 1890. Bruneians commute between the Temburong district and Bandar Seri Begawan in speedboats nicknamed 'flying coffins'.

Most of Brunei occupies a low alluvial coastal plain. There are four main rivers, flowing north into the South China Sea. The coastal lowlands and river valleys are characterized by a flat or gently undulating landscape, rarely rising more than 15 m above sea level. The coastline is mainly sandy except for a stretch of rocky headlands between Muara and Pekan Tutong. These cliffs rise to a height of about 30 m, where the north coastal hills meet the South China Sea. Further west, the Andulau Hills stand at the north end of a watershed that separates the drainage basins of the Belait and Tutong.

Towards the interior of West Brunei, along the border with Sarawak and in South Temburong district, it gets much hillier. In West Brunei there are two upland areas, comprised of sandstones and shale: the Ladan Hills run north to south between the Tutong and Limbang basins. Bukit Bedawan is the highest of these, at 529 m. In Belait district, near the border with Sarawak, are the Labi Hills – the highest being Bukit Teraja at 417 m. The south half of Temburong district is much more mountainous, with deep, narrow valleys and several hills of over 600 m. The highest of these is Bukit Pagon at 1850 m, although the summit itself is actually outside Brunei.

The Seria oilfield, the source of Brunei's liquidity, lies on a narrow anticline, a quarter of which is submerged by the sea. All the oil comes from a strip just 13 km long and 2.5 km wide. The oil is in fractured blocks of sandstone between 240 m and 3000 m below the surface. Some of the oil under the sea is accessed by wells drilled from the shore which reach more than 1.5 km out to sea.

Climate

Brunei is only five degrees north of the equator and so is characterized, like the rest of North and West Borneo, by consistently hot and sticky weather: uniform temperature, high humidity (average 82%) and regular rainfall.

Daily temperatures average at 28°C. Midday temperatures rarely exceed 35°C; at night it is unusual for the temperature to dip below 21°C. The average daily minimum temperature is 23°C, the maximum 32°C.

Rainfall is well distributed throughout the year but there are two distinct seasons: there is less rainfall between February and August, and the rainy season sets in during September and runs through to the end of January. The northeast monsoon peaks in December and January and is characterized by short-lived violent downpours. Even during the monsoon season, though, there is a 50% chance of it not raining each day and a daily average of seven hours of sunshine. The annual average rainfall is over 2500 mm a year, nearly five times that of London or more than double New York's annual rainfall. The south interior region, including Temburong district, is wetter, with up to 4060 mm a year. The west coast areas get between 2540 and 3300 mm of rainfall a year. In Bandar Seri Begawan, the average annual rainfall is 2921 mm.

Flora and fauna

Like much of the neighbouring Malaysian state of Sarawak, the low-lying areas of Brunei are characterized by peat swamp forest which is unsuited to agriculture. In parts the peat is up to 9 m thick and cannot support permanent agriculture. About 70% of Brunei is still covered in lush virgin jungle. If secondary forest – known as *belukar* – is included, about 80% of Brunei's land area is still forested.

Apart from the peat swamp forest, Brunei has areas of heath forest (*kerangas*) on sandy soils near the coast, and mangrove, which grows on the tidal mudflats around Brunei Bay and in the Belait and Tutong estuaries. The most common mangrove tree is the bakau, which grows to a height of about 9 m and has stilt roots to trap sediment. The *bakau* was the source of *cutch* – a dye made from boiling its bark, and used in leather tanning, which was produced at Brunei Bay until the 1950s. Bakau wood also made useful piles for stilt houses in Bandar Seri Begawan's Kampong Ayer as it is resistant to rotting, and excellent charcoal. Also on the coast, between Kuala Belait and Muara, are stretches of casuarina forest.

Away from the coastal plain and the river valleys, the forest changes to lowland rainforest – or mixed dipterocarp forest – which supports at least eight commercial hardwood species. The *Dipterocarpacae* family forms the jungle canopy, 30-50 m above the ground. Timber from Brunei's jungle is used locally – none is exported. By 1990, logging firms were required to use sustainable management techniques and within a year, felling was cut to half the 1989 level. Forest reserves have been expanded and cover 320,000 ha. Indeed, Brunei has some of Southeast Asia finest forests – despite its small size when compared with the neighbouring Malaysian states of Sabah and Sarawak and with Indonesian Borneo (Kalimantan).

Wildlife

Brunei's jungle has been left largely intact; thanks to its oil wealth there is no need to exploit the forest. Loggers and shifting cultivators have been less active than they have in neighbouring territories and the forest fauna have been less disturbed. Their only disruptions come from a few upriver tribespeople, a handful of wandering Penan hunter-gatherers, the odd scientist and the occasional platoon of muddied soldiers on jungle warfare training exercises.

Relatively few tourists venture into Brunei's jungle as Sarawak's nearby national parks are much more accessible and better known. The year of 1996, however, marked the opening of the Ulu Temburong National Park with its network of wooden walkways and a fantastic canopy walkway. What's more, Brunei is the best place for spotting the rare proboscis monkey (see box, page 295). For those who have access to a car, there are also several jungle trails on Brunei's doorstep.

Brunei boasts much of Borneo's jungle exotica. For oil explorers and their families in the early 1900s, some local residents proved more daunting than others. Up until the 1960s, encounters with large crocodiles were commonplace in Brunei, and in the oil town of Seria they posed a constant menace to the local community. In August 1959 Brunei Shell Petroleum was forced to recruit a professional crocodile catcher. Mat Yassin bin Hussin claimed to have caught and destroyed more than 700 crocodiles in a career spanning 40 years, the largest being a highly unlikely 8.5-m long man-eater that had devoured 12 Ibans south of Kuala Belait.

Mat Yassin's technique was to sprinkle gold dust into the river as part of a magic ritual, then to dangle chickens over bridges on baited rattan hooks. According to GC Harper, a Seria oilfield historian, Mat Yassin would wait until a crocodile jumped for the bait and then he would "blow down its snout with the aid of a blowpipe to make the strong reptile weak. It could then be dragged up the riverbank and its jaws tied before it was destroyed." Mat Yassin silenced cynics when he landed two man-eaters in as many days and said he had come across an old white crocodile which was considered sacred; he refused to touch it because it "could never be destroyed either by bullets or by magic".

Culture

People

Brunei 'Malays', who make up 67% of the sultanate's population, are mostly Kedayans or Melanaus, indigenous to north Borneo. There was no great migration of Malays from the peninsula. Similarly, few Iban migrated into what is modern Brunei, although in the 19th century, they pushed up to the middle reaches of Sarawak's rivers, which in those days came under the sultanate's ambit. Ibans, Muruts, Kedayans, Dayaks and even Dusuns are all represented in the 3% of the population labelled 'indigenous tribal groups' (for more detail on individual tribal groups, see page 370).

Today, most Bruneian Malays are well off and well educated; more than half of them have secure government jobs. Car ownership in Brunei is a telling indicator of Bruneians' affluence: the country has one of the highest car population ratios in the world. Recognizing that things might get out of hand, in 1995 the authorities introduced a new car tax to try and curb Brunei's love affair with the automobile. The standard of living is high by Southeast Asian standards although there are poorer communities living in Kampong Ayer and Kampong Kianggeh (near the open market). Many of these are recent immigrants – there is a high level of illegal immigration from the neighbouring states of Sabah and Sarawak as well as from Kalimantan.

The government policy of 'Bruneization' discriminates positively in favour of the Malays and against the Chinese, who make up 11% of the population. Most of the Chinese are fairly wealthy as they account for the vast majority of Brunei's private sector businesspeople. Unlike the Malays, the Chinese did not automatically become citizens of Brunei at Independence, even if they could trace their ancestry back several generations. The question of citizenship is very important as only Bruneian citizens can enjoy the benefits of the welfare state: free education, health care, subsidized housing and government jobs.

Religion

Brunei is a Sunni Muslim monarchy; the state motto, 'Always render service by God's guidance', is emblazoned on the crescent on Brunei's national flag. Islam appears to have been firmly established in the Sultanate by the mid-15th century. Today it is the official religion and a religious council advises the Sultan, who is head of the Islamic faith in Brunei, on all Islamic matters.

Arts and crafts

Brass is said to have been introduced into Brunei in the late 15th century, when the Sultanate became particularly famous for its brass cannon, which were used in battle and to convey messages between villages about deaths, births and festivities, such as the beginning and end of Ramadan. The 500 cannon and guns in the Brunei Museum are largely of local manufacture. Brass cannon and gongs were items of currency and barter and were often used in dowries, particularly among the tribal Belaits and Dusuns. Brassware is a prized family heirloom, and was the basis of fines in the traditional legal system. In 1908 there were more than 200 brass workers in Brunei, but by the mid-1970s their numbers had reportedly fallen to fewer than 10. Today, traditional casting by the 'lost wax' technique is being revived. Brunei's **silversmiths** have a good reputation for their intricate designs, betelnut boxes being a speciality. **Gold jewellery**, mostly 22 and 24 carat is also reasonable.

The best known local **textile** is *Kain Jong Sarat*, a cotton sarong, usually about 2 m in length, woven with more than 1000 gold threads on a handloom. Today Jong Sarat are only used on ceremonial occasions. The *Sukma-Indera* is distinguished by its multi-coloured floral patterns, while the *Tenunan* is woven with gold thread and worn by men round the waist on Hari Raya Aidil Adha; it can cost up to B$1000.

Contents

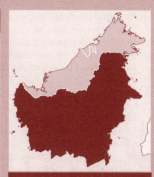

Footprint features

★ **Don't miss ...**
1 Banjarmasin, page 325.
2 Martapura jewellery shops and Cempaka diamond fields, page 328.
3 Tanjung Puting National Park, page 330.
4 Meratus Mountains, page 337.
5 Mahakam River, page 345.

*Celebes
Sea*

Semporna
Tawau
Nunukan
Tarakan
Tanjung Redeb
Sangkulirang

Tanjungselor
Partit Baru SABAH Kalabakan
Amo
Long Seridan
Bukit Batu
Bali (2082m)
Bario

BRUNEI
Tagala
Marudi
Long
Terawan
Limbang
Niah
Caves

Pelawanbesar
Sepasu
KALTIM
Muarawahau
Long Iram
Kutai
National Park
Tenggarong
Samarinda
Balikpapan

Pagatan
Pulau Laut

Muara
Muntai
Lempong
Meratus Mountains
KALSEL

SARAWAK
Belaga
Kapit
MALAYSIA
Long
Nawang
Muller
Range
Apo Kayan
Mahakam
Pegunungan

Amuntai
Martapura
Banjarmasin

Bintulu
Tatau
Mukah
Sibu
R Baling
Sariket
Bandar
Sri Aman
Kanowit
Sarikei

Putussibau
Luar
Lake
Sentarum
Lake
Sintang
Semitau

KALIMANTAN
INDONESIA
Olongiliko
Saripai
Seipinang

Palang
karaya
KALTENG
Sampit

Banjarmasin
1
2
4
5
3
Barito

*South
China
Sea*

Bako
Kuching
Serian
Pemarigkat
Singkawang
Sambas
Semantan
Liku

Ngabang
Sanggau
Sekadau
Schwaner Range
Kapuas

Pontianak

Sukaraja

Pangkalanbun
Tanjung Puting
National Park
Orang-Utan
Rehabilitation
Centre
Mount Palung
Wildlife Reserve

Kendawangan

*Natuna
Sea*

Java Sea

N

100 km
100 miles

322 • Kalimantan

Few tourists make it to Kalimantan: travel can be difficult and facilities, beyond the main cities, are not as well developed as elsewhere in Indonesia. But it offers a great deal: jungle trekking and whitewater rafting, orang-utans and proboscis monkeys, tribal villages and traditional cultures.

The island of Borneo has always held a mystical fascination for Westerners – it was a vast, isolated, jungle-covered island, where headhunters ran wild, and which, if romantic myths are to be believed, was rich in gold and diamonds. It is the third largest island in the world (after Greenland and New Guinea) and Kalimantan's 549,000 sq km (nearly 30% of Indonesia's total land area) form the major part. Most of the population is concentrated in a handful of coastal cities; the interior is populated by various Dayak tribes, whose villages are scattered along Kalimantan's riverbanks.

In the last 10 years it's also been a centre of ethnic conflict between the indigenous Dayak and business- and urban-orientated transmigrants from the crowded islands of Java and Madura. Kalimantan has also undergone environmental devastation. A large part of Indonesia's annual 20,000-30,000 sq km of deforestation takes place here, much of it illegal, sparking vast forest fires unseen on a global scale. Imagine an area the size of Italy stripped or burnt to a crisp within 30 years and you'll get an idea of the scale of the logging.

But hope is on the horizon with Brunei, Indonesia and Malaysia signing the Heart of Borneo Declaration in 2006, to put in place measures for conservation and sustainably managing 220,000 sq km of pristine forest, covering almost a third of Borneo.

South Kalimantan: Kalsel and Kalteng

The timber industry is an important source of revenue for Kalsel. Even with the cataclysmic fires of 1982-1983 and 1997 – which were concentrated in already logged areas rather than untouched forest – it is estimated that perhaps 40% of the province's 37,000 sq km is still officially forested. The area between the road and the coast, the Pegunungan Meratus, the range of mountains that forms the backbone of the state, is still covered in forest. It is too remote even for loggers, and much of the logging has been along the coast and on either side of the main road to Balikpapan.

To the west of this range is the Barito River, which has its headwaters deep in the interior. The coastal area is low lying and swampy; the name of the provincial capital, Banjarmasin, is from the Javanese 'saline garden'. Kalsel's coasts are dominated by rice land, where high-yielding varieties have been successfully introduced. The hybrid strains have been named after Kalsel's main rivers, the Barito and Negara. Over the past 50 years most of these rice fields have been reclaimed from the tidal swamps. Paddy seedlings are planted in the swamps during the dry season, and in the wet season they flood to a depth of 2-3 m. This padi air dalam *(deep water paddy)* is harvested from boats. These swamplands are also home to another oddity: the swimming buffalo of South Kalimantan. Herds of water buffalo paddle between grazing areas, sometimes swimming long distances. Farmers build log platforms (kalang) as resting places for their buffalo (kalang buffalo). In recent years the unchecked spread of water hyacinth has begun to threaten their grazing grounds. The best time to visit Kalsel is during the dry season from June to September.
➤ For listings, see pages 333-340.

Background

Legend has it that a kingdom centred on the southeast corner of Borneo was founded by Ampu-jatmika, the son of a merchant from India's Coromandel coast, who settled in the area in the 12th century. He called it Negara-dipa. It became a vassal state of Java's Hindu kingdom of Majapahit in the 13th century and from then on the city retained close cultural and trade links with Java, which led to its conversion to Islam in the 1540s. The city of Banjarmasin was founded by the Hindu ruler Pangeran Samudera (The Prince from the Sea) in 1526; it was he who first embraced Islam, changing his name to Pangeran Suriansyah in the process.

The Banjarese sultanate – which continued through a succession of 22 rulers – was the most important in Borneo (other than Brunei, on the north coast) and its tributary states included all the smaller sultanates on the west and east coasts of the island. However, in 1860, after several years of political turmoil, the Dutch abolished the sultanate altogether and installed its administrative headquarters, for all of what is now Kalimantan, in Banjarmasin. This sparked the four years' Banjarmasin War against the Dutch occupiers; long after the uprising was put down, the Dutch presence was deeply resented. The hero of the guerrilla struggle against the Dutch was Pangeran Antasari (his name immortalized in many Kalimantan street names), who was born in the nearby city of Martapura. He unified the Banjarese, the Dayaks and the Buginese against the Dutch and had a 100,000 guilder price on his head. He died in 1862, having evaded capture, and 106 years later was proclaimed an Indonesian national hero.

South Kalimantan or Kalsel is the smallest and most densely populated of the four provinces in Indonesian Borneo, with a population of 2.6 million. The population density is about 60 per sq km – low by Javanese standards, but high in comparison with

Kalimantan's other sparsely populated provinces. Kalsel used to include all of Central Kalimantan (Kalteng), until the latter's predominantly Dayak population won administrative autonomy from the Muslim Banjarese. The Banjarese are descended from a mixture of Dayak, Sumatran Malay, Javanese and Buginese stock, although their dialect is close to classical Malay.

Note Over the last few years the relative stability of Malaysia and Brunei has drawn tourists away from Kalimantan. This, coupled with a series of high-profile disasters and terrorist attacks, has hit the Indonesian tourism industry hard, forcing some well-established operators out of business. Bear this in mind when making plans for travelling in the region.

Banjarmasin → *For listings, see pages 333-340. Colour map 4, C3.*

In 1930 the provincial capital, Banjarmasin had a population of just 66,000, but this still made it the largest town on the island. Today the figure is about 750,000. Like several other cities in Asia, Banjarmasin has been dubbed the Venice of the Orient. It might be an overworked cliché, but if there is one city that deserves the epithet, this is it. Dominated by its waterways, most of Banjarmasin's population lives in pile houses and floating houses (*lanting*) on the sides of the Martapura, Barito, Kuin and Andai rivers, along and around which the city is built. These rivers – and the canals which link them – are the focus of everyday life in Banjarmasin. The waterways are alive with people bathing, swimming, fishing and washing their clothes; they clean their teeth in them, squat over them and shop on them.

Although Banjarmasin may be the largest urban centre in Borneo, it does not exude wealth in the same way that other cities do. Periodic outbreaks of cholera, and a shortage of drinking water in the dry season, means that wealthier potential inhabitants tend to live elsewhere, like Banjarbaru/Martapura some 40 km away.

Ins and outs

Getting there Syamsudin Noor airport ① *T0511-470 5277*, is 27 km east of Banjarmasin, Kalimantan's largest city. A taxi from the airport costs around Rp 75,000. Alternatively, walk the 1.5 km to the main highway and catch one of the constant *colts* (minibuses) that ply the road between Banjarmasin and Martapura. This will deliver you to the Km 6 terminal, from where you can catch a *bemo* into the city. Long-distance buses from Balikpapan, Palangkaraya and Samarinda arrive at **Taksi Antar Kota terminal** ① *Jln Pramuka*, 6 km from the town centre. Passenger ferries arrive at Bajaraya Pier from Palangkaraya and beyond. Speedboats from Palangkaraya arrive at the Dermaga pier in front of the Grand Mosque. Pelni (the Indonesian shipping company) ships arrive at the Trisakti port.

Getting around *Bemos* (small pickups) follow fixed routes while rickety *bajajs* (three-wheeled scooters) can be hired. *Ojeks* (motorcycle taxis), *becaks* (bicycle rickshaws) and taxis provide the full house of road-going public transport. More entertaining is to charter a *klotok* (motorized gondola) to explore Banjarmasin's waterways.

Tourist information Dinas Pariwisata Kalimantan Selatan ① *Jln Pramuka 34, T0511-326 3960, www.dispudar.kalselprov.go.id, Mon-Fri 0800-1500, closes at 1200 on Fri*, is the Kalsel provincial tourist office, which is located painfully far from the city centre. They aren't used to receiving foreign visitors, but have a small selection of local maps and guides and can help with the latest ferry timetables and information about travel to Loksado and beyond. The **City Tourist Office** ① *Jln Pasar Baru*, is next to the City Hall.

Note Travellers coming from Pangkalanbun and Java often spend their first few hours in the city wondering why all the clocks are wrong. Kalsel uses WIT (Waktu Indonesia Tengah), Central Indonesian Time, and is one hour ahead of Java, Kalbar and Kalteng (which use WIB or Waktu Indonesia Barat, Western Indonesian Time).

Sights

The number of tourists visiting Banjarmasin was growing fast for much of the early and mid-1990s; an estimated 30,000 every year, mostly from Java and Bali. However, this has since tailed off; the economic crisis, combined with the fires and the bad press that was

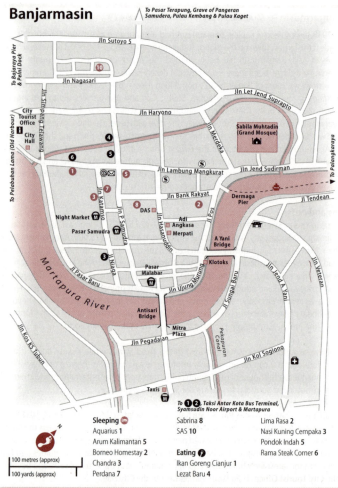

Banjarmasin

Sleeping
Aquarius 1
Arum Kalimantan 5
Borneo Homestay 2
Chandra 3
Perdana 7

Sabrina 8
SAS 10

Eating
Ikan Goreng Cianjur 1
Lezat Baru 4

Lima Rasa 2
Nasi Kuning Cempaka 3
Pondok Indah 5
Rama Steak Corner 6

Sasirangan tie-dyes: from shaman to shop shelf

The bright Banjar cloth is called *sasirangan* and was traditionally believed to hold magical powers capable of driving out evil spirits and curing illnesses. The cloth could be made only by shamans and was designed to cure medical problems. Patterns had particular significance to the spirit world. Colours were also important: the most common ones were yellow, green, red and purple.

When pharmaceuticals arrived in Banjarmasin, the shamans began to go out of business and with their demise, the *sasirangan* faded into obscurity. Local women, however, enthusiastically began to revive the dying art in the 1980s. Within a few years, hundreds of tiny cottage industries had sprung up across the town. The cloth was traditionally coloured with natural dyes: yellow came from turmeric root, brown from the areca nut and red from the karabintang fruit; today, chemical dyes are used, but the tie-dye procedure is lengthy: a simple *sasirangan* with basic motifs can take four days to produce, while complex ones are said to take several months.

generated by the communal violence of the late 1990s, understandably, directed people elsewhere. In more recent times, the global economic crisis and Indonesia's poor repuatation among many tourists has conspired to keep foreigners away from Banjarmasin in droves. Don't expect to hide in the anonymity of city life here; Banjarmasin offers a bewildering number of 'Hello Misters' down even the smallest of side streets. There is plenty to see in Banjarmasin, and much of the sightseeing can be done from a *klotok*.

The imposing **Sabila Muhtadin Mosque** (Grand Mosque), built in 1980, dominates the city's waterfront. Every Friday, 15,000 Muslims gather for prayer in its cool marbled interior; about 98% of Banjarmasin's population is Muslim. The Banjarese became Muslims when the local prince, Pangeran Samudera, converted to Islam around 1540, after which he became known as Pangeran Suriansyah. The city has more mosques per head of population than anywhere else in Indonesia, about one for every 40 families. Mosques, and their smaller equivalent *surau*, line the city's waterways; their domes and minarets, standing out among the parabola satellite dishes and television aerials on the skyline. Non-Muslims can enter the mosque, but should be dressed appropriately and avoid prayer times.

The highlight of most people's visit to Banjarmasin is the **Pasar Terapung** (floating market) ⓘ *early morning only, 0400-0900 or 1000*, which lies on the western outskirts of town on the Barito River. Unlike floating markets elsewhere in the region, this is far from being a tourist showpiece. The market is big and very lively, perhaps because sellers can actively pursue buyers, paddling after them in their sampans and canoes (*jukung*) or chasing them in their *klotoks*. The market includes a floating clinic (*posyandu*) and floating pharmacy; as well as *jukung* vendors selling rice, fish, fruit and vegetables, there are floating boutique shops, hardware shops, supermarkets, petrol stations and soup stalls. There is even a floating parking attendant, who extracts money from each of the stallholders. There are also delightful floating tea shops; these little covered sampans have their front sections covered in plates of sticky rice, doughnuts, cakes and delicacies, which customers draw up alongside and spear with a long harpoon-rod handed over by the teaman. When the sun comes up, the *tanggui* – the famous wide-brimmed Banjar hat – comes into its own as marketeers shelter from the heat under its lofty rim. The floating market starts early and finishes early, but there's little point getting there before 0700. By

0600 it is just light enough to see, so the river trip down canals to the market, as Banjarmasin is awakening, is fantastic.

En route to the floating market, from town, in Kuin village, is the **Grave of Pangeran Samudera** (see page 324). Next to the floating market and along the canals there are *pengger gajian* (small family-run **sawmills**), making sawn timber for the construction industry and the building of Bugis schooners. The main schooner building yards – in riverside dry docks called *alalak* – are just upstream from the floating market at the confluence of the Barito and Andai rivers. But the best place to see the schooners is at the **Pelabuhan Lama** (Old Harbour) on the Martapura River, not far from the town centre. The Orang Bugis, who still build their traditional beautiful sailing ships, live in little pockets along the Kalsel coast (there is another boat building yard at Batu Licin on the coast, 225 km east of Banjarmasin). The schooners, with their sweeping bows and tall masts, are known as *perahu layar* (sailing boats). These days, most of them have powerful engines too, so they are known as PLMs (*parahu layar motor*). The schooners are still in frequent use as trading vessels and most have a crew of about 30, living in quarters at the stern. On the opposite bank of the Barito River to the floating market there are some large plywood factories, some owned by the cronies of former president Suharto.

Pulau Kembang (Flower Island) ⓘ *just downriver from the floating market, in the middle of the Barito River, donation on arrival*, is better known as Monkey Island due to the troops of monkeys found there. Do not touch the big, male, long-tailed macaques; they can be vicious. A trip here is often included at the end of a tour to the floating market; alternatively, take a *klotok* from under A Yani Bridge.

About 12 km further down the Barito River is **Pulau Kaget**, also in the middle of the river. The river around the island is one of the best places to observe proboscis monkeys (see page 377), which are active on the shoreline at dawn and dusk. The local name for these is the *kera belanda*, the monkey that looks like a Dutchman. The round trip takes 1½ to two hours.

Around Banjarmasin → *Colour map 4, C3.*

Martapura and the Cempaka diamond fields
ⓘ *Martapura's diamond fields are shut on Fri, as are the stone-cutting and polishing workshops; most jewellery shops do, however, stay open. Fri, however, is the best day to see the Martapura market in full swing.*

The focus of Kalsel's gemstone mining industry, these diamond fields are near the village of **Cempaka**, 10 km from **Martapura**, about 40 km southeast of Banjarmasin. There, labourers dig 5-m-deep shafts using techniques little changed in over a century. The stony mud is handed to the top in bamboo baskets and then sifted and swilled in flowing water in the hope of striking lucky. If other precious stones are found in the pan, it indicates that a diamond is nearby. Many large diamonds have been unearthed at Cempaka over the past 150 years; the biggest was the 167.5-carat *Intan Trisakti* diamond, found in 1965.

Diamonds are traditionally believed to be benevolent spirits, with characters like virtuous virgins. The miners treat them with respect, referring to them as *Galuh* (Princess). A rigorously observed code of social conduct is in force in the diamond field so that nothing is done to frighten or offend 'her' in case 'she' refuses to appear. This includes the barring of sour-tasting food (said to be craved for by pregnant women), the banning of whistling (a vulgar means of attracting a girl's attention), and smoking is also taboo in case it offends Galuh. But there is also a saying: *Siapa yang mendapat batu besar, dia pasti susah nanti* (Whoever finds a big stone will eventually suffer). The problem is that large stones are so valuable that they overwhelm the local marketing system. And *orang kecil* (little people) should not hold such wealth in their hands. *Orang besar* (big men) in Banjarmasin quickly come to hear of these extraordinary finds and the miners find that wealth, if they get it, quickly turns sour. Other precious metals and stones mined at the site include gold, sapphires and amethysts. Cempaka is one of at least six diamond mining villages in the area. Cempaka can be reached from the *bemo* terminal in Martapura (take green minibuses to the diamond fields).

Around 30,000 people are employed in the gemstone industry, both in the mines and at Martapura. The latter is the gemstone cutting and polishing centre and there are many shops selling stones of all qualities. The best of Martapura's jewellery shops is **Kayu Tangi** ① *Jln Sukaramail 4/J*, it is the only one where stones are guaranteed. They have a good selection of precious and semi-precious stones, from diamonds to rough-cut lapis lazuli, but it is still important to bargain. Although this is the best shop in Kalsel for stones, they are not well finished and will probably require recutting and repolishing. There is a **polishing factory** ① *closed Fri*, next door and many stalls selling semi-precious stones, beads and jewellery – including *manik manik* stone necklaces – in the **Pasar Niaga** market ① *some shops close Fri*. There is a vast and very colourful **vegetable market** ① *next to Pasar Niaga, Mon-Sun, Fri market is the biggest*. Behind the vegetable market is a building with shops where silversmiths make rings.

Lambung Mangkurat State Museum ① *Tue-Thu and Sun 0830-1400, Fri 0830-1100, Sat 0830-1300, Rp 2000, take a taxi, minibus or bus (45 mins) from the intercity bus terminal or a speedboat from the Dermaga Pier in front of the Grand Mosque*, housed in a dubious modern version of a traditional Banjar-style building at Banjarbaru, near Martapura, has displays on Kalsel. There is a life-size ulin-wood (*belian* or ironwood) *tambangan* boat, the traditional Banjar river boat.

Kalteng → *For listings, see pages 333-340. Colour map 4, B2.*

The vast province of Kalteng is most easily reached from Banjarmasin, but few tourists go there. The domain of Dayaks and loggers, it is Borneo's Dayak heartland; the province was created in the late 1950s when the Dayak tribes sought autonomy from the Muslims of Banjarmasin. It covers nearly 154,000 sq km and has a population of 1.4 million. The north part of Kalteng is particularly remote and is fringed by the mountains of the Schwaner and Muller ranges. Southern Kalteng is virtually all marshland, with near-impenetrable mangrove swamps, reaching inland as far as 100 km.

Palangkaraya

This provincial capital was built virtually from scratch in 1957 and in 1991, at the time of the last census, had a population of 100,000. It has little to offer travellers. There is a small **state museum** ① *Jln Cilik Riwut, 2 km from town, Tue-Sun 0800-1200 and 1600-1800*, containing some Dayak heirlooms, mostly brass and ceramic jars. The only real tourist attraction here is the Tanjung Puting Orang-Utan Rehabilitation Centre, see page 330, which is still eight to 10 hours away by road.

Pangkalanbun

Few people bother to stay in this riverside town and if they do, it's probably not out of choice. However, it is necessary to make a stop in Pangkalanbun to obtain a permit to visit the Tanjung Puting National Park (see below), 25 km away. Park permits and guides are available at the **police headquarters** ⓘ *1 km from centre of town on Jln Diponegoro, daily 0700-1500. To get there, take a bemo from the Janan Kasamayuda-Jln Santrek intersection.* Most people move straight on to Kumai (see below), on the park boundary. Compared to the rough and chaotic nature of many towns in Indonesian Borneo, Pangkalanbun is very clean and well-organized, so if you're planning a longer stay in the area this is a good spot to relax, re-supply and meet some of the locals. The town has a distinctly Javanese feel to it, with the majority of residents being migrants from East Java and Madura and Friday lunchtimes see the town come to a virtual standstill as the menfolk pack the mosques for prayers. There are also some Balinese residents here and there's a small Balinese temple on the road out towards Sampit.

Pantai Kubu

Although it won't win any top 10 beach awards, this shallow, slightly muddy, stretch of oceanfront makes a good day trip from Pangkalan Bun or Kumai. At low tide it can be too shallow to swim on the main beach; nevertheless, swaying palms and a tranquil setting make this place attractive. A local fishing boat (*klotok*) can be chartered for Rp 50,000 to take you to the beach of Tanjung Kecuwan, with better swimming. You can hire a *bemo* from Pangkalanbun for the day for around Rp 200,000. Usman, a driver who often works for the Orang-Utan Foundation, is very reliable, T0813-5277 9684.

Tanjung Puting National Park

The 300,040-ha Tanjung Puting National Park was founded by Dr Birute Galdikas in the early 1970s in an area with a wild population of orang-utans. The park straddles several forest types, including swamp forest, heath forest and lowland dipterocarp rainforest. The unusual heath forest is found in the north of the park where stunted trees, many with undersized leaves, grow on impoverished white sand soils. The swamp forest is in the central portion of the park and many of the trees here are adapted to periodic flooding with stilt roots. Anyone who is ill is strictly barred from entering the centre. The park has experienced an almost constant annual increase in foreign visitors in the last nine years. 2008 saw 2392 foreign visitors heading upriver.

The **Orang-Utan Rehabilitation Centre** ⓘ *www.orangutan.org/facts/tanjing*, is smaller and less touristy than Sepilok in Sabah (see page 247) but has the same mission: to look after and rehabilitate orang-utans orphaned by logging or rescued from captivity. There is also a large population of other fauna in Tanjung Puting, including proboscis monkeys (see page 377), crab-eating macaques, clouded leopards, rare false gharial crocodiles, monitor lizards and over 200 species of bird.

There are two main stations in the park: **Camp Leakey**, the main research centre, and **Tanjung Harapan**, which was set up in the late 1980s as an overflow centre and is the one visited by most tourists. At Camp Leakey orang-utans are fed at 1500, 1600 and 1700. There is a proboscis monkey research programme at **Natai Lengknas**.

Permits A police permit must be obtained in Pangkalanbun (see above) before making the 25-km road trip to the small port of **Kumai**. From here, visitors should obtain a park permit from the **Conservation Office (PHPA Office)** ⓘ *T0532-61508, F61500, Mon-Thu and Sat 0800-1400, Fri 0900-1100, closed on Sun (tourists arriving on Sun, or outside office hours may be able to secure a permit through a guide), permits cost Rp 75,000 per day and a boat permit is another Rp 50,000 as a one-off charge, as of 2009. A photocopy of the police letter and*

Oiling the wheels

The bus trip from Pangkalanbun to Banjarmasin (see page 340) leaves a lasting impression of Kalimantan and the environmental changes that have befallen the island. The journey lasts 18-20 hours, and in this time you'll pass virtually no primary forest, just vast palm oil plantations and burnt roots.

Worldwide demand for biofuel – with palm oil one of its main sources – has soared over the past few years, as a renewable alternative to fossil fuels. The EU alone has set a target of 10% of its transport fuel being biofuels by 2020. Supporters of biofuel argue that their lower carbon emissions helps reduce global warming. However, palm oil production is accelerating the destruction of rainforest, especially in Brazil and Borneo, already under threat from the logging industry.

Over 80% of the world's palm oil currently comes from Malaysia and Indonesia and by 2030 demand for palm oil is predicted to be double that of 2000, with a production increase of 15 million tonnes expected between 2006 and 2016. Greenpeave points out that between 1996 and 2006 more than 5 million ha of palm concessions were created in Indonesia, a shocking equivalent to 50 football pitches an hour. As part of this expansion, a vast 1.8 million-ha plantation, half the size of the Netherlands and set to be the largest plantation in the world, was planned.

But in March 2007, the Indonesian government thankfully bowed to international pressure from environmental groups and revoked its scheme. In reaction to negative press reports on the country's palm oil plantations, the Indonesian government embarked on a PR campaign in October 2007 to deny claims that plantations 'degraded forests and killed orang-utans' and to promote their 'sustainable programme of oil palm plantations'.

In 2007 it was revealed that Indonesia stood to gain potentially billions of dollars on the international carbon market by preventing deforestation, and at the United Nations climate change conference in Bali, President Yudyhoyono unveiled an action plan to stabilize the orang-utan population by 2017, saying: "To save orangutans we must save the forests. By saving, regenerating and sustainably managing forests we are also doing our part in reducing global greenhouse gas emissions, while contributing to sustainable economic development of Indonesia".

The Roundtable on Sustainable Palm Oil (RSPO), www.rspo, has been created by producers, retailers and NGOs such as the WWF to promote sustainable production.

To read more on the destruction of rainforests in Indonesia, and the plight of the orang-utan see www.greenpeace.org/raw/content/usa/press-center/reports4/how-unilever-palm-oil-supplier.pdf.

---

a photocopy of the 1st page of your passport is required to secure the park permit. Guides are not required for exploring the park as the boatmen know the channels well. However, guides are available from the PHPA office in Kumai, in Pangkalanbun or from the ranger posts at Tanjung Harapan and Podok Tanggui (Rp 225,000 per day). Tours to the park can be organized from Banjarmasin.

Further fees payable at the Conservation Office include a one-off docking fee for the *klotok* (Rp 5000-Rp 25,000 depending on size) and camera fees (standard digital camera Rp 50,000, video camera Rp 150,000).

Guides Apart from organized tours (see page 337), it's possible arrange your own transport and wildlife trips into the park. It's a good idea to arrange a local guide, who should be able to help obtain park permits in Pangkalanbun and make arrangements in the park itself. Guides, who are mainly self taught, charge around Rp 225,000 per day, plus expenses. Contact the following guides through **Himpunan Pramuwisata Indonesia** (HPI; Indonesia Tourist Guide Association) ⓘ *T0852-4930 9250, www.hpionline.org*, or by asking locally in Pangkalanbun (PB) or Kumai: **Majid** (Kumai) ⓘ *600 Jln Haji Mohd Idris, T0852-4859 0487*; Thomas Sari (PB); Herry Roustaman (PB) and Anang Emen (Kumai) are all recommended.

Klotoks Hiring a slow-moving, African Queen-style *klotok*, chugging slowly upriver from Kumai, is almost as much a part of the Kalimantan experience as seeing the wildlife itself. Besides, the steadily narrowing branches of the Sekonyer River provide a good opportunity to spot animals, from huge silent reticulated pythons to proboscis monkeys crashing through the riverside foliage. Basic boat charges depend on the size of the vessel; a smaller boat big enough for two costs Rp 550,000 per day, and a larger boat with ample space for a party of four costs Rp 700,000 per day. These fees include payment for the captain and crew (except cook). Visitors are expected to pay for the food, which is bought in Kumai by the crew prior to departure. Food for a three-day trip costs around Rp 550,000, which includes enough for three meals a day, mineral water, juices and some light snacks. The fee for the cook is Rp 75,000 per day. Most *klotoks* can take up to four passengers and are good value, especially if you're sleeping on them (or in them) at night, as visitors are recommended to do. Make sure you check the *klotok* prior to booking a trip. The better *klotoks* are comfortable, with mattresses above and below deck, Western toilets and showers, electricity points and mosquito nets. It is custom for tourists to sleep above deck, where the air is much cooler. The sleeping space is covered, and should be fairly rainproof.

Most vessels can be hired for a minimum of three days, as it takes time to get anywhere interesting in the park. However, this being Indonesia, shorter trips can be negotiated. If visiting in the high season of June, July and August, it is recommended that visitors book a vessel in advance by telephoning the captain (or try the guide Majid listed above, he has excellent English and can organize trips efficiently).

Boats were charged a one-off *klotok* tax of Rp 50,000 per vessel in 2009. Boats are usually easy to contact in Kumai or Pangkalanbun. The following are recommended *klotoks* and their captains (boat name, captain name, address, telephone number): *Satria 2*, Suyono, Jln Haji Mohd, Idris 600, T053-261240; *Harapan Mina I*, Anang Alus, Jalan Bahari Kumai Hilir, T62-5326 1339; *Harapan Mina II* (Pak), Maslian, Jalan Bahari Kumai Hilir, T0813-4961 7210; *Efferedi*, Pak Abu, Jalan Bendahara Kumai, T0812-507 8534.

For Sleeping and Eating price codes and other relevant information, see Essentials pages 23-27.

☺ Sleeping

Banjarmasin *p325, map p326*

There aren't any particularly exciting places to stay in town, but there's a choice of lower mid-range options. Hoteliers often seem genuinely befuddled by foreign visitors.

A-B Arum Kalimantan, Jln Lambung Mangkurat, T0511-436 6818, F436 7345. This large white concrete block of a building looks a little shabby from the outside, but has a fairly plush interior and some good facilities including a fitness centre, pool and restaurant. The a/c rooms are carpeted and have soft mattresses, cable TV and attached bathroom with bathtub. It is a comfortable place to stay for those on expense-paid trips, but for the independent traveller it's distinctly overpriced.

B Aquarius, 32 Jln Lambung Mangkurat, T0511-336 2525, htlaquarius_mkt@yahoo.co.id. Smart hotel with a good selection of rooms. Pay more for a room with a window. The a/c rooms are neat and clean and have cable TV and fridge. Wi-Fi is available in the lobby and there's also a coffee shop. Recommended.

B-C SAS, Jln Kacapiring 2, T0511-335305. Fashioned as a traditional Banjarese house, this hotel has a good selection of a/c and fan rooms set in an alley off the busy streets. The atmosphere is peaceful and the rooms are cool, if a little dark. Rooms have a lot of bamboo and wood decor in line with the rest of the hotel's design. Couples may be asked to provide some proof of marriage here. Recommended.

C Chandra, 12 Jln Brig Jend Katamso, T0511-336 3990. Bog-standard hotel with sterile, clean a/c rooms with TV and attached bathroom with wonky doors. Not very exciting, but fair value nonetheless.

C Sabrina, 5 Jln Bank Rakyat, T0511-335 4442. This place is so popular with locals that unless you arrive at the crack of dawn you are unlikely to find a room. It's clean, but many of the a/c and fan rooms are dark. However, there are a couple of great rooms on the 2nd floor with a balcony overlooking the street. Cheaper rooms have shared bathrooms.

C-D Perdana, 8 Jln Brig Jend Katamso, T0511-335 3276, perdanahotel@plasa.com. Extraordinary hotel with a huge range of mind-boggling styles and colour mixed together in what has become an eccentric fusion. This is set to change as the hotel was undergoing extensive renovations at the time of writing with some promising new rooms being added to the front. There is a range of fan and a/c rooms, many windowless, but all have cable TV and include some good touches such as afternoon tea and cake. The 1400 checkout is handy. Recommended.

D Borneo Homestay, Jln Simpang Hasanuddin 33, T0511-66545, F57515. Situated down an alleyway off Jln Hasanuddin, this old-school travellers' haunt has miserable windowless rooms with grotty shared bathrooms. There are much better rooms available in town for slightly more money. The place is run by Johansyah Yasin who is an excellent source of local knowledge and offers tours including jungle treks, diamond mine tours and floating market cruises.

Palangkaraya *p329*

C Dandang Tingang, Jln Yos Sudarso 13, T0536-21805. A/c, restaurant and bar, multi-lingual staff. Best hotel around but a little out of town (take taxi bus C). Recommended.

D Mina, Jln Nias 17, T0536-22182. Some a/c, pleasant staff, clean rooms and a good place to stay at this price. It's popular so is often full.

D Yanti, Jln A Yani 82A, T0536-21634. A very clean little hotel. More expensive rooms have a/c, attached bathrooms and hot water.

Pangkalanbun *p329*

There is a surprising number of good-value, lower mid-range options here, making this an excellent place to base yourself and recover from the rigours of the road.

A Blue Kecubung, Jln Domba 1 (south of town), T0532-21211, www.bluekecubung hotel.com. The swishest place in town and sister hotel to the **Rimba Lodge** in Tanjung Puting (see below). Sparkling new business-class hotel with a cavernous and stylish lobby and comfortable sofas. A subterranean restaurant serves buffet breakfasts (included in price) and maintains a high standard. Rooms are spacious and en suite, with baths in the more expensive rooms. Minibars, TV and huge double beds in executive rooms make this hotel ideal for post-jungle pampering. Intriguing caveman-style Borneo Bar with live music. Free use of gym for residents.

B-C Bahagia, Jln Pangeran Antasari No 100, T0532-21226. Freshly painted with an icy fresh blue hue, this place has clean tiled rooms with TV, a/c and attached bathroom with squat toilet.

B-C Tiara, Jln Pangeran Antasari No 16, T0532-22717. Though the walls in this place could do with a lick of pain, the rooms are generally good value with cable TV and a/c in every room. Those on the 3rd floor are larger than those on the 2nd, although have a *mandi* rather than a shower. Breakfast is included in the price. Recommended.

B-D Abadi, Jln Pangeran Antasari 150, T0532-21021, F22800. Popular lodgings on the main drag with a good selection of clean, tiled a/c rooms. There are a couple of cheaper economy fan rooms. Most standard rooms have attached bathroom with TV and price includes breakfast. Fair value.

C City, Jln Kasamayuda (near the intersection of Jln Rangga Santerer), T0532-28569. New hotel offering a selection of gleaming large rooms with TV, a/c and attached Western bathroom. Most rooms are windowless.

D Losmen Hayati, Jln Diponegoro 4, T0532-24951. Old school *losmen* run by a friendly family. Rooms are somewhat rustic, but have TV and attached bathroom. No English spoken here. The owner can help with onward **Pelni** ferry bookings to Java.

D Yayorin Homestay, Jln Bhayangkara Km 1, T0532-29057, www.yayorin.org. Located next to the *kampong konservasi* (Rp 15,000 *ojek* ride from the town centre), run by the Yayorin (Yayasan Orangutan Indonesia) foundation on the edge on town, this place offers a great opportunity to learn about the forest, meet some wonderful local characters and gorge on organic produce from the foundation's sustainable agricultural development demonstration plots. Accommodation may not be the most luxurious in town, but the vibes more than make up for this. Highly recommended.

Tanjung Puting National Park *p330*
The best way to visit is to spend 2-3 nights on a 12-m *klotok*, sleeping and eating afloat. National park staff can help you to find a suitable boat. Rates vary depending on the size of the boat. A larger boat with ample space for 4 passengers costs Rp 700,000 a day, and a smaller boat for 2 costs Rp 550,000. Hiring a *klotok* often works out as a better deal than land accommodation, as the larger boats hold at least 4 passengers plus 3 crew members. All food is bought in Kumai and prepared by a cook, who is very friendly and welcoming. However, those travelling alone might find these costs prohibitive, in which case there are a couple of cabins in the park that can be booked through the Conservation Office in Kumai (page 330) and some rustic homestays. See Activities and Tours, page 337, for local guides and *klotoks*. For those needing more grounded accommodation, a wide variety is available in and around the park.

AL-A Rimba Lodge, T0532-671 0589, www.rimbalodge.com. If you need a little more privacy and comfort than the open deck of a *klotok*, this is the best option. On the north bank of Sekonyer River, these stylish timber rooms and bungalows blend pleasantly with the surrounding forest, which is home to large groups of macaques and proboscis monkeys. Rooms are connected by wooden walkways and there is a new if rather rickety walkway through the peat swamp to a birdwatching platform overlooking the river. Electricity is provided at night. Rooms vary, from individual bungalows, with vast and comfortable double beds, hot water and a/c (at night) to more basic rooms with fans and cold showers. The only downside is the location itself; just outside the park boundary, it's not ideal for spotting some of the region's rarer mammals. It's a few minutes by *klotok* to Tanjung Harapan village. As it's a few hours from the park's core at Camp Leakey, it can be a long day trip if you return to **Rimba** the same night. Some profits go to the Orang-Utan Foundation, www.orangutan.org.uk.

C Garuda, Jln Gerilya 377, Kumai, T0532-61145. Dark rooms but helpful staff, who help arrange park tours. Being modernized at the time of visit. Cable TV and good breakfast.

C Village homestays, Tanjung Harapan village. Head upriver for 1½ hrs in a *klotok* and you'll come to Tanjung Harapan, on the left bank of the river 10 mins before the **Rimba**. An interesting Dayak village in transition between old and new lifestyles, good for culture and a couple of relaxing days by the river, but there's little wildlife in the surrounding area. Several families offer homestays in the village; just turn up at the landing stage and ask. Rooms with attached bathrooms are surprisingly spacious and comfortable in semi-traditional wooden houses, breakfast is included. Also see PHPA cabins below.

D Aloha, Idris No 465, on the road from Pangkalabun, Kumai, T0813-4965 6177. One of the cheaper places to stay in this sleepy port at the edge of the park. Basic but clean. Owner Rusmin Aryadi speaks pretty good English and is quite helpful; he can help book ferry/boats to Java ports – economy cabin from Rp 125,000 to Samarang or Surubuya.

E PHPA cabins, book through the park office at Kumai. Basic accommodation in Tanjung Harapan (see **Village homestays**, above), just inside the park on the Sekonyer River. It's necessary to bring food and water upriver. River water must be thoroughly boiled before drinking.

🍴 Eating

Banjarmasin *p325, map p326*
The locals rave about their speciality, *soto banjar*, a delicious variant of *soto ayam*. For cheap food, visit the *warungs* (foodstalls) in the night market, off **Jln Lambung Mangkurat**, open to 0100, where you can eat for around Rp 5000 or less. For delicious local cakes (*kuey*) try **Minseng Bakery**, near the corner of Jln Pasar Baru and Jln Samudra.

🍴 **Ikan Goreng Cianjur**, 331 Jln A Yani Km 4.5, T0511-326 3979. You'll need to hop on an *ojek* to get to this place, not far from the bus terminal. This a/c restaurant is comfortable and serves tasty fried fish and chicken as well as numerous Sundanese and Javanese dishes.

🍴 **Lima Rasa**, 275 Jln A Yani Km 3.5, T0511-325 2153. A favourite with locals for authentic Banjar seafood dishes including *soto banjar* and some excellent baked and fried fish dishes. Recommended.

🍴 **Pondok Indah**, 22 Jln Pang Samudera, T0511-335 3191. Don't be fooled by the grimy kebab stand outside, as this comfortable a/c restaurant has a brilliant range of Sundanese and Javanese seafood dishes. The black pepper crab is excellent. For those not so keen on seafood, there are a few Javanese options such as *nasi timbel*.

🍴 **Rama Steak Corner**, Arjuna Plaza, Jln Lambung Mangkurat 62. Cosy restaurant with soft lighting. Imported Australian steaks cost twice the price of local ones.

🍴 **Shinta**, 115 Lambung Jln Mangkurat, T0511-335 7900. Comfortable restaurant serving good Indonesian fare. Recommended by locals.

🍴 **Lezat Baru**, Jln Pang Samudra 22. Part of a small chain of restaurants, with branches in Samarinda and Balikpapan, this place offers a huge Chinese menu with a good choice of seafood. Specials including excellent steamed crab and oysters done 10 different ways (when in season). Highly recommended.

🍴 **Nasi Kuning Cempaka**, 6 Jln Niaga Timur, T0511-336 0958. This is the spot for a solid working man's lunch with large portions of saffron-flavoured yellow (*kuning*) rice served with tender chicken or fish marinated in sweet soy sauce and served with sweet onion chutney and shaved coconut; it's delicious and filling. Recommended.

¶ Warung Yana Yani, 10-min *klotok* ride downriver from **Borneo Homestay** (see page 333), ask Johan to take you. This is the best riverside restaurant for *soto banjar*. For less than Rp 10,000 you'll get a huge bowlful and a long glass of *es teh* (iced tea).

Pangkalanbun *p329*
There are plenty of small *rumah makan* serving up some good fare. The **Blue Kecubung** hotel (page 334) is the only hotel serving good-quality international options.

¶¶ Meranti, 4 Jln Kasamayuda, T0532-27487. Swish local place with good, though slightly overpriced, local fare. Things to look out for include *ikan gurame bakar* (grilled carp), *sayur asem* (Javanese sour vegetable soup) and the delicious and refreshing *es kelapa muda* (iced young coconut milk). There are 2 menus; only one shows the prices, so ask to see that one. This place has a generator and escapes the power cuts that blight the town most days.

¶ Warung Sedap, 27 Jln Rannga Santrek, T0532-23744. Clean, spacious place offering duck-fried rice, juices and some Javanese noodle dishes. Just near here is the small **Warung Saté Solo** (¶), with cheap goat and chicken *saté*.

¶ WM Sandi, Jln Pankgalan Antasari (opposite the Tiara hotel). One of the best places in town for a cheap feed, this small family-run place has delightful *ikan pepes*, *lalapan* and freshly grilled chicken. It's a bit rough around the edges, but that only adds to the charm. Get there early as all the good stuff is gone by mid-afternoon.

Tanjung Puting National Park *p330*
¶ Indowarteg Prasmanan, No 224, on the waterfront side of main street, Kumai. Good spot for a cheap lunch – noodles, rice, chicken, veggies – all the local favourites. It gets crowded at lunchtime.

❀ Festivals and events

Banjarmasin *p325, map p326*
Mar/Apr Mappanre Tassi Buginese Fishermen's Festival (movable), 7-day festival on Pagatan beach (south of Batu Licin on the southeast coast, 240 km east of Banjarmasin) in which local Buginese fishermen sacrifice chickens, food and flour to the sea. Dancing and traditional songs, boat races and tug-of-war competitions. The festival climaxes on the last day. It is possible to stay overnight in the village where there are several *losmen* (cheap hotels); enquire at the tourist office or with tour operators as to how best to get to Pagatan. The Department of Tourism will transport visitors free of charge to the festival.

Aug/Sep Aruh Ganal (the big feast; movable) is the Hill Dayak harvest festival. (Another smaller harvest festival, **Aruh Halus**, is held in Jun, to celebrate the first of the twice-yearly rice crop.) Dancing all night from around 2000-0800; celebrated in the Hill Dayak longhouses in the Loksado and South Hulu Sungai districts.

Boat races (17 Aug) where teams compete in traditional *tanabangan* rowing boats on the river in front of the mosque – the course is from the government office to the Grand Mosque.

Sep/Oct Ramadan (movable) throughout the Islamic fasting month. When Banjaris break *puasa* after sundown, they indulge in local delicacies. Daily 1400-1800, in front of the Grand Mosque, the Ramadan Cake Fair is held, where people come to sell cakes for the evening feast. Traditional Banjari cakes are made from rice flour, glutinous rice, cassava and sago. Most are colourful, sweet and sticky.

Traditional **Banjarese wedding ceremonies** take place on Sun, in the auspicious month before Ramadan. Tourists are always welcome at these celebrations and do not require invitations. Traditional dances (such as the *hadrah* and *rudat*, which have Middle Eastern origins) are performed during wedding festivities.

O Shopping

Banjarmasin *p325, map p326*

Hill Dayak handicrafts include basketware and semi-precious stones from the Martapura mines. Many shops have good selections of Dayak knives (*mandau*) from Central Kalimantan; in South Kalimantan, these knives are called *parang*. One of the more unusual items on sale are Dayak war canoes/death ships, intricately carved from rubber. There are several art shops on Simpang Sudimampir and Pasar Malabar (near Antisari Bridge).

Toko Citra, Km 3.5 Jln Jend A Yani (towards the airport), is the best place in town for Sasirangan tie-dyes (see box, page 327). Also good for handicrafts are the markets, especially **Pasar Malabar**, next to Antasari Bridge (opposite side of the river from Mitra Plaza), and **Pasar Samudra**, on Jln Samudra/Jln Pangeran, which is good for sarungs and mosquito nets.

▲ Activities and tours

Banjarmasin *p325, map p326*
Tour operators

There are a few freelance guides in town who are tipped off about newly arrived foreigners by taxi drivers, so expect a visit within a few hours of arrival. One of the better guides is Makani (contact via **SAS** hotel, page 333), who offers early morning floating market tours, canal tours and trekking around Loksado.

Arjuna Tours, Arjuna Shopping Plaza, 62 Jln Lambung Mangkurat, T0511-335 8150. Efficient agency for domestic air ticketing.

Borneo Indo Tours, 45 Jln Brig Jend Hasan Basri, T0511-330 0050, www.borneo.indotours.co.id. Reputable agent offering Banajarmasin city tours, 3-day houseboat trips in Tanjung Puting (US$400 for 2, not including flights), 4-day trips to Loksado and areas to the north east of Banjarmasin including trekking, staying in a longhouse and bamboo rafting (US$410 for 2) and 5-day trips down the Mahakam (US$1055 for 2).

Indo Kalimantan Tours, see Borneo Homestay, page 333. Run by Johansyah Linus, it offers excellent canal tours (Rp 100,000), morning floating market tours (Rp 200,000 for 2), trips to Kaguet Island, Martapura and Cempaka, Loksado and further afield to Tanjung Puting Orang-Utan sanctuary.

PT Samudera Gemilang Angkasa, 96 Jln Pangeran Saumdera, T0511-335 0122. Air, ferry and bus ticketing. Friendly service.

Trekking

The best area for trekking is in the Meratus Dayak – or Hill Dayak – country around Loksado (on the Amandit River) and Mount Besar (1892 m), 190 km northeast of Banjarmasin in the **Pegunungan Meratus** range. There are more than 30 longhouses (*balai*) in and around Loksado, where trekkers can stay overnight. There are also caves in the area. The Kalsel tourism office produces a detailed list of treks between villages, with distances and approximate timings. To the southeast of Banjarmasin, at the south end of the range, there are jungle trails around Lake Riamkanan, accessible from Martapura/ Awang Bankal. It is necessary to take guides to both these areas (see Tour operators above), as few speak English; also, take mosquito repellent, torch and sleeping bag (temperatures drop sharply at night). The cheapest option is to hire a local guide in Loksado.

Whitewater rafting

From Loksado, it is possible to run the rapids on the Amandit by bamboo raft. There are many stretches of whitewater, of varying grades of difficulty.

Tanjung Puting National Park *p330*
Tour operators

Borneo Eco Tours, Jln Raya Pasir Panjang, T0532-25631, www.borneoecotour.com. Arranges a variety of tailored tours to Tanjung

Puting. It's more pricey than showing up in Kumai and organizing it yourself, but a fair option for those with limited time and an interest in seeing as much wildlife as possible. Includes packages staying at **Rimba Lodge**, page 334, and on a *klotok*.

Discovery Initiatives, 51 Castle St, Cirencester, Gloucestershire, GL7 1QD, UK, T+44 (0)1285-643333, www.discovery initiatives.com. This British-based company sometimes runs tours and volunteer programmes based on working with wild or rehabilitated orang-utans at the Orang-Utan Foundation in Tanjung Puting. Good for those with limited time who are interested in making a positive contribution to the area.

⊖ Transport

Banjarmasin *p325, map p326*
Air
Syamsudin Noor Airport is 27 km east of town. There are regular connections to **Sampit**, **Pangkalanbun**, **Ketapang** and **Pontianak** with Kal Star. Batavia flies daily to **Balikpapan**. Lion Air, Garuda, Sriwijaya and Batavia have daily flights to **Jakarta** and **Surabaya** (except Garuda). Mandala also flies to **Surabaya** and **Yogyakarta**.

Airline offices Batavia Air, Jln Letjend Haryono, T0511-335 4034. **Garuda**, 31 Jln Sultan Hasanuddin, T0511-335 2730. **Kal Star**, 53 Jln Jafri Zam Zam, T0511-620 9990. **Lion Air**, Jln A Yani (KM4.5), T0511-326 2680. **Mandala Airlines**, 78 Jln A Yani, T0511-325 1947. **Sriwijaya Air**, 7 Jln A Yani, T0511-327 1507.

Boat
Local For travelling on the waterways, the best place to hire a *klotok* is from under A Yani Bridge or Kuin Cerucuk (also known as Kuin Pertamina), to the northwest side of town on the Kuin River. Motorized *klotoks* (which can hold up to 8-10) cost about Rp 75,000 per hr. Speedboats cost Rp 100,000 per hr and leave from the Dermaga speedboat pier near the Grand Mosque.

Long distance Passenger boats leave for destinations upriver from **Bajaraya Pier**, at the far west end of Jln Sutoyo. The boats are double-deckers which, for trips beyond Palangkaraya, are equipped with beds (for rent) and even *warungs*. Behind the *warungs* there is a small prayer room and toilets and *mandi*. Reserve beds the day before if travelling long distances upriver. Boats have signs next to them with departure times. Most leave in the morning around 1100; ticket office open 0800-1400. To get to Bajaraya pier take a yellow *bemo* or *bajaj* from Pasar Malabar. **Palangkaraya**, 24 hrs; **Muara Teweh**, 48 hrs; and **Puruk Cahu**, 60 hrs. In the dry season big passenger boats cannot make it to Muara Teweh and Puruk Cahu; it's necessary to disembark at Pendang and take speedboats and motorized *klotoks* further upriver; to Muara Teweh, 3 hrs and Puruk Cahu, 8 hrs. **Pelni** ferries leave Banjarmasin's Trisakti terminal for other destinations in Indonesia. You can get to **Trisakti** by *bemo* from Jln Antasari. The *Egon* leaves for **Kumai** (for the Orang-Utan Sanctuary), every 2 weeks, 18 hrs. **Dharma Lautan Utama**, 4 Jln Yos Sudarso, T0511-441 0555, has boats leaving from Trisakti to **Surabaya** approximately every 3 days. Boats for **Makassar** depart from Batulicin (an 8-hr bus ride away) every Sat.

Bugis schooner to **Java**, enquire at **Kantor Syahbandar Pelabuhan I**, Jln Barito Hilir at Trisakti dock. The harbourmaster demands ID before allowing you to see the schooner. Mainly for special interest groups, journalists and photographers only. If you need assistance, contact Johan at **Borneo Homestay**, page 333.

Road
Local *Bajaj* congregate around Pasar Malabar (off Jln Samudra); they can be chartered. Yellow *bemos* leave from in front of the **Minseng Bakery** near the corner of Jln Pasar Baru and Jln Samudra. They follow fixed routes, but go all over town. *Bemos* can also be found on the corner of Jln Bank

Rakyat and Jln Hasanuddin, in front of the Corner Steak House. *Ojek* drivers seem to line to pavement every 5 m offering a ride. It costs around Rp 15,000 to get to the bus terminal.

The city taxi terminal is on Jln Antisari, next to the main market, Rp 50,000 per hr.

Bus Intercity buses leave from **Terminal Taksi Antar Kota** at Km 6. Overnight buses (with and without a/c) to **Balikpapan** leave at 1600-1700 (12 hrs, Rp 160,000). Overnight buses direct to **Samarinda** leave at the same time (15 hrs, Rp 175,000). There are plenty of buses plying the bumpy route to **Palangkaraya** (5 hrs, Rp 45,000) and onwards to **Sampit** and finally **Pangkalanbun** (18 hrs, Rp 165,000).

Car Vehicles can be chartered for a more comfortable overland journey upriver.

Taxis The taxis around Kalsel leave from the Terminal Taksi Antar Kota at Km 6. Airport taxi (Taxi Bandara), T0511-335 7060. Or try **Taxi Arya**, T0511-747 4567.

Palangkaraya *p329*
Air
The airport is just outside town; taxis into town cost Rp 25,000. Regular connections with **Jakarta** on Sriwijaya, Garuda and Batavia. Batavia also flies to **Surabaya**.

Boat
Canals, cut by the Dutch in the late 19th century, connect the Barito, Kapuas and Kahayan river systems. Boats travelling downstream leave from **Rambang Pier**; tickets are sold here. To **Banjarmasin**, the fast boat takes 6 hrs, the slow boat takes 18 hrs (travelling past **Pulang Pisau** and **Kuala Kapuas** en route). Boats travelling upstream to **Tewah** leave from **Dermaga Flamboyan** (or Flamboyant Pier). For journeys beyond Tewah you'll need to charter a boat.

Road
Buses and Kijangs frequently ply the bumpy route between Palangkaraya and **Banjarmasin**.

Bus connections with **Banjarmasin**, (5 hrs, Rp 45,000), **Pulang Pisau** and **Kuala Kapuas**.

Cars can be chartered for a more comfortable overland journey down river to **Banjarmasin**.

For jeeps: **Patas Tours**, Jln Yani 52, for twice daily travel to **Kuala Kapuas**, 4 hrs, or to **Sempas**, 7 hrs (in the dry season).

Pangkalanbun *p329*
Pangakalanbun is fairly well connected to nearby destinations in Kalimantan.

Air
Check your flight details thoroughly before booking your visit to Pangkalanbun and Tanjung Puting National Park. It is important to book and pay for flights out of Pangkalanbun before departing for trips to Tanjung Puting. Those with only reservations stand a good chance of being 'bumped'.

Kal Star has daily flights to **Ketapang** (30 mins, Rp 495,000), **Pontianak** (1 hr, Rp 595,000), **Sampit** (30 mins, Rp 495,000 and **Banajarmasin** (1 hr, Rp 600,000) on its 40-seater ATR42 300.

Transport to town by taxi or *bemo*.

Coming from Java and beyond By the time this book hits the shelves, **Trigana Airways**, T0532-22117, should be operating a thrice-weekly service between the north Javanese city of **Semarang** and Pangkalanbun for about US$95 one way. The airline also plans to link Pangkalanbun with **Surabaya** in the near future. Both Semarang and Surabaya airports offer VOA and can be accessed on flights from Singapore. However, new air routes come and go in Indonesia like lightning, so it's always worth checking the latest situation with travel agents.

Road
Local *Bemos* around town are cheap. Taxi from Pangkalanbun airport to town costs Rp 50,000. An airport pick-up, stop-off in Pangkalanbun on the way and drop-off in Kumai (pick-up point for *klotoks* to Tanjung Puting) costs Rp 100,000. The shorter ride from Pangkalanbun to Kumai is Rp 70,000 or Rp 30,000 by motorcycle taxi.

Long distance The road to **Palangkaraya** from Pangkalanbun is poor. *Kijang* taxis make the journey but it is long (about 10 hrs) and painful. Buses plough the bumpy road from Pangkalanbun to Banjarmasin (18-20 hrs, Rp 165,000), stopping in Palangkaraya. The trip to **Tanjung Puting**, by contrast, is short. Minibuses leave from the market area, 30 mins. Long-distance bus tickets can be bought from **Yessoe Travel** on Jln Rannga Santrek.

Tanjung Puting National Park *p330*
Air
The nearest airport is in **Pangkalanbun** (see above for details).

Boat
Local Speedboats can be chartered from **Kumai**, 45 mins to **Tanjung Harapan**, 1½ hrs to **Camp Leakey**. Contact (Pak) Udin T0813-4914 6485 or (Pak) Tarus T0852-4902 6930. Hire *klotoks* in Kumai for Rp 550,000-Rp 700,000 per day plus expenses for the crew; larger boats comfortable for 4 passengers plus 3 crew. See page 332 for recommended guides and *klotoks*. For travelling along the Sekonyer River, canoes (paddle powered) can be hired

from **Rimba**; it's the best and most peaceful way to see the forest and its wildlife.

Long distance **Kumai** is well connected to Semarang and Surabaya in Java with 3 sailings a week to **Semarang** (19 hrs) and 2 to **Surabaya** (24 hrs). Tickets can be bought at numerous agents in Kumai and Pangkalanbun.

ⓘ Directory

Banjarmasin *p325, map p326*
Banks BCA and BNI are both on Jln Lambung Mangkurat; avoid changing money with shifty characters on the street, rates are shocking. Instead, use the authorized money changer Haji La Tunrung, 17C Jln Pangeran Samudera, T0511-336 6119. **Internet** Kantor Pos (Post Office), Jln Lambung Mangkurat (0900-2000), Rp 3000 per hr. **Medical services** Suaka Insan Hospital, Jln Pembangunan (north side of town), T0511-335 3335. The best in Banjarmasin. **Post office** Jln Lambung Mangkurat/ Jln Samudra.

Pangkalanbun *p329*
Banks BNI, Jln Pangkalan Antasari (opposite Bahagia hotel), ATM. **Internet** Small cyber café on Jln Kusumayada, near the intersection with Jln Rannga Santerer. **Pharmacy** 31 Jln Pangkalan Antasari.

Tanjung Puting National Park *p330*
There are no ATMs in Kumai. Bring enough cash or you'll face a trip to Pangkalanbun.

East Kalimantan (Kaltim)

With its economy founded on timber (producing 70% of Indonesia's sawn timber exports), oil, gas and coal, Kaltim is the wealthiest province in Kalimantan. Its capital is Samarinda, the launch pad for trips up the Mahakam River. Balikpapan, an ugly oil town, is bigger than Samarinda and is the provincial transport hub. Indonesia's second largest province after Irian Jaya, Kaltim covers 211,400 sq km and has a population of barely more than two million. ▶▶ *For listings, see pages 350-358.*

Background

Archaeological digs on the East Kalimantan coast have uncovered stone *yupa* poles with Sanskrit inscriptions, suggesting Indian cultural influence possibly dating back to the fifth century or earlier. The province's first major settlement was founded by refugees from Java in the 13th century, who had fled from the Majapahits. They founded the kingdom of Kertanegara ('the lawful nation', which later became known as Kutai), believed to have been an important centre on the Java-China trade route. The word *kutai* is thought to have been used by Chinese traders, who knew it as 'the great

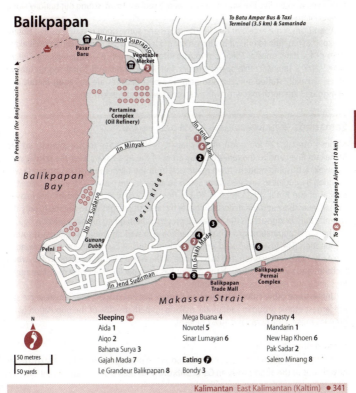

Balikpapan

To Batu Ampar Bus & Taxi Terminal (3.5 km) & Samarinda

Jln Let Jend Suprapto

Pasar Baru

Vegetable Market 3

Pertamina Complex (Oil Refinery)

Jln Minyak

To Penajam (for Banjarmasin Buses)

Balikpapan Bay

Jln SOR Yos Sudarso

Pasir Ridge

Gunung Dubb

Pelni

Jln Jend A Yani

1 6
2

3
4
5
6

Jln Gajah Mada

Jln Jend Sudirman

1 4 8 7

Balikpapan Trade Mall

Balikpapan Permai Complex

To 8 & Seppinggang Airport (10 km)

Makassar Strait

N

50 metres
50 yards

Sleeping
Aida 1
Aiqo 2
Bahana Surya 3
Gajah Mada 7
Le Grandeur Balikpapan 8

Mega Buana 4
Novotel 5
Sinar Lumayan 6

Eating
Bondy 3

Dynasty 4
Mandarin 1
New Hap Khoen 6
Pak Sadar 2
Salero Minang 8

land'. The imaginative Chinese traders also gave the Mahakam River its name (*mahakam* means big river).

Following Banjarmasin's conversion to Islam, Kutai became an Islamic sultanate in 1565. Disputes between Kutai and the Hindu kingdom of Martapura were settled by a royal marriage. In the 17th century, hostilities broke out again and Kutai was defeated and absorbed into the Martapura kingdom. The first Buginese settlers arrived from Sulawesi in 1701. As piracy in the Sulu Sea worsened, Kutai's capital moved inland, finally transferring to Tenggarong in 1781. Kutai remained intact as a sultanate until 1960.

Balikpapan → *For listings, see pages 350-358. See also map, page 341.Colour map 4, B5.*

Administrative headquarters for Kaltim's oil and gas industry, Balikpapan's population has tripled in 40 years to more than 300,000 today. At night, from the dirty beach along Balikpapan's seafront, the clouds are periodically lit up by the orange glow of flares from the offshore rigs in the Makassar Strait. Staff of **Pertamina**, the Indonesian national oil company, live mainly on Gunung Dubb, in Dutch colonial villas dating from the 1920s and overlooking the refinery. **Unocal** and **Total**, US and French oil companies, have their residential complexes on the opposite hill, on **Pasir Ridge**, overlooking the town. These foreign oil workers live like kings in Balikpapan, a soulless town, strung out untidily along several kilometres of road.

Apart from some excellent handicrafts shops and some good restaurants and hotels, Balikpapan has little to offer; it is a transit camp for visits to Samarinda and the Mahakam River or for Banjarmasin. There is a **tourist information office** ⓘ *Seppinggang Airport, T0542-21605, unpredictable opening hours*, but **Altea Benakutai Hotel** representative office is usually staffed and can also help. The best beaches are at **Tanah Merah** and **Manggar** (3 km north of town), which can be crowded at weekends.

Samarinda → *For listings, see pages 350-358. Colour map 4, A5.*

Kaltim's capital, 120 km north of Balikpapan, is the gateway to the interior, up the Mahakam River and to the remote Dayak areas of the Apo Kayan, near the border with Sarawak. A bustling modern town made rich from the timber industry, Samarinda was founded by Buginese seafarers from South Sulawesi in the early 1700s and became the capital of the Kutai sultanate. It is 40 km from the coast at the head of the splayed Mahakam estuary and the river is navigable by large ships right up to the town; only the recently built bridge across the Mahakam prevents them going further upriver.

The rapid population growth of Samarinda is based squarely on natural resource exploitation. The town produced almost three-quarters of East Kalimantan's plywood in the early 1990s and was reputed to have one of the world's highest densities of plywood factories and sawmills, although this output has since declined because of a shortage of logs and a stiff export tax on sawn timber.

Unlike some other cities in Indonesian Borneo, like Balikpapan, the Banjarese are still the largest ethnic group in Samarinda, making up perhaps 40% of the population (with 30% Javanese, 10% Bugis and 10% Chinese).

Ins and outs
Getting there and around Samarinda's airport is on the edge of town; take a taxi to town or walk out of the airport to Jalan Gatot Subroto and catch a *bemo* heading for the city.

There are long-distance buses from Balikpapan, Bontang and Tenggarong. **Pelni** vessels dock here on their fortnightly circuits through the archipelago and there are also boats that go up the Mahakam River. ▶ *See Transport, page 356.*

Bemos and minibuses, which follow set routes, are the main means of transport. There are also many *ojeks*.

Samarinda

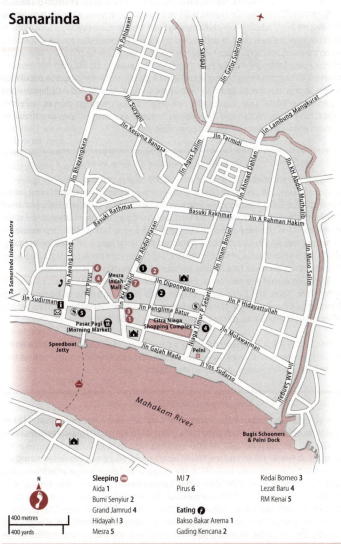

Tourist information **Dinas Pariwisate Kaltim (East Kalimantan Tourist Office)** ⓘ *22 Jln Jend Sudirman, T0541-736850*, has very limited printed information but can deal with basic queries. Travel agents are the best bet for the latest on flights and transport.

Sights

The only real 'sight' is the **Mahakam River** itself and it is well worth chartering a boat to cruise around for an hour. On the left bank, at the east end of town, is the harbour, where the elegant Bugis schooners dock. **Kampong Sulili**, further downriver from Samarinda, is built out over the river on stilts and backed by a steep hillside; there are lively scenes all along the riverbank. Small boats can be hired or speedboats can be chartered from any of the countless jetties behind the Pasar Pagi (morning market). Dominating the centre of town is Kalimantan's largest mosque, the Samarinda Islamic Centre, which also claims to be the largest mosque in East Asia with space for well over 40,000 worshippers and covering over 50,000 sq m. It is certainly one of Kalimantan's most extravagant buildings, with strong North African and Arab design features, including its towering minarets, Moorish arches and patternwork and clean open spaces.

Kutai National Park → *For listings, see pages 350-358. Colour map 4, A5.*

This park, 120 km north of Samarinda, is a 200,000-ha area of forest. The WWF believes it contains at least 239 species of bird. It is also home to a population of wild orang-utans (around Teluk Kaba) and proboscis monkeys. The park was first gazetted as a protected area before the Second World War, but has found itself gradually diminished in size as the government has allowed portions to be logged. In the early 1980s, 60% of the remaining protected area was devastated by a vast forest fire. Kutai park is reached via **Bontang**, which lies on the equator, and is the site of a large liquefied natural gas plant. Nearby, at Kuala Bontang, there is a Bajau fishing kampong built on stilts over the water.

Most people visit the park on an organized tour (see page 354). Regular buses run every three hours and there are passenger boats from Samarinda to Bontang. From Bontang (Lok Tuan or Tanjung Limau harbours), the park can be reached by speedboat in 30 minutes. Chartering boats can be expensive (around Rp 200,000).

Permits/guides It is necessary to obtain a permit from the Conservation Office (PHPA Office) in Bontang (no charge). The office can also advise on itineraries, organize boat trips to the park, provide guides and help arrange charter boats.

Tenggarong → *For listings, see pages 350-358. Colour map 4, A5.*

This was the last capital of the Sultanate of Kutai and is the first major town (45 km) upriver from Samarinda. The highlight of a visit to the town is the **Mulawarman Museum** ⓘ *Tue-Thu, Sat-Sun 0800-1600, Fri 0800-1100 and 1330-1600, Rp 2000*. It is housed in the Dutch-built former sultan's palace; his old wooden one, which was exquisitely furnished, burned to the ground in the mid-1930s. The museum contains a recreation of the opulent royal bedchamber, a selection of the sultan's *krisses* (knives), clothes, other items of royal regalia and his collection of Chinese ceramics. There are also replicas of the stone stelae bearing Sanskrit inscriptions, dating from the fourth or fifth centuries. The display of Dayak arts and crafts is poor, although there are some woodcarvings in the grounds, notably the tall Dayak *belawang* pole (with a carved hornbill on top) in front of the museum. A Dayak cultural show is often staged in the museum on Sunday. Near the museum is the **royal cemetery**, with graves of the founder of Tenggarong, Sultan Muslidhuddin and his descendants.

Mahakam River → *For listings, see pages 350-358. Colour map 4, A2-A5.*

The 920-km-long muddy Mahakam is the biggest of Kaltim's 14 large rivers and is navigable for 523 km. There are three main stretches. The Lower Mahakam runs from Samarinda, through Tenggarong to Muara Muntai and the three lakes; these lower reaches are most frequently visited by tourists. The Middle Mahakam stretches to the west from Kuara Muntai, through Long Iram to Long Bagun, where public riverboat services terminate. The Upper Mahakam, past the long stretch of rapids, runs from Long Gelat into the Muller Range; only a few adventure tours go this far. The Mahakam's riverbanks have been extensively logged, or turned over to cultivation. To reach less touristy destinations along the river you need plenty of time on your hands and, if on an organized tour (see page 354), plenty of funds as well. Many travellers just enjoy relaxing on the decks of the boats as they wind their way slowly upriver: one of the most important items for a Mahakam trip is a good, long book.

September to October, before the rainy season starts, is the best time to visit; it coincides with rice-planting rituals and the Erau festival, see page 353. Harvesting festivals are held from February to March. During the dry season (July to September), many of the smaller tributaries and shallow lakes are unnavigable except by small canoes; during the height of the wet season (November to January), many rivers are in flood and currents are often too strong for upriver trips. Most people travel up the Mahakam River on an organized tour, either from Samarinda or from Balikpapan.

Background

One of the first Western explorers to venture up the Mahakam was Carl Bock (1849-1932). Though born in Oslo, he went to England as a young man and from there to the Dutch East Indies collecting biological specimens for the collection of Arthur Hay, the Marquis of Tweeddale and president of the Zoological Society. Unfortunately, while frantically pillaging the flora and fauna of Sumatra, his patron died. A stroke of good fortune gave him a new mission: in Batavia (Jakarta) he met Governor-General Van Lansberghe, who asked him to mount an expedition to 'Koetai' (Kutai) and venture up the Koetai or 'Mahakani' River. He agreed, but immediately found a problem: no one would accompany him – even when the wages were so high they "amounted to a positive bribe" – because of the fear of cannibals. But perseverance and the governor-general's deep pocket allowed him to proceed and, accompanied by the Sultan of Kutai himself, Bock ventured upstream. In a sense, the expedition was a bit of a let down: he met no headhunters in six months, nor did he find the celebrated *Orang Buntut* (Tailed People) who were supposed to be the missing link between apes and humans. Nonetheless, he wrote up the account of the journey – with a literary flourish which did more for sales than his scientific credibility – that was published, in Dutch, in 1881. The book was translated into English and published as *The Headhunters of Borneo* (available as a 1985 reprint from OUP).

Today, when they're taking time out from their cultural performances for tourists, the Mahakam's Dayaks are not the noble savages, dressed in loincloths and hornbill feathers, painted by some tourist literature. Longhouses are quite commercialized and visitors are likely to be asked for money for photographs. Most villages on the lower and middle reaches of the river have been drawn, economically and socially, into the modern world over the past century. Although the traditional Kaharingan religion is still practised in some areas, many upriver Dayak groups have been converted to Christianity. Whereas in Sarawak, upriver tribespeople maintain their traditional lifestyles.

This is due historically to the policy of Sarawak's Brooke governments – the White Rajahs of Sarawak who attempted to protect the Orang Ulu (the upriver tribes) from the warring Ibans and Chinese traders. Other than trying to stamp out 'social vices' such as headhunting, they were largely left undisturbed. In Kalimantan, the Dutch colonial government did nothing to discourage the activities of Muslim and Christian missionaries, traders and administrators.

The Lower Mahakam: Samarinda to Muara Muntai

Tenggarong (see page 344) is the first major town upriver on the Mahakam from Samarinda, a trip of about 40 km. Upriver tours then pass through the villages of **Muara Kaman** and **Kota Bangun**, about six or seven hours upriver from Tenggarong. The lakes of **Semayang**, **Melintang** and **Jempang** – collectively known as the Mahakam Lakes – lie to the west and southwest of Kota Bangun. The lakes used to be known for their freshwater dolphins, which were sadly decimated during the drought and associated fire of 1982-1983. The lakes remain an important source of fish, though; it has been estimated that 30% of dried freshwater fish sold in Java come from these lakes. Other wildlife of the

Mahakam River

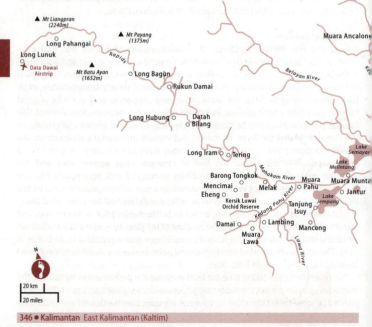

Mahakam here includes proboscis monkeys. **Muara Muntai** is the next village travelling upriver, built out over the riverbank on ironwood stilts.

The Dayak village of **Tanjung Isuy** is on the Mancong River, which feeds into Lake Jempang, the most southerly of the three main lakes; it takes about 2½ hours to reach the village from Muara Muntai. Tanjung Isuy is quite touristy, but is the best place on the Mahakam to witness traditional dance performances in full costume. The villagers of Tanjung Isuy have rejected longhouse living in favour of detached kampong houses, strung out along the riverbank. One of these rejected longhouses contains a government craft centre, which is also a hostel.

A worthwhile excursion from Tanjung Isuy is to visit the **Mancong longhouse**, about 10 km away, built as a tourist attraction in 1987. There are sometimes weaving demonstrations and traditional dance performances. But it is worth making the effort for the trip itself, rather than the destination; the chances of seeing wildlife, including proboscis monkeys and a profusion of water birds, are good.

The Middle and Upper Mahakam

Along the Mahakam, west of Muara Muntai, are many modern Dayak villages where the traditional Kaharingan religion is still practised. Funerals are particularly interesting affairs, involving the ritual sacrifice of water buffalo. Several more traditional villages are within reach of **Melak** (all are accessible by motorcycle), the largest settlement here. There is a scattering of *warungs* and Melak is also a good place to buy rattan goods.

Guides and transport are available, but the latter tends to be expensive.

Around 15 km southwest of Melak is the **Kersik Luwai Orchid Reserve**, which is best visited in January or February. Charter an *ojek* for the trip there and back. Northwest of the reserve is **Barong Tongkok**, a small community lodged near the centre of this plateau. From here, travel southwest to visit **Mencimai**, where there is a great little museum showing local farming methods. Beyond here is **Eheng**, with an exceptional Banauq longhouse, and local people selling handicrafts (the last stretch of road beyond Mencimai is not made up).

Towards **Long Bagun**, places become increasingly traditional, although some villages and tribal groups have embraced Christianity, and the long arm of the state and of modernity reaches far into the upper stretches of the Mahakam. Only a few public river boats go beyond **Long Iram**, partly due to lack of demand and also because travel in the dry season is difficult upriver from here. Long Iram is a small, pleasing town, with a relaxed atmosphere and a few architectural hangovers from the Dutch period.

Upriver from Long Iram is the domain of the **Tunjung** and **Benuaq Dayaks,** and a substantial number of Kenyah who have spilled over from the Apo Kayan, see page 349. The scenery becomes increasingly dramatic towards Long Bagun; there are many villages and it is always possible to stay somewhere. Past the long stretch of rapids to the west of Long Bagun is the upper Mahakam, which runs southwest and then twists north to its headwaters in the Muller Range, on the Sarawak border.

Tours

In the late 1990s around 15,000 tourists travelled up the Mahakam River annually. Today, however, it is a very different story. With reduced flights and a lack of interest by travellers regarding Indonesia in general, there is now a mere trickle of visitors and tour operators have very little custom. The vast majority of travellers go on organized tours that can be tailored to suit all budgets. Most tours are prohibitively expensive unless you're part of a group; costs fall dramatically with larger groups. Tour agents usually require a deposit of 50% upon booking. There is one major tour company in Balikpapan and some excellent ones in Samarinda offering similar deals (see page 354). There are also more adventurous trekking trips to the Apo Kayan (see below) and three- to four-day package deals to the Kutai National Park, north of Samarinda (see page 344). Independent travellers visiting the area alone will find tours very expensive. It would be better to try and find a travel partner or group to share costs with before turning up in Samarinda as there are very few foreign visitors in Samarinda nowadays.

Unlike neighbouring Sarawak, upriver tours on the Mahakam lasting less than a week will not get far enough to reach traditional longhouses; three- to four-day tours cost about US$150 per head per day (minimum two people) and travel to **Lake Jempang** and **Tanjung Isuy**; five- to nine-day tours continue upriver to **Tunjung**, **Bahau** and **Kenyah Dayak** villages west of Long Iram, costing from US$150 per head per day (minimum two people). A 14-day tour should reach **Long Baun** or beyond. A few operators offer a trans-Kalimantan trek starting off in Samarinda and finishing in Putussibau, Kalbar 19 days later. Costs for this are about US$3500 for two, all inclusive.

With Samarinda and Tarakan flights to Long Ampung now back on offer, tours to the Apo Kayan are possible. However, these need to be planned and flights need to be booked well in advance. It is possible to get there without flying but this but involves a convoluted process of long overland travel on expensive chartered longboats. All tours to the **Apo Kayan** area include the return flight from Samarinda to Long Ampung. Few are shorter than six days, most are about nine to 10 days. Expect to dig very deep into the pocket for the privilege of visiting this region.

Most tours involve a mix of trekking and river trips by longboat and canoe, visiting Long Nawang and nearby longhouses and waterfalls. Some offer a day's hunting with local Dayaks. Consult a tour operator in Samarinda for the latest costs, but expect it to be expensive.

Freelance guides tout around hotels looking for tourists wanting to go upriver. Some are good, others terrible: it is advisable to stick to those with tourist guide licences. (When planning a trip with a freelance guide, ask them to trace the intended route on a map; it soon becomes apparent whether they know what they are talking about.) Many of the good guides in Samarinda contract out their services to tour companies. An average daily rate for a freelance guide should be Rp 175,000.

The Apo Kayan → *For listings, see pages 350-358. Colour map 2, C1-2.*

This remote plateau region borders Sarawak and is the most traditional tribal area in Kalimantan. The inaccessible mountains and rapids have made the Apo Kayan non-viable from a commercial logger's point of view and the jungle is largely intact. The region has suffered from out-migration in recent decades and the tribal population has shrunk to a fraction, perhaps just a tenth, of what it was in the early 1900s. This migration has been spurred by well-paid work in the timber camps of Sarawak and East Kalimantan, combined with the prohibitive cost of ferrying and portering supplies from downriver. From the late 1980s the airstrip at Long Ampung was served by **DAS**, opening the area up and bringing the cost of freight and passenger fares down. Flights to the Apo Kayan died out in early 2009, but had life breathed back into them by Susi Air with fairly frequent connections on the company's Cessna Grand Caravans between Malinau, Tarakan, Samarinda and Long Ampung.

The Apo Kayan is divided into the **Kayan Hulu** (upriver) and **Kayan Hilir** (downriver) districts. The former has a much higher population (about 5000) and the vast majority are Kayan (see page 178), most, originally from Sarawak, driven upriver by Iban raids. Nearly all of them have converted to Christianity (most are Protestant). Until the 1920s the Kayan were the sworn enemies of Sarawak's Iban: in 1924 the Sarawak Brooke government convened a peace conference in Kapit (on the Rejang River), which was attended by Dayak groups from both sides of the border. This formally put a stop to upriver and cross-border headhunting raids.

During the Second World War, many Europeans in the coastal towns of East Kalimantan made their way upriver to what they considered the relative safety of Long Nawang, deep in the Apo Kayan, in the face of Japanese occupation. The Japanese troops followed them upriver and many were killed, having been forced to dig their own graves. Among those shot was a group of women and children, refugees from Kapit in Sarawak.

Most tours to the Apo Kayan involve treks and canoe trips from **Long Ampung** to **Long Nawang**, and visits to longhouses, like Nawang Baru and Long Betoah, and west of Long Ampung, along the Boh River, to Long Uro, Lidung Panau and Long Sungai Barang.

Tarakan → *For listings, see pages 350-358. Colour map 2, B2. Phone code: 0551.*

The oil-rich island of Tarakan, with over 81,000 inhabitants, has little to offer travellers, besides being a hopping-off point for neighbouring Sabah. In the closing months of the Second World War, a vicious battle was fought here as Australian forces spent several weeks trying to prise the Japanese out of their well-protected bunkers. They succeeded, but suffered many casualties. The legacy of the battle is still in evidence. Tarakan makes for a convenient place to arrive in Indonesia from Tawau, Sabah, and has good flight connections to Kalimantan and elsewhere in Indonesia.

Nunukan

A short hop from Tawau in Sabah, Nunukan offers very little for visitors: there are no beaches and it seems to be impossible to arrange even a canoe trip. On the plus side the people are friendly. There is one bank (**BNI**) on the main square, but it gives very poor exchange rates. Nunukan has a large sex industry, catering for Malaysian weekend visitors. **NB** VOA (Visa On Arrival) is not available at either Nunukan or Tarakan. Those wishing to enter Indonesia at either port should obtain a visa in advance from Tawau or KK.

⊙ East Kalimantan (Kaltim) listings

For Sleeping and Eating price codes and other relevant information, see Essentials pages 23-27.

⊝ Sleeping

Balikpapan *p342, map p341*

Largely because Balikpapan is an oil town and is geared to the needs of oil workers and government officials, there is woefully little accommodation for the budget traveller.

AL Le Grandeur Balikpapan, Jln Jend Sudirman, T0542-420155, www.legrandeur hotels.com. The most luxurious hotel in Kalimantan, with 189 rooms, set in extensive gardens overlooking the Makassar Strait, near a sandy beach. It has a/c, restaurants, a pool, fitness centre and business facilities, but with a 15-min drive to the town centre it's a bit inconvenient. Breakfast is included. Highly recommended.

AL-A Novotel, 2 Jln Brigjen Ery Suparjan, T0542-733111, info@novotelbalikpapan.com. This is the place to spot foreigners in Kalimantan, with a daily influx of business people working with the oil companies. The hotel positively gleams on a hill overlooking the town and the Straits of Makassar beyond. Rooms are sleek and elegant and the better ones have a sea view. Facilities at the hotel include a pool, restaurant, bar and spa. Internet access is available throughout the hotel, but it's expensive. Recommended.

A Bahana Surya, Jln Let Jend Suprapto 1, T0542-35845. 5 mins' drive from major oil company offices. A/c, 3 restaurants, pool, Balikpapan's next best after **Le Grandeur**, this is a large, modern hotel with a good range of facilities including in-house videos, satellite TV, sauna, billiards and Japanese shiatsu massage. Friendly staff. Recommended.

B-C Gajah Mada, 328 Jln Jend Sudirman, T0542-734634, F734636. Solid mid-range choice close to the heart of town and good eateries. There is a delightful open veranda at the back overhanging the sea. Rooms are clean with cable TV and attached bathrooms,

although some are a little dark. There are a couple of rooms at the back with sea views. Recommended.

C Aiqo, 9 Jln APT Pranoto, T0542-750288. New place with spotless rooms with cable TV and attached bathrooms. Rooms are on the small side, and some are windowless, so be sure to see a selection. Attached bathrooms have hot-water showers. Good value.

C Mega Buana, Jln Jend Sudirman Bl A 12, T0542 7203351. Popular place with sleepy staff. All rooms have cable TV and attached bathroom but they are not wildly exciting. There's also a restaurant.

C-D Aida, Jln Jend A Yani 1/12, T0542-421006. Sister hotel to its namesake in Samarinda (page 351). This place has a flash reception that leads onto a double terraced corridor of rooms. A lot of them are dark, but rooms here are kept clean and staff is friendly. All rooms have cable TV and attached bathrooms with *mandi* and squat toilet. The downside is its location, which is too far from good restaurants and shops. Breakfast is included.

C-D Sinar Lumayan, 05/49 Jln Jend A Yani, T0542-736092. A couple of doors down from **Aida**, this is another place that looks deceptively good from the outside. Rooms here are down an intensely blue-lit corridor and are small and dark. While rooms are clean and have cable TV and attached bathroom, they are small and cheerless.

Samarinda *p342, map p343*

AL-A Bumi Senyiur, Jln Diponegoro 17-19, T0541-741443, www.bumi.senyiurhotels. com. Excellent value hotel that will be enticing to those who need some pampering after tough times upriver. The lobby area is vast and contains an eccentric collection of classic cars and ancient motorbikes. Rooms are elegant and beautifully furnished with marble bathrooms, fluffy towels, soft lighting and cable TV. The hotel has some of the town's finest eateries, a huge pool, sauna and spa. Highly recommended for a splurge.

B Mesra, Jln Pahlawan 1, T0541-732772.
With a/c, restaurant, pool, golf course, tennis,
good bar and a choice of rooms, suites and
cottages, this place is good value for money.
Recommended.

C Grand Jamrud, 34 Jln Jamrud, T0541-
743828, F743837. Hotel set in a large pink
stucco villa located down quiet back lanes.
This is a good mid-range choice with small
but clean a/c rooms with cable TV.
Bathrooms here are pokey.

C MJ, 1 Jln K H Khalid, T0541-747689,
www.mjhotel.com. New place with flashy
reception area but slightly disappointing
rooms that need an upgrade. However, rooms
are clean and comfy, there's a café in the
reception and free Wi-Fi access in the lobby
and 1st floor rooms. Large discounts available.

C Pirus, Jln Pirus 30, T0541-731462. Large
pink block of a building with nonplussed staff,
but solid clean tiled a/c rooms with cable TV
and Wi-Fi access (with a pre-paid voucher,
available at reception). Good value.

C-D Aida, Jln K H M Temenggung, T0541-
742572. Located next to the *pasar pagi*, this
place has improved in recent years and now
has a good choice of clean, if dark, rooms
with cable TV, a/c and attached bathroom.
Cheaper fan rooms available. Rooms here
get filled by late morning, so an early arrival
is crucial. Fair value.

C-D Hidayah I, Jln KH Mas Temenggung,
T0541-732 1210, F737761. This is one of the
most popular places in town, undeservedly.
The owners have rested on their laurels and
the place seems to be falling apart at the
seams with damp rooms, stained bedding
and broken fittings. On the plus side, staff
are friendly and there is a decent balcony
area on the 1st floor. Rooms have a/c, cable
TV and attached bathrooms.

Kutai National Park p344
D Kartika, Jln Yani 37, Bontang, T0548-21012.
There are a number of rangers' posts in the
park with basic accommodation and food.
There is one on **Teluk Kaba** and others along
the **Sengata River** (**F**, Rp 3000 per meal).

Tenggarong p344
There are a handful of cheap *losmen*
(hotels) in town (a couple by the dock)
and a mid-range choice.

C Timbau Indah, Jln Muksin 15 (on the road
into town from Samarinda, on the river),
T0541-761367. A/c, restaurant, good rooms
but rather a trek from the town centre.

D Penginapan Anda II, Jln Sudirman 63
(over the bridge from the mosque), T0541-
61409. The best budget option. As well as
some cheap but clean fan rooms, this place
also has a/c rooms with attached *mandi*.

Mahakam River p345, map p346
The Lower Mahakam: Samarinda to Muara Muntai
C Sri Bangun Lodge, 10 mins' walk from
Mukjizat. Quite a comfortable place to stay.

D Penginapan Mukjizat, Kota Bangun,
facing the mosque. A welcoming place with
average to poor rooms but an above average
atmosphere and position. Also good source
of information on the Upper Mahakam.

E Hostel, Tanjung Isuy. In longhouse, with
private rooms and good beds.

The Middle and Upper Mahakam
There are several adequate places to stay in
Melak. **D Losmen**, Long Iram. There's also a
very good small restaurant here.

The Apo Kayan p349
It is possible to stay in the longhouses but it is
important to bring gifts (see box, page 124).
Independent travellers should pay around
Rp 40,000 per night to the longhouse
headman. Visitors should bring a sleeping
bag (it gets cold at night), insect repellent
and torch.

Tarakan p349
A Swiss Bel Hotel, 15 Jln Mulawarman,
T0551-21133, www.swiss-belhotel.com.
This is the place to splash some cash with a
full range of business facilities, a great pool
and the **Jasmine** restaurant offering good,
if somewhat expensive, fare.

B-C Tarakan Plaza, Jln Yos Sudarso 1,
T0551-21870. Recently renovated, although
still looking a little bit tired, this place has
helpful, friendly staff and offers some of the
best value lodging in town.
D Jakarta, Jln Sudirman 112, T0551-21704.
Rock-bottom rates for basic but clean rooms
and a friendly welcome.
D Taufiq, Jln Sudarso 26, T0551-21347.
Some a/c, rather basic but OK. It has a
certain ramshackle charm.

Nunukan *p349*

C-D Lenflin, 105 Jln TVRI, T0556-24178. Fair
value, clean digs, not very inspirational but
adequate for somewhere to crash for the night.
D Losmen Monaco, 5-min walk from the
port. One of several *losmen* in town. Clean
and reasonable value with shared *mandis*.

🍴 Eating

Balikpapan *p342, map p341*

🍴🍴🍴 **Bondy**, Jln Jend A Yani 7. One of the
better restaurants in town, entrance is
through a bakery with enticing smell of fresh
pastries, to the large open-air restaurant, set
around a courtyard. Here you'll find European
and local food, local and imported steaks and
a vast selection of sundaes and ice creams. It's
very popular with locals. Recommended.
🍴🍴🍴 **Square**, Novotel, page 350. With the
tinkling of the grand piano, and ballads from
a crooner, you could almost forget you're in
Borneo here. This eatery is popular with expats
and has good Asian and Western fare on offer.
Also here is **Colors Bar and Restaurant**, with a
weekly poolside barbecue on Fri.
🍴🍴 **Dynasty**, Jln Jend A Yani 10/7. Chinese
food and seafood, huge menu, deep-fried
crab claws, prawns fried with *rambutan*,
shellfish and *saté*. Recommended.
🍴🍴 **Lezat Baru**, Pasar Baru Blok A, Jln Jend
Sudirman 1, Komplex Pertokoan. Part of
the Kalimantan chain, huge Chinese
menu with a good choice of seafood,
specials include oysters.

🍴🍴 **Mandarin**, Jln Jend Sudirman,
T0542-739053. Halal Chinese fare in a/c
comfort with an emphasis on Cantonese
cuisine and seafood. Popular.
🍴🍴 **New Hap Khoen**, Jln Jend Sudirman 19.
Huge Chinese menu, good seafood selection,
specialities include crab curry, chilli crab and
goreng tepung (squid fried in batter).
Recommended.
🍴 **Pak Sadar**, Jln Jend A Yani (5 mins downhill
from **Sinar Lumayan** hotel). Popular hangout
for students and young mums, this *warung*
eats to a soundtrack of Indonesian rock, and
has menu if *bakso* and *mie ayam*.
🍴 **Salero Minang**, 14 Jln Jend Sudirman.
Right next to **Hotel Gajah Mada**, this place
is held in high regard by locals for its tasty
nasi Padang meals.
   There is an excellent **foodcourt** (🍴) on
the 3rd floor of the Balikpapan Trade Mall
featuring cuisine from all over the
archipelago, from Manado to Betawi fare.
Free Wi-Fi access, good fresh juices and
football on a large screen at the weekends.

Foodstalls

There are stalls in the Balikpapan Permai
complex on the road to the airport and
more at the vegetable market, **Kebun Sayur**,
the Chinatown of Balikpapan.

Samarinda *p342, map p343*

🍴🍴🍴 **Chong Palace**, Bumi Senyium hotel,
page 350. This place doesn't have a
particularly interesting interior but is one of
the town's best bets for Chinese food with an
array of Cantonese and Sichuan dishes with
an unmistakeable Indonesian influence.
🍴🍴🍴 **Daisaku**, Bumi Senyium hotel, page 350.
Upmarket Japanese restaurant with massive
bottles of sake, solid standard fare including
teppanyaki as well as a couple of interesting
Korean options.
🍴🍴🍴 **Gading Kencana**, top floor of **Hotel Gading
Kencana**, Jln Pulau Sulawesi 4, T0541-722456.
Beautifully decorated with ikats, baskets and
Dayak handicrafts and soft lighting. It doesn't
fill up until after 2000. Romantic breezy

balcony available for dining. It serves freshwater (*ikan mas*) and saltwater fish (*ikan bawal, terkulu, bandeng* and *kakap*), also Mahakam River prawns. Highly recommended.

¶¶ Lezat Baru, Jln Mulawarman 56. See page 352. Extensive menu of Chinese fare, loads of good seafood. Recommended.

¶¶ RM Kenai, 6 Jln Sudirman, T0541-716789. Informal place set off the busy main thoroughfare. Good spot to come for its signature crab dishes, prepared myriad ways. There are also plenty of prawn and fish dishes.

¶ Bakso Bakar Arema, Jln Diponegoro. A bright red place with a strange mixture of fresh seafood dishes, plates of *bakso* cooked every conceivable way and for the adventurous, chewy fried cow's lung.

¶ Kedai Borneo, Jln Abdul Hasan (opposite Mesra Indah Mall). Blink and you'll miss this tiny cupboard of a place. The menu is limited to a couple of winning dishes including excellent *soto banjar* and *nasi kuning*.

Tarakan *p349*
¶ Antara, Jln Yos Sudarso. Good *ikan bakar* fish.

¶ Bagi Alam, Jln Yos Sudarso. Another place worth visiting for its *ikan bakar*.

¶ Kepeting Saos, Jln Sudirman. Excellent crab dishes.

☺ Entertainment

Balikpapan *p342, map p341*
Balikpapan's status as an oil town, with a good number of testosterone-charged men, means that it has a lively nightlife. The major hotels have bars and discos and their popularity changes with the seasons. The Novotel's **Colors Bar** has a long happy hour on Fri from 1830 to accompany its weekly barbecue, and down in the basement there is a good lounge bar with theme nights such as Ladies' Night on Wed.

Samarinda *p342, map p343*
Being a rough and ready town, it is no surprise that Samarinda has plenty of sin on offer. **Dejavu** and **Platinum** on Jln Panglima Batur are popular spots for ogling girls in very short skirts, downing tumblers of spirits and crooning on the karaoke machine. Those in search of a more sedate drink will find the lounge bar at the **Bumi Senyium** hotel a fitting venue (Rp 50,000 minimum order). **Tepian Mahakam**, Jln Untung Suropati, T0541-34204. Floating disco playing a mix of chart hits and traditional Indonesian love songs is in a barge moored next to the bridge; cover charge. Recommended.

Cultural performances
Every Sun at 1400 there is a cultural performance of the Kenyah Dayaks at Pampang, 22 km from Samarinda. These Kenyah Dayak migrated here from the Apo Kayan and have made this a permanent fixture on the local calendar. Expect to pay Rp 15,000 to photograph one of the Kenyah participants.

⊛ Festivals and events

Tenggarong *p344*
23-28 Sep Erau Festival, traditionally celebrated at the coronation of a new Sultan of Kutai, this festival used to go on for 40 days and nights. Today it lasts for 5 days. Festivities include traditional Dayak dances, where the different tribes dress in full costume, and sporting events such as *behempas* (where men fight with braided whips and rattan shields), *sepak takraw* (top spinning), *lomba perahu* (boat races) and blowpipe competitions. Following the final *ngulur naga* ceremony – in which a large colourful dragon is floated down the Mahakam – the festival degenerates into a water fight (water in which the dragon has swum is lucky water and should be shared – in bucketfuls). Dayak rituals are performed during the festival, including the *belian* healing ceremony and *mamat*, which traditionally welcomed heroes back from war and headhunting trips, and during which a buffalo is slaughtered.

O Shopping

Balikpapan *p342, map p341*
Arts, crafts and antiques
There is a vast array of handicrafts shops here and it is perhaps the best place in Kalimantan to buy Dayak handicrafts; 'antiques' may not, however, be as old as they seem. A new shopping centre, **Balikpapan Plaza**, is on the seafront, at the bottom of Jln Jend A Yani. There are lots of arts and crafts shops above the vegetable market (Kebun Sayur/Pasar Inpres) on Jln Let Jend Suprapto, at the north end of town.

Bahati Jaya Art Shop, Jln May Jen Sutoyo 9. A good range of tribal handicrafts and antiques.
Borneo Art Shop, Jln Jend A Yani 34/03. One of the best selections of handicrafts, Dayak antiques, ceramics and gemstones.
Iwan Suharto Batik Gallery, Hotel Benakutai, Jln Jend A Yani. Excellent selection of original batik paintings (traditional and modern), much of it from Java, but also some interesting Dayak designs.
Kalimantan Art Shop, Blok A1, Damai Balikpapan Permai, Jln Jend Sudirman 7. The undisputed king of Balikpapan's antiques, and Dayak arts and crafts shops, textiles, beads, porcelain, etc. Proprietor Eddy Amran is friendly and knowledgeable.
Syahda Mestika, Jln Jend A Yani 147. A vast selection of tribal arts and crafts, Chinese porcelain and antiques.

Shopping centres
Balikpapan Plaza, Jln Sudirman. Open 0930-2200. Standard Indonesian shopping mall with boutiques, **Excelsio** coffee shop, **Gramedia** bookshop, supermarket and fast-food outlets. Next door is the newer **Balikpapan Trade Mall** with a huge supermarket, an excellent food court and stalls selling mobiles, DVDs and cheap clothing.

Samarinda *p342, map p343*
The **Pasar Pagi** (morning market) is in the middle of town and is busy most of the day.

The area around the modern **Citra Niaga** shopping complex, between Jln Yos Sudarso and Jln P Batur, is lively in the evenings with musicians, fortune tellers, quack doctors and dentists.

Arts, crafts and antiques
Samarinda has many small handicrafts shops along Jln Martadinata, mostly selling Dayak items, but they are not as good as Balikpapan. Always bargain; be wary of 'antiques'.
Dewi Art Shop, Mesra Indah Mall. Antiques, tribal arts and crafts, good selection of postcards and T-shirts.
Fatmawati, Mesra Indah Mall. Good selection of semi-precious stones and rings.

▲ Activities and tours

Balikpapan *p342, map p341*
Tour operators
With so few tourists arriving in the region, tour operators running trips up the Mahakam are few and far between in Balikpapan. You're better off booking something in Samarinda.
Bayu Buana, Kompleks Rucco Bandar Blk 18, Jln Jend Sudirman, T0542-720 3389. Well-established operator. Recommended.
Musi, Jln Dondang (Antasari) 5A, T0542-24272, F24984. A variety of package tours, mainly up the Mahakam River. Recommended.

Samarinda *p342, map p343*
DeGigant Tours, 21 Jln Martadinata, T0541-7778648, www.borneotourgigant.com. Run by Lucas, a Dutch guy with over 18 years experience leading tourists around the region.
Eco Borneo Tours, 87 Jln Martadinata, T0541-747376. Reliable outfit offering houseboat tours up the Mahakam, trans-Kalimantan treks and overnight trips to Kutai.
PT Millda Tirta Tour and Travel, 37 Jln Panglima Batur, T0541-747089.
Waperisma Tour and Travel, 38 Jln KH Khalid, T0541-732 590.

Mahakam River *p345, map 346*
Ayus Wisata, Jln Argamulyo 83, Samarinda, T0541-743771, F732080. Adventure tourism specialist with a/c boats and experienced guides. Recommended.

Tour operators
Freelance guides When hiring a local guide, ensure that you have consulted a couple and have an idea of the different prices and experiences on offer. Cheaper tours up the Mahakam involve using public boats, nowhere near as comfortable as the private houseboats on offer. Guides usually linger around the **Aida** and **Hidayah** hotels, and hotel staff tip off guides when new foreign visitors arrive in town.
Jailani, T0813-4633 8343, www.geocities.com/visit_Kalimantan; Fajri, T0852-5009 8887; and their Dayak friend **Marten**, T0813-5482 4004, can arrange cheaper tailor-made trips upriver to Muara Muntai and Malak over 3-5 days, via houseboat and canoe for around US$150 per person per day (minimum 2 people) including all food, sheets, mosquito nets and guide. They also offer tours to Kutai, treks to longhouses and treks over the border to East Kalimantan.
Contact **Suriyadi**, another recommended guide, through **Hidayah I Hotel**. Damianus, T0812-4633 1194, is a Flores-born guide working for Dinas Pariwasata on Jln Sudirman. He can arrange a number of tours around the region and claims to offer treks to experience life with the Penan people near the Sarawak border.

Tarakan *p349*
Angkasa, Jln Sebengkok 33, T0551-21130.
Wisma Murni Travel, Hotel Wisata, T0551-21697.

☉ Transport

Balikpapan *p342, map p341*
Air
Sepinggang Airport (T0542-766886) is 10 km from Balikpapan. Airport facilities include a post office, souvenir shop, money changer and restaurant. Fixed-price taxis run from the airport to town (Rp 50,000, less from town to the airport). The cheapest way to travel from town to the airport is to catch a yellow *bemo* No 2 and then change onto a green *bemo* No 7. *Ojeks* do the run for around Rp 25,000.
Note VOA (Visa On Arrival) is available at Sepinggang Airport.

Direct daily flights to **Jakarta** with Garuda, Mandala, AirAsia, Lion Air and Sriwijya, **Surabaya** with Mandala, Citilink and Wings Air, **Makassar** with Merpati and Garuda and **Yogya** with Mandala.

International There are daily flights to **Singapore** with Silk Air. Prices for these flights are quite high and those on a budget are advised to book tickets with **AirAsia** or Sriwijaya and transit in Jakarta.
Kalimantan Balikapan is well connected to destinations in Kalimantan. **Kal Star** flies daily to **Samarinda, Berau, Nunukan** and **Tarakan**. Batavia flies daily to **Banjarmasin, Tarakan** and **Berau**. Susi Air flies to **Melak, Samarinda** and on to **Long Ampung** in the Apo Kayan. Mandala and Batavia also fly to **Tarakan**.
Airline offices Batavia, BDI Jln MT Haryono, T0542-739230. **Garuda**, Jln Jend A Yani 19, T0542-422301. **Kal Star**, Airport, T0542-737473 **Mandala**, Jln Jend Sudirman, T0542-410708. **Sriwijaya**, Jln Jend Sudirman, T0542-749422. **Susi Air**, Jln Pupuk Raya 33, T0811-211 3086.

Boat
Pelni ships *Dobonsolo, Kelimutu, Fudi* Tidar and *Nggapalu* dock at the harbour west of the centre, off Jln Yos Sudarso, and call at various places around the archipelago. Useful destinations include **Makassar, Tarakan, Tanjung Priok** and ports in **Papua** for those looking for some more jungle action. The **Pelni** office is at No 1 Jln Yos Sudarso, T0542-424171.

Road

Local *Bemo* trips around town cost Rp 3000. They take a circular route, down Jln Jend A Yani, Jln Jend Sudirman and past the Pertamina complex on Jln Minyak. They can be hailed at any point; shout 'Kiri!' (literally 'Left!') when you want to alight. *Ojeks* charge around Rp 7000 for a short journey and can also be chartered for a minimum Rp 40,000 per hr.

Bus Regular long-distance connections with Samarinda and Banjarmasin. Express buses to **Samarinda** leave frequently between 0530-2000 from Batu Ampar terminal at Km 3.5 on the Samarinda road (2½ hrs, Rp 21,000). (To get to Batu Ampar terminal take a Kijang taxi to Rapak, the junction with the Samarinda Rd. From Rapak, taxis and *bemos* leave for Batu Ampar when full; alternatively, take an *ojek*.) Buses to **Banjarmasin** (12-14 hrs, Rp 155,000) also leave from the Batu Ampar terminal or from Penajam, on the other side of the bay. Boats cross to Penajam from Pasar Baru at the north end of town on Jln Monginsidi, 10 mins.

Taxi Saloon taxis for up to 7 also go to **Samarinda** from Batu Ampar bus terminal. You can charter an a/c taxi to Samarinda.

Samarinda *p342, map p343*
Air
The airport is on the northeastern outskirts of town. A new airport is under construction further away from the town centre and is due for completion at the end of 2010. Currently, **Kal Star** flies from Samarinda to **Balikpapan**, and onwards to **Nunakan**, **Tarakan** and **Berau**. **Susi Air** has 4 flights a week to **Long Ampung** on Wed, Thu, Sat and Sun; book as far in advance as possible.

Airline offices Kal Star, 80 Jln Gatot Subroto, T0541-742119. Susi Air have no office in Samarinda, but one in Balikpapan; see above.

Boat
Sapulidi speedboat from the end of Jln Gajah Mada (near the post office). Terminal Feri, Jln Sungai Kunjang, is the launchpad for **Mahakam River tours**. To get there, take a green bemo (Rp 3000). There are 2 daily departures up the Mahakam at 0700 calling at Melak, Long Irum and Long Bagun (40-plus hrs, Rp 250,000). Boats are fairly comfortable, sleeping quarters are fan-cooled and travellers are provided with a mattress.

The **Pelni** vessel *Binaiya* calls here on its fortnightly circuit between ports in Kalimantan and **Java**. The *Binaiya* has a useful to connection to **Sampit** for those wishing to head to **Tanjung Puting**. Pelni office, 76 Jln Yos Sudarso, T0541-741402.

Road
Local Minibuses: as in Balikpapan, these are called taxis. Red ones head to Terminal Lempakek, 5 km from the town centre and congregate around Mesra Indah Komplex, Rp 3000. Green ones go to **Sungai Kunjang** (for upriver trips and express buses to Balikpapan). *Bemos* are colour coded to different destinations. For *bemos* to the north, wait on Jln Awang Long; for those travelling west, Jln Sudirman or Jln Gajah Mada.

Ojeks congregate around the Pasar Pagi (Morning Market); Rp 7000 around town (can be chartered for Rp 40,000 per hr).

Bus Southbound buses arrive and depart from Seberang on the outskirts of town on the south bank of the river: **Banjarmasin** (15 hrs, Rp 175,000). The terminal can be reached by green taxis (see Local above) or by boat – a pleasant trip from Pasar Pagi (Rp 2000, boats leave when full); the station is immediately behind the ferry terminal. Buses to **Bontang Sengagata** (for **Kutai**) and **Berau** leave from Terminal Lempakek, 5 km to northeast of town. Express buses to **Balikpapan** (2½ hrs, Rp 21,000), **Tenggarong** (1 hr) and **Melak** leave from Terminal Sungai Kunjang.

Taxi Taxis to **Balikpapan** leave from Sungai Kunjang; to **Bontang** from Terminal Segeri.

Tenggarong p344

Boat

Travelling by public transport (staying in *losmen* and longhouses en route) gives you more contact with locals and costs a fraction of the price of a package tour. However, these boats are much less comfortable than the big houseboats operated by tour companies. There are regular connections from Sungai Kunjang in Samarinda to all settlements upriver to Long Bagun (in the wet season) and Long Iram (in the dry season). Boats leave from Sungai Kunjang in the early to mid-morning: **Kota Bangun**, 9 hrs, **Tanjung Isuy**, 14 hrs, **Muara Muntai**, 12-14 hrs, **Melak**, 24 hrs, **Long Iram**, 36 hrs, **Long Bagun**, 40 hrs. It's possible to charter a longboat anywhere along the river for a cruise.

Road

The **Petugas** terminal is outside town; *bemos* ferry passengers into the centre. Regular connections by **Taksi kota** (*colts*) with **Samarinda**, 1 hr, or take the ferry; Tenggarong lies 3 hrs upstream from Samarinda.

Mahakam River p345, map 346

The Lower Mahakam: Samarinda to Muara Muntai

There are daily bus connections from Kota Bangun to Samarinda. There are boat connections with Samarinda from **Muara Muntai** (12-14 hrs on the express boat), as well as public boats upriver to **Tanjung Isuy**, 2½ hrs. Boats from Samarinda to Tanjung Isuy every Mon and Thu. From Tanjung Isuy, **Mancong** is 3 hrs' walk (one way); 2½ hrs canoe (one way), or you can get there by hired motorcycle.

The Middle and Upper Mahakam

It takes about 25 hrs from Samarinda by boat to **Melak**. Few tours make it as far as Long Iram, 1½ days from Samarinda; it is possible to go further upriver, but this usually means chartering a longboat, which is expensive.

The Apo Kayan p349

Air

There are 4 weekly flights to/from **Tarakan** (Mon, Wed, Fri, Sat) via Malinau on Susi Air, and 4 weekly flights to/from **Samarinda** (Wed, Thu, Sat and Sun). Flights from both places take 1½-2 hrs and need to be booked as far in advance as possible as seats on these tiny Cessnas are limited. Book through the **Susi Air** office in Balikpapan, T0811-211 3086.

Tarakan p349

Air

Regular connections to **Balikapan** with Mandala, Batavia and Merpati. Kal Star has frequent flights to **Nunukan**, **Balikpapan**, **Berau** and **Samarinda**. Susi Air flies to **Long Ampung** in the Apo Kayan 4 times weekly via Malinau (Mon, Wed, Sat and Sun).

Taxis to town from the airport charge Rp 25,000 or chartered *bemo* charge about Rp 15,000.

Airline offices Batavia Air, 11 A Jln Yos Sudarso, T0551-23385. DAS, Jln Sudirman 9, T0551-51578. Kalstar, Juwata Airport. MAF, Jln Sudirman 129 (Hotel Barito Timur), T0551-51011. Mandala, 10 Jln Yos Sudarso, T0551-22929. Merpati, Jln Yos Sudarso 8, T0551-21875.

Boat

The **Pelni** office is at the main port, at the south end of Jln Yos Sudarso. The **Pelni** ships *Dobonsolo*, *Umsini* and *Tidar* call here on their way to **Java** and **Sulawesi**, and ports in Kalimantan including **Balikpapan**. Daily ferries to **Nunukan**. There is a daily ferry (except Sun) to **Tawau** in Sabah (4 hrs, RM140).

Road

Bemos around town charge Rp 300.

Nunukan p349

Air

Kal Star offers regular flights to **Berau**, **Samarinda**, **Balikpapan** and **Tarakan**.

Boat
Twice daily connections by ferry (which are packed) with **Tawau** in Sabah (1 hr, RM75). Also daily ferries to **Tarakan**. The Pelni ships *Dobonsolo, Tidar, Awu,* and *Umsini* dock here. The Pelni office is at 11 Jln A Yani, T0556 21309.

❸ Directory

Balikpapan *p342, map p341*
Banks There are lots of banks along Jln A Yani and Jln Jend Sudirman including BNI, Lippo Bank and BCA. The best place to change money is at the authorized money changer Haji La Tunrong, 73 Jln A Yani. Rates here are fair and there is no commission.
Internet There's a pleasant a/c internet café: **Data Net**, 12 Jln Jend Sudirman, 0900-2200, Rp 6000 per hr. Free Wi-Fi access

is available at the foodcourt in the 3rd floor of Balikpapan Trade Mall. **Medical services** Public Hospital, Jln Yani, T0542-872222. International Hospital, Jln MT Haryono.

Samarinda *p342, map p343*
Banks Banks can be found on Jln Sudirman and include DBS, Lippo Bank and BCA.
Internet There's a comfortable place next to Kedai Borneo (opposite Mesra Indah Mall) on Jln Abdul Hasan, Rp 3000 per hr. Free Wi-Fi is available at the foodcourt on the 3rd floor of Mesra Indah Mall.
Telephone 24-hr telephone on Jln Awang Long; also in Citra Niaga Plaza.

Tarakan *p349*
Banks Bank Dagang Negara, Jln Yos Sudarso, for TCs and cash.

West Kalimantan (Kalbar)

Kalbar attracts few tourists as it is cut off from Kalimantan's other provinces. It occupies a fifth of Kalimantan (146,800 sq km) and is mostly very flat. The Kapuas River, Indonesia's longest at 1243 km, runs east to west through the middle. Its headwaters, deep in the interior, are in the Muller range, fringing the northeast and east borders of Kalbar.

The Kapuas River is navigable for most of its length, which – as with the Mahakam River in East Kalimantan – has allowed merchants and missionaries to penetrate the interior over the past century. There are small towns along the river and the surrounding forest has been heavily logged. For tourists, the Kapuas is less interesting than the Mahakam River and those in neighbouring Sarawak. As few foreign visitors make the trip, however, the Kapuas River is certainly not touristy.

To the north, the province borders Sarawak, and the east end of this frontier runs along the remote Kapuas Hulu mountain range. The southeast border with Central Kalimantan province follows the Schwaner Range.

About two thirds of West Kalimantan's jungle (a total of some 95 000 sq km) is classed as production forest; most of the remaining 30 000 sq km is protected, but it is such a large area that it is impossible to guard against illegal loggers. The timber industry is the province's economic backbone, but Kalbar is also a major rubber producer. ▶▶ *For listings, see pages 364-368.*

Background

History
At about the time Java's Hindu Majapahit Empire was disintegrating in the mid-1300s, a number of small Malay sultanates grew up along the coast of West Kalimantan. These controlled upriver trade and exploited the Dayaks of the interior. When Abdul Rahman, an

Arab seafarer-cum-pirate, decided to set up a small trading settlement at Pontianak in 1770, he crossed the paths of some of these sultans. This prompted the first Dutch intervention in the affairs of West Kalimantan, but they did not stay long and for the next 150 years their presence was minimal: Borneo's west coast ranked low on the colonial administration's agenda. A gold rush in the 1780s brought Hakka Chinese immigrants flooding into the Sambas area. Their descendants – after several generations of intermarriage with Dayaks – make up more than 10% of West Kalimantan's population today, most living in Pontianak. In the 19th century, the Dutch were worried about the intentions of Rajah James Brooke of Sarawak as he occupied successive chunks of the Sultanate of Brunei. In response, the Dutch increased their presence but any threat that Brooke posed to Dutch territory never materialized. During the Second World War, the people of Kalbar suffered terribly at the hands of the Japanese Imperial Army, who massacred more than 21,000 people in the province, many at Mandor in June 1944.

People

West Kalimantan's 3.9 million inhabitants are concentrated along the coasts and rivers. Malay Muslims make up about 40% of the population, Dayaks account for another 40%, Chinese 11% and the remainder include Buginese (originally from Sulawesi) and Minangkabau (originally from Sumatra). West Kalimantan has also received large numbers of transmigrants from Java. Most were originally resettled at Rasau Jaya, to the south of Pontianak, but many have come to the metropolis to find work as labourers – while others have simply resorted to begging. Tribal people also come to Pontianak from settlements upriver on the Kapuas; they have usually fared better than the transmigrants and a number hold important jobs in the provincial administration.

Tourism

In 1986 only 5000 foreign tourists arrived in Kalbar; by 1990 this had quadrupled and, following the opening of the Entikong border crossing on the Sarawak frontier, the number of tourists rose by around 50%. The vast majority of these were curious Malaysians. Westerners account for less than a tenth of Pontianak's tourist arrivals; up to 2000 a year according to provincial government figures. The main reason for this is that the province is rather lacking in tourist sites and receives little attention in the national tourism promotion literature. True, Kalbar has jungle, rivers, ethnic minorities and offshore islands, but these can also be found in countless other more accessible places in Indonesia.

English is not widely spoken in Kalbar: visitors are advised to learn some basic Bahasa, particularly those heading upriver. Tourist literature produced by the provincial tourism office waxes lyrical about Kalbar's many beautiful islands and national parks. But it fails to mention that few of these have any facilities for tourists and most are very difficult to get to. Visitors who want to immerse themselves in Dayak culture and visit traditional longhouses will not find much of interest in Kalbar; only a few tribal groups still live in longhouses on the upper reaches of Kapuas River and its tributaries.

Pontianak → *For listings, see pages 364-368. Colour map 3, A1.*

Living in Pontianak would be like a European living in a city called Dracula; the name literally translates as 'the vampire ghost of a woman who dies in childbirth'. Apparently, hunters who first came to this area heard terrible screams in the jungle at night and were so scared by them that they dubbed the area 'the place that sounds like a *pontianak*'. But modern Pontianak is no ghost town. It is a thriving, prosperous town with a satellite dish on almost every rooftop. A third of the population of 387,000 is Chinese. Other ethnic groups are Melayu (26%), Bugis (13%), Javanese (12%) and Dayaks (3%).

The confluence of the Kapuas and Landak rivers, where the Arab adventurer Abdul Rahman founded the original settlement in 1770, is strongly Malay. This area, which encompasses several older kampongs, is known as Kampong Bugis. The commercial heart of Pontianak is on the left bank of the Kapuas, around the old Chinese quarter. The other side of the river is called Siantan and is distinguished only by its bus terminal, a few rubber-smoking factories (whose choking smell permeates the air) and the pride of Pontianak: the Equator Monument. Like other cities in Kalimantan, Pontianak derives much of its wealth from timber – there seem to be scores of plywood factories and sawmills close to the city. The second string to Pontianak's economic bow, so to speak, is Siam orange production, of which it is Indonesia's largest grower.

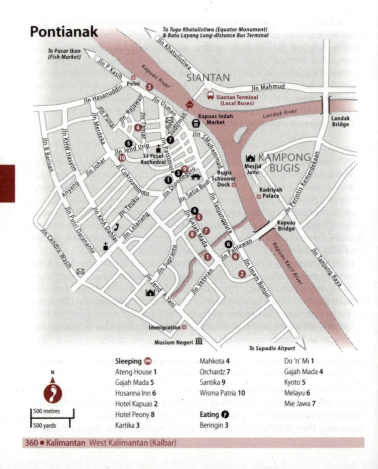

Pontianak

Sleeping
Ateng House **1**
Gajah Mada **5**
Hosanna Inn **6**
Hotel Kapuas **2**
Hotel Peony **8**
Kartika **3**
Mahkota **4**
Orchardz **7**
Santika **9**
Wisma Patria **10**

Eating
Beringin **3**
Do 'n' Mi **1**
Gajah Mada **4**
Kyoto **5**
Melayu **6**
Mie Jawa **7**

N

500 metres
500 yards

Modern-day Pontianak is a fairly grim city, hot and humid and with little to recommend it to tourists. Roads are choked with waspish motorbikes and crossing from one side to the other could test the patience of a saint. Foreign visitors are few and far between and primarily visit the city as a stopover between Sarawak and Tanjung Puting in Kalimantan's south.

Tourist information The **Department of Posts and Telecommunications** (Parpostel) ① *Jln Sutan Syahril 17, T0561-739444*, has information on travelling around Kalbar, but not much English is spoken. The **tourist information office** is at the airport (and at Entikong border crossing) and the **Tourist Promotion Office** (Kalbar) ① *Jln Achmad Sood 25, T0561-736172*, is out of town.

Sights

The **Musium Negeri** ① *southern end of Jln Jend A Yani, Tue-Sun 0900-1300*, the state museum, contains good models of longhouses and a comprehensive display of Dayak household implements, including a collection of tattoo blocks; weapons, from blowpipes to blunderbusses; one sad-looking skull; masks; fish traps and musical instruments. There are examples of Dayak textiles, ikat, *songket* and basketry. There is also a model of a Malay house and a collection of typical household implements. The Dayak and Malay communities are represented in the huge relief sculptures on the front of the museum. But there is absolutely nothing on or in it acknowledging the presence of the large Chinese population other than some Chinese ceramics. Nor, unfortunately, are any of the objects labelled in English. To get there take an *oplet* (pickup) from Kapuas Indah covered market. Just past the museum is the huge whitewashed West Kalimantan governor's office. There is a replica Dayak longhouse near the museum, off Jalan Jend A Yani, built in 1985 to stage a Koran-reading contest.

The ironwood *istana* or *kraton*, **Kadriyah Palace** ① *open 0900-1730, admission by donation*, was built at the confluence of the Landak and Kapuas rivers by the town's Arab founding father, Abdul Rahman, shortly after he established the trading settlement. The palace was home to seven sultans; Sharif Yusof, son of the seventh, looks after it today. His uncle married a Dutch woman whose marble bust is one of the eccentric collection of items which decorate the palace museum. Among the fascinating array of odds and ends are two 5 m-tall decorated French mirrors, made in 1923; these face each other across the room and Sharif's party trick is to hold a lighter up to create an endless corridor of reflected flames. There is also a selection of past sultans' *bajus* and *songkoks*, a jumble of royal regalia, including two thrones, tables of Italian marble and a photograph of the sixth sultan and his heir, who were murdered by the Japanese in a mass killing during the Second World War.

Next to the palace, the **Mesjid Jami** (mosque), or Mesjid Abdurrahman, was built soon after the founding of the city in the late 1700s, although it has been renovated over the years. It is a beautiful building with tiered roofs, standing at the confluence of the two rivers, with its lime-green, turret-like minarets and its bell-shaped upper roof. The Kapuas riverbank next to the mosque is a pleasant place to sit and watch life on the river – the elegant Bugis schooners berth at the docks on the opposite bank. The sky over the mosque and palace is alive with kites flown by the children in Kampong Bugis.

Over the Landak Bridge and past the stinking Siantan rubber smokehouses, which line the right bank of the Kapuas, is the **Tugu Khatulistiwa** (Equator Monument). During the March and September equinoxes, the column's shadow disappears, which is an excuse for a party in Pontianak. In 1991, the old *belian* (ironwood) equator column was encased in a new architectural wonder, a sort of concrete mausoleum where it is intelligently hidden from the sun. There is a 6-m column on top.

The heart of the city, around **Kapuas Indah** indoor market, is an interesting and lively part of town. There are a number of *pekong* (Taoist temples) around the market area; the oldest, **Sa Seng Keng**, contains a huge array of gods. The **Dwi Dharma Bhakti Chinese Temple** on Jalan Tanjungpura is notable for its location in the middle of the main street.

The **Pasar Ikan** (Fish Market), downriver from town on Jalan Pak Kasih, is a great place to wander in the early morning; the stallholders are just as interesting as the incredible variety of fish they sell. One of the best things to do in Pontianak is to hire a **sampan** for a couple of hours and just potter along the river, taking in all the activity.

Around Pontianak

Tourist facilities and sights are limited outside Pontianak. Some areas along the northwest coast, including offshore islands, can be visited in day-long excursions from Pontianak, and these have been listed under the separate sections, see below.

A couple of Pontianak's tour operators offer city tours and short package tours along the west coast to Singkawang and Sambas regencies, as well as offshore islands. Longer upriver trips on the Kapuas can be arranged, as can adventure tours with jungle trekking and whitewater rafting. **Berjaya Tour** offers whitewater rafting trips to rapids on the Pinoh River.

Singkawang and the northwest coast → *For listings, see pages 364-368.*
Colour map 3, A1.

Singkawang was originally settled by Hakka Chinese in the early 1800s and was the main town servicing the nearby gold rush shanty at Mantrado. It is now an important farming area and is named after a local turnip. About 7 km south of Singkawang is a **pottery** village, where replicas of antique Chinese ceramics are fired in a big kiln.

Facilities are being developed on **Pulau Randayan**, a 12-ha island with good coral. It's two hours by boat from Pasir Panjang and you can stay overnight. Trips to the island are organized by Mr Sukartadji, owner of the **Palapa Hotel** in Singkawang. Alternatively, Berjaya Tour in Pontianak can arrange a trip.

Pulau Temajo, 60 km south of Singkawang (off the coast from the village of Sungai Kunyit), is an island with white-sand beaches and good coral. There is some accommodation available on the island. **Ateng Tours & Travel** in Pontianak (see page 366) can advise on the best way to get there; the company also runs one-day package tours to the island, supplying food and skin-diving equipment.

Kapuas River → *For listings, see pages 364-368. Colour map 3, A1-A3.*

The first European to venture up the 1243-km-long Kapuas River was a Dutchman, Major George Muller, who reached the site of present-day Putussibau in 1822 and who lent his name to the mountains to the east. Four years later, while attempting to cross these mountains from the upper Mahakam to the Kapuas, he had his head taken by Dayaks. The Dayaks of the upper Kapuas were themselves terrorized by Iban headhunters, mostly from the Batang Lupar in Sarawak, although some Iban settled in the area to the north of the Kapuas. Few Dayak communities (except those in more remote areas) live in traditional longhouses or observe tribal rituals today. Those who did not turn to Islam (under the influence of the coastal Malays) converted to Christianity: there is a large number of Roman Catholic and Protestant evangelists working throughout the Kapuas Basin; Christians (mainly Catholics) make up about 28% of Kalbar's population.

There is still a lot of gold panning along the Kapuas – using *palong dulang* pans – and larger operations have turned some areas of jungle into a moonscape. Many Dayaks are also employed in the logging industry. Although it is possible to take a *bandung* barge all the way up the river from Pontianak (four or five days to Putussibau, Rp 40,000), most tourists opt to travel to Sintang by road, which branches off the coast road from Sungai Pinyuh, 50 km northwest of Pontianak.

Pah Auman and north of the river

Between Pontianak and Ngabang (120 km from Pontianak, en route to Entikong), Pah Auman is the nearest village to Kamung Saham longhouse (12 km by road). This 30-door Kendayang (or Kenatyan) longhouse is one of the most traditional longhouses remaining in Kalbar, despite not being particularly remote. You can ask the Kepala Desa's (village head's) permission to stay here overnight. Travellers think that the further they go into the interior, the further they will get from civilization, but Kalbar is not like neighbouring Sarawak. The area north of the Kapuas River was a focus of the *Konfrontasi*, the brief war between Indonesia and Malaysia from 1963 to 1965. The West Kalimantan Communist Party was also active in the area in the late 1960s, before being crushed.

Sintang and further east

Sintang (245 km, eight hours east of Pontianak) is at the confluence of the Kapuas and Melawi rivers. About 18 km from town is Mount Kelam (Dark Mountain), which at 900 m affords good views of the surrounding plains and rivers. Guides can be hired in Sintang (two hours' walk to the summit). Sintang is a mainly Chinese town, founded by traders dealing with the Dayaks of the interior. On the upper reaches of the Melawi – and its tributary, the Pinoh – there are some traditional Ot Danum (upriver) Dayak groups (the equivalent of Sarawak's Orang Ulu), notably the Dohoi on the upper Melawi. The two rivers begin in the Schwaner Range.

Sentarum, Luar and Sumpa lakes

From **Semitau**, halfway between Sintang and Putussibau, it's possible to visit Sentarum, Luar and Sumpa lakes. The lake area is mainly settled by Ibans, who originally came upriver from the Batang Lupar in Sarawak; other tribal groups include Maloh Dayaks (famed for their skill as silversmiths and goldsmiths) and the Kantuq.

Putussibau

Putussibau is the last noteworthy settlement on the Kapuas before the Muller Range, which divides the watersheds of the Kapuas and Mahakam (in East Kalimantan). In the 1800s, when Chinese traders first visited the Upper Kapuas, the settlement was often raided by Iban headhunters from the Batang Lupar in Sarawak. The Malays along the Upper Kapuas are mainly Dayaks who converted to Islam. Despite Putussibau's remoteness, few Dayaks in the area live in traditional longhouses, the exception being the Taman Kapuas Dayaks. Two Taman Kapuas longhouses are accessible from Putussibau: **Melapi I** and **Semangkok**, the latter being more traditional; it is possible to stay overnight at both (see also box, page 124). Longboats for expeditions further upriver are very expensive to charter; regular passenger boats link main towns.

South of Pontianak → *Colour map 3, B2.*

There are few tourist attractions in the southern **Ketapang** regency, except for the 90,000-ha **Mount Palung Wildlife Reserve**, which encompasses most forest types and contains a wealth of flora and fauna, including orang-utans and proboscis monkeys. It is difficult – and expensive – to get to and is mainly a scientific research centre; there are, however, basic facilities at nine camps within the park. Permits must be obtained from the **Conservation Office (PHPA)** ⓘ *Jln Abdurrahman Saleh 33*, in Pontianak. If you would like to visit the reserve, contact Ricky or Helena at **Berjaya Tours**, page 366, whose company can organize the tortuous travel arrangements.

◉ West Kalimantan (Kalbar) listings

For Sleeping and Eating price codes and other relevant information, see Essentials pages 23-27.

⬤ Sleeping

Pontianak *p359, map p360*
Pontianak has a good range of mid-range accommodation. There are a couple of fair choices for more budget-minded travellers.
A Mahkota, Jln Sidas 8, T0561-736022, www.grandmahkotahotel.com. Not far from the port, this swish hotel has modern rooms with Wi-Fi access. Facilities at the hotel include a café, karaoke lounge and business centre. Rack rates here are overly expensive and lack of custom sees discounts of up to 35%. Good buffet breakfast included in the price.
A Santika, 46 Jln Diponegoro, T0561-733777, www.santika.com. Popular business hotel offering some excellent discounts. Rooms are clean and comfortable with cable TV, Wi-Fi access and slick bathrooms. **Bamboo Café** serves good Indonesian and Chinese cuisine. Prices are generally too high compared to other choices in town. A pool is to be added in the near future.
A-B Orchardz, 89 Jln Gajah Mada, T0561-768999, www.pontianak.orchardzhotel.com. Sprawling hotel with 148 modern rooms with earthy relaxed hues, modern decor and tasteful artwork adorning the walls. The rooms have LCD TVs, free Wi-Fi access and some offer excellent city views. Recommended.
B Gajah Mada, 177 Jln Gajah Mada, T0561 761598, www.hotelgajahmada.com. Smart

hotel popular for meetings and conventions. The 'moderate' rooms are stuck in the basement car park and are to be avoided at all costs. An extra Rp 50,000 gets a spacious modern room with TV and Wi-Fi access (chargeable). This is a solid mid-range option, though not as nice as its sister hotel, **Hotel Peony**. Breakfast included.
B Hotel Kapuas, 889 Jln Gajah Mada, T0561-736122, www.hotelkapuas.com. Massive hotel with endless corridors and plenty of 1960s concrete charm. Rooms are huge and comfortable with cable TV and attached bathroom with tub. There is a decent-sized pool at the back with sun loungers and a good restaurant serving mainly Indonesian fare. Wi-Fi available (chargeable – expensive).
B Hotel Peony, 86 Jln Gajah Mada T0561-732878, www.hotelpeony.com. Plenty of clean lines and minimalist decor are the themes at this excellent option. The city view rooms are worth the money, offering beautiful city views. Rooms are well equipped with Wi-Fi access (chargeable), cable TV and comfy beds. Great café on the 5th floor, **Rooftop**. Breakfast included. Highly recommended.
B Kartika, Jln Rahardi Usman, T0561-734401. Old hotel near the port with spacious clean and functional a/c rooms with TV, fridge and nasty blue carpets. Wi-Fi is available (chargeable at a steep Rp 55,000 for 10 hrs). Good restaurant and friendly staff. Better rooms offer views over the river.

C-D Ateng House, 201 Jln Gajah Mada (above Ateng Tours), T0561-732683, atenghouse@yahoo.com. Fair budget option with bright, slightly tatty a/c rooms with TV. The twin rooms are a bit cramped.

C-D Hosanna Inn, 224 Jln Pahlawan (above Berjaya Tour), T0561-735052, www.hosannainn.com. Excellent guesthouse with a selection of clean a/c rooms with TV. Almost all rooms are windowless and have shared bathroom. There's a pleasant communal area with TV and Wi-Fi access and the staff here are friendly and helpful. Breakfast included in the price. Highly recommended.

D Wisma Patria, Jln Hos Cokroaminoto 497 (Jln Merdeka Timur), T0561-736063. A/c, Sprawling old homestay option with plenty of broken doors and toilets without seats. Rooms are some of the cheapest in town, and standards are fairly spacious with TV and a/c. Economy rooms are grim. There's also a small café downstairs.

Singkawang and the northwest coast
p362

B Mahkota, Jln Diponegoro 1, Singkawang, T0562-631244. A/c, restaurant, pool, sister hotel to Mahkota in Pontianak with equally good range of facilities.

B Palapa Beach, 17 Jln Padang Pasir, Singkawang T0562 633402. Cottage-style, beachside hotel, with a/c, restaurant, pool, tennis court and water sports.

C Wisata, Jln Diponegoro 59, Singkawang, T0562-632047. Clean rooms and good English-speaking receptionist.

Sintang *p363*

D Flamboyan. Some a/c and some baths, a notch up from the Sasean.

D Sasean, Jln Brig Jend Katamso on the river. Welcoming.

⦿ Eating

Pontianak *p359, map p360*

🍴 **Gajah Mada**, Jln Gajah Mada 202. Big Chinese-run restaurant with a landscaped interior offering very high-quality food, particularly seafood and freshwater fish. Specialities include: *jelawat* (West Kalimantan river fish), *hekeng* (chopped, deep-fried shrimp), *kailan ca thik pow* (thinly sliced salted fish), crab *fu yung* and sautéed frog. Recommended.

🍴 **Kyoto**, 33 Jln Jendral Urip. Open 1000-2300. Pseudo-Japanese joint with staff dressed like extras from a 1980s kung fu movie. Nevertheless, the ambience is pleasant, with lanterns and low tables and the food is fairly priced with good set teriyaki and teppanyaki meals, ramen and plenty of deep-fried treats.

🍴 **Rooftop**, Hotel Peony, 86 Jln Gajah Mada. Lovely rooftop café with a menu of burgers, Asian dishes and some excellent fresh juices – the apple and ginger is very refreshing. A night-time visit offers views over the dimly lit city and a nice environment for a chilled beer.

🍴🍴 **Restoran Pondok Sunda**, 36 Jln Suprapto, T0561-768303. Open 1000-2200. Set in a leafy neighbourhood, this lime green villa has a pleasant outdoors seating area at the back and makes for a pleasant venue to escape the bustle of the city. The cusine is mainly Sundanese (West Java) with a lot of good seafood. Recommended are the prawns or the crab. There are also excellent value set lunches. Recommended.

🍴 **Beringin**, Jln Diponegoro 113 and 149. 2 Padang restaurants within 40 m of each other. These restaurants are held in high regard by locals for their superb, cheap West Sumatran dishes. Apart from the standard rendang and *ayam gulai* dishes, try the *sambal sotong* and *sate Padang* here. Highly recommended. Other good *nasi Padang* places to look for include **Seri Bundo** and **Sintaro** (both on Jln Tunku Umar), both highly recommended by locals.

Do 'n' Mi, Jln Pattimura. Well-known bakery held in high regard by the city's middle classes. The cakes and buns are baked Indonesian style, fresh in ovens on the pavement outside. The cakes and breads are nothing exciting, but offer a break from Indonesian food.

Mie Jawa, Jln Nusa Indah 1. A/c restaurant popular with the city's youth. The menu offers good Indonesian staples including *pangsit*, *bakso* and bowls of steaming spicy noodle soup. Good value.

Pinang Merah Restoran, Disko dan Singing House, Jln Kapten Marsan 51-53 (behind Kapuas Indah), down the alleyway past the **Wijaya Kusuma Hotel**. Very cool and pleasant place for a drink in the early evening, on wooden walkway next to the river. Seafood and Chinese dishes.

Melayu, Jln Pahlawan (opposite Damri office). Great spot for a cheap local dinner with a large selection of *nasi campur* treats. The *ikan asam pedas* and *tempe* here are tasty.

Foodstalls

Bobo Indah, opposite the **Wijaya Kusuma Hotel** next to the colourful cinema hoardings. There are also some stalls next to the river. In the mornings there are hawker stalls selling breakfast fishballs and *mee kepitang* (noodles and crab) along Jln Nusa Indah II. In the evenings, on the south side of Jln Diponegoro, there are lots of hawker stalls that sell a range of cheap Chinese, Padang and Batawi (Jakarta) food.

Fruit market, at the top of Jln Nusah Indah, next to St Yosef Katholik Kathedral. Excellent selection, including *jeruk* oranges from around Tebas, north of Singkawang. Their greeny-yellow appearance makes them look rather unappetizing, but they are very sweet. Good durians when in season in Jul and Aug.

Coffee shops

Warung kopi are the hubs of Pontianak social life. They serve not just good coffee, but also tasty snacks such as *pisang goreng* (deep-fried banana) and local patisseries.

Around Pontianak p362

Sea Food Garden, Kakap. About 30-mins' drive west of Pontianak, on the coast, in a village famous for its seafood. Local farm crabs, lobsters, shrimps and fish, recommended by locals.

✱ Festivals and events

Pontianak p359, map p360

1 Jan West Kalimantan Anniversary, commemorating its accession to the status of an autonomous province in 1957. Folk art exhibitions and dance.

21 Sep Naik Dango Festival (rice storage), when the sun is directly overhead at noon.

Nov Trans-Equator Marathon; in the past this has been a full 42-km event; in 1992 it became a quarter marathon (10 km).

◯ Shopping

Pontianak p359, map p360

Due mainly to its large Chinese population, Pontianak is full of gold shops. Dayak handicrafts, porcelain, textiles (including *ikat* and *songket*) and antiques sold, but it is more limited than Balikpapan and Samarinda. There's a row of stalls on Jln Pattimura selling *ikat*, basketware and sarongs.

Leny Art Shop, Jln Khattulistiwa, at the roundabout opposite the Equator Monument (also branch at 1A Blok D, Jln Nusa Indah III). Interesting antique Dayak pieces including stone axes, medicine boxes, knives, *ikat*, basketware and Chinese ceramics.

▲ Activities and tours

Pontianak p359, map p360

Tour operators

Ateng Tours & Travel, Jln Gajah Mada 201, T0561-732683. Recommended.

Berjaya Tours, 224 Jln Pahlawan, T0561-737325.

Citra Tour & Travel, Jln Rahadi Usman, T0561-736436.
Insan Worldwide Tours & Travel (ITT), Jln Tanjungpura 149.

Spas

Travellers in need of some pampering after the bumpy roads of Kalimantan are advised to check into **Martha Tilaar Spa**, 20 Jln A Yani, T0561-761080. This renowned relaxation centre also has branches in Jakarta, KL and Singapore.

⊖ Transport

Pontianak *p359, map p360*
Air

Supadio Airport is 20 km from town. Taxis between the airport and town cost Rp 35,000, although ticket agents in town should be able to book one for less. Illegal minivan taxis are plentiful and charge Rp 60,000 for a trip to the airport. Regular connections on **Garuda**, **Mandala**, **Sriwijaya**, **Batavia Air** and **Lion Air** to **Jakarta**. Batavia Air also flies from Pontianak to **Yogyakarta**, **Semarang**, **Batam** (for Singapore) and **Surabaya**. Pontianak is poorly connected with other desinations in Kalimantan. **Kal Star** uses small 40-seater ATRs to connect with destinations in Kalimantan including **Ketapang** (daily, Rp 495,000), **Pangkalanbun** (via Ketapang, daily, Rp 600,000) and **Banjarmasin** (daily, Rp 1,000,000).

International The only international flight departing Pontianak these days is the thrice-weekly hop over to **Kuching** in Sarawak (1 flight on Tue, Thu and Sun, 50 mins, Rp 600,000). Travellers wishing to head to **Singapore** are advised to take the **Batavia Air** flight to Batam from where it is a short 30-min ferry ride from Batam's Sekupang to Singapore.

Airline offices Batavia Air, Jln HOS Cokroaminoto 278A, T0561-732179; **Garuda**, Jln Rahadi Usman 8A, T0561-741441; **Kal Star**, 429 Jln Tanjung Pura, T0561-739090;

Lion Air, Airport, T0561-7066110; **Mandala**, Jln Ahmad Dahlan, T0561-766447; **Sriwijaya**, 10 Jln Gajah Mada, T0561-768777.

Boat

A comfortable a/c express launch departs for Ketapang (south of Pontianak) every odd date (21st, 23rd etc) at 0700. The only vessel doing the trip is the *Ekspress Bahari*. Prices start at Rp 150,000 for *economi* up to Rp 200,000 for *eksekutif* class.Tickets can be bought at numerous agents along Jln Pahlawan and Jln Gajah Mada. A good agent to try is **Berjaya Tour**, 224 Jln Pahlawan. *Bandong*, Kalbar's ungainly big river cargo barges, go from near the Hotel Wijaya Kusuma, Pontianak, to **Putusibau** (4 days, 3 nights), from Sep-Apr when the water level is high. Several **Pelni** ships call into Pontianak on their fortnightly circuits. The KM **Lawit** connects Pontianak with **Semarang** and eventually **Jakarta** (after a long trawl to Sibolga in Sumatra). The KM **Bukit Raya** heads to **Sampit** in KalTeng before crossing to **Surabaya** in Java. The KM **Leuser** sails from Pontianak to **Tanjung Priok** via **Tanjung Pandan**.

Pelni office, 17 Jln S Abdurachman, T0561-748124. There are loads of agents around the port that sell Pelni tickets. A good place to start in Jln P Kasih.

Road

Local Buses (*bis kota*) around the Pontianak area leave from Sintian terminal on the north side of the river (regular ferries cross the river from Jln Bardan to the terminal). *Ojeks* are a good way to see the sights; the easiest place to pick up an *ojek* is along Jln Tanjungpura. *Oplets* leave from Jln Kapten Marsan in front of the Kapuas Indah indoor market, next to the *warungs*; special demarcated routes to most destinations around town. There are also *oplet* stations on Jln Sisingamangaraja and Jln Teuku Cik Ditiro. **Taxis** (saloons): congregate around Jln Tanjungpura and Jln Pahlawan.

Long distance Buses travel as far as **Kota Kinabalu**, **Bandar Seri Begawan** and **Miri**, although these are not journeys to be undertaken lightly. There is no central long-distance terminal and buses leave and arrive outside their offices in town. Good companies include **Biaramas**, 165 Jln Diponegoro, T0561-765081; **Damri**, 220 Jln Pahlawan, next to Hosanna Inn; and **Bintang Jaya**, 310A Jln Tanjung Pura, T0561-6597402. Buses to **Kuching**, Malaysia, depart all morning and cross at **Entikong** (Rp 165,000, 10 hrs). **Damri** have regular buses to **Singkawang**, 3½ hrs, **Sambas**, **Sintang** (on the Kapuas River), 10 hrs, **Meliau**, **Tayan**, **Sekadan** and **Ngabang**.

Travellers coming from Malaysia will need to buy a visa at the border (US$25 for 30 days). Those who wish to stay longer in Indonesia can purchase a 60-day visa at the Indonesian consulates in Kuching or Kota Kinabalu. The visa situation in Indonesia is volatile. Check the latest situation before travelling.

Car Car hire is available from **Berjaya Tour**.
Taxi Long-distance taxis are available from the taxi office by the **Kartika Hotel**.

Singkawang and the northwest coast *p362*
Road 143 km north of Pontianak. There are regular connections with **Pontianak**.

Pah Auman and north of the river *p363*
Pah Auman can be reached on any east-bound bus from **Pontianak**'s Batu Layang bus station.

Sintang *p363*
Regular buses from **Pontianak**. There are regular passenger boats leaving Sintang for **Putussibau**. MAF flies between Sintang and **Putussibau**.

ⓘ Directory

Pontianak *p359, map p360*
Banks There are several banks along Jln Tanjungpura and Jln Gajah Mada (including **BCA Bank Danamon** and **Lippo Bank**). There are lots of money changers along Jln Tanjungpura and Jln Diponegoro.
Consulates Malaysia, 21 Jln Sutan Syahir, T0561-736 986. **Immigration offices** Jln Sutoyo, T0561-767655, for Pontianak.
Internet Internet is available at countless places in the town and most hotels (Rp 3000 per hr). Wi-Fi is available in most of the mid-range hotels, but is chargeable. Also, try the GPO, Mon-Thu, Sat, Sun 0800-1400, Fri 0800-1100. **Medical services** Dr Sudarso Hospital, Jln Adisucipto; Sei Jawi Hospital Centre, Jln Merdeka Barat. **Post office** Jln Rahadi Usman 1 and Jln Sultan Abdul, Rakhman 49, open 0800-2100. Poste restante available.
Telephone Department of Posts and Telecommunications (Parpostel), Jln Sutan Syahril 17, T0561-739444. **Telkom office**, Jln Teuku Umar 15, open 24 hrs.

Background

History

Borneo was first visited by Europeans in the early 16th century, most notably by Antonio Pigafetta, the official chronicler on the Portuguese explorer Ferdinand Magellan's expedition, which called in on the Sultan of Brunei in 1521. The Ibans of Sarawak maintain that the name Borneo derives from the Malay *buah nyior* (coconut) while the Malays had another, less well-known name for the island: Kalimantan. This appears to have been the name of a species of wild mango "and the word would simply mean 'Isle of Mangoes'". This was the name chosen by Indonesia for its section of the island; it is generally translated as River of Diamonds, probably because of the diamond fields near Martapura in the south.

The outside world may have been trading with Borneo from Roman times and there is evidence in Kaltim (East Kalimantan) of Indian cultural influence from as early as the fourth century. Chinese traders began to visit Borneo from about the seventh century; they traded beads and porcelain in exchange for jungle produce and birds' nests. By the 14th century, this trade appears to have been flourishing, particularly with the newly formed Sultanate of Brunei. The history of the north coast of Borneo is dominated by the Sultanate of Brunei from the 14th to 19th centuries. The Europeans began arriving in the East in the early 1500s, but had little impact on North Borneo until British adventurer James Brooke arrived in Sarawak in 1839.

To the south, in what is now Kalimantan, a number of small coastal sultanates grew up, many of which were tributary states of Brunei and most of which are thought to have been founded by members of the Brunei nobility. The upriver Dayaks were left largely to themselves. In the 16th century, following the conversion of Banjarmasin to Islam, the religion was embraced by these other sultanates. The Dutch, who first tried to control Banjarmasin's pepper trade in the late 1500s, were unsuccessful in Kalimantan until 1817 when they struck a deal with the Sultan of Banjarmasin.

In the last 20 years Kalimantan has hit world headlines for all the wrong reasons, with illegal logging contributing to a choking haze that caused havoc in parts of Southeast Asia. However, it was the images of beheaded corpses and tales of tribal violence that really caught the world's attention, as Kalimantan was rocked by a series of ultra violent eruptions in the late 1990s and early 2000s. Transmigrants from Madura, an island off Java, were the targets of this Dayak-led pogrom. The Madurese settled in Kalteng in great numbers, making up 21% of the population, and quickly became fairly affluent from their business interests in the logging and plantation industries. They also imported Islam into areas where the Christian faith of the Dayaks had once dominated. Violent eruptions occurred in Kalbar in the late 1990s and in 2001, huge clashes broke out in Sampit leaving over 500 Madurese dead, and 100,000 more fleeing the province, many from boats heading to Java from Kumai. Many believe the Dayak violence to be a direct result of the transmigration scheme, settling people from crowded Java and Bali to the outlying islands without thinking through the consequences of the potent ethnic cocktails and the potential for seething resentments that were being created. See also box, page 371.

Culture

People

The vast majority of Borneo's population is concentrated in the narrow coastal belt; the more mountainous, jungled interior is sparsely populated by Dayak tribes. While Dayak communities are represented in all state and provincial governments in Borneo, they only have one province of their own: Kalimantan Tengah (Central Kalimantan), with its capital at Palangkaraya. The Dayaks lived in self-sufficient communities in the interior until they began to come under the influence of Malay coastal sultanates from the 14th and 15th centuries. Some turned to Islam and, more recently, many have converted to Christianity, as a result of the activities of both Roman Catholic and Protestant missionaries. Few Dayaks, other than those in the remoter parts of the interior, still wear their traditional costumes.

Dayaks throughout Borneo have only been incorporated into the economic mainstream relatively recently. Relations with coastal groups were not always good and there was also constant fighting between groups. Differences between the coastal peoples and inland tribes throughout Borneo were accentuated as competition for land increased. Today, however, Dayak groups have relatively good access to education and many now work in the timber and oil and gas industries, which has caused out-migration from their traditional homelands.

The Kalimantan Dayaks can be broadly grouped by region. Kalsel (South Kalimantan) and Kalteng (Central Kalimantan) groups are collectively known as the **Barito River Dayaks** and include the 'Hill Dayaks' of the Meratus Mountains, northeast of Banjarmasin. The **Ngaju** live in Kalteng; they were the first Dayak group in Kalimantan to assert their political rights, by lobbying (and fighting) for the creation of Kalteng in the 1950s. The province was later separated from Kalsel, which was dominated by the strictly Islamic Banjarese. Other Dayak groups in Kalteng include the **Ma'anyan** and the **Ot Danum**, who live along the rivers on either side of the Schwaner Range.

Bugis This group, whose name means sea gypsy people, lives along Kalimantan's coasts and are originally from South Sulawesi. They are famous shipbuilders and their schooners are still made in Kalsel, South Kalimantan (see page 328).

Iban Dayak communities in Kalbar (West Kalimantan) include the Iban. But the Iban are far better known as the largest tribal group in East Malaysia than they are in Kalimantan. Groups related to the Iban include the Seberuang, Kantuq and Mualang. ▶▶ See also box, page 176.

Kadazan Living in the border areas of East Kalimantan, the Kadazan traditionally inhabited longhouses but these are rare now and most live in Malay-style houses. All Kadazan share a common language, although dialects vary. ▶▶ See also box, page 279.

Kayan and Kenyah The main groups living in East Kalimantan are the Kayan and Kenyah, who live in the Apo Kayan region and near the Mahakam River. They are also found on the Mendalam River in West Kalimantan. ▶▶ See also box, page 179.

The **Bahau**, related to the Kayan, live in the upper Mahakam region, upriver from Long Iram; the majority are Roman Catholics. The other groups living in the upper Mahakam area include the **Modang** (they are mainly Catholic and are a subgroup of the Kenyah who migrated south), the **Bentian** and the **Penihing**. The **Tanjung Dayaks** live in the middle reaches of the Mahakam; some remain animist although large numbers have converted

Ayo! Transmigrasi!

A visit to Kalimantan often shatters the illusion of dreamy encounters with noble savages with feathered hair. Under the Transmigration scheme many areas of coastal Kalimantan has been heavily populated by settlers from Java, Madura and to a lesser extent, Bali. The settlers brought their religion, food and housing, making a stay in a place like Pangkalan Bun akin to a visit to a tidy Javanese town. The aim of the scheme has been to reduce pressure on heavily populated areas of the country and to provide a hard-working workforce capable of utilizing the abundant natural resources of places like Kalimantan.

More cynical critics of the scheme argue that the Indonesian government has used *transmigrasi* as a means to colonize areas with Javanese, thus reducing the possibility of separatist uprisings by indigenous groups.

Billboards in crowded Javanese cities tower over streets displaying pictures of grinning happy migrants surrounded by spacious lush green fields, a small nicely painted house and the words *Ayo! Transmigrasi!* (Let's go! Migrate!). As the government attempts to relocate around 15,000 families a year, many migrants have found themselves in areas with soil poorer than that of fertile volcanic Bali and Java, and little help in learning the skills necessary to utilize the land effectively. Worse still, the bloody ethnic killings in Sampit in 2001 meted out on Maduruse transmigrants by the indigenous Dayaks show that these newcomers are not always welcome.

to Christianity (both Roman Catholic and Protestant). The other main group on the middle Mahakam are the **Benuaq**; Tanjung Isuy (see page 347) is a Benuaq village, for example. They are also Roman Catholic.

Kelabit The Kelabit live in the mountains close to the Sarawak border and the headwaters of the Baram river. The Kelabit-Murut are distinct culturally and linguistically from the Murut of Northeast Kalimantan. ►► *See also box, page 178.*

Murut The Murut live in Northeast Kalimantan. ►► *See also box, page 280.*

Penan Perhaps Southeast Asia's only remaining true hunter-gatherers, the nomadic Penan live mainly in the upper Rejang and Limbang areas of Sarawak, but there is also a small population in the Apo Kayan of Kalimantan. They hunt wild pigs, birds and monkeys in the forest and make their staple food – sago flour – from sago palms. The Penan are seen as jungle experts by other inland tribes. Living in the cool, shady forest, they were virtually unseen by outsiders until the 1960s. ►► *See also box, page 107.*

Dance

Dayak tribes are renowned for their singing and dancing, and the most famous is the hornbill dance. In her book, *Sarawak*, Hedda Morrison writes: "The Kayans are probably the originators of the stylized war dance now common among the Ibans, but the girls are also extremely talented and graceful dancers. One of their most delightful dances is the hornbill dance, when they tie hornbill feathers to the ends of their fingers which accentuate their slow and graceful movements. For party purposes everyone in the longhouse joins in led by musicians and a group of girls who sing." On these occasions, drink flows freely. With the Ibans, it is *tuak* (rice wine), with the Kayan and Kenyah it is *borak*, a bitter rice beer. After being entertained by dancers, a visitor is under compunction to drink a large glassful, before bursting into song and doing a dance routine themselves. The best guideline for visitors on how to handle such occasions is provided by Redmond O'Hanlon in *Into the Heart of Borneo*. The general rule of thumb is to be prepared to make an absolute fool of yourself, throwing all inhibition to the wind. This will immediately endear you to your hosts.

Music

Gongs range from the single large gong, the *tawak*, to the *engkerumong*, a set of small gongs, arranged on a horizontal rack, with five players. An *engkerumong* ensemble usually involves between five and seven drums, which include two suspended gongs (*tawak* and *bendan*) and five hour-glass drums (*ketebong*). They are used to celebrate victory in battle or to welcome home a successful headhunting expedition. The Bidayuh also make a bamboo gong called a *pirunchong*. The *jatang uton* is a wooden xylophone which can be rolled up like a rope ladder; the keys are struck with hardwood sticks.

The Bidayuh make two main stringed instruments: a three-stringed cylindrical bamboo harp called a *tinton* and the *rabup*, a rotan-stringed fiddle with a bamboo cup. The Kenyah and Kayan play a four-stringed guitar called a *sape*. It is the most common and popular lute-type instrument, whose body, neck and board are cut from one piece of softwood. It is used in Orang Ulu dances and by witchdoctors. It is usually played by two musicians, one keeping the rhythm, the other the melody. Traditional *sapes* had rotan strings; today they use wire guitar strings and electric pick-ups. Another stringed instrument, more usually found in Kalimantan than Sarawak, is the *satang*, a bamboo tube with strings around the outside, cut from the bamboo and tightened with pegs.

One of the best-known instruments is the *engkerurai* (or *keluri*), the bagpipes of Borneo, which is usually associated with the Kenyahs and Kayans. It is a hand-held organ in which four vertical bamboo pan-pipes of different lengths are fixed to a gourd, which acts as the wind chamber. Simple *engkerurai* can only manage one chord; more sophisticated ones allow the player to use two pipes for the melody, while the others provide a harmonic drone. The Bidayuh are specialists in bamboo instruments and make flutes of various sizes; big thick ones are called *branchi*, long ones with five holes are *kroto* and small ones are called *nchiyo*.

Arts and crafts

Basketry A wide variety of household items are woven from rotan, bamboo and bemban reed, as well as nipah and pandanus palms. Basketry is practised by nearly all the ethnic groups in Borneo and they are among the most popular handicrafts. A variety of baskets are made for harvesting, storing and winnowing paddy, as well as for collecting and storing other items.

The Penan are reputed to produce the finest rattan sleeping mats – closely plaited and pliable. The Kayan and Kenyah produce four main types of basket. The *anjat* is a finely woven jungle rucksack with two shoulder straps; the *kiang* is also a rucksack-type affair but with a rougher weave, and is stronger and used for carrying heavier loads; the *lanjung* is a large basket used for transporting rice; while the *bakul* is a container worn while harvesting rice, so that the pannicles drop in. The *bening aban* is the famous baby carrier; it is woven in fine rattan, has a wooden seat and is colourfully decorated with intricate beadwork. Many of the native patterns used in basketry come from Chinese patterns and take the form of geometrical shapes and stylized birds. The Bidayuh also make baskets from either rotan or sago bark strips. The most common Bidayuh basket is the *tambok*, which is simply patterned and has bands of colour; it also has thin wooden supports on each side.

Beadwork Among many Kenyah, Kayan, Bidayuh and Kelabit groups, beads have long been symbols of status and wealth; necklaces, skull caps and girdles are handed down from generation to generation. Smaller glass – or plastic – beads (usually imported from Europe) are used to decorate baby carriers, baskets, headbands, jackets, hats, sheaths for knives, tobacco boxes and handbags. Beaded baby carriers are mainly used by the Kelabit, Kenyah and Kayan, and often have shells and animals' teeth attached which make a rattling sound to frighten away evil spirits. Rounded patterns require more skill than geometric patterns, the quality of the pattern used to reflect the status of the owner. Only upper-classes are permitted to have beadwork depicting 'high-class' motifs such as human faces or figures. Early beads were made from clay, metal, glass, bone or shell (the earliest have been found in the Niah Caves.)

Blowpipes Blowpipes are usually carved from hardwood – normally *belian* (ironwood). The first step is to make a rough cylinder about 10 cm wide and 2.5 m long. This rod is tied to a platform, from which a hole is bored through the rod. The bore is skilfully chiselled by an iron rod with a pointed end. The rod is then sanded down to about 5 cm in diameter. Traditionally, the sanding was done using the rough underside of macaranga leaves. The darts are made from the nibong and wild sago palms, and the poison itself is the sap of the *upas* (Ipoh) tree (*Antiaris toxicari*) into which the point is dipped.

Hats Kalimantan's Dayak hats are called *seraung* and are made from biru leaves; they are conical and often have colourful *ta-ah* patchwork cloth sewn onto them, or they might be decorated with beads. The Kenyah – like their relations across the Sarawak border – wear distinctive grass-plaited caps called *tapung*.

Textiles The Benuaq Dayaks of the Mahakam are known for their ikat weaving, producing colourful pieces of varied designs. They are woven with thread produced from pineapple leaves. While traditional costumes are disappearing fast, it is still possible to find the *sholang*, colourful appliqué skirts, which have black human figures and dragon-dogs (*aso/asok*) sewn on top. The traditional sarong worn by Dayak women is called a *ta-ah*, which is a short, colourful, patchwork-style material.

The weaving of cotton *pua kumbu* is one of the oldest Iban traditions, and literally means 'blanket' or 'cover'. The weaving is done by the women and is a vital skill for a would-be bride to acquire. There are two main methods employed in making and decorating *pua kumbu*: the more common is the ikat tie-dyeing technique, known as *ngebat* by the Iban. The other method is the *pileh*, or floating weft. The Ibans use a warp-beam loom which is tied to two posts, to which the threads are attached. There is a breast-beam at the weaving end, secured by a back strap to the weaver. A pedal, beneath the threads, lowers and raises the alternate threads, which are separated by rods. The woven material is tightly packed by a beater. The material is tie-dyed in the warp. Because the *pua kumbu* is made by the warp-tie-dyeing method, the number of colours is limited. The most common are a rich browny-brick-red colour and black, as well as the undyed white sections; blues and greens are used in more modern materials. Traditionally, *pua kumbu* were hung in longhouses during ceremonies and were used to cover images during rituals. The designs and patterns are representations of deities which figure in Iban myths and are believed to protect individuals from harm; they are passed down from generation to generation. Such designs, with deep spiritual significance, can only be woven by wives and daughters of chiefs. Other designs and patterns are representations of birds and animals, including hornbills, crocodiles, monitor lizards and shrimps, which are either associated with worship or are sources of food. Symbolic representations of trees, plants and fruits are also included in the designs as well as the events of everyday life. A typical example is the zigzag pattern which represents the act of crossing a river – the zigzag course is explained by the canoe's attempts to avoid strong currents. Many of the symbolic representations are highly stylized and can be difficult to pick out.

Weapons The traditional Dayak headhunting knife is called a *mandau*. It is a multi-purpose knife with practical and ritualistic uses. The different tribes have different-shaped *mandau* blades, which are made of steel; their handles are carved in the shape of a hornbill's head from bone. Human hair was traditionally attached to the end of the handle. Other Dayak weapons include the *tombak* hunting spear, made from ironwood, with a steel tip. The *sumpit*, or blowpipe, was used for hunting, but now plays a largely ceremonial role during rituals and festivals. The Dayak battle shield (*kelbit*) is made from cork, and is shaped like an elongated diamond.

Woodcarvings Many of Borneo's tribal groups are skilled carvers who can produce everything from huge burial poles to small statues, masks and other decorative items and utensils. The traditional Kenyah masks, which are used during festivals, are elaborately carved and often have large protruding eyes. Eyes are always emphasized, as they are to frighten the enemy. Other typical carved items include spoons, stools, doors, walking sticks, *sapes* (guitars), ceremonial shields, tops of water containers, tattoo plaques and the hilts of *parang ilang* (ceremonial knives). The most popular Iban motif is the hornbill, which holds an honoured place in Iban folklore (see page 378), being the messenger for the sacred Brahminy kite, the ancestor of the Iban. Another famous Iban carving is the sacred measuring stick called the *tuntun peti*, used to trap deer and wild boar; it is carved to represent a forest spirit. The Kayan and Kenyahs' most common motif is the *aso*, a dragon-like dog with a long snout with religious and mythical significance. The Kenyah and Kayan carve huge burial structures, or *salong*, and small earrings made of hornbill ivory.

Small carved statues, or *hampatong*, are commonly found in handicraft shops. They are figures of humans, animals or mythical creatures and traditionally have ritual functions. They are often kept in Dayak homes to bring good luck, good health or good harvests. They are divided according to the Dayak cosmology: male figures (human and animal) are associated with the upper world, female figures (human and animal) with the lower world, while hermaphrodite figures symbolize the middle world. Large *hampatong* are associated either with death or headhunting, while others, usually placed as a totem outside a village, will serve as its protector. Another group of large *hampatong* are the *sapundu*, to which sacrificial victims were tied before being put to death.

Land and environment

Geography

The highest peak in Kalimantan is Gunung Rajah (2278 m) in the Schwaner Range, to the southwest; the two biggest rivers are in Kalimantan: the Kapuas, which flows west from the centre of the island, and the Mahakam, which flows east.

Kalimantan itself is divided into four provinces. South Kalimantan (or Kalimantan Selatan) is usually called Kalsel and is the smallest of the four and is also the highlight of most tourists' visits to Kalimantan. To the west is Central Kalimantan (Kalimantan Tenggah), known as Kalteng, a vast province with a tiny population; few foreign tourists venture here; its only real tourist attraction is a remote orang-utan rehabilitation centre near the swampy south coast. East Kalimantan (Kalimantan Timur) is known as Kaltim and is the richest of the four provinces because of its timber, oil and gas resources. Its main attraction is the Mahakam River that penetrates deep into the interior from the provincial capital, Samarinda. West Kalimantan (Kalimantan Barat) – or Kalbar – is, like neighbouring Kalteng, visited by few tourists. It is cut off from the rest of Kalimantan by the mountainous, jungled interior and can only be reached by air, although some east coast tour operators offer two-week trans-Borneo treks. The longest river in Indonesia, the 1243-km-long Kapuas, reaches far into the interior from Kalbar's capital, Pontianak.

Tourists usually come to Kalimantan in search of two things: jungle and jungle culture in the form of the Dayak forest tribes. It sometimes comes as a shock that loggers have beaten them into the jungle, particularly in the more accessible areas along the coasts and rivers. For quite long distances on either side of the riverbanks, the primary forest has all been 'harvested'. Kalimantan's powerful rivers (the Kapuas, Mahakam and Berito) have been the arteries of commerce and 'civilization'; the riverbanks are lined with towns and villages as far as they are navigable.

Missionaries and traders have also beaten tourists into the tribal interior. Many Dayak tribes have been converted to Christianity and most people have completely abandoned their cultures, traditions and animist religion. The majority of upriver people, apart from those in the remoter parts of the Apo Kayan in Kaltim, prefer to wear jeans and T-shirts, and many have relatively well-paid jobs in the timber industry.

That said, it is still possible to visit traditional longhouses in Kalimantan (in the hills of Kalsel and the upper reaches of the Mahakam and Kenyah rivers in Kaltim) and trek through tracts of virgin rainforest. But trips to these areas take time and cost money. There are several experienced adventure tourism companies in Kalimantan, mostly based in Balikpapan and Samarinda.

Climate

Borneo has a typical equatorial monsoon climate: the weather usually follows predictable patterns, although in recent years it has become less predictable. Temperatures are fairly uniform, averaging 23-33°C during the day and rarely dropping below 20°C at night, except in the mountains, where they can drop to below 10°C. Most rainfall occurs between November and January during the northeast monsoon; this causes rivers to flood, and there are many short, sharp cloudbursts. The dry season runs from May to September. It is characterized by dry southeasterly winds and is the best time to visit. Rainfall generally increases towards the interior; most of Borneo receives about 2000-3000 mm a year, although some upland areas get more than 4000 mm. Note that there are significant variations in the pattern of rainfall across Kalimantan.

Flora and fauna

Borneo's ancient rainforests are rich in flora and fauna, including between 9000 and 15,000 species of seed plant (of which almost half may be endemic), 200 species of mammal, 570 species of birds, 100 species of snake, 250 species of freshwater fish and 1000 species of butterfly. Despite years of research the gaps in scientists' knowledge of the island's flora and fauna remain yawning, and if anything are becoming more so. For a significant proportion of the flora of Borneo, scientists have barely any information on their geographic distribution, let alone details of their ecology.

Borneo's forests hit the news for the wrong reasons in 1997: a series of fires scorched millions of hectares of land and shrouded an area the size of Western Europe, with a population of around 100,000,000, in what became euphemistically termed 'the haze'.

As late as the 1850s, the great bulk – perhaps as much as 95% – of Borneo was forested. Alfred Russel Wallace, like other Western travellers, was enchanted by the island's natural wealth and diversity: "ranges of hill everywhere", he wrote, "covered with interminable forest". But the jungle is fast disappearing and since the mid-1980s there has been mounting international environmental campaigning against deforestation.

The best-known timber trees fall into three categories, all of them hardwoods. Heavy hardwoods include selangan batu and resak; medium hardwoods include *kapur*, *keruing* and *keruntum*; light hardwoods include *madang tabak*, *ramin* and *meranti*. There are both peat-swamp and hill varieties of meranti, which is one of the most valuable export logs. *Belian*, or Bornean ironwood (*Eusideroxylon zwageri*), is one of the hardest and densest timbers in the world. It is thought that the largest *belian* may be 1000 years or more old. They are so tough that when they die they continue to stand for centuries before the wood rots to the extent that the trunk falls.

The main types of forest include: lowland rainforest (mixed dipterocarp) on slopes up to 600 m. Many of the rainforest trees are an important resource for Dayak communities. The jelutong tree, for example, is tapped like a rubber tree for its sap ('jungle chewing gum'), which is used to make tar for waterproof sealants – used in boat-building. It also hardens into a tough but brittle black plastic-like substance used for *parang* (machette) handles. Montane forest occurs at altitudes above 600 m, although in some areas it does not replace lowland rainforest until considerably higher than this. Above 1200 m mossy forest predominates. Montane forest is denser than lowland forest, with smaller trees of narrower girth. Moreover, dipterocarps are generally not found, while flowering shrubs like magnolias and rhododendrons appear. In place of dipterocarps, tropical latitude oaks, as well as other trees that are more characteristic of temperate areas, such as myrtle and laurel, make an appearance.

The low-lying river valleys are characterized by peat swamp forest – where the peat is up to 9 m thick – which makes wet-rice agriculture impossible.

Heath forest or *kerangas* – the Iban word meaning 'land on which rice cannot grow' – is found on poor, sandy soils. Although it mostly occurs near the coast, it is also sometimes found in mountain ranges, but almost always on level ground. Here trees are stunted and only the hardiest of plants can survive. Some trees have struck up symbiotic relationships with animals – such as ants – so as to secure essential nutrients. Pitcher plants (*Nepenthes*) have also successfully colonized heath forest. The absence of bird calls and other animal noises make heath forest rather eerie, and it also indicates their general biological poverty.

Along beaches there are often stretches of casuarina forest; the casuarina grows up to 27 m and looks like a conifer, with needle-shaped leaves. Mangrove occupies tidal mud flats around sheltered bays and estuaries. The most common mangrove tree is the bakau (*Rhizophora*), which grows to heights of about 9 m and has stilt roots to trap sediment. Bakau wood is used for pile-house stilts and for charcoal.

Orang-utan (*Pongo pygmaeus*) Borneo's great red-haired ape is known as 'man of the jungle' after the translation from the Malay: orang (*man*), utan (*jungle*). It is endemic to the tropical forests of Sumatra and Borneo. The Sumatran animals tend to keep the reddish tinge to their fur, while the Borneo ones go darker as they mature. It is Asia's only great ape; it has four hands, rather than feet, bow-legs and no tail. Males of over 15 years old stand up to 1.6 m tall and their arms span 2.4 m. Adult males (which make loud roars) weigh 50-100 kg, about twice that of adult females (whose call sounds like a long, unattractive belch). Orang-utans are said to have the strength of seven men but they are not aggressive; they are peaceful, gentle animals, particularly with each other.

Orang-utans mainly inhabit riverine swamp forests or lowland dipterocarp forests. They are easily detected by their nests of bent and broken twigs, which are woven together, in much the same fashion as a sun bear's, in the fork of a tree. They are solitary animals and always sleep alone. Orang-utans have a largely vegetarian diet consisting of fruit and young leaves, supplemented by termites, bark and birds' eggs. They are usually solitary, but the young remain with their mothers until they are five or six years old. Two adults will occupy an area of about 2 sq km and are territorial, protecting their territory against intruders. They can live up to 30 years and a female will have an average of three to four young during her lifetime. The gestation period is nine months. After giving birth, they do not mate for around another seven years.

Estimates of the numbers of orang-utan vary considerably. What is certain is that the forest is disappearing fast, and with it the orang-utan's natural habitat. Orang-utans' favoured habitat is lowland rainforest and this is particularly under threat from logging. The black market in young apes in countries like Taiwan means that they fetch relatively high returns to local hunters.

Proboscis monkey (*Nasalis larvatus*) The proboscis monkey is an extraordinary-looking animal, endemic to Borneo, which lives in lowland forests and mangrove swamps all around the island. Little research has been done on proboscis monkeys; they are notoriously difficult to study as they are so shy. Their fur is reddish-brown and they have white legs, arms, tail and a ruff on the neck, which gives the appearance of a pyjama-suit. Their facial skin is red and the males have grotesquely enlarged, droopy noses; females' noses are shorter and upturned. To ward off intruders, the nose is straightened out, 'like a party whoopee whistle', according to one description. Recently a theory has been advanced that the nose acts as a thermostat, helping to regulate body temperature. But it also tends to get in the way: old males often have to resort to holding their noses up with one hand while stuffing leaves into their mouths with the other.

Proboscises' penises are almost as obvious as their noses – the proboscis male glories in a permanent erection, which is probably why they are rarely displayed in zoos. The other way the males attract females is by violently shaking branches and making spectacular – and sometimes near-suicidal – leaps into the water, in which they attempt to hit as many dead branches as they can on the way down, so as to make the loudest noise possible.

The proboscis is a diurnal animal, but keeps to the shade during the heat of the day. The best time to see them is very early in the morning or around dusk. They can normally be heard before they are seen; they make loud honks, rather like geese; they also groan, squeal and roar. Proboscis monkeys are good swimmers; they even swim underwater for up to 20 m – thanks to their partially webbed feet. Males are about twice the size and weight of females. ▸▸ *See also box, page 295.*

Other monkeys Other monkeys found in Borneo include various species of leaf monkey – including the grey leaf monkey, the white-fronted leaf monkey and the red-leaf monkey. One of the most attractive members of the primate family found in Borneo is the tubby slow loris or *kongkang*. And perhaps the most difficult to pronounce – at least in Dusun – is the tarsier, which is locally known as the *tindukutrukut*.

Hornbill There are nine types of hornbill in Borneo, the most striking and biggest of which is the rhinoceros hornbill (*Buceros rhinoceros*) – or *kenyalang*. They can grow up to 1.5 m long and are mainly black, with a white belly. The long tail feathers are white too, crossed with a thick black bar near the end. They make a remarkable, resonant 'geronk' call in flight, which can be heard over long distances; they honk when resting. Hornbills are usually seen in pairs and are believed to be monogamous. After mating, the female imprisons herself in a hole in a tree, building a sturdy wall with her own droppings. The male bird fortifies the wall from the outside, using a mulch of mud, grass, sticks and saliva, leaving only a vertical slit for her beak. She remains incarcerated in her cell for about three months, during which time the male supplies her and the nestlings with food – mainly fruit, lizards, snakes and mice. Usually, only one bird is hatched and reared in the hole, and when it is old enough to fly, the female breaks out of the nest hole. Both emerge looking fat and dirty.

The 'bill' itself has no known function, but the males have been seen duelling in mid-air during the courting season. They fly straight at each other and collide head-on. The double-storeyed yellow bill has a projection, called a casque, on top, which has a bright red tip. In some species the bill develop wrinkles as the bird matures: one wrinkle for each year of its life. For this reason they are known in Dutch, and in some eastern Indonesian languages as 'year birds'.

Most Dayak groups consider the hornbill to have magical powers and the feathers are worn as symbols of heroism. In tribal mythology the bird is linked with the creation of mankind and is a symbol of the upper world. The hornbill is also the official state emblem of Sarawak. The best place to see hornbills is near wild fig trees as they love the fruit and play an important role in seed dispersal. The helmeted hornbill's bill is heavy and solid and can be carved like ivory. These bills were highly valued by the Dayaks and have been traded for centuries. The third largest hornbill is the wreathed hornbill that makes a yelping call and a loud – almost mechanical – noise when it beats its wings. Other species in Borneo include wrinkled, bushy-crested, white-crowned and pied hornbills.

Contents

Useful words and phrases

Bahasa Malaysia and Bahasa Indonesia are mutually intelligible but not the same; the list below gives the word in Malay with the Indonesian version in the third column if the difference is significant. ▸▸ *See also page 40.*

Basic phrases

Yes/No	*Ya/tidak*	
Thank you	*Terimah kasih*	
Good morning	*Selamat pagi*	
Good afternoon (early)	*Selamat tengahari*	*Selamat siang*
Good afternoon (late)	*Selamatpetang*	*Selamat sore*
Good evening/night	*Selam at malam*	
Welcome	*Selamat datang*	
Goodbye (said by the person leaving)	*Selamat tinggal*	
Goodbye (said by the person staying)	*Selamat jalan*	
Excuse me/sorry	*Ma'af saya (Ma'af)*	
Where's the ...?	*Dimana ...*	
How much is this ...?	*Ini berapa?*	*Berapa harganya?*
I [don't] understand	*Saya [tidak] mengerti*	

Sleeping

How much is a room?	*Bilik berapa?*	*Kamar berapa harga?*
Does the room have air conditioning?	*Ada bilik yang ada air-con-kah?*	*Ada kamar yang ada AC-nya?*
I want to see the room first please	*Saya mahu lihat bilik dulu*	*Saya mau lihat kamar dulu*
Does the room have hot water?	*Ada bilik yang ada air panas?*	*Ada kamar yang ada air panas?*
Does the room have a bathroom?	*Ada bilik yang ada mandi-kah?*	*Ada kamar yang ada kamar mandi?*

Travel

Where is the railway station?	*Stesen keretapi dimana?*	*Dimana stasiun ketera api?*
Where is the bus station?	*Stesen bas dimana?*	*Dimana stasiun bis?*
How much to go to ...?	*Berapa harga ke ...?*	
I want to buy a ticket to ...	*Saya mahu beli tiket ke ...*	*Saya mahu beli karcis ke ...*
Is it far?	*Ada jauh?*	
Turn left/turn right	*Belok kiri/belok kanan*	
Go straight on!	*Turus turus!*	*Terus saja*

Days

Monday	*Hari Isnin*	*Hari Senin*
Tuesday	*Hari Selasa*	
Wednesday	*Hari Rabu*	
Thursday	*Hari Khamis*	
Friday	*Hari Jumaat*	
Saturday	*Hari Sabtu*	
Sunday	*Hari Minggu*	
Today	*Hari ini*	
Tomorrow	*Esok*	*Hari besok*

Numbers

1 *satu*	9 *sembilan*	101 *se-ratus satu ...etc*
2 *dua*	10 *sepuluh*	150 *se-ratus limah puluh*
3 *tiga*	11 *se-belas*	200 *dua ratus*
4 *empat*	12 *dua-belas ...etc*	1000 *se-ribu*
5 *lima*	20 *dua puluh*	2000 *dua ribu*
6 *enam*	21 *dua puluh satu ...etc*	100,000 *se-ratus ribu*
7 *tujuh*	30 *tiga puluh*	1,000,000 *se-juta*
8 *lapan*	100 *se-ratus*	

Basic vocabulary

In Malay, with the Indonesian version in parenthesis if the difference is significant.

a little *sedikit*
a lot *banyak*
all right/good *baik*
bank *bank*
beach *pantai*
beautiful *cantik*
bed sheet *cadar*
big *besar*
boat *perahu*
bus *bas (bis)*
buy *beli*
can *boleh*
cheap *murah*
chemist *rumah ubat (apotek)*
clean *bersih*
closed *tutup*
day *hari*
delicious *sedap (enak)*
dentist *doktor gigi*
dirty *kotor*

doctor *doktor*
eat *makan*
excellent *bagus*
expensive *mahal*
food *makan*
hospital *rumah sakit*
hot (temperature) *panas*
hot (spicy) *pedas*
I/me *saya*
island *pulau*
market *pasar*
medicine *ubat ubatan (obat)*
open *masuk*
please *sila*
police *polis (polisi)*
police station *pejabat polis (stasiun polisi)*
post office *pejabat pos (kantor pos)*

restaurant *kedai makanan (rumah makan)*
room *bilik (kamar)*
sea *laut*
ship *kapal*
shop *kedai (toko)*
sick *sakit*
small *kecil*
stop *berhenti*
taxi *teksi (taksi)*
that *itu*
they *mereka*
toilet – female/male *tandas – perempuan/ lelaki (WC, 'way say')*
town *bandar (kota)*
very *sangat (Sekali)*
water *air*
what *apa*

Glossary

A

Adat custom or tradition

Amitabha the Buddha of the Past (see Avalokitsvara)

Atap thatch

Avalokitsvara also known as Amitabha and Lokeshvara, the name literally means 'World Lord'; he is the compassionate male Bodhisattva, the saviour of Mahayana Buddhism and represents the central force of creation in the universe; usually portrayed with a lotus and water flask

B

Bahasa language, as in Bahasa Malaysia and Bahasa Indonesia

Bajaj three-wheeled motorized taxi

Barisan Nasional National Front, Malaysia's ruling coalition

Batik a form of resist dyeing

Becak three-wheeled bicycle rickshaw

Bodhi the tree under which the Buddha achieved enlightenment (*Ficus religiosa*)

Bodhisattva a future Buddha. In Mahayana Buddhism, someone who has attained enlightenment, but who postpones nirvana to help others become enlightened

Brahma the Creator, one of the gods of the Hindu trinity, usually represented with four faces, and often mounted on a *hamsa*

Brahmin a Hindu priest

Budaya cultural (as in Muzium Budaya)

Bumboat small wooden lighters, now used for ferrying tourists in Singapore

C

Cap batik stamp

Chedi from the Sanskrit *cetiya*, meaning memorial. Usually a religious monument (often bell-shaped) with relics of the Buddha or other holy remains. Used interchangeably with stupa

Cutch see Gambier

D

Dalang wayang puppet master

Dayak/Dyak tribal peoples of Borneo

Dharma the Buddhist law

Dipterocarp family of trees characteristic of Southeast Asia's forests

Durga the female goddess who slays the demon Mahisa, from an Indian epic story

G

Gambier also known as *cutch*, a dye derived from the bark of the bakau mangrove and used in leather tanning

Gamelan Malay orchestra of percussion instruments

Ganesh elephant-headed son of Siva

Garuda mythical divine bird, with predatory beak and claws, and human body; the king of birds, enemy of naga

Gautama the historic Buddha

Geomancy feng shui

Godown Asian warehouse

Goporum tower in a Hindu temple

Gunung mountain

H

Hamsa sacred goose, Brahma's mount; in Buddhism it represents the flight of the doctrine

Hinayana 'Lesser Vehicle', major Buddhist sect in Southeast Asia, usually termed Theravada Buddhism

I

Ikat tie-dyeing method of patterning cloth

Indra the Vedic god of the heavens, weather and war; usually mounted on a three-headed elephant

J

Jataka(s) birth stories of the Buddha, of which there are 547

K

Kajang thatch
Kala (makara) literally, 'death' or 'black'; a demon ordered to consume itself; often sculpted over entranceways to act as a door guardian, also known as *kirtamukha*
Kampong or kampung, village
Kerangas from an Iban word meaning 'land on which rice will not grow'
Kinaree half-human, half-bird, usually depicted as a heavenly musician
Klotok motorized gondolas of Banjarmasin
Kongsi Chinese clan house
Kris traditional Malay sword
Krishna an incarnation of Vishnu
Kuti living quarters of Buddhist monks

L

Laterite bright red tropical soil/stone
Linga phallic symbol and one of the forms of Siva
Lokeshvara see Avalokitsvara
Lunggyi Indian sarong
Losmen guesthouse

M

Mahabharata a Hindu epic text written about 2000 years ago
Mahayana 'Greater Vehicle', major Buddhist sect
Mandi Indonesian/Malay bathroom with water tub and dipper
Maitreya the future Buddha
Makara a mythological aquatic reptile, a little like a crocodile and sometimes with an elephant's trunk; often found, along with the *kala*, framing doorways
Mandala a focus for meditation; a representation of the cosmos
MCA Malaysian Chinese Association
Meru the mountain residence of the gods; centre of the universe, the cosmic mountain
MIC Malaysian Indian Congress
Mudra symbolic gesture of the hands of the Buddha
Musium museum

N

Naga benevolent mythical water serpent, enemy of Garuda
Naga makara fusion of *naga* and *makara*
Nalagiri the elephant let loose to attack the Buddha, who calmed him
Nandi/Nandin bull, mount of Siva
Negara kingdom and capital, from Sanskrit
Negeri also negri, state
Nirvana enlightenment, the Buddhist ideal

O

Ojek motorcycle taxi

P

Paddy/padi unhulled rice
Pantai beach
Pasar market, from the Arabic 'bazaar'
Pasar malam night market
Pelni Indonesian state shipping line
Perahu/prau boat
Peranakan mixed race, usually applied to part-Chinese and part-Malay people
Pradaksina pilgrims' clockwise circumambulation of a holy structure
Prang form of stupa built in the Khmer style
Prasat residence of a king or of the gods (sanctuary tower), from the Indian *prasada*
Pribumi indigenous (as opposed to Chinese) businessmen
Pulau island
Pusaka heirloom

R

Raja/rajah ruler
Raksasa temple guardian statues
Ramayana the Indian epic tale
Ruai common gallery of an Iban longhouse, Sarawak
Rumah adat customary or traditional house

S

Sago multi-purpose palm
Sakyamuni the historic Buddha
Sal the Indian *sal* tree (*Shorea robusta*), under which the historic Buddha was born

Silat or *bersilat*, traditional Malay martial art

Singha mythical guardian lion

Siva one of the Hindu triumvirate, the god of destruction and rebirth

Songket Malay textile interwoven with supplementary gold and silver yarn

Sravasti the miracle at Sravasti when the Buddha subdues the heretics in front of a mango tree

Sri Laksmi the goddess of good fortune and Vishnu's wife

Stele inscribed stone panel or slab

Stucco plaster, often heavily moulded

Stupa see Chedi

Sungai river

T

Tamu weekly open-air market

Tanju open gallery of an Iban longhouse, Sarawak

Tara also known as Cunda; the four-armed consort of the Bodhisattva Avalokitsvara

Tavatimsa heaven of the 33 gods at the summit of Mount Meru

Theravada 'Way of the Elders'; major Buddhism sect also known as Hinayana Buddhism ('Lesser Vehicle')

Tiffin afternoon meal – a word that was absorbed from the British Raj

Timang Iban sacred chants, Sarawak

Tong or *towkay*, a Chinese merchant

Totok 'full blooded'; usually applied to Chinese of pure blood

Towkay Chinese merchant

Triads Chinese mafia associations

Tunku also *tuanku* and *tengku*, prince

U

Ulama Muslim priest

Ulu jungle

UMNO United Malays National Organization

Urna the dot or curl on the Buddha's forehead, one of the distinctive physical marks of the Enlightened One

Usnisa the Buddha's top knot or 'wisdom bump', one of the physical marks of the Enlightened One

V

Vishnu the Protector, one of the gods of the Hindu trinity, generally with four arms holding the disc, the conch shell, the ball and the club

W

Waringin banyan tree

Warung a foodstall – a simple place to eat on the street. The alternative Malay name is *Kedai Makan*. The word originally comes from Indonesia.

Wayang traditional Malay shadow plays

Food glossary

For more information on cuisine, see page 25.

assam sour; tamarind
ayam chicken
babek duck
babi pork
belacan hot fermented prawn paste
buah fruit
daging meat
es krim ice cream
garam salt
gula sugar
ikan fish
kacang tanah peanut
kambing mutton
ketupat cold, compressed rice
kopi coffee
lombok chilli
manis sweet
mee noodles
minum drink
nasi rice
roti bread, pancake
sambal spicy relish side dish
sayur vegetables
sejuk crab
susu milk
tahu beancurd
telur egg
udang prawn

Rice dishes

nasi biryani saffron rice flavoured with spices and garnished with cashew nuts, almonds and raisins (Sarawak).
nasi campur Malay curry buffet of rice served with meat, fish, vegetables and fruit.
nasi dagang glutinous rice cooked in coconut milk and served with fish curry, cucumber pickle and sambal.
nasi goreng rice, meat and vegetables fried with garlic, onions and *sambal*.
nasi lemak a breakfast dish of rice cooked in coconut milk and served with prawn sambal, *ikan bilis*, hard-boiled egg, peanuts and cucumber.

nasi puteh plain boiled rice.
nontong rice cakes in a spicy coconut milk topped with grated coconut and sometimes bean curd and egg (Sarawak).
rijsttafel Indonesian meal consisting of a selection of rice dishes, to which are added small pieces of meat, fish, fruit and pickles.

Soup

lontong cubed, compressed rice served with mixed vegetables in coconut milk. Sambal is the accompaniment. Popular for breakfast.
soto ayam a spicy chicken soup served with rice cubes, chicken and vegetables, popular for breakfast in Sarawak.
sup manuk on hiing chicken soup with rice wine (Sabah).
sup terjun jumping soup – salted fish, mango and ginger (Sabah).

Meat, fish and seafood

hinava marinated raw fish (Sabah).
pan suh manok chicken cooked in bamboo cup, served with *bario* (Kelabit mountain rice) (Sarawak).
satay chicken, beef or mutton marinated and skewered on a bamboo, barbecued over a brazier. Usually served with *ketupat*.
Sayur masak lemak deep-fried marinated prawns (Sarawak).
tapai chicken cooked in rice wine (Sabah).
ternbok fish, which has been either grilled or steamed (Sarawak).

Noodles

kway teow flat noodles fried with seafood, egg, soy sauce, beansprouts and chives.
laksa johor noodles in fish curry sauce and raw vegetables.
mee goreng fried noodles.
mee jawa noodles in gravy, served with prawn fritters, potatoes, tofu and beancurd.
mee rebus noodles with beef, chicken or prawn with soybean in spicy sauce. In Sarawak, it's yellow noodles served in a thick

sweet sauce made from sweet potatoes and garnished with sliced hard-boiled eggs and green chillies.

mee siam white thin noodles in a sweet and sour gravy made with tamarind (Sarawak).

Curries

longong vegetable curry made from rice cakes cooked in coconut, beans, cabbage and bamboo shoots.

Salad

gado-gado cold dish of bean sprouts, potatoes, long beans, tempeh, bean curd, rice cakes and prawn crackers, topped with a spicy peanut sauce.

rojak Malaysia's answer to Indonesia's *gado gado* – mixed vegetable salad served in peanut sauce with *ketupat*.

Vegetables

kang-kong belacan water spinach fried in chilli-shrimp paste.

pakis ferns, which are fried with *belacan* and mushrooms. Sometimes ferns are eaten raw, with a squeeze of lime (*sayur pakis limau*) (Sabah).

sayur manis sweet vegetables; vegetables fried with chilli, *belacan* and mushrooms.

Sweets (kueh)

apam steamed rice cakes.

es delima a dessert of water chestnut in sago and coconut milk.

hinompula a dessert made from tapioca, sugar, coconut and the juice from screwpine leaves (Sabah).

ice kachang similar to Chinese *chendol*, a cone of ice shavings topped by syrup and other ingredients, but with evaporated milk instead of coconut milk.

nyonya kueh Chinese *kueh*, among the most popular is *yow cha koei* – deep-fried kneaded flour.

pulut inti glutinous rice served with sweetened grated coconut.

Index → *Entries in bold refer to maps*

Credits

Footprint credits

Project Editor: Jo Williams
Layout and production: Emma Bryers
Colour section: Rob Lunn
Maps: Kevin Feeney
Proofreader: Jen Haddington

Managing Director: Andy Riddle
Commercial Director: Patrick Dawson
Publisher: Alan Murphy
Publishing Managers: Jo Williams,
Felicity Laughton
Digital Editor: Alice Little
Series design: Mytton Williams
Marketing: Liz Harper, Hannah Bonnell
Sales: Jeremy Parr
Advertising: Renu Sibal
Finance and administration:
Elizabeth Taylor

Photography credits

Front cover: Chris Mattison/Alamy
Back cover: Chris Hellier/Alamy
Opener: ppart/Shutterstock
Introduction: Mark Eveleigh/Alamy
Montage: pic 1 John Frumm/Hemis.fr,
pic 2 Lonely Planet Images/Alamy,
pic 3, 4, 6 Robert Harding/SuperStock,
pic 5 Juriah Mosin/Shutterstock,
pic 7 Photononstop/Superstock,
pic 8 Hanne & Jens Eriksen/Nature PL,
pic 9 Khoroshunova Olga/Shutterstock,
pic 10 Mayumi Terao/iStock

Printed in India by Nutech.

Footprint feedback

We try as hard as we can to make each
Footprint guide as up to date as possible
but, of course, things always change. If you
want to let us know about your experiences –
good, bad or ugly – then don't delay, go to
footprinttravelguides.com and send in
your comments.

Publishing information

Footprint Borneo
3rd edition
© Footprint Handbooks Ltd
September 2010

ISBN: 978 1 907263 06 4
CIP DATA: A catalogue record for this book
is available from the British Library

® Footprint Handbooks and the Footprint
mark are a registered trademark of Footprint
Handbooks Ltd

Published by Footprint
6 Riverside Court
Lower Bristol Road
Bath BA2 3DZ, UK
T +44 (0)1225 469141
F +44 (0)1225 469461
footprinttravelguides.com

Distributed in the USA by Globe Pequot Press,
Guilford, Connecticut